State and Local Government

Politics and Public Policies

EIGHTH EDITION

David C. Saffell
Ohio Northern University

Harry Basehart
Salisbury University

Mc
Graw
Hill

Boston Burr Ridge, IL Dubuque, IA Madison, WI New York
San Francisco St. Louis Bangkok Bogotá Caracas Kuala Lumpur
Lisbon London Madrid Mexico City Milan Montreal New Delhi
Santiago Seoul Singapore Sydney Taipei Toronto

Higher Education

STATE AND LOCAL GOVERNMENT
Politics and Public Policies, Eighth Edition

Published by McGraw-Hill, an imprint of The McGraw-Hill Companies, Inc., 1221 Avenue of the Americas, New York, NY 10020. Copyright © 2005, 2001, 1998, 1993, 1990, 1987, 1982, 1978 by The McGraw-Hill Companies, Inc. All rights reserved. No part of this publication may be reproduced or distributed in any form or by any means, or stored in a database or retrieval system, without the prior written consent of The McGraw-Hill Companies, Inc., including, but not limited to, in any network or other electronic storage or transmission, or broadcast for distance learning.

1 2 3 4 5 6 7 8 9 0 DOC / DOC 0 9 8 7 6 5 4

ISBN 0-07-286901-1

Editor-in-chief: *Emily Barrosse*
Publisher: *Lyn Uhl*
Sponsoring editor: *Monica Eckman*
Editorial assistant: *Kimberly McGrath*
Marketing manager: *Katherine Bates*
Media producer: *Sean Crowley*
Production editor: *Brett Coker*
Senior production supervisor: *Richard DeVitto*
Design manager and cover designer: *Preston Thomas*
Art editor: *Emma Ghiselli*
Senior photo research coordinator: *Nora Agbayani*
Cover photo: © *Kevin R. Morris/Corbis*
Compositor: *GAC Indianapolis*
Typeface: *10/12 Times Roman*
Paper: *45# New Era Matte*
Printer and binder: *RR Donnelley, Crawfordsville*

Photo Credits
p.1, © Peter Menzel/Stock Boston; p. 36, © Corbis; p. 67, © Steve Miller/AP Wide World Photo; p. 105, © Kenneth James/Corbis; p. 146, © Bob Daemmrich/Stock Boston; p. 180, © Ronen Zilberman/AP Wide World Photo; p. 225, © Getty; p. 268, © Chuck Nacke/Woodfin Camp & Associates; p. 294, © Michael S. Yamashita/Corbis; p. 323, © A. Ramey/Woodfin Camp & Associates

Chapter opening photos
Chapter 1, Capitol Building for the state of Utah; Chapter 3, Connecticut Secretary of State Susan Bysiewicz with her daughter Ava at the Connecticut Democratic Party Convention held in Hartford, Connecticut, July 2002; Chapter 4, California Governor Gray Davis supporters rally outside the California Broadcasters Association debate held at Sacramento State University; Chapter 5, Floor of the Texas state legislature; Chapter 6, Linda Lingle being sworn in as Hawaii's sixth governor and the first woman to hold the state's highest office

Library of Congress Cataloging-in-Publication Data

Saffell, David C., 1941–
   State and local government : politics and public policies / David C. Saffell,
Harry Basehart. — 8th ed.
    p. cm.
   Includes bibliographical references and index.
   ISBN 0–07–286901–1 (softcover)
   1. State government—United States. 2. Local government—United States. I. Basehart,
Harry. II. Title.

JK2408.S17 2004
320.8'0973—dc22

                                   2003066608

The Internet addresses listed in the text were accurate at the time of publication. The inclusion of a Web site does not indicate an endorsement by the authors or McGraw-Hill Higher Education, and McGraw-Hill does not guarantee the accuracy of the information presented at these sites.

www.mhhe.com

Contents

About the Authors

DAVID C. SAFFELL is professor emeritus of political science at Ohio Northern University. He received his Ph.D. in political science from The University of Minnesota. He is the coauthor (with Harry Basehart) of *Governing States and Cities* (1997); the coeditor (with Harry Basehart) of *Readings in State and Local Government: Problems and Prospects* (1994); and the author of several other textbooks on American government. Professor Saffell has been teaching state and local government to undergraduate students for thirty years.

HARRY BASEHART is professor of political science and codirector of the Institute for Public Affairs and Civic Engagement at Salisbury University in Salisbury, Maryland. He received his Ph.D. in political science from The Ohio State University. Professor Basehart is the author or coauthor of articles on state legislatures that have appeared in *American Politics Quarterly* and *Legislative Studies Quarterly*. He recently served on the Governor's Special Committee on Voting Systems and Election Procedures in Maryland.

Preface

Beginning with its first edition in 1978, *State and Local Government: Politics and Public Policies* has attempted to present up-to-date, readable analysis about the structure and operation of state and local government. Although the book has remained a concise treatment of subnational politics, we have always included discussion of a reasonably wide range of policy issues and we have attempted to incorporate current research in the field.

Our discussion of political parties, interest groups, political participation, elections, legislatures, executives, bureaucrats, and courts centers on state governments, but it also includes considerable analysis of political behavior and government structure in cities, counties, and other units of local government. At all levels, the reader is reminded about the impact of political culture, tradition, and economic development on government structure and policy making.

Over the years we have chronicled the evolution of state and local government from serious financial problems in the early 1980s through a "resurgence" in the early 1990s and budget surpluses of the late 1990s. With this edition, we look at ways in which most states are dealing with their most severe financial crisis since World War II. Even in this downturn, we are impressed by the continuing vitality of state governments as they find ways to maintain their tradition of innovation.

We continue to employ a variety of pedagogical devices in all chapters. These include points to consider, chapter summaries, key terms, and summaries of state-local differences. All chapter-opening stories are new or revised and websites have been updated and expanded.

The existence of an extraordinary number of outstanding websites makes the study of state and local government more exciting than ever. It has never been easier to study the politics of the fifty states, and even hundreds of cities. At the end of each chapter, under "Interesting Websites," we identify several websites that have useful information if you decide to pursue some of the chapter's topics in more depth; however, the best overall website for state government is Stateline.org at www.stateline.org. This site is operated by the Pew Center on the States, a research organization administered by the University of Richmond and funded by the Pew Charitable Trusts. Once you are at the home page of Stateline.org, click on "State News Roundup" and you will have access to the major story of the day in each of the states. If you want to look at issues, click on one you're interested in, such as "Environment and Energy," and you'll be connected to recent news stories on this issue from several states. Under "States," you can choose a state and discover background information and the latest news stories. Finally, you should consider registering for "My Stateline." My Stateline provides easy access to stories relating to your state and/or issue interests. News alerts are available if you want to be notified by e-mail when there is an important news story or an important development regarding an issue tracked by Stateline.org. Enjoy!

In addition to updating statistics in graphs and tables and information about current political behavior and elections, this edition contains new or expanded material on a variety of subjects. Major additions include discussion of population change among the states in the 1990s; Supreme Court federalism decisions, including *Bush v. Gore*; an evaluation of devolution under presidents Clinton and Bush; growth of the Republican Party in the South; divided government in the states and its impact on public policy; lobbying ethics; the Voting Rights Act of 1975 and the Chicano movement; impact of the National Voter Registration Act; state efforts to improve voting systems after the 2000 presidential election in Florida; the changing nature of judicial elections; public financing of state elections and Clean Election Reform; the role of money in the initiative process; legislative districting after the 2000 census; new challenges to state legislatures; gubernatorial pardons; affirmative action in state bureaucracy; activism by state attorneys general; the impact on the legal system of the increasing numbers of women and minority judges; why crime rates and rates of imprisonment have declined recently; gambling and American Indian casinos; the economic recession and the drop in state revenues; the effects of e-commerce on sales tax revenues; economic and political diversity among suburbs; smart growth strategies; population growth in rural areas; education reform, charter schools, and the role of the federal government in public education; and successes and failures of welfare reform.

Preparation of this edition was greatly aided by the thoughtful comments of many people. As always, several anonymous (to us) reviewers of the last edition of the book helped bring to our attention numerous places for improvement. Reviewers included: J. Theodore Anagnoson, California State University, Los Angeles; Charles A. Hantz, Danville Area Community College; Lori Klein, Harding University; Rick S. Kurtz, Central Michigan University; Phillip W. Roeder, University of Kentucky.

Others who helped enrich this edition and helped us avoid errors of commission and omission include Timothy G. O'Rourke, Dean, Fulton School of Liberal Arts, Salisbury University; David A. Warner, Maryland Department of Legislative Services; and staff at the Knight Library and the John E. Jaqua Law Library of the University of Oregon.

As with past editions of this book, we had superb editorial direction from Monica Eckman and we benefited greatly in this edition from the hands-on management of Angela Kao. Excellent copyediting by Sheryl Rose greatly improved the clarity and accuracy of the book.

David C. Saffell

Harry Basehart

CHAPTER 1

The Setting of State and Local Government

POINTS TO CONSIDER

- How state government activities have been affected by the decline of the national economy, the threat of terrorism, and the war in Iraq.
- How state policy is influenced by economic factors, physical setting, political culture, sectionalism, and racial/ethnic diversity.
- The impact of immigration on California and many other states during the last thirty years. Should the United States reduce the number of immigrants admitted annually to the country?

- The nature of population change in states and cities, especially in the Sunbelt, and how this has affected public policy in the past forty years.
- The projected impact of changes in United States population by region and in terms of race and ethnicity in the next twenty-five years. How is life in the United States likely to change when whites no longer are the majority group?
- The composition of state constitutions and their historical evolution.
- The legal position of cities and how this affects their policy making.
- The process by which state constitutions are amended. What is the best way to accomplish significant constitutional change?

STATES IN THE TWENTIETH CENTURY

The states dominated American government in the nineteenth century and the first decade of the twentieth century. However, several events in the first half of the twentieth century relegated the states to a position of secondary importance. Ratification of the Sixteenth Amendment (relating to income tax) in 1913 gave the federal government much greater ability to raise money and to centralize policy making. The Depression showed the weaknesses of the states in responding to the nation's economic problems and led to greater focus on the president as the center of government. World War II further strengthened the authority of the president and the centralization of power in Washington.

The American States: United or Divided?

As the American population is becoming more diverse—whites will comprise about 50 percent of the nation's population in 2050—minority groups are becoming more concentrated regionally. Nearly 55 percent of all blacks live in the South, about half of all Hispanics live in the West, and nearly 55 percent of all Asians in the West. As black and white middle-class suburbanites from the North move to the Sunbelt states (South Atlantic Coast plus Texas and California) and as Hispanics and Asians move to New York, Florida, Texas, and California, new voting blocs are emerging. In the North, the political power of groups left behind (older whites) has increased.[1]

Increasingly, as in 2000, presidential candidates carefully craft their political messages to appeal to, and not to offend, dominant groups in various regions around the country. As regions become more demo-graphically distinct, presidential campaigns become more like balancing acts and less like acts of leadership. In particular, what candidates say in presidential primary races can vary greatly from South Carolina to Michigan.

In this chapter we will look at differences in policy making in various regions of the country, and we will consider how migration and immigration are affecting the American political system. This has been an ongoing process since the beginning of the nation.

Is present-day regional division by race and ethnicity a dangerous trend? If so, how is it likely to affect American politics in the coming years? What incentives are there for presidential candidates, especially in primary elections, *not* to pander to the interests of regional voting blocs?

State reform has been taking place since the early twentieth century, but the negative image of corrupt and incompetent state government persisted (and with good reason) into the early 1960s.[2] Since the mid-1960s, more than forty states have ratified new constitutions or made significant changes in existing ones. Governors' terms have been lengthened and their powers increased. Legislatures have become more professional (see Chapter 5) and more representative of urban interests, and nearly all meet in annual sessions. Court systems have been unified (see Chapter 7), and intermediate appellate courts have been added in many states. State bureaucrats are more professional, and the number of state employees under some form of merit system has increased from 50 percent in 1960 to nearly 80 percent, with nearly all state employees covered by merit systems in nearly three-fourths of the states (see Chapter 6). An increase in party competition in the states, followed by the election of energetic governors and the relaxation of federal directives, have led to more innovative state policies. In addition, cuts in federal aid have caused local governments to look more to the states for financial help (see Chapter 2).

This resurgence of the states was well under way when Ronald Reagan was elected president in 1980. Reagan believed that the federal government had done too much and that more responsibility for policy making should be turned over to the states. In addition, federal categorical grants-in-aid (see Chapter 2) were criticized by congressional conservatives and by state and local officials for their red tape and insensitivity to local problems. The timing of Reagan's changes in policy and philosophy thus caught the states at a point at which they were the most capable of assuming new policy making responsibilities. Unfortunately, the states also found themselves without some of the financial assistance they had come to expect from the national government. By 1990, states and localities faced severe financial pressures brought on by the recession and cuts in federal funds. A majority of states raised taxes, spending was cut, and employees were furloughed or fired in the early 1990s.

By the mid-1990s the financial position of most states and cities had improved as the national economy rebounded. Many states cut taxes and boosted spending for social services and infrastructure, and some put money away for a "rainy day." But the boom years for virtually all governments ended with the dawn of the new century. As the bubble burst on high-technology companies, stock values plummeted, unemployment rose, and state and federal budget surpluses turned to deficits (see Chapter 8).

Following federal tax cuts in 2001, dozens of states that tied their tax codes to federal rates had to make major code changes to avoid the loss of tax revenue. States also have had to absorb increases of about 10 percent annually in Medicaid costs. When they turned to the federal government, whose policies were adding to their woes, for financial help, states found that the Bush administration was preoccupied by its war on terrorism and that the federal budget surplus of 2000 had disappeared. Congress and the president promised to help pay for the training of "first responders" to deal with another terrorist attack, but the funds have not been authorized.

President Bush's 2003 budget called for more tax cuts and no significant direct assistance to the states. When the war against Iraq began, financial pressures on the federal government made assistance to states even less likely. At the same time, state and local security expenses grew, and many local police were called up to military service.

As a result of the combination of a sluggish domestic economy, international terrorism, and war, states faced what the National Governors Association called "the worst crisis in state finances since World War II." Only a few states, such as New Mexico and Wyoming, where there was a natural gas boom, were exempt from the crisis.

By 2002 nearly all states reported revenues below forecasts, with a gap of nearly $50 billion between revenues and projected spending. The gap was projected to be even greater in the next two years. States across the country responded by cutting spending, canceling capital projects (such as roads and bridges), and closing some state parks.[3] So-called rainy-day funds soon were depleted. At the same time that Congress approved a $330 billion package of rebates and tax cuts in 2003, it provided only $20 billion in aid to states and cities over the next two years. Of that, $10 billion was directed to Medicaid assistance.

CONTINUED STATE VITALITY

In 1998 Garry Wills commented, "States and localities are manifesting a new energy, almost a frenzy, in starting, altering, or killing programs."[4] In education, Wills noted that states had developed charter schools, introduced vouchers for private schools, retrenched in the use of bilingual education, and ended affirmative action in colleges. To fight crime, they had reintroduced the death penalty and passed "three strikes and you're out" laws. In politics, they had enacted term limits for legislators and created public financing of campaigns. In welfare, many states were ahead of the federal government, establishing "from welfare to work" programs. In the areas of welfare reform, the environment, and health care the states reversed a trend for most of the last century in which the federal government centralized programs and controlled resources.

Despite the array of financial problems we have outlined above, states have managed to maintain their vitality as we move into the twenty-first century. This is especially true in the area of regulation of business, where Congress and the president have been conspicuously reluctant to take effective regulatory action.

New York State's attorney general, Elliot Spitzer, has been in the forefront of taking legal action against Wall Street securities firms, reminiscent of the state action against tobacco companies in the 1990s. In 2001 and 2002 several state attorneys general joined Spitzer's investigation of the cozy relationship between securities companies and large corporations. Spitzer won a $100 million settlement with Merrill Lynch and he sued other brokerage firms. In 2003 Spitzer moved against mutual fund managers.

Peter A. Harkness notes that in 2002 the California legislature passed legislation forcing automobile companies to reduce greenhouse emissions and to make cars and trucks more fuel efficient.[5] Because the vehicle market in California is so large, it gives the state unusual power over major automotive corporations. In addition, nine other states challenged the federal court settlement of an antitrust action against Microsoft.

State vitality was evident in the ways in which states and local governments across the country quickly responded to the terrorist attacks of September 11, 2001. Although state-level intergovernmental cooperation worked well, there often was an absence of effective coordination among federal agencies and between federal agencies and state and local officials. With the creation of the Department of Homeland Security, coordination improved among government agencies. The Iraq war put more pressure on state and local governments to devise new ways to deal with security issues.

Current state vitality is part of a long history of innovative policy making by state governments. Wisconsin serves as a classic example: In 1900–1914, that state initiated the direct primary, civil service regulations, a state income tax, conservation laws, and a variety of state regulatory commissions. Studies done in the 1960s indicated that larger, wealthier, industrialized states were the most innovative.[6] Still, states that were innovative in one area were not necessarily innovative in other areas.[7] More recently, political scientists have found that innovation often comes in response to fiscal crisis. Other factors affecting state innovation include the influence of other states in their region and response to federal financial incentives.

In pioneering research, Jack L. Walker and others defined *innovation* as the adoption of laws modeled after those in other states. Other definitions of innovation looked at the creation of new programs, and they went beyond the enactment of legislation to consider executive actions and administrative programs.

While recognizing that there is a certain amount of follow-the-leader **diffusion of policy innovation,** recently political scientists have suggested that the pattern of diffusion more often resembles a convoy in which states as a group head in a common direction. Some states may break away from the convoy, but no state wants to fall too far behind those states in front of it. Even among states that adopt a broadly defined type of innovation, specific differences may exist, and some states may never adopt a given policy. For example, thirty-seven states created a wide variety of charter school programs in the 1990s, while thirteen states did not make any serious effort to adopt this innovation (see chapter 10).[8] When convoys become very compact, that is, when many states have nearly identical policy, the pattern is said to resemble a "pack."

As we will see in Chapter 6, a host of cities and counties across the country have been busy "reinventing government" by changing their budget processes; moving to prevent problems, such as crime and pollution, instead of treating symptoms; empowering citizens to manage public housing; privatizing public services; and establishing enterprises that make money. For example, some sewerage facilities are transforming sludge into fertilizer and selling it at a profit.

Much more so than federal government policy, what states and localities do directly affects everyday life. These governments not only have the major responsibility for education, crime, AIDS and other health problems, and welfare administration, but also they determine public university tuition, the price of subway fares, where and when we can purchase alcoholic beverages, whether soda bottles are returnable, and how much we pay for electricity. Most of these issues, even those that may appear trivial, generate strong political reactions from groups that have economic or ideological interests in public policy outcomes.

Political activity within the states is another indication of vitality. The activities of political parties and the management of campaigns and elections occur mainly in state and local settings. All elected public officials, except the president, are selected by voters within the states. Political parties have their organizational base in the states, with their power lodged most firmly in county committees and city organizations. Many members of the U.S. Congress initially held state or local office. Once elected, many senators and representatives devote much of their time (and the time of their staff members) to "casework"—that is, representing the interests of their local constituents in dealing with federal agencies. In election campaigns they often focus their attention on local issues. In electing a multitude of state and local officials (plus participating in federal elections) and in deciding special ballot issues, such as higher tax rates for schools, voters experience a nearly continuous process of campaigns and elections. By holding the first presidential primary, New Hampshire exerts a disproportionate influence on national politics. In the 2000 presidential election, Republican governors played a major role in the nomination of fellow-governor George W. Bush.

STATE POLICY MAKING

Economic Factors

Public policy making is affected by a variety of factors operating outside the formal structure of state and local governments. A state's economic characteristics—including levels of urbanization, personal income, and education—influence political decision making as well as the nature of political participation and party competition.[9]

One example of the effects of economic factors on policy making is funding for education. Wealthy, urbanized states, such as Michigan, New Jersey, and New York, spend considerably more per capita on education than do less prosperous, rural, southern states. Although wealthy states can obviously afford to spend more money per capita on social services than can poor states, their willingness to spend should be differentiated from their ability to spend. In education, some relatively poor states, such as Iowa and Vermont, make a stronger effort to assist their schools than do some rich states (i.e., their educational spending as a proportion of personal income is greater than that of wealthier states). Still, those poor states with relatively high tax rates are unable to match the per-pupil expenditures of wealthier states where the tax effort (or burden) is less. The term *tax burden* refers to taxes as a percentage of personal income; it expresses a relation between total taxes and total income in a state. The tax burden is lower than the national average in New Jersey because personal income is high and tax rates are relatively low.

The willingness to spend money often is tied to such political factors as the role of political parties, the influence of public opinion, and the leadership of the governor. These political factors help to explain why differences in spending levels exist among rich states and why some poor states make substantially greater efforts than other poor states. As we will see later in this chapter, willingness to spend money also is related to political culture and state tradition.

As far as political participation is concerned, party competition usually is stronger in the more wealthy, urbanized states, and voter turnout tends to be higher in those states as well. A few interest groups are more likely to dominate government in poor states, such as South Carolina and West Virginia, whereas in wealthier states a variety of interest groups tend to balance one another. The economically well-developed states also have been the most likely to adopt new policy ideas. Although there are many exceptions to economic explanations (see the sections that follow), they do provide us with one of several useful approaches to understanding state politics.

Physical Setting

In a country as diverse as the United States, the physical environment affects the decisions of the state governments in many ways. Geographically large states have huge rural legislative and congressional districts that make political campaigning and representation much different from those of the small districts of New Hampshire. Large states, such as Wyoming and Montana, often spend significantly more per capita to maintain their highways than do smaller states, such as Maryland and Massachusetts. In addition, the presence of natural resources may affect state policies significantly. Oil and natural gas interests have had a major impact on government in Oklahoma and Texas. For most of the twentieth century the Anaconda Company (copper) was the dominant political force in Montana. When it was unable to comply with new environmental standards in the 1970s, Anaconda ended all mining operations in Montana.[10] The distribution of water rights has had a tremendous influence on politics in such western states as Arizona and California. Water shortage is a permanent circumstance in Los Angeles, where the annual rainfall is a scant nine inches. Farms and cities from Salt Lake City to San Diego are literally drinking the Colorado River dry. In many western states nearly 90 percent of water is used by agricultural interests. This can create strong conflict when, as in Arizona, urban populations outnumber traditionally powerful rural interests. The existence of such geographical features as mountains, deserts, and lakes within a state may cause special problems and influence the allocation of state resources. Historically, physical features influenced the flow of migration and helped shape political institutions. For example, Utah is one of the most geographically isolated states, and Mormons chose to settle there largely for that reason.

Alaska is as large as the combined area of the twenty-two smallest states. Rural states such as Alaska, Montana, Wyoming, and the Dakotas have state legislative districts that are much larger than congressional districts in most states. While their representatives must travel great distances to see their constituents, state legislators in New England states practice a kind of neighborhood, personal style of politics.

Consider some of the physical features of California—features that subject its political decision makers to contrasting pressures from interest groups as well as force them to acquire knowledge about a wide array of technical matters. The state stretches for 650 miles, from the Mexican border to the Oregon state line. The Sierra Nevada Mountains extend for about 400 miles along the eastern border of the state. Temperatures range from harsh cold and deep snow in the High Sierras to unbearable heat in Death Valley. Northern California has ample water, but southern California must import its water. The same state that has produced the Los Angeles freeway system also has the agriculturally rich Central Valley where 90 percent of all fresh vegetables consumed in the U.S. are grown.

California is so physically and culturally diverse that since it achieved statehood in 1850 nearly thirty propositions have been made in its state legislature to split up the state. The latest, in 1992, calls for three states: a predominantly rural Northern California, Central California with San Francisco and Sacramento, and Southern California with Los Angeles and San Diego.[11] Rural, northern Californians argue that unfunded state mandates and unfair legislative districting have helped push their counties toward bankruptcy. They also contend that their political power has been weakened by legislative redistricting that strengthened urban areas. The 1992 proposal by Assemblyman Stan Statham of Shasta County passed in the Assembly, but died in the Senate Rules Committee.

For nearly a hundred years a group of northern California and southern Oregon counties have pushed for the creation of the state of Jefferson. In both states, residents of rural counties contend they often are forgotten by remote legislators in their state capitals.

Another secessionist movement in California has involved residents of the San Fernando Valley who want to split from the city of Los Angeles. Separated from the rest of the city by the Santa Monica Mountains, the Valley has nearly 1.5 million people and about half the land area of Los Angeles. Its residents contend that they have been short-changed on a variety of city services and that with Los Angeles sprawling over 467 square miles it is just too big for a single government to be effective. After years of complaining, secessionists succeeded in getting the issue on the 2002 ballot and at the same time there was a separate vote for Hollywood to secede from Los Angeles. Under California law, a vote to secede must be approved by a majority of the area that wants to secede *and* by a majority of the entire city.[12] The San Fernando Valley vote failed when 66 percent of the total city voters said no (among Valley residents the secessionist vote was split nearly 50-50). Sixty-eight percent of the residents of Hollywood voted against secession. Before the election, the city built new parks and roads in the Valley and pushed a program to give more policy making power to neighborhood councils. Following the vote, the *Los Angeles Times* suggested in its lead editorial that Valley residents "claim victory and come home" to Los Angeles.

Under the U.S. Constitution, a state can be divided if its legislature and Congress agree. Historically, Vermont, Maine, Massachusetts, and Kentucky were carved out of existing states. Because Texas was an independent nation when it was annexed to the United States, it was given the right to divide itself into as many as five states.

Population size and the presence of large metropolitan areas also have important effects on state politics. In the mid-1970s, the financial problems of New York City threatened the fiscal stability of New York State and involved the governor in extended negotiations with private bankers and the federal government to help "save" New York City. In the early 1990s the state's budget deficit led to cuts for projects in New York City. City dwellers demand more services—health care, welfare, sanitation, recreation, slum clearance, public housing—than do residents of small towns. These demands are transmitted to state legislative and gubernatorial candidates, who cannot ignore city voters as they campaign for office. In New York, Illinois, Pennsylvania, and Michigan, to name a few, serious conflicts between major cities and the rest of the state have long existed within state government. In Illinois nearly two-thirds of the state's population lives in the Chicago metropolitan area.

The Impact of Immigration

Largely because of their geographical location, a few states have attracted large numbers of immigrants who both benefit those states' economies and add to the cost of public services. Throughout the 1990s, about 1 million immigrants entered the United States each year, more than were admitted to all other countries in the world combined. The

2000 census showed that about 31 million Americans came from abroad. This was 11.3 million more than in 1990. Large numbers of people continue to enter the country illegally each year, and they are not included in these official figures. The percentage gain in the decade of the 1990s was the second largest in the twentieth century, exceeded only by the increase in immigrants from 1900 to 1910.[13] The United States has become the most racially diverse country in the world.[14]

Immigration has continued to surge since 2000, swelling the nation's foreign-born population to more than 33 million in 2003. The number of legal and illegal immigrants is largely independent of American economic conditions because life is so much worse in immigrant-sending countries. However, increased security checks have somewhat reduced the numbers of immigrants.

Of the 3.3 million immigrants who came to the United States in the first fifteen months of the twenty-first century, about 1 million were from Mexico. Money sent back to Mexico by illegal immigrants keeps entire villages financially afloat. "Regularization" (amnesty for illegals) was backed by the Mexican government and President Bush, but after September 11, 2001, immigration reform was put aside. In 2004 President Bush proposed granting legal status to undocumented workers in the United States.

In 2000 there were about 7 million illegal immigrants in the United States, up from an estimated 5.8 million in 1996. Mexicans comprised 69 percent, or 4.8 million, of the illegal immigrants, with 2.2 million of them living in California. California was home to about one-third of the nation's illegal immigrants, down from 42 percent of the total in 1990. In 1960 the United States was nearly 90 percent white; in 2000 it was 71 percent white; and by 2050 it is estimated that whites will be a bare majority of the population. In 2001 Hispanics became the largest minority group in the United States, with 37 million people, compared to 36.2 million African Americans. The Hispanic population is projected to increase from about 12 percent in 2000 to 25 percent in 2050, and the Asian population will increase from 4 to nearly 10 percent of the U.S. population. In 2050 African Americans will comprise about 13 percent of the American population, about the same percentage as in 2000 and only 2 percent more than in 1900. There will be about 40 million more Hispanics than blacks in 2050.

In the 1990s about half of all foreign-born immigrants settled in five states—California, Texas, New York, Florida, and Illinois—and nearly 70 percent of the nation's foreign-born population lives in those states.[15] Eight large metropolitan areas—New York City, Los Angeles, San Francisco, Chicago, Miami, Dallas, Houston, and Washington, D.C.—were home to nearly 60 percent of the foreign-born population in 2000. Curiously, California, New York, and Illinois had net losses of both foreign-born immigrants and domestic immigrants to other states in the 1990s. Overall, the United States population is projected to increase by 50 percent by 2050, but without immigration population would slowly decline in the next half century.

As noted in the chapter-opening box, the influx of new foreign-born immigrants, along with domestic migration, has a significant impact on regional politics. For example, in the six **"Melting-Pot"** states (Figure 1-1) non-Hispanics constituted 61 percent of the voting population in 2000, compared to 71 percent of the voting population overall in the United States.[16] Continued migration of whites and the return of blacks to the South has created a group of **"White-Black Gainer"** states in the southeast. The addition of northern suburban whites should keep that region politically conservative, but

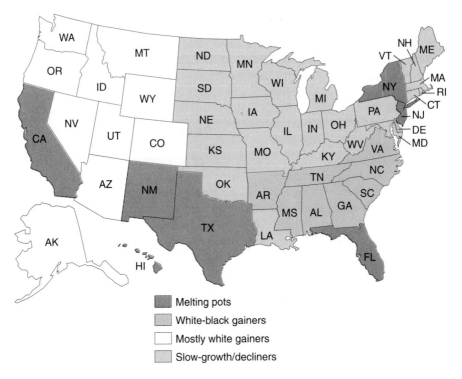

Melting pots
White-black gainers
Mostly white gainers
Slow-growth/decliners

FIGURE 1-1 Voters on the move.

Source: William H. Frey, "The New, Regional U.S. Politics," *Population Today* (October 2000), p. 1. Analysis of U.S. Census Bureau sources by William H. Frey. Used with permission of the Population Reference Bureau.

the increase in black voters will likely make the South overall more liberal than in the past.

The **"Mostly White Gainer" states** in the West are experiencing significant in-migration of whites; for example, Californians moving to Nevada and Colorado. The majority of the states (29) are in the interior of the country where there has been little population gain. Still, the 2000 Census represented the only time in the twentieth century in which all states in the nation gained population. The **"Slow-Growth/Decliner" states** in the interior of the country are 81 percent white and 12 percent black, with little domestic or international in-migration.

The influx of immigrants has rekindled debate about the economic and social impact of the nation's immigration policy. Although states bear much of the costs, immigration policy is set by the federal government. The debate has been most intense in California, where the number of immigrants in the 1990s was nearly double that of the second state, Texas. From 2000 to 2001 there were about 270,000 immigrants to California, or one-fourth the total for the United States.

A study prepared by the Rand Center for Research on Immigration Policy concluded that California's economy has benefited from these new low-paid, productive employees. Still, the heavy concentration of refugees and low-income immigrants has created heavy users of public services.[17] The impact has been greatest on California's public education system. In addition, as the state's economy shifts to higher-skilled technology, job prospects for newly arriving immigrants decrease.

California voter resistance to higher taxes to support public services for immigrants led to passage in 1994 of Proposition 187, which barred illegal aliens from receiving welfare, education, and nonemergency health care.* Proposition 209, approved in 1996, ended affirmative action in state education and employment. This measure was seen as a backlash against Hispanics, whose large voter turnout helped make the margin of victory less than expected. Proposition 227, approved in 1998, ended bilingual education in California schools.

Washington state voters approved an anti-affirmative action initiative in 1998, and since the 1980s more than twenty states have passed English-only laws, which clearly are aimed at Spanish-speaking immigrants. Curiously, these actions are very similar to those taken by the states near the end of the nineteenth century and in the early twentieth century when, for example, the Wisconsin and Illinois legislatures prevented public schools from teaching any foreign languages.

The Rand Center suggests that the number of legal immigrants admitted to the United States annually should be reduced and that better balance should be found between low-skilled people admitted for family reasons and skilled immigrants admitted for economic reasons. If that seems like too much social engineering, they recommend that the federal government provide financial assistance to those states most affected by immigration. The nation, Rand suggests, should help pay the bills for California because federal policies created the problems.

Political Culture

Although explanations based on economics and physical characteristics are helpful in understanding state politics, there remain a significant number of exceptions to the rule. Economic conditions do not explain the high levels of voter turnout in Montana, Idaho, Wyoming, and Utah, where levels of income and urbanization are below the national average. Some states with low levels of personal income, such as West Virginia and Kentucky, provide surprisingly high welfare benefits. In contrast, while Nevada ranked fifteenth in personal income per capita in 2000, it ranked fiftieth in welfare spending as a percentage of income and forty-fifth in education spending as a percentage of income. In this section, we note some of the vast differences that exist even among states within the same geographical area.

Sometimes states that have similar economic and demographic characteristics are very different politically. A case in point is the adjacent states of Michigan and Ohio. They are alike in terms of population, industrialization, and urbanization. Both have many small towns and rich farmland. In both states, there is significant party competition. In both, organized labor is a strong political force. Yet Michigan has been a much more progressive state than Ohio. It has allocated proportionately greater expenditures for social welfare services, and it has experienced significantly less corruption in gov-

*Proposition 187 immediately was challenged in federal court, where it was overturned. The state appealed that decision, but in 1999 dropped its legal action, meaning that only a few minor provisions of Prop. 187 were enforced.

ernment. In Ohio, on the other hand, the **spoils system,** in which political parties give public jobs to their supporters, has been more prevalent than in Michigan.

Another example is the neighboring states of Vermont and New Hampshire. Both are small and predominantly rural. Yet Vermont, the poorer of the two states, ranks among the highest in terms of tax burden, whereas New Hampshire ranks among the lowest. Vermont has been a center of public-spirited activism, but New Hampshire is characterized as a stronghold of stingy government. The former Socialist mayor of Burlington, Bernie Sanders, has been Vermont's Independent U.S. Representative since 1991. Much of the reason for these differences appears to lie in the political cultures of the two states.

Political culture is defined by Daniel Elazar as "the particular pattern of orientation to political action in which each political system is embedded." Elazar notes that "the study of political culture is related to the study of culture as a whole."[18] Culture refers to a "way of life": It is learned behavior based on communication within a society. Political culture, says Elazar, sets limits on political behavior and provides subtle direction for political action. In the following analysis, political culture is understood to encompass political tradition and the rules governing political behavior. For students of state government, political culture helps explain differences in political attitudes and government concerns from state to state. In large part, political culture determines what policies can be expected from state government, the kinds of people who become active in political affairs, and the way in which the political game is played in particular states and their communities.

Each state has its own history and traditions that are reflected in differences in its population's concerns and attitudes toward political life. In many states, differences among nationalities are important to understanding politics. For example, Irish Catholics in Massachusetts and Jews in New York have played major roles in forming distinctive patterns of political participation in those states. The Civil War and Reconstruction left a lasting mark on the political systems of Southern and border states. The **Progressive movement** early in this century had a major impact on the political processes in Wisconsin, Minnesota, and the Dakotas. In particular, Progressivism created an intense distrust of party organizations and reliance on widespread citizen participation. Alaska and Hawaii have truly unique histories and cultures because of their geographical isolation and their mixtures of racial and ethnic groups. Residents of some states have a strong sense of identity with their state, but it has been suggested that the dominant fact of political life in New Jersey is that residents do not and never did identify with their state.[19]

Elazar identifies three political cultures that can be found throughout the United States—**individualistic, traditional,** and **moralistic.**[20] These cultures have their roots in the three geographic regions of colonial America. The individualistic culture developed in the business centers of New York, Philadelphia, and Baltimore; the traditional culture developed in the plantation society of the Old South; and the moralistic culture arose out of the tradition of Puritanism and town meetings in New England. As waves of settlers moved westward, these three cultures spread throughout the United States. In many instances, two or three cultures met, meshed together, and produced a variety of state and sectional cultural strains. In Illinois, Indiana, and Ohio, this mixing of political cultures produced complex politics and caused conflicts that have persisted over decades.

Political scientist Daniel Elazar uses the concept of cultural "geology" to illustrate how the three political subcultures (moralistic, traditionalistic, and individualistic) spread across the United States and subsequently were modified by local conditions.[21] In Elazar's descriptive words, as great streams of immigrants moved west and stopped in various places, they deposited their relatively clear-cut political cultures. In many cases, other populations stopped in the same locations and deposited their cultures. Sometimes these "deposits" were side by side, in other cases they were on top of each other; and in some cases they overlapped. Over time, external events, such as economic depressions, eroded these cultural traditions, or they may have modified or strengthened them. At any rate, the result was something like strata in exposed rock that's been blasted out for an interstate highway—a look into the past and present.

Politics in the three political cultures can be described with respect to (1) degree of political participation, (2) development of government bureaucracy, and (3) amount of government intervention in society. Of the three dimensions, degree of political participation (i.e., voter turnout and suffrage regulations) is the most consistent indicator of political culture. In individualistic political cultures, participation is limited because politics is viewed as just another means by which individuals may improve their economic and social position. Because corruption is accepted as a natural part of politics, its disclosure is unlikely to produce public protest. In moralistic cultures, political participation is regarded as the duty of each citizen in a political setting where government seeks to promote the public welfare of all persons. In traditional cultures, voter turnout is low and voting regulations are restrictive. Here government is controlled by an elite whose family and social position give it a "right" to govern. In many cases citizens are not even expected to vote. Corruption tends to be even more widespread in traditional than in individualistic states because politics is not oriented toward the **public interest,** and it is expected that payoffs will occur.

In regard to the development of government bureaucracy, individualistic cultures limit government functions and provide only those few basic services demanded by the public. Bureaucracy is distrusted because of its potential to encroach on private matters, but it often is used to advance the personal goals of public officials and in the past the spoils system provided government jobs to political supporters. In moralistic cultures, bureaucracy typically is permitted to expand to provide the public with the wide range of services it demands. Here government commitment to the public good, honesty, and selflessness leads to low levels of corruption. Traditional cultures tend to be antibureaucratic, because a professional bureaucracy would interfere with the established pattern of personal relations developed by politicians.

In regard to government intervention into community affairs, both individualistic and traditional political cultures strive to protect private activities by limiting government intrusions. Government action in the individualistic political culture is largely limited to encouraging private economic initiative. In traditionalistic cultures government's role is limited to maintaining the existing social order. The moralistic culture, in contrast, fosters a definite commitment to government intervention; government is viewed as a positive force.

Those who represent the moralistic political culture may oppose federal aid to some local projects because they favor community responsibility for local problem solving. **Communitarianism** (communal activism) often results in innovative new approaches to problems that may not be perceived by the general population. Communitarians are both liberal *and* conservative. Although they favor liberal programs, such as public housing, that support equality, they also favor conservative programs, such as mandatory testing for AIDS, that seek to impose social order in communities.

The moralistic political culture also differs from the other two cultures in that its political campaigns are marked by an emphasis on issues rather than personalities. Parties and interest groups are organized to direct policy in the public interest.

Each culture has made both positive and negative contributions. Elazar notes that the moralistic culture, although it has been a significant force in the American quest for the good society, tends toward fanaticism and narrow-mindedness—roughly parallel to groups that claim to have found the "true religion." In spite of widespread corruption, the individualistic culture of the Northeast and many large Midwestern cities did facilitate the assimilation of immigrant groups into American society. Moreover, some corruption occurs in all states, and it does not necessarily affect the delivery of public services. Although the predominant traditional culture in the South has helped sustain racial discrimination and second-rate demagogues, it also has produced a significant number of first-rate national leaders and effective governors.

Elazar's theory has been subjected to vigorous investigation from critics who charge that it is static and impressionistic. But most of his conclusions linking policy to political culture have been confirmed. Political scientist Joel Lieske has refined Elazar's three categories, using race, ethnicity, and religion to identify a number of subcultures within a single state.[22] Other researchers have found greater policy innovation in moralistic states than in states with other subcultures. When people move, those raised as moralists tend to remain moralistic, while those raised as traditionalists or individualists are more likely to adapt to their new cultures.[23]

One significant departure from Elazar's work is a study by Rodney E. Hero and Caroline J. Tolbert that argues that much of state politics and policy is a product of racial/ethnic diversity.[24] They suggest that Elazar's categories may be largely a function of diversity. For example, moralistic states are the least ethnically diverse and individualistic states are the most ethnically diverse. Hero and Tolbert found a number of strong relationships between diversity and policy. For example, as state minority diversity increases, African Americans have higher school graduation rates and state Medicaid expenditures are lower.

As we have noted, political culture has been found to have a strong impact on political participation: It is higher in moralistic states. Moralistic states also are more likely to support social programs that are generous to the poor, and public officials in those states are less corrupt than in traditionalistic and individualistic states. Although there is independent evidence linking political culture with policy making and citizen participation, other factors that we explain in this chapter—economic factors, physical setting, and sectionalism—also affect state politics. Often it is difficult to isolate the impact of any one factor. Because economic factors are easier to quantify (that is, we have lots of economic data to examine), political culture often is used to explain state political behavior when social or economic factors are inadequate.

There is some evidence to suggest that distinctive state and local cultures are weakening because of population mobility, especially in the **Sunbelt** states—the fifteen states extending from southern California through Arizona, Texas, Florida, and up the Atlantic coast to Virginia. The change has arisen because of the growing importance of the news media, especially television, nationwide and because federal grants have encouraged states to enact a variety of programs under which they can receive matching funds. As we noted in earlier discussions of policy diffusion, national movements are likely to be enacted differently, or not at all, among the states depending on their political cultures.

Sectionalism

Adjacent states tend to share some persistent political similarities. States within particular areas, sharing a common cultural, economic, and historical background, exhibit clearly identifiable political tendencies. This is known as **sectionalism.** Major sections as defined by the U.S. Bureau of the Census are the Northeast, the North Central states, the South, and the West. Within each section we can identify several regions, such as the Southwest (West) and the Middle Atlantic (Northeast). The component states of the various sections and regions define problems and formulate public policy in a similar manner.

The *South*, which includes the eleven former Confederate states plus the border states of West Virginia, Kentucky, Delaware, Oklahoma, and Maryland, has long been the most clearly identifiable section of America. Throughout most of the South, there is widespread poverty, levels of educational attainment are generally low, and government functions are centralized at the state level. In the South, state governments often perform many of the government functions typically carried out by cities and counties in other sections of the country. As in other sections, it often is difficult to tell whether policy is influenced more by geographical location or by economic factors. Moreover, as in other sections, major exceptions to the general rule can be identified. For example, West Virginia has had a high level of interparty competition; considerable wealth exists in parts of Texas, Virginia, and Florida; and politics in Atlanta is vastly different from politics in Yazoo County, Mississippi. Florida's large Cuban population and its high percentage of northern-born whites make it different from other southern states.

From the Civil War until after World War II, the South remained solidly Democratic. Southern states began to vote for Republican presidential candidates in the 1950s and steadily elected more Republican governors, state legislators, and U.S. Congress members during the next three decades. In 1994, Republicans won a majority of U.S. House and Senate seats in the South. Republicans also have made unprecedented gains in southern state legislatures since 1994. Except for Democratic gains in 1998, Republicans continued to gain strength in the South through the 2000 elections. In 2002 a firm political shift in power was evident as Georgia elected a Republican governor for the first time since Reconstruction. In 1965 there was only one Republican governor (in Oklahoma) in the sixteen census-defined southern states; following elections in 2003 there were ten Republican governors. In 2003 Republicans controlled both houses of the Texas legislature and the governor's office for the first time since 1870.

Although the South has undergone dramatic political and social change, "the Southern way of life" continues to bind southerners, black and white, together. Despite great urban growth, traditional courthouse politics in small-town county seats continues to characterize the South more than any other section of the country.[25]

In the *Northeast* (the six New England states plus the Middle Atlantic states of New York, Pennsylvania, and New Jersey), most states share problems of congestion and industrialization. Levels of party competition and voter turnout are comparatively high. There is an emphasis on local government decision making stemming from the New England tradition of town meetings. As a result, government functions are much less centralized than in the South. On a regional basis, Boston continues to be the economic and educational hub of New England, and New York City dominates the Middle Atlantic states in terms of culture and business. In many northeastern states a substantial number of children attend parochial schools. Yet major differences exist between the northern northeastern states, which have been predominantly rural and Protestant (Maine, New Hampshire, and Vermont), and the southern northeastern states, which have been predominantly urban and Catholic (Rhode Island, New York, Connecticut, Massachusetts, Pennsylvania, and New Jersey). There is a great contrast between the wealth of suburban Connecticut and the poverty of rural Maine and Vermont. Without military installations or large public works projects, northeastern states lack a highly visible federal presence.

The eleven states of the *West* (including the Rocky Mountain, Desert, and Pacific Coast states), which comprise nearly 60 percent of the land mass of the continental United States, share problems of natural resource development, population diffusion, and water distribution. Most western states have relied heavily on resource extraction with little economic diversity. This has produced a history of boom-or-bust economic cycles. Despite their political conservatism and dislike of the federal government, the western states have depended heavily on federal aid, and government is the major employer in several of these states.[26] In fact, no other section of the country is more dependent on federal aid, which provides water, rangeland, and fire control assistance that keeps much of the West from becoming a desert. In eleven of the western states, the federal government owns at least 28 percent of the land. The federal government owns 83 percent of the land in Nevada and 48 percent in California. As noted, there can be great geographical diversity in just one state, such as California, and there are vast cultural differences between residents of San Francisco and those of Salt Lake City. Geographically, California is about the same size as Japan and its population is comparable to that of Argentina. As with other sections of the country, we need to be careful about stereotyping the West. Although there have been great population increases in metropolitan areas, such as Los Angeles, Las Vegas, Phoenix, and Seattle, other parts of the West have experienced population decline since the 1970s. For example, Wyoming lost 3.4 percent of its population in the 1980s and became the nation's least populous state, and in the 1990s its population increased by less than the national average.

Typically, the western states are marked by high levels of voter turnout and relatively weak party organizations. Although Democratic–Republican competition is keen in state elections, these states have been strongly Republican in presidential elections. In the 1968 and 1972 presidential elections, Richard Nixon carried every western state (except Washington in 1968). In 1976, Gerald Ford lost only Texas and Hawaii among all states west of Minnesota. In 1980 and 1984, Ronald Reagan carried all the western states. And in 1988, George Bush carried all the western states except Washington and Oregon. Bill Clinton broke the trend by carrying a majority of the eleven Rocky Mountain and Pacific Coast states in 1996, but in 2000 George W. Bush won seven of those eleven states.

The *North Central* (Great Lakes and Great Plains) states each have a blend of agricultural, industrial, and urban areas. There is strong two-party competition and above-average wealth, particularly in the Great Lakes states. However, the twelve North Central states are the least homogeneous of the four sections. Because the North Central section borders on each of the other three sections, some of its regional areas share the characteristics found in other sections. As with the other sections, there are major internal contradictions. Politics in Indiana, Ohio, and Missouri often has centered on patronage, jobs, and personalities (a reflection of their Southern heritage), but in Minnesota, Wisconsin, and Michigan it has been issue-oriented and government has been essentially corruption-free.[27]

The Great Plains region includes parts of ten West and North Central states, extending south from Montana and North Dakota to New Mexico and Texas. It is where rainfall begins to lessen and the tall grasses of the prairies become shorter. This area, with very hot summers and cold winters, has been called the Empty Quarter. Recently there has been a movement in North Dakota to change the state's name to "Dakota" in an effort to alter the state's image as a cold, inhospitable place and attract new residents and businesses.[28] No state has ever changed its name, and this issue is not likely to go much beyond a debating topic in Fargo.

The Great Plains comprises about 20 percent of the territory of the lower forty-eight states, with a population of about 6.5 million people. Nearly 40 percent of the counties in this region have been losing population continuously since 1950. In the 1990s, forty-seven of North Dakota's fifty-three counties lost population, and throughout the Great Plains many counties lost more than 20 percent of their population. In 1990 Kansas had more "frontier land"—counties with less than six people per square mile—than it had in 1890. Ninety percent of Nebraska and South Dakota was frontier in 1890 and remained that way in 2000.

Although the Great Plains are emptying and many counties are becoming nearly all white (all but three of the 767 residents of Slope County, North Dakota, were white in 2000), there are more American Indians and bison in the Plains than at any time since the 1870s.[29] In the 1990s the Indian populations in North Dakota, South Dakota, and Nebraska grew by 12 to 23 percent. Even as Indians return, they still comprise less than 10 percent of the population in South Dakota and Oklahoma, the states with the highest percentages of Indians.

POPULATION SHIFTS AMONG SECTIONS

Americans are a highly mobile people, and movement from the cities to the suburbs and from one region to another has added a dynamic dimension to state politics. In 2000 about 80 percent of Americans lived in one of the 353 **metropolitan statistical areas (MSAs)** in the United States. There were only 170 MSAs in 1950. As defined by the Census Bureau since 1983, a county may qualify as an MSA if it contains a city of at least 50,000 population or if it contains an urbanized area of 50,000 or more population and a total metropolitan population of 100,000 or more. An MSA can be one county or group of counties. There is at least one MSA in every state. There are twenty **consolidated metropolitan statistical areas (CMSAs)** that encompass two or more adjoining

MSAs and have at least 1 million people (see Table 1-1). New Jersey is completely within MSAs and seven other states are more than 90 percent metropolitan. That the United States is becoming increasingly metropolitan can be seen in statistics showing that 56 percent of the population in 1950 lived in metropolitan areas, and nearly 90 percent of the nation's population growth since 1980 has occurred in the forty largest metropolitan areas.

The density, heterogeneity, and interdependence of urban life have created obvious political problems in the areas of health, housing, and crime. The spread of the suburbs (in extreme cases creating vast, sprawling developments—as along the East Coast, southern California, and southern Lake Michigan)—has fragmented government and

TABLE 1-1 The 25 Largest Metropolitan Areas, 1990–2000

Rank	Metropolitan Area	Population in 1990	Population in 2000	Percent Change, 1990–2000	Rank in 1990
1.	New York-Northern N.J.-Long Island, N.Y.-N.J.-Conn.-Pa. (CMSA)	19,549,649	21,199,865	8.4%	1
2.	Los Angeles-Riverside-Orange County, Calif. (CMSA)	14,531,529	16,373,645	12.7	2
3.	Chicago-Gary-Kenosha, Ill.-Ind.-Wisc. (CMSA)	8,239,820	9,157,540	11.1	3
4.	Washington-Baltimore, D.C.-Md.-Va.-W.Va. (PMSA)	6,727,050	7,608,070	13.1	4
5.	San Francisco-Oakland-San Jose, Calif. (CMSA)	6,253,311	7,039,362	12.6	5
6.	Philadelphia-Wilmington-Atlantic City, Pa.-N.J.-Del.-Md. (CMSA)	5,892,937	6,188,463	5.0	6
7.	Boston-Worcester-Lawrence, Mass.-N.H.-Me.-Conn. (CMSA)	5,455,403	5,819,100	6.7	7
8.	Detroit-Ann Arbor-Flint, Mich. (CMSA)	5,187,171	5,456,428	5.2	8
9.	Dallas-Fort Worth, Tex. (CMSA)	4,037,282	5,221,801	29.3	9
10.	Houston-Galveston-Brazoria, Tex. (CMSA)	3,731,131	4,669,571	25.2	10
11.	Atlanta, Ga. (MSA)	2,959,950	4,112,198	38.9	13
12.	Miami-Fort Lauderdale, Fla. (CMSA)	3,192,582	3,876,380	21.4	11
13.	Seattle-Tacoma-Bremerton, Wash. (CMSA)	2,970,328	3,554,760	19.7	12
14.	Phoenix-Mesa, Ariz. (MSA)	2,238,480	3,251,876	45.3	19
15.	Minneapolis-St. Paul, Minn.-Wisc. (MSA)	2,538,834	2,968,806	16.9	15
16.	Cleveland-Akron, Ohio (CMSA)	2,859,644	2,945,831	3.0	14
17.	San Diego, Calif. (MSA)	2,498,016	2,813,833	12.6	16
18.	St. Louis, Mo.-Ill. (MSA)	2,492,525	2,603,607	4.5	17
19.	Denver-Boulder-Greeley, Colo. (CMSA)	1,980,140	2,581,506	30.4	21
20.	Tampa-St. Petersburg-Clearwater, Fla. (MSA)	2,067,959	2,395,997	15.9	20
21.	Pittsburgh, Pa. (MSA)	2,394,811	2,358,695	−1.5	18
22.	Portland-Salem, Ore.-Wash. (CMSA)	1,793,476	2,265,223	26.3	23
23.	Cincinnati-Hamilton, Ohio-Ky-Ind. (CMSA)	1,817,571	1,979,202	8.9	22
24.	Sacramento-Yolo, Calif. (CMSA)	1,481,102	1,796,857	21.3	26
25.	Kansas City, Mo.-Kans. (MSA)	1,583,000	1,778,000	12.2	25

Source: Bureau of the U.S. Census, *Metropolitan Areas Ranked by Population: 2000:* MSAs, CMSAs, and PMSAs as defined by the Office of Management and Budget, June 30, 1999, revised 1990 census population counts.

made metropolitan planning and coordination extremely difficult. There are forty-nine MSAs that have more than 1 million population and two with populations that exceed 10 million (Table 1-1). The increasing metropolitanization of the U.S. population masks the fact that Americans in this century have become less likely to live in large cities. For example, the percentage of our population living in cities over 1 million peaked in 1930. Currently a smaller percentage of people live in cities over 1 million than was the case in 1900. The least metropolitan state is Vermont (27.8 percent).

Particularly during the 1950s and 1960s, great numbers of lower-income southern blacks and Appalachian whites moved into northern cities such as Chicago, Detroit, and New York, greatly compounding the financial problems of those city governments. Since the 1980s there has been a large increase in the number of Asians and Hispanics in many American cities. About two-thirds of immigrants to the United States from 1980 to 2000 settled in ten metropolitan areas. The population of New York City increased by 685,000 in the 1990s, but without immigrants it would have lost over 350,000 people.

In the 1990s there was a record black migration to the South. Atlanta led all the metropolitan areas in total black population gains in the 1990s, and there were large black increases in Miami, Houston, and Dallas. High rates of black migration are projected to continue through 2025. As noted in the chapter-opening box, these patterns of migration have led to increasing regional concentrations of minority groups, and they are changing the nature of national political campaigns.

GROWTH IN THE SUNBELT

In 1976 the Census Bureau reported for the first time that a majority of the U.S. population lived in the South and the West, and by the 2000 census nearly 60 percent of the nation's population lived in southern and western states. Nevada has been the fastest-growing state in every decade since 1970. From 1990 to 2000 it had by far the fastest growth of any state—66 percent. Across the southern part of the United States, from California to Virginia, only two states in the nation's Sunbelt grew by less than 10 percent in the 1990s (see Figure 1-2).

From 1940 through 2000, the population of Houston grew from 385,000 to 1,954,000; that of Phoenix from 65,000 to 1,321,000; San Diego and San Antonio each have gained more than one million people in the past sixty years. At the same time, Chicago lost nearly 800,000 people and St. Louis saw its population cut in half. In 2000 Detroit became the nation's first city to lose more than 1 million people. Its population peaked in 1950 with nearly 2 million. Philadelphia has lost 500,000 people since 1950 and currently has an inventory of 31,000 vacant lots and 26,000 abandoned residential structures.[30] Five of the nation's twenty-five largest cities lost population in the 1990s, and all of them except Washington, D.C. were in the Midwest and Northeast (see Table 1-2).

Many of the fastest-growing cities since 1970 have been mid-sized suburbs, close to interstate highways, located in the Sunbelt. For example, from 1970 to 2000 the population of Coral Springs, Florida, ballooned from 1,000 to 118,000; Gilbert, Arizona,

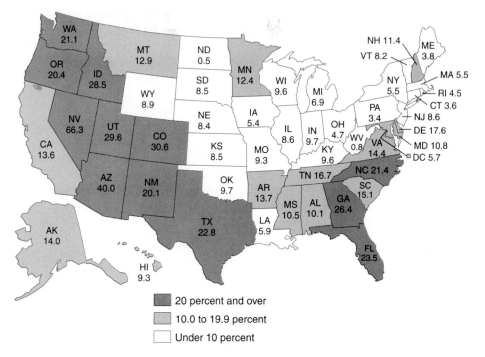

FIGURE 1-2 Percent population change: 1990 to 2000.

Source: *Statistical Abstract of the United States: 2001* (Washington: U.S. Government Printing Office, 2001), p. 7.

from 2,000 to 110,000. Las Vegas was by far the fastest-growing city in the 1990s, increasing by 113 percent and moving from the sixty-third to the thirty-second largest city in the country. All large cities that grew by more than 10 percent in the 1990s were in the Sunbelt. Still, some Sunbelt cities, such as New Orleans and Jackson, Mississippi, lost population in the last decade.

Population growth has been especially strong in state capitals and in university towns across the country in the past twenty years. Sunbelt state capitals with large state universities, such as Austin and Tallahassee, had especially strong growth. In many cases, state government generates jobs and helps the economy of an entire metropolitan area. In several instances, urban public universities have spurred economic growth and have become community social leaders. For example, the University of Alabama at Birmingham is the largest employer in the state.

In his groundbreaking book, *Power Shift,* Kirkpatrick Sale described the political implications of the major population shift to the South and West.[31] Sale argued that by the early 1970s America's southern rim, or Sunbelt, had come to dominate American politics as population, manufacturing, and capital moved from the North to the South. From 1960 to 2002, New York lost twelve seats in Congress and Florida gained thirteen. In 1960 California had thirty-two electoral votes, the same number as Pennsylvania; in 2002 California had fifty-five electoral votes, Pennsylvania only twenty-one.

TABLE 1-2 The 25 Largest Cities, 1990–2000

Rank	Population in 1990	Population in 2000	Percent Change 1990–2000	Rank in 1990
1. New York	7,322,564	8,008,278	9.4%	1
2. Los Angeles	3,485,398	3,694,820	6	2
3. Chicago	2,783,726	2,896,016	4	3
4. Houston	1,630,553	1,953,631	19.8	4
5. Philadelphia	1,585,577	1,517,550	−4.3	5
6. Phoenix	983,403	1,321,045	34.3	9
7. San Diego	1,110,549	1,223,400	10.2	6
8. Dallas	1,006,877	1,188,580	18	8
9. San Antonio	935,933	1,144,646	22.3	10
10. Detroit	1,027,974	951,270	−7.5	7
11. San Jose	782,248	894,943	14.4	11
12. Indianapolis*	741,952	791,926	6.7	12
13. San Francisco	723,959	776,733	7.3	14
14. Jacksonville*	635,230	735,617	15.8	15
15. Columbus	632,910	711,470	12.4	16
16. Austin	465,622	656,562	41	27
17. Baltimore	736,014	651,154	−11.5	13
18. Memphis	610,337	650,100	6.5	18
19. Milwaukee	628,088	596,974	−5	17
20. Boston	574,283	589,141	2.6	20
21. Washington, D.C.	606,900	572,059	−5.7	19
22. Nashville*	510,784	569,891	11.6	23
23. El Paso	515,342	563,662	9.4	22
24. Seattle	516,259	563,374	9.1	21
25. Denver	467,620	554,636	18.6	26

Source: U.S. Bureau of the Census.
*Consolidated city-counties. In 1990 Cleveland ranked 24th and New Orleans 25th.

Congressional redistricting for 2002 resulted in a switch of twelve seats. All the gainers, except Colorado (one seat) were in the Sunbelt, and most of the losers were concentrated in a nearly unbroken line from Massachusetts west to Illinois. Arizona, Georgia, Texas, and Florida each gained two seats.

Population projections suggest that the South and West combined will account for about 80 percent of United States growth between 2000 and 2025. Texas passed New York to become the nation's second largest state in the mid-1990s and Florida soon will replace New York as the third largest state. New York was the nation's largest state until the mid-1960s. California, Texas, and Florida contain nearly one-fourth the total United States population. Nevada's population gain in the 1990s exceeded the population of each of the six smallest states and California's gain of about 6 million people in the 1990s was greater than the population of about half the states.

CONSTITUTIONAL AND LEGAL LIMITS ON STATE ACTION

The U.S. Constitution on the one hand provides certain guarantees to the states and on the other hand imposes certain restrictions on state actions. For example, political integrity is protected by federal constitutional provisions that states cannot be divided or consolidated without state legislative consent. In addition, amendments to the Constitution must be ratified by three-fourths of the states. The Constitution limits state action by denying to the states the power to coin money or pass **ex post facto laws.** Treaties with foreign nations are binding on the states as the law of the land; and the Constitution and all laws made under it are the supreme law of the land.

The American system of federalism (discussed in detail in Chapter 2) distributes power in such a way as to deny the central government authority in only a few areas. However, the central government must rely on the cooperation of state and local governments to achieve most of its objectives. As a result, there is a great deal of sharing in policy making between the states and the federal government. Because the constitutional division of power between the states and the federal government is not precise, a dynamic relationship exists that allowed the federal government to move into many areas traditionally reserved to the states. Federal administrative actions, congressional statutes, and court decisions have imposed national standards that in some instances replace previously controlling local standards. Specifically, federal grants-in-aid (see Chapter 2) have given the national government the means to exercise powers concurrent with the states in many areas of policy making.

Federal court decisions have limited state action from the earliest days of the republic. In **McCulloch v. Maryland (1819)** and **Gibbons v. Ogden (1824),** the Supreme Court supported the supremacy of national law and broadly interpreted congressional power in interstate commerce (these decisions are discussed in Chapter 2). In the 1960s, decisions in the areas of civil rights, school integration, rights of criminal defendants, and voting qualifications expanded federal authority while limiting that of the states. As an instrument of the national government, the Supreme Court, under Chief Justice John Marshall and in most instances from the late 1930s through the 1980s, broadly construed the implied powers of Congress vis-à-vis the states and ignored the so-called reserved powers of the states (see the **Tenth Amendment**). However, as we will see in Chapter 2, the Court rediscovered the Tenth Amendment in the 1990s and consistently ruled against federal intrusion into state affairs.

STATE CONSTITUTIONS

Historical Development

State constitutions prescribe the structure of government, the powers granted various public officials, terms of office and means of election, and the way in which constitutional amendments shall be enacted.[32] Of course, provisions of the U.S. Constitution take precedence over state laws that may conflict with them. Some powers granted to the national government, such as regulation of interstate commerce, are denied to the states. However, other powers are reserved to the states and, as we will see in Chapter 2, many powers are shared by the states and the federal government.

It is difficult to generalize among the fifty state constitutions (Table 1-3). The oldest is that of Massachusetts, adopted in 1780; Georgia, Illinois, Louisiana, Montana, and Virginia have adopted new constitutions since 1970. The 1982 constitution in Georgia replaced a document well known for its excessive length (48,000 words) and excessive amendments. The new Georgia constitution eliminated approximately 1,200 local amendments added by voters over the years. Georgia has had ten constitutions and Louisiana has had eleven. The charters of the thirteen original states, which in most cases were extended into their constitutions, were only about five pages long. The U.S. Constitution has about 8,700 words. Among the states, only Vermont's is shorter (8,295 words). Alabama's constitution is more than three times longer than any other state's. Vermont has added fifty-two amendments to its 1793 constitution, and California has added over 500. The typical unamended state constitution is over three times longer than the federal constitution and has an average of 120 amendments.[33] Although nineteen states have their original constitution, most have had three or more.

Most state constitutions were written in the nineteenth century, when government power was distrusted. Only eighteen are twentieth-century documents. The reform movement of the early twentieth century focused on rooting out political corruption and bringing more popular participation through the initiative, recall, referendum, and direct primary.

Framework of Constitutions

In spite of their differences, a general framework of state constitutions can be presented. Most constitutions have a separate section that affirms the doctrine of separation of powers. All state constitutions have a preamble and a bill of rights. Like the United States Constitution, state preambles identify the source of authority (the people) and the purposes the constitution is intended to serve. Although preambles do not have legal authority, they serve as concise statements of basic principles envisioned by the state's founders. Often these sections contain obsolete provisions. For example, according to the Pennsylvania and Tennessee preambles, a state officeholder must not only believe in God but also in a future state of rewards and punishments. And in seven of the bills of rights, the honorable art of dueling is at issue. Many of these provisions, such as a belief in God, have been declared unconstitutional by the Supreme Court and others have been overturned by state law. Because of that, and because most of these provisions have not been enforced for many years, state legislators feel little political pressure to clean up obsolete language.

The newer constitutions, such as Alaska's and Hawaii's, omit any specific reference to the mutual exclusiveness of legislative and executive functions. Legislative articles have been strengthened since the 1960s so that most legislatures are considered to be in continuous session and empowered to meet annually. Executive articles limited the power of governors by creating large numbers of boards and commissions whose members often were independent of the governor. For example, before Michigan wrote a new

TABLE 1-3 General Information on State Constitutions
(As of January 1, 2002)

State or Other Jurisdiction	Number of Constitutions*	Dates of Adoption	Effective Date of Present Constitution	Estimated Length (number of words)	Number of Amendments	
					Submitted to Voters	Adopted
Alabama	6	1819, 1861, 1865, 1868, 1875, 1901	Nov. 28, 1901	310,296 (a) (b)	986	711 (c)
Alaska	1	1956	Jan. 3, 1959	15,988 (b)	40	28
Arizona	1	1911	Feb. 14, 1912	28,876	235	130
Arkansas	5	1836, 1861, 1864, 1868, 1874	Oct. 30, 1874	59,500 (b)	183	88 (d)
California	2	1849, 1879	July 4, 1879	54,645	842	504
Colorado	1	1876	Aug. 1, 1876	45,679	290	140
Connecticut	4	1818 (f), 1965	Dec. 30, 1965	16,608 (b)	30	29
Delaware	4	1776, 1792, 1831, 1897	June 10, 1897	19,000	(e)	136
Florida	6	1839, 1861, 1865, 1868, 1886, 1968	Jan. 7, 1969	52,421 (b)	117	87
Georgia	10	1777, 1789, 1798, 1861, 1865, 1868, 1877, 1945, 1976, 1982	July 1, 1983	37,849 (b)	75 (g)	57 (g)
Hawaii	1 (h)	1950	Aug. 21, 1959	20,774 (b)	116	97
Idaho	1	1889	July 3, 1890	24,232 (b)	204	117
Illinois	4	1818, 1848, 1870, 1970	July 1, 1971	13,700	17	11
Indiana	2	1816, 1851	Nov. 1, 1851	10,315 (b)	75	43
Iowa	2	1846, 1857	Sept. 3, 1857	12,616 (b)	57	52 (i)
Kansas	1	1859	Jan. 29, 1861	12,246 (b)	122	92 (i)
Kentucky	4	1792, 1799, 1850, 1891	Sept. 28, 1891	23,911 (b)	72	38
Louisiana	11	1812, 1845, 1852, 1861, 1864, 1868, 1879, 1898, 1913, 1921, 1974	Jan. 1, 1975	54,112 (b)	157	107
Maine	1	1819	March 15, 1820	13,500	200	168 (j)
Maryland	4	1776, 1851, 1864, 1867	Oct. 5, 1867	46,600 (b)	251	215 (k)
Massachusetts	1	1780	Oct. 25, 1780	36,700 (l)	148	120

State	Number	Dates	Effective date	Length	Col6	Col7
Michigan	4	1835, 1850, 1908, 1963	Jan. 1, 1964	27,649 (b)	59	23
Minnesota	1	1857	May 11, 1858	11,547 (b)	213	118
Mississippi	4	1817, 1832, 1869, 1890	Nov. 1, 1890	24,323 (b)	155	121
Missouri	4	1820, 1865, 1875, 1945	March 30, 1945	42,600 (b)	158	100
Montana	2	1889, 1972	July 1, 1973	13,145 (b)	45	25
Nebraska	2	1866, 1875	Oct. 12, 1875	20,048	328 (m)	219 (m)
Nevada	1	1864	Oct. 31, 1864	31,377 (b)	208	129
New Hampshire	2	1776, 1784	June 2, 1784	9,200	283 (n)	143
New Jersey	3	1776, 1844, 1947	Jan. 1, 1948	22,956 (b)	67	54
New Mexico	1	1911	Jan. 6, 1912	27,200	266	140
New York	4	1777, 1822, 1846, 1894	Jan. 1, 1895	51,700	288	215
North Carolina	3	1776, 1868, 1970	July 1, 1971	11,000	38	30
North Dakota	1	1889	Nov. 2, 1889	20,564	254	141 (o)
Ohio	2	1802, 1851	Sept. 1, 1851	36,900	264	160
Oklahoma	1	1907	Nov. 16, 1907	79,133 (b)	321 (p)	161 (p)
Oregon	1	1857	Feb. 14, 1859	63,372 (b)	456 (q)	227 (q)
Pennsylvania	5	1776, 1790, 1838, 1873, 1968 (r)	1968 (r)	27,503 (b)	34 (r)	28 (r)
Rhode Island	2	1842 (f)	May 2, 1843	10,908 (b)	105	59
South Carolina	7	1776, 1778, 1790, 1861, 1865, 1868, 1895	Jan. 1, 1896	22,300	668 (s)	483 (s)
South Dakota	1	1889	Nov. 2, 1889	27,703 (b)	213	111
Tennessee	3	1796, 1835, 1870	Feb. 23, 1870	13,300	57	34
Texas	5 (t)	1845, 1861, 1866, 1869, 1876	Feb. 15, 1876	93,000	583 (u)	409
Utah	1	1895	Jan. 4, 1896	11,000	148	98
Vermont	3	1777, 1786, 1793	July 9, 1793	8,295 (b)	210	52
Virginia	6	1776, 1830, 1851, 1869, 1902, 1970	July 1, 1971	21,319 (b)	44	36
Washington	1	1889	Nov. 11, 1889	50,237 (b)	166	94
West Virginia	2	1863, 1872	April 9, 1872	26,000	117	68
Wisconsin	1	1848	May 29, 1848	14,392 (b)	181	133 (i)
Wyoming	1	1889	July 10, 1890	31,800	112	69

See footnotes at end of table.   *(continued)*

TABLE 1-3 (concluded)

State or Other Jurisdiction	Number of Constitutions*	Dates of Adoption	Effective Date of Present Constitution	Estimated Length (number of words)	Number of Amendments	
					Submitted to Voters	Adopted
American Samoa	2	1960, 1967	July 1, 1967	6,000	14	7
No. Mariana Islands	1	1977	Jan. 9, 1978	11,000	55	51 (v)(w)
Puerto Rico	1	1952	July 25, 1952	9,281	6	6

Source: Survey conducted by Janice May, The University of Texas at Austin, March 2002.

*The constitutions referred to in this table include those Civil War documents customarily listed by the individual states.

(a) The Alabama constitution includes numerous local amendments that apply to only one county. An estimated 70 percent of all amendments are local. A 1982 amendment provides that after proposal by the legislature to which special procedures apply, only a local vote (with exceptions) is necessary to add them to the constitution.

(b) Computer word count.

(c) One Alabama amendment not counted in 1998 has been added to the total of proposals because the legal dispute has been resolved.

(d) Eight of the approved amendments have been superseded and are not printed in the current edition of the constitution. The total adopted does not include five amendments proposed and adopted since statehood.

(e) Proposed amendments are not submitted to the voters in Delaware.

(f) Colonial charters with some alterations served as the first constitutions in Connecticut (1638, 1662) and in Rhode Island (1663).

(g) The Georgia constitution requires amendments to be of "general and uniform application throughout the state," thus eliminating local amendments that accounted for most of the amendments before 1982.

(h) As a kingdom and republic, Hawaii had five constitutions.

(i) The figure includes amendments approved by the voters and later nullified by the state supreme court in Iowa (three), Kansas (one), Nevada (six) and Wisconsin (two).

(j) The figure does not include one amendment approved by the voters in 1967 that is inoperative until implemented by legislation.

(k) Two sets of identical amendments were on the ballot and adopted in the 1992 Maryland election. The four amendments are counted as two in the table.

(l) The printed constitution includes many provisions that have been amended. The length of effective provisions is an estimated 24,122 words (12,400 annulled) in Massachusetts, and in Rhode Island before the "rewrite" of the constitution in 1986, it was 11,399 words (7,627 annulled).

(m) The 1998 and 2000 Nebraska ballots allowed the voters to vote separately on "parts" of propositions. In 1998, 10 of 18 separate propositions were adopted; in 2000, 6 of 9.

(n) The constitution of 1784 was extensively revised in 1792. Figure represents proposals and adoptions since the constitution was adopted in 1784.

(o) The figures do not include submission and approval of the constitution of 1889 itself and of Article XX; these are constitutional questions included in some counts of constitutional amendments and would add two to the figure in each column.

(p) The figures include five amendments submitted to and approved by the voters which were, by decisions of the Oklahoma or U.S. Supreme Courts, rendered inoperative or ruled invalid, unconstitutional, or illegally submitted.

(q) One Oregon amendment on the 2000 ballot was not counted as approved because canvassing was enjoined by the courts.

(r) Certain sections of the constitution were revised by the limited convention of 1967–68. Amendments proposed and adopted are since 1968.

(s) In 1981 approximately two-thirds of 626 proposed and four-fifths of the adopted amendments were local. Since then the amendments have been statewide propositions.

(t) The Constitution of the Republic of Texas preceded five state constitutions.

(u) The number of proposed amendments to the Texas Constitution excludes three proposed by the legislature but not placed on the ballot.

(v) By 1992 49 amendments had been proposed and 47 adopted. Since then, one was proposed but rejected in 1994, all three proposals were ratified in 1996 and in 1998, of two proposals one was adopted.

(w) The total excludes one amendment ruled void by a federal district court.

Source: Book of the States 2002 (Lexington, KY: Council of State Governments, 2002), pp. 14–15. Used with permission of the Council of State Governments.

constitution in 1963, the executive branch consisted of the governor, six major elected officials, twenty-three executive departments, four elected boards, sixty-four appointed boards and commissions, six ex officio boards, and five retirement boards. Judicial articles typically have been marked by detail, multiplicity of courts, and overlapping jurisdictions. Here, too, many amendments have been added to establish new courts, alter the way in which judges are selected, and create a unified state judicial system.

Other constitutional articles deal with suffrage and elections, local government, particular economic interests (such as farming), and amendments. Although most rules and regulations regarding voting have been established by the states, a series of amendments to the U.S. Constitution (Fifteenth, Seventeenth, Nineteenth, Twenty-third, Twenty-fourth, and Twenty-sixth) have provided a degree of uniformity throughout the nation. Nevertheless, a few interesting examples may be cited. In Vermont, for example, the constitution requires "quiet and peaceable behavior" as a voting qualification. In some southern states before 1965, a person of "good character" might have been excused by the local voting registrar from taking a literacy test or complying with other regulations specifically established to disenfranchise African Americans.

Most newer state constitutions have separate articles on policy areas, such as education and welfare. In the 1980s and 1990s several states made changes to eliminate gender bias language in their constitutions. Most constitutions have a miscellaneous or general provisions article to lay out provisions that do not fit elsewhere or that apply to more than one section of the constitution. Eighteen states have an equal rights amendment, similar to the national amendment that failed to be ratified.

There were fewer constitutional amendments in the 1990s than in the 1970s and 1980s, but the number of changes brought out by the initiative process was at a record high. Mississippi became the eighteenth state to permit the constitutional initiative, and Rhode Island and New Jersey authorized the recall in the 1990s.

In contrast to the U.S. Constitution, most state constitutions are long, detailed, and heavily amended. There is a strong feeling that much of their detail should have been left to legislatures to determine by passing bills. Although length and detail are not necessarily bad, these characteristics have had great political significance in the operation of state government. Excessive detail is due in part to the successful efforts of interest groups to have constitutions specifically recognize and protect their economic concerns. Indeed, constitutions are longest in those states with the strongest interest groups. Unless amended, these provisions may hinder government regulation as changes in society occur. Duane Lockard notes that the complexity of state constitutions invites litigation and thus plays into the hands of those resisting change.[34] Opponents can often challenge new laws on the grounds that some detail of constitutional procedure was not properly followed. State courts have often tended toward a narrow interpretation of state constitutions, particularly limiting legislative and executive authority. Indeed, Lockard suggests that courts often have been so opposed to change that they reach beyond specific to general provisions to invalidate laws.

Since the 1970s, state supreme courts have been forces for change, not obstruction. In what is referred to as judicial federalism (see Chapter 2), many state courts have interpreted their own constitutions independently of the U.S. Constitution, especially in civil rights cases to support reformist goals. We need to remember that state constitutions are changed by judicial interpretation as well as by amendments. Very detailed constitutions make it more likely that amendments will be added as circumstances change and explicit provisions leave less leeway for change through interpretation. As a result, length and detail beget greater length through amendments.

Model Constitutions

Many state constitutions reveal a strong suspicion of government power, and they act as roadblocks to change. In particular, constitutional restrictions on gubernatorial power have made activist government in the twentieth century difficult. In many of the constitutions written in the nineteenth century, governors were limited to two-year terms; legislatures met as infrequently as every other year and only for a limited period (sixty to ninety days); legislative salaries were specified; most state officials, such as the attorney general and auditor, were elected rather than appointed by the governor; significant restraints were placed on borrowing; many special interests were exempt from taxation; and reapportionment in some cases required constitutional amendment. As noted in Chapter 6, much of the history of state governors can be written in terms of constitutional amendments to give them powers comparable to those of the president of the United States.

An effective state constitution—that is, one allowing government to take an active role in the initiation and implementation of policy—should include the following three fundamental characteristics:[35]

1. It should be brief and to the point. Constitutions are not legislative codes; all they should do is establish the basic framework within which state officials can act.
2. It should make direct grants of authority so that the governor and legislators can be held accountable by the voters for their actions.
3. It should be receptive to orderly change. The amendment process should not be too cumbersome, and the constitution should include enforceable provisions on redrawing legislative districts. Unfortunately, legislators often have a built-in resistance to change, and voters often defeat new constitutions at the polls when they are asked to accept or reject in total a new constitution.

To most people, state constitutions are painfully boring documents. They are not read by those seeking examples of stirring phrases or eloquent prose style. However, as we shall see throughout this book, there are few, if any, problems of state government for which the suggested solution will not sooner or later run headlong into constitutional prohibitions, restrictions, or obstructions. Constitutions are necessarily conservative documents that limit the exercise of political power. Because of the nature of state constitutions, there was a strong movement in the twentieth century to pass constitutional amendments aimed at increasing the power of legislators, governors, and judges and at providing an independent basis of power for local governments.

Probably the most unusual of all state constitutions was a proposal for the new state of New Columbia, which was approved by voters of the District of Columbia in 1982; a revised document was submitted to Congress in 1987. The proposed government structure called for a unicameral legislature, permitted public employees to strike, guaranteed a right to employment, and gave state benefits to persons unable to work because of pregnancy. It was rejected by Congress.

Constitutional Status of Cities

Because cities and counties are not mentioned in the U.S. Constitution, they fall under the control of states. This means that local powers are provided by state constitutions or by acts of state legislatures and that cities and counties are not given any protection against state interference.

Local governments are clearly subordinate to the state. In a classic statement, Judge John F. Dillon formulated **Dillon's Rule** (1868), which says that municipal corporations can exercise only those powers expressly granted by state constitutions and laws and those necessarily implied from granted powers. If there is any question about the exercise of power, it should be resolved in favor of the state. Guided by Dillon's Rule, many state legislatures passed legislation that affected only one or two cities, and they often enacted policy that concerned minor local matters. Although this rule has been accepted by the U.S. Supreme Court, Daniel Elazar notes that more than 80 percent of the states have rejected Dillon's Rule or have changed it to recognize the residual powers of local government.[36]

The powers that cities have under state law are spelled out under general statutes or in **city charters.** Until the 1850s, legislatures issued a special act or specific charter to explain the structure of government for individual cities. Because this was a time-consuming process, state legislatures moved to establish classified charters in which cities are put in general classes according to population. Under this system larger cities typically have a broader range of powers than smaller cities. Many states use optional charters in which voters can choose among several plans—mayor-council, manager-council, or commission—when a new city is incorporated.

Most states now provide **home rule charters** for cities (in 48 states) and counties (in 37 states), and two-thirds of cities with populations over 2,500 have adopted home-rule charters. Home rule modifies the traditional subordinate relationship of cities to states by permitting cities to draft and approve their own charters, and it limits the ability of states to act on certain local matters. Home rule cities are free to enact their own laws so long as they are not contrary to state law. There also is the recognition of implied powers for cities to do anything so long as it is not prohibited by state law. Variations in home rule provisions among the states mean that in some states there is extensive local discretion and in others local choices are very limited. In states with constitutional home rule, cities can adopt whatever form of charter they wish without getting legislative approval to spell out details. In other states, legislative home rule can be withdrawn or amended by a vote of the legislature. A few states have "self-enforcing" home rule provisions that permit cities to bypass state legislatures and enact home rule for themselves. In the other cases, cities must get legislative approval to have home rule. Broader grants of local self-rule mean that long, detailed provisions for cities in state constitutions can be shortened. In response to the passage of abusive nineteenth-century legislation aimed at a specific city, forty-one states prohibit passage of special laws unless a local government requests it.[37]

Curiously, in some states home rule has been resisted. David R. Berman notes that interest groups often oppose grants of power to local governments, preferring to deal with a single state legislature.[38] There also are regional differences; for example, the tradition of local authority in the South has limited the use of home rule. Home rule cities typically have more authority than do home rule counties. Only one in ten cities eligible to adopt a home rule charter has done so.

Amending Constitutions

There are four methods of changing state constitutions: legislative proposal, constitutional initiative, constitutional commission, and constitutional convention. **Legislative proposal** is available in all states, and it is by far the most commonly used means of change. In most states, a two-thirds or three-fifths vote of the legislature is required as the first step in approving an amendment. In seventeen states, only a majority vote is necessary. Although most states require approval in only one legislative session, twelve require approval in two consecutive sessions. Following legislative approval, the amendment is typically placed on the ballot, where a majority vote is needed for ratification. Only Delaware does not require voter approval of amendments, and New Hampshire requires a two-thirds majority vote. State legislators initiate nearly 90 percent of all proposed amendments. Voters approve about 75 percent of legislative proposals submitted to them.

The **constitutional initiative** can be used in eighteen states. It allows proponents of reform to have suggestions for limited change placed on the ballot. The process is time-consuming and often expensive for reform groups, especially in large states. Still, the number of constitutional initiatives rose to all-time highs during the 1980s and 1990s. Proponents must first get signatures on an initiative proposal. In California, for example, the number required is 8 percent of the total number of voters for governor in the last election. In a few states, the signatures must come from people distributed across the state. In Massachusetts no more than one-fourth can come from any one county. As a final step, there is a referendum vote, in which most states require a majority vote on the amendment for it to be approved.

Eighteen states use a constitutional initiative in which citizens by petition propose amendments that go directly to the voters. Only Massachusetts and Mississippi employ an indirect initiative, which is submitted to the legislature before it is placed on the ballot. Thirteen of the states employing the initiative are west of the Mississippi River. The initiative process is discussed in more detail in Chapter 3.

In the mid-1990s two state constitutional amendments approved by the initiative process were struck down by the Supreme Court. In *Romer v. Evans* (1996) a six-member majority overruled a Colorado amendment that nullified existing civil rights protection for homosexuals and barred passage of new laws by the state or localities that protected homosexuals. In 1995 the Court ruled against state-imposed term limits on U.S. Congress members.

Constitutional commissions, available in all fifty states, may be formed to study the state constitution and make recommendations for change, or their purpose may be to make arrangements for a constitutional convention. Only in Florida can a constitutional commission initiate and refer amendments to the voters. Most commissions have acted as study groups that turn their work over to state legislatures. As a result, they operate under less media and public scrutiny than do constitutional conventions. Commission size varies from as few as five members to as many as fifty. Members are usually appointed by the governor, legislative leaders, and chief justice of the highest court in the state.

Constitutional conventions are the oldest method of changing constitutions. Conventions are called by state legislatures, and in some cases they must be authorized to meet by the voters. Fourteen states require a vote on the question of calling a convention. In several states a vote must occur every ten years; in one case it is every twenty years. This means that voters at least will be reminded about constitutional reform on a regular basis. If constitutions were extensively changed even every ten years (which they aren't), it might reflect dangerous short-term responses to shifts in public opinion. Delegates to conventions usually are elected on a nonpartisan basis from state legislative districts. In most instances delegates have been white, middle-aged, professional men. In some cases the state legislature convenes as a constitutional convention.

Rhode Island (1986) was the last state to hold a constitutional convention. Its delegates were selected in nonpartisan elections in each of the state's 100 House districts. One delegate was elected governor four years later and several were elected to the legislature. The convention made structural changes, deleted old language, and included as constitutional provisions material that had been added as amendments. Before this it was said that the only way to read the Rhode Island constitution was backwards, starting with the amendments. Following the convention, voters approved eight of fourteen proposals made by the delegates. A different approach was taken in 1967 when New York's constitutional convention met for six months and in an up-or-down vote the state's voters defeated a new constitution.

Conventions may approve amendments, or they may propose completely new constitutions. Not surprisingly, less extreme changes in constitutions are more likely to be approved by voters than entirely new documents. The most recently adopted new constitution was in Georgia in 1982 where a constitutional convention was employed.

In 2000–2001, constitutional changes were proposed in forty states, the lowest number in forty years.[39] Nearly half occurred in three states—Alaska, Oregon, and Texas. Of the 212 total amendments, 180 were by legislative proposal (a significant decline from recent decades) and thirty-two (comparable to recent years) were by constitutional initiative. Seventy-eight percent of the legislative proposals were adopted, and 40 percent of the initiatives were successful.

THE STATES CONTRASTED AND COMPARED

This chapter has pointed out the great diversity among the states in terms of culture, socioeconomic characteristics, population, and geography. In the chapters that follow, the reader should develop a clearer picture of *similarities* among the states. Most states have virtually the same patterns of government structure—they have bicameral legislatures organized by parties and by committees; their governors exercise similar constitutional powers in such areas as the budget and veto; and their judicial systems are organized in a common three- or two-tier arrangement of trial and appellate courts.

Although personalities differ and unique styles can be identified, political campaigns and elections proceed in the same general pattern in all the states. Particular circumstances dictate how each state and community will respond to demands for public policy. Yet every state must confront common problems in education, housing, transportation, welfare, health, and safety. Differences in political culture are becoming less distinct as people grow more mobile, as means of communication improve, and as an international economy develops.

Comparative analysis of politics in the fifty states reveals both similarities and differences. Because the states are alike in many ways, they offer social scientists the opportunity to make a wide range of comparisons. Because there also is great variety among the states and the thousands of local governments, it gives us the opportunity to study why structural and behavioral differences occur at particular times and under particular conditions.

Comparative state politics provides an excellent means to introduce the study of political science.[40] As we have noted, states have similar government structures and the variations in matters such as voter turnout and economics are interesting, but relatively limited. Moreover, state and local governments are primarily responsible for those public issues that most directly affect our lives—education, public safety, and transportation. Because most students come to their first course on state government with a considerable amount of general information, the study of comparative state politics is much more manageable than the study of international relations.

As noted at the beginning of this chapter, states have continued to be policy innovators even in financially troubled times. All of us should pay more attention to state governments because they determine most issues, big and small, that affect our daily lives. These include: "whether customers can smoke in restaurants and bars, whether children can be tried as adults . . . how many minority students will be admitted to state universities, how difficult it will be for women to get abortions, (whether) dog groomers (or) veterinarians (have) the right to brush a dog's teeth, . . . how much you will pay to get your car insured, how fast you can drive it, . . . whether your 10-year-old child legally can buy an assault weapon (yes in Arkansas)." And states control much of what cities can do. "Albany decides whether New York City subway trains have one crew member or two . . . and New Jersey has seized control of . . . schools (in Newark, Jersey City, and Paterson) and begun running them itself."[41]

SUMMARY

There has been a resurgence of state government, beginning with constitutional reform in the 1960s and extending into the twenty-first century as the predominant political mood in the country has favored the return of power to the states. Helped by a strong national economy and their own reform initiatives, states experienced budget surpluses in the late 1990s. But because of a decline in the national economy and the preoccupation of Congress and the president with fighting terrorism, most states have seen their surpluses disappear and have responded by increasing taxes and cutting services.

The nature of public policy varies greatly among the fifty states. Even states with similar economic and geographic circumstances may differ markedly in the amount of money they devote to particular policy areas. Differences in public policy making are explained by examining the impact of the following factors on the states: levels of economic development, physical setting, political culture, sectionalism, public opinion, and race and ethicity.

Shifts in population—to metropolitan areas, to suburbs, and to the South and West—have had major impacts on state policy making since the end of World War II. Projections are that these population trends will continue well into this century and that regional racial and ethnic diversity will have an impact on national politics.

Public policy making also is affected by state constitutions, which are conservative documents that have hindered change. Constitutional change mainly comes from legislative proposals for amendments and from direct initiatives in which the general public may recommend and approve amendments.

KEY TERMS

city charters
communitarianism
consolidated metropolitan statistical
   area (CMSA)
constitutional commission
constitutional convention
constitutional initiative
diffusion of policy innovation
Dillon's Rule
ex post facto law
Gibbons v. Ogden (1824)
home rule charters
individualistic culture
legislative proposal
McCulloch v. Maryland (1819)

Melting-Pot states
metropolitan statistical area (MSA)
moralistic culture
Mostly White Gainer states
political culture
Progressive movement
public interest
sectionalism
Slow-Growth/Decliner states
spoils system
Sunbelt
Tenth Amendment
traditional culture
White-Black Gainer states

SUMMARY OF STATE/LOCAL DIFFERENCES

Issue	States	Local Governments
Vitality	Innovations in education, health care, and welfare	Innovations in policing, controlling sprawl, and fighting illegal drugs
Political culture	Traditionalistic in the South, moralistic in the Northeast, individualistic in Mid-Atlantic states and spreading across the country	Individualistic culture tends to flourish in cities that are business centers
Population shifts	Gains in the Sunbelt, losses in the Great Plains, little change in the Midwest and Northeast	Gains in most Sunbelt cities, large losses in many Midwest cities, such as Detroit
Legal documents	Constitutions that prescribe the structure of state government	Cities and counties are legal creatures of the states, which control the kinds of charters they can have

INTERESTING WEBSITES

www.census.gov. U.S. Census Bureau's website. Lots of information; the "State & County QuickFacts" is particularly good. Also, find "Subjects A to Z" and click on the letter "G" to find the "Census of Governments" and other reports on state and local governments.

www.loc.gov/global/state/stategov.html. A Library of Congress Internet resource page that has links to state and local government information and to websites in each state.

www.law.cornell.edu/statutes.html. This website has links to the fifty state constitutions. Scroll down to "Constitutions, Statutes, and Legislative Information—By State."

NOTES

1. William H. Frey, "The New, Regional U.S. Politics," *Population Today* (October 2000), p. 1.
2. Larry Sabato, *Goodbye to Goodtime Charlie*, 2d ed. (Washington, D.C.: Congressional Quarterly Press, 1983), p. 8.
3. William T. Pound, "The Fiscal State of the States," *New York Times* (January 14, 2002), p. A15.
4. Garry Wills, "The War Between the States . . . and Washington," *New York Times Magazine* (July 5, 1998), p. 26.
5. Peter A. Harkness, "States of Amazement," *Governing* (June 2002), p. 4.
6. See Jack L. Walker, Jr., "The Diffusion of Innovations in the American States," *American Political Science Review* (September 1973), pp. 880–899.
7. See Virginia Gray, "Innovation in the States: A Diffusion Study," *American Political Science Review* (December 1973), pp. 1174–1185.
8. Greg M. Shaw and Tari Renner, "Patterns of State Policy Diffusion: Convoys, Packs, and Clusters." Paper presented at the Midwest Political Science Convention, Chicago, April 2002, p. 3.
9. See Thomas R. Dye, *Understanding Public Policy*, 9th ed. (Englewood Cliffs, N.J.: Prentice-Hall, 1998).
10. Thomas Payne, "Montana: From Copper Fiefdom to Pluralist Polity," in *Interest Group Politics in the American West,* Ronald J. Hrebenar and Clive S. Thomas, eds. (Salt Lake City: University of Utah Press, 1987), p. 77.
11. Charles Price, "The Longshot Bid to Split California," *California Journal* (August 1992), pp. 387–391. Also see Margo Price and Stephen Birdsall, *Regional Landscapes of the United States and Canada* (New York: John Wiley, 1999).
12. Joseph Kahn, "Valley Girls (and Guys) Push to Secede from Los Angeles," *New York Times* (April 20, 2002), pp. A1, 14.
13. Peter T. Kilborn and Lynette Clementson, "Gains of the 90's Did Not Lift All, Census Shows," *New York Times* (June 5, 2002), p. A20.
14. Joel Liske, "Race and Diversity," P.S.: *Political Science and Politics* (June 1999), p. 217.
15. William H. Frey, "U.S. Census Shows Different Paths for Domestic and Foreign-Born Migrants," *Population Today* (August/September 2002), p. 4.
16. William H. Frey, "The New, Regional U.S. Politics," pp. 1–3.
17. Kevin F. McCarthy and George Vernez, *Immigration in a Changing Economy: California's Experience* (Santa Monica, Calif.: Rand Corporation, 1997).

18. Daniel J. Elazar, *American Federalism: A View from the States,* 3rd ed. (New York: Harper & Row, 1984), p. 109.
19. Maureen Moakley, "New Jersey," in *The Political Life of the American States,* Alan Rosenthal and Maureen Moakley, eds. (New York: Praeger, 1984), pp. 219–220.
20. Elazar, *American Federalism,* pp. 114–122.
21. Elazar, *American Federalism,* pp. 122–141; and Elazar, *The American Mosaic* (Boulder, Colo.: Westview Press, 1994), pp. 237–252.
22. Joel Lieske, "Regional Subcultures of the United States," *Journal of Politics* (November 1993), pp. 888–913.
23. Russell L. Hanson, "The Political Acculturation of Migrants in the American States," *Western Political Quarterly* (June 1992), pp. 355–384.
24. Rodney E. Hero and Caroline J. Tolbert, "A Racial/Ethnic Diversity Interpretation of Politics and Policy in the States of the U.S.," *American Journal of Political Science* (August 1996), p. 853. Also see Rodney E. Hero, *Faces of Inequality: Social Diversity in American Politics* (New York: Oxford University Press, 1998).
25. Elazar, *The American Mosaic,* p. 140.
26. See Hrebenar and Thomas, eds., *Interest Group Politics in the American West,* p. 144.
27. See John H. Fenton, *Midwest Politics* (New York: Holt, Rinehart and Winston, 1966).
28. Mark Singer, "True North," *New Yorker* (February 18 & 25, 2002), p. 118.
29. Timothy Egan, "Indians and Bison Returning to Plains Others Abandoned," *New York Times* (May 27, 2001), p. A1.
30. Rob Gurwitt, "Betting on the Bulldozer," *Governing* (July 2002), p. 30.
31. Kirkpatrick Sale, *Power Shift: The Rise of the Southern Rim* (New York: Random House, 1975).
32. See Albert L. Strum, "The Development of American State Constitutions," *Publius* (Winter 1982).
33. G. Alan Tarr, *Understanding State Constitutions* (Princeton, NJ: Princeton University Press, 1998), p. 10.
34. Duane Lockard, *The Politics of State and Local Government,* 3d ed. (New York: Macmillan, 1983), chap. 4.
35. See National Municipal League, *Model State Constitution,* 6th ed. (New York: National Municipal League, 1968).
36. Elazar, *American Federalism,* p. 203.
37. Joseph F. Zimmerman, "Evolving State-Local Relations," *Book of the States 2002* (Lexington, Ky.: Council of State Governments, 2002), p. 33.
38. David R. Berman, "State-Local Relations: Authority, Finances, Partnerships," *Municipal Year Book 2001* (Washington: International City Management Association, 2001), p. 63.
39. Janice C. May, "State Constitutions and Constitutional Revision, 2000–2001," *Book of the States 2002* (Lexington, Ky.: Council of State Governments, 2002), pp. 3–4.
40. Christopher Z. Mooney, "Why Do They Tax Dogs in West Virginia? Teaching Political Science Through Comparative State Politics," *P.S.: Political Science and Politics* (June 1998), pp. 199–203.
41. All quotes from Charles S. Layton and Mary Walton, "Missing the Story at the Statehouse," *American Journalism Review* (July/August 1998), p. 46.

CHAPTER 2

Intergovernmental Relations

POINTS TO CONSIDER

- How has the United States system of federalism evolved since its creation?
- How should power be divided among levels of government? Is devolution a good thing? What domestic responsibilities should be the primary responsibility of the federal government?
- Compare and contrast the positions on federalism taken by presidents since the 1960s.
- Are block grants better than categorical grants? If so, why aren't there proportionately more block grants?

- In what sense does federalism "mean war" these days in the Supreme Court?
- Should the national government and the states be permitted to approve *any* unfunded mandates?
- Would you have been more satisfied if Congress or the Florida supreme court, rather than the U.S. Supreme Court, had determined the outcome of the 2000 presidential election?

FEDERALISM AS A POLITICAL CONCEPT

Most textbooks in the past discussed federalism in terms of structure and legal principles. This approach stressed the constitutional division of authority and functions between the national government and the states. As such, it was a static view of power being assigned to units of government and remaining fixed over a long time. The current approach suggests a much more dynamic notion of intergovernmental relations.

The U.S. Supreme Court v. The Florida Supreme Court

On December 12, 2000, by a 5-4 vote, the United States Supreme Court reversed a ruling of the Florida supreme court that had ordered a manual statewide recount of votes where no vote for president was machine recorded. The opinion was based on the lack of standards regarding how the manual recount would be conducted and the impossibility of completing the recount by the deadline provided by Florida law. This unprecedented intrusion into a state's election process by the Supreme Court effectively ended the overtime presidential election, giving George W. Bush Florida's twenty-five electoral votes and raising his total electoral votes to 271—one vote more than required for a majority.

Had the Supreme Court refused to rule in the case of *Bush v. Gore,* the matter would have been returned to the Florida supreme court, which ultimately would have had to rule on the validity of recounted votes, thus conceding the election to George W. Bush or Al Gore.

In the prolonged battle following the November election, Gore won twice in the Florida supreme court and Bush won twice in the United States Supreme Court. Critics on both sides of the issue point to the fact that all seven members of the Florida supreme court had been appointed by Democratic governors and that all five members of the Supreme Court majority had been appointed by Republican presidents. The decision caused many Americans to consider the political motives of judges.

In dissent, Justice Stevens criticized what he called George W. Bush's "unstated lack of confidence" in the Florida courts. Justice Ginsburg chided the majority for not deferring to state courts' interpretations of their own laws and, she said, "Were the other members of this Court as mindful as they generally are of our system of dual sovereignty, they would affirm the judgment of the Florida supreme court."

In this chapter we will discuss the Supreme Court's interpretation of "dual sovereignty," noting a series of opinions since the early 1990s that have limited federal authority and protected state sovereignty—that is, the ability of states to act without federal interference. After you read that section you can decide if *Bush v. Gore* was out of character for the Rehnquist Court.

Thus interpretation focuses not on *structure* but on *politics*. According to this view, levels of government share authority and power in an interdependent and constantly changing relationship of joint action. Federalism is regarded, in part, as a state of mind. For example, although the national government has the *legal* authority to take a wide range of actions, it is constrained by political and social forces that support state autonomy and resist centralization. As we will see in the chapters that deal with education, welfare, crime, and economic development, the decentralized nature of our system has a powerful impact on how money is spent and how problems are addressed.

We need to be reminded that there never was a time when federal, state, and local government affairs were completely separate. The traditional analogy of the American federal system as a "layer cake," with clear divisions between layers of government, was never true. Instead, it is more accurate to speak of the federal system as a "marble cake," in which government functions are shared by all levels.[1] Cooperative efforts by federal, state, and local governments have become increasingly necessary since the 1960s. A vast system of about 85,000 local governments fits together to serve a wide range of functions. In 2000 there were 3,043 counties, 19,279 municipalities, 16,656 towns or townships, 14,222 school districts, and 31,555 special districts. A suburban Pittsburgh resident, for example, may come under the jurisdiction of and pay taxes to nearly a dozen governments. The number of local government units per state ranges from four in Hawaii to more than 6,700 in Illinois.

In many ways states are at the center of an elaborate web of relationships among governments in our federal system.[2] States mediate differences among local governments and the national government. They manage affairs among their local governments. And through trade missions, states act as intermediaries between private businesses and foreign governments.

This sharing of functions is most clearly seen in federal grants-in-aid (which are discussed in detail later in this chapter). Most Americans favor the decentralization of power. At the same time, they want to solve problems. Grants-in-aid are a practical solution: The programs are funded by the national government but administered by state and local governments and even by nonprofit business firms. Virtually every function of local government has a counterpart federal program. As we shall see in this chapter, fiscal federalism provides the means by which the congressional majority's sense of basic policy needs directs and shapes public policy making in states and cities.

The Reagan administration believed that the expansion of grants-in-aid in the 1960s and 1970s represented a serious overreaching of federal authority. It was concerned that the state and local governments had become too dependent on federal funds and that federal regulations had become too intrusive. The Reagan administration also was convinced that state and local aid was taking too high a percentage of the federal budget (it had reached an all-time high of 17 percent of all federal spending in 1978). Although President George H.W. Bush continued to support the Reagan philosophy of limiting federal expenditures and giving more management responsibility to states and cities, funding for grants-in-aid increased substantially while he was in office.

Under President Clinton and a Republican-controlled Congress, power continued to flow to the states. New block grants, begun in the 1980s, gave states more flexibility to manage their affairs. In particular, the conversion of the nation's welfare system (formerly known as Aid to Families with Dependent Children) into a block grant

(Temporary Assistance to Needy Families) signaled a major change away from power in Washington.

The welfare system could be changed more easily than some other social programs because it had never been fully centralized. The George W. Bush administration has continued to support the idea of greater state flexibility, but as we will see at the end of this chapter, there may have been less devolution of authority to the states since 1992 than policy makers would have us believe.

As noted in Chapter 1, the reemergence of a federal budget deficit and preoccupation with fighting terrorism and the war in Iraq have led both Congress and the president to short-change states since 2001. Across the nation, states have struggled to find ways to deal with critical budget shortfalls. As a result, some of the attention of governors and legislators has been redirected from policy innovation to innovative ways to cut spending and increase revenue.

CREATION OF THE AMERICAN FEDERAL SYSTEM

The decision by the framers of the Constitution in 1787 to create a federal system of government may be viewed as a compromise between those who wanted to continue with a confederate form of government and those who wanted to change to a centralized system as existed in England. Under the Articles of Confederation, the national government lacked the authority to manage effectively the economic and international affairs of the nation. The population had strong loyalties to the states, and there was a general fear of centralized authority as it had been manifested in colonial America. A federal system offered unity without uniformity. By reserving to the states considerable power, it lessened the likelihood of centralized tyranny. A federal system seems appropriate for many developing countries because it is flexible and permits changes in the distribution of power among government units and in the balance of power without changing the fundamental charter of government.

A **federal system** may be distinguished from a **confederacy** in the following ways: (1) in a federal system, the central government is stronger than its member states in regard to the size of its budget and the scope of its jurisdiction; (2) in a federal system, national law is supreme; (3) in a federal system, the central government acts directly upon individuals in such matters as taxation and raising an army, whereas in a confederacy, the central government must act indirectly through the states when dealing with individual citizens; and (4) in a federal system, states may not withdraw from the union, but in a confederacy, they may secede. The most basic problem faced by confederations is that they must rely on member states to provide revenue voluntarily to the central government.

But federations often face many of the problems confronted by confederacies. Recently several federations, most notably the Soviet Union and Yugoslavia, have been pulled apart by regional conflict. Canada has faced a strong secessionist movement in Quebec for several decades.

A less flexible sort of system is the **unitary nation-state,** in which local governments can exercise only those powers given them by the central government. Unitary government exists in such nations as Great Britain, France, and Israel. In physically small countries, a unitary structure provides efficiency in dealing with national problems and ensures that national values will prevail. Because most nondemocratic nations have unitary systems, it means that only about twenty nations in the world are federations. Curiously, as American federalism has devolved power to the states in the last twenty years, so too have British and French unitary systems given more power to their subgovernments.

The relationship between states and cities in the United States is unitary. Legally, cities are creatures of the states, meaning that states have much greater control over cities than the federal government has over states. For example, state legislatures determine which taxes cities can impose and what the rate will be and what forms of government cities can have. Among the fifty states there are vast differences in how much authority cities are permitted to exercise.

Relations among states are **confederal,** meaning that all states are equal to each other. In a real sense their relations with each other are like relations among sovereign nations. As a result, when state representatives interact with each other they proceed diplomatically, recognizing others as their legal equals.

As discussed in Chapter 1, the U.S. Constitution provides guarantees to the states and imposes limits on their actions. The powers of the states are limited because substantial powers are delegated to Congress, and the supremacy clause makes very clear the subordinate relationship of the states to the national government:

> This constitution, and the laws of the United States which shall be made in pursuance thereof; and all treaties made or which shall be made under the authority of the United States shall be the supreme law of the land; and the judges in every state shall be bound thereby, anything in the constitution or laws of any state to the contrary notwithstanding.

The Constitution created a system of **dual sovereignty** in which the national government has the exclusive power to act in its sphere of influence, for example, in interstate commerce. At the same time certain constitutional powers are reserved to the states. These include ownership of property, regulation of domestic relations, prosecution of most crimes, and control of local government. As we will see later in this chapter, the line between national and state authority is not clearly drawn. This has led to disagreement among Supreme Court justices as to what is "truly local" and what is within the proper sphere of the national government.

To underline the limits of federal authority, the **Tenth Amendment** states: "The powers not delegated to the United States by the Constitution, nor prohibited by it to the States, are reserved to the States respectively, or to the people." Recent Supreme Court decisions regarding the Tenth Amendment are discussed later in this chapter.

THE EVOLUTION OF AMERICAN FEDERALISM

Relationships among governments in the United States have been dynamic, rather than stable. Figure 2-1 illustrates the changes in the distribution of power between the states and the federal government, and the general expansion of government from its creation to near the end of the twentieth century and projected into the near future. This

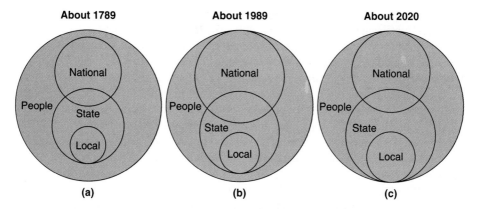

FIGURE 2-1 The distribution of constitutional authority in the United States.

Source: Russell L. Hanson, "Intergovernmental Relations," in Virginia Gray, Russell L. Hanson, and Herbert Jacob, *Politics in the American States,* 7th ed. (Washington: Congressional Quarterly Press, 1999), p. 39. Used with permission.

projection shows a reduced role for the national government and enlarged spheres for both state and local governments. As conceived by the framers (Figure 2-1a), federal authority was limited largely to foreign affairs, whereas state authority was relatively broad, and there was little overlap or cooperation between the two levels of government. Over time (Figures 2-1b and 2-1c), both federal and state authority have expanded, and federal activities are now greater than those of the states. The overlap in power between the states and the federal government also has increased greatly. The loss of power has been in those areas originally reserved to the people. Expanded government activity and regulation in such areas as environmental control and occupational safety inevitably limit the authority of private persons and businesses.

The increase in federal authority has been the result of various factors. In some cases states have encouraged Congress to enact national standards to prevent unfair economic competition. In the area of civil rights Congress has enacted legislation, and presidents have supported broad federal enforcement of laws and constitutional provisions. This, in turn, has led to a series of challenges in federal courts. As a result, federal courts (especially the Supreme Court) have acted as umpires in the federal system to decide where power should reside. As part of the national government, the Supreme Court most often in United States history has supported federal power over state power. However, in a series of decisions the Court since the early 1990s has limited the reach of federal law, restricting the ability of Congress to pass laws that were binding on the states.

Early Nineteenth-Century Federalism

McCulloch v. Maryland (1819) was the first examination by the Supreme Court of state-federal relations. The background of the case is as follows: Maryland had levied a tax on notes issued by all banks not chartered by the state of Maryland. McCulloch, the cashier in the Baltimore branch of the United States Bank, refused to pay the tax, and Maryland brought suit against him. After losing in Maryland state courts, McCulloch (as directed by the secretary of the treasury) appealed and the case was reviewed by the Supreme Court, headed by Chief Justice John Marshall.

Regarding the first issue—"Does Congress have the authority to charter a bank?"—the Court ruled that although this was not among the enumerated powers of Congress, it could be implied from the **"necessary and proper" clause** of the Constitution. Marshall reasoned that although the chartering of a bank was not absolutely indispensable in the performance of delegated Congressional responsibilities, it was, nevertheless, "convenient or useful to another objective." On the second issue—"Can the states tax an instrument of the national government?"—the Court ruled no. The power to tax, said the chief justice, is the power to destroy, and states cannot interfere with operations of the national government.

Shortly after *McCulloch,* the Marshall Court had another opportunity to rule in favor of a broad interpretation of national authority. *Gibbons v. Ogden* (1824) concerned the desire of New York and New Jersey to control shipping on the lower Hudson River. The states argued that the definition of **commerce** should be narrowly construed so as to include only direct dealings in commodities. Thus the regulation of shipping on inland waterways would be beyond the constitutional power of Congress. Marshall, however, ruled that the power of the national government to regulate commerce included all commercial activity. The Court stated: "This power, like all others vested in Congress, is complete in itself, may be exercised to its utmost extent, and acknowledges no limitations other than are prescribed in the Constitution."

The first federal money grants to states were made in 1837, when surplus funds were sent to the states with no restrictions regarding their use. Before that, federal land grants had been made to assist in the construction of schools, canals, roads, and railroads. The first Morrill Act, passed in 1862, provided land to states to establish agricultural colleges; these institutions became land-grant universities. Terms of the legislation foreshadowed more modern grants-in-aid because they required colleges to make annual reports and required governors to account for the use of federal funds.

Of course, the most serious threat to national authority came with the Civil War. Prior to 1860, John C. Calhoun proposed the concept of **concurrent majority.** In Calhoun's model each interest group (or state) had the right to decide independently whether to accept or reject national policy affecting it. Calhoun's idea was similar to the doctrine of **nullification,** under which each state could veto national legislation with which it disagreed.* Ultimately, the Southern states seceded from the Union. After the issue had been decided on the battlefield, the Supreme Court ruled in *Texas v. White* (1869) that: "Ours is an indestructible union, composed of indestructible states."

Dual Federalism

Between the Civil War and 1937, the Supreme Court followed the doctrine of **dual federalism** (the "layer cake" analogy), in which the distribution of powers between the federal government and the states was seen as fixed. In particular, the Court narrowly

---

*Following the passage of the Alien and Sedition Acts of 1798, the Jeffersonians developed the idea of "interposition." Under this doctrine, states were given the power to "interpose" themselves between their citizens and the national government if they believed that a national law affecting their citizens was unconstitutional. The Alien and Sedition Acts were repealed in 1801, and interposition was never reviewed by the courts.

defined commerce so as to exclude manufacturing. The effect was to prevent the state and national governments from regulating such matters as wages, hours, and child labor. Court opinions discouraged joint federal–state programs, and they kept the federal government out of most areas of domestic policy.

Dual federalism had its roots in the **compact theory of federalism** that was used as an argument for states' rights in the pre–Civil War period. As formulated by John C. Calhoun, this theory stated that the framers had created a system in which the United States was composed of sovereign states united through a compact. Power was given to the national government by the states, but the states could reclaim power by nullifying, or vetoing, laws passed by Congress that affected them. Thus the states operated separately from the national government.

Acting under the theory of dual federalism, the federal government in the 1920s turned away from social concerns supported by President Wilson, and the states were left to take action regarding such problems as care of dependent children. Federal domestic programs in the late 1920s were so limited that state spending was double federal spending.[3] States also were dominant over cities as policy makers, spending about three times as much money as local governments.

From 1860 until 1932 only two Democrats, Grover Cleveland and Woodrow Wilson, were elected president. When Franklin D. Roosevelt became president in 1932 the Supreme Court was dominated by conservative justices who had been appointed by Republican presidents. With a majority of its members continuing to apply the theory of dual federalism, the Supreme Court repeatedly overturned New Deal legislation from 1933 to 1937.

Cooperative Federalism

President Roosevelt's transformation of the Supreme Court began with his first appointment of a justice in 1937 (he ultimately appointed eight justices). With new members and a change of heart by some moderate justices, the Court reverted to the views of the Marshall era that the national government has broad authority under its implied powers and that the reserved powers under the Tenth Amendment do not limit national action. As a result the Court approved New Deal legislation that supported social and economic regulation, such as the federally prescribed minimum wage and a very broad interpretation of the power of Congress over interstate commerce. By the early 1940s, says Martin Shapiro, "The New Deal Court had effectively announced the constitutional demise of federalism as a limit on the power of the national government."[4]

State dominance quickly changed with the coming of the Great Depression. Cities, states, and private charities were overwhelmed by high unemployment rates that led to the homeless constructing tent cities and out-of-work men trying to sell apples on street corners. Faced with depleted budgets and fearing social rebellions, governors and mayors begged the federal government to come to their assistance. The election of Franklin D. Roosevelt in 1932, and the beginning of New Deal programs the next year, ushered in a new era in intergovernmental relations. Federal domestic spending tripled in the years leading up to World War II.

The size of state bureaucracy also increased from the 1930s through the 1960s.[5] This was because much of the increased federal aid was transferred to the states. In turn, state aid to cities (much of it federal aid passed on to local governments) stimulated a growth in city bureaucracy.

This era in intergovernmental relations has become known as **cooperative federalism.** Unlike dual federalism, in which there were differences between state and federal power and responsibilities, under cooperative federalism the system looked more like a "marble cake" in which federal power and responsibilities were intermingled. State and federal agencies undertook joint projects and power was shared, even as the role of the federal government expanded.

The modern-day structure of categorical grants-in-aid came into being in the 1930s when federal aid was provided almost exclusively to states.[6] Congress required states to submit plans for the use of the funds, to provide matching funds, and to allow federal audit and review of the programs. Under President Harry Truman, more federal aid went directly to local governments. Federal grants continued to expand under President Dwight Eisenhower, although there was some concern about the proper division of responsibility between Washington and the states. Federal aid tripled from 1952 to 1961 (reaching $7.3 billion), but dramatic change in the federal system did not occur until the mid-1960s.

In the 1960s and 1970s the Supreme Court became a nationalizing power itself, upholding provisions of the Voting Rights Act that called for federal registrars to replace state officials in several southern states. It ordered apportionment of both houses of state legislatures on the basis of population; and it ordered busing to achieve racial integration of public schools where segregation had been imposed by state law.

From 1965 to 1969 federal aid to state and local governments nearly doubled, to $20.2 billion. Under President Lyndon Johnson's **"creative federalism,"** more than 200 new grant programs were created. Johnson, who saw himself as a protege of Franklin D. Roosevelt, wanted to be remembered as the health, education, and welfare president. His "War on Poverty" program significantly increased the federal presence among the states. In many cases, states were bypassed and aid went directly to cities, counties, school districts, and nonprofit organizations. Although the first two block grants (explained later in this chapter) were created in 1966 (Partnership in Health Act) and 1968 (Safe Streets Act), the Johnson administration relied heavily on categorical grants (grants made for a specific purpose) to further national objectives.

Creative federalism evolved into another subset referred to by political scientists as **"coercive federalism."** As the number of federal grants grew, so too did federal rules attached to them. With the lure of grant money the federal government was able to coerce states and cities into complying with various regulations that they found unduly restrictive.

New Federalism

In the 1968 presidential campaign, Richard Nixon stressed his commitment to return power to the states and to cut administrative red tape. Americans seemed to be tiring of "big government" at home and abroad as the 1960s ended and conservatives were gaining political power in Washington. In fact, however, federal grants grew from $24 billion in 1970 to nearly $50 billion in 1975. Nearly 100 new categorical grants were created under the Nixon and Ford administrations as political pressure on individual members of Congress remained strong to send federal dollars to their districts. Nixon's **"new federalism"** did, however, establish general **revenue sharing,** which gave state and local governments greater discretion and flexibility in spending federal funds. Three new block grants giving recipients more freedom also were established.

The 1970s were marked by several significant changes in intergovernmental relations. We have noted the continued growth of federal grants. Grant eligibility was extended to virtually all local governments and many nonprofit organizations. As a result, by 1980 about 30 percent of all federal aid bypassed state governments, compared with 8 percent in 1960. Federal aid became available for a host of projects (e.g., libraries, historic preservation, snow removal, and development of bikeways) that had previously been state and local responsibilities. Thus state and local reliance on the federal government grew significantly. More procedural strings were attached to grants-in-aid, and more substantive strings were added to block grants. As a result, a coercive federal presence persisted and Nixon's "new federalism" failed to alter the relative power of the federal governments and the states.

As president, Jimmy Carter spoke of a "new partnership" in referring to intergovernmental relations. This was a return to Johnson's policies and a retreat from Nixon's new federalism. Carter called for a greater urban focus, expanded intergovernmental programs, and a leadership role for the federal government. Categorical grants remained dominant, and the federal government maintained direct access to local governments. It is significant that there was a clear shift in federal aid policy in the second half of Carter's term. Carter pulled back from his urban aid proposals, and the national political mood (as evidenced in "tax revolts" across the country) began to call for cuts in government programs. This shift became a focal point of the Reagan administration.

Under Ronald Reagan's "new federalism" plan, the first substantial effort was made to reduce the tide of centralization that had been growing since the 1930s. After his first year in office, Reagan cut federal aid to state and local governments by about $6.5 billion. About sixty categorical aid programs were dropped, and more than seventy-seven others were consolidated into block grants. Essentially, the administration sought to retrench by cutting the federal budget and to "devolve" domestic programs back to state and local governments.

At the beginning of his second year in office, President Reagan announced plans to shift most domestic programs to state and local governments by 1990. Reagan's new "new federalism" program, if enacted, would have given the federal system its most dramatic change since the New Deal brought big government to Washington in the 1930s. In his 1982 State of the Union message, the president declared, "In a single stroke we will be accomplishing a realignment that will end cumbersome administration and spiraling costs at the federal level while we insure these programs will be more responsive to both the people they are meant to help and the people who pay for them." President Reagan called for the federal government to take full financial responsibility for Medicaid, while the states would take full responsibility for food stamps.

However, the proposal was not even given serious considerations by Congress, and it was strongly attacked by Democrats and minority groups. In his 1983 State of the Union message, the president dropped the idea of transferring major federal programs to the states. By its second term the Reagan administration had lost much of its enthusiasm for radical reform of intergovernmental relations. Emphasis shifted to more conventional reform, such as reducing federal regulations regarding grant applications and evaluation.

The relative lack of success of Reagan's proposals can be attributed to several factors.[7] One was bad timing. The national recession and runaway inflation in 1982 diverted attention away from debate about the nature of American federalism, and it also put additional financial pressure on the states. Politically, many liberals in Congress wanted to maintain control over federal programs, and they resisted cuts in social services when the president was asking for money for military spending. At the state and local levels, governors called for a federal takeover of the Aid to Families with Dependent Children (AFDC) program, rather than devoting it to the states. They feared the Reagan proposal would increase the tax needs and burdens of the states. Mayors feared that states would not deliver federal funds that were designed to be used to finance the turnback programs. Politically, the administration was not able to build a coalition broad enough to support a revolutionary restructuring of our federal system, and it had less control over Congress after 1982.

A major legacy of the Reagan and Bush administrations was the huge federal debt. Although the federal budget had a deficit every year since 1969, the rate of growth was particularly steep in the 1980s. The size of the debt and the antitax sentiment of the Reagan and Bush years made it very difficult to initiate new domestic programs in the 1990s. In response to these financial and political restraints, Congress effected change largely through unfunded mandates that required spending by state and local governments. At the same time, states were surprisingly willing to fund programs cut by Congress.

A Devolution Revolution?

As a former governor and personal friend of many sitting governors, President Bill Clinton was expected to identify closely with the intergovernmental problems faced by states. During his first year in office President Clinton met frequently with state and local officials, and he placed Vice President Al Gore in charge of a review of relations between the federal government and the states. In his 1996 State of the Union Address President Clinton seemed to align himself with the **"devolution revolution"** when he stated, "The era of big government is over."

Although President Clinton issued an executive order on unfunded mandates shortly after he took office, he found mandates and preemptions convenient ways to support his domestic programs when the federal deficit made it difficult to find additional funding. For example, the Handgun Violence Prevention Act of 1993 (the Brady Act) requires local law-enforcement officers to conduct background checks on handgun purchasers, but it does not provide any money to cover the added expense. As noted earlier, that provision was struck down by the Supreme Court. The Americans with Disabilities Act of 1993 requires state and local governments to make all new and renovated facilities accessible to the disabled, but it is an underfunded mandate that provides only part of the cost of compliance.

Vice President Gore's National Performance Review (NPR) proposed more than 100 recommendations for change in federal-state relations in 1993. The broad goals of the NPR sounded a definite "reinventing government" theme (see Chapter 6) that included "cutting red tape, putting customers first, empowering employees to get results, cutting back to basics."[8] The NPR noted that, "In a perfect world, we would consolidate the 600 federal grant programs into broad funding pools, organized around major goals and desired outcomes—for example, safe and secure communities."

Specifically, the NPR called for a **"bottom-up solution"** to the problem of grant fragmentation. It cited the failure of previous "top-down" proposals aimed at revamping all 600 federal grant programs from offices in Washington. Instead, state and local officials would be trusted to design solutions from the citizen-customer perspective. The NPR noted, for example, that there were more than 140 federal programs assisting children and their families, with funding coming from ten federal departments and two independent agencies. The NPR called for ways to simplify and streamline procedures for state and local governments to comply with federal grant regulations.

The NPR called for improved management and performance with federal monitoring of states and more state flexibility. But it did not envision a basic restructuring of intergovernmental relations.[9] In fact, the number of categorical grants increased in 1993–94, and proposals were made by the president to expand the federal role in areas such as health care and education. This haphazard reform, which also occurred under President Bush, is referred to by David B. Walker as "slouching toward Washington."[10]

During the 1994 congressional election campaign, public support for devolution grew and the Republican Party's Contract With America supported several changes, including reform of unfunded mandates (the first item). The newly elected Republican majority in Congress acted quickly to devolve much more power to the states than had occurred under President Reagan in the 1980s. An early Republican plan would have consolidated nearly 350 existing programs into ten broad block grants. Had that been approved, it would have brought about a true "devolution revolution." Still, Congress approved and Clinton signed into law several significant measures, beginning with the Unfunded Mandates Act (1995) and including a package of block grants plus welfare reform in 1996. Mandate reform will be discussed later in this chapter and welfare reform is discussed in detail in Chapter 10.

Evaluating the Clinton administration's reinventing government programs, federalism expert John Kincaid concludes that it produced little increased discretion for state and local governments.[11] Indeed, Kincaid refers to the period since 1969 as the "era of coercive or regulatory federalism." Although cooperation continues between the states and the federal government, Kincaid suggests that it is "under conditions often dictated by Congress and presidents."[12]

Later in this chapter we will look at mandates, preemptions, and conditions attached to federal grants. All of them have been used recently at historically high levels by Congress and the president to regulate state governments.

Waivers of federal regulations for welfare policy by the Clinton administration did permit state experimentation, but rules attached to the major welfare reform program, Temporary Assistance for Needy Families (TANF), have meant that devolution has delivered less than expected.[13] The Unfunded Mandates Reform Act slowed mandates, but Congress has continued to attach them to legislation.

Like President Clinton, President Bush, as a former governor, philosophically supports devolution of power to the states. He supports block grants and has placed three former governors (Christine Whitman of New Jersey, Tommy Thompson of Wisconsin, and Tom Ridge of Pennsylvania) in top administration positions. However, Bush's education bill, "No Child Left Behind," supports *more* federal intervention in setting standards for curriculum, testing, and teacher qualifications than was made in any other proposals since President Lyndon B. Johnson. The 2001 federal tax cut, as noted in Chapter 1, hurt those states whose tax systems were tied to the federal system. And preoccupation with fighting terrorism and the war in Iraq have resulted in making federalism issues a low priority for the Bush administration.

Following the 2000 presidential election and revelations about serious voting irregularities in Florida and several other states, more than fifty voting reform bills were introduced in Congress. Many of them would have substantially increased federal control over a policy area traditionally controlled by the states. In *Bush v. Gore* the Supreme Court noted that nationwide an estimated 2 percent of ballots in 2000 did not register a vote for president. State voting reforms are discussed in Chapter 4.

Political scientist Martha Derthick's evaluation of American federalism at the end of the Clinton administration concluded that in the areas of electoral politics, welfare, education, and criminal justice the picture of devolution remains "murky." Considerable decentralization has occurred since the 1980s, but in each of the policy areas noted above, Presidents Clinton and Bush took actions that have increased the federal role. For example, in the area of criminal justice, which traditionally has been dominated by the states, Derthick notes that federal law on matters such as carjacking and church burning has "grown explosively."[14] With passage of the Homeland Security Act, federal police power to detain and question American citizens has mushroomed. And in 1999 the Republican Congress passed legislation barring states from collecting sales tax on Internet transactions.

As we will see in the following section, even after more than a decade of Supreme Court decisions that consistently have supported the states against the federal government, the devolution picture as framed in Court opinions is far from clear.

Supreme Court Federalism Since the 1970s

Federalism cases, involving interpretation of the historically obscure Tenth and Eleventh Amendments, may not seem very exciting when compared to more controversial cases on abortion or criminal rights that regularly are decided by the Supreme Court. But since the 1990s, the Supreme Court has become strongly polarized in a series of 5–4 opinions that brought federalism to the forefront of constitutional issues. As a result, the Court changed the federal-state balance of power and placed states outside the reach of several federal laws.

As noted earlier, the Tenth Amendment reserves to states all powers not specifically granted to the national government or prohibited to the states. It has been resurrected from its earlier obscurity to serve as the legal basis for striking down federal laws that the Court majority believes interfere with powers reserved to the states. The **Eleventh Amendment** prohibits suits against states by citizens of another state. Recently, it has been interpreted to shield states from being sued by their citizens in federal and state courts for alleged violations of federal law.

Since the mid-1970s, the Supreme Court has decided several significant cases involving interpretation of the Tenth Amendment. In *National League of Cities v. Usery* (1976) the Court overturned congressional action that had extended federal minimum wage and overtime provisions to state and local government employees. Using the Tenth Amendment, the Court held that federal laws could not impinge on traditional state functions. After struggling to define "traditional state functions," the Court reversed itself in *Garcia v. San Antonio Metropolitan Area Transit Authority* (1985), stating that "the Constitution does not carve out express elements of state sovereignty that Congress may not employ its delegated powers to displace." Although *Garcia* has not been overruled, the Court often has ignored it in decisions since the early 1990s that limit federal authority.

When Congress passed the National Minimum Drinking Age Act in 1985, it included a provision that states would get reductions in federal highway funds if they did not raise the legal age for purchasing alcoholic beverages to 21. This was challenged as a violation of the Twenty-first Amendment (repeal of Prohibition), which some contended returned absolute control of alcoholic beverages to the states. In *South Dakota v. Dole* (1987) the Supreme Court held that, even though Congress lacked the authority to raise the drinking age, it could attach an age requirement to a grant proposal because state participation was voluntary. To others it seemed coercive because states could not afford to give up sizable federal revenue. Although South Dakota would have lost $8 million in 1988, Texas would have forfeited $100 million in highway aid. All states raised their drinking age to 21. In dissent, Justice Sandra Day O'Connor believed the legislation violated the Twenty-first Amendment, and she stated that the drinking age was not "sufficiently related to highway construction to justify conditioning funds appropriated for that purpose." This was the last time Justice O'Connor found herself in the minority in a major federalism decision.

Using a "state autonomy" argument based on the Tenth Amendment and the Constitution's guarantee to the states of a "republican form of government," O'Connor authored the Court's opinion in *Gregory v. Ashcroft* (1991), upholding a mandatory retirement age for judges in Missouri, despite the federal Age Discrimination in Employment Act. In another approach to the Tenth Amendment, the Court in *New York v. United States* (1992) struck down a federal law governing the disposal of radioactive waste. In that opinion Justice O'Connor noted that the federal government could not "commandeer" the states "into the service of Federal regulatory purposes." The commandeering or conscription argument was used by the Supreme Court to strike down the provisions of the Brady gun control law that required local sheriffs to perform background checks on would-be gun purchasers. In *Printz v. United States* (1997) the Court extended its prohibition on commandeering beyond federally mandated policy to a statute that obligated state law enforcement officials to "make a reasonable effort" to determine if pending gun purchases would be illegal.

In *United States v. Lopez* (1995) a five-person majority for the first time since 1936 overturned a federal law on the ground that it exceeded the Constitution's grant of authority to Congress to regulate interstate commerce. In *Lopez* the Court declared unconstitutional the Gun-Free School Zones Act of 1990 that made it a federal crime to possess a gun in close proximity to a school. The majority held that this was the responsibility of states, noting that many states already had approved gun-free zones around schools and that the law had "nothing to do with commerce." In *United States v. Morrison* (2000), the Court invalidated a provision of the Violence Against Women Act as an overreach of the commerce clause. Here Congress had based the law on the idea that violence against women has effects on the nation's economy.

Employing yet another pro–states' rights strategy, in 1996 the Supreme Court turned to the obscure Eleventh Amendment to strike down part of the Indian Gaming Regulatory Act, which set terms by which Indian tribes could conduct gambling on their reservations. Despite the nearly complete power Congress has to control Indian affairs, the decision in *Seminole Tribe v. Florida* overturned part of a federal law that permitted Indian tribes to sue states to bring them to the bargaining table over terms to open casinos.

The same concept of states' **sovereign immunity** was used to prevent private parties from suing states for monetary damages under the Americans with Disabilities Act (*Board of Trustees of the University of Alabama v. Garrett,* 2001). And in *Federal Maritime Commission v. South Carolina* (2002), the Court held that sovereign immunity under the Eleventh Amendment means that state governments are not subject to the jurisdiction of the Federal Maritime Commission. Justice Thomas argued that the opinion upheld the "dignity" of the states as dual sovereigns with the federal government.

All the major federalism decisions since the early 1990s have been supported by the Supreme Court's "Federalism Five": Justices O'Connor, Rehnquist, Scalia, Kennedy, and Thomas. With the passage of time, disputes within the Court regarding the nature of our federal system have grown more intense. As *New York Times* Supreme Court reporter Linda Greenhouse has noted, "These days federalism means war."

As noted at the beginning of this chapter, the same 5–4 majority that has ruled in favor of state governments in federalism cases overruled the Florida supreme court's interpretation of its state's law in *Bush v. Gore* in 2000. That decision, handed down thirty-five days after election day, ended the recount and, in effect, gave the election to Bush. The United States Supreme Court rejected the option of remanding the case to the Florida supreme court and then waiting to see if the manual recount of votes could be completed within the specified time of six days. By intervening the Court also removed Congress from ruling in what might have been defined as a political dispute.

There have been several other recent decisions in which the Court has not favored state power. For example, in 2000–01 the Court ruled against police roadblocks to check, at random, for drugs in Massachusetts, and it ruled against a California law that exempted the private medical use of marijuana from criminal prosecution. In 2003 the Court held that provisions of the Family and Medical Leave Act apply to state employees.

Linda Greenhouse argues that the Supreme Court has been more concerned about the balance of power between the Court and Congress than between the states and the federal government.[15] Some academics believe the Court is treating Congress as if it were a bad lower court. In defense of the Court, Jonathan Walters notes that Congress has been passing laws and writing regulations without much thought about their constitutionality, thus inviting review by the Supreme Court.[16] Viewed in this light, the Supreme Court's federalism decisions seem less supportive of a "devolution revolution" than if we were to construct a scorecard of how often the Court sides with the states in federalism cases.

It may be, as Timothy Conlan and Franco de Chantal conclude, that the Rehnquist Court's "Federalism Five" views its role as a stabilizer of the national-state balance of power in the United States.[17] From this perspective, the Court seeks to prevent either side from becoming too strong. But balance is a judgment call and depending on how much the Court's membership changes in the next few years, it could end up supporting a "devolution revolution."

FEDERAL-STATE FUNDING ARRANGEMENTS

The evolution of American federalism shows that the nation has moved from separate levels of government, acting almost as sovereign entities, to levels of government that interact and cooperate in an increasingly interdependent system. Intergovernmental relations involve interactions between the federal government and the states, between states, and between states and their localities.

Grants-in-Aid

We have briefly examined the changing relationships between the national government and the states. In large part, **grants-in-aid** have been the vehicle by which federal authority has greatly expanded since the early 1950s. **Fiscal federalism**—grants of money from the national government to the states and from the states to local governments—is at the center of intergovernmental relations and enables Congress to exert considerable influence over the states. For example, the threat of withholding funds from the states allowed Congress to set such national standards as the 55 mph speed limit and led to increasing the legal age for drinking alcoholic beverages. These so-called crossover sanctions give Congress substantial power over the states. Despite concerns about devolving power, since the 1960s Congress has continued to increase conditions attached to grants.

One argument for increased federal involvement in traditional state and local activities has been that it provides a degree of national uniformity (in the form of minimal standards) in a system divided by interstate competition. Also, because of great differences in state wealth, spending for such programs as education and public assistance varies greatly from one part of the country to another. Federal aid can make things more equal and provide more nearly uniform benefits by transferring money from rich states to poor states (the "Robin Hood effect"). As a result, the federal grants-in-aid program has provided a politically acceptable way of providing needed money to state and local governments while keeping the formal structure of federalism.

Increasingly in the 1950s and 1960s, both state and local governments were faced with pressing demands to solve social problems at a time when their financial base was either dwindling or expanding only a little. Cities often found state legislatures unwilling or unable to come to their aid. As a result, they turned directly to Congress for help. Congress responded to cities and states by greatly expanding the grants-in-aid programs already existing while keeping state and local administration of government programs. Grants provide the means by which the federal government exerts some effect on state programs without taking over the entire function and removing it from state or local control.

The federal grant program also grew as a result of the formation of **vertical coalitions.**[18] As explained by Thomas J. Anton, groups that were too weak politically to get what they wanted from local governments joined with similar groups across the country to persuade Congress to enact legislation that would support their goals. Anton comments that these relatively loose vertical coalitions, or alliances, often were able to demonstrate that a "problem" existed and to convince Congress to "spend some money and see what happens." The alliances received grants and members of Congress could take credit for responding to needs in their districts. As a result, everyone—Congress members and administrators at several levels of government—seemed to benefit.

Grants-in-aid are by no means new. They began with the Land Ordinance Act of 1785, which provided land grants for public schools in the developing Western territory. Throughout the nineteenth century, grants were made available for railroads and canals. However, they did not become politically significant until after World War II. In 1950, federal grants to state and local governments amounted to only $2 billion annually. By 1970, there were 530 grants-in-aid programs paying out about $24 billion every year. In spite of President Nixon's campaign oratory about decentralizing government, about 100 grant programs were created by the Nixon and Ford administrations. The federal grant program continued to increase sharply under the Carter administration.

In fiscal 1982, federal grants had their first absolute decline in more than twenty-five years. As noted, this was consistent with President Reagan's desire to cut federal spending and reduce government regulation. However, total grant-in-aid outlays doubled in the 1990s, from $153 billion in 1991 to $308 billion in 2000. Federal grants in 2000 were about $1,120 per capita nationwide. By far the largest category of grants (about 63 percent of the total in 2000) went for education. Public welfare (10 percent) and highways (4 percent) were second and third. Throughout the 1990s grants represented about 24 percent of total federal expenditures. Table 2-1 shows how federal grants are distributed among the states. As percentages of all state revenue, federal grants ranged from a high of 25 percent in North Dakota to a low of 10.4 percent in

TABLE 2-1 Federal Aid to States and Localities

	State & Local Total (in millions)	State Share (vs. Local)	Total per Capita	Per Capita Rank	Federal Aid as % Total Revenue	% Total Revenue Rank
Alabama	$5,087	93.3%	$1,144	13	19.8%	8
Alaska	1,411	84.9	2,250	1	13.4	39
Arizona	4,475	85.8	872	41	16.1	20
Arkansas	2,823	95.9	1,056	24	20.4	6
California	38,476	87.5	1,136	16	14.2	34
Colorado	3,711	88.4	863	45	12.5	46
Connecticut	3,674	92.2	1,079	21	14.2	35
Delaware	830	95.0	1,059	23	13.3	41
Florida	11,718	84.5	733	48	12.7	42
Georgia	7,070	90.7	864	44	14.3	33
Hawaii	1,294	86.8	1,068	22	15.2	28
Idaho	1,150	93.0	889	40	15.2	29

TABLE 2-1

	State & Local Total (in millions)	State Share (vs. Local)	Total per Capita	Per Capita Rank	Federal Aid as % Total Revenue	% Total Revenue Rank
Illinois	$10,791	86.0%	$ 869	43	13.4%	40
Indiana	5,169	92.7	850	47	15.8	22
Iowa	2,885	91.2	986	31	16.8	19
Kansas	2,482	95.3	923	37	15.3	26
Kentucky	4,595	94.0	1,137	15	18.2	15
Louisiana	5,070	93.3	1,134	17	18.7	11
Maine	1,630	94.9	1,279	10	19.1	9
Maryland	4,609	87.3	870	42	13.6	38
Massachusetts	6,439	84.3	1,014	27	14.0	36
Michigan	10,331	88.7	1,040	25	14.7	30
Minnesota	4,769	91.9	970	33	12.3	47
Mississippi	3,528	94.9	1,240	11	21.2	5
Missouri	5,628	92.5	1,006	28	17.8	17
Montana	1,306	90.9	1,448	7	23.1	2
Nebraska	1,710	90.1	1,000	29	14.7	31
Nevada	1,233	81.0	617	50	10.4	50
New Hampshire	1,062	93.6	859	46	15.3	27
New Jersey	7,883	92.7	937	36	12.6	44
New Mexico	2,398	88.9	1,319	9	18.3	13
New York	29,249	89.6	1,541	4	15.5	24
North Carolina	9,051	89.0	1,125	18	17.9	16
North Dakota	1,126	86.5	1,753	3	25.0	1
Ohio	10,933	90.0	963	34	13.7	37
Oklahoma	3,181	93.1	922	38	17.0	18
Oregon	5,233	88.4	1,530	5	18.3	14
Pennsylvania	12,498	84.1	1,018	26	15.5	23
Rhode Island	1,196	91.2	1,142	14	16.1	21
South Carolina	4,377	92.6	1,091	20	18.7	12
South Dakota	869	89.8	1,151	12	20.3	7
Tennessee	6,321	94.4	1,111	19	18.8	10
Texas	18,576	89.2	891	39	15.4	25
Utah	2,172	86.4	973	32	14.5	32
Vermont	903	97.1	1,483	6	22.5	4
Virginia	5,010	86.1	708	49	11.3	49
Washington	5,828	87.4	989	30	12.6	45
West Virginia	2,489	95.0	1,377	8	23.1	3
Wisconsin	5,059	91.6	943	35	11.8	48
Wyoming	891	94.7	1,804	2	12.7	43
DC	1,748	—	3,056	—	27.4	—
US	291,950	88.8	1,037	—	15.0	—

Source: U.S. Census Bureau, FY 2000. *State and Local Sourcebook 2003.* Supplement to *Governing,* p. 30.

Nevada. Relative to the amount of federal taxes paid by the states, smaller, rural states such as Vermont and Wyoming tend to receive the most money back in federal grants.

There are several ways in which the federal government sends money to the states and some ways give states more control than others. **Categorical grants** are made for specific purposes, such as job training, highway safety, prevention of juvenile delinquency, and agricultural extension. The recipient of such a grant has little choice about how the money is to be spent, so the federal government retains more control. In 2002, the nearly 670 categorical grants made up about 95 percent of all federal grants. Throughout the 1990s, federal aid to states consistently made up slightly more than 20 percent of their total revenues.

Block grants are much broader in their scope. They allow greater choice by the recipient, and they reduce or end matching requirements. For example, Community Development Small Cities Block Grants create a "package" of grants to deal with a series of problems previously covered by separate, categorical grants. As discussed earlier, President Reagan's "new federalism" program stressed the development of block grants, and the Republican-controlled Congress has since 1995 strongly favored the use of block grants as a way to return power to the states. In 1996 Congress took a major step in the direction of devolving power to the states when it passed a welfare reform bill (see Chapter 10) that provided block grants to the states. Still, there were only 24 block grants in 2002.

Another way of categorizing grants is according to their terms for distribution. **Formula grants** are distributed automatically to all eligible recipients on the basis of established guidelines. For example, a formula grant in a highway bill might provide for funds to be distributed on the basis of the number of miles of highway in a state. Controversy with this type of grant involves what formula should be used.

When Congress creates **project grants** it makes funds available for a specific purpose, and state or local governments must apply to the agency in charge of administering the grant to get approval. This introduces competition among potential recipients, and it may be that governments with the ability to write the best proposals are the ones that are funded. As a result, "grantsmanship"—knowing what grants are available and how best to complete the application forms—may determine who gets the money.

More recently, combined **formula/project grants** have been developed. These grants are competitive, but they also are based on a formula. For example, only so much money may be awarded to a state or region.

A balance sheet evaluating the grants-in-aid system would contain the following advantages and disadvantages:

Advantages	Disadvantages
1 Provide funds needed by state and local governments.	1 Large number and complexity of grants imposes administrative burdens on recipients and leads to the development of large bureaucracies.
2 Help equalize resources in rich and poor states.	2 Uncoordinated grants often overlap or are at odds with one another.

3 Encourage local initiative and experimentation.	**3** They dull local initiative and distort planning by directing attention to available grants rather than proposing solutions for problems in fields not covered by grants.
4 Are based on the progressive tax structure of the federal government.	**4** Duration of grants is often too long or too short.
5 Can concentrate attention in a problem area and provide valuable technical assistance.	**5** They encourage "grantsmanship"— the ability to fill out the forms in a way that pleases federal officials.
6 Allow introduction into the federal system of national values and standards.	**6** Categorical grants leave little room for state and local discretion regarding expenditures and require increased federal supervision. Local elected officials have little control of the programs.

Although states have the option of *not* participating in the grants-in-aid programs, there is strong pressure to take advantage of the opportunity to get programs for half cost or less. This, in turn, places a great financial burden on states (particularly poor ones) to earmark much of their discretionary money as matching funds for grants-in-aid. This fiscal federalism also puts strong pressure (some would say coercion) on the states to comply with federal regulations. Earlier we said that states were pressured by Congress into raising the drinking age to 21. As also noted, more recent decisions by the Supreme Court have given states much more judicial protection against federal policy making than had been the case from the late 1930s until the early 1990s.

In the past twenty-five years there has been a marked shift in federal aid from places to persons. About 63 percent of federal aid now goes to individuals (persons), much of it for health care and welfare. This leaves a much smaller percentage of aid going to places, meaning states have less federal money to spend for investment in capital projects such as bridges, sewers, and roads. It also means that states and cities often are treated just like other interest groups seeking funds from the federal government.

Let us look at the *economic rationales* that support the entire grants-in-aid system. As noted, it is easier to raise revenue at the national level than at the state and local levels because the federal tax structure is more elastic than that of the state and local governments. Federal revenues rise in direct proportion to overall economic growth in the United States. As a result, federal revenue expands greatly without any increase in tax rates. In contrast, state and local taxes are less elastic; they do not respond well to economic growth. Thus city councils and state legislatures must create new taxes or raise existing tax rates to get added funds necessary to respond to their constituents' demands for more services. In addition, federal taxes are more *progressive* than state and local taxes. (Chapter 8 deals more specifically with state and local financing.)

A second economic rationale for grants-in-aid is what some observers refer to as **spillover benefits.** This means that the benefits obtained from a program administered in one government area may extend into other government areas. Thus it seems fair that all who benefit should share in the cost. Education is an example of how spillover benefits work. If a person educated in New York or New Jersey, where per capita spending is far greater than the national average, moves to a state such as Tennessee, where per capita spending for education is lower, the second state benefits from educational programs for which it has not paid. Federal grants that support education make certain that all states share in the cost of any single program by the national government.

An additional benefit of federal grants is that they have helped reduce corruption by requiring review of state and local financial records by federal auditors. A final economic rationale is that grants reduce unnecessary administrative expense by requiring recipients to improve their administrative structures.

Regarding *political* expediency, it may be easier to mount a national campaign for a mixed federal-state program than to manage campaigns throughout the fifty states. Labor, for example, has its membership centered in about one-third of the states. It therefore has little effect in many of the other state capitals. Yet labor's strong influence in urban, industrial states gives it a great deal of bargaining power with Congress and the president. It also exerts pressure on the national government to respond to such problems as poverty, community mental health, and environmental protection—problems that otherwise would not receive political support because of the unresponsiveness of local political elites. From another perspective, political scientist David Mayhew argues that categorical grants provide "particularized benefits" to congressional constituencies and thus allow members of Congress to claim credit for benefits in their districts.[19] As this helps their chances for being reelected, it is not surprising that members of Congress are reluctant to cut categoricals.

More and more, traditional state and local political problems can be viewed as having national implications. With an interdependent economy, including transportation and communications systems, most problems do not have a purely local impact. As a result, the federal system involves plans in which federal and state officials join in fighting such problems as air pollution and urban decay. Federal grants allow Congress to form national objectives, which are put into effect through cooperation between federal officials and state and local governments. Such grants also have been an effective way for strong presidents, such as Franklin D. Roosevelt and Lyndon Johnson, to centralize their political aims.

Duplication in grant programs abounds. For example, the Clinton administration's NPR stated that ten departments and two independent agencies administered over 140 programs designed to help children and their families. Each program has its own set of rules and regulations. Because of competing, and often conflicting, federal rules, states are not free to integrate programs in a general service area to fit the special needs of residents. As a result, programs are operated by different agencies, often in different locations, by different people with varying degrees of expertise, and in accordance with different sets of rules and regulations.

The complex grant delivery system increases the administrative costs of states and localities. Over $20 billion of federal grant funds is used to reimburse states for direct and indirect administrative costs. Procedures could be greatly simplified to reduce costs. The NPR reported that states and localities must comply with eighteen cross-cutting federal requirements for each grant application, and there are other requirements not contained in the standard forms.

Federal Mandates and Preemptions

Federal mandates are legal orders from Congress or administrative agencies that require state or local governments to perform a certain activity or to provide a service. Condition-of-aid provisions in categorical grants can be avoided by states and localities by simply not applying for the grant, but mandates legally cannot be avoided, and they can be enforced in court. Nearly all mandates in United States history have been enacted since 1969. A mandate problem began to occur in the late 1980s because of the cumulative effect of an increased number of mandates since the mid-1960s and because an increasing percentage of mandates are unfunded. Cities get a double hit from mandates imposed by Congress and by state legislatures. In addition, some federal mandates are placed on states that, in turn, pass them through to local governments.

Two bills passed by Congress in 1993 show the financial impact of mandates on state and local governments. First, the Family and Medical Leave Act requires private and public employers with fifty or more employees to allow up to twelve weeks of unpaid leave in any twelve-month period. Second, the National Voter Registration Act ("Motor-Voter Bill") mandates that state and local governments establish procedures to permit voter registration where individuals apply for drivers' licenses or by mail. It also permits, but doesn't require, state and local governments to use offices that provide public assistance, unemployment compensation, and services to the disabled at voter registration locations. As noted earlier, a mandate in the Brady Handgun Control Act, also passed in 1993, was struck down by the Supreme Court.

Joseph F. Zimmerman notes that environmental mandates are the most expensive federal requirements imposed on local governments, and they have increased dramatically since the early 1970s.[20] For example, new Environmental Protection Agency (EPA) standards in 1991 required cities to lower by tenfold the level of lead in drinking water. In many cases, water suppliers have to replace service lines, and this imposes significant costs, especially on small local governments. At the other extreme, New York City constructed a $600 million plant to comply with federal water filtration requirements. Other expensive mandates for states and localities include those dealing with underground storage tanks, asbestos abatement, and persons with disabilities.[21]

Unfunded mandates were the biggest source of conflict between states and the federal government in the 1990s. Nearly thirty statutes were enacted in the 1980s that imposed new regulations or significantly expanded existing mandates. By the early 1990s, more than 170 pieces of federal legislation imposed mandates on state and local governments. Alice Rivlin observed that:

> The federal government's own fiscal weakness has not made it any less eager to tell states and localities what to do. Indeed, when its ability to make grants declined, the federal government turned increasingly to mandates as a way of controlling state and local activities without having to pay the bill. . . . Mandates add to citizen confusion about who is in charge. When the federal government makes rules for state and local officials to carry out, it is not clear to voters who should be blamed, either when the regulations are laxly enforced or when the cost of compliance is high.[22]

In response to widespread criticism about mandates, President Clinton issued an executive order on unfunded mandates. One of the first actions taken by the 104th

Congress after Republicans gained control of the House and Senate in the 1994 elections was to pass the so-called unfunded mandates bill. The bill had broad support among Republicans and Democrats, and it was backed by President Clinton. The bill forces Congress to define the costs and to vote on individual mandates, but it does not prohibit Congress from imposing new mandates. It does not apply to existing legislation, and it will not apply to bills, such as the Clean Water Act, when they come up for reauthorization. Although Congress has passed fewer unfunded mandates since 1995, the total cost to states of unfunded mandates has remained nearly constant. Congress continues to pass mandates, in part as a way to satisfy interest groups without having to fund projects. As a result, states were successful in modifying how new mandates are implemented, but not in limiting new mandates.[23] To the extent that Congress will be less likely to impose regulations if it has to pay the costs, mandate reform is a part of a broader Republican Party attack on federal power.

In addition to mandates, restraints, and restrictions in federal grants, **preemption** is another means of federal intervention into state and local affairs. Here Congress nullifies certain state and local laws totally or partially. Congress enacted only thirty preemption statutes before 1900, and the number remained low until the 1970s. The major increase came when President Reagan signed into law over ninety preemption bills in the 1980s.

Various types of total preemption range from those such as the Americans with Disabilities Act that remove all regulatory power from states to those that encourage states to cooperate in enforcing a statute. As Zimmerman notes, "The states have been stripped of their powers to engage in economic regulation of airlines, buses, and trucking companies, establish a compulsory retirement age for their employees except for policy-makers, or regulate bankruptcies."[24]

Since the mid-1960s, partial preemption statutes have had a greater impact on federal-state relations than total preemption statutes. Congress has enacted minimum standards for partial preemption to give a framework for new regulatory programs. This has increased the interdependence of states and the federal government because states develop regulations and then negotiate with federal officials to implement the plans within minimum standards set by a federal agency, such as the EPA. Only if a state fails to carry out regulation will the federal government step in to assume complete control. States are free to adopt more stringent standards, but weaker standards are preemptively blocked by Congress. Many partial exemptions are in the area of environmental regulation.

Although federal aid as a percentage of all state and local expenditures declined from an all-time high of 27 percent in 1978 to 15 percent in 2000, the federal government actually became *more* intrusive in state and local affairs. This is due to the increase in mandates and preemptions plus the fact, as noted, that federal aid increasingly has bypassed state and local governments to go directly to individuals.

HORIZONTAL FEDERALISM: INTERSTATE COOPERATION

As noted earlier, relations among states are confederal, meaning that states must negotiate with each other as political equals.

The U.S. Constitution attempts to encourage cooperation among the states in the following ways:

1. States are to give *"full faith and credit . . .* to the public acts, records, and judicial proceedings of every other state." This clause requires a state to recognize the validity of actions among private citizens, such as a contract for sale of property, which originate in another state. In the area of domestic relations—divorce, child custody, alimony—the situation is complicated by state refusal on occasion to accept as binding civil judgments of other states. Recent same-sex marriages and civil unions performed in several states raise the question whether the full faith and credit clause should make them binding in other states.

2. States are to extend to residents of other states all **"privileges and immunities"** granted their own residents. This includes allowing residents of one state to acquire property, enter into contracts, and have access to the courts in a second state. It does not include the extension of political rights such as voting and jury service. The Supreme Court has held that some kinds of discrimination against nonresidents, such as charging them higher tuition at state universities and higher hunting and fishing fees, does not violate the privileges and immunities clause.

3. The interstate rendition clause requires states to return to another state fugitives who have fled from justice. It is the governor who signs **extradition** papers to deliver a fugitive to the state having jurisdiction over the criminal act. Although governors usually comply with requests for extradition, the Supreme Court during the Civil War ruled that this was a matter of executive discretion and that a governor may refuse to deliver a fugitive upon request from another state. More recently the Court held that states must return fugitives. In 1934, Congress made it a federal crime to cross state lines to avoid prosecution or imprisonment.

4. States may enter into **compacts** (a kind of treaty arrangement) with one another provided that Congress approves. There has been only one case in which congressional approval of a proposed interstate compact was denied. A state cannot withdraw from a compact unless the other-party states agree. The provisions of compacts take precedence over any state laws that conflict with their provisions.

The most significant use of interstate compacts has developed since World War II. Only thirty-six compacts were created between 1789 and 1920.[25] There were fifty-eight by 1940. Between 1941 and 1975, however, more than 100 compacts were enacted, and the coverage was broadened. Now there are about 120 compacts in effect, dealing with the management of problems that cross state lines, such as transportation, environmental protection, taxes, and health care. In recent years there has been a decline in the number of compacts enacted, but an increase in interstate administrative agreements. The latter are entered into by administrative officials as a way to improve interstate cooperation in areas such as criminal identification and motor vehicle law enforcement.

The best known interstate compact is the Port Authority of New York, established in 1920 between New York and New Jersey. The Port Authority controls much of the transportation in greater New York City. It manages marine terminals and tunnels, leases airports, and is responsible for a rapid transit system that carries 70 million passengers annually.

Beginning with the Delaware Basin Commission in 1961, the federal government has joined with states—here Delaware, New York, New Jersey, and Pennsylvania—in "federal-interstates." More than thirty compacts are open to participation nationwide, and others are organized on a regional basis. Although the growth of interstate compacts has slowed, new compacts have been formed since 1980 dealing with such areas as hazardous waste and natural resources management. In most instances compacts are viewed as a way to improve problem solving without involving the federal government.

States also cooperate by exchanging information. An ever-growing number of associations—governors, attorneys general, welfare officials, lieutenant governors—hold regular conferences. Many of these organizations are associated with the Council of State Governments, which provides a framework of organization and also publishes materials (including *The Book of the States*) on a wide range of state government issues. State and local police cooperate with each other and with the FBI in the exchange of information regarding criminals. Some states have developed reciprocal programs in higher education. For example, residents of northwestern Ohio can attend Eastern Michigan University and pay Michigan in-state tuition. In turn, residents of southeastern Michigan can attend the University of Toledo and pay Ohio in-state tuition.

In spite of the availability of formal means of cooperation, interstate relations often are marked by *competition* and *conflict,* rather than by accommodation. In the field of taxation, states sometimes cite their low tax rates as a means of luring businesses from other states. Increasingly, environmental issues are causing interstate conflict. These include disposal of hazardous waste, dumping of pollutants in waterways, and acid rain in New England that is caused by air pollution in the Midwest.

Although there is greater uniformity in state laws now than there was fifty years ago, significant differences in areas such as child support remain. Even though legislators and attorneys general attend regular conferences, and even though the National Conference of the Commissioners on Uniform Law has existed since 1892, there remains a significant lack of uniformity in commercial law. Differences also exist in divorce laws, legal marriage age, and voting residency requirements. At one time, California legislators attempted (unsuccessfully) to bar paupers from moving into their state. In 1999 the Supreme Court rejected a California plan to limit first-year residents to the welfare benefits they would have received had they stayed in their former states. Truckers are confronted with a variety of state rules regulating lights, load limits, and licensing as they travel cross-country. One might expect that in a "reasonable" system such confusion would have been eliminated by now. However, in the name of federalism Americans continue to support state and local autonomy and are therefore willing to live with the inconveniences that inevitably result.

STATE-LOCAL RELATIONS

As seen, states and cities in the United States exist in a unitary relationship. Thus, unlike the federal government's relations with the states, each state can coerce its cities to comply with policy objectives. While states often can resist national directives, local governments are legally bound to follow state policy. As a result, there are many more

state mandates to local governments than there are federal mandates to the states. And some expensive federal mandates are passed on to localities by states.

Many mandates are enacted to promote uniformity across the state, and there is general agreement that they are beneficial. For example, the length of the public school year and the permissible number of bad-weather days off generate little controversy. Problems arise because local governments may disagree with the goals of state legislators and, like the states' reactions to federal mandates, they object to the cost imposed on them to implement the programs. Whenever one level of government can push a costly responsibility down to another level, it nearly always does so.

As in Congress, a majority of states have enacted laws restricting mandates by requiring extramajority votes in the legislature or, as in California and New Hampshire, requiring the state to pay the full cost of mandates. Still, as in Congress, although the number of unfunded mandates has declined, they are far from being eliminated. At the extremes, a recent study showed that one in four laws passed in Tennessee imposed unfunded mandates on local governments.

As in Congress, state legislatures also preempt and prohibit local governments from taking certain actions. Preemptions are especially prevalent in the areas of smoking bans, rent control, and gun control. Tobacco interests often have successfully pressured legislatures to enact state clean-indoor-air regulations that are less stringent than city ordinances. In about a dozen states the National Rifle Association has succeeded in getting legislatures to prohibit cities from suing gun makers to recover the costs of gun-related violence.

Although state legislators criticize federal control of states, both Republican and Democratic legislators resist turning over political power to cities and counties, in part because business groups (refer to preemptions) prefer to deal with one government rather than fight battles across the state.

Federal *and* state mandates illustrate the mistrust between levels of government in our federal system. Federal officials mistrust the ability of the states to make good decisions, especially when it comes to protecting the interests of the poor, and, in turn, state officials don't trust city and county governments to act in the best interests of the public. States criticize the federal government, and cities and counties criticize the states, both arguing that remote officials in Washington and in state capitals do not understand what it is like to govern on a daily basis.

Local governments turn to their states for help because limited resources make them unable to respond to local demands for more and better services. And, as we have noted, state mandates put additional financial pressure on local governments. In some states, notably in Michigan, governors have opposed local autonomy if that means mayors could ignore the states' general strategy, even as governors decry centralization of power in Washington.

As federal aid to cities leveled off in the 1980s and early 1990s, state aid to cities increased. State payments to local governments nearly doubled from 1986 to 1996.[26] More than half of all state aid to localities was for education, with welfare, highways, and health the next largest categories. This picture changed drastically after 2000. As state budget shortfalls grew, aid to cities and counties was cut. Cities also suffered because property tax rollbacks approved by state legislatures in the 1990s were depriving them of revenue.[27]

As we would expect, there are wide variations among the states in levels of state aid. State per capita payments to counties, municipalities, and townships in 2000 ranged from about $1,500 in Alaska, California, Michigan, and New York to lows of $125 in Hawaii and $400 in New Hampshire.

Much of the difference is explained by the degree of state centralization of services. Some states historically have centralized services with state legislative control; others have permitted services to be decentralized at the local level and have provided aid to assist localities in delivering those services.

Hawaii gives so little intergovernmental aid because the state totally administers and finances its elementary and secondary education system. Education is largely a local responsibility in New Hampshire, but state per capita assistance in New Hampshire is the second lowest in the country. At the other extreme, California provides five times as much financial aid per capita as does New Hampshire for education and, in general, few government services are centralized in the state. Alaska and Wyoming rank first and third in the per capita state aid for education, reflecting the need to serve widely dispersed populations and the availability to the state government of severance tax revenue to fund programs.

As noted earlier, increases in state power mean more power for local governments because states work through localities in most instances and their bureaucracies are enlarged. Russell Hanson notes that the trend across the country is for greater state assistance to localities, rather than states taking over functions.[28] States provide money to localities and offer technical advice, but they tend to respond to public opinion that favors decentralization. Because two or more governments often have responsibility for delivery of the same service, states have enacted legislation to improve coordination among local governments.

FEDERALISM EVALUATED

Critics of federalism offer a number of serious charges. Some suggest that, because it gave Southern states independent power, federalism helped foster racism in America;[29] that the states cannot deal effectively with social problems that cross state boundaries; that relations between states are marked more by conflict than by cooperation; that the unequal distribution of wealth among the states creates a system in which social benefits vary greatly from state to state; and that with more than 80,000 units of government, duplication of effort is unavoidable and makes it difficult for citizens to hold officials accountable for their actions.

In this chapter we have examined the lack of cooperation and the unequal distribution of social services among the states. We have noted that states have delayed and often obstructed national policy directions. Perhaps federalism means that too much attention is directed to local matters. What level of government should address specific societal problems has been the most persistent and divisive fundamental political issue throughout American history.

Americans are questioning more and more the growth and centralization of government authority. Smaller units of government permit more citizens to participate and make possible greater economic control for residents of urban areas. Although few

people would favor conversion to a confederate form of government, since the early 1980s there has been a strong movement led by the political right to reduce the centralization of power that has occurred in our federal system. The evolution of American federalism shows periodic movement along a continuum that extends from very centralized to very decentralized (that is, state-centered) federalism.

There is a need to sort out responsibilities between the states and the federal government in a way that clearly would limit federal authority. During the Clinton transition period of 1992–1993, David Osborne argued that the federal government should not act unless (1) the problem needs an interstate solution, (2) uniform national standards are required, (3) the absence of national standards would lead to "destructive competition" among the states, or (4) redistribution across state lines is required to solve local problems.[30] Osborne's recommendation to eliminate 100 federal aid programs and devolve control over 400 others was not acted upon by the Clinton administration. The Bush focus has been almost entirely on foreign affairs.

Federal systems offer a number of benefits.[31] These include the flexibility to respond to regional differences; the prevention of abuse of power because no single group is likely to gain control of government at the state and local levels; the encouragement of innovation by testing new ideas at the local level; the creation of many centers of power to resolve conflict and to handle administrative burdens; the stimulation of competition among levels of government that encourages policy innovation; and, as James Madison predicted, the prevention of abuse of power because it is nearly impossible for a single group to gain control of government at all levels. Of course, most of these benefits will occur only if state and local governments are energetic and respond to public demands. As we shall see throughout this book, there is strong evidence that the states have made the necessary structural changes and that elected officials have sufficient personal commitment to enable them to respond effectively to policy needs, but only if they have sufficient revenue and citizen support for expanded programs.

SUMMARY

American federalism has evolved from a decentralized (state-centered) system at the time of its creation until the first part of the twentieth century, to a much more centralized system. This expansion of power in Washington reached its high point in the 1960s and 1970s. President Reagan's call for a "new federalism" in the 1980s and the Clinton and Bush administrations' efforts at devolution of power, which were accelerated by demands for "less government" by congressional Republicans, have led to a shift of government responsibilities to the states and to reductions in federal spending for many domestic programs. Still, a "devolution revolution" has not occurred because even as reform legislation is approved, federal control continues to be exercised.

Since the early 1990s, the Supreme Court most often has ruled against Congress in cases where states have resisted federal authority. Interpretation of the Tenth and Eleventh Amendments by the Court's "Federalism Five" has been applauded by political conservatives and criticized by liberals, who fear the balance of power in the federal system will be pushed too far in favor of the states.

Much of the increase in federal power in the 1960s, 1970s, and 1980s was accomplished by the expansion of federal grants-in-aid and by the use of unfunded federal mandates. The use of block grants, beginning in the 1970s and expanded in the 1990s, cuts in categorical grants, and congressional action to limit unfunded mandates have helped reduce federal power.

Relations among states and between states and cities also have been marked by conflict and by the centralization of power in state capitals. After increasing in the 1960s, state aid to localities has declined as states struggle to balance their budgets. Like Congress, states also have used unfunded mandates to require certain actions by cities and counties. Parallel to state-federal relations, there has been a move to protect localities from unfunded mandates and to give cities more flexibility to manage their own affairs.

KEY TERMS

block grants
bottom-up solution
categorical grants
coercive federalism
commerce
compacts
compact theory of federalism
concurrent majority
confederacy
confederal
cooperative federalism
creative federalism
devolution revolution
dual federalism
dual sovereignty
Eleventh Amendment
extradition

federal system
fiscal federalism
formula grants
formula/project grants
grants-in-aid
"necessary and proper" clause
"new federalism"
nullification
preemption
"privileges and immunities"
project grants
revenue sharing
sovereign immunity
spillover benefits
Tenth Amendment
unitary nation-state
vertical coalitions

SUMMARY OF STATE/LOCAL DIFFERENCES

Issue	States	Local Governments
U.S. Constitutional status	Certain powers are reserved to the states and others are shared with the national government (a federal relationship)	No mention is made of cities or counties
State constitutional status	Free to write and amend their constitutions	Forms of government are prescribed by the state; home rule charters give some autonomy (a unitary relationship)
Grants-in-aid	Categorical and block federal grants to states	Categorical state grants to localities
Mandates	States have gotten some relief from unfunded federal mandates	Localities have gotten some relief from state mandates
Devolution	More responsibilities have been transferred from the federal government to the states	More responsibilities have been transferred from state governments to localities

INTERESTING WEBSITES

http://supct.law.cornell.edu/supct. Federal-state issues frequently are resolved in the federal courts, and this is a good site to access U.S. Supreme Court decisions. If you don't know the name of a case, click on "By topic."

www.ncsl.org. Website of the National Conference of State Legislatures. Click on "Policy Issues," then "Issue Areas—L thru Z," then "State-Federal Relations."

http://ww2.lafayette.edu/~meynerc/. The Meyner Center for the Study of State and Local Government has several resources on American federalism, and even information on "International Federalism."

www.nga.org. Website of the National Governors' Association. Go to the site directory and click on "Key State-Federal issues."

NOTES

1. See Morton Grodzins, "Centralization and Decentralization in the American Federal System," in Robert A. Goldwin, ed., *A Nation of States* (Chicago: Rand McNally, 1963).
2. Russell L. Hanson, "Intergovernmental Relations," in *Politics in the American States,* 7th ed., Virginia Gray and Herbert Jacob, eds. (Washington, D.C.: Congressional Quarterly Press, 1999), p. 34.
3. Ibid., p. 40.
4. Martin Shapiro, "The Supreme Court from Early Burger to Early Rehnquist," in *The New American Political System,* 2d version, Anthony King, ed. (Washington: American Enterprise Press, 1990), p. 66.
5. John E. Chubb, "Federalism and the Bias for Centralization," in *The New Direction in American Politics,* John E. Chubb and Paul E. Peterson, eds. (Washington: Brookings Institution, 1995).
6. Richard P. Nathan, Fred C. Doolittle, et al., *Reagan and the States* (Princeton, N.J.: Princeton University Press, 1987), p. 31.
7. Peter M. Benda and Charles H. Levine, "Reagan and the Bureaucracy: The Bequest, the Promise, and the Legacy," in *The Reagan Legacy: Promise and Performance,* Charles O. Jones, ed. (Chatham, N.J.: Chatham House, 1988), p. 123.
8. *Creating a Government That Works Better and Costs Less* (Washington, D.C.: U.S. Government Printing Office, 1993), p. 1. Also see Bill Clinton and Al Gore, *Putting People First* (New York: Times Books, 1992); and William A. Galston and Geoffrey L. Tibbets, "Reinventing Federalism: The Clinton/Gore Program for a New Partnership Among the Federal, State, Local, and Tribal Governments," *Publius* (Summer 1994), pp. 23–48.
9. Timothy J. Conlon, *From New Federalism to Devolution: Twenty-Five Years of Intergovernmental Reform* (Washington: Brookings Institution, 1998), p. 224.
10. David B. Walker, *The Rebirth of Federalism: Slouching Toward Washington,* 2d ed. (Chatham, N.J.: Chatham House, 1999).
11. John Kincaid, "The State of U.S. Federalism 2000–2001: Continuity and Crisis," *Publius* (Summer 2001), p. 20.
12. John Kincaid, "State-Federal Relations: Continuing Regulatory Federalism," *Book of the States 2002* (Lexington, Ky.: Council of State Governments, 2002), pp. 26–28.
13. Ann O'M Bowman, "American Federalism on the Horizon," *Publius* (Spring 2002), p. 12.
14. Martha Derthick, "American Federalism: Half-Full or Half-Empty?" *Brookings Review* (Winter 2000), p. 26.

15. Linda Greenhouse, "The High Court's Target: Congress," *New York Times* (February 25, 2001), Sec. 4, p. 3.
16. Jonathan Walters, "Leaving It to the Court," *Governing* (September 2002), p. 14.
17. Timothy J. Conlan and Franco Vergniolle de Chantal, "Courting Devolution: The Rehnquist Court and Contemporary American Federalism." Annual Meeting of the American Political Science Association, Washington, 2000.
18. See Thomas J. Anton, *American Federalism and Public Policy: How the System Works* (New York: Random House, 1989), pp. 83–85.
19. David Mayhew, *Congress: The Electoral Connection* (New Haven, Conn.: Yale University Press, 1974), p. 129.
20. Joseph F. Zimmerman, "Financing National Policy through Mandates," *National Civic Review* (Summer–Fall, 1992), p. 366.
21. John Kincaid, "Developments in Federal-State Relations, 1992–93," in *Book of the States, 1994–95* (Lexington, Ky.: Council of State Governments, 1994), p. 580. Also see Timothy J. Conlon and David R. Beam, "Federal Mandates: The Record of Reform and Future Prospects," *Intergovernmental Perspective* (Fall 1992), pp. 7–11.
22. Alice Rivlin, *Reviving the American Dream* (Washington, D.C.: The Brookings Institution, 1992), p. 107.
23. See Paul L. Posner, "Unfunded Mandates Reform Act: 1996 and Beyond," *Publius* (Spring 1997), pp. 53–71.
24. Joseph F. Zimmerman, "Congressional Regulation of Subnational Governments," *PS: Political Science & Politics* (June 1993), p. 179. Also see Joseph F. Zimmerman, "Federal Preemption under Reagan's New Federalism," *Publius* (Winter 1991), pp. 7–28.
25. Joseph F. Zimmerman, *Interstate Relations* (Westport, Conn.: Praeger, 1996), p. 41.
26. *The Book of the States 1998–99* (Lexington, Ky.: Council of State Governments, 1998), p. 432.
27. Peter T. Kilborn, "As State Budgets Break, Pain Trickles Down," *New York Times* (December 13, 2000), pp. 1, 30.
28. Hanson, "Intergovernmental Relations," p. 61.
29. William H. Riker, *Federalism: Origin, Operation, Significance* (Boston: Little, Brown, 1964), p. 155.
30. David Osborne, "A New Federal Compact: Sorting Out Washington's Proper Role," in *Mandate for Change,* Will Marshall and Martin Schram, eds. (New York: Berkley Books, 1993).
31. See David C. Nice and Patricia Fredericksen, *The Politics of Intergovernmental Relations,* 2d ed. (Chicago: Nelson-Hall, 1995), pp. 15–20.

CHAPTER 3

Political Parties and Interest Groups

POINTS TO CONSIDER

- Are political parties unregulated private associations?
- What factors caused the decline of urban political machines?
- Describe the activities of today's Democratic and Republican parties at the state and local level.
- What types of primaries are used in the states?
- Are the Democratic and Republican parties becoming more competitive in state elections?
- What is the effect of party competition and divided government on state policies?

- How do political parties differ from interest groups?
- What tactics do interest groups use in state capitals?
- Can lobbyists buy influence?
- What interest groups are found in cities?
- What are the approaches to the study of community power?

POLITICAL PARTIES AS ORGANIZATIONS

Legal Basis of Parties

The U.S. Constitution does not mention political parties, and Congress has made little effort to pass laws affecting them. As a result, states are relatively free to restrict party organizations and activities by provisions in their constitutions and laws. On occasion, however, the U.S. Supreme Court has found some state regulations unconstitutional.

State regulation of parties can be divided into three periods. The first period, from the adoption of the U.S. Constitution through the beginning of the 1880s, contained no regulation. Parties were considered to be private political associations. Early national leaders such as George Washington and James Madison feared the effects of parties and viewed them as necessary evils, at best. Nevertheless, parties developed quickly because they were effective in mobilizing voters to elect candidates.

Is There Anyone Else I Can Vote For?

A frequent complaint about American politics is found in the words of a citizen in Minnesota who said, "I didn't feel my political philosophy was represented," referring to the candidates for governor in the 2002 general election.[1] Her views reflect those of millions of Americans, not just those in Minnesota.

Minnesota voters had the same feelings in 1998 when they elected Jesse Ventura as their governor. Ventura, former pro wrestler and radio talk show host, did not run as a Democrat[2] or a Republican but was the candidate of the Reform Party. Nationally, Ross Perot created the Reform Party after his strong showing as an independent candidate in the 1992 presidential election. Ventura spent less money than his Democratic and Republican opponents. He made extensive use of the Internet to reach his supporters, and his outsider candidacy and message of

"Retaliate in '98" was a perfect fit with the attitudes of a large number of Minnesota's voters, especially young adults.

Ventura did not run for reelection in 2002, but Tim Penny, a former conservative Democratic member of Congress, did run as an Independence Party candidate. Penny could not duplicate Ventura's success; he received only 16 percent of the vote. Minnesota voters switched back to the two traditional parties, electing as governor Republican Tom Pawlenty, with the Democratic candidate coming in second place.

Even with substantial public dissatisfaction with the two major parties—and much of it is justified—they have demonstrated amazing resilience. Their importance to elections and governing, especially at the state level, is one of the principal topics to examine in this chapter.

By the 1880s, with the widely held view that parties were under the control of corrupt party bosses, a second period began. It was one of extensive regulation that lasted into the 1970s. The first of these laws, voter registration and the Australian ballot, affected the conduct of elections. **Voter registration** created a list of eligible voters in advance of the election date and was useful in combating fraudulent voting practices such as the same person voting more than once.[3] Prior to the Australian ballot, voters would deposit in the ballot box, in full public view, a ballot that had been printed by one of the parties and contained only the names of its candidates. This practice allowed for voter intimidation or bribery. The new **Australian ballot** system consisted of a single official ballot that was prepared by the state and listed all parties and candidates. Voters were provided a booth so they could mark their ballot in secret.[4] Later reforms, adopted during the Progressive movement (1900–1920), were directed at regulating the parties' internal structures and procedures, requiring, among other things, the use of primary elections to nominate candidates. Many of these reforms will be discussed in more detail later in this chapter.

During this second period of regulation, state laws and party practices that prevented minority groups from voting in primaries in many southern states were appealed to the U.S. Supreme Court. For example, the practice of excluding African Americans from the Texas Democratic primaries was declared unconstitutional (1944), as was the practice of Democrats in a Texas county that excluded African Americans from participating in a preprimary straw poll of an informal group known as the Jaybird Democratic Association (1953).[5] (Although these cases are significant, it should be remembered that at this time most African Americans in southern states were prevented from voting because of discriminatory provisions in voter registration laws. See Chapter 4.)

The third period of state regulation, which began in the 1970s and continues today, is a trend toward deregulation, that is, returning to the earlier view that political parties are private associations. This is not to say that states no longer regulate parties; they do.[6] The U.S. Supreme Court has again entered the picture and declared some state laws unconstitutional because they violate a party's First Amendment right of freedom of association. A Connecticut law that limited participation in a party's primary election to voters registered only with that party is a good example. The Republican Party of Connecticut challenged the law because it wanted to allow voters registered as independents to vote in Republican primaries. Republicans hoped that if independents voted in their party's primary they would also vote for Republican candidates in the general election and that some of these voters might eventually join the party, resulting in a stronger organization. The Court concluded in 1986 that the Republican Party's decision on who could vote in its primary was a private matter, and not one that could be overturned by state law.[7] In another important Court decision (1989), a major obstacle to party activity in California was eliminated when laws prohibiting parties from endorsing candidates in primary elections and regulating various details of internal governance of the parties were overturned.[8]

How far will this deregulation trend go? Will political parties be completely deregulated? This seems unlikely because party officials have frequently persuaded state legislatures to enact laws that give some protection to the two major parties, even though the general thrust of state laws, as described above, was designed to restrict parties.

Sore-loser laws, for example, help the Democratic and Republican Parties by prohibiting a candidate who loses in a primary election from running in the general election as an independent or as the nominee of another party. And the U.S. Supreme Court recently upheld a Minnesota law that prohibits "fusion" candidacies for elected office. "Fusion" candidacies occur when a minor party, in this instance the Twin Cities Area New Party, chooses as its candidate an individual who is already the candidate of another party. Supporters of minor parties believe that "fusion" candidates will help them gain an electoral foothold because minor party voters can point to their votes for the "fusion" candidate and, consequently, expect the winning candidate to be responsive to some of their policy views. But the Court majority decided that Minnesota had a valid state interest in preserving the stability of its political system by enacting laws that may favor the existing two-party system.[9] It appears that even the Supreme Court does not want to invalidate all state laws regulating parties.

Urban Political Machines

Perhaps the best example of traditional party organizations occurred not at the state level but at the local level. Around 1850, urban political machines started spreading rapidly among many cities, primarily those located in the Northeast and Midwest. In a handful of cities such as Chicago, they were influential even into the late 1970s. An **urban political machine** was a cohesive and unified party organization led by a strong leader usually called the boss. The machine controlled city or county government because voters loyal to the machine voted for its candidates on election day. The machine gained and kept the loyalty of voters mainly through patronage.[10] **Patronage** refers to the distribution of material rewards, especially public jobs, to the politically faithful. Control of public payroll jobs and influence over hiring for some jobs in private business was always the machine's greatest source of power.

In terms of organizational structure, the political machine was based on city blocks, precincts, and wards. (A **precinct** is the smallest unit for voting in elections and usually contains up to 1,000 people and one polling place. To elect members to the city council, precincts frequently were joined together to form election districts called **wards.**) Each precinct was headed by a precinct captain and each ward by a ward leader. Precinct captains were responsible for delivering the votes for the boss; they frequently held city jobs and could lose those jobs if the vote was lower than expected.[11] (See Figure 3-1.)

Council elections by wards helped machines by focusing elections on small areas where an ethnic group beholden to the machine often constituted a majority of the population. Although the boss was often the mayor and ward leaders were often members of the city council, sometimes they were party officials who operated behind the scenes to control local government.

But why did political machines emerge and thrive? Fred I. Greenstein and Frank Feigert state that their development in the second half of the nineteenth century was caused by a number of factors, including the following:

1. The population of American cities experienced dramatic growth as the nation's economy shifted from agriculture to industry. In 1850, only one American city had a population over 250,000; in 1890 eleven cities had more than 250,000 and three had over a million.

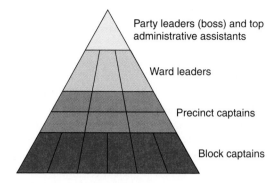

FIGURE 3-1 Political machine organization chart.

Source: Bernard H. Ross and Myron A. Levine, *Urban Politics: Power in Metropolitan America,* 5th ed. (Itasca, Ill.: F. E. Peacock Publishers, 1996), p. 147. Reproduced by permission of the publisher.

2. The structure of city government, marked by mayors with little power and many elected officials, made it almost impossible to manage the challenges of urban growth.
3. More than 25 million immigrants came to the United States, and most of them settled in cities. They were an important source of cheap labor for American industry. Local governments, however, were ill-equipped to aid in their transition to a new culture.
4. Businesses increasingly needed services from government in the form of construction permits, roads paved or upgraded, and water and sewerage services, among others. Also, utility producers and transit companies were interested in obtaining city franchises that gave them the exclusive right to provide a service within the city's boundaries.[12]

It was city political machines that rushed to fill many of these needs. The machine centralized public decision making and provided much needed social services at a time when government assumed little responsibility for social welfare. Most importantly, in terms of votes that the machine needed to survive, it assisted immigrants. As William J. Crotty puts it, the machine "figuratively and literally met people at their boats, helped them settle in ethnic neighborhoods, provided them with gift baskets of food or clothing or coal at Christmas and Thanksgiving . . . occasionally got them jobs, and acted as an intermediary with government agencies."[13] The machine saw to it that immigrants became naturalized citizens and voters. In some cities, machines created new voters almost as needed because the clerk of a local court, an office easily influenced by the machine, could certify naturalization.[14]

Although immigrants were important to political machines, it should be remembered that machines dominated many southern and midwestern cities early in the twentieth century where there were relatively few new immigrants. In these cases, machines relied on the working-class poor for much of their support.

For city policies to be carried out, it was absolutely critical that the boss put his stamp of approval on them. Bosses were usually brokers who chose among alternatives developed by others. They had little interest in political ideology and seldom developed broad policy goals. An exception to this general rule was in Boston where Mayor James M. Curley's machine went beyond providing basic services to build parks, modernize roads, and redevelop the city.

Reform Movement

As powerful as political machines were, they also engaged in corrupt activities such as kickbacks and payoffs in city contracts. Election fraud was common, including, for example, inaccurate counting of votes, fictitious voters, and "repeaters," people who voted several times in the same election.[15] As the nineteenth century turned into the twentieth century, the Progressive movement grew in influence not only at the national and state levels but also at the local level. **Good-government organizations** sprang up everywhere, advocating and eventually winning structural reforms of local government, including merit systems for hiring city employees (civil service), professional city managers, nonpartisan elections, and at-large elections. The National Municipal League was formed and held national conferences at which local reform leaders would meet and discuss ways of changing city government.[16] The National Municipal League is still in existence, now known as the National Civic League.

All of these reforms were direct attempts to eliminate, or at least reduce, the influence of political machines. The change to a merit system (civil service) for hiring most public employees hit the machines especially hard because it reduced their most important source of patronage. George Washington Plunkett, a member of New York City's machine known as Tammany Hall, denounced civil service as "the curse of the nation." Still, some patronage jobs continued to be available for decades, especially in cities such as Chicago. Beginning in the 1970s, three Supreme Court decisions dealt a serious blow to a party's ability to reward its supporters with jobs. The Court held that *non–civil service* employees in the sheriff's office in Cook County (Illinois) could not be fired simply because they did not support the party of the newly elected sheriff.[17] In another case from Illinois, the Court also decided that party affiliation could not be a factor in hiring, promoting, or transferring state employees.[18] This decision affected the treatment of 60,000 employees in Illinois and caused changes in personnel practices in several states and cities. In *O'Hare Truck Service v. City of Northlake* (1996) the Court extended this protection from jobs to businesses that contract their services to a city. The case came from the city of Northlake, Illinois, where O'Hare Truck Service was taken off the city's list of towing contractors because its owner refused to contribute to the incumbent mayor's reelection campaign and displayed at his place of business a campaign poster supporting the mayor's opponent. In all of these cases ruling against patronage, the Court has argued that it is supporting the individual's right of political association.[19]

The creation of city manager positions meant the hiring of professional, nonpolitical administrators who were *not* dependent on the machine. Nonpartisan and at-large elections also reduced the influence of machines to elect their favorite candidates. In **nonpartisan elections** candidates are prohibited from listing their party affiliation on the ballot. The machine cannot *officially* select or *formally* endorse a candidate. (Informally, of course, parties could still try to influence elections.) Over 70 percent of all cities in the United States use nonpartisan elections. In **at-large elections,** *all* council members are elected by voters of the entire city. There are no wards or districts from which individual council members are elected. Reformers hoped that the switch to at-large elections would elevate the tone of elections, produce better candidates, break the local bias of ward elections, and eliminate the "building blocks of the machines."[20] Today about 60 percent of all cities have at-large elections.

Although these changes in the structure of local government had significant adverse effects on political machines, several other factors combined to weaken them. In the 1920s, federal government policy severely limited immigration. Without new arrivals, machines lost their supply of new voters. Meanwhile, second- and third-generation im-migrants moved into the middle class and lost their ties to the machines. Even among lower-class residents, the availability of federal welfare programs, beginning in the 1930s, eliminated another machine resource. No longer able to attract voters by giving out food baskets, the most machines could do was to help people apply for public assis-tance or to take political credit for government programs.[21]

As urban residents became better educated and better off financially, the patronage machines could provide loyal voters ceased to be attractive. Individuals began to place a greater value on their vote and were less willing to tolerate corruption in government. It was a combination of structural reforms *and* changing economic and social conditions that brought down many machines.

In many instances Progressive (structural) reformers had little faith in the ability of the people to make good judgments about their government. They wanted cities to be run by an educated, upper-class elite. Only a few reformers at the beginning of the twen-tieth century were *social reformers* who sought to help the working class. Social re-formers included two colorful mayors: Samuel "Golden Rule" Jones in Toledo, Ohio, advocated an eight-hour day for city employees and services for poor citizens that in-cluded playgrounds, public baths, and free kindergartens. Hazen Pingree, mayor of Detroit, Michigan, battled the privately owned phone, gas, and light utilities in an effort to keep prices low and initiated work-relief programs for the city's poor.

Years later, reforms frequently have unanticipated consequences, and this is the case with the switch from ward or district elections of city council members to at-large elections. Researchers agree that minorities have better representation in the unreformed district election system. A study of ten Texas cities concludes that under district systems more Mexican Americans seek and win election to city councils. The presence of Mexican Americans on the councils, at least in these cities, had a policy impact in that more Mexican Americans were hired as city employees, salaries of Mexican Americans were increased, and more Mexican Americans were appointed to city boards and commissions.[22]

One machine that thrived long after other machines had disappeared was the Democratic Party organization in Chicago, known as the Daley Machine (1955 to 1976). As mayor of Chicago and chairman of the Cook County Democratic Party, Richard J. Daley controlled as many as 30,000 public jobs and perhaps 10,000 private jobs. Chicago's civil service was notoriously weak, with many permanent jobs filled with "temporary" employees, which allowed the hiring process to bypass civil service procedures. Not only was Mayor Daley powerful in Chicago, Democratic presidential candidates visited him on a regular basis seeking his support in their quest for the Democratic nomination. Although several of his associates went to jail in the 1970s for graft, Daley did not fall victim to personal greed. Still, the Daley machine eventually lost power. While Chicago won national praise as "the city that works," a growing African-American population, representing almost 35 percent of Chicago's residents in 1977, believed that their needs were being ignored in favor of policies that favored the older white ethnic wards. African Americans were demanding "open housing" policies that would attack Chicago's segregated housing market.

Daley was elected to his sixth term in 1975, but died a year later. After his death, the Democratic Party leadership splintered and racial division and animosity increased in what became a chaotic period for Chicago politics. Jane Byrne won the next regularly scheduled election and became the city's first woman mayor; she was *not* backed by the Democratic machine. Byrne was defeated after one term by Harold Washington, an African-American member of the U.S. Congress, who won with a strong turnout by African-American voters and additional support from Latinos and white liberals. Washington was reelected but died in office in 1988.[23] Richard M. Daley, son of the former mayor, won a special election in 1989 and has held the office since then. He was most recently reelected in 2003, with almost 80 percent of the vote.

Party Organization Today

An example of how one state party (Kansas Democrats) is organized is found in Figure 3-2. Precinct committees are at the bottom, county committees are in the middle, and the state committee and chairperson are at the top. The Kansas Democratic Party also has congressional district committees and members on the Democratic National Committee. Although all state parties have members on their national committees, congressional district party organization is not found in all states. State party organization is not a true hierarchical structure, in which power flows from the top to the bottom; instead each level operates somewhat independently of those units above and below it.

Most political scientists agree that it is the *local* party organizational units, especially county committees, that are vital to a strong party. Sarah McCally Morehouse and Malcolm E. Jewell suggest that the county committee is important because the county as a governmental unit elects a large number of public officials; its officials still control some patronage, although significantly less than in the past; the boundaries of many larger electoral units, such as congressional and state legislative districts, frequently follow county lines; and county chairpersons usually serve as members of the state committee.[24] The structure of parties at the county level varies among the states. In most states a precinct committeeperson (or captain or chair) is elected by voters in the primary election or by a precinct caucus. (A **precinct caucus** refers to a meeting where voters registered with the party get together and as a group elect the committeeperson.) The committeeperson becomes a member of the county committee, which elects the county party chairperson. In another pattern members of a county committee are the lowest level of elected party officials, and if precincts are organized it is done by the appointment of the county chairperson.

Great diversity is found in the actual strength and activity of county party organizations. A very few are well funded with a paid executive director and permanent headquarters, but almost all are part-time, voluntary operations without even a telephone listing.[25] Sometimes just finding an intelligent and energetic person to become Republican or Democratic county chairperson is a difficult task. Activity is cyclical,

DNC Representatives

The state chair, vice chair, committeeman and committeewoman represent Kansas at the Democratic National Committee.

Kansas Representatives to the Democratic National Committee

| State Chair | State Vice Chair |
| National Committeeman | National Committeewoman |

| State Treasurer | State Secretary |

Kansas Democratic State Committee

State committee elects officers. Members of the state executive committee are indicated with a red line. (The Hispanic Caucus is an example of an affiliated organization.)

Kansas Democratic State Committee

| 7 chairs of affiliated organizations | Federal and statewide elected officials and senate and house leadership |

28 delegates (14 men/ 14 women)

- District Chair
- District Vice Chair
- District Secretary
- District Treasurer

Congressional District Committees

Each of the four district committees elects officers and additional delegates to represent the district on the state committee.

4 Congressional District Committees

Additional delegates (based on population)

- County Chair
- County Vice Chair
- County Secretary
- Country Treasurer

County Central Committees

Central committees elect officers (chair, vice chair, secretary, and treasurer). Additional delegates may be elected to represent the county on their congressional district committee.

105 County Central Committees

Precinct committeemen and committeewomen in over 3200 precincts in Kansas

Election of Precinct Committeepersons

At the statewide primary Democrats vote to elect one man and one woman to the county central committee.

All registered Democrats in Kansas

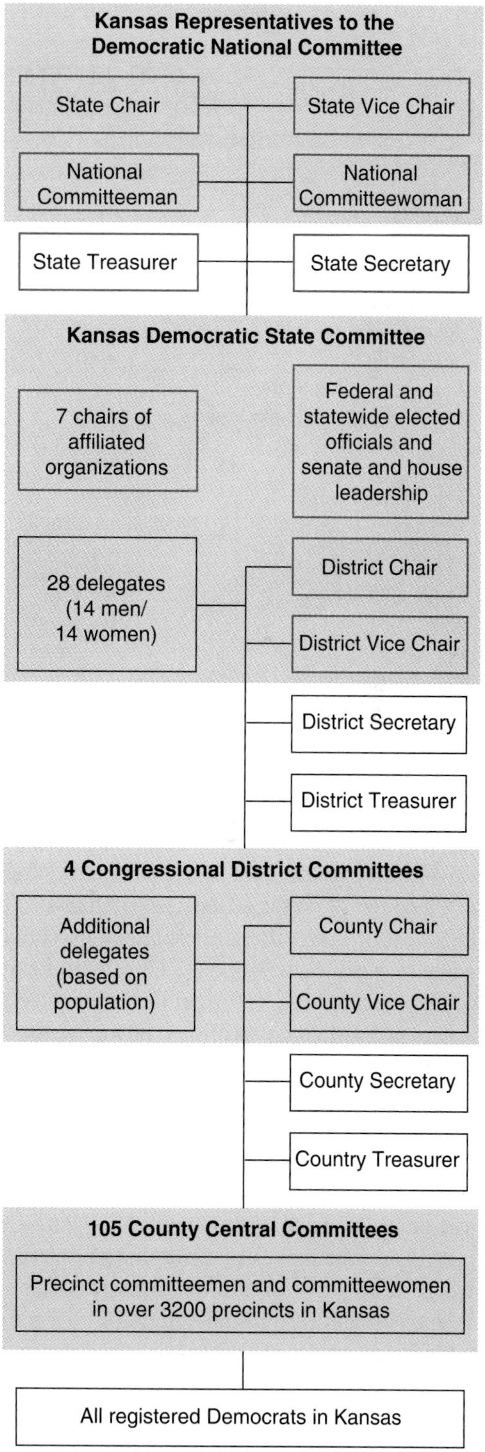

FIGURE 3-2 Democratic party organization in Kansas.

Source: Adapted with the permission of the Kansas Democratic Party. The organizational chart is available from the Kansas Democratic Party at www.ksdp.org. Accessed January 15, 2003.

TABLE 3-1   Campaign Activity Levels of Local Party Organizations in Southern States *(Percentages)*

Activity	Democrats		Republicans	
	Chair	Member	Chair	Member
Organized canvassing	29.7	25.8	31.9	30.6
Organized campaign events	66.7	29.9	70.0	33.8
Arranged fundraising	57.2	25.4	60.6	28.1
Sent mailings	40.5	33.0	53.8	47.1
Distributed literature	72.9	60.5	78.7	71.4
Organized phone banks	45.6	29.1	56.8	38.6
Purchased billboards	8.4	4.5	9.2	5.4
Distributed posters	70.8	52.2	79.7	65.3
Contributed money	77.2	59.8	85.4	72.9
Registration drives	35.1	20.3	33.6	23.0
Utilized surveys	12.8	9.1	16.5	12.5
Dealt with media	60.9	18.0	64.0	22.6
(N)	(619)	(4981)	(611)	(4246)

Source: John A. Clark, Brad Lockerbie, and Peter W. Wielhouwer, "Campaign Activities," in *Party Organization and Activism in the American South*, Robert P. Steed, John A. Clark, Lewis Bowman, and Charles D. Hadley, eds. (Tuscaloosa, Ala.: The University of Alabama Press, 1998), p. 123. Reproduced by permission of The University of Alabama Press.

peaking in the years of election campaigns. Table 3-1 identifies the frequency at which local Democratic and Republican parties in southern states engage in certain campaign activities.

Turning to the state level, state party chairs and committees are selected according to state laws or, in the absence of such laws, party rules. In more than forty states, members of state committees are selected by committee members at local levels or by delegates to party conventions. The remaining states select state committee members in primary elections. The formal means of selecting state party chairs are by the state committee or by state conventions; however, the state's governor frequently influences the actual choice.

A general revitalization of state-level party organization started in the 1980s; however, it is important to keep this heralded revitalization in the context of history and region. There is little doubt that both the Democratic and Republican state parties are stronger in southern states where previously the Republicans were a hopeless minority and the dominance of the Democratic Party "produced a politics of faction rather than party, and state party organizations were largely irrelevant."[26] The same is true in states where the Progressive movement was strong; from the upper midwestern states of Wisconsin and Minnesota extending to Pacific Coast states, party organizations were typically weak. On the other hand, in older industrial states, reaching from New England to Illinois, most state party organizations are stronger today than they were at their low point in the early 1970s, but they will probably never be as strong at the state or local level as they were in the early part of the twentieth century.

State parties in almost all states now have permanent headquarters, annual budgets in election years that average more than $2 million, and a professional staff organized into several sections such as finance, political, communications, field operations, and clerical. In addition to the position of state party chair, which is usually not a paid position, there is a paid, full-time executive director in all of the state parties. The headquarters of the Florida Republican Party, one of the best organized and funded, "operates with a budget of $6 million and is packed with computer hardware, telephone banks, and printing facilities."[27]

John Bibby calls today's state parties "service-oriented" organizations that provide important services to local parties and candidates.[28] Party-building activities include regular programs to raise money, maintaining voter identification lists, and conducting public opinion polls for the development of campaign strategy. Candidates' personal campaign organizations, especially in statewide races, make most of the decisions about individual campaigns, but state parties are increasingly providing services to candidates: training of campaign volunteers, assistance in polling, and get-out-the-vote drives.

How many and how well these activities are performed by a state party depend in part on the relationship between the party chairperson and the governor, when they are of the same party. Frequently, a governor will be responsible for the election of a chairperson, and when this happens, he or she serves as the governor's agent and tries to control the party and have it fight the governor's battles.[29] Sometimes the chairperson is more independent of the governor, especially if the office was achieved on his or her own efforts. Although this chairperson may cooperate with the governor, he or she will devote more time to broad-based party activities. Of course, half of the chairpersons are members of the party that does not control the governor's office (the outparty) and also tend to engage in party-building activities.

Activities presently performed by state and local parties appear to be routine, and one may wonder whether they affect the outcomes of elections. Overall, studies show that a well-organized county party has a positive, though minor, effect on the share of the vote received by its candidates. However, in certain situations a well-organized party can make a greater difference. This is true in counties where the party occupies a minority status, that is, a party that wins few or no elections. In these counties, the better organized parties will run candidates for every elected office on the ballot (a full slate of candidates), resulting in an increase in the number of votes their candidates receive, even at the congressional level. Also, it is likely that a minority party with a strong organization may have a greater effect on election results when longtime incumbents retire or a sudden swing in the mood of the voters goes against the dominant party.[30] A well-organized minority party is capable of taking advantage of these situations. Finally, party organization is an important factor in determining how close the parties are in contesting statewide offices: The better organized the parties, the more competition there is between the Democratic and Republican Parties.[31]

People active in a political party, from precinct committeepersons to state party chairs, often are classified as professionals or amateurs. **Amateurs** are more reform-minded, more interested in advocating certain issue positions and supporting candidates who take the same positions. They enter politics because of their desire to further particular political causes. **Professionals** are more interested in winning elections and are therefore more willing to compromise issue positions if that is what it takes to win. They are less concerned about their parties' candidates taking clear positions on the issues. (See Table 3-2.) The Christian Coalition is a recent example of an issue-oriented group

TABLE 3-2 Professionals and Amateurs: A Typology

	Professionals	Amateurs
Political style	Pragmatic	Purist
Incentives for activism	Material (patronage, preferments)	Purposive (issues, ideology)
Locus of party loyalty	Party organization	Officeholders, other political groups
Desired orientation of party	To candidates, elections	To issues, ideology
Criterion for selecting party candidates	Electability	Principles
Desired process of party governance	Hierarchical	Democratic
Support of party candidates	Automatic	Conditional on issues, principles
Recruitment path	Through party	Through issue, candidate organizations
SES level	Average to above average	Well above average

Source: Paul Allen Beck and Majorie Randon Hershey, *Party Politics in America*, 9th ed. (New York: Addison-Wesley Educational Publishers, Inc., 2001), p.102. Reproduced by permission of Addison-Wesley Educational Publishers.

that has won control of party committees in several states so that it can advance a conservative agenda, especially on social issues such as abortion. The Christian Coalition has gained considerable influence in the Republican party in Iowa, Minnesota, New Mexico, Oregon, South Carolina, and Texas.[32]

Because the amateur style emphasizes issues over party, there has been speculation that it might severely weaken party organizations, but there is no real evidence that this has occurred.[33] In fact, politically active groups would not try to gain control of party organizations if they didn't think they were important in the political process. Nevertheless, differing styles are a source of tension and conflict within party organizations.

PARTIES AND THE NOMINATION OF CANDIDATES

The importance of the nomination process to political parties is summed up by the statement: "Who can make nominations is the owner of the party."[34] During the latter half of the nineteenth century, statewide nominations were formally made by state party conventions composed of delegates selected earlier at county conventions. And, as mentioned previously, party bosses frequently controlled nominations that were made at the local level. Primary elections changed forever the role of party organizations in the nomination of candidates.

The Direct Primary

In 1903, Wisconsin adopted the first direct primary law to nominate candidates for statewide offices and by 1917, a majority of states had adopted it. The **direct primary** is an election in which voters decide the parties' nominees for the general election. In other words, voters are directly involved in the nomination process, unlike party conventions where only delegates to the convention vote on nominees. The spread of the direct primary weakened party organizations. Of course, this is just what its advocates, members of the Progressive movement, intended. They wanted to open the nominating process by removing the monopoly of power held by party leaders to handpick candidates and even to direct their behavior once they were elected to office. Today, no state uses only the convention method to nominate candidates, but a few southern states (Alabama, Georgia, South Carolina, and Virginia) allow the party to choose each election year whether to use a convention or a primary.[35] Although laws regulating nominations and primary elections vary among the fifty states, they all must cover who is allowed to vote in the primary and how a person places his or her name on the ballot as a candidate for the party's nomination.

Types of Primaries

Who is allowed to vote in primary elections? One might think all registered voters are eligible to vote in primary elections, but this is usually not the case. One view is that voters who participate in the Democratic primary must be registered as Democrats in advance of the primary election and voters who participate in the Republican primary must be registered as Republicans, again in advance of the primary election. Others argue that voters should have the freedom to vote for the person they perceive as the best candidate, and that the party affiliation of the voter and candidate is immaterial. In devising primary laws, states have sided with one or the other of these two views, and some have managed to fall in between. Political scientists have developed elaborate schemes to classify state primaries. Nevertheless, the familiar terms of *closed primary* and *open primary,* along with the less familiar *blanket primary* and the *open elections* procedure, make for the simplest presentation.

Closed primaries are used in twenty-six states. In a **closed primary,** voters declare a party preference in advance and can vote only in that party's primary. States vary in terms of how far in advance voters need to declare their party preference or affiliation. Most require voters who want to change their party to do so several months in advance of the primary. Others have more flexibility in changing parties. Iowa, for example, allows voters to switch registration on the day of the election, although a record is kept of the party a voter registers with. States that allow voters to change registration on election day are very similar to open primaries.

Open primaries are used in twenty states. In an **open primary,** voters do not declare a party preference in advance and may choose either a Republican or a Democratic ballot, that is, vote in either party's primary. Although some states require voters to express publicly a preference for the ballot of a party at the polls, in other states voters can decide which party's primary they will vote in in the privacy of the voting booth. (Either way it is possible for the supporters of one party to vote in the other party's primary. When this happens it is called *crossover voting.*)

For several decades, a blanket primary has been used in Alaska and Washington. A **blanket primary** gives registered voters maximum choice in selecting candidates. It goes a step further than open primaries by allowing voters to decide office by office which primary they will vote in. A voter can vote in the Democratic primary for governor and then in the Republican primary for attorney general, for example, moving back and forth between the parties by office; however, it is not permissible to vote in both parties' primary for the same office. In 1996, California switched from a closed primary to a blanket primary when voters approved a ballot initiative titled the "Open Primary Initiative." (Although it was called an open primary, it was actually a blanket primary.)[36] At the present time, the continued use of the blanket primary is problematic. The U.S. Supreme Court in *California Democratic Party v. Jones* (2000)[37] concluded that a political party has a right, protected by the First Amendment, to determine which voters may participate in the nomination of its candidates for public office. As in the Connecticut case mentioned earlier, the Court is saying that state laws cannot mandate the type of primary a party must use. California returned to the closed primary system, which it had used prior to 1996. Political parties in Alaska also have changed to closed primaries for all political parties in the state. (As of this writing, Washington has not moved to a different type of primary.)

A unique **open elections** procedure,[38] adopted in 1975, is used in Louisiana. All candidates for an office, regardless of party affiliation, are required to appear on the same ballot. Candidates may, and usually do, list their party affiliation. If one of the candidates receives a majority of the votes cast, that candidate is declared elected and the general election is canceled. If no one has a majority, the general election is held and the top two candidates run against each other. This allows for the possibility that the two candidates could be affiliated with the same party, two Democrats or two Republicans. This happened in the 1987 gubernatorial race when two Democrats ran against each other. (The election was won by Charles "Buddy" Roemer, who changed his affiliation to the Republican Party while in office.) The effect of this system in state legislative races has been to help incumbents, who, because of their name recognition, frequently win a majority in the first election. Also, at least initially, the law resulted in fewer Republicans—the minority party in Louisiana—contesting state legislative contests. More recently, the Republican Party has done better in gubernatorial races, with Republican Mike Foster elected in 1995 and winning reelection in 1999 in the primary election. Nevertheless, the fact that a minority party may not have a chance to contest general elections makes the open elections a bad choice; it discourages the development of two strong parties.

In most states the winner of the primary is the candidate who receives the most votes (plurality), even if it is not a majority. In many southern states, however, a majority vote is required. This has led to **runoff primaries**, a second primary between the top two candidates if no one received a majority in the first primary. The runoff primary was instituted in the South when the Democratic Party was dominant and winning the Democratic primary was tantamount to winning the general election. The runoff required a candidate to receive support of a majority of the Democrats. The rise of the Republican Party has put more importance on the general election and decreased participation in the Democratic primary.[39] Some civil rights organizations have claimed that runoff primaries discriminate. They argue that fewer whites voting in the

Democratic primary has increased the importance of the African-American vote. And if there is one African-American candidate and several white candidates on the ballot, it is possible for the African-American candidate to win a plurality, but not a majority, of the votes in the *first* primary if white voters split their votes among all of the white candidates. In the ensuing runoff primary, with an African-American candidate facing a white candidate, white voters may coalesce around the white candidate who will then have a majority to win the nomination. A study of a number of primary elections in the South found that the number of African-American candidates who led in the first primary fell by 50 percent in the runoff primary, giving some support to the belief that runoff primaries have a discriminatory effect.[40] Thus far, courts have not declared runoff primaries unconstitutional.

At the local level, elections are frequently nonpartisan, and when that is the case, the primary election is nonpartisan and the two candidates receiving the most votes in the primary will face each other in the general election. In some cities and towns, the general election is canceled if a candidate receives a majority of votes in the primary.

Access to the Primary Ballot

Candidates normally gain access to the primary ballot by obtaining signatures on a petition or paying a modest filing fee. Seven states, however, use this stage of the nominating process as an opportunity for parties to gain back some of the influence they have lost over nominations with the adoption of the direct primary. They do this by allowing preprimary endorsements of candidates for governor by state party conventions. It is a procedure that is written into law in these states. The specifics vary, with parties playing a rather strong role in Utah where a candidate receiving more than 70 percent of the convention vote is declared the nominee and no primary is held. Otherwise, the top two candidates in convention voting are placed on the primary ballot. In other states, the names of the endorsed candidates will appear automatically on the primary ballot while others who seek to be the nominee will have to gather signatures on petitions. Sometimes the endorsement is simply an endorsement and does not affect access to the ballot.

During the 1960s and 1970s, these endorsements had substantial influence in determining the nominee (endorsed candidates won contested primaries close to 80 percent of the time). The success rate of endorsed candidates between 1980 and 2000 has dropped to the 50 percent level. Malcolm Jewell suggests there is no single explanation for the decline in success of party-endorsed candidates. But some of the endorsed candidates have lost to opponents who had little political experience, which is actually appealing to many voters at this time, or had ample campaign funds to spend on television ads to counter the party-endorsed candidate.[41] It also has happened that a well-organized faction in a party will elect a majority of state convention delegates and endorse a candidate whose policy positions are too extreme for voters who normally support the party. (Occasionally, as few as 12,000 voters will participate in the convention delegate selection process.) This appears to have happened in Minnesota in 1994, when the Republican state convention did *not* endorse the incumbent Republican governor, Arne Carlson. The convention endorsed a candidate with more conservative political views, Allen Quist, who lost to Carlson in the primary.[42] In 1998, in Minnesota, the candidate endorsed by the Democrat-Farmer-Labor party lost in the primary to Hubert H.

Humphrey, III. Stephen I. Frank and Steven C. Wagner suggest that one reason Jesse Ventura was elected governor was that he was able to "capitalize on the dissatisfaction of the voters with the Republican and DFL endorsement and primary process and made a successful appeal to them."[43] Preprimary endorsements of candidates by convention delegates that are unrepresentative of a party's supporters will be of little help to them in winning the primary.

PARTY COMPETITION IN THE STATES

Political scientists have devoted considerable attention to the level of party competition in the states. **Party competition** is present when candidates of the two major parties (Democrats and Republicans) have an almost equal chance of winning the governor's office and a majority of seats in the state legislature.

Classifying the States

Regardless of measurement techniques employed to determine the degree of competition, states are usually grouped into a number of categories that identify those where Republicans dominate elections, those with competitive elections, and those where Democrats dominate elections. Our classification is for 1988 through 2002 elections and is based on definitions developed by Malcolm Jewell and David Olson that we have modified to take into account the large number of competitive states that have emerged recently.[44] Jewell and Olson, analyzing the 1965–1988 time period, identified thirty-two states as competitive. Because the competitive category is so large, Jewell and Olson's single competitive category has been expanded to three categories so we can classify states as competitive or as leaning to one party or the other. Fewer one-party dominant and one-party majority states allow the merger of these two categories into one. For Figure 3-3, states were classified as follows:

> *Dominant/majority.* In majority party states, one party is consistently more successful in winning elections to state offices. Both parties seriously contest elections for the governor's office and for control of the legislature. However, the majority party controls the governor's office more than two-thirds of the time, and its candidates usually receive approximately 60 percent of the vote. The majority party also controls the senate and house more than two-thirds of the time, and the proportion of the seats it wins is usually less than three-fourths of the total. Also in this category are a few states labeled "one-party dominant." In these states, one party always or almost always wins the election for governor with more than two-thirds of the total vote cast and always wins control of the state legislature with a majority that frequently exceeds three-fourths of the total number of seats.
>
> *Competitive leaning.* Both parties win elections to state offices, but one party does just slightly better. Typically, in these states the Democratic and Republican Parties divide control of the governor's office, but one is more consistent in winning control of the legislature. Competitive leaning states are classified as competitive Democratic or competitive Republican to indicate which party has a slight advantage.

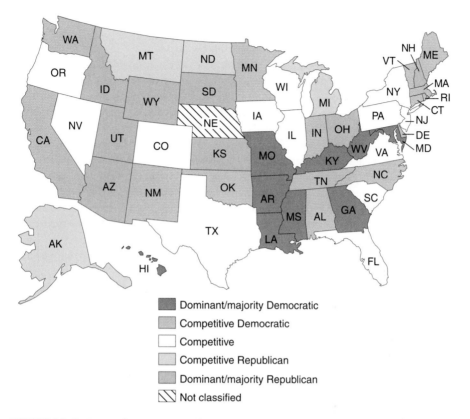

FIGURE 3-3 Patterns of party competition in the states, 1988–2002.

Source: Authors' update of a map of party competition that appeared in Malcolm E. Jewell and David M. Olson, *Political Parties and Elections in American States,* 3d ed. (Chicago: The Dorsey Press, 1988), p. 29.
Note: Nebraska is not classified because its state legislative elections are nonpartisan.

Competitive. Both parties come close to sharing equally the winning of state offices. Democratic and Republican Parties divide control of the governor's office close to one-half of the time. Even control of both houses of the legislature is frequently divided between the parties, as is the membership in each chamber. New Jersey is an unusual example of a state in which recent party competition has been so keen that for a four-year period the Democratic Party controlled the governor's office and the lower house of the legislature, while membership in the senate was evenly divided between the two parties. This even division required senate co-presidents, one from each party, serving as presiding officers. Also labeled as competitive are states in which the parties split control of the executive and legislative branches, with one party consistently winning the governor's office and one party consistently winning control of both houses of the legislature.

Generally, competitive and competitive leaning states are described as two-party states and states in the dominant/majority category are called one-party states.

The Trends Toward Competition

Today, competition between the two major parties at the state level continues to be widespread. A close look at Figure 3-3 reveals that there are thirteen states classified as competitive, and an additional nineteen states are classified as slightly less competitive because they tilt toward the Democratic Party (fifteen states) or the Republican Party (four states). Nine Democratic states and eight Republican states are in the dominant/ majority category, and only a few of them have one party that is dominant; most are one-party majority states. Democratic dominant states include Hawaii and Kentucky; Republican dominant states include Utah and South Dakota. The process by which party competition develops in a state can be described as follows: (1) voters who consistently supported the dominant party begin to split their tickets and vote for some minority party candidates in national and state elections; (2) voters (especially younger persons) begin to shift their party identification, perhaps first to independent and then to the minority party; and (3) voters shift their party registration.

This is not an automatic process, and a wide variety of factors may work to retard change. In states with closed primaries, voters will be more hesitant to change registration because the winner of the dominant party's primary almost always wins the general election, meaning that the only real choice a voter has is in this party's primary. Republicans have been frequently frustrated in the South because Democratic incumbents compile fairly conservative records, giving the people little incentive to switch parties. Earl and Merle Black note that southern Democratic candidates for statewide office try to distance themselves from the liberal image of the national Democratic Party. They campaign on platforms that are both conservative (support of budgetary restraint and school prayer) and progressive (support for improving the educational system and environmental protection).[45]

However, recent elections have reduced, if not eliminated, the Republican Party's frustration in the South. In the 1994 elections, an antigovernment, anti-Democratic tide swept the Republicans to control of both houses of the U.S. Congress for the first time in forty years and caused equally historic gains for Republican candidates to state offices in the South. For the first time in the twentieth century, the party won control of a majority of the governors' offices in the South. Although Democrats still controlled almost all of the state legislatures, the Republicans won a majority of the seats in North Carolina's House of Representatives and the Florida Senate, again for the first time in the twentieth century. Another indication of growing Republican strength was that two of the Republican governors elected in 1994 were previously members of the Democratic Party. In fact, both had been elected as Democrats: Fob James, Jr., was Democratic governor of Alabama (1979–1983), and David Beasley was a Democratic member of the South Carolina state legislature.

Has the Republican Party expanded on these gains in more recent elections? The answer is yes. Republicans achieved a significant breakthrough in Florida (1996) where, for the first time since Reconstruction, they won control of both legislative houses in a southern state. Georgia, clinging to its tradition of Democratic governors longer than any other southern state, was the big prize in the 2002 elections. Georgia voters elected a Republican governor and Republican candidates won a majority of seats in the Georgia state senate; in legislative district races they defeated the Democratic speaker of the house and the Democratic senate majority leader.[46] After the 2002 elections, eight southern states had Republican governors and eight had Democratic governors. The Democratic Party controls both houses of the state legislatures in eight states, but Republicans have a majority of both houses in five states and control is split between the parties in three states. (If the South is defined as the eleven former Confederate states, seven states have Republican governors and only four have Democratic governors!) John H. Aldrich concludes that in the South, "the Republican Party has become a serious and sustained competitor to the Democrats for essentially any and all national and state-level offices, and quite often at lower levels as well."[47]

Although the Republican Party was very successful in the 2002 elections, the overall pattern in the states is clear: Two competitive parties are present in most of the fifty states. After the 2002 elections, there were twenty-six Republican governors and twenty-four Democratic governors. Democrats won in big industrial states, taking the governor's office for the first time in a number of years in Pennsylvania, Michigan, Wisconsin, and Illinois. Democrats also won in some Republican western strongholds such as Arizona, Kansas, Oklahoma, and Wyoming. (In Illinois, it was twenty-six years between Democratic governors.) The Republican Party held onto the governor's offices in New York, Ohio, and Texas. Republicans increased their control of both state legislative chambers from sixteen to twenty-two states, but Democrats still have control in sixteen states and eleven states are split between the parties (Nebraska has a nonpartisan legislature).

Third Parties

The Democratic and Republican Parties have a near monopoly on state politics, but not a complete monopoly. Third-party candidates and independents, candidates not affiliated with any party, have occasionally been elected. During the 1990s, four states had independent or third-party governors: Alaska, Connecticut, Maine, and Minnesota. Some states have a history of active minor parties. Minnesota's Farmer-Labor party won gubernatorial elections early in the twentieth century and eventually merged with the Democratic Party. The official name of the Democratic Party in Minnesota is still the Democrat-Farmer-Labor Party (DFL). In recent years, support in New York for gubernatorial candidates of the Liberal and Conservative Parties has been as high as 9 percent. In 1998, the Libertarian Party offered gubernatorial candidates in sixteen states, but its most successful candidate, John Cashin in Georgia, received only 3.4 percent of the vote. A pro-environment party, known as the Green Party, has been active in some western states, notably New Mexico.

PARTY COMPETITION AND PUBLIC POLICIES

Two-Party States

Although it is generally taken for granted that competitive, two-party states are preferable to one-party states, political scientists disagree regarding the effects of competition on government performance. V. O. Key framed the debate in his classic book, *Southern*

Politics in State and Nation.[48] Key analyzed the politics of southern states in the late 1940s, noting that the South's one-party politics did not raise important issues during election campaigns, discouraged voter participation, and resulted in governments adopting policies that ignored the needs of the "have-nots" (lower socioeconomic groups).[49] Two-party politics, Key believed, would raise more important issues because the parties would tend to represent different socioeconomic classes. The presence of these issues in elections and governing would increase voter participation. In addition, close electoral competition between the parties would force one of the parties to offer some policies favored by the "have-nots" so as to win their votes.

Some political scientists adapted Key's framework by using interparty competition to study all fifty states, but they did not always agree with his conclusions. Studies by Thomas R. Dye indicate that education, welfare, taxation, and highway programs appear to be more closely related to economic factors in the states than the degree of party competition. In other words, states with greater wealth spend more money on various programs regardless of levels of competition. Dye concludes, "Party competition itself does not necessarily cause more liberal welfare policies."[50] In fact, some observers even went so far as to argue that politics was really unimportant in the making of policy.

Unfortunately, analyzing all fifty states, although a good idea, frequently pushes researchers to rely on a few statistical indicators of each state's politics and policies that in all likelihood do not accurately reflect its political history and perhaps not even the current context of policy making. And in doing so they underestimate the important role of political parties. However, additional research is providing new evidence that parties do affect policy making.

Robert D. Brown concludes that greater state policy benefits for the have-nots are found in states where the electoral base of the Democratic Party tends to be a coalition of low-income persons, union members, and Catholics.[51] Using a similar approach in a study of California and New York, Diana Dwyre and her associates add more evidence for the importance of parties in policy making when they have different electoral bases. This study concludes that the "disorganized" decision-making process in California is the principal cause of policies that have placed a greater state and local tax burden on low-income groups (have-nots) than in New York, where the process is more "organized." California's decision-making process is one where parties are minor actors. Many decisions are made through the use of ballot initiatives (see Chapter 4) with temporary coalitions forming around them. These coalitions are composed of various interests but not political parties; they exist for that single issue and then disappear. In New York's decision-making process parties are major actors having clear differences in their electoral bases, with the Democratic Party representing the interests of the have-nots.[52] Party members in the legislature are reasonably cohesive in advancing the interests of their electoral base. Brown and Dwyre and her associates, by examining the electoral bases of parties, are focusing on a crucial and frequently neglected part of Key's arguments.

Another problem with studies that have found economic factors of prime importance in policy making is that they were usually cross-sectional; that is, the data were collected for fifty states at one point in time and then the states were compared with each other. James Garand utilized a longitudinal approach, collecting data on each state at different points. In other words, the data reflect characteristics of each state at several points during a twenty-year period. As a result, he was able to examine the effect of political changes on policy within states. Garand finds, for example, that a change in the party that controls state government does have a substantial impact on spending priorities, especially on the money spent for education.[53]

Further evidence that parties matter in the making of policy comes from a study that finds state party elites have different **ideologies,** that is, beliefs about the purpose and role of government. Although it is frequently claimed that there is not a "dime's worth" of difference between the Democratic and Republican Parties, this bit of conventional wisdom appears to be wrong. Robert Erikson, Gerald Wright, and John McIver have developed a "party elite ideology" score for both parties in forty-six states.[54] The term "party elite" refers to Democrats and Republicans who occupy reasonably high-level positions such as national convention delegates, local party chairpersons, and state legislators.

The attitudes of state party elites on various issues result in a conservative/liberal classification scheme. These traditional labels in American politics have defined **liberals** as those favoring an active role for government and **conservatives** as favoring a limited role for government, definitions that are probably too simple for today's complex issues. Today's liberals believe government should act to assist the economically disadvantaged and racial minority groups, but they are less willing to have government take an active role intervening on moral and social issues such as abortion and prayer in public schools. Conservatives still oppose government intervention in economic areas and in actively assisting minority groups, but they favor government action on many moral and social issues, for example, making abortions illegal and requiring prayer in public schools.

Overall, Erikson, Wright, and McIver conclude that Republican Party elites tend to be conservative and Democrats tend to be liberal. Variations exist by state and region. This is noticeable in the Democratic Party where a number of southern state party elites are classified as "conservative." The largest concentration of "most liberal" Democratic Party elites is in the Northeast. In the Republican Party, the "most conservative" are found in the South and West. No state Republican Party is classified as liberal, not even in the more liberal Northeast. Differences within the parties also are evident. Ideologically, Connecticut Democrats ("most liberal") have about as much in common with Georgia Democrats ("conservative") as they do with Connecticut Republicans ("conservative").[55]

Although these variations are important, it should be remembered that in each state the Republican Party is always more conservative than the Democratic Party. State Democratic and Republican Party elites do have different beliefs on public policy issues.

The Question of Divided Government

Divided government at the national level—when the presidency and the Congress are controlled by opposite political parties—is a frequent occurrence. For example, while Bill Clinton was president the Democratic Party controlled both houses of Congress for only two of eight years (1993 and 1994). **Divided government** in the states occurs when one or both houses of the legislature is controlled by the opposite party of the governor. **Unified government** occurs when one party controls the governor's office and both houses of the state legislature. (Control in each house of a legislature is determined by identifying the party to which a majority of its members belong. The importance of political parties in state legislatures will be discussed in Chapter 5.)

Since the middle of the twentieth century the number of states with divided government has increased steadily; beginning in the 1980s and continuing through the most recent elections, it has been as common as unified government. As can be seen in Table 3-3, after the 2002 elections the number of states with divided government was thirty-one and with unified government, eighteen. During the 1980s and early 1990s, states with divided governments increased as more Republicans were elected as governors, but the Democratic Party still controlled one or both houses of the state legislature.[56] After the 1994 elections, the trend of divided government states continued, but unified Republican government states are outnumbering the states with unified Democratic government. Again, a look at Table 3-3 confirms this: Republicans have eleven unified government states and the Democrats have only seven; and the Democratic divided government states outnumber Republicans, seventeen to fourteen.

To further complicate matters, there has been an increase in the number of states with split control of the legislature—one party controls one house and the other party

TABLE 3-3 Unified and Divided Party Government in the States, 2003		
UNIFIED GOVERNMENT	18 STATES	
Republican governor and legislature	11 states	Alaska, Florida, Idaho, Montana, New Hampshire, North Dakota, Ohio, South Carolina, South Dakota, Texas, Utah
Democratic governor and legislature	7 states	California, Illinois, Mississippi, New Mexico, Oklahoma, Tennessee, West Virginia
DIVIDED GOVERNMENT	31 STATES	
Republican governor and Democratic legislature	8 states	Alabama, Arkansas, Connecticut, Hawaii, Louisiana, Maryland, Massachusetts, Rhode Island
Republican governor and split legislature	6 states	Colorado, Georgia, Minnesota, New York, Nevada, Vermont
Democratic governor and Republican legislature	9 states	Arizona, Iowa, Kansas, Michigan, Missouri, Pennsylvania, Virginia, Wisconsin, Wyoming
Democratic governor and split legislature	8 states	Delaware, Indiana, Kentucky, Maine, New Jersey, North Carolina, Oregon, Washington

Source: The authors collected the data for this table.

Note: Nebraska, with a nonpartisan legislature, is not included. New Jersey seems to fit best in the Democratic governor and split legislature category; the lower house has a Democratic majority, but in the state senate the Democrats and Republicans jointly share power because the chamber membership is split equally between the two parties.

controls the other house. Table 3-3 gives a complete picture. Almost half of the states with divided government are classified that way because of split legislatures.

Is it of any importance that a state has divided government rather than unified government? The most often suggested negative consequence is that divided government will make it impossible for the governor and the legislature, since they represent different parties, to get anything accomplished, in other words, gridlock. However, a number of studies at the national level conclude that the prevalence of gridlock has been exaggerated and that a close look at legislative accomplishments indicates that unified governments were no more likely than divided governments to produce important or significant laws.[57] It needs to be pointed out that no consensus exists among scholars as to the exact effect of divided government in national politics.

A number of political scientists have studied the effects of divided government in the states. Generally, they conclude that divided government has important consequences for a state's politics. Cynthia J. Bowling and Margaret R. Ferguson take a comprehensive look at all fifty states. They discover that gridlock from divided government is unlikely to occur on every type of issue; rather, it is most likely to occur on those issues that have a high potential for partisan conflict, such as welfare, education, crime, and the environment. Divided government encourages "gridlock as the two parties wrestle with the difficult policy challenges or ideological symbolism surrounding these high conflict areas."[58] Another important finding is that the normal way of thinking about divided government—one party controlling the governor's office and the other party controlling the legislature—has the least impact on gridlock. Gridlock is more likely to occur when one party controls *one* house of the legislature and the other party has the other legislative chamber and the governor's office. (Again, Table 3-3 shows that this kind of divided government occurs frequently.)

In another useful study, Laura A. van Assendelft looks at the politics of four southern states, two with divided government (Mississippi and Tennessee) and two with unified government (Georgia and Tennessee). She concludes that the principal effect of divided government is not on the number of bills passed by the legislature, but on what the governors place on their agendas, that is, the priorities they establish from among numerous competing policy alternatives. Governors in unified states are more likely to place controversial issues on their agendas. For example, Ned McWherter, Democratic governor of Tennessee (1987–1995), obtained legislative approval of a very unpopular state income tax to pay for an educational reform proposal. Governors in divided states have less party support in the legislature and are less likely to pursue controversial issues. A legislator from South Carolina described the effect of divided government on the governor's agenda this way:

> . . . a lot of times you may think about introducing something, but you know good and well that it is never going to pass. So to keep from being publicly defeated you just don't introduce it. That's what the difference is. You temper what you put out based on the audience that is there.[59]

Finally, Robert C. Lowry, James E. Alt, and Karen E. Ferree, researching gubernatorial and state legislative elections between 1968 and 1992, determine that voters are more likely to hold elected officials responsible for taxing and spending policies in states with unified government than in states with divided government.[60] In other words, divided government makes it harder for voters to figure out who is responsible for, in particular, budget deficits and surpluses. This improved accountability is an important benefit of unified government.

INTEREST GROUPS IN THE STATES

Political parties and interest groups are important links between citizens and their government; both seek to move public policies in a particular direction by influencing who is nominated and elected to public office, as well as the specific decisions made by these officials. The principal difference between parties and interest groups revolves around the emphasis given to furthering a specific interest or policy versus winning elections. Jeffrey M. Berry puts it this way: Interest groups are *policy maximizers;* they offer citizens "a direct, focused, and undiluted way of supporting advocacy on the issue they care most about."[61] Political parties, on the other hand, are *vote maximizers;* their primary concern is to win elections so their candidates control important positions in state and local governments. Interest groups are concerned about a single policy or at most a very limited number of policy areas, while the Democratic and Republican Parties take positions on a large number of social and economic issues. Frequently, in attempting to appeal to a broad spectrum of the electorate, political parties will have weak or even ambiguous policy positions, just the opposite of interest groups.

Only about 25 percent of American adults have ever worked for a political party or for a candidate in an election, and fewer than 10 percent have been members of a political club or organization. In contrast, about 60 percent of the American people are members of organized interest groups, which take stands on various public issues and try to affect government decisions and policies.

Since the 1960s, there has been a significant expansion in virtually all states in the number of groups that are politically active. Although interest groups representing business, labor, and agriculture continue to be important, new groups are becoming active and influential; the interests they represent "range from environmentalists to women's groups to gay rights and victims' rights groups to hunting and fishing groups to anti-poverty and senior citizens' lobbies."[62] Greater economic diversity in the states (such as the growth of the telecommunications industry) also has caused the creation of new groups in the private economic sector. Education unions and public employee unions have become much more politically active and powerful in the states.

Power of Interest Groups

No state today is run by one or two interests, as once was the case in Montana with the Anaconda Copper Company. Nevertheless, Clive S. Thomas and Ronald J. Hrebenar believe that the increased number of interest groups and the fragmentation of the business community have not lessened the overall power of interest groups. In addition, the need for more campaign money, and the rise of PACs to furnish it, have increased the power of interest groups.

One way to look at interest group power is to compare interest groups to political parties. In other words, are interest groups or political parties dominant in making and implementing policy in a state? It should be assumed that interest groups are always important in making policy and the real question is the extent of their power, or dominance.[63] Strong political parties can exert some control over the process of making policy and reduce the ability of interest groups to dominate it. Because parties represent broader constituencies than interest groups, it is also more likely that the public can have a voice in policy deliberations. Table 3-4 classifies the states according to the impact on policy making by interest groups. States with the "dominant" classification have an interest group system that has overwhelming influence on policy making.

TABLE 3-4 Classification of the States According to the Overall Impact of Interest Groups in 2002, with Comparison to 1985 Classification				
Dominant (5)	Dominant/ complementary (26)	Complementary (16)	Complementary/ subordinate (3)	Subordinate (0)
Alabama	− Alaska	Colorado	− Michigan	
Florida	Arizona	+ Connecticut	Minnesota	
+ Montana	Arkansas	+ Delaware	− South Dakota	
+ Nevada	California	− Hawaii		
West Virginia	Georgia	Indiana		
	Idaho	Maine		
	+ Illinois	Massachusetts		
	+ Iowa	New Hampshire		
	+ Kansas	New Jersey		
	Kentucky	New York		
	− Louisiana	North Carolina		
	+ Maryland	North Dakota		
	− Mississippi	Pennsylvania		
	+ Missouri	+ Rhode Island		
	Nebraska	+ Vermont		
	− New Mexico	Wisconsin		
	Ohio			
	Oklahoma			
	Oregon			
	− South Carolina			
	− Tennessee			
	Texas			
	Utah			
	Virginia			
	Washington			
	Wyoming			

Source: Clive S. Thomas and Ronald J. Hrebenar, "Interest Groups in the States," in Virginia Gray and Russell L. Hanson, eds. *Politics in the American States: A Comparative Analysis,* 8th ed. (Washington, D.C.: CQ Press, 2004), p. 122. Reproduced by permission of CQ Press.

Note: + or − indicates movement one category up or down since the first survey in 1985.

Interest groups in "complementary" states have to work with other participants such as political parties. The "subordinate" category is where interest groups have little impact on policy making; no state fits into this category. The two mixed categories ("dominant/complementary" and "complementary/subordinate") contain states that alternate between the two categories or are evolving from one to the next.

Interest Group Tactics

Interest groups are involved in all stages of political activity but usually focus on state legislatures where they work to have bills adopted or defeated. A 1990 Associated Press survey found that registered lobbyists outnumbered legislators by a margin of 6 to 1.[64] Before discussing specific tactics, it should be noted that in many instances the most successful interest groups are those that can use a defensive strategy: They wish to preserve the status quo against those who are trying to bring about change. Many legislators live by the adage, "If it ain't broke, don't fix it." The status quo represents previous political compromises. As a consequence, interest groups advocating a new policy must first show that something is so wrong that it must be fixed before they can effectively argue for their proposed solution. For convenience, interest group tactics may be divided into three categories: public relations campaigns, electioneering, and lobbying.

Public Relations Campaigns

Interest groups can use public relations campaigns to help create a favorable image of themselves and to generate support on specific issues. These campaigns include press conferences, advertising, radio and television interviews, and news releases. Because there is a close connection between public relations campaigns and commercial advertising, groups representing the business community have an advantage in expertise and available personnel, not to mention money. The advantage of money is partially offset because the media frequently give favorable coverage to groups that take positions—such as protecting the environment—that are popular with the public. A little creativity can also help. Alan Rosenthal reports that an environmental group in New Jersey received considerable media attention when it announced the results of pollution studies at contaminated waste sites rather than in an office conference room.[65]

Electioneering

Interest groups may participate in political campaigns by providing assistance to political parties or individual candidates. Some groups may assume a position of neutrality and support candidates from both parties if they support the group's goals. Others may be closely tied to partisan politics. Labor unions, for example, are usually connected to the Democratic Party in most of the large, industrial states, such as California, Illinois, Michigan, New Jersey, New York, Ohio, and Pennsylvania.

Interest groups provide an opportunity for candidates to acquire friendships and build reputations. Most candidates are members of several groups, and they believe they can translate friendship into votes. Candidates may be invited to appear before the group, or they may respond to questionnaires that seek to identify candidates' positions on issues that are of concern to the group. More directly, interest groups may provide staff assistance in running a campaign. Mailing lists of members, office material, and equipment also can be made available for candidates' use.

Money is probably the most important resource an interest group can provide candidates. Many states still allow corporations and labor unions to contribute money legally to campaigns. And **political action committees (PACs),** which are sponsored by interest groups and are created specifically to raise and distribute money to political campaigns, have expanded in the states just as they have at the national level. There are an estimated 12,000 PACs in the states, and they have become the dominant source of campaign funds as election campaigns have become more and more expensive. According to Rosenthal, PACs contribute money to political campaigns to (1) help elect candidates who are considered friends; (2) show support for those who are likely to be reelected, especially if they are in a legislative leadership position such as committee chair; and (3) gain or improve access to legislators.[66]

PACs raise money through personal contact and direct mail appeals. Some corporations and labor unions even use voluntary payroll deduction; teachers' unions are particularly good at raising money. The Minnesota Education Association automatically receives $10 from every member each year, unless he or she indicates otherwise.[67] Incumbents are the prime beneficiaries of PAC money, sometimes receiving up to 80 percent of PAC contributions. Frequently, PACs ignore party labels, give money to incumbents of both parties, and "go with the power."

Lobbying

Interest groups use **lobbying** to communicate specific policy goals more directly to legislators. Communication may be in the form of testimony before legislative committees or, more indirectly, by establishing contacts in a social setting. In state legislatures with a large professional staff it is often as important to communicate with the members of the legislator's staff as it is with the legislator. If lobbyists can convince a staff member that their policy position is the correct one, then the staff member may be able to convince his or her boss.

Thomas and Hrebenar have identified five categories of lobbyists in the states:[68]

1. *In-house.* Employees of organizations who have titles such as vice president of public affairs or director of government relations and as part of their job devote at least some of their time to lobbying. They represent only one client, and that is their employer. Examples are state chambers of commerce or large corporations. This category represents nearly 40 to 50 percent of all state lobbyists.
2. *Government or legislative liaisons.* Employees of state, local, and federal agencies that, as part of their job, represent their agencies to the legislature. These are sometimes called the "hidden lobbies" because many states do not require government employees to register as lobbyists. State universities, for example, usually have a vice president of state relations (or a similar title) whose real job is to lobby the legislature. This category contains 25 to 40 percent of all lobbyists.
3. *Contract.* Also known as independent lobbyists or "hired guns." They are hired for a fee to lobby and will represent a number of clients, ranging from fewer than ten to thirty or forty. Contract lobbyists sometimes work by themselves or with partners

in law firms; either way they are a growing presence in state capitals. They represent 15 to 25 percent of all lobbyists.

4. *Citizen, cause, or volunteer.* These lobbyists represent citizen or community organizations on a part-time and volunteer basis. They rarely represent more than one organization at a time. Perhaps 10 to 20 percent of all lobbyists fit into this category.

5. *"Hobbyists."* These are self-styled lobbyists, private individuals, who act on their own behalf to support pet projects and are not designated to act on the behalf of any organization. The number of "hobbyists" (perhaps 5 percent) is hard to estimate because few are required to register by law.

After laws are passed, interest-group activity continues as lobbyists contact executive branch administrators, who are usually given considerable discretion in executing the law. Administrators interact very little with the general public, and they have a tendency to identify very closely with the goals of the groups they are supposed to oversee. As noted in Chapter 1, detailed state constitutions invite litigation by opponents charging that a new law violates part of the constitution. This provides yet another tactic for interest groups that hope to negate laws or render their provisions meaningless through narrow judicial interpretation. Beginning in the 1980s, interest groups have increased their participation in state court litigation, and a greater variety of interest groups are using litigation as a means of shaping policy. Business, religious, and civil rights organizations are continuing to use litigation strategies, and educational and health groups are using it more than they have in the past.[69] In some states, pro-smoking groups are going to court to challenge the legality of government regulations banning smoking in various places such as work areas. The Brady Center to Prevent Gun Violence has joined more than twenty cities in suing gun manufacturers, alleging that the design, marketing, and distribution of firearms makes it too easy to purchase guns, especially for criminals. They are seeking millions of dollars in liability damages from gun manufacturers.

Ethics of Lobbying

Can lobbyists buy a state legislator's vote? It does occur, but not often. In the 1990s, a few legislators were involved in scandals and found guilty of taking money from lobbyists for introducing and working for the passage of legislation that would benefit the lobbyists' clients. Prosecutions occurred in Arizona, California, Indiana, Kentucky, and South Carolina. Many of these indictments and convictions were the result of federal investigations. Still, given the large number of lobbyists (close to 43,000) and legislators (7,382), the actual number of instances of bribery is very small. However, this is not to underestimate the importance of influence buying because its effect on public confidence and trust in government can be devastating. After a corruption probe in Arizona was made public, a statewide survey found that more than 70 percent of the people interviewed believed that a legislator would take a bribe if offered one![70]

If the actual buying of influence is infrequent, lobbying activities that have the *appearance* of buying influence are widespread, at least in the public's perception. One of the more dominant images of lobbying is that of legislators accepting from lobbyists gifts and free entertainment, including dinners and drinks during the legislative session, tickets to sporting events, and hunting and golf trips. And this image certainly has a basis in reality. Alan Rosenthal reports that during one session of the Colorado legislature, members "were invited to forty-eight cocktail parties, forty-four lunches, forty breakfasts, nineteen dinners, and twenty-three other functions during their six-month session."[71]

What do gifts and free entertainment buy, if anything? One view is that lobbyists are only buying access to legislators; they want to ensure that when they need five minutes with a legislator, they can get it. Or when a legislator has twenty phone messages, their call is one of the three that will actually be returned. Tickets to games and free food and drinks at receptions, it is argued, are not given with the expectation that lobbyists are actually buying a vote; they are only buying access. An alternative view is that access is close to influence. And if money is needed to have access, then interest groups that can mount a well-financed lobbying operation have an advantage over groups with less money. According to Common Cause, the "result is that public policy decisions may be based solely on who has money and access to government officials, rather than on whether the policy is in the public's interest."[72]

In the past few years, most state legislatures, reacting to real scandals and the appearance of influence buying, have adopted increasingly strict regulations that cover almost all aspects of the lobbyist-legislator relationship. Lobbying activities can be regulated, but they cannot be eliminated because lobbying falls under the right of the people to "petition the Government for a redress of grievances," guaranteed by the First Amendment to the U.S. Constitution and provisions in state constitutions as well. All states and the District of Columbia require lobbyists to register with a state ethics commission or a similar agency; accompanying registration will be the requirement to report lobbying expenditures. This type of regulation provides "public information and illuminate[s] group activities."[73] Approximately half of the states require lobbyists to identify legislative and administrative actions that the lobbyists seek to influence. Lobbying on a contingency fee basis, which means that lobbyists are paid only if they are successful, is prohibited in almost all states; it is believed that lobbyists are more likely to attempt to exert "improper influence" if they have to win to be paid. All but a few states prohibit lobbyists from making campaign contributions during the legislative sessions.[74]

Regulation of gifts from lobbyists to legislators has received the greatest attention in the states. As can be seen in Figure 3-4, states are taking different approaches. The most restrictive states are those that have "zero tolerance." These states also are called "no cup of coffee states" because a lobbyist cannot give *anything* to a legislator, including a cup of coffee. States with the "bright line test" allow gifts up to a certain dollar value, for example, $3 per day in Iowa; dollar limits vary considerably among the states. Quite a few states restrict gifts but allow exceptions for food and entertainment under certain conditions such as inviting all members of the legislature to a reception. Finally, a number of states have no monetary limits, but prohibit gifts if they influence a legislator's official actions.[75] Unfortunately, this is not enough guidance for lobbyists and legislators and does little to reduce the appearance of buying influence.

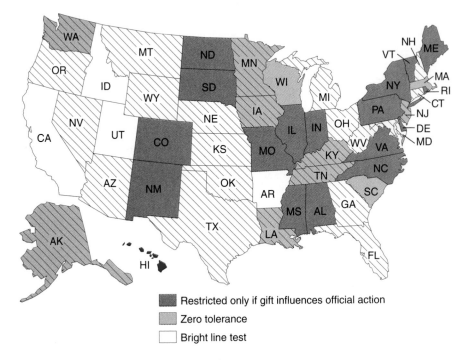

FIGURE 3-4 Gift restrictions on state legislators.

Source: National Conference of State Legislatures, *The State of State Legislative Ethics: A Look at the Ethical Climate and Ethics Laws for State Legislators.* (Denver, Colo.: National Conference of State Legislatures, 2002), p. 54. Reproduced by permission of National Conference of State Legislatures.

Note: States with slanted lines exempt food and beverages from gift restrictions under certain circumstances, as explained in the text.

URBAN INTEREST GROUPS

Interest groups operate in much the same way in large cities as in state legislatures. The difference is that the same groups are not equally active in state capitols and city halls. Real estate groups and downtown merchants have been more influential at the city level than at the state level.

Types and Tactics

Urban interests groups may be classified as follows:

Business and economic interests. Groups are organized on the basis of common economic interests. Examples of specific interests are boards of realtors, downtown merchants associations, and local manufacturing associations. Active and influential in almost all cities and towns are local chamber of commerce associations; with membership open to all businesses, they seek to represent business interests generally. Although the interests of labor organizations tend to be with national and state issues (occupational safety and minimum wage, for example), the presence of a large, unionized workforce in the private sector in many cities in the Midwest and East does lead to more labor union activity in local politics. Individual labor unions in a city usually come together to form a *labor council* to represent labor's interests much in the same way that a chamber of commerce represents business interests.

Neighborhood interests. A neighborhood is usually thought of as the houses in the immediate vicinity of one's own house. At a more general level, a neighborhood can be thought of as an area where housing is of a similar type and market value. It is at this more general level that neighborhood organizations and homeowner associations form for political action. Neighborhood organizations frequently form, as Terry Christensen says, when they "find themselves trying to prevent something from happening to their area that they perceive as a threat, either to their local quality of life or to property values."[76] Anything from construction of a new Wal-Mart to group homes for the developmentally disabled can lead to a negative neighborhood reaction that is labeled by the acronym **NIMBY,** "Not in My Backyard."

Good-government interests. As noted, the municipal reform movement that started in the late nineteenth century was aided by a number of so-called good-government groups. The desire for local government reform is still alive and so are some of the original reform groups. The League of Women Voters, for example, is active in many cities and towns and emphasizes contemporary reforms such as ethics in public service, campaign financing, and opening government meetings to the public.[77] Other, more conservative groups have advocated for term limits for elected political leaders and for limits on property tax increases.

The strength of interest groups comes from their willingness to take action and their resources (organization, leadership, number of members, and money), all factors that are found in abundance in the business community. And there are plenty of local issues for businesses to be concerned with, including taxes, parking, zoning restrictions, building and housing regulations, and policies toward economic development and growth.

Many interest groups adopt the tactics of state-level interest groups and apply them to the local level, such as providing testimony at public hearings of the city council or some other governing body, lobbying elected and appointed officials in private meetings, and supporting favored candidates in their election campaigns. Citizens without traditional political resources may adopt different tactics. African Americans, other minority groups, and low-income neighborhood associations frequently use nonviolent protests such as demonstrations, rallies, and marches to influence decision makers. (See Chapter 4.)

Community Power Studies

Another approach by scholars seeking to understand the various groups that compete for influence in cities and towns, especially those representing economic interests, is to ask this important question: Who really has power? This seemingly simple question has been looked at from a number of perspectives and has stirred decades of debate. Political scientists and sociologists have studied community power structures and their conclusions are nearly as numerous as the individual cities and towns studied. Generally speaking, researchers fall into one of two categories: the **elitists** (usually sociologists who find that a few top leaders form a power structure that dominates decision making) and the **pluralists** (usually political scientists who view power as a process that is shared by a variety of competing groups).

In the classic elitist studies, such as Robert and Helen Lynd's work on Middletown[78] (actually Muncie, Indiana) and Floyd Hunter's examination of Regional City[79] (actually Atlanta, Georgia), power is believed to be concentrated in the hands of a few old families and business leaders. Community leadership is viewed as a rigid system in which those at the top are a relatively permanent group. There is a one-way flow of power, with the elite dictating policy to subordinates. In many cases, the "power elite" does not exercise control openly but operates by manipulating more visible public officials. Although there are occasional disagreements among the elite membership, their common economic interests unite them on most basic issues. In such a system, public opinion and elections have little effect on policy making.

Critics charge that there is more conflict among top business leaders than the Lynds or Hunter suggest.[80] Still, at the time these studies were made, their conclusions, if a bit exaggerated, may have been correct. Many U.S. cities—such as Pittsburgh, Atlanta, and Gary, Indiana—early in this century were dominated by a single industry or small group of business persons, or even by a single family. As urban populations have become more heterogeneous, we would expect power relationships to change.

Pluralist studies such as Robert Dahl's analysis of New Haven, Connecticut, conclude that power is shared by a variety of groups that are in conflict with one another.[81] The groups are often short-lived—they form around an issue and then disappear. Thus pluralists do not see a stable power structure; rather, they perceive a fluid system of leadership. Persons or groups who dominate decision making in one area are seldom equally effective in other areas. In the pluralist model, public decisions are influenced by public opinion, and elections are an important means of transferring power from one group to another.

As one might expect, elitists and pluralists are critical of each other's methodology. Pluralists charge that elitists begin by assuming the existence of power relations. Elitists often rely on an interview method in which the respondents are asked, "Who has power in Gotham City?" Such a *reputational* approach, suggest the pluralists, often results in confusing groups with high potential for power (i.e., groups that have high status) with groups that actually exercise power. A great many people believe that "they"—bankers, merchants, old families—run cities, so the elitist argument has strong appeal: It is simple, dramatic, and "realistic."

Elitists argue that the pluralist method of focusing on decision making has some major drawbacks. They contend that "key decisions" are not easily selected for analysis. Furthermore, elitists note that political influence is not always seen in the public decision-making process. Those with power may be able to exclude an issue from public discussion altogether and thus exercise control by blocking decision making. For example, wealthy landlords might prevent a city council from proposing laws that would require landlords to maintain their rental property and expose them to fines if they violate the law. The ability to keep issues off local political agendas is, of course, the ultimate power that individuals or groups can exercise.

No definitive answer that applies to all cities can be given to the question "Who has power?" Particular mixtures of social, economic, and cultural patterns clearly influence the distribution of power in different cities. Furthermore, cities that are characterized by citizen activism on community issues are less likely to have power concentrated in the hands of a few.[82] We turn to the topic of political participation in the next chapter.

SUMMARY

Political parties and interest groups are important to democratic societies because they help to link citizens to their government. Political parties are regulated by the states, but the U.S. Supreme Court has declared some of these regulations unconstitutional. Urban political machines, a traditional party organization, dominated many cities in the past. By exchanging material rewards for voter support, machines controlled who was elected to local government offices. Too often, however, they became corrupt. Reformers attacked political machines by changing the structure of local government so it was difficult for them to thrive. Even then, a few machines such as Mayor Richard J. Daley's in Chicago survived well into the 1970s.

Contemporary state party organization has enjoyed a revitalization after experiencing a low point during the 1970s. They provide more services to candidates running for elected offices, even though they may never again control the nominating process the way traditional party organizations did. Local party organizations still vary a great deal in terms of organizational strength and level of activity. In almost every state, political parties use some type of primary election to nominate their candidates for elected state-level positions, but only the closed primary requires a voter to register with a party before voting in its primary.

Fewer states are dominated by one party; the trend is toward two competitive parties in an increasing number of states. The Democratic Party's grip on the South is rapidly weakening, especially in races for the governor's office and even in state legislative races. This is of some importance because recent research concludes that changes in party control of state government affect some state policies.

Divided government in the states, when one or both houses of the legislature are not controlled by the governor's party, is now more common than unified government. Under divided government, governors must compromise with legislative leaders and they may not place controversial issues on their agenda; sometimes gridlock occurs. In addition, the accountability of elected leaders to the voters is weakened in divided government.

Accompanying the growth of state government in policy making has been the growth in the number of interest groups and the variety of interests they represent. Interest groups use various tactics to present their views to legislators in the hope of having favorable policies enacted. Often, groups find that having their own lobbyist or hiring one may be the most effective way to influence decisions. Media attention on the money interest groups contribute to political campaigns and spend on entertaining legislators has pushed many states to enact new laws that further regulate what lobbyists can do.

Local interest groups primarily reflect business and economic interests, along with neighborhood and good-government interests. Community power studies look beyond the more visible aspects of local politics and ask the question: Who really has power? Some researchers find an elite power structure and others find a pluralist one. Recent research concludes that the amount of citizen activism on community issues can affect the extent to which power is concentrated in the hands of an elite.

KEY TERMS

amateurs	**direct primary**
Australian ballot	**divided government**
at-large elections	**elitists**
blanket primary	**good-government organizations**
closed primary	**ideology**
conservatives	**liberals**

lobbying
NIMBY
nonpartisan elections
open elections
open primary
party competition
patronage
pluralists
political action committees (PACs)

precinct
precinct caucus
professionals
runoff primary
unified government
urban political machine
voter registration
ward

SUMMARY OF STATE/LOCAL DIFFERENCES

Issue	State Level	Local Level
Political parties	Paid executive director and staff at headquarters, conduct opinion polls and party-building activities	Volunteers serve on party committees, distribute campaign literature, and conduct get-out-the-vote drives
Nominations	Voters choose a party's nominee in a primary election	Nonpartisan primaries are used more frequently
Interest groups	Great diversity in interests that are represented in state capitals	Groups representing business are more active and influential

INTERESTING WEBSITES

www.ballot-access.org. This is a nonpartisan website that focuses on the difficulties independent and third-party candidates have in placing their names on national, state, and local ballots.

www.commoncause.org. Common Cause is a national interest group that "works against corruption in government and big money special interests." Click on "States." You can look at "Features" or "Select a State" to see reports on ethics and lobbying, along with information on campaign finance reform.

www.democrats.org. Official website for the Democratic National Committee. Click on "Get local" for links to state Democratic Parties.

www.ncsl.org/program/ethics. The Center for Ethics in Government is sponsored by the National Conference of State Legislatures. Up-to-date information on ethics issues in government generally, and state legislatures in particular.

www.rnc.org. Official website for the Republican National Committee. Click on "State Parties" for information on state Republican Parties.

NOTES

1. Steven Thomma, "Some Americans, Fed Up with Both Parties, Turn to Independents," Knight Ridder/Tribune News Service, October 20, 2002, lexisnexis@prod.lexisnexis.com (accessed January 7, 2003).
2. In Minnesota, the Democratic party's official name is the Democrat-Farmer-Labor Party, which was created in 1944 when the Democratic Party and the Farmer-Labor Party merged.
3. A. James Reichley, *The Life of the Parties: A History of American Political Parties* (New York: The Free Press, 1992), pp. 207–209.
4. Ibid.
5. Leon Epstein, *Political Parties in the American Mold* (Madison, Wisc.: The University of Wisconsin Press, 1986), pp. 174–179. The two U.S. Supreme Court cases are Smith v. Allright, 321 U.S. 649 (1944) and Terry v. Adams 345 U.S. 461 (1953).
6. An excellent analysis of the effect of state laws on political parties can be found in Kay Lawson, "How State Laws Undermine Parties," in *Elections American Style,* A. James Reichley, ed. (Washington, D.C.: The Brookings Institution, 1987), pp. 240–260.
7. Tashjian v. Republican Party of Connecticut, 479 U.S. 208 (1986).
8. Eu v. San Francisco County Democratic Central Committee, 489 U.S. 214 (1989).
9. Timmons v. Twin Cities Area New Party, 520 U.S. 351 (1997).
10. William J. Crotty, "Urban Political Machines," in *Parties and Politics in American History: A Reader,* L. Sandy Maisel and William G. Shade, eds. (New York: Garland Publishing, 1994), p. 134.
11. Samuel J. Eldersveld, *Political Parties in American Society* (New York: Basic Books, Inc., 1982), pp. 150–152.
12. Fred I. Greenstein and Frank Feigert, *The American Party System and the American People,* 3d ed. (Englewood Cliffs, N.J.: Prentice-Hall, Inc., 1985), pp. 60–63.
13. Crotty, "Political Machines," p. 137.
14. John Allswang, *Bosses, Machines and Urban Voters*, rev. ed. (Baltimore: Johns Hopkins University Press, 1986), p. 52.
15. Crotty, "Urban Political Machines," p. 141.
16. Dennis R. Judd and Todd Swanstrom, *City Politics: Private Power & Public Policy* (New York: HarperCollins College Publishers, 1994), p. 79.
17. Elrod v. Burns, 427 U.S. 347 (1976).
18. Rutan v. Illinois Republican Party, 497 U.S. 62 (1990).
19. See O'Hare Truck Service v. City of Northlake, 518 U.S. 712 (1996). A good review of these patronage cases can be found in Cynthia Grant Bowman, "The Supreme Court's Patronage Decisions and the Theory and Practice of Politics," in *The U.S. Supreme Court and the Electoral Process,* 2d ed., David K. Ryden, ed. (Washington, D.C.: Georgetown University Press, 2002), pp. 126–43.
20. Terry Christensen, *Local Politics: Governing at the Grassroots* (Belmont, Calif.: Wadsworth Publishing Company, 1995), p. 125.
21. Bernard H. Ross and Myron A. Levine, *Urban Politics: Power in Metropolitan America,* 5th ed. (Itasca, Ill.: F. E. Peacock Publishers, 1996), p. 147.
22. J. L. Polinard, Robert D. Wrinkle, Tomas Longoria, and Norma E. Binder, *Electoral Structure and Urban Policy: The Impact in Mexican American Communities* (Armonk, N.Y.: M. E. Sharp, Inc., 1994).
23. For a comprehensive analysis of Chicago's mayors, see Paul M. Green and Melvin G. Holli, eds., *The Mayors: The Chicago Political Tradition,* rev. ed. (Carbondale, Ill.: Southern Illinois University Press, 1995).

24. Sarah McCally Morehouse and Malcolm E. Jewell, *State Politics, Parties, & Policy,* 2d ed. (Lanham, Md.: Rowman & Littlefield, 2003), pp. 116–17.
25. John F. Bibby, *Politics, Parties, and Elections in America,* 3d ed. (Chicago, Ill.: Nelson-Hall, 1996), pp. 111–113.
26. A. James Reichley, *The Life of the Parties: A History of American Political Parties* (New York: Free Press, 1992), p. 382.
27. John F. Bibby, "State Party Organizations: Coping and Adapting," in *The Parties Respond: Changes in American Parties and Campaigns,* 2d ed., L. Sandy Maisel, ed. (Boulder, Colo.: Westview Press, 1994), p. 30; Reichley, *The Life of the Parties,* p. 388.
28. Bibby, "State Party Organizations," p. 29.
29. Robert J. Huckshorn, "State Party Leaders," in *Political Parties and Elections in the United States: An Encyclopedia,* L. Sandy Maisel and Charles Bassett, eds. (New York: Garland Publishing, 1991), pp. 1059–1060.
30. John P. Frendreis, James L. Gibson, and Laura L. Vertz, "The Electoral Relevance of Local Party Organizations," *American Political Science Review* 84 (March 1990), pp. 228–233.
31. Samuel C. Patterson and Gregory A. Calderia, "The Etiology of Partisan Competition," *American Political Science Review* 78 (September 1984), pp. 701–703.
32. Sidney Blumenthal, "Letter from Washington: Christian Soldiers," *The New Yorker* (July 18, 1994), pp. 31–37.
33. Bibby, *Politics, Parties, and Elections,* pp. 116–118.
34. E. E. Schattschneider, *Party Government* (New York: Holt, Rinehart and Winston, 1942), p. 1, quoted in Bibby, *Politics, Parties, and Elections,* p. 8.
35. Bibby, *Politics, Parties, and Elections,* p. 131.
36. http://www.ss.ca.gov/executive/press_releases/open_primary_qa.htm.
37. California Democratic Party v. Jones, 530 U.S. 567 (2000).
38. Louisiana's nomination process is sometimes classified as "nonpartisan," meaning no party names are on the ballot. (Also, "nonpartisan" is placed in quotes indicating that it is somehow different from the normal nonpartisan election.) This seems incorrect for Louisiana because party names are allowed in both the first and second elections. The open elections name has been used by Kazee and Hadley and is more appropriate. See Charles D. Hadley, "The Impact of the Louisiana Open Elections System Reform," *State Government* 58, no. 4 (1986), pp. 152–156; Thomas A. Kazee, "The Impact of Electoral Reform: 'Open Elections' and the Louisiana Party System," *Publius* 13 (Winter 1983), pp. 131–139.
39. Bibby, *Politics, Parties, and Elections,* p. 137.
40. Ibid., p. 139.
41. Malcolm E. Jewell, "State Party Endorsements of Gubernatorial Candidates Declining in Effectiveness," *Comparative State Politics* 16 (June 1995), pp. 10–12.
42. James P. Melcher, "Party Endorsements in Minnesota in the Wake of the 1994 Elections: Reform Strikes Out," *Comparative State Politics* 16 (December 1995), pp. 1–13.
43. Stephen I. Frank and Steven C. Wagner, *"We Shocked the World!" A Case Study of Jesse Ventura's Election as Governor of Minnesota* (New York: Harcourt College Publishers, 1999), p. 6.
44. Malcolm Jewell and David Olson, *Political Parties and American States,* 3d ed. (Chicago, Ill.: The Dorsey Press, 1988), pp. 28–30.
45. Earl Black and Merle Black, *Politics and Society in the South* (Cambridge, Mass.: Harvard University Press, 1987), p. 287.
46. Jonathan Allen and Rebecca Adams, "States' Priorities vs. Funds," *CQ Weekly* (November 9, 2002), pp. 2945–46.
47. John H. Aldrich, "Southern Parties in State and Nation," *Journal of Politics* 62 (August 2000), p. 647.

48. V. O. Key, Jr., *Southern Politics in State and Nation* (New York: Vintage Books, 1949), pp. 15–18, 298–311. For an analysis of Key's work, see *V. O. Key, Jr., and the Study of American Politics,* Milton C. Cummings, ed. (Washington, D.C.: American Political Science Association, 1988). David Mayhew's "Why Did V. O. Key Draw Back from His 'Have-Nots' Claim?" in the Cummings monograph is excellent.

49. Key, *Southern Politics,* pp. 307–310.

50. Thomas R. Dye, *Politics in States and Communities,* 7th ed. (Englewood Cliffs, N.J.: Prentice-Hall, 1991), p. 135.

51. Robert D. Brown, "Party Cleavages and Welfare Effort in the American States," *American Political Science Review* 89 (March 1995), pp. 23–33.

52. Diana Dwyre, Mark O'Gorman, Jeffrey M. Stonecash, and Rosalie Young, "Disorganized Politics and the Have-Nots: Politics and Taxes in New York and California," *Polity* 27 (Fall 1994), pp. 26–27.

53. James C. Garand, "Partisan Change and Shifting Expenditure Priorities in the American States, 1945–1978," *American Politics Quarterly* 13 (October 1985), pp. 370–371.

54. Robert S. Erikson, Gerald C. Wright, and John McIver, *Statehouse Democracy: Public Opinion and Policy in the American States* (New York: Cambridge University Press, 1993).

55. Ibid., p. 103.

56. Morehouse and Jewell, pp. 209–10.

57. Morris Fiorina, *Divided Government,* 2d ed. (Boston, Mass.: Allyn & Bacon, 1996), pp. 85–110.

58. Cynthia J. Bowling and Margaret R. Ferguson, "Divided Government, Interest Representation, and Policy Differences: Competing Explanations of Gridlock in the Fifty States," *Journal of Politics* 63 (February 2001), p. 187.

59. Laura A. van Assendelft, *Governors, Agenda Setting, and Divided Government* (Lanham, Md.: University Press of America, 1997), p. 202.

60. Robert C. Lowry, James E. Alt, and Karen E. Ferree, "Fiscal Policy Outcomes and Electoral Accountability in American States," *American Political Science Review,* vol. 92 (December 1998), pp. 759–774.

61. Jeffrey M. Berry, *The Interest Group Society,* 3d ed. (New York: Longman, 1997), p. 46.

62. Clive S. Thomas and Ronald J. Hrebenar, "Who's Got Clout? Interest Group Power in the States," *State Legislatures* (April 1999), p. 31.

63. Clive S. Thomas and Ronald J. Hrebenar, "Interest Group Power in State Politics: A Complex Phenomenon," *Comparative State Politics* 15 (June 1994), pp. 13–15.

64. Associated Press, June 25, 1990, quoted in Common Cause, *State Issue Brief: Lobby Disclosure Reform in the States* (Washington, D.C.: Common Cause, 1993), p. 4.

65. Alan Rosenthal, *The Third House* (Washington, D.C.: Congressional Quarterly Press, 1993), p. 170.

66. Ibid., p. 136.

67. Ibid., p. 134.

68. Clive S. Thomas and Ronald J. Hrebenar, "Interest Groups in the States," in *Politics in the American States,* 5th ed., Virginia Gray, Herbert Jacob, and Robert B. Albritton, eds. (Glenview, Ill.: Scott, Foresman/Little, Brown, 1990), pp. 149–151; Alan Rosenthal, *The Third House,* pp. 21–23.

69. Lee Epstein, "Exploring the Participation of Organized Interests in State Court Litigation," *Political Research Quarterly* 47 (June 1994), pp. 341–348.

70. Susan Biemesderfer, "Making Laws, Breaking Laws," *State Legislatures* (April 1991), p. 18.

71. Rosenthal, *The Third House,* p. 95.

72. Common Cause, *State Issue Brief: Lobby Disclosure,* p. 2.

73. Morehouse and Jewell, *State Politics,* p. 88.

74. *The State of State Legislative Ethics: A Look at the Ethical Climate and Ethics Laws for State Legislators* (Denver, Colo.: National Conference of State Legislators, 2002), pp. 92–110.

75. Ginger Sampson and Peggy Kerns, *Gift Restrictions: Laws for Legislators—It's Not a Physics Lesson.* National Conference of State Legislatures, Center for Ethics in Government, Eye on Ethics, Briefing Papers on Important Ethical Issues, www.ncsl.org/programs/ethics/legisbrief-gifts.

76. Terry Christensen, *Local Politics: Governing at the Grassroots* (Belmont, Calif.: Wadsworth, 1995), p. 228.

77. Ibid., p. 234.

78. Robert Lynd and Helen Lynd, *Middletown* (New York: Harcourt, Brace, and World, 1929), and Robert Lynd and Helen Lynd, *Middletown in Transition* (New York: Harcourt, Brace, and World, 1937).

79. Floyd Hunter, *Community Power Structure* (Chapel Hill: University of North Carolina Press, 1953).

80. Nelson Polsby, *Community Power and Political Theory* (New Haven: Yale University Press, 1963).

81. Robert A. Dahl, *Who Governs?* (New Haven, Conn.: Yale University Press, 1961).

82. Lawrence, J.R. Herson and John M. Bolland, *The Urban Web* (Chicago, Ill: Nelson-Hall Publishers, 1995), p. 194.

CHAPTER 4

Political Participation and Elections

POINTS TO CONSIDER

- How can people participate in politics?
- What is the goal of a strong democracy?
- Discuss changes in voter registration procedures, especially those that affected the voting rights of African Americans, Hispanics, and other minority groups.
- What factors affect voter turnout in state elections?
- What are the important factors determining the winner of a gubernatorial election?
- How do judicial election campaigns differ from other campaigns?
- What do election campaigns cost?

- What is public financing of election campaigns and what factors determine its success?
- Highlight differences among the initiative, referendum, and recall.
- What are the pros and cons of the initiative process?

POLITICAL PARTICIPATION

Political scientists approach **political participation** as "actions through which ordinary members of a political system influence or attempt to influence outcomes."[1] For this definition, voting in elections is one example, but so are other acts such as contributing money to candidates or interest groups, signing petitions, protesting, and writing letters to government officials. The concept of political participation refers to actions of average citizens, not those involved in politics and government in elected positions or as a career.

How Americans Participate

Much of what political scientists know about political participation is a result of **survey research,** which is a way of collecting information by asking a relatively small number

---

Internet Voting—Is it a Better Idea?

Would you like to vote from your own personal computer in the next election in your state? It would be pretty difficult for a person, especially a college student, to answer "no" to this question.

Internet voting has the potential to solve a number of problems with elections today; one is that voter participation, usually called voter turnout, in state and local elections is low. If people could vote without traveling to the polls or standing in long lines, voting would be easier and perhaps more people would vote. Also, Internet voting would prevent the problem of spoiled ballots that occurred in Florida in the 2000 presidential election, would eliminate the need for thousands of election day workers at polling places, and would allow for the quick reporting of election results.[2]

Internet voting may be in our future, but it will not be any time soon. Even today, many people do not have home computers, and there are legitimate concerns about the security and reliability of the Internet. But let's assume that these two drawbacks could be eliminated (and surely they will be). Would voting on the Internet still be the way to go?

Comments by critics of vote-by-mail systems, which are now used for all elections in Oregon, seem to apply to Internet voting as well and should be considered before we decide to adopt it. Critics see disadvantages in being able to vote at home. First, it is argued, at a traditional polling place a voter is properly identified by poll workers, and the voter is guaranteed a place to mark his or her ballot in secret and uninfluenced by others. Second, doing away with a formal election day and precinct voting "removes an important ritual of democracy that ties voters together as participants in a common act of governance."[3] Both of these criticisms should be weighed over the next few years as Internet voting technology improves. This chapter focuses on the ways people participate in politics in the United States, with special attention to voting.

of people that are representative of a larger population questions about their political attitudes or behavior. Sidney Verba and Norman Nie, in their classic study, *Participation in America*, identify four general categories or modes of political participation. The first is *voting* in elections. The second is *campaign activity* such as working for a party or to elect a candidate. The third, *citizen-initiated contacting,* occurs when a person contacts a government official with a particular concern relating to that person or his or her immediate family; an example would be calling a city official to complain about potholes on the street in front of your house. In the fourth, *cooperative activity,* citizens act as members of a group or organization to influence government to solve a social or political problem in the state or community.[4]

But how much do Americans participate? The Social Capital Benchmark Survey,[5] completed in 2000, asked a national sample of 3,000 people questions concerning their civic involvement and the ways they participate in politics. The data, shown in Table 4-1, are worth discussing in some detail.

Eighty percent of the survey respondents reported that they were registered to vote. This percentage is far larger than those reported for other acts of participation. (Of course, registering to vote is not the same as voting, and everyone knows that participation in the actual act of voting is much lower than this; usually around half of the voting age population actually votes in presidential elections. More will be said about voter turnout in state and local elections later in this chapter.) Beyond registering to vote, participation drops dramatically. Still, a sizeable number of respondents report

TABLE 4-1 Level of Individual Political Participation During a Twelve-Month Period

	Yes	No
Are you currently registered to vote?	80	20
Have you . . .		
Signed a petition?	35	65
Attended a political meeting or rally?	16	84
Worked on a community project?	38	62
Participated in demonstrations, protests, boycotts, or marches?	7	93
Have you taken part in any sort of activity with a . . .		
Neighborhood association, like a block association, a homeowner or tenant association, or a crime watch group?	20	80
Other public interest groups, political action groups, political clubs or party committees?	9	91
Did any of the groups that you are involved with take any local action for social or political reform?	18	82

Source: These data are from the Social Capital Benchmark Survey, which was conducted as a project of the Saguaro Seminar: Civic Engagement in America, John F. Kennedy School of Government, Harvard University. A description of the project and the survey can be found at http://www.cfsv.org/communitysurvey.

that they have worked on a community project (38 percent) or signed a petition (35 percent). Participation is much lower for taking part in a neighborhood association (20 percent) and attending a political meeting or rally (16 percent). Coming in at the bottom is participation in other public interest groups or political clubs (9 percent) or demonstrations and protests (7 percent). And only 18 percent of the respondents reported that any of the groups they were involved with advocated local action for social or political reform. Participation in most political acts is low.

Before leaving this overview of ways Americans participate in politics, a closer look at protest is required because controversy surrounds it as a means of political participation. Nonviolent protests such as marches, rallies, and demonstrations are protected by the First Amendment of the U.S. Constitution, and were especially prominent during the civil rights movement of the 1950s and 1960s. Specific causes of protests in urban areas have ranged from public housing conditions to police practices. Protests are aimed not only at decision makers but also at gaining support from public opinion, which may help influence those who make policies.

Protest also can be violent, as were the urban riots of the 1960s and the 1992 Los Angeles riot that occurred after a jury refused to find four police officers guilty of any wrongdoing for their beating of Rodney King while they were arresting him. Whether these urban riots are a form of political participation or are simply the work of habitual lawbreakers "who shoot, loot, and burn for strictly nonpolitical motives"[6] is still a hotly debated question. Although riots often have been touched off when seemingly routine contact between the police and African Americans went awry, the underlying cause of riots in several cities during the 1960s has been traced to long-standing racial discrimination and the resultant feeling of powerlessness on the part of inner-city African Americans. This is not to say that all rioters were politically motivated; certainly some rioters were participating for the possibility of stealing material goods.

Do political leaders respond to the demands of protestors? The answer is mixed. Of course, the civil rights movement is an example of the successful use of peaceful protest, especially demonstrations and marches, over a period of several years to achieve changes in laws. To be effective, protests must focus on specific policy goals that decision makers can act on rather than simply express general discontent.[7] After much debate, the U.S. Congress responded to the 1992 Los Angeles riots with financial assistance that was used to reopen destroyed businesses and provide summer jobs for youths. It also financed a Weed and Seed program, favored by President Bush, that would "weed lawbreakers out of neighborhoods and seed these areas with enrichment services for children."[8] However, protests, especially those that are violent, always risk the possibility of creating a backlash against the actions and demands of protestors that reduces the likelihood they will achieve anything. Lawrence Herson and John Bolland conclude that the "lack of positive outcomes and the plethora of negative outcomes"[9] are the best way to describe the results of urban riots of the 1960s. Negative outcomes include increased police expenditures and the election in several cities of mayors who ran on law-and-order platforms.

Strong Democracy

The New England town meeting, citizens coming together to make decisions for the community, is the ideal of democratic decision making. Today, however, the size of most local governments and the complexity of issues they face make it impractical for everyone to come together at one time to make decisions. Nevertheless, a number of political scientists and governmental leaders think that ways must be found to increase citizen participation in government, that is, create strong democracy.[10] They argue that this may not be possible in national and state politics because of problems of distance and size, but that it is possible in local governments. The goal of **strong democracy** is to rebuild citizenship in the United States, which means getting people to participate in "public forums where they can work with their neighbors to solve the problems of their community."[11]

Of course, the many demands on people's time lead one to question whether they would participate in these forums. Jeffrey Berry, Kent Portney, and Ken Thomson, after studying five cities, conclude that effective citizen participation can occur through neighborhood-based associations, containing 2,000 to 5,000 people, if they meet the criteria of breadth and depth. (These neighborhood associations would be more formal in terms of organization and function than those referred to in Table 4-1 and in the context of local interest groups in Chapter 3.)

Breadth of participation is the extent to which every citizen is offered the opportunity to take part in the deliberations of their neighborhood association. This involves conducting an extensive outreach effort detailing information on the time and place of meetings and issues to be discussed. Efforts to keep citizens informed should be continuous, perhaps involving the publication of a monthly neighborhood newspaper describing the association's activities. This type of effort requires a commitment of financial resources and staff from the local government that the associations are a part of. *Depth of participation* is the extent to which citizens, working through associations, actually influence local governmental policies. Citizens should have a say, at least, in how land is used and how government funds are spent in their neighborhoods.[12]

Again, at the heart of strong democracy is the idea that citizenship involves people participating in the making of decisions that affect themselves and their community. Neighborhood assemblies, it is believed, "conducted as an open and ongoing forum for the discussion of a flexible and citizen generated agenda,"[13] can provide an institutional framework for effective citizen participation.

VOTING

Although voting participation has been declining, it is still the act of political participation most often studied by political scientists. Sidney Verba, Kay Schlozman, and Henry Brady point to the vote as a unique political act because "casting a ballot is, by far, the most common act of citizenship in any democracy and because election returns are decisive in determining who shall govern."[14] However, before citizens can vote, they must register by filling out a voter registration application form for the local board of elections; this results in their names being placed on a list of eligible voters and their assignment to a polling place. This sounds simple enough, but voter registration procedures in the states have involved considerable controversy over the years.

African Americans and the Right to Vote

Historically, procedures and requirements in southern states in particular made it difficult for African Americans to register; in essence they discriminated against African

Americans and other minority groups. Underlying this legal framework in most places in the South was the reality of threats and intimidation that prevented the vast majority of African Americans from even thinking about registering to vote. This has changed greatly since the mid-1960s. Sometimes states changed on their own; other times, only after being pressured by the federal government.

Beginning in the 1890s, southern states enacted various laws, including a literacy test requirement, aimed at preventing African Americans from registering to vote but still allowing all whites to register. Over the years these laws became quite complex in the procedures used to accomplish this goal. Basically, local registration officials were given considerable discretion so they could register whites, but not African Americans. Illiterate whites could register because an "understanding clause" allowed potential voters to interpret a section of the Constitution after it was read to them. And for whites their interpretation was always correct. African-American citizens who were literate and who correctly interpreted the Constitution could still be kept from registering if, in the opinion of the registration official, they failed a "good character" requirement.[15] The civil rights movement in the 1960s was concerned about finding ways so African Americans could register. In 1965, the need for federal action was dramatized when civil rights activists, marching for the right to vote in Alabama, were arrested and beaten by state troopers using night sticks and tear gas.

Federal action came quickly with the U.S. Congress adopting the **Voting Rights Act of 1965,** which suspended literacy tests as a requirement of registering to vote. The Voting Rights Act covered a county or state if it met the guidelines of a "triggering formula": (1) A literacy test was in use as of November 1, 1964, and (2) fewer than 50 percent of the eligible voters were registered or cast ballots in the 1964 presidential election. If a county or state met these conditions, and those in the South almost exclusively did, the U.S. attorney general was empowered to suspend the literacy tests and replace local registration officials with federal agents who would register voters under federal procedures. The act effectively ended literacy tests, and they were permanently banned nationwide in 1975. Because of eventual voluntary compliance in registering voters, federal registrars were sent to only a few counties in the South.

Section 5 of the Voting Rights Act, which was to grow in importance during the ensuing years, prohibits covered jurisdictions from making any changes affecting voting unless they are approved by the U.S. attorney general or the U.S. District Court for the District of Columbia. Proposed changes are *not* approved if they deny or abridge the right to vote on account of race. This means that changes such as drawing new district lines for members of state or local legislatures, annexing additional land by a city that changes its racial composition, or changing the location of polling places have to go through a process known as **preclearance** at the federal level before they can be implemented.[16]

The results of the Voting Rights Act are impressive: Nearly 1 million African Americans were added to voter registration lists in Deep South states. From 1964 to 1968, for example, the percentage of voting-age African Americans registered in Mississippi increased from 6.7 to 59.4. The U.S. Justice Department, charged with implementing the act, estimated that within five years after its passage as many African Americans had registered in Alabama, Mississippi, Georgia, Louisiana, North Carolina, and South Carolina as in the previous one hundred years.[17]

Voting Rights Today

The main provisions of the Voting Rights Act of 1965 were viewed as temporary but were extended by Congress, sometimes with important changes, in 1970, 1975, and 1982. The last reauthorization was for twenty-five years; the Voting Rights Act will come up again for congressional review in 2007.

An important change was adopted in the Voting Rights Act Amendments of 1975. Mexican Americans in southwestern states had suffered discrimination in their efforts to register and vote similar to, although not as severe as, that suffered by African Americans. And in the 1960s the **Chicano movement,** a "surge of militant activity among the younger generation of Mexican Americans that quickly spread throughout the Southwest,"[18] focused national attention on discrimination against Mexican Americans. As a result, coverage of the Voting Rights Act was extended to language minorities, such as Asian Americans, American Indians, Alaska natives, and Hispanic Americans. To be covered by the law, a language minority had to make up at least 5 percent of the voting-age population in a state or local jurisdiction, usually a county. In addition, election information including registration forms, voter information sample ballots, and actual ballots had be available in the minority language.

Prior to the renewal of the Voting Rights Act in 1982, a debate exploded over whether those suing under the act had to prove that a defendant had intended to discriminate. Civil rights groups protested that intent would be difficult to prove and that, in any case, discrimination, even if it is not deliberate, still adversely affects African Americans, Hispanics, and other minorities. The 1982 amendments resolved this controversy by prohibiting any voting practice or procedure, regardless of intent, that results in discrimination. As a consequence, the Voting Rights Act today deals with subtle forms of discrimination such as minority vote dilution. **Minority vote dilution** occurs when election laws and racial bloc voting combine to keep minorities from winning elective positions. It has occurred in state and local governments throughout the United States, and not just those in the South. Examples of minority vote dilution are especially evident at the local level where city or county councils use at-large elections (see Chapter 3). For example, if voting in a county with a population 51 percent white and 49 percent one or more minority groups is polarized—minority voters vote for minority candidates, and white voters vote for white candidates—100 percent of the council members will be white. All white candidates will be elected with 51 percent of the vote, and all minority candidates will lose, with 49 percent of the vote. Even though the minority population is almost as large as that of the whites, no minorities will be elected to the council. After being sued under the Voting Rights Act, many local governments with at-large elections and a history of no minorities running in or winning these elections have been forced to adopt single-member districts. These districts increase the likelihood of members of minority groups winning office because boundary lines are drawn so that the minority will be a majority of the voters in at least one or more districts.

Have these voting rights changes significantly empowered minority groups? There is little doubt that the number of African Americans and Hispanics in elected local offices has steadily increased. For example, in 1997 more than 5,000 African Americans were serving as mayors and members of city or county councils, an increase of 44 percent since 1985. The number of Hispanics—the second largest minority in the United

States, who comprise 10 percent of the total population—in similar positions was just over 2,000 in 1994, an increase of 67 percent since 1985.[19]

Still, these increases in office holding, especially for Hispanics, do not indicate numerical equality or parity, that is, the proportion of minority officials in most local governments is less than the proportion of minorities in the population. Representation is improving, but recent studies show that **political incorporation,** where minorities are part of the dominant city policy making coalition on minority-related issues, is the exception rather than the rule.[20] Political scientist Clarence N. Stone has noted that greater representation by minorities has not meant either greater access to government for lower-class African Americans or that poor inner-city neighborhoods have benefited from new public works projects.[21]

Additional Changes in Voter Registration

In the past twenty-five years, other registration requirements such as living in a state for at least one year and appearing in person at the election board's headquarters to register were changed. States changed residency requirements to only ten to thirty days before an election, and more than half the states adopted mail-in registration. A few states gave voters the opportunity to register when they obtain or renew their drivers' license ("motor-voter" registration) or apply for certain types of public assistance such as food stamps and Medicaid (agency-based registration).[22] Although many states were easing registration procedures, Congress in 1993 enacted the **National Voter Registration Act (NVRA)** that required all states to adopt mail-in, "motor-voter," and agency-based registration procedures. In addition, state laws that purge voters, that is, cancel their registration solely for failure to vote at least once during a specified time, are prohibited. This act expanded federal control over voter registration.[23]

During 1999–2000, state motor vehicle offices handled 38 percent of the 45.6 million registration applications or transactions processed nationwide; the next most popular way of taking care of registration transactions was through the mail, 31 percent of the total. Transactions include people registering to vote for the first time, changing their place of registration because they moved into a new county, or changing their name or local address.[24] States reported more than 156 million registered voters in 2000, over 76 percent of the voting-age population. However, NVRA has not raised the percentage of registered voters, disappointing many of its advocates.[25]

And contrary to a long-standing fear of Republicans, it is not a bonanza for the Democratic Party. Voters are registering as independents much more frequently than expected. In the South, in particular, many voters are registering as independent and "may well represent partial conversions by people abandoning traditional Democratic ties but simply unwilling to jump all the way over to the Republican side in one step."[26]

Another question is whether new voters that registered through the relatively easy motor-voter process will have enough interest to vote on election day. Raymond E. Wolfinger and Jonathan Hoffman have examined this question with data from Current Population Surveys of the U.S. Census Bureau. Voter turnout for the 1996 presidential election, by registration status, is presented below.[27]

70 percent—state motor vehicle offices.

51 percent—state public assistance agencies.

82 percent—other new registrants.

84 percent—pre-1995 registrants.

The highest turnout is among those who were registered to vote prior to 1995 or were new registrants that used some other method of registration. The lowest turnout is among those who registered through motor vehicle offices or public assistance agencies. (Overall, 83 percent of all registered voters voted in 1996.) Wolfinger and Hoffman conclude that "while registration may be the greatest cost of voting, it is not the only hurdle that must be surmounted."[28] Still, given the millions of registration transactions that take place every year, it makes sense to make these transactions as convenient as possible for citizens.

Five states have gone about as far as you can go in easing registration requirements: Idaho, Minnesota, New Hampshire, Wisconsin, and Wyoming allow Election Day registration (EDR); NVRA exempted EDR states from its coverage. Registration and voting become a one-step process completed at the same time. EDR was an important factor in Jesse Ventura's election as governor of Minnesota. Approximately 15 percent of the voters registered on Election Day, and many of them were new, young voters who voted overwhelmingly for Ventura.[29] A study of EDR states concludes that on average the voter turnout rate is 5 percent higher than in states that do not have a one-step process.[30] Nevertheless, concern about the potential for voting fraud has prevented most states from adopting it.

Voting Systems

State and local governments have many accomplishments, but there is no doubt that the state of Florida failed to meet its responsibilities of ensuring fair elections and accurate counting of every vote in the 2000 presidential election. After much analysis of election procedures throughout the nation, however, it became clear that what happened in Florida could just as easily have happened in a number of other states. In fact, election procedures and **voting systems,** defined as any device for casting and tabulating ballots or votes, were an accident waiting to happen. One fact the 2000 presidential election brought to everyone's attention is that holding an election is not a simple event. In this election, more than 100 million voters cast ballots on over 700,000 voting machines in over 200,000 polling places that were managed by approximately 22,000 election officials and 1.4 million part-time election-day workers![31]

What happened in Florida? Of the 6 million ballots that were cast in the presidential election, more than 175,000 ballots were "spoiled," that is, they were rejected and not counted. Ballots were rejected because of "overvotes," where voters voted for more than one candidate for president, or "undervotes," where the voter's choice was not recorded. The common factor in the "spoiled" ballots is that the vast majority was cast on punch card voting systems that were used in a number of Florida counties. In this system, which has been around since the 1960s, voters mark their ballots by punching holes in paper cards. When the election is over and polling places close, the cards are fed into computerized counting machines to tally the votes. The requirements of the punch card voting system and the large number of presidential and vice presidential candidates (a total of ten) that qualified for Florida's ballot caused problems with ballot design and instructions that led to confusion among a large number of voters. In Duval

County, for example, the first page of the ballot listed the names of five presidential candidates and their running mates, and the second page had the names of the remaining five candidates and their running mates. The first page also had a printed instruction that read, "Turn page to continue voting." And that's exactly what many voters did, and in the process they voted for two presidential candidates and disqualified their ballot. Undervotes were caused when voters did not cleanly punch a hole in the card beside the name of the candidate they were voting for. If the hole isn't punched cleanly, a small piece of paper called a chad will remain. The counting machine will not read it, and the vote will be rejected. Overvotes in Florida numbered approximately 110,000, undervotes slightly over 60,000.[32]

Recognizing that the right to vote is one of the most important rights people have in a democracy, special commissions or committees were quickly established in many states to study the act of voting and determine what changes needed to be made. The goal of Maryland's committee was typical: "[to] ensure that all votes are counted accurately and that voting is easily understood and as convenient as possible."[33] Florida was the first state to enact comprehensive election reform, which included the following provisions:

- All voting jurisdictions were mandated to switch from punch card, mechanical lever, and paper voting to optical-scanning systems. Optical scan ballots are similar to Scantron forms used for tests in colleges and universities. Voters indicate their choice by filling in an oval or connecting the middle part of an arrow beside a candidate's name.
- State funds were made available to counties to help pay for the purchase of new voting systems and to upgrade training of poll workers.
- A uniform, statewide ballot design was required.
- Uniform, statewide standards for the conduct of election recounts were mandated.[34]

Florida and a number of other states acted more quickly than the federal government, but Congress soon passed and President Bush signed into law the **Help America Vote Act of 2002.** One of the more important provisions of HAVA will provide federal grant money to the states to assist in improving election administration, replace punch card voting systems, and improve access to polling places for persons with disabilities. Federal financial assistance is particularly important because the cost just for replacing punch card systems is high; $100 million was the estimate for Los Angeles County, the nation's most populous voting jurisdiction.[35] HAVA requires states to develop and maintain a single statewide voter registration list. This will eliminate county-maintained registration lists and should ensure a more accurate and up-to-date list of voters. As is often the case with federal laws, a few states on their own initiative have made significant progress in reaching these requirements. Finally, HAVA establishes a Help America Vote College Program that will encourage high school and college students to volunteer as poll workers on election day.

Voter Turnout in Gubernatorial Elections

Voter turnout figures are calculated in a number of ways. A popular way is based on survey research: Respondents are simply asked to report their frequency of voting. The

U.S. Bureau of the Census conducts this type of research every two years, but only asks about participation in national elections. For a number of reasons, voter turnout percentages from survey research are always slightly higher than the percentages arrived at by defining voter turnout as the percentage of the citizens of voting-age population that actually votes in an election; that is, the number of ballots counted by election officials divided by the number of a state's registered voters or voting-age population.

Table 4-2 shows voter turnout percentages in recent gubernatorial elections. A couple of methodological points: First, beginning in 2000, the Census Bureau provides a voting-age population estimate that includes citizens only; of course, citizenship is a requirement for voting, so the citizen voting-age population, rather than the total population that is eighteen and older, is the denominator for calculating the percentages in Table 4-2. Second, we are interested in looking at the level of participation. This means that citizen voting-age population is a better denominator than registered voters because it provides a clearer idea of the level of participation. In all but a few states, if you are not registered, you cannot vote; it's not unusual to find that 20 percent of a state's population is not registered to vote. Using this definition, turnout in recent gubernatorial elections has ranged from a low of just under 20 percent in Kentucky to a high of over 60 percent in Minnesota. (For comparative purposes, remember that approximately 50 percent of the voting-age population has been voting in recent presidential elections.)

A close examination of Table 4-2 reveals several patterns:

1. The timing of elections is important for turnout. States that elect governors in the same years as presidents (2000) are elected have higher turnout than states that elect governors in nonpresidential years. All but one of the states that held elections in 2000 had over 50 percent turnout, while less than 15 percent of the states with elections in nonpresidential years reached that level. Presidential elections stimulate voter interest, increasing the number of people who go to the polls and the number of people who vote in governors' races.
2. The effect of presidential elections also can be found in New Hampshire and Vermont, where two-year gubernatorial terms allow elections to alternate between presidential and nonpresidential years. Both states have a much higher percentage of people voting for governor when they also are voting for president.
3. Although the relationship between voter turnout and region is not perfect, states in the South and Southwest have the lowest turnout, with midwestern and New England states having the highest turnout.

As noted in Chapter 1, political culture affects voter turnout, also. States with a moralistic culture consistently lead the nation in rates of turnout. Another factor that affects turnout is the closeness of the election; down-to-the-wire contests usually increase turnout.

Voter Turnout in Local Elections

Voter turnout is even lower in local (county and city) elections—usually less than 30 percent of the voting-age population. Surveys show that the decline of voter turnout over time is greater in local than in presidential elections. A variety of factors are responsible, including the lack of media attention paid to these elections, the absence of

TABLE 4-2 Voter Turnout in Recent Gubernatorial Elections
(Percentages)

1999	2000	2001	2002	
41.9 Louisiana	65.9 New Hampshire	41.7 New Jersey	64.3 Minnesota	44.9 Oregon
38.2 Mississippi	65.1 Vermont	38.4 Virginia	62.9 South Dakota	44.8 Idaho
19.9 Kentucky	65.0 North Dakota		51.0 Illinois	44.3 Kansas
	63.1 Montana		50.4 Iowa	43.5 Maine
	60.6 Washington		50.2 Wyoming	43.2 Oklahoma
	59.6 Delaware		49.6 New Hampshire	42.1 Arkansas
	58.9 Missouri		49.5 Alabama	40.5 Tennessee
	55.3 Utah		49.5 Alaska	40.1 Pennsylvania
	55.1 North Carolina		49.2 Florida	39.0 Ohio
	50.6 Indiana		48.8 Vermont	38.2 Nevada
	46.4 West Virginia		48.7 Massachusetts	37.9 South Carolina
			48.3 Hawaii	37.4 Nebraska
			46.9 Wisconsin	36.9 New Mexico
			46.0 Rhode Island	36.1 New York
			45.9 Maryland	35.5 Georgia
			45.6 Connecticut	32.5 California
			45.4 Colorado	32.4 Texas
			45.0 Michigan	29.4 Arizona

Note: Percentages were calculated by dividing the total number of votes cast by the citizen voting-age population.

Source: Compiled by the authors. Citizen voting-age population is based on estimates from the Current Population Reports of the U.S. Bureau of the Census. Citizen voting-age population for 2000 is from *Voting and Registration in the Election of November 2000* (Washington, D.C.: U.S. Bureau of the Census, 2002); available at www.census.gov/population/socdemo/voting/p20-542 (accessed February 11, 2003). Election statistics for 2002 were obtained from "RGA Election Coverage 2002" at http://election2002.rga.org (accessed February 11, 2003). Election statistics for 2000, 2001, and 2003 were obtained from the website of each state's secretary of state.

116

opponents to challenge incumbents in many races, and frequently the large number of positions that are filled by election. In most cases, there is little excitement because local officials deal largely with such noncontroversial issues as road repair and other basic services. In most small towns, officials avoid controversy and support the status quo. Campaigns are low-key events and center on name identification.

Nonpartisan elections, widely used at the local level, also lower voter turnout. This happens because the partisan identification of candidates that are displayed during the campaign and the party name on the election ballot lower the information costs of voting decisions by providing citizens with easily accessible information about candidates—whether they are Democrats or Republicans. And in most cities this information will provide voters with some ideas about the candidates' beliefs concerning the role of government. Also, some voters have feelings of loyalty to their party and they will be motivated to support their party's candidates on Election Day. Brian Schaffner, Matthew Streb, and Gerald Wright, in a well-designed study, compared voter turnout in nonpartisan elections in Champaign, Illinois to partisan elections in neighboring Urbana, Illinois. Both cities are in the same congressional district so turnout in these two local elections was compared to turnout in a partisan congressional election. The results were very clear: Turnout in both cities was lower in the local elections than in the congressional, but turnout in Champaign dropped by 43 percent and in Urbana by only 33 percent. Turnout in the nonpartisan election dropped by an extra 10 percentage points.[36] In addition, without party labels incumbent candidates have an even greater electoral advantage. Schaffner, Streb, and Wright state "that without partisan cues voters rely on the next most obvious low cost voting cue—incumbency—which represents some combination of candidate name familiarity, less uncertainty about the candidate, and satisfaction with performance in office."[37]

A typical 30 percent voter turnout means that election outcomes can be determined by a little over 15 percent of the voting-age population. Given that those with low incomes are less likely to vote than those with higher incomes and more education, an upper-class elite often exercises great power in local elections.

ELECTION CAMPAIGNS

Running for Governor

State constitutional amendments that created four-year terms for governors and moved their election to the middle of the U.S. president's term have caused gubernatorial elections, and elections to other state offices, to become increasingly autonomous affairs, that is, separate from the issues and personalities of presidential elections. These midterm elections have made it unlikely that voters' evaluation of the parties' presidential candidates will affect their choice for governor. During the 1980s, for example, voters were prone to elect Republican presidents in presidential elections and Democratic governors two years later.[38]

As often happens, just about the time political scientists develop an important generalization, a political event occurs that is an exception. In this case, the event was the 1994 midterm elections during President Clinton's first term. As noted in Chapter 3, 1994 elections resulted in huge losses for the Democratic Party. Not only did the

Republican Party win new majorities in the U.S. Senate and House of Representatives, but it also made significant gains in governors' offices and state legislative seats. It is hard to escape the conclusion that voters were intent on throwing out Democrats at the national *and* state level. In 1994, voters' evaluations of the national scene affected their votes at the state level.

As with all elections, it is important to consider the effect of incumbency. Data gathered by Thad Beyle between 1970 and 2002 show that incumbent governors were eligible to seek another term in 76 percent of the elections. (Remember, most governors are subject to two four-year terms. See Chapter 6.) What happened in these elections? Basically, 78 percent of the incumbents decided to run, and 76 percent of the incumbents who decided to run were reelected.[39] These two percentages are not as high as those found for members of the U.S. House of Representatives, which are normally in the 80–90 percent range and sometimes even higher. Nevertheless, the percentages for governor are moderately high.

Incumbent reelection success for a shorter and more recent time period, between 1999 and 2002, is presented in Table 4-3. The percentage of incumbents eligible to run is lower than it is in the thirty-year period for which Beyle collected data (62 percent versus 76 percent); an unusually large number of governors could not run because of term limits. However, the percentage of incumbents who were eligible and actually ran (75 percent) and the percentage that were reelected (79 percent) are almost identical to those reported by Beyle.

Peverill Squire and Christina Fastnow compared the election environment of incumbent governors and U.S. senators and concluded that it is different. Voters are more likely to know and have an opinion of their governor than of their senators. News about governors appears much more frequently in newspapers than news about senators. But better known does not translate into better liked: Governors receive less favorable job performance ratings than senators. Consequently, voters are more likely to vote for a challenger to an incumbent governor than for a challenger to an incumbent senator.[40]

A recurrent question in the study of gubernatorial elections is the role of taxes in determining the outcome of the election. The specific question is this: Are candidates who raise taxes while they are in office punished by the voters, that is, do they lose votes in the next election? Obviously, it's possible to lose enough support among the voters to

TABLE 4-3   Incumbent Reelection Success in Gubernatorial Elections, 1999–2002

Year	Number of Races	Eligible to Run	Ran	Won
1999	3	2 (67%)	2 (100%)	2 (100%)
2000	11	7 (64%)	6 (86%)	5 (83%)
2001	2	0	—	—
2002	36	23 (64%)	16 (70%)	12 (75%)
Totals for 1999–2002	52	32 (62%)	24 (75%)	19 (79%)

Sources: Data for 1999, 2000, and 2001 are from Thad Beyle, "Governors: Elections, Powers and Priorities," *Books of the States 2002* (Lexington, Ky.: Council of State Governments, 2002), p.136. Data for 2002 were compiled by the authors from "RGA Election Coverage 2002," at http://election2000.rga.org (accessed February 11, 2003).

lose the election. Brian Stults and Richard F. Winters have taken a comprehensive look at this question of electoral retribution in gubernatorial elections from 1990 to 1998.[41] The most important factors are incumbency, party affiliation, the type of tax that was raised, and the state of the economy. Conventional wisdom predicts that governors who raise taxes will be defeated at the next election. According to Stults and Winters, the picture is much more complicated than this. First, governors who raise state *sales* taxes are much more likely to lose support among the voters than governors who raise income taxes. (For a discussion of state taxes see Chapter 8.) The sales tax has "a unique ability to inspire voter ire" because it is levied on most purchases voters make and they are reminded daily of the increase.[42]

Another finding suggests that voter retribution is greater for *nonincumbent* gubernatorial candidates who belong to the same party as the governor who raised taxes than it is for the incumbents who actually raise taxes and then run for reelection. This relationship exist because many incumbents who raise taxes may decide not to run for reelection because they see their chances of success as being very low. Other incumbent governors will do the opposite. They take on the challenge of explaining to the voters why a tax increase was necessary and overcome or at least reduce its negative impact on electoral support. When an incumbent leaves the race and decides not to run, the candidate who is nominated is the target of greater electoral retribution. Party affiliation of candidates also has an effect, with voters showing greater displeasure toward Democratic candidates than Republican candidates. This may be because the Democratic Party is frequently viewed as the "tax and spend" party, but the evidence is not clear on this. Finally, in economic hard times governors may have to raise taxes to maintain programs and services, but it's not a reason that finds favor with the voters. Governors who raise taxes in hard times, especially the sales tax, face electoral retribution.[43]

Research by Thomas M. Carsey reminds us that gubernatorial elections are more than factors and variables. They involve many campaign decisions made by real candidates who are communicating with real voters, hoping to earn the support of a majority of them on election day. Carsey states that gubernatorial candidates can choose between three strategies regarding the information they communicate to voters. Briefly, the strategies are the following:

1. Candidates can change their own position on an issue that is salient to the voters by adopting a new position that is closer to the one held by most of the voters.
2. Candidates can try to persuade voters to change their position on a salient issue and to adopt the candidates' position.
3. Candidates can try to shift voters' attention to another issue that is more beneficial to them.[44]

Although candidates have used each strategy, Carsey believes that the third one is the best. The first strategy has problems. Candidates that change their position and move to where most of the voters are may end up losing their more partisan and ideological backers that want their candidate to stand for something, whether it be, for example, liberalism or conservatism. Also, candidates that change position usually are accused of flip-flopping on the issue. Voters wonder about the candidates' credibility. The second strategy of trying to convince voters to change their position and move closer to the candidate may occasionally work, but it usually won't because voters are being asked to admit that they have been mistaken in their thinking, something that is unlikely to happen during a campaign that lasts only a few months. But the third strategy, of trying to redefine the issues that are salient to the voters during the campaign, is an approach that avoids the pitfalls of the first two strategies. Carsey concludes:

> . . . the campaign becomes a struggle between candidates providing information to voters as they try to define for voters the important issues in that particular election. One candidate might focus on economic concerns while the other stresses social issues. Which candidate wins will depend in part on who is better able to make their campaign theme more salient for voters.[45]

The 2002 gubernatorial election in Michigan is one for which this framework works well. The Republican nominee was Lieutenant Governor Dick Posthumus. His Democratic opponent was Jennifer M. Granholm, who was elected as Michigan's attorney general in 1998. Granholm's mix of "brains and movie-star looks" had propelled her to a strong lead over Posthumus in early polls. (Granholm is a Harvard Law School graduate and had spent several years in Los Angeles as an aspiring actress.) The Posthumus campaign tried to shift voters' attention from Granholm's personal characteristics by pointing to his twenty years of experience in Michigan government as better qualifying him to lead the state. His campaign accused Granholm of being light on substance and that the Democratic Party was running a "Spice Girls" ticket. Granholm countered with fifty-eight pages of position papers on her campaign's website and called for "new leadership" in the state after twelve years of Republican control of the governor's office.[46] Both candidates attempted to define the central campaign issues for the voters in ways that would benefit them; Granholm won the election.

Running for the State Legislature

Every two years, upwards of 10,000 candidates may be running for approximately 5,000 seats in the lower houses of state legislatures, and as many as 2,600 candidates may be running for almost 1,300 seats in the state senates. Most have had a long-term interest in politics, and many come from politically active families. A 1998 study of legislative candidates found that almost half the candidates were "encouraged" to run, that is, they had been thinking of running when officials in the local party or local elected officials approached them, asking them to run. Approximately one-third of the candidates were "self-starters" who said that it was entirely their own idea to run. The smallest group of candidates was the "persuaded," who had not seriously thought about running until someone else suggested it to them.[47] Candidates frequently mention public service and, more than in the past, commitment to issues as reasons for running.[48] In almost all states, but especially large states where party control for a majority of legislative seats is close, parties have created legislative campaign committees. According to Gary Moncrief, Peverill Squire, and Malcolm Jewell, **legislative campaign committees** are controlled by legislative party leaders and provide financial support to both incumbent and nonincumbent candidates; they also are frequently active in recruiting candidates. These committees usually target districts, that is, identify districts that are crucial for the party to win and allocate most of their assistance to these districts. In addition, some legislative leaders have their own PACs that are used to support candidates.[49]

A study of ten states finds that close to half of the candidates are from *broker careers;* that is, they are in occupations that require them to negotiate, bargain, and persuade. Examples of such private careers are lawyers, teachers, real estate agents, and owners and operators of business establishments.[50] Candidates consciously weigh their opportunity costs. The risks, including some sacrifice of their private careers and of time spent with their families, are balanced against increases in social esteem and political influence. Of course, the opportunity costs include the chances of winning, the presence of an incumbent, and the financial cost of running a campaign.[51]

Individual campaigns differ greatly depending on the nature of the district, the strength of political parties, and the presence of an incumbent. District size varies from about 846,000 people in California senate districts and 423,000 in California house districts to 16,000 in Wyoming senate districts and 3,000 in New Hampshire house districts. Of course, urban house districts are smaller geographically, whereas many rural senate districts are very large. The level of professionalism in campaigns varies across the country. In states with a large population, such as California and New York, legislative races often are professionally managed and use "wholesale" advertising techniques such as television and radio to reach large numbers of voters.[52]

In most states, however, legislative campaigns are "retail" in nature, that is, they involve face-to-face contact between candidates and voters. With weak political parties and insufficient funds to hire professional campaign managers, candidates are pretty much on their own and need to develop a personal following that will volunteer for campaign work. Candidates will go door-to-door to drop off their campaign literature and meet voters. Mass advertising techniques include billboards, yard signs, and direct mail. Direct mail, usually done by a professional, is increasing in popularity because voters can be targeted according to their party affiliation, the frequency with which they vote, and when they registered to vote.

Political scientists value campaigns because they provide an opportunity, though not always fulfilled, for candidates to educate voters on the issues of the day. Tom Loftus, former speaker of the Wisconsin State Assembly, argues that campaigns, especially those involving face-to-face contact with the voters, also educate the candidate:

> All the handshaking, all the pleasantries exchanged, help make a politician representative. If you talk with people at their doors, on the threshold of their homes, and glimpse their families and perhaps their furniture and the pictures on the walls, you will begin to see their dreams realized and not realized, and you will begin to understand your prospective constituents.[53]

The number of members who leave a legislature at the end of their term and are replaced by newly elected members is called **membership turnover.** Turnover rates have been on a long-term decline in almost all states since the early 1960s; the fifty-state average in 1996 was 20 percent (2002 turnover rates are in Table 4-4). A drop in the proportion of members that leave voluntarily, that is, simply decide not to run again, is the most likely cause of this decline. A study of eighteen states from 1978 to 1986 found that it is not unusual for 70 to 80 percent of incumbents to run for reelection and typically 90 percent are reelected. Incumbent legislators also are less likely to face an opponent in the general election than they were a few years ago.[54] Challengers of incumbents face a tough battle.

TABLE 4-4 Membership Turnover in the Legislatures: 2002

State or Other Jurisdiction	Senate			House		
	Total Number of Members	Number of Membership Changes	Percentage Change of Total	Total Number of Members	Number of Membership Changes	Percentage Change of Total
Alabama	35	5	14	105	24	23
Alaska	20	7	35	40	15	38
Arizona	30	8	27	60	33	55
Arkansas	35	15	43	100	33	33
California	40	6	15	80	15	19
Colorado	35	7	20	65	19	29
Connecticut	36	5	14	151	28	19
Delaware	21	2	10	41	6	15
Florida	40	16	40	120	30	25
Georgia	56	18	32	180	57	32
Hawaii	25	7	28	51	16	31
Idaho	35	10	29	70	19	27
Illinois	59	19	32	118	34	29
Indiana	50	3	6	100	18	18
Iowa	50	20	40	100	43	43
Kansas	40	2	5	125	29	23
Kentucky	38	3	8	100	11	11
Louisiana	39	1	3	105	5	5
Maine	35	11	31	151	69	46
Maryland	47	12	26	141	42	30
Massachusetts	40	4	10	160	22	14
Michigan	38	29	76	110	55	50
Minnesota	67	21	31	134	42	31
Mississippi	52	1	2	122	0	0
Missouri	34	12	35	163	90	55

State						
Montana	50	19	38	100	30	30
Nebraska	49	7	14		—Unicameral—	38
Nevada	21	4	19	42	16	37
New Hampshire	24	11	46	400	149	29
New Jersey	40	9	23	80	23	
New Mexico	42	2	5	70	12	17
New York	62	10	16	150	24	16
North Carolina	50	16	32	120	35	29
North Dakota	47	5	11	94	13	14
Ohio	33	7	21	99	21	21
Oklahoma	48	9	19	101	17	17
Oregon	30	7	23	60	20	33
Pennsylvania	50	4	8	203	23	11
Rhode Island	38	2	5	75	7	9
South Carolina	46	2	4	124	19	15
South Dakota	35	14	40	70	24	34
Tennessee	33	6	18	99	21	21
Texas	31	6	19	150	37	25
Utah	29	5	17	75	16	21
Vermont	30	10	33	150	40	27
Virginia	40	2	5	100	3	3
Washington	49	7	14	98	19	19
West Virginia	34	7	21	100	20	20
Wisconsin	33	8	24	99	16	16
Wyoming	30	6	20	60	21	35

Source: Book of the States 2004 (Lexington, Ky.: Council of State Governments, 2003). Reproduced by permission of the Council of State Governments. The authors wish to thank Keon Chi for making this table available to us prior to its publication.

Note: Turnover is calculated after the 2002 legislative elections. Sixteen states have legislative term limits: Arizona, Arkansas, California, Colorado, Florida, Louisiana, Maine, Michigan, Missouri, Montana, Nebraska, Nevada, Ohio, Oklahoma, South Dakota, and Wyoming. Term limits are discussed in Chapter 5.

Some states have adopted legislative term limits that may increase turnover (see Chapter 5). It is important, however, to point out that if a state legislative chamber has 100 members and 80 percent run for reelection and 90 percent are reelected, there will be twenty-eight new members, that is, a membership turnover of 28 percent, which is still quite a few new members. In other words, if a number of members leave voluntarily, turnover rates can still be reasonably high even with a large percentage of incumbents being reelected.

Running for Judge

Two types of judicial elections can be found in the states: One is the type of election we usually think of in which citizens use their votes to fill an elected office in government, in this case a judge, by choosing from two or more candidates. The second type is called a **retention election.** In this election, the name of an incumbent judge, whose term of office is about to expire, is placed on the ballot and voters can decide whether the judge should be retained in office for another term. By law, no opposing candidate can be on the ballot. (It is important to point out that not all judges are elected. Judicial selection methods, along with additional information on retention elections, are discussed in Chapter 7.)

In the past few years there have been indications that the election of judges, especially those who are members of a state's highest court (usually called the state supreme court), is undergoing tremendous change, at least in a few states. Before looking at this possible trend, we will summarize the main patterns of judicial elections. One noteworthy finding is that incumbent judges frequently do *not* face a challenger when they run for reelection; this is especially true of nonpartisan elections, which are more common in the election of judges. Studies of a few states have shown that judges on major trial courts are opposed only about 25 percent of the time. Incumbent trial judges are rarely defeated. However, elections for a state's highest court are usually contested, winning candidates have smaller margins of victory, and incumbents are more likely to be defeated.[55]

Judicial elections are much less visible to voters and receive much less media coverage than elections to the U.S. Congress and the governor's office. Consequently, some voters who go to the polls vote for the higher offices and skip over lower offices; this is known as **ballot roll-off.** Voters in judicial elections usually have little information about the candidates. An in-depth study of Ohio found that voters' decisions between competing candidates rest on name recognition (which gives incumbents an advantage), party affiliation, and gender (a large number of women voters said they voted for a woman). It is important to remember that many of the voters interviewed could not articulate reasons for their choices and that some could not recall whom they had voted for.[56]

Two recent developments may change the above description as it applies to state supreme court elections. First, elections in some states such as Alabama, California, Kentucky, Ohio, Texas, and Wisconsin have become "nastier, noisier, and costlier."[57] In most of these states, the elections have changed as the battle over the amount of damages awarded in civil liability suits has grown more intense and spilled from the courtroom to the electoral arena. Personal injury lawyers are on one side and business groups, especially insurance companies, and their lawyers are on the other side. Both sides are seeking to elect judges who will be more likely to decide in their favor; at stake are millions of dollars in lawsuits. In the 2000 election, supreme court candidates raised over $45 million for their campaigns, double what was raised in 1994. Much of this money is spent on expensive television advertising; interest groups frequently run their own ads to support or attack candidates. In the 2002 election, the Michigan Chamber of Commerce spent almost $350,000 in support of two candidates who were running for reelection. Some observers believe that judicial candidates airing television ads and interest groups supporting or attacking judicial candidates in their own television ads will weaken the public's faith in the courts.[58]

A recent U.S. Supreme Court decision also has the potential to affect the nature of judicial campaigns and elections, which traditionally have been regulated by state laws based on the judicial ethics codes of the American Bar Association. These laws limit what judicial candidates can say during election campaigns concerning their future conduct in the courtroom. The most common limitation is that candidates cannot make statements that indicate how they will decide on cases, issues, or controversies that are likely to come before the court. Many states go further and provide that candidates should not "make pledges or promises in office other than the faithful and impartial performance of the duties of the office."[59] A candidate for Minnesota's supreme court challenged Minnesota's version of these regulations. The U.S. Supreme Court in *Republican Party of Minnesota v. White* (2002)[60] ruled that Minnesota's "announce clause," which prohibited candidates from announcing their views on disputed legal or political issues, violated the First Amendment that guarantees freedom of speech. Future elections will allow judges to speak more freely about their views on contentious issues. What is unknown is how this will affect the public's confidence in judicial decision making. Will judges be perceived as approaching cases before them in a fair and impartial manner?

Running for Mayor

Because of the great diversity of cities, it is difficult to generalize about mayoral campaigns. For example, running for mayor of Chicago differs greatly from running for mayor of Small Town, U.S.A. Small-town campaigns in one-party areas or with nonpartisan elections obviously are very different from highly partisan elections in large or medium-size cities. Timing of local elections is different from federal and sometimes even different from state elections. Local elections are usually held in odd-numbered years or in late spring of even numbered years so the contests will be decided on local issues and candidates. Because nearly 70 percent of cities have nonpartisan elections, the personality of the candidates is even more important than in gubernatorial elections. In addition, many cities with nonpartisan elections also have city managers and few, if any, patronage jobs. This means that mayoral candidates must rely on volunteer campaign workers who cannot be promised jobs or other special favors if their candidate is elected.

Mayoral candidates in large cities are using many of the same techniques—polling, television advertisements, direct mail—as gubernatorial candidates to build their images. The hiring of political consultants to manage campaigns is common in most big-city elections. As a result, campaign costs have increased. In large northern cities, party organizations have lost power because candidates can use television effectively to go directly to the voters. The use of these techniques has been particularly helpful to Republican candidates running in cities where their party never had a strong organization.

CAMPAIGN FINANCING

Cost of Campaigns

Gubernatorial races are, of course, the most expensive. Thad Beyle reports that the total expenditures for elections held between the1998–2001 election cycle were $694 million. In the 1977–1980 cycle, total expenditures were $465 million, an increase, controlling for the effects of inflation, of 49 percent. The largest increase in expenditures was between elections held during the 1977–1980 cycle and those during 1987–1990, expenditures were fairly steady during the 1990s. Gubernatorial races, including primary and general elections, have cost as much as $135 million in California in 1998 and as little as $800,000 in Wyoming in the same year, when the incumbent governor won reelection.[61] Recently, wealthy businessmen have spent huge sums of money to elect themselves governor; although they have not always been successful, they do run up the total cost of gubernatorial elections. Al Checchi spent close to $39 million in 1998 in a failed attempt to win the Democratic nomination in California. And in the 2002 election in New York, Rochester billionaire businessman Thomas Golisano spent $73.9 million of his own money on a third party bid to become governor; he lost to incumbent George Pataki, who spent only $45 million! Mark Warner was elected governor in Virginia in 2001, spending a total of $22 million; approximately $5 million was from his own pocket.

Figure 4-1 shows the amount of money raised by the majority party for the 2000 general election. Most of the time the candidate that raises the most money wins the election; only two winning candidates in Figure 4-1spent less money than their opponents. Incumbent governors, because they already are in power and make decisions that literally affect all interests, have no problem raising more money than their opponents; challengers must overcome the name recognition and fundraising advantage that incumbents have. (It's interesting to note that in the 2000 general elections, the gubernatorial candidates in most states were almost even in the amount of money they raised.)

State legislative candidates in 2000 (almost 14,000 filed to run) raised $700 million for their campaigns! State by state variation is enormous, with heavily populated urban districts such as in California costing many times more than lightly populated rural districts in Kansas. Average total campaign contributions to California house and senate districts were $309,000 and $720,000, respectively; in Kansas the amounts are $13,000 and $47,000, respectively.[62] Robert E. Hogan, examining legislative candidates in twenty-seven states, has identified several factors affecting campaign spending. Candidate-level factors such as being an incumbent, holding a leadership role in the legislature, and being a member of the legislative majority are associated with raising and spending more money. District-level factors, number of opponents in the primary, and a high rate of spending by the general election opponent also increase campaign spending; however, prior competitive elections in a district have a positive but weak effect on

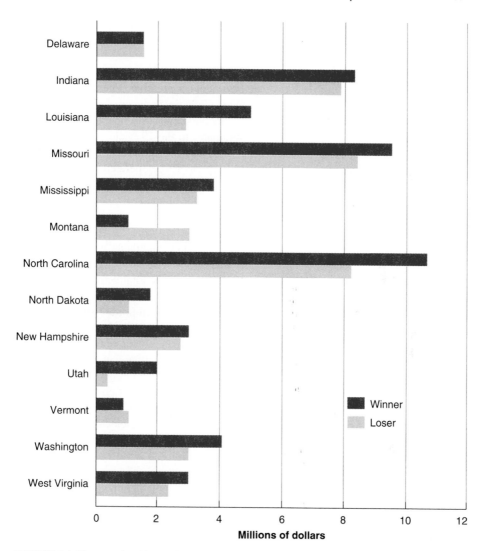

FIGURE 4-1 Money raised by major party gubernatorial candidates, 2000 general election.

Source: The Institute on Money in State Elections, *2000 State Election Overview*, p. 8. www.followthemoney.org. Accessed Feb. 17, 2003. Reprinted with permission of The Institute on Money in State Politics.

spending. Finally, the average campaign amount spent per voter of 98 cents is lowered by 18 cents if a state has public financing of elections.[63] (Public financing of elections will be discussed later in this chapter.)

Money, even if it's only $20,000 for a state legislative race, is difficult to raise in individual contributions of $10 and $20, so candidates typically turn to the business community (if they are Republicans) or to labor unions or teachers' associations (if they are Democrats). Unlike federal elections, corporations do not always have to establish PACs because about half the states permit corporations to make campaign contributions directly from their profits. Many states allow labor unions to make contributions directly from their treasuries, also. Candidates also use fundraising dinners and coffees and mail solicitations to raise money, especially in smaller states where campaigning is not as expensive.

As noted in Chapter 3, PACs have distributed greater and greater amounts of money to campaigns since the mid-1980s. A study of state legislative candidates in several states found that on average, PAC contributions made up anywhere from 13 to 43 percent of the total funds candidates raised. PACs are particularly strong in Alabama, where they contributed $9.3 million to *winning* candidates in the 1998 election; that was 70 percent of the $13.2 million that they received. The two most active PACs were A-Vote, of the Alabama Education Association, and Progress PAC, operated by the Business Council of Alabama.[64]

Research on campaign contributions at the local level are few and far between, but a study by Arnold Fleischmann and Lana Stein helps to fill the gap. They examined itemized contributions in recent elections in two cities, St. Louis, Missouri and Atlanta, Georgia. (Itemized deductions are required to be listed in candidates' campaign finance reports and are $101 and larger.) In Atlanta, candidates for mayor and city council collected $3.3 million for the 1989 election and in St. Louis the total was $1.9 million. In both cities, business interests were the most important source of itemized contributions, accounting for approximately 75 percent. PACs are not an important source because corporations and labor unions are allowed to make donations directly to campaigns in Missouri and Georgia. Contrary to findings in other cities, a wide range of businesses were contributors, not just those interested in development and land use such as real estate and construction firms. In council races, money was *not* an important predictor of election winners, indicating that "shoe leather" campaigns are still possible in districts that are small in size.[65] Labor unions, especially the American Federation of State, County, and Municipal Employees, have been a major force in elections through endorsements and financial contributions in many cities; however, this was not true in Atlanta and St. Louis.

Campaign Contributions: Disclosure and Limits

Efforts to regulate more closely the financing of campaigns originated as a response to a number of developments: the national Watergate scandal in the early 1970s, the public's view that politicians were too beholden to campaign contributions from special interests, and, occasionally, campaign financing scandals in individual states.

Disclosure laws, one of the first reforms adopted, require that candidates disclose the source of their campaign funds (contributions) and expenditures. With disclosure, the public can learn what interests are supporting a candidate before elections are held. If all contributors and the size of contributions are made public, ideally, voters have the opportunity to vote against a candidate who is receiving money from groups they don't support. Disclosure might even reduce the influence of special interests because candidates may not want to act in ways that appear to be responding to interest groups that gave them money. All states have disclosure laws, but their quality varies. To be useful, disclosure reports must contain information on the amount of money contributed, the contributor's occupation, and his or her place of employment. Although some agencies responsible for collecting disclosure reports still hand-enter candidates' written information into a computer, many states are moving to electronic filing for candidates.

Michael Malbin and Thomas Gais, in a major study of the real-world experience of state campaign finance reform, are skeptical that disclosure laws have achieved their goal. One problem is that the average voter will only learn about the information if it is reported by the news media, but very few newspapers have even one reporter analyzing rather complex campaign finance documents.[66]

Contribution limits are another way states regulate campaign financing. Thirty-six states have **contribution limits** that set a maximum on the amount of money individuals can contribute to campaigns. These limits usually fall in the range of $1,000 to $5,000 per gubernatorial candidate per election and force candidates to raise smaller amounts of money from a greater number of people, reducing dependence on a few contributors that donate large sums. Limits are usually smaller for state legislative candidates. States that allow labor unions and corporations to make contributions usually place limits on them as well. Most states limit PAC contributions, and a few have placed limits on the percentage of a candidate's contributions that can come from PACs.

Public Financing of Campaigns

Public financing, the use of money from taxpayers to finance candidates' campaigns or political parties, is a reform idea being tried in almost half of the states. States rely on the voluntary participation of individual income taxpayers to generate revenues to fund campaigns. The most popular method is an "add-on" tax, whereby a taxpayer donates, depending on the state, anywhere from $1 to $25; this adds to the taxes an individual must pay. Other states use the "tax checkoff," which allows voters to designate $1 to $5 of their taxes to public financing. The contribution is not added to their taxes but is taken out of what they already owe.

New Jersey adopted one of the first public financing laws in the nation. This law covers only gubernatorial candidates, but covers them in both primary and general elections. To qualify for public funds, a candidate must raise $260,000 (no single contribution can be larger than $2,600) from private sources; then he or she receives $2 in public funding for every $1 from private sources. By accepting public funds, candidates agree to **expenditure limits,** that is, to limit how much money their campaigns spend. Candidates also are required to participate in two televised debates during the general election campaign. In the 2001 election, three candidates qualified for funding for the primary election and two qualified for the general election. Both of the general election candidates qualified for the maximum public funds they were entitled to: $5.6 million. Total expenditures for each candidate were limited to $8.4 million. Public financing in New Jersey has reduced the importance of special interest money and has encouraged candidates to run in the primary who might not have done so without the promise of public funds.[67] It should be noted that in states with public financing, candidates do *not* have to accept the money. If they choose, they can run their campaigns entirely from private contributions.

The question of expenditure limits for campaigns, or spending caps as they are sometimes called, is a confusing one that needs to be addressed. First, the Supreme Court in *Buckley v. Valeo* (1976) decided that expenditure limits imposed by state legislatures or Congress are unconstitutional. The Court ruled that spending money in a political campaign was a form of speech and was therefore protected by the First Amendment to the U.S. Constitution and could not be regulated. Second, the Court provided for an exception by saying that expenditure limits are constitutional if they are a condition of accepting public financing. In other words, the only constitutional way to limit spending is to tie it to public funds. Some states are devising stronger ways to encourage candidates to accept public financing and/or the accompanying expenditure limits. In Kentucky, if a gubernatorial candidate using private contributions exceeds the expenditure limit, the candidate receiving the public financing subsidy is allowed to exceed the limit and will continue to receive $2 in public money for every $1 in private contributions. This plan was upheld in a federal appeals court and the Supreme Court refused to hear the case, meaning the appeals court decision stands.

Public Financing Evaluated

Public financing laws are not a universal success in the twenty-seven states that have them. Of course, public financing is not possible if funds are not available, and that is one of the problems. Another problem is that if candidates who accept public financing are required to adhere to unrealistically low expenditure limits, then they simply may decide that funding their campaigns from private sources with no expenditure limits is the wiser course. Public financing will not work if candidates refuse to participate.[68] These problems and possible solutions will be reviewed below.

Taxpayer participation in the "add-on" tax and the "tax checkoff" is low. No "add-on" state has had participation higher than 2 percent of its taxpayers; participation is higher in "tax checkoff" states, around 16 percent.[69] Participation in Hawaii, in the 20 percent range, has been the highest. This means that little money is raised to distribute to candidates, and until recently, only New Jersey and Minnesota were willing to use money from their general fund budgets to supplement taxpayer-designated funds. (Minnesota and New Jersey also use the "tax checkoff.")

Maryland has had an on-again, off-again relationship with public financing and shows what can happen with inadequate funds. In the post-Watergate period, it passed a comprehensive law but repealed it when several years of the "add-on tax" did not yield enough money to offer public financing to gubernatorial candidates until the 1994 election. The Republican candidate, Ellen Sauerbrey, accepted public funds and unexpectedly won the primary and almost won the general election. Then in 1995, concluding that public financing might be a good idea, the legislature readopted it, along with the "add-on tax." If the past is any guide, it could take close to ten years to raise enough money to finance one gubernatorial election.

Within the past several years, four states—Arizona, Maine, Massachusetts, and Vermont—have adopted clean election reform laws. (In Massachusetts the law has been surrounded by controversy and has not been fully implemented.) Under **clean election reforms,** which are now being considered in a number of states, candidates who forego large private contributions and agree to strict expenditure limits will receive a fixed amount of money for their campaigns from a publicly financed election fund.[70] Let's look at how clean elections work in Maine, the first state to adopt this plan. Candidates for a seat in the state senate, for example, are allowed to raise $1,500 from private sources; "seed money" as it's called. This "seed money" must include $5 donations from at least 150 people, and no single contribution can exceed $100. All qualifying candidates are given campaign funds for the primary and general elections based on the average amount spent in similar races in the two previous election cycles. Money for public financing comes from a Clean Election Fund, which receives money from three sources: qualifying contributions raised by candidates, "tax checkoff" on tax returns, and an appropriation from the state's general fund. Of course, candidates can finance their campaigns from private sources if they choose to. But the law has two additional provisions designed to discourage this: First, contribution limits are very low, $250 per donor. This means that a candidate will have to work hard to contact a large number of donors to obtain adequate campaign funds. Second, if publicly financed candidates are being outspent by privately financed candidates, they will receive funds to match the amount being spent by their opponents, up to double what they were initially authorized. Again, both of these provisions are designed to make public financing more attractive to candidates.

Minnesota's public financing system, which covers both gubernatorial and state legislative elections, may well be the most successful in the nation. Its key elements are as follows:

1. Expenditure limits for candidates that accept public funds are higher than in most states and indexed to inflation.
2. Grants to candidates from the $5 checkoff are supplemented by money from the state treasury if the checkoff does not provide enough revenue.
3. Individual contributors to *publicly financed* candidates are eligible for state refunds of up to $50 for individuals and $100 per couple per calendar year.

Kenneth Mayer's examination of public financing in Minnesota notes that participation is nearly universal for both incumbents and challengers. For example, in recent state senate races, 98 percent of the general election candidates used public funds. Mayer concludes that Minnesota's public financing of legislative races "can dramatically increase competition levels, by reducing incumbent fund-raising advantages and giving potential challengers an incentive to enter races."[71]

It is ironic that public displeasure with candidates raising money from special interests has not produced public willingness to support a system of public financing based on relatively small contributions from all or almost all taxpayers. An average-size state with 1 million taxpayers and a $25 "tax checkoff" could raise $25 million a year, more than enough to finance gubernatorial elections every four years and perhaps state legislative elections as well.

INITIATIVE, REFERENDUM, AND RECALL

State and local governments differ from the federal government in that their constitutions or charters often permit the use of techniques of direct democracy known as the initiative, referendum, and recall. Although they were occasionally used in colonial America and their use can be traced back to ancient Greece, direct democracy in the United States is largely a product of the Progressive movement in the early twentieth century. As noted in Chapter 3, these reformers distrusted political machines and party bosses and wanted to have a way for citizens to *directly* check governmental corruption and incompetence.

TABLE 4-5 Initiative, Referendum, and Recall in the States

Initiative, Referendum, and Recall	Initiative and Referendum	Initiative	Referendum	Recall	None*
Alaska	Arkansas	Mississippi	Kentucky	Georgia	Alabama
Arizona	Florida		Maryland	Kansas	Connecticut
California	Illinois		New Mexico	Louisiana	Delaware
Colorado	Maine			Minnesota	Hawaii
Idaho	Massachusetts			New Jersey	Indiana
Michigan	Missouri			Wisconsin	Iowa
Montana	Nebraska				New Hampshire
Nevada	Ohio				New York
North Dakota	Oklahoma				North Carolina
Oregon	South Dakota				Pennsylvania
Washington	Utah				South Carolina
	Wyoming				Tennessee
					Texas
					Vermont
					Virginia
					West Virginia

Sources: Compiled by the authors from the following: *I&R FactSheet,* Initiative and Referendum Institute, www.iandrinstitute.org/factsheets; Minnesota House of Representatives Research Department, *Recall of State Elected Officials: A Proposed Minnesota Constitutional Amendment,* October 1996, p. 6, www.house.leg.state.mn.us/hrd/pubs/recall96.pdf.
*This category refers to states that do not have any form of the initiative, do not have the popular referendum, and do not have the recall. All states, except Delaware, use a legislative referendum for proposed constitutional amendments.

Briefly stated, a **ballot measure** is a generic term that refers to anything on the ballot other than candidates for office. The initiative, referendum, and recall are ballot measures. More specifically, the **initiative** is a procedure whereby citizens can propose new laws or changes in state constitutions and determine by their votes in an election whether the proposal will be adopted. The **referendum** gives voters the opportunity to have the final say on a bill that their legislature already has approved. In both the initiative and referendum, proposed laws are actually placed on the ballot for voter approval. The **recall** is a procedure to remove an elected public official from office before his or her term officially ends. States using these techniques today are identified in Table 4-5. It's important to note two additional points: First, of the three, the initiative, because voters actually *propose* laws, receives the most attention from the public, the media, and academic researchers; it also will be the focus of this section. Second, the initiative, referendum, and recall are available in thousands of counties, cities, and towns and are actually used more frequently at the local level than at the state level; many states that do not have the statewide initiative allow its use at the local level.

What Kinds of Issues Are on the Ballot?

It has been approximately 100 years since South Dakota became the first state to adopt the initiative procedure, and since Oregon became the first state to have a statewide initiative on the ballot. During this time voters have decided the fate of slightly more than

2,000 initiatives. Over 60 percent of these initiatives have appeared on the ballots of just six states: Arizona, California, Colorado, North Dakota, Oregon, and Washington.[72] Initiative activity also varies by decade. The last two decades of the twentieth century had high levels of usage, with a record high of 389 initiatives on the ballot during the 1990s. The resurgence of interest in the initiative can be traced to California in 1978 when voters passed Proposition 13, which significantly reduced property taxes. (See Chapter 8.) This successful initiative was followed by similar measures in other states, demonstrating its effectiveness. In recent years, voters have proposed and voted on the following:[73]

- Allow casino gambling (Florida, 1986, failed).
- Prevent public funding of abortions (Arkansas, 1988, passed).
- Prohibit sport hunting of mountain lions (California, 1990, passed).
- Impose term limits for state legislatures (Oklahoma, 1990, passed).
- Allow physician-assisted suicide (Washington, 1991, failed; Michigan, 1998, failed).
- Impose "three strikes, you're out" sentences for major criminals (Washington, 1993, passed).
- Eliminate property tax exemptions for religious and nonprofit organizations (Colorado, 1996, failed).
- Permit use of marijuana for medicinal purposes (Arizona, 1996, passed).
- End racial preferences in state programs (California, 1996, passed).
- Decriminalize the use of marijuana (Alaska, 2000, failed).

In the 2002 election, 202 statewide measures were on the ballots in forty states; fifty-three were placed on the ballot through the initiative process, the smallest number since 1986. The most successful initiatives in this election were those dealing with education, causing one news reporter to call this the "education election."[74] In Florida voters passed a measure to ensure that every four-year-old be offered "a high quality pre-kindergarten learning opportunity." Voters also approved a proposal to limit class size in public schools; for example, classes in high school could have no more than twenty-five students, and the limit would be even smaller in lower grades. Parents, frustrated with portable classrooms and large classes, helped to pass this initiative even though Governor Jeb Bush, who won reelection, campaigned against it. California voters approved a proposal that would increase state funding of before and after school programs. Movie actor Arnold Schwarzenegger backed this measure. Initiatives dealing with drug policies did not fare well. Ohio voters voted against allowing treatment instead of jail for nonviolent drug offenders, and Nevadans voted down a proposal that would have legalized marijuana for recreational purposes. Animal rights activists were successful in outlawing cockfighting in Oklahoma, but failed to change animal cruelty from a misdemeanor to a felony in Arkansas. Efforts to bring election day voter registration to California and Colorado failed.[75]

The Initiative Process

Two forms of the initiative are used in the states: The **direct initiative** allows voters to bypass the legislature and place proposals directly on the ballot. Citizens in twenty-one states can use the direct initiative to propose new laws and in eighteen states citizens can propose changes in the constitution. The vast majority of these states are located west of the Mississippi River, where political parties are weaker and nonpartisan good-government groups have been stronger.[76]

There are three stages in winning voter approval of a direct initiative. Elisabeth Gerber classifies them as follows: drafting, qualifying, and campaigning.[77] In the drafting stage, a group of citizens research and write the proposed law that will appear on the ballot. Once the proposal is drafted it must be submitted to a state official, usually the secretary of state or attorney general, where it is reviewed and an official title and summary are written.

During the qualifying stage, supporters of the initiative must show support among the state's citizens; they do this by asking registered voters to sign petitions, which contain the official title and summary of the proposal. If a certain percentage of registered voters (usually about 10 percent) sign within a specified period of time (150 days in California, eighteen months in Wyoming), the proposal will be on the ballot in the following election. Laws regulating how petitions can be circulated are an important factor in determining the level of difficulty in using the initiative. A requirement that a person gathering signatures must actually witness each person signing the petition means that signature gathering will consume a large amount of time and money. The process is easier in states such as California, where signatures may be collected by mail, and in Washington, where petitions may be printed in newspapers. However, these methods are not trouble free because they frequently yield a high number of invalid signatures, that is, signatures of people who are not registered voters.[78]

If the initiative qualifies, the third stage is the campaign, the process of educating voters about the initiative and persuading them that they should vote for it. Of course, opponents will want to defeat it and they will try to convince voters to vote "no." Initiative campaigns differ from campaigns between candidates for elected offices in that there are *no limits* on the size of contributions that can be made to initiative campaign committees by individuals, corporations, labor unions, or interest groups; there are no limits on expenditures made by the campaign committee or by any group, either. The U.S. Supreme Court has ruled in a number of cases, including *First National Bank of Boston v. Bellotti* (1978) and *Citizens Against Rent Control v. City of Berkeley* (1981), that any limits violate the First Amendment to the Constitution.[79]

Another type of initiative is the **indirect initiative,** whereby a proposal with the required number of signatures must first be submitted to the legislature rather than going directly to the voters. If the legislature fails to act within a specified time, the proposal is then placed on the ballot for voter approval or disapproval. This procedure gives the legislature a chance to act, acknowledging its role in policy making. In Mississippi, if the legislature considers and amends an initiative, both the original initiative and the amended version are placed on the ballot. The indirect initiative is used in eight states, including five that also have the direct initiative. A total of nine states use the indirect initiative for statutes; two of these states also have the direct initiative. Only two states use the indirect initiative for proposing constitutional amendments.

The Referendum Process

Twenty-four states have a **popular referendum:** After voters gather the required number of signatures on petitions, a newly enacted law must win the approval of the voters at the next election. If the voters do not approve the law, it does not go into effect. The popular referendum, because of citizens signing petitions and citizens voting on a measure, is easily confused with the direct initiative. The important difference between the two is the source of the issue that appears on the ballot. With the direct initiative, a new law proposed by citizens is being voted on. With the popular referendum, the proposal being voted on is a law that was just approved by the legislature and signed by the governor.

The more common referendum procedure is submission by the legislature or **legislative referendum.** Here the legislature, after adopting a law, directs that it be placed on the ballot for final approval or disapproval by the voters. Some proposals, in a slight variation of the submission by the legislature process, may be *required* by state constitutions or local charters to go automatically to the voters. Examples are amendments to state constitutions and financial (tax and bond) issues.

The Recall Process

The recall is the least used, the least available, and, until the successful recall of California Governor Gray Davis in 2003, the least recognized of the three techniques of direct democracy. Eighteen state constitutions include a provision for the recall of their states' elected officials. These states tend to be the states that also have the initiative and referendum because the recall is the product of the same Progressive movement that was based, in part, on distrust of politicians. Generally, recalls occur more frequently, although they still are the exception rather than the rule, in local politics where the targets are mayors and members of city councils and school boards. It can be argued that the recall could impair the independence of the judiciary (see Chapter 7); nevertheless, a majority of these states allow the recall of judges. Prior to the recall of Gray Davis, only one governor had been recalled, Lynn Frazier of North Dakota in 1922. (Frazier, however, made a comeback shortly after he was recalled. North Dakota voters elected him to the U.S. Senate, where he served until he was defeated in a 1940 reelection bid.)

Supporters of a recall are required to gather signatures of registered voters on petitions that clearly call for the removal of an elected official. A signature requirement of 25 percent of the vote cast in the last election is fairly typical; this is higher than the percentage needed for an initiative. Signatures must be gathered within a specified period of time, for example, ninety days. In California, the signature requirement is only 12 percent and recall supporters have 160 days to circulate the petitions; because of these lenient rules California is one of the easiest states in which to attempt a recall. If a sufficient number of signatures are collected, a special election is usually called, rather than waiting for the next regular election. To remove the official from office, a majority of the voters must vote "yes" on the recall question. A successor may be chosen on the same ballot as the recall or in a subsequent special election. The former procedure was used in California, where voters first voted on the recall of Gray Davis and then, in the event that the recall was approved, voted for a new governor from among 135 candidates who qualified for the ballot! Arnold Schwarzenegger, of *The Terminator* and other movies, Cruz Bustamante, lieutenant governor of California, and Tom McClintock, a California state senator, were the only competitive candidates. The recall was approved with 55.4 percent of the vote, and Schwarzenegger won with 48.6 percent of the vote. If the recall had failed, the second vote would have had no meaning.

What are the grounds for recalling an elected official? A few states (e.g., Alaska, Georgia, and Minnesota) specify incompetence, neglect of duties, failure to perform duties prescribed by law, or violation of the oath of office. And some of these states provide for a court review to determine whether the allegations against an elected official, if they are true, satisfy the state's legal requirements for a recall election. Procedures in other states (e.g., California and Colorado) require that voters be informed through a "statement of reasons" for the recall, but do not identify the specific grounds that must be included in the statement. A majority of the recall states (e.g., Louisiana and Michigan) are completely open, requiring neither specific grounds nor a statement of reasons.[80]

In states where no specific grounds must be cited, a recall can be started by simple voter dissatisfaction with an elected official; however, even after the extensive national press coverage given to the California recall, it is important to remember that attempted recalls of state elected officials, as mentioned before, are still rare. Although no one is keeping track on a regular basis, one study found that between 1970 and 1995, only eleven recall elections of state officials were held in the entire country. (They were held in just five states: California, Wisconsin, Idaho, Michigan, and Oregon.) In eight of these elections, the officials lost their office (all were state legislators). In most cases it was not incompetence or wrongdoing that caused these successful recalls, but rather an official's position or vote on a controversial issue.[81] Until the California recall in 2003, one of the most politically significant recalls occurred in 1984 when Michigan voters, unhappy with an income tax increase, successfully recalled two state senators, and as a result also changed party control of the senate.[82]

Will the successful recall of California Governor Gray Davis be repeated in other states? Many political movements start in California and frequently spread across the nation, but this may not be one of them. The factors leading to Davis's recall and the election of Arnold Schwarzenegger may not be easily duplicated in other states. Consider the following: First, Governor Davis, for a number of reasons, including having to deal with the largest budget deficit among the fifty states, was unpopular with California voters. His job performance ratings were extremely low; at times the percentage of Californians giving him favorable approval ratings dipped into the low 20s. Second, opponents of Davis had ample money to finance the recall petition drive; Republican Congressman Darrell Issa used $1 million of his own money to bankroll the petition drive. Third, Schwarzenegger's candidacy offered voters an attractive nonpolitician to turn to; his candidacy probably made it much easier for voters to recall Davis.

The Direct Initiative Evaluated

One of the arguments for the direct initiative is that it is a way to counter the influence of special interests on legislators and to give citizens more control over the making of laws. However, some question whether today's practice of direct democracy is actually achieving these goals. To support their position they cite the fact that interest groups, not grassroots organizations composed of average citizens, are the dominant users of the initiative and referendum. Just organizing and financing a petition drive is expensive. Even a moderate-sized state such as Oregon required 75,630 petition signatures for 2003 through 2006. Not an easy task for the most dedicated of volunteers! It is not hard to see why professional assistance might be needed. The total amount of money spent to qualify initiatives for the ballot more than doubled between 1992 and 1996, from $1.8 million to $4 million; in California it takes at least $1 million to place an initiative on the ballot.[83] Of course, interest groups are well equipped with organizing skills and financial resources. And they do not have to know a lot about running an initiative campaign because they can hire "professional managers, petition circulators, media consultants, pollsters, direct-mail specialists and lawyers."[84] Paid petitioners frequently work with at least three separate initiatives, approaching citizens and asking them to sign as many as they agree with. Charles Price reports that in California two professional petitioning organizations, usually referred to as signature companies, were responsible for 75 percent of the initiatives on the California ballot between 1982 and 1992.[85] Thirty-two American Indian tribes in California, after unsatisfactory negotiations with Governor Pete Wilson, qualified an initiative proposal for the ballot that would legalize video slots, blackjack, and off-track betting at reservation sites in less than thirty days. The tribes hired National Petition Management and paid the premium rate of $1.50 per name. Of course, professional signature gatherers first asked people to sign the petition paying the most.[86]

Colorado, and several other states, tried to limit this practice by requiring that people who circulate petitions be registered voters of the state and requiring initiative proponents to file reports disclosing whom they paid to circulate petitions and how much each individual was paid. The U.S. Supreme Court declared these requirements unconstitutional, a violation of the First Amendment, in *Buckley v. American Constitutional Law* (1999).

Evidence is strong that money is an important resource in getting initiatives on the ballot. However, an important question remains: Does the amount of money spent by supporters and opponents during the campaign stage determine whether initiatives are approved by the voters? Before looking at this question, it is important to note that in the hundred-year history of initiatives in the U.S., voters approved *less than half* (41 percent) of the initiatives that actually made it to the ballot. Overall, the passage rate is not high. (Table 4-6 has more details on the number of initiatives proposed and passage rates.) The most recent research on passage rates is from Elisabeth Gerber. She examined more than 160 initiatives in several states, comparing the success of initiatives backed by economic interest groups and citizen interest groups. Economic groups such as trade associations and corporations have greater financial resources for campaign spending, but they are *less* successful than citizen interest groups such as the League of Women Voters and the Sierra Club in obtaining voter approval of proposals they support. About one-third of initiatives supported by economic interests are approved by the voters, compared to one-half of those supported by citizen groups. However, economic interests are slightly more successful in defeating proposals they oppose.[87]

These groups are not the only actors in initiative politics; wealthy individuals have single-handedly put up the money for some ballot initiatives. Billionaire George Soros, an international financier-philanthropist, bankrolled the initiatives that legalized medical marijuana in Arizona and California. Ron Unz, a Silicon Valley millionaire, conceived and largely financed the California initiative requiring all public school instruction to be in English. But not all efforts by those in the exclusive "zillionaire club" are successful. Ron Unz's campaign finance reform initiative was defeated in

TABLE 4-6 Statewide Initiative Passage Rates

	Number Proposed	Number Adopted	Passage Rate
DECADES WITH THE HIGHEST NUMBER OF BALLOT INITIATIVES			
1991–2000	389	188	48%
1911–1920	293	116	40%
1981–1990	271	115	42%
DECADES WITH THE LOWEST NUMBER OF BALLOT INITIATIVES			
1901–1910	56	25	45%
1961–1970	87	37	41%
1951–1960	114	45	39%
STATES WITH THE HIGHEST NUMBER OF BALLOT INITIATIVES			
Oregon	325	115	36%
California	279	98	35%
Colorado	183	65	36%
North Dakota	168	76	45%
Arizona	154	64	42%

Source: This table is modeled after a table by M. Dane Waters, "A Century Later—The Experiment with Citizen-Initiated Legislation Continues," in Everett Carll Ladd, ed., *America at the Polls, 1998* (Storrs, Conn.: The Roper Center for Public Opinion Research), p. 128. The table has been updated with information from Initiative & Referendum Institute, *General Election Post Election Report* (Washington, D.C.: Citizen Lawmaker Press, 2002), pp. 7–8, www.ianrinstitute.org.

2000, and efforts to pass school choice initiatives (see Chapter 10), which were supported by Dick DeVos, founder of Amway, were defeated. A recent twist is that elected officials occasionally become advocates of an initiative so they can associate their name with an initiative that appears to have great popular support, calculating that it may give their popularity a boost or help them in a reelection bid. Also, individuals who hope to be elected have used the process to gain statewide name recognition or build a reputation that legitimizes their interest in state policies to help in a later run for political office. Such was the case with Arnold Schwarzenegger's Proposition 49 mentioned earlier. Prior to the California recall election, he had hoped to use the successful adoption of this initiative to launch a campaign to become California's governor in 2006.

There are also examples of private citizens who, through great determination, use the initiative process successfully. One such person is Helen Hill of Oregon, who in 1998 almost single-handedly won voter approval of Measure 58, which required the state to issue upon request an "unaltered, original and unamended certificate of birth" to any adopted person over 21. Although Hill was adopted, her primary motivation came from the fact that her father learned late in his life that he had been adopted, also. Hill's personal torment led her to use the initiative to seek a change in Oregon's adoption laws. Richard Ellis calls Hill's story "a model citizen initiative."[88] Supporters of her proposal spent $17,000, raised from small contributions, and most of it went for a full-page newspaper ad in the *Oregonian*. Opposition to the proposal was neither well organized nor well financed. Still, even in this case money was important. During the crucial qualifying stage Hill used some of the money she inherited from her father to hire a professional signature-gathering organization to complete the task of gathering the required number of signatures; this cost approximately $100,000.[89]

Arguments over the direct initiative could easily fill a book of this size. Detractors argue that the average voter cannot be expected to read voter information pamphlets that sometimes total nearly one hundred pages (California, 1994) and vote intelligently on as many as fourteen ballot propositions, including both initiatives and referendums (Arizona and New Mexico, 2002). Richard Ellis says that the reason we elect political leaders is not to have them simply "mirror public preferences but to engage in reasoned debate about the public interest."[90] Advocates argue that citizens voting on public policy issues, actually making decisions, is what democracy is all about.[91] This may be one of those debates in which there is some truth on both sides. Certainly, representative government, in the form of legislatures, is needed. Citizens cannot be well informed on every issue and make all decisions required in today's complex world. On the other hand, citizen consideration of a reasonable number of initiatives during an election can give them a direct say in issues affecting their lives.

SUMMARY

American citizens can participate in state and local politics in a number of ways—from voting to contacting a public official about a specific problem. Advocates of strong democracy focus on ways of increasing citizen participation through neighborhood forums to solve at least some of the problems of their community.

Voter registration requirements that discriminated against minorities were eliminated by the Voting Rights Act of 1965. The Voting Rights Act has been amended to prohibit more subtle forms of discrimination such as minority vote dilution. Although more African Americans and Hispanics are elected to state and local offices, it does not always follow that they dominate city policy making decisions on minority-related issues.

Even before the passage of the 1993 National Voter Registration Act, many states had made voter registration less burdensome by adopting mail and "motor-voter" procedures. Many states and the federal government have taken steps to improve voting systems and election administration after serious problems in the presidential election in Florida in 2000. States that elect governors in presidential election years have higher turnout than those that do not. Local elections have lower turnout than state elections; and turnout is even lower if the elections are nonpartisan.

The advantage of holding state elections at a different time than presidential elections is that voters are less likely to be influenced by how they view the national political scene. However, the 1994 midterm election illustrates that it still is possible for national politics to affect state races.

Incumbent governors face a reelection environment that is less favorable than that of U.S. senators, but if they are eligible for reelection most of them will run and most will be reelected. Tax increases and how candidates define the issues for the voters are important factors in determining who is elected governor.

Campaigns for a seat in the state legislature differ greatly because the size of legislative districts varies so much. States such as California or New York that have districts with a large population frequently have professionally managed campaigns; in most states races are informal and involve face-to-face contact between candidates and voters.

There are two types of judicial elections: One allows voters to select whom they want to fill a judgeship, and the other allows voters to vote yes or no on whether an incumbent judge should continue in office. Legal ethics that restrict what judicial candidates can say during a campaign have been weakened by the Supreme Court.

Running for mayor in large cities involves modern campaign techniques of polling, television advertisements, and direct mail. Most cities have nonpartisan elections, and the personalities of the candidates are important in determining who the winner is.

Political campaigns are increasingly expensive, especially in large states. Even before the start of this explosive growth, states attempted to regulate the influence of large financial contributors through laws that limited the size of contributions and required candidates to disclose information about the source of contributions and expenditures. Public financing of campaigns, which could reduce a candidate's reliance on private contributors, has had limited success because most states rely on the "add-on" tax to generate funds, and taxpayer participation has been very low.

The initiative, referendum, and recall procedures allow citizens to propose laws, make decisions on laws that they or their legislatures have proposed, and remove elected officials from office before they have finished their terms. Progressive Era reformers hoped that these direct democracy techniques would be a way for ordinary citizens to enact laws without the influence of special interests that characterizes legislatures. It is clear that money is important in qualifying initiatives for the ballot; however, economic interest groups are less successful than citizen interest groups in obtaining voter approval for their proposals once they are on the ballot. In the hundred-year history of the initiative, voters have approved less than half of the initiatives that they voted on. The direct initiative has both strong supporters and critics.

KEY TERMS

ballot roll-off
ballot measure
Chicano movement
clean election reforms
contribution limits
direct initiative
disclosure laws
expenditure limits
Help America Vote Act of 2002
indirect initiative
initiative
legislative campaign committee
legislative referendum
membership turnover

minority vote dilution
National Voter Registration Act (NVRA)
political incorporation
political participation
popular referendum
preclearance
public financing
recall
referendum
retention election
strong democracy
survey research
Voting Rights Act of 1965
voting systems

SUMMARY OF STATE/LOCAL DIFFERENCES

Issue	State Level	Local Level
Elections and voting	Midterm, partisan elections in most states. Voter turnout is in 40–59 percent range.	Elections, usually nonpartisan, are held at a variety of different times. Voter turnout is frequently under 30 percent.
Campaign financing	Excellent comparative studies. PACs play an important role. Public financing plans have been adopted in almost half of the states, but are successful in only a few.	Few comparative studies. Little public financing. "Shoeleather" campaigns are still possible.
Direct democracy	Initiatives are regularly on the ballot in a few states such as Oregon, California, and Colorado. In many states, the referendum is used more frequently.	Initiative procedures are not common. Referendums are used widely, especially for proposals for the construction of new public school buildings.

INTERESTING WEBSITES

www.azclean.org. The Clean Elections Institute advocates campaign finance reform and focuses on the progress of "clean election" laws, which have been adopted in Arizona and Maine and are under consideration in other states.

www.ballot.org and *www.iandrinstitute.org.* Good websites for the initiative and referendum. They have historical databases and lots of current information on what's happening with direct democracy in the states, with emphasis on the initiative.

www.bettercampaigns.org. Alliance for Better Campaigns seeks to improve elections and campaigns, especially political discourse on television. Click on "State Partners."

www.followthemoney.org. National Institute on Money in State Politics offers state-by-state information. Summaries of each state's campaign finance laws are available as well as information on how much money candidates received in campaign contributions and where it came from. Some state reports can take a year or longer to process before they are available from the website.

NOTES

1. Jack H. Nagel, *Participation* (Englewood Cliffs, N.J.: Prentice-Hall, 1987), p. 1.
2. Rachel Gibson, "Elections Online: Assessing Internet Voting in Light of the Arizona Primary," *Political Science Quarterly* (2001–02), pp. 561–583.
3. Margaret Rosenfield, *All-Mail-Ballot Elections* (Washington, D.C.: National Clearing House on Election Administration, 1995), p. 39.

4. Sidney Verba and Norman H. Nie, *Participation in America: Political Democracy and Social Equality* (New York: Harper & Row, 1972), pp. 66–67.
5. The Social Capital Benchmark Survey was designed by the Saguaro Seminar: Civic Engagement in America, a project at the John F. Kennedy School of Government at Harvard University. The principal investigator for this project was Robert D. Putnam. Putnam is author of *Bowling Alone: The Collapse and Revival of American Community* (New York: Simon & Schuster, 2000).
6. Lawrence J. R. Herson and John M. Bolland, *The Urban Web* (Chicago, Ill.: Nelson-Hall Publishers, 1990), p. 171.
7. Terry Christensen, *Local Politics: Governing at the Grassroots* (Belmont, Calif.: Wadsworth Publishing, 1995), p. 239.
8. Dennis E. Gale, *Understanding Urban Unrest* (Thousand Oaks, Calif.: Sage Publications, 1996), p. 121.
9. Herson and Bolland, *Urban Web*, p. 172.
10. The term *strong democracy* is frequently found in the literature on citizen participation in the affairs of local communities. The idea is presented fully in Benjamin R. Barber, *Strong Democracy* (Berkeley: University of California Press, 1984).
11. Jeffrey M. Berry, Kent E. Portney, and Ken Thomson, *The Rebirth of Urban Democracy* (Washington, D.C.: The Brookings Institution, 1993), p. 2.
12. Ibid., pp. 54–70.
13. Ibid., p. 270.
14. Sidney Verba, Kay Lehman Schlozman, and Henry E. Brady, *Voice and Equality: Civic Voluntarism in American Politics* (Cambridge, Mass.: Harvard University Press, 1995), p. 23.
15. V. O. Key, Jr., *Southern Politics in State and Nation* (New York: Alfred A. Knopf, 1949), pp. 556–577.
16. Chandler Davidson, "The Recent Evolution of Voting Rights Law Affecting Racial and Language Minorities," in *Quiet Revolution in the South,* Chandler Davidson and Bernard Grofman, eds. (Princeton, N.J.: Princeton University Press, 1994), p. 31.
17. Chandler Davidson, "The Voting Rights Act: A Brief History," in *Controversies in Minority Voting,* Bernard Grofman and Chandler Davidson, eds. (Washington, D.C.: The Brookings Institution, 1992), p. 21.
18. Robert Brischetto, et al., "Texas," in *Controversies in Minority Voting*, Bernard Grofman and Chandler Davidson, eds. (Washington, D.C.: The Brookings Institution, 1992), p. 241.
19. *Statistical Abstract of the United States: 1998* (Washington, D.C.: Bureau of the Census, 1998), tables 479–480.
20. Rodney E. Hero, *Latinos and the U.S. Political Pluralism: Two-Tiered Pluralism* (Philadelphia, Pa.: Temple University Press, 1992), pp. 131–154; and Rodney Hero, *Latinos and U.S. Politics* (New York: HarperCollins, 1995), pp. 14–20. This term was first discussed by Rufus P. Browning, Dale R. Marshall, and David H. Tabb in *Protest Is Not Enough* (Berkeley: University of California Press, 1984).
21. Clarence N. Stone, "Race and Regime in Atlanta," in Rufus P. Browning et al., eds., *Racial Politics in American Cities* (White Plains, N.Y.: Longman, 1991), pp. 125–139.
22. Frances Fox Piven and Richard A. Cloward, "Northern Bourbons: A Preliminary Report on the National Voter Registration Act," *PS: Political Science and Politics* 29 (March 1996), pp. 39–40. An "active"/"passive" classification of state mail-in and "motor-voter" laws, as they existed prior to the National Voter Registration Act, is contained in Stephen Knack, "Does 'Motor Voter' Work? Evidence from State-Level Data," *Journal of Politics* 57 (August 1995), pp. 800–801.
23. Richard G. Smolka and Ronald D. Michaelson, "Election Legislation, 1992–93," in *Book of the States, 1994–95* (Lexington, Ky.: Council of State Governments, 1994), pp. 204–208.

24. Federal Election Commission, "The Impact of the National Voter Registration Act on Federal Elections 1999–2000," www.fec.gov/nvrareport2000/nvrareport2000.htm.

25. Raymond Wolfinger and Jonathan Hoffman, "Registering and Voting with Motor Voter," *PS: Political Science and Politics* (March 2001), p. 85.

26. Geoff Earle, "Motor Trouble for Democrats," *Governing* 9 (August 1995), p. 26.

27. Wolfinger and Hoffman, "Registering and Voting with Motor Voter," p. 89.

28. Ibid., p. 90.

29. Stephen I. Frank and Steven C. Wagner, *"We Shocked the World!" A Case Study of Jesse Ventura's Election as Governor of Minnesota* (New York: Harcourt College Publishers, 1999), pp. 6–7.

30. Mark J. Fenster, "The Impact of Allowing Day of Registration Voting on Turnout in U.S. Elections from 1960 to 1992," *American Politics Quarterly* 22 (January 1994), p. 84.

31. Special Committee on Voting Systems and Election Procedures in Maryland, *Report and Recommendations*, February 2002, p. 4.

32. Of the numerous studies of what went wrong in Florida's 2000 election, one of the best is Dennis Cauchon and Jim Drinkard, "Florida Voter Errors Cost Gore the Election," *USA Today* (May 4, 2001), http://www.usatoday.com/news/washington/2001-05-10.

33. Special Committee, p. 55.

34. The Election Reform Information Project, "Ready for 2002, Forgetting 2000" (January 2000), pp. 8–12, http://www.wlwctionline.org/site/docs (accessed February 24, 2003).

35. Ibid.

36. Brian F. Schaffner, Matthew J. Streb, and Gerald C. Wright, "A Rule That Works: The Nonpartisan Ballot in State and Local Elections," presented at the 1999 Annual Meeting of the Midwest Political Science Association, April 15–17, 1999, Chicago, Ill.

37. Brian F. Schaffner, Matthew Streb, and Gerald Wright, "Teams Without Uniforms: The Nonpartisan Ballot in State and Local Elections," *Political Research Quarterly* (March 2001), p. 25.

38. Mark E. Tompkins, "Have Gubernatorial Elections Become More Distinctive Contests?" *Journal of Politics* 50 (1988), pp. 192–205.

39. Thad L. Beyle, "2002 Gubernatorial Elections," *Spectrum: The Journal of State Government* (Winter 2003), p. 12.

40. Peverill Squire and Christina Fastnow, "Comparing Gubernatorial and Senatorial Elections," *Political Research Quarterly* (September 1994), pp. 705–720.

41. Brian Stults and Richard F. Winters, "The Political Economy of Taxes and the Vote," presented at the 2002 Annual Meeting of the Midwest Political Science Association, April 25–28, 2002.

42. Ibid., p. 10.

43. Ibid., p. 36.

44. Thomas M. Carsey, *Campaign Dynamics: The Race for Governor* (Ann Arbor: The University of Michigan Press, 2000), p. 11.

45. Ibid., p. 15.

46. Paul West, "Michigan Woman's Star Rising on Political Stage," *Sun* (Baltimore), September 16, 2002, p. 1A.

47. Gary F. Moncrief, Peverill Squire, and Malcolm E. Jewell, *Who Runs for the State Legislature?* (Upper Saddle River, N.J.: Prentice-Hall, 2001), pp. 38–43.

48. Lillian C. Woo, "Today's Legislators: Who They Are and Why They Run," *State Legislatures* (April 1994), p. 29.

49. Moncrief, Squire, and Jewell, *Who Runs,* pp. 53–57.

50. Emily Van Dunk, "Who Runs for State Legislative Office? A Look at Candidates for Citizen and Professional Legislatures," presented at the 1994 Annual Meeting of the Midwest Political Science Association, April 14–16, Chicago, Ill.

51. Alan Rosenthal, *Legislative Life* (New York: Harper & Row, 1981), pp. 101–112.
52. Moncrief, Squire, and Jewell, *Who Runs,* p. 86.
53. Tom Loftus, *The Art of Legislative Politics* (Washington, D.C.: CQ Press, 1994), p. 10.
54. David Breaux and Malcolm Jewell, "Winning Big: The Incumbency Advantage in State Legislative Races," in *Changing Patterns in State Legislative Careers,* Gary F. Moncrief and Joel A. Thompson, eds. (Ann Arbor: The University of Michigan Press, 1992), p. 104.
55. G. Alan Tarr, *Judicial Process and Judicial Policymaking* (St. Paul, Minn.: West Publishing Company, 1994), p. 70.
56. Lawrence Baum, "Electing Judges," in Lee Epstein, ed., *Contemplating Courts* (Washington, D.C.: CQ Press, 1995), pp. 33–36.
57. Roy A. Schotland, "Comment," *Law and Contemporary Problems* 61, no. 3 (Summer 1998), p. 150.
58. "A Brief History of Judicial Selection in State Courts," in Reports of the Task Forces of Citizens for Independent Courts, *Uncertain Justice: Politics and America's Courts* (New York: The Century Foundation, 2000), pp. 107–113.
59. Brennan Center for Justice, "Republican Party of Minnesota v. White: What Does the Decision Mean for the Future of State Judicial Elections?" www.brennancenter.org/programs/prog (accessed March 4, 2002).
60. *Republican Party of Minnesota v. White,* 536 U.S. 765 (2002).
61. Thad Beyle, "Governors: Elections, Powers and Priorities," *The Book of the States 2002,* pp. 139–141.
62. The Institute on Money in State Politics, "2000 State Election Overview," August 2002, www.followthemoney.org (accessed March 4, 2003).
63. Robert E. Hogan, "The Costs of Representation in State Legislatures: Explaining Variations in Campaign Spending," *Social Science Quarterly* 81, no. 4 (December 2000), pp. 941–956.
64. Frederick M. Hermann and Ronald D. Michaelson, "Financing State and Local Elections: Recent Developments," in *Book of the States, 1994–95,* p. 229. This information is based on William E. Cassie, Joel A. Thompson, and Malcolm E. Jewell, "The Pattern of PAC Contributions in Legislative Elections: An Eleven State Analysis," presented at the Annual Meeting of the American Political Science Association, 1992, Chicago, Ill. Also see John Archibald and Michael Sznajderman, "PACs Fill Campaign Coffers," *Birmingham News,* March 14, 1999; www.al.com.news.birmingham/Mar1999.
65. Arnold Fleischmann and Lana Stein, "Campaign Contributions in Local Elections," *Political Research Quarterly* 51 (September 1998), pp. 673–689.
66. Michael J. Malbin and Thomas L. Gais, *The Day After Reform: Sobering Campaign Finance Lessons from the States* (Albany, N.Y.: The Rockefeller Press, 1998), pp. 45–49.
67. Herbert E. Alexander, *Reform and Reality: The Funding of State and Local Campaigns* (New York: The Twentieth Century Fund Press, 1999), pp. 30–32.
68. Robin Wallace, "States Struggle with Public Funding of Elections," Fox News Channel (February 25, 2002), www.foxnews.com (accessed March 6, 2002).
69. Alexander, *Reform,* p. 42.
70. Marc Breslow, Janet Groat, and Paul Saba, *Revitalizing Democracy: Clean Election Reform Shows the Way Forward* (Money and Politics Implementation Project, 2002), p. 3.
71. Kenneth R. Mayer, *Public Financing and Electoral Competition in Minnesota and Wisconsin* (Los Angeles, Calif.: Citizens' Research Foundation, 1998), p. 12.
72. Initiative & Referendum Institute, *November 5, 2002 General Election Post Election Report* (Washington, D.C.: Citizen Lawmaker Press, 2002), p. 7, www.iandrinstitute.org (accessed March 11, 2003).
73. Initiative & Referendum Institute, "A Brief History of the Initiative and Referendum Process in the United States," www.iandrinstitute.org (accessed March 11, 2003). This paper is largely

based on David Schmidts's *Citizen Lawmakers* (Philadelphia, Penn.: Temple University Press, 1989).

74. Tamar Lewin, "The Education Election," *New York Times,* November 10, 2002, www. nytimes.com (accessed March 11, 2003).

75. Initiative & Referendum Institute, "A Brief History."

76. Charles M. Price, "The Initiative: A Comparative Analysis and Reassessment of a Western Phenomenon," *Western Political Quarterly* 28 (June 1975), p. 59.

77. Elisabeth R. Gerber, *The Populist Paradox: Interest Group Influence and the Promise of Direct Legislation* (Princeton, N.J.: Princeton University Press, 1999), pp. 38–44.

78. David Kehler and Robert M. Stern, "Initiatives in the 1980s and 1990s," in *Book of the States, 1994–95,* pp. 279–281.

79. First National Bank of Boston v. Bellotti, 435 U.S. 765 (1978) and Citizens Against Rent Control v. City of Berkeley, 454 U.S. 290 (1981).

80. Minnesota House of Representatives Research Department, *Recall of State Elected Officials: A Proposed Minnesota Constitutional Amendment* (October 1996), pp. 6–7, www.house.leg.state.mn.us/hrd/pubs/recall96.pdf (accessed March 12, 2003).

81. Ibid., p. 9.

82. Jack C. Plano and Milton Greenberg, *The American Political Dictionary,* 9th ed. (Orlando, Fla.: Harcourt Brace Jovanovich, 1993), p. 102.

83. Charles Mahtesian, "Grassroots Charade," *Governing (*November 1998). www.governing.com.

84. Martha Angle, "Initiatives: Vox Populi or Professional Ploy," *Congressional Quarterly Weekly Report,* October 15, 1994, p. 2982.

85. Charles Price, "Signing for Fun and Profit: The Business of Gathering Petition Signatures," *1994–1995 Annual—California Government and Politics* (Sacramento: California Journal Press, 1994), p. 76.

86. David B. Broder, "Collecting Signatures for a Price," *Washington Post,* April 12, 1998, p. A01.

87. Elisabeth R. Gerber, *The Populist Paradox,* pp. 110–115.

88. Richard J. Ellis, *Democratic Delusions: The Initiative Process in America* (Lawrence, Kan.: University Press of Kansas, 2002), p. 14.

89. Ibid., pp. 8–9.

90. Ibid., p. 200.

91. Charles M. Price, "Direct Democracy Works," *State Government News* (June/July 1997), pp. 14–15, 35.

CHAPTER 5

State and
Local Legislatures

POINTS TO CONSIDER

- What was the Reapportionment Revolution and why was it important?
- How do professional and amateur state legislatures differ?
- Describe the legislative term limits movement.
- Compare the influence of committees, parties, and leaders in the state legislative lawmaking process.
- What are the challenges state legislatures face today?
- Describe the characteristics of city councils.
- How are county, township, and town governments organized?

STATE LEGISLATURES

Between 1960 and the early 1990s, state legislatures have come almost full circle. At the beginning of this period, they were dominated by rural political interests and frequently were described as holdovers from the nineteenth century, when many state constitutions were written and the public wanted a limited role for state government. Most legislators met every other year; only twenty had annual sessions. Being a legislator was a part-time activity for individuals who viewed themselves as **citizen legislators.** They had few staff and usually did not even have offices in the state capitol building. A large number of members voluntarily left after serving one or two terms. By the beginning of the 1960s, however, state legislatures were criticized as "sometime governments: their presence is rarely felt or rarely missed."[1]

Change began in 1965, following the U.S. Supreme Court's rulings on legislative apportionment, which diminished the legislative representation of rural areas and increased the representation of cities and their suburbs. Furthermore, studies conducted by universities and especially the Citizens Conference on State Legislatures recommended significant reforms, including more frequent and longer sessions, higher salaries for members, and more staff assistance.[2] Being a legislator, in other words, should be a full-time job; **professional legislators,** not citizen legislators, were needed. In the 1980s, President Reagan's "new federalism" also helped to energize state legislatures by reducing the federal government's role in domestic policy. Legislatures were becoming the focal point for initiatives in areas such as education, the environment, and welfare.

It was not too long, however, before the public was dismayed. By 1990, professional legislators were present in many states, but now they were viewed by the public as more interested in advancing their own legislative careers than pursuing the interests of the people who elected them. The most visible manifestation of the public's mood was the term limits movement that wanted to keep legislators accountable to voters by

Willie Brown and Term Limits

Willie Brown, an African American and Democrat, was elected speaker by majority vote of the members of the California Assembly in 1980. He held this position through the end of 1995, a record-breaking fifteen years. During this time, Brown became one of the most powerful politicians in the country. He was praised by many who viewed him as an expert in legislative procedures for using his knowledge and power to protect core Democratic constituencies and programs when they were under attack from Republican governors. Others viewed Brown as someone who only wanted to ensure that he continued as speaker. And in

pursuing this goal, they argued, he spent too much of his time raising and distributing campaign funds to help elect Democratic legislative candidates. With a Democratic majority in the Assembly, Brown was almost guaranteed to be reelected speaker. Then, in 1995, with still another year to serve in his legislative term, Willie Brown decided to run for mayor of San Francisco. He won.[3]

Why did Willie Brown decide to leave an office that at one time he said he wanted to hold for life? In part, the answer can be discovered in how state legislatures developed and changed during the last few decades.

allowing only a few terms of service, thus no professional or career legislators. As will be discussed later, California was one of the first states to adopt term limits. In fact, if Willie Brown had not decided to run for mayor of San Francisco, his last year as a member of the California Assembly would have been 1996. (Brown was reelected mayor in 1999; his second term will be his last because the mayor's office has a two-term limit!)

Apportionment and Districting

Before legislators can be elected, there must be districts containing voters they can represent. Creating legislative districts is accomplished through apportionment and districting. Some confusion exists in the meaning of these terms, so a brief definition of each is needed. **Apportionment** refers to how the number of seats in a legislative body is distributed within a state's boundaries. Historically, population and units of local government (such as counties) were the most important factors in apportionment. **Districting** is the process of drawing boundaries on a map that delineates the geographic areas—the districts—from which representatives will be elected.[4] These are not terms we see in newspapers or hear on television every day. But they are used frequently after each federal decennial census (the most recent was in 2000), when states are required to *redistrict* their state legislatures using new population figures.[5]

The Reapportionment Revolution

Before 1962, the state legislatures were described as malapportioned. Simply put, **malapportionment** meant that legislators from some districts represented more people than legislators from other districts. In part, this problem was caused by the legislatures' failure to change boundaries as population growth and shifts occurred; some state constitutions required reapportionment on a regular basis, but these provisions were ignored. As a result, cities were underrepresented in legislatures that were dominated by rural and small town interests. Before 1962, for example, Alabama and Tennessee had not reapportioned since 1901, and Vermont's house and senate apportionment had not been changed since the adoption of the state constitution in 1793!

Of the two legislative chambers, the state senates were more malapportioned because representation in the senates frequently was apportioned to counties. In eight states, each county was guaranteed equal representation in the senate. This meant that counties, regardless of population, would have the same number of senators. (Vermont was the only state that guaranteed to each town equal representation in the lower house.)

Illustrations of malapportionment could easily fill an entire book, but a few examples will do. Some legislative chambers were so malapportioned that the population represented by a majority of the legislators was only a fraction of the state's total population. In California, 10.7 percent of the state's population elected a majority of the members of the state senate: One senator represented 6 million people and another represented only 14,294 people. In Vermont, 11.9 percent of the state's population elected a majority of the members of the state's lower house: One representative served a district with twenty-four people and another served a district with 35,531 people!

The federal courts were of no help to those who wanted states to reapportion. The Supreme Court had ruled that malapportionment was a political question, meaning that change would have to come through the action of legislators themselves rather than by decisions from federal or state courts. This, of course, had the practical effect of producing no change as legislators were unlikely to risk voting themselves out of a job by adopting a new apportionment scheme.

In ***Baker v. Carr***[6] (1962), however, the Supreme Court changed course and ruled that federal courts have jurisdiction in cases challenging malapportionment. The Court concluded that malapportioned state legislatures could violate the equal protection clause of the Fourteenth Amendment. The reapportionment revolution was started. *Baker v. Carr* opened the floodgates, and suits challenging apportionment schemes that had been used for decades quickly appeared in every state. But it was not clear what would be acceptable to the Court. Would states be required to make extensive changes? In ***Reynolds v. Sims***[7] (1964), the Court answered this question by ruling that both houses of the state legislatures must be apportioned on the basis of population—that is, "one person, one vote." The Court stated that "legislators represent people, not trees or acres." By including state senates, the Court rejected the use of the federal analogy as justification that one house of a state legislature, like the U.S. Senate, could be apportioned on the basis of geography or governmental units rather than population. The Court held that counties and cities within the states are not "sovereign entities" as are the states themselves, consequently, they are not entitled to representation.

Although the Supreme Court demands almost exact population equality in the drawing of districts for the U.S. Congress, it permits greater flexibility in state legislative redistricting. In ***Mahan v. Howell***[8] (1973), the Court approved a Virginia plan in which the number of people in one district was 6.8 percent under the average size of all house districts and one district was 9.6 percent over. The Court suggested that strict application of the "absolute equality" test to state legislative districts could conflict with other legitimate state goals. An example of a legitimate goal is that of maintaining the integrity of political subdivisions, that is, attempting to create districts that do not unnecessarily split counties and cities into different districts. Nevertheless, the population deviations in this case approached the limits of what the Court would accept.

By 1968, every state had reapportioned at least one house of its legislature since the *Baker v. Carr* decision, and redistricting was implemented again in every state following the 1970 census. What were the effects of the Reapportionment Revolution? First, as expected, representatives from urban and especially suburban areas increased markedly. In some southern states where cities had been grossly underrepresented, urban representation increased by a factor of ten. These new legislators were younger, better educated, and had less political experience than those elected prior to reapportionment. There also was a significant increase in the number of African-American legislators in both the North and the South.

Second, most political scientists are more cautious in regard to the policy implications of reapportionment because they may not have been as great as many observers anticipated. However, there appears to have been a trend toward more active state government. Some statistical studies indicate that reapportionment was associated with higher spending for education, public health, hospitals, and highways. And state legislators believe that policy has become more liberal and more urban oriented.[9]

A major factor limiting the impact of reapportionment on policy making is that within metropolitan areas, legislators are often strongly divided between city and suburbs, African Americans and whites, Republicans and Democrats, and end up not voting as a bloc. In contrast, rural legislators are more homogeneous (white, Protestant, and conservative) and thus constitute a much more effective voting bloc than metropolitan legislators. In a few states new suburban legislators actually joined with rural legislators in opposing liberal social policies.

Legislative Redistricting Today

Although federal and state courts are important actors in the redistricting process, it needs to be remembered that the responsibility of drawing district lines does *not* belong to the courts. In most states, it is the state legislature that must draw the new lines. As noted, this means that those who will be directly affected by where lines are placed also are the ones who draw them. Districting plans are contained in a bill and go through the normal legislative process of passage by both houses and approval of the governor before becoming law. This is done in the first or second year of each decade, as soon as population figures are available from the federal decennial census. However, before looking closer at how states actually redraw district lines, two more Supreme Court decisions must be discussed. One is concerned with political parties and the other with race.

If one party controls the governor's office and both houses of the legislature, it will be able to create districts as it wants them—probably protecting members of its party and attempting to win a few seats from the minority party. Drawing lines in this manner is called **gerrymandering.** With computer technology and sophisticated databases, creating districts nearly equal in population and still helping your party's candidates is not difficult. The Supreme Court ventured into the partisan gerrymandering question in *Davis v. Bandemer*[10] (1986). For the first time, the Court held that gerrymandering could violate the Constitution. However, in this instance (the case involved a districting plan for the Indiana legislature) the majority held that relying on a single election was inadequate to make a judgment that unconstitutional gerrymandering had occurred. Because the decision did not set definite guidelines for defining a gerrymander, it left the matter very unclear. *Davis v. Bandemer* places a heavy burden of proof on those seeking to show that a particular gerrymander violates the Constitution.

Legislative redistricting plans also are subject to the Voting Rights Act of 1965 as amended, discussed in Chapter 4. Plans that dilute the voting strength of minority groups are prohibited.[11] To avoid court challenges after the 1990 census, most states with a substantial minority population drew a number of districts in which members of a minority group were in the majority. This is frequently referred to as "racial gerrymandering." The most interesting Supreme Court decision in the 1990s, *Shaw v. Reno*[12] (1993), involved *not* a state legislative redistricting plan but one the state of North Carolina had drawn for its twelve members of the U.S. House of Representatives. The *Shaw v. Reno* decision concludes that under certain conditions the creation of majority minority districts is a form of reverse discrimination and is unconstitutional. The Supreme Court did not say that all majority minority districts are unconstitutional. But if race is the sole factor in drawing a district's lines, and if other districting standards such as compactness and respect for local governmental boundaries are ignored, the district is probably unconstitutional. Because of *Shaw v. Reno,* initial districting plans of at least two state legislatures, Georgia's and South Carolina's, were changed to reduce the number of majority minority districts before lower federal courts would approve them.[13] Obviously, there is tension between the Voting Rights Act goal of protecting minority voting rights and recent court decisions limiting race as a factor in drawing new district lines.

Early analysis of redistricting after the 2000 census shows no lessening, and perhaps even an increasing presence, of partisan gerrymandering.[14] And there still is no indication that the Supreme Court will declare any of these plans unconstitutional. In fact, in another North Carolina congressional redistricting case, a plaintiff's legal challenge to *racial* gerrymandering failed on appeal to the Supreme Court. The court decided, in *Easley v. Cromartie*[15] (2001), that because the district lines were really designed to further the interests of the Democratic Party, and not to create an African-American district, it was an example of a partisan gerrymander, which was constitutional.

Redistricting of the Texas state legislature provides one of the best examples of partisan gerrymandering. The Texas legislature has the constitutional authority to draw new lines immediately following the release of census numbers. However, the Texas constitution also states that if the legislature is divided and cannot reach agreement, which happened in 2001, the task falls to a five-member Texas Legislative Redistricting Board. The members of the board include officials from the state's executive branch such as the attorney general and the lieutenant governor, and only one legislator, the Speaker of the Texas House of Representatives. In 2001, the board was composed of four Republicans and one Democrat, giving Republicans an opportunity for partisan gerrymandering. Figure 5-1 shows what happened to one district in the Texas House of Representatives. District 128, in Houston, elected a Democratic representative in the 2000 election; the Republican Party did not run a candidate. During the redistricting process, the geographic center of this district was shifted south of Interstate 10 to include more Republican voters. In the 2002 election, the Democratic incumbent decided not to run for reelection and district 128 elected a Republican. Three Houston-area districts with Democratic representatives were reconfigured to increase the likelihood that Republicans would be elected in 2002; Republicans were elected in two of the three.[16]

The final plans were approved on a 3-2 vote, and observers predicted that the Republican Party would expand its control in the senate and gain a majority in the house. The Mexican American Legal Defense and Educational Fund and other groups, including the Democratic Party, challenged the plan. The U.S. Justice Department, acting under the Voting Rights Act, requested changes in the House plan so as to improve Latino majorities in a few districts. When all was said and done, lower federal court judges approved the Legislative Redistricting Board's plan along with the Justice Department's changes.[17] After the 2000 election Republicans increased their numbers in the thirty-one-member senate from sixteen to nineteen and in the 150-member house from seventy-two to eighty-eight. This was the first time since 1870 that the Republican party in Texas controlled both houses of the legislature and the governor's office.[18]

California and New York reveal different redistricting outcomes when the legislature is in charge of the process. In California, the Democratic Party controlled the governor's office and both houses of the legislature in 2001. Of course, the Democrats had an opportunity to draw new legislative maps to further their control of the legislature, but they took the unusual step of making a deal with the Republican Party. Democratic legislators agreed to forego drawing more Democratic-leaning districts and to draw

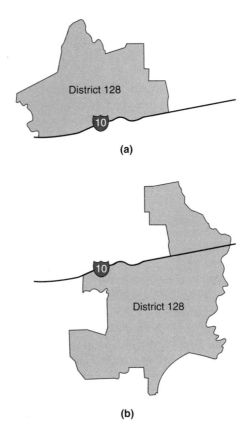

(a)

(b)

FIGURE 5-1 (a) Texas house district 128, 2000, before gerrymandering by Republican Party; (b) Texas house district 128, 2002, after gerrymandering by Republican Party.

Source: The map for 2000 is adapted from William Lilley, III, Laurence J. DeFranco, and William M. Diefenderfer, III, *The Almanac of State Legislatures* (Washington, D.C.: Congressional Quarterly, Inc., 1994), p. 287. Reproduced by permission of *Congressional Quarterly.* The map for 2002 is adapted from the Texas Legislative Council.

lines that reflected the existing partisan makeup of the legislature. In other words, lines were drawn to preserve incumbents of both parties and to maintain the status quo. In exchange, Republican legislators agreed not to challenge the districting plan in the courts or through a referendum.[19] After the 2002 election, the Democrats actually lost two seats in the assembly (the lower house) and one seat in the senate. In the state of New York, approximately two decades of divided control of the legislature have led to an arrangement whereby the district lines are drawn by the party with a majority in each house; the Democrats draw lines for the assembly and the Republicans draw lines for the senate. Then each house approves the work of the other, and the governor signs the bill. The governor has a small role or no role in this process. Drawing lines to protect incumbents (sometimes called "incumbent gerrymandering") is a frequent outcome when divided legislatures draw the lines. It was estimated that more than 85 percent of New York's legislative districts gave one party (Democratic or Republican) at least 10 percent more voters than the other party.[20]

A few state constitutions place authority over legislative redistricting with a commission, not the legislature. States have various ways of selecting commission members and usually some of the members are legislators, but the legislature as an institution has no formal role to play in the process.[21] Generally, commissions yield bipartisan gerrymandered plans that protect the incumbents of both parties. This is especially likely to occur in states such as Pennsylvania, where a commission has four members appointed by the majority and minority leaders of the senate and house of representatives, with each party ending up with two members. These four then select the fifth member, who serves as the chairperson.[22]

Iowa has a unique approach. The Legislative Service Bureau, a nonpartisan legislative office, prepares a new districting plan following such specific legal criteria as that districts should be composed of contiguous territory connected by roads and that the unity of county and city boundaries should be respected. Also, districts *cannot* be drawn to favor a political party or incumbent legislator; this means that information on party affiliation of registered voters, home addresses of incumbents, and elections results cannot be used in drawing lines. The legislature, along with the governor, still retains approval, but in a series of steps. The first plan proposed by the bureau must be accepted or rejected by the legislature. If it is rejected, the bureau develops a second plan that again can be accepted or rejected. If it is rejected, a third plan is presented, which the legislature can accept, reject, or modify.[23] The advantage of this process is that the proposed plans carry some weight with the public and the news media because they come from a neutral office using neutral criteria to draw the lines. In addition, the majority party, or the majority party in cooperation with the minority party, would be subject to criticism for rejecting three plans only to end up writing and adopting their own. In 2001, the state senate rejected the bureau's first plan; however, the second plan was approved by the legislature and signed by the governor. Iowa's procedures, in fact, do not protect incumbent legislators; thirty-nine of one hundred house members and twenty-five of fifty senate members were placed in districts with at least one other incumbent; although an incumbent will run against another incumbent, other choices are available, including deciding not to run or moving to a nearby district where there is no incumbent legislator.[24]

In those states where the legislatures draw new district lines every ten years, there is always a fair amount of criticism of the way in which it is handled. In general, redistricting is criticized because it is perceived to be undemocratic, or at least unfair; as Michael P. McDonald says, "It provides politicians a chance to choose voters, rather than allowing voters to choose politicians."[25] Are these states likely to change and take redistricting away from their legislatures? The answer is no. Changes in redistricting require amending state constitutions, and legislatures are unlikely to approve any amendment that gives redistricting to someone else. Change is more likely in states where voters can use the initiative process (see Chapter 4) to propose constitutional amendments. In the 2000 election, voters in Arizona passed an initiative that transferred redistricting from the legislature to the Arizona Independent Redistricting Commission (Proposition 106). This proposition also identified a number of criteria for the commission to follow in drawing new district lines; one of these criteria is to create competitive districts, as long as that does not hinder meeting other goals such as population equality, compactness, and contiguousness. Arizona may be the first state to recognize competitive districts as an explicit criterion for the redistricting process.

A PROFILE OF LEGISLATORS AND LEGISLATURES

Legislators

According to a survey of 900 state legislators, the average legislator is 49.4 years old, is married, has 2.4 children, and first ran for office at the age of thirty-eight. More than 80 percent are college graduates, and one-third have an annual family income between $60,000 and $85,000. Most continue to live in the state where they were born, and many live in the cities and towns where they grew up.[26] Attorney is the most common occupational background (about 16 percent). This figure is approximately six percentage points lower than it was in 1976.

Although most legislators are white males, the number of African-American and women legislators has increased significantly since the 1970s. Today more than 20 percent of legislators are women, and close to 8 percent are African American (Figure 5-2). The number of women is five times as many as in the 1960s, and the number of African Americans has doubled since then. The increase in Hispanic legislators has been gradual, although more substantial gains have been made in states with a large Hispanic population such as California, Florida, and Texas.

Another important distinction is how legislators themselves view their job. Do they see themselves as full-time (professional) legislators or as part-time (citizen) legislators? In a 1993 study 15 percent of those queried reported that being a legislator was their sole occupation, up from 3 percent in 1976. If legislators who listed themselves as retirees, students, and homemakers are included, the number of full-time lawmakers jumps to 24 percent. More than half of the legislators in Massachusetts, Michigan, New York,

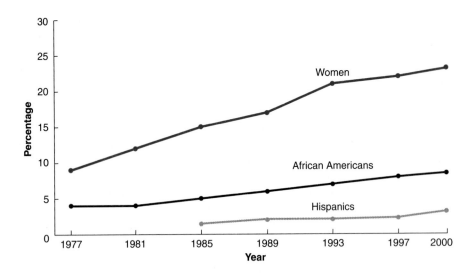

FIGURE 5-2 African Americans, Hispanics, and women in state legislatures.

Sources: Percentages for African-American legislators are from the Joint Center for Economic and Political Studies, www.jointcenter.org/whatsnew/beo2000; percentages for Hispanic legislators are from *Statistical Abstract of the United States: 2002* (Washington, D.C.: U.S. Census Bureau, 2002), p. 252; percentages for women legislators are from "CAWP Fact Sheet: Women in State Legislatures: 2000," *Center for American Women and Politics*, www.cawp.rutgers.edu/pdf/stleghist/stleg00.pdf. (both sites accessed March 1, 2003).

Pennsylvania, and Wisconsin consider themselves professional or career legislators. (Keep in mind that this study is reporting how legislators describe the legislative job. A categorization of state legislatures according to degree of institutional professionalization will be presented.)

Basic Structure

With the exception of Nebraska, every state has a **bicameral** (two-house) legislature. Official names of the two houses are the Senate and the House of Representatives; however, in some states the lower house is called the Assembly or the House of Delegates.

The strong bicameral tradition originated when most legislatures in colonial America adopted the upper- and lower-house model of the British Parliament. The U.S. Constitution, of course, provides for two chambers, a House and Senate, and this has influenced the states. In the early years, many state legislatures included an economic class factor, in which extra property requirements were imposed for service in the state upper chamber. Concern over a **unicameral** (one-house) legislature is reflected in John Adams's warning that "a single assembly is liable to all the vices, follies, and frailties of an individual; subject to fits of humor, starts of passion, flights of enthusiasms, partialities or prejudices, consequently productive of hasty results and absurd judgments."

It also is significant that separation of powers did not exist in early state governments. Governors had little power and often were appointed by the legislature. Legislatures exercised broad powers of economic management and occasionally even overrode the courts in some property-dispute cases. In such circumstances, a bicameral legislature offered greater protection against the abuse of power and undue influence by strong interest groups.

Nebraska adopted a unicameral legislature in 1934, largely due to the well-organized campaign by George Norris, a popular U.S. senator from Nebraska and important leader of the Progressive movement. (Nebraska also is the only legislature that elects its legislators on a nonpartisan ballot.) Although no state has followed Nebraska's lead, it is not outlandish to suggest that unicameral plans could be adopted in other states. A study comparing the Nebraska and Minnesota legislatures concludes that the operating cost of Nebraska's unicameral legislature is considerably less. Although a number of factors contribute to this, it's clear that a smaller number of legislators (Nebraska's forty-nine senators versus Minnesota's sixty-seven senators and 134 representatives) and a consequently smaller legislative staff are important causes. To meet the criticism that two chambers are required to reduce the possibility of hasty consideration of bills, rules and procedures in Nebraska require lengthy and repeated consideration of bills during debate in the full senate. The process is described as "unusually full, exacting and methodical."[27] The case for unicameralism has been made at several recent state constitutional conventions. Although the idea appears logical to many academics and as a cost-savings measure should be attractive to citizens demanding more efficient and less costly government, arguments for unicameralism usually have failed to move politicians who fear radical change and the loss of a large number of legislative seats.

In 1999, Minnesota's governor, Jesse Ventura, proposed combining Minnesota's 134-seat house and sixty-seven-seat senate into a unicameral body of 135 members. Ventura argued that two houses cause too much partisan bickering and allow "legislators to duck accountability by saying that shortcomings were caused by members of the other house."[28] The proposed constitutional amendment, which also called for nonpartisan legislative elections, failed to pass the Minnesota legislature.

The number of members of state legislatures varies. The senates have the smaller membership, of course. The size of upper houses varies from twenty in Alaska to sixty-seven in Minnesota. New Hampshire has 400 members in its lower house who represent a total of 1.2 million people, while the California lower house has eighty members who represent more than 32 million people. In a majority of states (thirty), the lower house has 100 or more members, and in several others, the number is ninety-eight or ninety-nine. In thirty-four states, the upper house has at least thirty-five members.

Although most students of state government conclude that legislatures are too large, it is difficult to say what the ideal size should be because there are advantages and disadvantages to both. Large bodies often become impersonal and more dedicated to staging debates than to taking action. On the other hand, in larger bodies the representational function, to be discussed shortly, is generally improved as legislators represent smaller numbers of people. There also is evidence that larger legislatures are more efficient because of their greater specialization in committees. A disadvantage of small legislatures is that members have a tendency to become too cozy in a kind of social club atmosphere. Moreover, racial and ethnic minorities are less likely to be represented among the members of small legislatures.

As a practical matter, the size of legislative bodies does not change very often. Nevertheless, marginal changes will occasionally be made to facilitate reapportionment and redistricting. Rhode Island voters took an unusual action in 1994 when they reduced the size of the senate from fifty members to thirty-eight and the house from 100 to seventy-five. (This change took place in 2002, the first election after the census in 2000.)

Length of terms also varies among the states. The most common pattern is for representatives to serve two-year terms and senators four-year terms. Terms in the senate are usually staggered with half of the members elected every two years. Maryland is an exception to the normal pattern. In Maryland, all members of both houses, along with the governor, are elected for four-year terms at the same election; this provides voters the opportunity, if they desire, to vote in a large number of new faces in one single election.

Professional or Citizen?

As mentioned at the beginning of this chapter, a shift from citizen to professional legislators started in the mid-1960s. At the institutional level, this involved changes in state constitutions and in rules and procedures. A **professional legislature** would have the capability to deal with problems as a coequal of the governor. The usual quantitative indicators of professionalization have been higher legislative salaries, longer legislative sessions, and more legislative staff. Although political scientists have placed great emphasis on the importance of this shift, Karl Kurtz reminds us that much diversity still exists among state legislatures and that many states have citizen legislatures. The idea of **citizen legislatures,** composed of men and women with full-time jobs who leave their hometowns for a couple of months to become lawmakers in the state capital, is an important component of America's political culture. Kurtz compares all fifty state

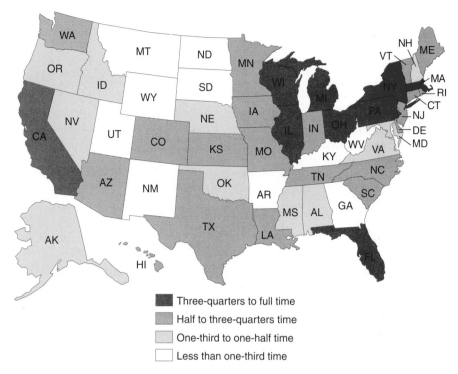

Three-quarters to full time
Half to three-quarters time
One-third to one-half time
Less than one-third time

FIGURE 5-3 Time demands of legislative work.

Source: Alan Rosenthal, Burdett A. Loomis, John R. Hibbing, and Karl T. Kurtz, *Republic on Trial: The Case for Representative Democracy* (Washington, D.C.: CQ Press, 2003), p. 73. Reprinted by permission of CQ Press.

legislatures and finds that citizen legislatures are as common as professional legislatures, with most states falling into a hybrid or in-between category.[29] Figure 5-3 is based on the amount of time required to serve in the legislature, one indicator of the citizen-professional dimension. The length of legislative sessions, the actual time legislators are at the state capital, varies greatly, from two months during a two-year period (Kentucky and Wyoming) to almost year-round (California and Massachusetts). But the job includes more than attending legislative sessions; for example, meeting with constituents is a year-round activity, and participating in committee meetings to study state problems during the interim is important in many states.[30] (The interim is the time period between official, regularly scheduled sessions.) Examples of professional, hybrid, and citizen legislatures are shown in Table 5-1.

In Figure 5-3, it is clear that a state's population affects whether its legislature is full time or close to full time, that is, a professional legislature. California and New York, along with states in the Great Lakes region, have large populations. States with smaller populations, especially those in the Rocky Mountains and New England, tend to have legislatures that meet for less than one-third time and are classified as citizen legislatures. Hybrid states are found in all regions, especially in states whose population is medium-sized. Political culture is important, too. Southern states, with the exception of Florida, are absent from the professional category, even though Texas ranks second in

TABLE 5-1 Diversity of State Legislatures			
	Professional	Hybrid	Citizen
State	New York	Maryland	Arkansas
Annual salary	$79,500	$31,509	$12,796
Legislative sessions	Annual session, no limit on length	Annual session, 90-day limit	Biennial session, 60-day limit
Staff	3,428	965	493

Sources: Annual salaries and legislative sessions information are from *Book of the States 2002* (Lexington, Ky.: Council of State Governments, 2002), pp. 69–70, 86–87. We wish to thank Brian Weberg, National Conference of State Legislatures, for making the staff figures available to us.

population and Georgia and North Carolina are in the top twelve states. This is due in part to traditionalist political cultures and a desire for limited government.

Large and diverse states probably need professional legislators who can devote full time or close to full time to the problems of governing, but small and medium-size states may get along fine with part-time legislators. And it is frequently argued today that people who combine being a legislator for part of the year with another occupation will be more in touch with their constituents and better able to represent them. (The term limits movement, which takes this argument even further, will be discussed next.) The National Conference of State Legislatures concludes that the desire for more full-time, professional legislatures must be balanced with the benefits of part-time citizen bodies.[31]

TERM LIMITS

State legislators, like most public officials and the institutions they are a part of, did not escape the public's strong dissatisfaction with government during the 1990s, as already noted. Professional legislators frequently are viewed as part of the problem. The **term limits movement,** a nationwide effort to limit the number of terms state legislators could serve, thrived in this environment. (Limiting the terms for members of Congress was another goal of this movement.) In 1990, term limit initiatives were placed on the ballot and approved by voters in California, Colorado, and Oklahoma. Other western states, where the initiative process is widely used, quickly followed.

Eventually, a total of twenty states adopted legislative term limits; at this time sixteen states still have them. (See Table 5-2.) Term limits usually were proposed through the initiative process, requiring voter initiation and approval, as amendments to state constitutions. Only Louisiana and Utah adopted term limits as statutory law, following the normal legislative process of approval by both the legislature and the governor. It's much easier to gain support from voters than it is from legislators; obviously, few legislators would approve limits on their terms that might force them from office before they are ready to leave.

Term limits adopted by Oklahoma voters are among the most restrictive, limiting a legislator during his or her lifetime to no more than twelve years of service in either or

TABLE 5-2 States with Legislative Term Limits

State	Year Enacted	House		Senate		Nature of Limit
		Limit	Impact Year	Limit	Impact Year	
California	1990	6	1996	8	1998	Lifetime
Colorado	1990	8	1998	8	1998	Consecutive
Oklahoma	1990	12-year combined total for both houses. Impact year 2002.				Lifetime
Arizona	1992	8	2000	8	2000	Consecutive
Arkansas	1992	6	1998	8	2000	Lifetime
Florida	1992	8	2000	8	2000	Consecutive
Michigan	1992	6	1998	8	2002	Lifetime
Missouri	1992	8	2002	8	2002	Lifetime
Montana	1992	8	2000	8	2000	Consecutive
Ohio	1992	8	2000	8	2000	Consecutive
South Dakota	1992	8	2000	8	2000	Consecutive
Wyoming	1992	12	2006	12	2006	Consecutive
Maine	1993	8	1996	8	1996	Consecutive
Louisiana	1995	12	2007	12	2007	Consecutive
Nevada	1996	12	2010	12	2010	Lifetime
Nebraska	2000	n/a		8	2006	Consecutive

Source: Information for this table is from National Conference of State Legislatures, www.ncsl.org/programs/legman/about/states.htm and the Council of State Governments, www.csgwest.org/misc/state_legislative_term_limits_limits.html.
Note: Term limits in Maine were retroactive; the effective date was January 1, 1996, thus prior years of service counted for legislators who were serving when term limits were adopted.

both houses. California law allows no more than six years in the Assembly and eight years in the senate. In almost all states, terms served in the legislature prior to the adoption of the law did not count toward the number of allowable terms.

Although the idea of term limits has strong support among voters and has been approved by overwhelming margins in initiative states, political scientists are divided as to whether it will improve the governing process. The proponents argue that limiting the length of time individuals can serve will break up the "culture of ruling" that is present in state capitals. This culture is based on the interaction of legislators with other legislators, lobbyists, and executive branch officials, all of whom are in the "business of regulating other people's lives or spending other people's money."[32] The professional legislature has provided the means for members to become career legislators: longer sessions, higher salaries, and more staff and office space. Of course, legislators must be reelected or it is not a career, but this is not a problem, say the proponents of term limits, because PACs and other special interests provide ample campaign funds. This culture has a harmful impact because legislators are primarily interested in winning reelection. To do this they cater to interest groups and other special interests, and the interests of the voters they are elected to represent are forgotten.

Opponents argue that term limits violate one of the basic principles of democracy, that "the people choose their representatives and tell them when to leave."[33] People, not arbitrary limits, should make this decision. Aside from this normative argument, opponents state that experienced legislators can develop a knowledge of issues that frequently makes them as much as an expert, perhaps even more, than the governor and other members of the executive branch. This expertise helps the legislature to make decisions independently, that is, without relying too much on the executive branch.

Arguments as to how term limits will affect the influence of interest groups are of particular importance, and here the two sides disagree completely. Proponents have argued that term limits will *reduce* the influence of special interests: Legislators, not planning on a legislative career, will have less interest in winning future elections and less interest in doing the bidding of special interests because they do not need a continuous supply of campaign funds. Opponents argue that special interests will be *more* influential under term limits: What will really happen is that legislators will have to rely on the lobbyists' knowledge of issues. Of course, their knowledge is always based on their clients' perspectives.[34] Thus, the influence of special interests will only increase.

Research on the types of changes that term limits actually cause in legislatures is just beginning to appear in the political science literature. At this time, it is difficult to tell which side will be more accurate in their predictions, term limits' proponents or opponents. Many states experienced the first impact of term limits in the 2000 election, and some states will not be affected until even later. (See Table 5-2.) The only states that have lived with term limits for at least a few years are California, Colorado, Maine, and Michigan.

Nevertheless, a brief review of some initial findings provides some clues as to what will happen in "termed" states. Research by Richard J. Powell examines whether legislators in "termed" states are less interested in political careers for themselves, one of the goals of the term-limits movement. He examines legislators (180 out of a total of 198) who left office in 1998 because term limits prevented them from running again; more than half of these legislators *did* run for another elective office, and about half of those who ran won their election. A few legislators were candidates for the U.S. Congress, but many ran for local offices such as county or city councils. Powell also finds that almost as many legislators moved into nonelective political positions. These include appointed positions within the executive branch, especially if legislators were members of the same political party as the governor, or lobbying or political consulting positions in the private sector. These individuals appear to view their position as legislators "as a resume-builder for non-elective political positions, either inside or outside government."[35] James M. Penning reports a similar finding for the state of Michigan: Legislators play a game of "political musical chairs," moving from one government position to another, with many of them ending up in a position in Lansing, the state capital.[36] In other words, even though "termed" legislators are forced out of their careers in the state legislature, a majority of them do not return to a nonpolitical career but find a way to continue a career in politics. Right now, considerable evidence exists to support this generalization.

How term limits will affect the actual legislative process and the legislature's relations with the governor, lobbyists, and legislative staff are even more important questions. What is known with certainty is that with greater membership turnover, members' legislative experience will decline, as will their knowledge of the process and of issues. This will be true for the rank-and-file members as well as for committee chairs and other legislative leaders. Research by George Peery and Thomas H. Little surveys the attitudes of legislative leaders in "termed" and "untermed" states to determine if they perceive that the balance of power is shifting away from the legislature to other actors. Leaders in "termed" states, when compared to those in "untermed" states, are more likely to say that the governor, the executive branch bureaucracy, and the staff of legislative committees have gained influence in the last five years. They perceive that the legislature has lost influence to the governor and the executive branch; within the legislature, they believe that individual legislators have lost influence to legislative staff. Legislative leaders are attempting to adjust to or counter these changes by instituting presession orientations so new members can more quickly understand the legislative process and the issues facing the states. Some states are creating mentoring programs that pair a new member with a senior member. To provide more stable and experienced leadership, a few states are selecting a "leader in waiting" before the term of the current speaker has ended.[37] Again, it will take extensive research over the next few years to determine the actual effect of term limits. It's safe to say that although there will be some patterns across the states, the uniqueness of each state also will cause variations in the effects of term limits.[38]

All in all, it is ironic that the term limits movement targeted state legislatures. If these legislatures were out of touch with their constituents, it was not for a lack of new members. A healthy rate of turnover has existed in most states for a long time, even though turnover has been declining for a number of years (see Chapter 4). One study found that in 1979 more than 70 percent of the legislators, from both lower and upper houses, were not members ten years later, a time period that is only two years longer than most of the limits that have been adopted. Similar turnover exists among legislative leaders. During a recent ten-year period, the turnover rate of senate presidents and house speakers was close to 90 percent.[39]

Constitutional challenges to state legislative term limits have been raised. In most cases, term limits have survived these challenges. The U.S. Supreme Court refused to hear a challenge to California's law. However, state supreme courts of Massachusetts, Nebraska, and Washington found term limits unconstitutional. In Washington, the court's decision focused not on the substance of term limits but on the fact that it was adopted as an ordinary statute rather than an amendment to the state constitution. The court said that term limits are a qualification for office and, since qualifications for office are in the state constitution, they can only be changed through the constitutional amendment process. Five states have abolished legislative term limits. (See Table 5-3.)

TABLE 5-3 States That Adopted, Then Abolished Legislative Term Limits

State	Year Enacted	Year Abolished	Abolished by . . .
Oregon	1992	2002	State supreme court
Utah	1992	2003	State legislature
Washington	1992	1998	State supreme court
Idaho	1994	2002	State legislature
Massachusetts	1994	1997	State supreme court

Source: Information for this table is from the National Conference of State Legislatures, www.ncsl.org/programs/legman/about/states.htm.

It should be noted that the antigovernment mood that spawned term limits also had a small effect on the other two key components in the professionalization of state legislatures: session length and size of staff. Voters have approved a reduction in the length of sessions in Alaska, Colorado, and Oklahoma. There even has been some discussion that legislatures should return to biennial sessions. The growth of legislative staff has slowed, and in some cases declined. California's Proposition 140, which established term limits, also mandated a $115 million ceiling on legislative expenditures, resulting in a 38 percent cut in the legislature's budget and the elimination of 600 staff positions.

FUNCTIONS OF STATE LEGISLATURES

Representation

What is representation? This deceptively simple question has been debated since the early beginnings of representative government. Edmund Burke, a member of the British House of Commons in the late eighteenth century, in a speech to the electors of Bristol, placed the controversy on the meaning of representation in what is now a classic formulation:

> Should (must) a representative do what his constituents want, and be bound by mandates or instructions from them; or should (must) he be free to act as seems best to him in pursuit of their welfare?[40]

Contemporary political scientists refer to this question as the mandate-independence controversy, or the delegate-trustee controversy. Alan Rosenthal, in an in-depth discussion of representation, asked a small number of Florida legislators to rank themselves on a 10-point scale. Point 1 was for legislators who followed the mandate/delegate role, point 5 was for legislators who act as they think constituents would want, unless they receive instructions to the contrary, and point 10 was for legislators who follow their own judgment regardless of constituent demands (independence/trustee). The Florida legislators fell into a clear pattern between points 5 and 9. Twelve definitely placed themselves toward the trustee end of the scale, but no one was at point 10. Five legislators were in the middle.[41]

Why is there an absence of legislators at the mandate-delegate side of the scale? One reason is that on some issues legislators will have strong beliefs and those beliefs will determine how they vote on a particular issue, even if they do not reflect the views of their constituents. This will occur on only a few issues during a legislative session, but many legislators are direct in saying that their beliefs and knowledge of issues are more important than the views of their constituents. Of course, this behavior makes it very unlikely that any legislator will select the mandate/delegate role. Another reason the mandate/delegate role is not selected is that legislators learn very quickly that more often than not it is difficult to discover what constituent opinion is on the wide range of issues they must deal with. On some issues, constituents may have no opinions and on other issues, especially in heterogeneous districts, there are differing opinions. It is true that legislators receive phone calls and mail from their constituents, but much of it is at the instigation of special interests and may not accurately express the interests of all or at least a majority of their constituents.

This is *not* to say that legislators can completely ignore their constituents; elections impose limits that prevent this. "Elections are the mechanisms by which representatives are held accountable. If legislators stray too far afield, they risk challenge and defeat at the polls."[42]

Policy Making

The most important function of the state legislature is to participate in making policy by passing laws. Any self-respecting legislature should not be content merely to deal with the governor's legislative program or routinely approve members' bills. It has a responsibility to initiate action and to deliberate on a wide variety of proposals dealing with the most important and controversial problems of the day, such as abortion, crime, gun control, welfare, and education, to name a few. In fact, legislators are confronted with issues that can range from the trivial (whether the ladybug should be designated the "state insect" in Ohio) to the enormously complex (annual general expenditures for the state of Texas in 2000 was over $60 billion).

In reality, policy initiation, that is, priorities and ideas for legislation, remains largely in the hands of state governors. The lawmaking process is best for deliberation, discussion, marginal changes, and even the defeat of bills rather than the initiation of policy. Under the best of circumstances, legislators share their lawmaking power with the governor. More will be said of the governor's role in policy making and influence on the legislature in Chapter 6.

Thousands and thousands of bills are introduced in state legislatures during their regular sessions, but only a small percentage (approximately 20 percent) actually become law. Minnesota is on the high side: More than 4,900 bills were introduced in 2001; 208 became law (less than 5 percent). Delaware, a much smaller state than Minnesota, had 624 bills introduced in the same year with 212 becoming law (34 percent). A state closer to the average is North Carolina where 2,587 bills were introduced and 544 became law (21 percent). A few states have adopted various rules to limit the number of bills that are introduced. One approach is to simply put a limit on the number of bills each legislator can introduce; in the Florida house of representatives the limit is six bills. In Colorado the limit is five bills, but a Committee on Delayed Bills may grant permission for a legislator to exceed the limit. The idea behind these limits is to ensure that legislators have more time to consider important legislation by reducing what many consider to be superfluous bills that legislators introduce only because they please a constituent or an interest group. Others argue that these limits hinder members from carrying out their legislative responsibilities as they see fit.[43]

In general, all state legislatures follow a similar procedure for passing bills into laws. (Of course, in Nebraska bills are considered by one house.) Once a bill has been introduced in the upper or lower house, it is assigned to a committee. The committee holds public hearings, and then committee members meet to discuss and possibly amend the bill. If committee action is favorable, the bill is reported out and placed on the chamber's calendar.

The bill is then given a second reading on the floor (its introduction constitutes a first reading), following which there is debate, amendments are offered, and a vote is taken on passage. After a usual delay of one calendar day, a third reading occurs and a final vote is taken. If the vote is affirmative, the bill then moves to the other legislative chamber, where the process of committee and floor action is repeated. If the second chamber approves the bill without amendment, it goes to the governor for his or her signature. If the bill is approved in a different form by each house, a conference committee is appointed to work out an agreement, and both houses must approve the conference report before the bill is sent to the governor (Figure 5-4).

Legislative Oversight

With the growth of gubernatorial power and the expansion of state administrative bureaucracies, legislatures have struggled to find ways to check executive authority. Because their attention tends to be focused on immediate policy issues, legislators find it difficult to conduct long-range review of the executive branch. Generally, **legislative oversight** is review by the legislature of the performance of executive branch agencies in administering the laws and programs approved by the legislature. The purpose is to ensure that public services are delivered to citizens in an effective manner.

Legislative oversight takes many forms.[44] Constituents constantly ask legislators for help in dealing with state agencies. In responding to a particular request, legislators may be prompted to review in more general terms how an agency is performing. In the budget process, several committees—appropriations, ways and means, and finance—review requests for money from state agencies, and this allows legislators to examine how well the agencies are performing. A majority of the states have enacted **"sunset laws,"** which call for the termination of executive branch agencies unless the legislature formally reviews and extends their programs. These reviews are required at regular intervals, frequently every five years. Generally, the agencies that have been terminated have been minor and had lost their usefulness. Numerous other agencies have been consolidated or their authority and responsibilities clarified. A number of states have repealed or suspended their "sunset laws" because they required an excessive amount of time of both legislators and staff.

Today, almost every state legislature has a specific office—similar to the federal government's General Accounting Office—that has primary responsibility for legislative oversight. These offices vary in their official names; in Illinois it is the Office of the Auditor General, Nebraska has the Legislative Program Evaluation Unit, and in Florida it is the Office of Program Policy Analysis and Government Accountability. These offices vary in size, organization, and activities; however, their focus is the same: to conduct research and produce reports that evaluate whether agencies are properly implementing government programs and to identify ways to improve these programs.[45]

LEGISLATIVE POLITICS

Committees

The state senates have approximately fifteen standing committees, and the lower houses have approximately twenty. (Standing committees are permanent committees that are created by a chamber's legislative rules.) These committees are established on a subject-matter basis to consider bills introduced by legislators and to monitor the activities of

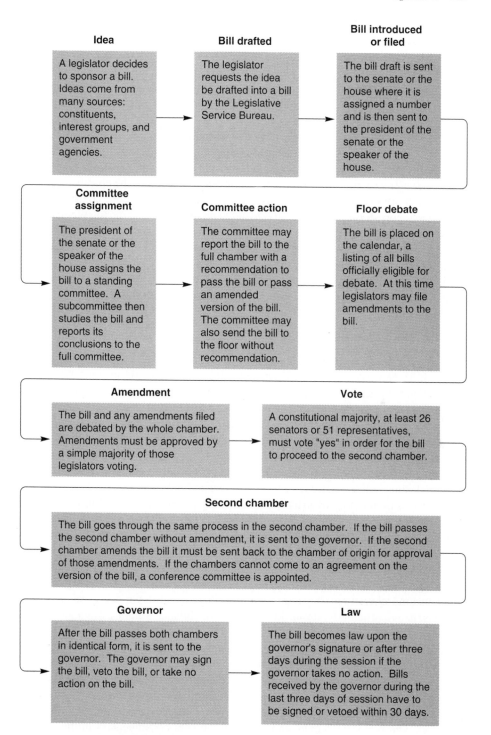

Idea

A legislator decides to sponsor a bill. Ideas come from many sources: constituents, interest groups, and government agencies.

Bill drafted

The legislator requests the idea be drafted into a bill by the Legislative Service Bureau.

Bill introduced or filed

The bill draft is sent to the senate or the house where it is assigned a number and is then sent to the president of the senate or the speaker of the house.

Committee assignment

The president of the senate or the speaker of the house assigns the bill to a standing committee. A subcommittee then studies the bill and reports its conclusions to the full committee.

Committee action

The committee may report the bill to the full chamber with a recommendation to pass the bill or pass an amended version of the bill. The committee may also send the bill to the floor without recommendation.

Floor debate

The bill is placed on the calendar, a listing of all bills officially eligible for debate. At this time legislators may file amendments to the bill.

Amendment

The bill and any amendments filed are debated by the whole chamber. Amendments must be approved by a simple majority of those legislators voting.

Vote

A constitutional majority, at least 26 senators or 51 representatives, must vote "yes" in order for the bill to proceed to the second chamber.

Second chamber

The bill goes through the same process in the second chamber. If the bill passes the second chamber without amendment, it is sent to the governor. If the second chamber amends the bill it must be sent back to the chamber of origin for approval of those amendments. If the chambers cannot come to an agreement on the version of the bill, a conference committee is appointed.

Governor

After the bill passes both chambers in identical form, it is sent to the governor. The governor may sign the bill, veto the bill, or take no action on the bill.

Law

The bill becomes law upon the governor's signature or after three days during the session if the governor takes no action. Bills received by the governor during the last three days of session have to be signed or vetoed within 30 days.

FIGURE 5-4 How a bill becomes law in Iowa.

Source: Iowa General Assembly, "Chart of How a Bill Becomes a Law," www.legis.state.ia.us/Pubinfo/Chart.gif (accessed April 23, 2003).

particular administrative agencies. The trend in recent years has been to reduce the number of committees. Nevertheless, a considerable range still exists among the states: Maryland has the fewest committees, six in the senate and eight in the house; New York has the highest number of committees in a senate, thirty-two, and Missouri the highest in the house, forty-eight. Joint committees, that is, members of both the senate and house serving on the same committees, can be found in Connecticut, Maine, and Massachusetts.

The actual influence committees have in determining the fate of bills varies among the states, and sometimes even between chambers in the same state. Committees have more influence in those states where the rules permit them to let bills die in committee without taking any action. This is the case for about 75 percent of the chambers; examples are Michigan, Ohio, and Rhode Island. In the remaining chambers, committees are required to report all bills referred to them, based on the belief that the full membership should have an opportunity to vote on proposed bills rather than allow bills to be bottled up in committee. Illinois has one of the weakest committee systems; committees are expected to ratify decisions made by the leadership and majority-party caucus (discussed below). On occasion, proposed bills have been placed on a "fast track" and were sent to a committee dominated by the leadership to ensure prompt action.[46]

Political Parties

A basic goal of political parties in a legislature is to produce the votes necessary to pass specific bills. However, the degree to which parties are successful in controlling their members' votes varies greatly among the states. In urban, industrial states with strong two-party systems, party control of voting behavior clearly is evident. Frequently, in these states, parties will caucus on a regular basis to determine a party position on various pieces of legislation and to mobilize support of its members for the party's position. In state legislatures, a **caucus** is the name given to a meeting of legislators who are members of the same political party. Daily caucuses occur in about 15 percent of the states, and about half the states have weekly caucuses.

Partisanship in voting on legislation, according to Sarah McCally Morehouse and Malcolm Jewell, is strongest where the Democratic and Republican parties "represent significantly different constituencies."[47] For example, in many states in the Northeast and Midwest, Democratic legislators are elected from working-class and some middle-class districts in urban areas, with a significant percentage of racial and ethnic minorities living in many of these districts. Republican legislators tend to be elected from higher income districts in suburban areas and from small-town and rural districts. Partisanship is particularly strong in Connecticut, Indiana, Illinois, Michigan, New York, and Pennsylvania, as well as California, Colorado, and Washington in the West. Partisanship is less important in most western states, for example, Montana and Oregon. Greater legislative partisanship is emerging in many southern states where the Republican Party is becoming more competitive and winning a larger share of seats in the legislature, for example, Florida, Georgia, and North Carolina. Research by Shannon Jenkins confirms the importance of constituency in voting on legislation by noting that legislators who represent people who make up the core constituencies in their party show more support for their party; and legislators who represent people who are atypical of their party's supporters are less likely to vote with their party. In other words,

Democratic legislators with a high percentage of African Americans or Hispanics in their districts will have high support for their party; and Democratic legislators with a very small percentage of minority groups in their districts will tend to have lower support for their party. Of course, only a few Democratic legislators will be elected from these districts because they really are more typical of the Republican Party.[48]

Political parties do more than affect the voting behavior of legislators. The role of parties is particularly strong in the selection of legislative leaders, which we turn to next.

Leaders

In the lower house, a speaker, elected by a vote of the entire membership, is the presiding officer. Each party nominates its own candidate for speaker, and the nominee of the majority wins in a straight party-line vote. The speaker is the presiding officer *and* the effective leader of the majority party, even though the speaker's party has a position with the title of majority leader.

More than half of the state legislative chambers have an even number of members, and on occasion—about one chamber in every election year recently—a tie with an equal number of Democratic and Republican legislators winning office will occur. When this happens neither party has enough votes to elect the leaders. The usual solution is a negotiated agreement between the two parties to share power. Under one type of agreement the parties select co-leaders and committee co-chairs and alternate, sometimes daily, when they preside. Another approach is to divide power between the parties. One party selects the presiding officer, and members of the other party chair the most powerful committees such as appropriations and ways and means. These agreements, although not perfect, have prevented complete deadlock in the legislative process.[49] After a tie in the 2001 election in New Jersey, a power-sharing agreement provided for the rotation between the two parties at specified intervals of the senate presidency and committee chairs.

Identifying the most important leader in a state senate is more difficult than in the house. In over half of the states the lieutenant governor presides over the senate, following the federal arrangement where the vice president is the president of the Senate. Because the voters elect the lieutenant governor, his or her influence in the senate is usually minimal, and the effective leader is the president pro tem, who is elected by the majority party. If the lieutenant governor has no constitutional responsibilities in the senate, the presiding officer is elected by the entire membership, usually in a party-line vote, and has the title of president of the senate.

How do these leaders affect the legislative process? Malcolm Jewell and Marcia Whicker, in a major study of legislative leadership in the states, identify a number of roles:

1. *Gatekeepers* in the lawmaking process who can use their power to delay or block the adoption of a proposed law.
2. *Coalition builders* and *negotiators* who can put together majority support for a proposal that will determine whether it is enacted in the form it was introduced or becomes a "watered-down" version.
3. *Communicators* who explain legislative intent to the public. By communicating their own interpretations of the how and why of new laws they can aid public understanding and acceptance.[50]

Legislative leaders have a considerable number of specific powers they can rely on in performing these roles. A major one is control over appointing legislators to committees. This can be used to reward members who have been loyal to the leadership, assigning them to the more important committees. Committee assignments also have a policy dimension because leaders can appoint members to a committee who have policy views similar to theirs on bills that come before that committee. Leaders can also decide not to reappoint legislators to a committee, because most states do not have a written or unwritten rule that gives legislators the right to reappointment.

Legislative leaders also appoint committee chairs. Because chairs owe their position to the leaders, they are much more likely to cooperate with them in speeding or slowing the movement of key bills through their committees and in keeping unwanted amendments from being adopted.[51]

Traditionally, state legislative committees have been viewed as being less independent in the making of laws than their U.S. Congress counterparts. For the most part, this has been true because state legislative leaders' appointing power is much greater than that of congressional leaders. However, committees in state legislatures that have become more professional also have become stronger, making them more like Congress. Lower turnover allows members to stay on the same committees for a longer time and to develop expertise on bills that come before them. The same is true for committee chairs. When this happens, committees tend to become more independent of party leaders. Even though the leaders still control committee appointments, it may give them only "influence over the broad direction in which the committee moves . . . the leader cannot solve differences over specific legislation by a constant threat to remove members from the committee."[52] (It also is worth noting that committees in the U.S. House of Representatives may not be as independent as they have been. This is because after the 1994 congressional elections, the newly elected speaker, Republican Newt Gingrich, and subsequent speakers, played a major role in appointing new committee chairs.)

Generally, Jewell and Whicker conclude that legislative leadership style is changing. **Leadership style** is the extent to which leaders desire to control the behavior of other members and how they react to conflict. The command style of leadership is not as common as it used to be. Command-style leaders limit decision making to a single small group, minimize participation by rank-and-file legislators, and have a high need to control the behavior of others. Conflict is viewed as a challenge to their leadership. They are likely to use the threat of punishment (for example, removal from a committee) to pressure members to support the party line.

More prevalent today are the coordinating and consensus leadership styles. Coordinating-style leaders usually harmonize the decision making of various small groups of leaders. When conflict occurs, this type of leader tries to resolve it through negotiation and is more likely to use rewards rather than the threat of punishment. Rank-and-file legislators occasionally participate in decision making. Consensus-style leaders have a low need to control the behavior of others and use accommodation to resolve conflict. Rank-and-file legislators are encouraged to participate in decision making. Debate, discussion, and developing a consensus that a large number of party members can support replace the use of rewards and punishment to gain adherence to the party line.[53]

Another reason the consensus style is becoming prominent is that more women are moving into leadership positions and women are more likely to be consensus-style leaders. In 2001, women occupied at least one-third of the committee chair positions in seven states, including Colorado and Washington. Two women were presiding officers: the senate president in Iowa and the speaker of the house in Connecticut. Overall, women held 13 percent of the leadership positions (including presiding officers and other legislative leaders such as majority and minority leaders) and 19 percent of the committee chairs.[54] Recall that 23 percent of all state legislators are women.

Challenges to State Legislatures

State legislatures, along with representative democracy, face two challenges today. One challenge is from public distrust of legislatures, which frequently reaches the level of cynicism. The second challenge is from the techniques of direct democracy, especially when combined with the possibilities for political action that are presented by the Internet.

Since the early 1970s, survey after survey of American citizens has found distrust and lack of confidence in American political institutions, as was noted at the beginning of this chapter. (After the 9/11 terrorist attacks in New York City and Washington, D.C., levels of trust and confidence increased, but this is undoubtedly a "rally around the flag" effect and is likely to be temporary.) Although distrust is a fairly generalized phenomenon, its level may be even higher among young adults, ages 18 to 24. A 1998 survey of this age group by the National Association of Secretaries of State found that 57 percent agreed with the statement "You can't trust politicians because most are dishonest," and 64 percent agreed that "Government is run by a few big interests looking out for themselves, not for the benefit of all."[55] Americans' perceptions of politics and politicians are largely negative.

Is American politics really as terrible as the public perceives? The National Conference of State Legislatures and several well-known political scientists are attempting to show that these perceptions are inaccurate. Alan Rosenthal, Karl Kurtz, John Hibbing, and Burdett Loomis have come forward to defend and explain how state legislatures and representative government work—in essence, they believe that a new "civic education" is required. Their approach is to compare public perceptions of state legislatures with the reality of the legislative process. For example, most people believe that a state's citizens "agree on what is right and necessary, so the legislature should just pass the laws that the people want."[56] But this view is not realistic because there is disagreement among citizens over what the most important problems facing a state or the nation are, and even more disagreement over the best way to solve these problems. We live in a diverse society with less agreement on issues than we think, and it is "the job of the legislature to resolve the clash of values, interests, and claims."[57]

A related public perception is that the "lawmaking process doesn't work well because of politics, unprincipled deal making and needless conflict." Rosenthal, Kurtz, Hibbing, and Loomis argue that this view is incorrect because the legislative process is normally not an orderly one; dissension, debate, and conflict, sometimes heated and intense, are a natural part of the process. To resolve the conflict, compromise is also part of the process; compromise is not the same as "selling out." It is unlikely that any group will get all of what it wants. We may not always like these decisions, "but we should understand why they came about and recognize that this frustrating process and these imperfect decisions are what democracy is all about."[58] Overall, these advocates of the importance of "civic education" want to communicate this idea: "Representative democracy does work—by no means perfectly, but reasonably well."[59]

A related challenge to state legislatures is the concept of direct democracy that we discussed in Chapter 4. Direct democracy, especially as embodied in the initiative process, allows citizens to propose laws and then decide their fate. With modern computer technology and the Internet, it is easy to imagine not only the gathering of initiative petition signatures but also voting on these initiatives by a simple keystroke from home computers. And why have elections on initiatives only once a year? Every week it would be possible for citizens to decide any number of issues affecting their state, county, and city. Elected representatives would be unnecessary; people would make their own decisions. An expanded system of direct democracy would replace legislative institutions that are the heart of representative government. There is no doubt that we will confront these questions, and probably sooner than many expect.

But representative government has important advantages that should be weighed and considered. Richard J. Ellis says it well:

> The ideal was not just to mirror public preferences but to engage in reasoned debate about the public interest. The point of having selected individuals study, discuss, and debate public policy in a face-to-face forum was that they might reach a judgment that was different from the opinion or prejudice with which they began. Expert testimony might lead them to revise their beliefs, or the intense pleas of affected groups might unsettle their convictions. The rival interests of other constituencies would need to be heard and considered; compromises would need to be reached.[60]

LOCAL LEGISLATURES

If it is dangerous to make generalizations about fifty state legislatures, the pitfalls clearly are multiplied when presenting an overview of close to 40,000 local legislatures found in counties, cities, townships, and towns. On two characteristics, however, local legislatures are different from their state counterparts: local legislatures are *unicameral*. And membership in local legislatures is a part-time job with low salaries and minimal staff assistance, except in cities and counties with very large populations.

Counties

The **county** is a major unit of local government in the United States that exists as an agent for the state and as a unit of local governance. (Counties are called "parishes" in Louisiana and "boroughs" in Alaska.) There were 3,066 counties in 2002; eighty had a population of over 1 million and 696 had populations of less than 10,000. Loving County in Texas has a population of only seventy people!

County governments are found in all states except Connecticut and Rhode Island. Counties have never been important in the New England states, where the town remains the basic unit of local government. The size and number of counties vary greatly.

Delaware and Hawaii have only three counties each, whereas Texas has 254. San Bernardino County, California (20,000 square miles), is larger than Vermont and New Hampshire combined. Counties are the creatures of the state, and their existence often is spelled out in state constitutions. (Keep in mind that within most counties, there will be a number of cities and towns that provide general local government for people living within their boundaries; they may receive some county services but most will come from the city or town.)

Counties traditionally have performed a wide variety of functions in the areas of health, welfare, education, criminal justice, maintenance of roads, and record keeping. They have been given additional functions as the administrative units for various federal and state programs. Although counties have traditionally been the most important unit of government in rural areas, urban counties have been gaining significant authority. In some states, home-rule charters allow counties to perform functions that previously were city responsibilities. These include water supply, library services, sewage disposal, flood control, and management of airports. This has been especially true in southern states where counties traditionally have been more powerful than cities.[61] As will be discussed in Chapter 9, strong urban counties can serve as a kind of metropolitan government by providing a wide range of services traditionally associated with cities.

Counties that are neither urban nor rural—so-called 50–50 areas (they are fifty miles from a metropolitan area, and they have populations around 50,000)—are experiencing new demands from affluent families who are moving away from cities but still want many urban services.

Traditionally, three- or five-member boards of commissioners have administered most counties. In a few states, such as Illinois and Wisconsin, there are large governing boards with ten or more members. Commissioners often share administrative duties and some legislative responsibilities with independently elected officials that include auditors, treasurers, clerks-of-court, sheriffs, engineers, prosecutors, and coroners. Commissioners' legislative functions include adopting a budget and setting tax rates. As executives they appoint some county employees and supervise county roadwork. Although the Voting Rights Act has prompted more district elections in counties, the more common pattern is at-large election of commissioners.

The organization of county government has been widely criticized.[62] The absence of a chief executive often has meant inadequate supervision and coordination of the numerous county departments. A system designed for rural, small-town America has not had the flexibility to adapt to the needs of urbanized, metropolitan populations.

Reformers have favored alternative forms of county government with appointed or elected executives. Change has come because the home-rule movement has allowed counties to pick among several types of structures that centralize administrative responsibility. Nearly one-fourth of all counties, including many urban counties, have a *commission-administrator* form of government in which the commissioners appoint an administrator; or they have a *council-elected executive* with two branches of government; voters elect the executive and the council. County administrators are sometimes called county managers, chief administrative officers, or executive directors. They serve at the pleasure of the board. Administrators' powers vary and include budget preparation, appointment of some department heads, and supervision of some departments. Executives who are elected by the voters have more substantial powers, which may include the ability to veto legislation approved by the county board. Elected executives are found in about one-fourth as many counties as administrators. Typically, voters elect fewer county officials under this structure than under the commission form of government.

Cities

City councils vary in size: cities with a large population also have larger councils. For example, cities with over 1 million people have councils with an average of thirty-three members, cities with 500,000 to 1 million people have an average of eleven council members, and cities between 50,000 to 99,999 have seven council members.[63] Members of larger councils are elected by districts, sometimes called wards. (The councils discussed in this section are associated with a type of local government known as a municipality. A **municipality** provides general government for a defined geographic area. The state grants it a charter that defines its powers, as explained in Chapter 1. A municipality can be a city, town, or village; however, "town" has a special meaning in the New England states and a few states in the Midwest. This will be explained below.)

Susan MacManus explains that council members must be both generalists and specialists because the issues that arise in communities vary widely:

> land use, availability of housing and services, tax policy and tax rates, service delivery . . . , buildings and facilities, economic development, the environment, public safety, recreation, cultural opportunities, and more.[64]

In close to 75 percent of the cities, council members (in larger cities they are sometimes called aldermen) devote only part of their time to city affairs and continue their full-time employment as business executives, employees in service industries, and teachers, or, in large cities, as lawyers. Their pay reflects this part-time service and ranges from $1 to $39,000 annually, typically $10,000. Only in the largest cities are council members full time and well paid, from $63,000 to $90,000.[65]

When council members are part time, it is easier for the mayor or city manager to dominate their decision making. The degree of council participation in decision making is greatly affected by the form of city government (see Chapter 6). Where there is a weak-mayor system, the council will have considerable formal authority. In cities with strong mayors or managers, the basic function of council members often is to act as representatives to bring complaints to the attention of city hall. In most cities, councils are passive and seldom act as policy innovators. Their most common role is to oppose rather than to propose policy. Because turnover is high and voter participation low, it is difficult to hold council members accountable by threatening to defeat them in the next election. Many retire before the end of their term, allowing the mayor or council to appoint a successor. In such a situation, the general public's ability to influence public policy through legislative representatives is more difficult.

A few large cities, Dallas, Los Angeles, New York, and Washington, D.C., have term limits for city council members, usually two terms, but they are the exception. Victor DeSantis and Tari Renner found that among cities with populations over 25,000, only 8.4 percent of cities reported having term limits. Term limits are not needed because of the higher rate of turnover among local officials, compared to state legislators and members of Congress. Nearly half of the council members in the surveyed cities were in their first term. (And the average tenure for mayors was 5.4 years. The turnover of city managers was 29 percent in a one-year period. See Chapter 6.)

The high level of turnover among local officeholders can be attributed to several factors. As DeSantis and Renner note:

> The advantages of incumbency, for example, may not be as strong given that incumbents' name recognition is likely to be lower, their constituencies smaller, and campaign costs lower than at other levels. It may be comparatively easy (from both an organizational and financial perspective) to successfully challenge an incumbent under these circumstances. It is also possible that the tendency for local public service positions to be part-time and volunteer, rather than full-time and career, results in more voluntary turnover of incumbents and less longevity than at other levels of government.[66]

In small cities, council sessions may be once or twice a month, and in large cities, councils meet at least once a week. The use of committees and professional staff in large cities has been increasing because councils are facing more complex problems, but it is nowhere close to the level present in state legislatures. About one-half have committees and one-third have a professional staff. Staff are usually hired to serve the entire council and not individual committees or members. In the past, small-town councils, in particular, often resolved issues at an informal and private meeting before the scheduled session, and then voted unanimously in public sessions. State **"sunshine laws"** have forced councils to have open meetings on nearly all matters.

The composition of large and many medium-size city councils is changing as more minorities and women are elected. African Americans make up just over 5 percent of all city council members, Hispanics 2.5 percent, Native Americans 0.7 percent, and Asian Americans 0.3 percent.[67] The fact that many small and medium-size cities have a small minority population hides the gains of minority groups on city councils in large cities with ethnically diverse populations. Nationally, women constitute about 20 percent of city council members, up from 10 percent in the mid-1970s. Women are most likely to be underrepresented in southern cities, where one study reported that 73 percent of medium to large cities in Alabama did not have any women on their councils.[68] Much of the increase of minorities on city councils has been caused by the change from at-large elections to single-member districts that was caused by the Voting Rights Act. Many observers thought that lower campaign costs in single-member districts would make it easier for women to run and win, but research does not support this; in fact, at-large elections have produced slightly more women council members.

Townships and Towns

The **township,** basically a subdivision of a county, is a form of government found in Middle Atlantic and midwestern states. In much of the Midwest, townships were carefully laid out in six-mile squares, with 36 one-mile square sections. These surveyor's townships did not become political townships until later when local government was organized. As a result, all political townships are not neat six-mile squares. Midwest counties were designed so that no one would be more than a day's driving time from the county seat, and the township hall was within an hour's buggy ride. Unlike towns, townships are primarily rural, not a combination of rural and urban areas. Townships also are not the principal unit of government in any state in which they are found. They exist throughout many states such as Ohio, Kansas, and Pennsylvania in the Midwest and Middle Atlantic, but only parts of other states such as Illinois and the Dakotas have townships. A few townships have annual meetings that are similar to New England town meetings, but most elect trustees to act as legislators, as well as administrators. Some elect a chief executive, commonly known as a supervisor. Many rural townships have transferred much of their authority (e.g., repair of roads and bridges) to counties.

In most midwestern states all land area not incorporated into municipalities lies within the jurisdiction of townships. The township, typically with three elected trustees, may levy taxes and sue and be sued. In a few wealthy suburban areas (in Pennsylvania and Kansas, for example) townships have gained powers nearly equal to those of cities. Township powers can grow as new businesses locate in unincorporated areas adjacent to cities and as the population of those areas increases.

Collectively, townships may have surprising political power in a state. When we consider that many midwestern counties are divided into more than a dozen townships, this means that some states have over 1,000 townships, with over 3,000 trustees. Because annexation presents a direct threat to their power, townships have lobbied in Ohio for a requirement that township land cannot be annexed without trustee approval. Of course, counties also have statewide organizations to lobby, and cities join state municipal leagues that present a unified effort to represent their interests in the state legislature.

The **town** continues to be the basic form of local government in New England states. In colonial America, a "town" included a village and surrounding farms. Over time, some New England urban areas have incorporated and withdrawn from towns, but towns as governmental units continue to be a combination of urban areas and the surrounding countryside. For example, New Hampshire has only ten counties and thirteen municipalities, but it has 221 towns. It is here that the fabled town meeting convenes annually to levy taxes, determine how money will be spent, and elect the next year's "selectmen." The selectmen acted in a manner similar to county commissioners to oversee the administration of schools, roads, health, and welfare.

Because attendance at many town meetings has declined, a representative town meeting plan has been devised in some towns whereby voters choose a large number of citizens (around 100) to attend the town meeting and represent their views.

SUMMARY

For state legislatures, the reapportionment revolution was a landmark event. Supreme Court decisions in the 1960s ruled that both the lower and the upper houses of state legislatures were to be apportioned on the basis of population. With the resulting shift in legislative power from rural to urban and suburban areas, many states began a process of professionalizing their legislatures. After each federal decennial census, new legislative district lines are drawn in the states. The only clear guideline is that districts must be substantially equal in population. The protection or enhancement of the number of seats held by the majority party or racial minorities or incumbents may be important factors in this redistricting process.

State legislators are usually white men, but the number of legislators who are women, African Americans, and members of other minority groups has increased substantially since

1975. As institutions, state legislatures are quite diverse. Some are professional and have longer sessions, higher salaries for their members, and a larger staff. At the other extreme are legislatures with short sessions, lower salaries, and a smaller staff; their members are usually called citizen legislators. The term limits movement, to some extent an expression of the public's dissatisfaction with government and career politicians, has limited the number of terms an individual can serve in the legislatures of sixteen states. The effects of term limits are still unfolding. An early finding is that "termed" legislators usually continue their political careers in positions outside the state legislature and do not return to life as ordinary citizens, as was hoped by the advocates of term limits.

State legislatures have a number of functions, including representation (individual legislators representing the interests of their constituents), lawmaking (making policy through the passage of laws), and legislative oversight (reviewing the performance of executive branch agencies). Governors are important in lawmaking because they play a key role in the initiation of policies considered by the legislature.

Decision making in legislatures centers around committees, parties, and leaders. Leaders perform a number of roles and have powers such as control over the appointment of committee chairs that allow them to influence the making of decisions, even with the general decline in the strength of allegiance legislators have to their parties. Today's legislative leaders use a coordinating and consensus style of leadership more than a command style.

Public cynicism and the initiative process present challenges to state legislatures and representative democracy. One response is a "civic education" approach that emphasizes a realistic understanding of how representative institutions work and their benefits.

Generally, the most important local legislatures are city councils and county boards of commissioners. In most cities, being a council member is a part-time job, and the council is often dominated by the mayor or city manager. County boards of commissioners have both legislative and executive responsibilities, and the latter frequently are shared with independently elected officials, such as the sheriff and engineers. The absence of a chief executive in county government is a frequent criticism. A few counties now have an elected chief executive or an appointed county administrator.

The town is an important unit of local government in New England. Many towns continue to have annual town meetings that serve as a legislative body and make decisions for the town. In many midwestern states, townships provide a few services for rural areas. Township trustees are elected by the voters to act as legislators and administrators.

KEY TERMS

apportionment	malapportionment
Baker v. Carr	municipality
bicameral	professional legislators
caucus	professional legislatures
citizen legislators	*Reynolds v. Sims*
citizen legislatures	*Shaw v. Reno*
county	"sunset laws"
Davis v. Bandemer	"sunshine laws"
districting	term limits movement
gerrymandering	town
leadership style	township
legislative oversight	**unicameral**
Mahan v. Howell	

SUMMARY OF STATE/LOCAL DIFFERENCES

Issue	State Level	Local Level
Structural characteristics of legislatures	Bicameral (except Nebraska), larger number of members and committee system.	Unicameral, smaller number of members, and usually no committee system.
Degree of professionalization of legislatures	More likely to be viewed as full-time job, lower turnover, generally higher salaries.	More likely to be viewed as part-time job, higher turnover, generally lower salaries.
Legislative term limits	Adopted by one-third of the states.	Generally, have not been adopted, for example, used by less than 10 percent of city councils.

INTERESTING WEBSITES

The National Conference of State Legislatures in Denver, Colorado maintains an excellent website at *www.ncsl.org*. Be sure to click on "Policy Issues" for reports on timely state issues and "State Legislatures," where you can find a link to each state's legislature.

www.termlimits.org. U.S. Term Limits is an advocacy group for "limiting the terms of politicians at the local, state and congressional levels."

www.naco.org. The National Association of Counties maintains this site. It has all kinds of county information—issues to demographics—plus data on individual counties.

NOTES

1. See John Burns, *The Sometime Governments* (New York: Bantam Books, 1971), p. 32.
2. Rich Jones, "State Legislatures," *The Book of States, 1994–95* (Lexington, Ky.: Council of State Governments, 1994), p. 98.
3. The following are helpful sources on Willie Brown's career: Ken DeBow and John C. Syer, *Power and Politics in California*, 5th ed. (Boston, Mass.: Allyn and Bacon, 1997), pp. 160–163; Douglas Foster, "The Lame-Duck State," *Harper's Magazine* (February 1994), pp. 65–74.
4. Leroy Hardy, Alan Heslop, and George S. Blair, "Introduction," in *Redistricting in the 1980's,* Leroy Hardy, Alan Heslop, and George Blair, eds. (Claremont, Calif.: Rose Institute of State and Local Government, 1993), pp. 1–4.
5. Newspaper and television reporters frequently use the term *redistricting* to refer to the drawing of new congressional district boundaries and *reapportionment* to refer to the drawing of new state legislative district boundaries. Although this usage is not exact, it conveniently distinguishes the two processes.
6. Baker v. Carr, 369 U.S. 186 (1962).
7. Reynolds v. Sims, 377 U.S. 533 (1964).

8. Mahan v. Howell, 410 U.S. 315 (1973).
9. See Timothy O'Rourke, *The Impact of Reapportionment* (New Brunswick, N.J.: Transaction Books, 1980); and David C. Saffell, "Reapportionment and Public Policy: State Legislators' Perspectives," *Policy Studies Journal* 9 (Special #3 1980–1981), pp. 916–936.
10. Davis v. Bandemer, 478 U.S. 109 (1986).
11. Laughlin McDonald, "1982 Amendments of Section 2," in *Controversies in Minority Voting: The Voting Rights Act in Perspective,* Bernard Grofman and Chandler Davidson, eds. (Washington, D.C.: The Brookings Institution, 1992), p. 69.
12. Shaw v. Reno, 509 U.S. 630 (1993).
13. Two good studies of minority voting rights are Charles S. Bullock, III, "The Opening Up of State and Local Processes," in *American State and Local Politics: Directions for the 21st Century,* Ronald E. Weber and Paul Brace, eds. (New York, N.Y.: Chatham House Publishers, 1999), pp. 212–240 and Richard K. Scher, Jon L. Mills, and John J. Hotaling, *Voting Rights & Democracy: The Law and Politics of Districting* (Chicago, Ill.: Nelson-Hall Publishers, 1997).
14. First attempts to present an overview of the post-2000 census redistricting can be found in Richard L. Engstrom, "The Post-2000 Round of Redistricting: An Entangled Thicket Within the Federal System," *Publius: The Journal of Federalism* (Fall 2002), pp. 51–70; and Ronald E. Weber, "State Legislative Redistricting in 2001–2002: Emerging Trends and Issues in Reapportionment," *Book of the States* (Lexington, Ky.: Council of State Governments, 2002), pp. 233–238.
15. 532 U.S. 234.
16. Patty Reinert, "High Court Backs Texas Remap Plan; Hispanic Challenges Fail," *Houston Chronicle,* June 18, 2002, p. 1A, http://web.lexis-nexis.com (accessed March 25, 2003).
17. Laylan Copelin, "Districts Likely Set for 2002 Election: Federal Judges Largely Accept GOP-Backed Maps for Texas House, Senate," *Austin American Statesman,* November 29, 2001, p. A1. http://web.lexis-nexis.com (accessed March 25, 2003).
18. Tim Storey, "2002 State Legislative Elections," *Spectrum: The Journal of State Government* (Winter 2003), p. 9.
19. Steve Lawrence, "Davis Signs Bills Aimed at Status Quo in Legislature, Congress," Associated Press State & Local Wire, September 27, 2001; and Dan Walters, "A Self-Serving Redistricting Process," *Sacramento Bee,* October 19, 2001, p. B-9. http://web.lexis-nexis.com/universe (accessed March 25, 2003).
20. "Redistricting Disgrace; Governor Pataki Signs Off on a Plan That Serves the Interests of the Majority Parties," *Times Union* (Albany), April 24, 2002, p. A12, http://web.lexis-nexis.com/universe (accessed March 26, 2003).
21. An excellent analysis of the different types of redistricting commissions and redistricting processes generally can be found in Michael P. McDonald, "United States Redistricting and the Decline of Competitive Congressional Districts." Paper presented at the George Mason Center for Public Choice, Fairfax, Virginia, April 2, 2003.
22. Harry Basehart, "Pennsylvania," in *Redistricting in the 1980's,* Hardy, Heslop, and Blair, eds., pp. 217–221.
23. Rex Honey and Douglas Deane Jones, "Iowa," in *Redistricting in the 1980's,* Hardy, Heslop, and Blair, eds., pp. 97–102.
24. Mike Glover, "Moving Vans Fire Up After New Districts Approved," Associated Press State & Local Wire, June 20, 2001, http://web.lexis-nexis.com/universe (accessed March 28, 2003).
25. McDonald, p. 46.
26. Lillian C. Woo, "Today's Legislators: Who They Are and Why They Run," *State Legislatures* (April 1994), p. 29.

27. Tom Todd, "Nebraska's Unicameral Legislature: A Description and Some Comparisons with Minnesota's Bicameral Legislature," *Journal of the American Society of Legislative Clerks and Secretaries* (Spring 1998). AASLCS home page, http://www.ncsl.org/programs/legman/aslcs/cshome.htm (accessed March 25, 2003).

28. B. Drummond Ayres Jr., "Political Briefing. Ventura's Mission: Turning Two into One," *New York Times,* August 22, 1999, p. 22.

29. Karl Kurtz, "Understanding the Diversity of American State Legislatures," *Extension of Remarks* (June 1992), p. 3. Kurtz uses Red, White, and Blue as names of the categories to avoid any judgment that one category is better than another.

30. Alan Rosenthal, Burdett A. Loomis, John R. Hibbing, and Karl T. Kurtz, R*epublic on Trial: The Case for Representative Democracy* (Washington, D.C.: CQ Press, 2003), p. 72.

31. Kurtz, "Understanding," p. 3.

32. Edward H. Crane, "Six and Twelve: The Case for Serious Term Limits," *National Civic Review* (Summer 1991), pp. 252–253.

33. Cal Ledbetter, Jr., "Limiting Legislative Terms Is a Bad Idea," *National Civic Review* (Summer 1991), p. 244.

34. Charles Price, "Advocacy in the Age of Term Limits: Lobbying after Proposition 140," in *1994–1995 Annual California Government and Politics,* Thomas R. Hoeber and Charles M. Price, eds. (Sacramento, Calif.: California Journal Press, 1994), p. 56.

35. Richard J. Powell, "The Unintended Effects of Term Limits on the Career Paths of State Legislators," in *The Test of Time: Coping with Legislative Term Limits,* Rick Farmer, John David Rausch, Jr., and John C. Green, eds. (Lanham, Md.: Lexington Books, 2003), p. 144; Richard J. Powell, "The Changing Career Paths of State Legislators in an Era of Term Limits," Midwest Political Science Association Annual Meeting, Chicago, Ill., April 3–6, 2003.

36. James M. Penning, "Michigan: The End Is Near," in *The Test of Time: Coping with Legislative Term Limits,* Rick Farmer, John David Rausch, Jr., and John C. Green, eds. (Lanham, Md.: Lexington Books, 2003), p. 41.

37. George Peery and Thomas H. Little, "Views from the Bridge: Legislative Leaders' Perceptions of Institutional Power in the Stormy Wake of Term Limits," in *The Test of Time: Coping with Legislative Term Limits,* pp. 105–118.

38. A major study, the Joint Project on Term Limits, is underway to examine the effects of term limits, sponsored by the National Conference of State Legislatures, Council of State Governments, and the State Legislative Leaders Foundation. Information is available at www.ncsl.org.

39. Thad Beyle and Rich Jones, "Term Limits in the States," in *The Book of the States 1994–95* (Lexington, Ky.: Council of State Governments, 1994), p. 31.

40. Edmund Burke, quoted in Malcolm E. Jewell, *Representation in State Legislatures* (Lexington, Ky.: University Press of Kentucky, 1982), p. 11.

41. Alan Rosenthal, *The Decline of Representative Democracy: Process, Participation, and Power in State Legislatures* (Washington, D.C.: CQ Press, 1998), pp. 2–11.

42. Ibid., p. 25.

43. National Conference of State Legislatures, "Bill Introduction Limits," www.ncsl.org (accessed April 11, 2003).

44. Alan Rosenthal, "Legislative Oversight and the Balance of Power in State Government," *State Government* 56, no. 3 (1983), pp. 93–95.

45. National Legislative Program Evaluation Society, "Ensuring the Public Trust: How Program Policy Evaluation Is Serving State Legislatures" (July 2000), http://www.ncsl.org/program/nlpes.

46. Tommy Neal, *Lawmaking and the Legislative Process: Committees, Connections, and Compromises* (Phoenix, Ariz.: Oryx Press, 1996), pp. 56–57; and Alan Rosenthal, *Representative Democracy,* pp. 141–145.

47. Sarah McCally Morehouse and Malcolm E. Jewell, *State Politics, Parties, & Policy,* 2d ed. (Lanham, Md.: Rowman & Littlefield, 2003), p. 227.

48. Shannon Jenkins, "Party Voting in State Legislatures," *Spectrum: The Journal of State Government* (Fall 2002), pp. 10–13.

49. National Conference of State Legislatures, "Legislative Deadlock: What If It Happens to You?" www.ncsl.org/programs/press/2000/tiedexpl.htm (accessed April 11, 2003).

50. Malcolm E. Jewell and Marcia Lynn Whicker, *Legislative Leadership in the American States* (Ann Arbor: The University of Michigan Press, 1994), pp. 58–59.

51. Ibid., pp. 89–95.

52. Ibid., p. 96.

53. Ibid., pp. 125–130.

54. Center for American Women and Politics, "Women State Legislators: Leadership Positions and Committee Chairs 2001," www.cawp.rutgers.edu (accessed April 11, 2003).

55. National Association of Secretaries of State, "New Millennium Survey: American Youth Attitudes on Politics, Citizenship & Voting," National Questionnaire, p. 15, www.stateof thevote.org/survey (accessed April 12, 2003).

56. Alan Rosenthal, Karl T. Kurtz, John Hibbing, and Burdett Loomis, *The Case for Representative Democracy: What Americans Should Know About Their Legislatures* (Denver, Colo.: National Conference of State Legislatures, 2001), p. 18. Also see Rosenthal, Loomis, Hibbing, and Kurtz, *Republic on Trial.*

57. Rosenthal, Kurtz, Hibbing, and Loomis, *Case for Representative Democracy,* p. 18.

58. Ibid., p. 32.

59. Rosenthal, Loomis, Hibbing, and Kurtz, *Republic on Trial,* p. 215.

60. Richard J. Ellis, *Democratic Delusions: The Initiative Process in America* (Lawrence, Kan.: University Press of Kansas, 2002), p. 200.

61. See David R. Berman, ed., *County Government in an Era of Change* (Westport, Conn.: Greenwood Press, 1993).

62. See Herbert S. Duncombe, *Modern County Government* (Washington, D.C.: National Association of Counties, 1977), chap. 2.

63. Evelina R. Moulder, *Profile of the City Council, 1996* (Washington, D.C.: International City/County Management Association, 1996).

64. Susan MacManus, "The Resurgent City Councils," in Ronald E. Weber and Paul Brace, *American State and Local Politics: Directions for the 21st Century* (New York, N.Y.: Chatham House, 1999), p. 181.

65. Ibid., pp. 175–176.

66. Victor S. DeSantis and Tari Renner, "Term Limits and Turnover Among Local Officials," in *The Municipal Yearbook 1993* (Washington, D.C.: International City/County Management Association, 1993), p. 36.

67. MacManus, "City Councils," p. 187.

68. Susan A. MacManus and Charles S. Bullock, "Women on Southern City Councils: A Decade of Change," *British Journal of Political Science* (Spring 1989), pp. 32–49.

CHAPTER 6

Governors, Bureaucrats, and Mayors

POINTS TO CONSIDER

- Should governors' power of clemency be constitutionally restricted?
- How has the power of governors evolved over the past two hundred years?
- How does the formal power of governors differ among the fifty states?
- What are some informal ways in which governors exercise control over legislatures?
- How has government benefited or suffered from the use of affirmative action?
- What are the goals of the "reinventing government" movement, what reforms are recommended to achieve these goals, and to what extent have states put these reforms into practice?

- Compare and contrast the roles of mayors in four different systems of municipal government.
- What difference does it make to have significantly more women and minority mayors than was the case twenty years ago? What is the approach of "second-generation African-American mayors"?

HISTORICAL DEVELOPMENT OF THE GOVERNOR'S OFFICE

When the early state constitutions were written, all governmental power was distrusted, but executives were particularly suspect because of the colonial experience under King George III of England. Consequently, the legislative branch dominated early state government. In most of the original states the legislature chose the governor, who served a one-year term. Pennsylvania and Georgia had plural executives, that is, leadership by committee. In only one state did the governor have the veto power, and Virginia did not elect its governor until 1851.

During the **Jacksonian democracy era,** which began with the election to the presidency of Andrew Jackson in 1828, the prestige of chief executives was enhanced. Jacksonian democracy emphasized political and social equality, government by the "common man" over government by an aristocracy, that is, those who inherited their

Mass Clemency in Illinois

As a member of the Illinois legislature in 1977 George Ryan voted to resume the use of the death penalty in his state. In 2003 Governor Ryan cleared the Illinois death row, saying that the 167 people residing there had been sentenced to die by an "immoral" system.

In 2000, one year after taking office, Ryan issued a moratorium on executions in Illinois. This was prompted by the realization that since 1977 thirteen condemned men had been found innocent—one just forty-eight hours before his scheduled execution—and only twelve had been executed.

Ryan appointed a commission that completed an exhaustive study of the capital punishment system in Illinois. When Ryan announced his clemency action, he criticized the state legislature for failing to act on any of the commission's eighty-five recommendations. Few legislators wanted to take a position that later could be used to suggest they were soft on crime.[1]

Critics of the governor argued that his clemencies and the focus on capital punishment were only ways to divert attention from scandals that plagued his entire term in office. Ryan left office the day before opening statements were expected in the racketeering trial of his former chief of staff and of his campaign committee. About a year later, Ryan was indicted on charges of taking payoffs to steer state business to friends while he was governor.

Considering Ryan's scandal-filled four years as governor and agreeing with his clemencies, the *New York Times* commented, "Nothing became Governor George Ryan's term in office like leaving it."[2] Ryan's successor, Democrat Rod Blagojevich, announced in 2003 that he would continue the moratorium on executions.

wealth and social position. Popular election was viewed as the best way to fill other executive offices, such as attorney general and treasurer. Pushed by the disclosure of legislative corruption and incompetence, states extended the terms of governors, usually to two years, and added the veto power. Toward the end of the nineteenth century, legislatures, responding to urban residents who were demanding more services, created new executive branch agencies. In New York, there were only ten state agencies in 1800; by 1900 the number had increased to eighty-one. Typically, these agencies were administered by boards and commissions, at least some of whose members were appointed by the legislature.[3] The executive branch of state government was becoming an administrative nightmare.

Many twentieth-century government reforms fall under the heading of **administrative efficiency,** meaning to centralize administrative authority and responsibility in the hands of one person—the governor. Boards and commissions were consolidated into a more manageable number of departments headed by a secretary appointed by the governor. Urbanization, the Great Depression, and the growth of federal programs administered by the states placed increasing burdens on state governments. To meet these responsibilities, governors have been given stronger budget authority and four-year terms. Changes were made by state constitutional conventions or by legislative action. Reapportionment reduced the influence of rural legislators, who historically were hostile toward executive authority. Another factor helping to strengthen the role of governors has been the general acceptance of the view that chief executives should maximize their powers in the manner of Franklin D. Roosevelt. The presidential model still continues to have a strong influence on people's willingness to support strong executive authority at the state level and on people's expectations that governors should be able to solve problems. Since the 1980s, the retreat of the federal government has resulted in a more dominant role for governors as policy makers, especially in the areas of health and welfare.

WHO BECOMES GOVERNOR?

The traditional image of the typical governor as a white male lawyer in his late forties is still fairly accurate, but it should not obscure the slowly increasing diversity of political leaders who are now becoming governors. Beginning in the twentieth century, several women were elected governor to succeed their husbands. But it was not until 1974 that a woman (Ella Grasso in Connecticut) was elected governor on her own. Although there were six women governors in 1991, by the mid-1990s there was only one woman governor—Christine Whitman in New Jersey. In 2002 four female wins set a record in one election year, and with the election in 2003 of Kathleen Blanco as governor of Louisiana there was a record high of seven women governors.

Most observers felt that gender issues were less significant than budget deficits in states where women were running for governor in 2002. In Hawaii, the win by Republican Linda Lingle, a former mayor of Maui, was the first for a Republican gubernatorial candidate since Hawaii's first year of statehood. Five women nominated for governor by a major party lost in 2002.

Since the mid-1970s an African American and three Hispanics have been elected governor. In 1996, Gary Locke of Washington became the first Asian-American governor on the U.S. mainland. The first and only African-American elected governor was

L. Douglas Wilder of Virginia (1989–1993). Jerry Apodaca, Toney Anaya, and Bill Richardson in New Mexico and Bob Martinez in Florida are the only Hispanics to serve as governor since the mid-1970s. The major barrier faced by minority candidates for governor is that in no state do African Americans or Hispanics comprise more than 40 percent of the population.

In states with strong party organizations (e.g., Illinois and Massachusetts), a pattern of service in the state legislature or in another statewide elected position, such as attorney general, has been a common background for governors. Among governors serving in 1998, about half had statewide elective and service experience.[4] However, statewide officials, such as the lieutenant governor and secretary of state, when running for governor have lost about 70 percent of the time. Because of limits on consecutive terms, an increasing number of former governors are among those running for governor. Although nearly all governors have had some previous experience in government, some like Ronald Reagan and George W. Bush were elected in their first try for public office. A measure of the increased status of governors is that since 1980 an increasingly larger number of people have left Congress to run for governor.

Gubernatorial specialist Thad Beyle argues that governors who have worked their way up from local to statewide elective office are the most successful in office. In contrast to governors with limited political experience, these governors understand better how to form effective political alliances. If they held administrative posts, those skills add to their gubernatorial success. In the 320 gubernatorial races between 1977 and 2001, Beyle found, fifty-six were won by candidates who had held statewide office.[5]

As noted in Chapter 4, in recent years about three-fourths of governors who were eligible for reelection decided to run and about three-fourths of them were successful. In the thirteen states that held gubernatorial elections in 2000 and 2001, six incumbents sought reelection. Only one, Cecil Underwood of West Virginia, who was 74 years old, lost. Four of sixteen incumbent governors seeking reelection in 2002 were defeated. In large part because of term limits, in twenty states the incumbent did not run for reelection. This, of course, resulted in the election of new governors in nearly half the states. Unlike Congress, where nearly 90 percent of House seats were considered safe in 2002, there were competitive races in about three-fourths of the thirty-six states holding gubernatorial elections. The inability of the party in power to deal effectively with state budgets led to unusually high (50 percent) turnover in party control in those states. The overall closeness of party competition was reflected in the 26–24 Republican advantage in governorships in 2003.

INSTITUTIONAL POWERS OF THE GOVERNOR

In a much-cited analysis of governors, Joseph A. Schlesinger studied formal gubernatorial powers and developed an overall measure of the relative power of governors in the fifty states.[6] **Formal powers** are those powers that can be found in a state's constitution or statutes. The more important powers are those dealing with tenure potential, appointment of executive branch officials, control over preparing the budget, and ability to veto legislation.

Thad Beyle has updated and expanded Schlesinger's work on the formal powers of the governor.[7] Beyle includes the four powers discussed, adds two more—the number of separately elected officials in the executive branch and the party that controls the legislature—and then compares the *institutional* powers of the governors in all fifty states. States are rated on a scale of 1 to 5, with 5 representing governors who have the strongest power. The results, including an overall average for each state, are in Table 6-1.

TABLE 6-1	Governors' Institutional Powers, 2003							
	SEP	TP	AP	BP	VP	PC	Total	Score
AL	1	4	3	3	4	2	17	2.8
AK	5	4	3.5	3	5	4	24.5	4.1
AZ	2.5	4	4	3	5	1	19.5	3.2
AR	2.5	4	3	3	4	2	18.5	3.1
CA	1	4	4	3	5	4	21	3.5
CO	4	4	3.5	3	5	4	23.5	3.9
CT	4	5	2.5	3	5	2	21.5	3.6
DE	2.5	4	3.5	3	5	3	21	3.5
FL	3	4	2.5	3	5	4	21.5	3.6
GA	1	4	2	3	5	3	18	3.0
HI	5	4	2.5	3	5	2	21.5	3.6
ID	2	4	2	3	5	5	21	3.5
IL	3	5	3	3	5	4	23	3.8
IN	3	4	2.5	3	2	3	17.5	2.9
IA	3	5	3	3	5	2	21	3.5
KS	3	4	3	3	5	2	20	3.3
KY	3	4	4	3	4	3	21	3.5
LA	1	4	3.5	3	5	2	18.5	3.1
ME	5	4	3.5	3	2	4	21.5	3.6
MD	4	4	2.5	5	5	2	22.5	3.7
MA	4	5	3.5	3	5	1	21.5	3.6
MI	4	4	3.5	3	5	2	21.5	3.6
MN	4	5	2.5	3	5	3	22.5	3.7
MS	1.5	4	2	3	5	4	19.5	3.2
MO	2.5	4	3	3	5	2	19.5	3.2
MT	3	4	3	3	5	4	22	3.7
NE	4	4	3	4	5	3	23	3.8
NV	2.5	4	3.5	3	2	3	18	3.0
NH	5	2	3	3	2	4	19	3.2
NJ	5	4	3.5	3	5	3	23.5	3.9
NM	3	4	3	3	5	4	22	3.7
NY	4	5	3.5	4	5	3	24.5	4.1
NC	1	4	3.5	3	2	3	16.5	2.7
ND	3	5	3.5	3	5	4	23.5	3.9
OH	4	4	3.5	3	5	4	23.5	3.9
OK	1	4	1	3	5	4	18	3.0
OR	2	4	3	3	5	3	20	3.3

TABLE 6-1 (concluded)

	SEP	TP	AP	BP	VP	PC	Total	Score
PA	4	4	4	3	5	2	22	3.7
RI	2.5	4	3	3	2	1	15.5	2.6
SC	1	4	2	2	5	4	18	3.0
SD	3	4	3.5	3	5	4	22.5	3.1
TN	4.5	4	4	3	4	4	23.5	3.9
TX	2	5	1	2	5	4	19	3.2
UT	4	5	3	3	5	5	25	4.2
VT	2.5	2	3.5	3	2	2	15	2.5
VA	2.5	3	3.5	3	5	2	19	3.2
WA	1	5	3.5	3	5	3	20.5	3.4
WV	2.5	4	4	5	5	4	24.5	4.1
WI	3	5	2	3	5	2	20	3.3
WY	2	4	3.5	3	5	2	19.5	3.2
50 avg	2.9	4.1	3.1	3.1	4.5	3.1	20.7	3.4

SEP—Separately elected executive branch officials: 5 = only governor or governor/lieutenant governor team elected; 4.5 = governor or governor/lieutenant governor team, with one other elected official; 4 = governor/lieutenant governor team with some process officials (attorney general, secretary of state, treasurer, auditor) elected; 3 = governor/lieutenant governor team with some process officials, and some major and minor policy officials elected; 2.5 = governor (no team) with six or fewer officials elected, but none are major policy officials; 2 = governor (no team) with six or fewer officials elected, including one major policy official; 1.5 = governor (no team) with six or fewer officials elected, but two are major policy officials; 1 = governor (no team) with seven or more process and several major policy officials elected. [Source: CSG, The Book of the States, 2000–2001 (2000): 33–38.]

TP—Tenure potential of governors: 5 = 4-year term, no restraint on reelection; 4.5 = 4-year term, only three terms permitted; 4 = 4-year term, only two terms permitted; 3 = 4-year term, no consecutive reelection permitted; 2 = 2-year term, no restraint on reelection; 1 = 2-year term, only two terms permitted. [Source: CSG, The Book of the States, 2000–2001 (2000): 31–32.]

AP—Governor's appointment powers in six major functional areas: corrections, K–12 education, health, highways/transportation, public utilities regulation, and welfare. The six individual office scores are totaled and then averaged and rounded to the nearest .5 for the state score. 5 = governor appoints, no other approval needed; 4 = governor appoints, a board, council or legislature approves; 3 = someone else appoints, governor approves or shares appointment; 2 = someone else appoints, governor and others approve; 1 = someone else appoints, no approval or confirmation needed. [Source: CSG, The Book of the States, 2000–2001 (2000): 34–37.]

BP—Governor's budget power: 5 = governor has full responsibility; legislature may not increase executive budget; 4 = governor has full responsibility, legislature can increase by special majority vote or subject to item veto; 3 = governor has full responsibility, legislature has unlimited power to change executive budget; 2 = governor shares responsibility, legislature has unlimited power to change executive budget; 1 = governor shares responsibility with other elected official, legislature has unlimited power to change executive budget. [Source: CSG, The Book of the States, 2000–2001 (2000): 20–21 and NCSL, "Limits on Authority of Legislature to Change Budget" (1998).]

VP—Governor's veto power: 5 = has item veto and a special majority vote of the legislature is needed to override a veto (3/5's of legislators elected or 2/3's of legislators present); 4 = has item veto with a majority of the legislators elected needed to override; 3 = has item veto with only a majority of the legislators present needed to override; 2 = no item veto, with a special legislative majority needed to override it; 1 = no item veto, only a simple legislative majority needed to override. [Source: CSG, The Book of the States, 2000–2001 (2000): 101–103.]

PC—Gubernatorial party control: The governor's party—5 = has a substantial majority (75% or more) in both houses of the legislature; 4 = has a simple majority in both houses (under 75%), or a substantial majority in one house and a simple majority in the other; 3 = split control in the legislature or a nonpartisan legislature; 2 = has a simple minority (25% or more) in both houses, or a simple minority in one and a substantial minority (under 25%) in the other; 1 = has a substantial minority in both houses. [Source: NCSL Web page and report on the 2001 legislative elections.]

Total—sum of the scores on the six individual indices. Score—total divided by 6 to keep 5-point scale.

Source: Thad Beyle (12/30/02). Available on the website, www.unc.edu/~beyle.

The states with the strongest governors in 2003, as measured by the Beyle scale, are Utah (4.2), Alaska (4.1), and New York (4.1). The weakest state was Vermont (2.5), with Alabama, Indiana, North Carolina, and Rhode Island all under 3.0. From 1960 to 2002 the overall institutional powers of governors, as measured by the Schlesinger-Beyle index, increased by 20 percent. The greatest increase was in veto power (61 percent). Budget power was the only category that showed a decline, but this was largely due to increased legislative powers, even though some governors had their budget authority increased.

Some governors with relatively weak constitutional powers, such as in Oklahoma and South Carolina, are helped by the fact that their party is especially strong in the legislature. In contrast, Pennsylvania's governor has very strong constitutional powers, but his legislative party is relatively weak.

Tenure Potential

As noted earlier in this chapter, governors historically have had short terms of office. In ten of the original thirteen states, the governor was limited to a term of one year. States moved first to two-year terms (by the 1840s) and gradually to four-year terms, which today can be found in forty-eight states. Recently, Arkansas and Rhode Island switched to four-year terms, leaving only New Hampshire and Vermont with two-year terms. As far as length of term is concerned, governors with four-year terms are high on tenure potential.

Another side of tenure potential is term limits, which has recently been an important issue with state legislators (see Chapter 5). Some states follow the model of the Twenty-second Amendment to the U.S. Constitution, which says that a person can be elected only twice to the presidency. In these states, governors can serve only two terms; for obvious reasons this type of term limitation is known as an absolute two-term limit. Other states limit the number of *consecutive* terms, usually two, so that it is possible to serve two four-year terms, leave the office for one term, and then serve another two terms. Of course, other examples of restraints can be found. Washington prohibits its governor from serving more than eight years out of a fourteen-year period. Utah allows three consecutive terms. Only Virginia has a one-term limit. Overall, governors are relatively equal in tenure potential: Thirty-eight states have four-year terms and some form of restraint on reelection. Nine four-year term states and the two states with two-year terms have no restraint of any kind on reelection. Of course, governors with four-year terms and no restraint on reelection have the highest tenure potential.

Tenure potential is a measure of the possible number of years a governor could stay in office. Why is tenure potential important to a governor's power? The ability to succeed oneself in office means that the governor will not become a **lame duck,** that is, have diminished power because he or she will soon leave office and cannot run again. Legislators cannot ignore a governor in the fourth year of his or her term if he or she may run for reelection and win and be around another four years. Shorter tenure lessens the ability of governors to attain leadership positions in groups such as the National Governors Association that can have an influence on public policy issues vital to the states. Also, a four-year term allows governors time to prove themselves: Policies enacted during their first two years (e.g., something controversial such as a tax increase) can be evaluated by reelection time two years later (whether any benefits have been produced by the tax increase).

In forty-nine states governors can have their terms ended by impeachment. Typically, the process is similar to presidential impeachment and removal, where action begins in the House and the Senate holds a trial in which a two-thirds vote is required for removal. Only four governors were impeached and removed in the twentieth century, the last in 1987 (Arizona). Governors also can have their tenure ended by recall (see Chapter 4), but only two governors, including Gray Davis of California in 2003, have been recalled.

Appointing Power

Governors' **appointing power** is strongest when they alone can name people to head (usually called a secretary or director) the more important agencies in the executive branch such as corrections, public safety, education, agriculture, environment, and economic development. Appointive power diminishes when one or two houses of the legislature must approve appointments or if the appointment is made by a department director. If the position is elective or is filled by a board or commission, then the governor's formal power is reduced.

Gubernatorial appointive power grew from weak beginnings, and it still varies greatly among states. Almost all appointments by the governor of Virginia must be approved by both houses of the legislature. In New Jersey governors appoint the secretary of state and other officials normally elected statewide, plus they appoint judges, county prosecutors, and hundreds of members of state commissions. There is variation not only among states but also within states. Even in states where the governor's appointing authority is strong, some appointments will need the approval of the senate and some will probably be made by a board or commission acting on its own.

A strong appointing power is important because governors free to appoint officials to top-level posts in the executive branch can select people whose political views are similar to theirs and who will feel a sense of obligation to the governor who appointed them. This will help a governor obtain action on his or her priorities. Although strong appointment power is the most effective means for governors to control state bureaucracy, most governors' power to appoint falls in the middle range on the Beyle scale.

Budgetary Power

Early in the twentieth century, most states instituted an **executive budget.** This means that the governor and officials appointed directly by the governor have full responsibility to *prepare* the state budget. Governors' staffs almost always include a budget director and professional assistants. As noted, the budget staff reviews requests for funds from all state agencies and, with the governor exercising final approval, prepares a budget that is then acted upon by the legislature. In only a few states, including Mississippi, Florida, and Texas, does the governor share responsibility for budget preparation with the state legislature or with other elected executive branch officials.

Even when governors have strong formal powers, they find that their control does not give them complete discretion in proposing where money should be spent because more than 50 percent of the budget must provide funds for specific purposes (such as gasoline taxes for highway construction and maintenance). Also, the growth of federal mandates has limited states' ability to control their expenditures.

Only in West Virginia does the governor have full budget power. In most other states legislatures have unlimited power to change it. In many states legislatures prepare their own budgets and in a few they draft the initial budget bill.[8] As noted in Chapter 5, state legislatures have been trying to assert more power in the budget process through oversight procedures.

Veto Power

Governors are participants in the legislative process because they must sign bills passed by the legislature before they can become state law. After voters in North Carolina approved a veto referendum in 1996, all governors now have the power to veto legislation. Curiously, as of 2002, no veto had been cast by the governor of North Carolina. Governors **veto** a bill by returning it to the legislature unsigned, along with their objections. The veto makes the governor a participant in the legislative process. If the legislature votes to override a veto, the bill becomes law without the governor's signature.

Budget problems, growing out of the Great Depression, brought an expansion of veto power that gave governors a way to avoid the difficult choice of accepting or rejecting an entire appropriations bill. The power of the **item veto** permits governors in forty-three states to veto individual items in appropriation bills. Governors in eleven states have a reduction veto for reducing specific items in appropriations bills without vetoing the line item entirely. In fifteen states governors can veto bills but indicate legislative changes that would make them acceptable. If the legislature agrees, then the governor will sign the bills. Like the president, governors in fifteen states can use a **pocket veto:** They do not take any action on a bill near the end of a legislative session, and then if the legislature adjourns the bill is considered vetoed.

An extreme example of the veto power was found in Wisconsin where Republican Governor Tommy Thompson (1987–2001), taking literally his constitutional power to veto appropriation bills "in whole or in part," changed the meaning of sentences by vetoing words such as "shall" and "not." Thompson even struck out individual letters to make new words, and new laws. Local commentators labeled this the "Vanna White veto" (named after Vanna White, who appears on the television show "Wheel of Fortune"). In the early 1990s a federal court found the partial veto "quirky," but not unconstitutional. However, a constitutional amendment has somewhat lessened the veto power of the governor in Wisconsin. As state legislatures have become stronger policy making bodies, able to challenge the governor on nearly every issue, the use of the item veto has increased. As a result, governors are more likely to veto bills to remove policy directives than to impose fiscal restraint. Overuse of the item veto can wreck havoc with legislative appropriations, and it greatly increases formal confrontations between governors and legislatures.

Typically, the governor's veto must be overridden by at least a two-thirds vote of the elected membership of both houses of the legislature (some states specify two-thirds of the members present on an override vote rather than elected membership). This means that the governor's veto will be sustained if he or she can persuade only a small percentage of the legislators in one house not to vote to override. A two-thirds vote is normally required to override an item veto.

Governor Tommy Thompson holds a record with more than 1,500 partial vetoes in his first eight years in office.[9] Although the number of vetoes across the country has increased a little in recent years, governors veto only about 5 percent of the bills that pass the legislature, and very few (5 percent) of these vetoes are overridden by the legislature. The number of vetoes increases dramatically if the governor's office and legislature are controlled by different parties. James Thompson, Republican governor of Illinois (1977–1991), vetoed one out of every three bills sent to him by a Democratic legislature. Governor Pete Wilson (1991–1999) of California vetoed about 20 percent of all bills sent to him and none was overridden. At the other extreme, in 1992–1993 the governor of Tennessee signed all bills sent to him.[10] In most states, if the governor's party has at least one-third of the seats, it is unlikely that vetoes will be overridden. As legislatures have become more assertive in the last 20 years, the percentage of vetoes overridden has increased.

Often a governor's threat of a veto can cause legislators to change the content of a bill before they finish acting on it. Unfortunately, no statistics are compiled on the number of times governors threaten to veto and with what success, but it is another tool a skillful governor can use to persuade legislators to modify bills so that they are more to the governor's liking.

Separately Elected Officials

Although states have steadily enacted reforms to reduce the number of separately elected officials, most continue to elect about a half dozen statewide officials plus the governor. These range from attorneys general in forty-three states to such positions as the heads of agriculture, education, and insurance in a few states. Problems arise when separately elected officials have partisan policy differences with the governor and choose to pursue their own agendas.

Only five states employ the presidential model in which only the governor and lieutenant governor are elected statewide. As with many other issues of gubernatorial power, the two newest states, Alaska and Hawaii, give their governor strong authority and follow the presidential model of statewide elections. At the other extreme, Beyle reports that in eight states, typically in the South, seven or more process and major policy officials are elected.

Party Control

Increasingly, voters have elected a governor of one party and the majority of at least one legislative chamber of the other party. Similar to politics at the national level, divided party control can lead to stalemated state government when, as noted, the governor's use of the veto increases. However, in most cases political scientists have found that divided government does not reduce legislative productivity.[11] Voters seem to like the restraint that divided government brings and, as noted in Chapter 3, governors can overcome partisan differences by their willingness to negotiate and compromise with legislative leaders.

Other governors seem to relish confrontation. In his first term, New Mexico's Republican governor, Gary Johnson, vetoed about half the 400 bills passed by the Democratically controlled legislature. Johnson cut the state budget unilaterally and made it clear he did not intend to compromise with anyone in state government. In 1996, Alan Ehrenhalt stated, "The result (of Johnson's actions) has been ineffectual administration, a string of overridden vetoes, and a two-year shouting match between the governor and the legislature."[12] In 1998 Johnson was reelected with 54 percent of the vote, while Democrats controlled the senate 25–17 and the house 42–28. After being reelected, he said, "You have not elected a kinder, gentler Johnson when it comes to the legislature." Still, even Johnson admitted his policy accomplishments were limited and that "none of my good ideas get anywhere." Term-limited, Johnson left office in 2003.

Of course, Independent and third-party governors (as in Alaska, Connecticut, Maine, and Minnesota in the 1990s) always must deal with legislatures controlled by opposition political forces. Some of them, like Lowell Weicker of Connecticut (1991–1994) have been very effective legislative leaders. Others may be less adroit.

Following Ross Perot's bids for president in 1992 and 1996, Jesse Ventura ran for governor of Minnesota in 1998 on the Reform Party ticket. He was elected with 37 percent of the vote, getting strong support from young voters and those who previously had not been politically active. The colorful former professional wrestler had to deal with a legislature in which party control of the house and senate was split between Democrats and Republicans. Early in 2000 Ventura broke from the Reform Party to become an Independent. Then with his popularity declining, he chose not to run for reelection in 2002. With the 2002 election of a Republican in Minnesota and a Democrat in Maine, all governors represented one of the two major parties.

ROLES OF THE GOVERNOR

Chief Legislator

Identifying formal powers of governors is important, but it does not reveal what happens when men and women use these powers during their tenure, especially in their relationship with the legislative branch where only one of the formal powers—the veto—can be used directly. Also, lists of formal powers measure only *potential* effectiveness. Bad economic times, for example, may seriously limit the initiatives taken by a governor, even though he or she may have considerable formal power. But the most effective opposition to a governor's efforts to change policies resides right in the capitol building with the governor—the state legislature. Governors must persuade the legislature that what they want to accomplish is what the legislature, or at least a majority of its members, should want to accomplish also. The size of governors' margins of victory and their personal style (their style of speaking and how well they fit the state's political culture) help governors control the legislature and gain public support.

Like the president, governors bring a different political perspective to office than do legislators. Unlike individual legislators, governors represent the entire state and they are full-time public officials. Although power may be diffused among 100 legislators in most states, it is centralized in the governor.

Alan Rosenthal suggests a number of additional powers, some formal and some informal, that contribute to a governor's success as a legislative leader: the power of initiation, the power of publicity, and the power of party.[13] Informal powers are not found in constitutional or statutory law. **Informal powers** refer to things such as the skill a governor brings to negotiating and bargaining and the ability to communicate through the media.[14] In many cases governors with weak formal powers can be strong leaders in their states. This is accomplished by a combination of personal skills of persuasion that enable governors to lead their legislatures, skillfully manage administrative tasks, and effectively appeal to the public.

State constitutions authorize governors to recommend measures to the legislature that they think should become law. This may seem to be rather innocuous, but it is the basis of the power of initiation. Initiation is the ability to set the policy agenda for the state, that is, to identify those issues that need to be addressed first. Governors begin the process of setting the agenda in their inaugural address, delivered at the start of their term. In this address governors can set out broad themes and goals for their new administration and, because of media attention to the event, can communicate to the people. Annual "state of the state" messages from the governor to the legislature are more specific than inaugural addresses. These messages contain the governor's priorities for the upcoming legislative session and are referred to as the governor's legislative program. These proposals are general statements that will have to be drafted into bills and introduced by legislators, usually members of the leadership, and then considered by both houses. The fact that a bill is part of the governor's legislative program guarantees that it will receive serious consideration by the legislature and, in most cases, increases the likelihood that the bill will become law. Governors may also focus attention on a particular issue by calling the legislature into special session to deal with politically difficult problems. Because many legislatures meet for short regular sessions, the ability to call members back into session gives governors a means of exerting considerable pressure on legislators who are reluctant to face an issue.

Governors, such as George Pataki of New York, tend to be most effective when they limit the number of their legislative priorities. For example, each legislative session, Zell Miller of Georgia (1991–1998) tried to present three or four proposals that had strong public support. In contrast, Mario Cuomo of New York proposed about 150 measures in 1989. Cuomo laid out an ambitious agenda and then abandoned it.[15]

Governors can influence the agenda through the creation of commissions or task forces to study a problem and make recommendations to solve it. Members of this type of commission are appointed by the governor and represent the governor's office and relevant interest groups. They may also contain key legislators and distinguished private citizens. Commission recommendations usually support the policy direction the governor wants to take: After all, it is the governor who created the commission. Because the commission works over several months, it is quite likely that it will attract media attention, which also may create some public support for its final product. In addition, members of the commission can be helpful in lobbying for legislative approval of the recommendations. The commission approach sounds easy, but it takes a skillful governor to balance the membership so that it is not viewed as a group that will simply get out the rubber stamp and "approve" everything the governor wants. If this is the case, the commission will be viewed as too one-sided, and it will be of little help in gaining legislative support of the governor's ideas. Rosenthal notes that commissions were popular in many public education reforms in the 1980s. Bill Clinton, as governor of Arkansas, used recommendations from a legislatively created committee on educational standards, chaired by his wife, Hillary Rodham Clinton, to pass a tax increase to pay for improvements in primary and secondary education.[16]

The power of publicity is similar to the power of initiation in that it sounds easy to do. Every governor should simply go directly to the public and, with public backing, get most everything he or she wants through the legislature. But it is not that easy, even if governors have the requisite communication skills. Rosenthal cautions that governors cannot "make use of this power on each and every issue; to do so would be self-defeating, for at some point they would no longer be taken seriously by the press or public."[17] Governors cannot continuously try to drum up public support and expect that the public will always respond. Still, governors are much more effective than legislators in getting media attention.

In a manner similar to the president, all governors are party leaders, though not in the sense that they occupy a formal position in their party's organization. Rather, they are the informal head of their party by virtue of the fact that they occupy the highest elected position in the state. At one time governors working with the chairperson of their state party could maintain party discipline in the legislature through the use of patronage appointments to fill state jobs and the promise of help from the party in primary and general elections. But those days are long gone in most states: Patronage appointments are fewer, and candidates frequently run for the legislature without the help of anyone in their party.

Not too long ago governors often controlled the selection of legislative leaders. One extreme example was that before 1966 the governor of Georgia picked the house speaker and committee heads. In Louisiana, legislative leaders still are selected with the governor's consent.[18]

Legislators are more likely to support governors of their own party and oppose governors who belong to the other party. Members of the party share a common association, frequently share similar ideas on the role of government, and sometimes share specific policy preferences.[19] Even with more and more legislative candidates running their own campaigns, a governor who runs strongly at the top of the ticket in the general election can pull some of the party's candidates along to victory. And after the election is over, legislators in the governor's party have some incentive to support the governor's proposals so that he or she is able to do something other than squabble with the legislature, which will drive down the governor's popularity and could harm the reelection chances of the legislators as well as the governor. It is in their interests to have their governor look good to the public. On the other hand, if the governor's popularity drops, party support can quickly erode.

Chief of State

As chief of state, the governor performs a variety of ceremonial functions and acts as official spokesperson for the people of the state. Ceremonial functions include dedicating new highways and bridges, attending funerals and weddings, greeting distinguished visitors to the state capitol, proclaiming special days or weeks, and attending football games. Although much of this activity appears trivial and undoubtedly bores many governors, it does reap political rewards in terms of publicity and image building. Next to working with the legislature, ceremonial duties are the most time-consuming activity for most governors.

In this role of official spokesperson, the governor can speak in a highly moralistic tone. This approach was effective in the area of civil rights when governors were able to promote social justice by their actions as well as by their words. For example, in his inaugural speech, Governor Jimmy Carter of Georgia (1971–1975) stated, "I say to you quite frankly that the time for racial discrimination is over." Carter went on to appoint African Americans to important positions in state government and to place a portrait of Martin Luther King, Jr., in the statehouse.

Governors act as economic advocates for their states, expending time and energy to lure business and manufacturing concerns from other states and to encourage plant investment from foreign corporations. At the urging of governors, legislatures have offered major economic concessions to foreign automobile manufacturers to build assembly plants in their states.

Following President Clinton's controversial pardons as he left office, there has been more scrutiny of gubernatorial **clemency orders.** Some 2,000 orders are issued annually by governors. They include **pardons** that release a person convicted of a crime from the legal penalties, and commutations that reduce the severity of punishment for a crime. Most of the controversial actions are done as governors prepare to leave office and/or they involve clemency that appears to have been motivated by friendship or political advantage. Governors in about two-thirds of the states have broad authority to issue pardons. In the other states gubernatorial power is shared with a state clemency board or exercised by a board whose members are appointed by the governor.

As noted in the chapter-opening story, in 2003 outgoing Governor George Ryan of Illinois pardoned four condemned men outright and commuted the sentences of the remaining 164 men and four women on death row. Ryan was the fourth governor in American history to empty death row as he departed office, but the numbers involved in Illinois dwarfed all other clemency actions.

Commander-in-Chief

Although governors do not command a navy with nuclear-powered submarines or an air force with intercontinental ballistic missiles, they do have a commander-in-chief role as head of their state's National Guard (formerly called the state militia) until it is called into service by the president. The U.S. Constitution provides for a cooperative system in which states appoint officers (the state adjutant general is their commander) and Congress organizes, arms, and finances the Guard. Since 1916, the former militias have been organized as an auxiliary of the regular army subject to substantial national control. As its civilian commander-in-chief, the governor may call the Guard into service for such emergencies as floods, tornadoes, or urban riots. The president may also call the Guard into service, at which time state control ends. Control of the Guard allowed some governors to become involved in foreign affairs by refusing to send their state troops to Central America for training exercises in 1986. In response, Congress passed a bill to prohibit governors from interfering with troop deployment overseas.

The record of the Guard in responding to civil disturbances has ranged from adequate to disastrous. Prior to World War II, the Guard often was used brutally to break up racial disturbances, labor strikes, and prison riots. Since then the most noteworthy incident occurred in Ohio in 1970 when Ohio National Guardsmen killed four students and injured others in responding to a demonstration against the Vietnam War at Kent State University. On a more positive note, the Guard has been effective (often invaluable) when dealing with natural disasters. Also, after two days of rioting in Los Angeles in 1992, when the Los Angeles police clearly had lost control of the situation, Guardsmen were posted on nearly every corner, and looting quickly diminished.

Chief Administrator

As chief administrator, the governor is responsible for the management of all state administrative agencies. As noted, the governor's administrative authority in the early part of the twentieth century was not equal to the responsibility associated with a person who is a chief executive. Agencies in the executive branch were actually controlled by boards or commissions with several members. This meant that, if a governor wanted an agency to take some action, he or she would first have to convince the members of the board, because it was the board that had direct control over the agency's activities. This awkward administrative arrangement occurs less frequently today because administrative efficiency reforms have eliminated boards and commissions and reduced the number of agencies by consolidating them into a smaller number of departments. Nearly all states have a **cabinet** form of executive branch organization that concentrates authority and responsibility in the hands of the governor and creates a cabinet of department secretaries appointed by the governor who individually administer a department and collectively advise the governor. Cabinet size varies from thirty-eight in Arizona to six in Vermont.

Because of the increasing complexity of state government and the ever-broadening responsibilities of their office, governors have surrounded themselves with expanding numbers of *staff personnel* who provide both political and administrative assistance. In a large state a governor's staff of perhaps 100 people will include a press secretary, an executive secretary, a legal adviser, a speechwriter, a director of the budget, a commissioner of administration, and others assigned by the political party. Some staff will work as liaison with state, local, and federal agencies and as liaison to the state legislature to help guide the governor's program through the legislative process. Staff personnel tend to be young (in their thirties) and politically ambitious. Many are lawyers, and most staff members previously worked in the governor's campaign or in the campaigns of other candidates in their party.

In addition to serving in an administrative capacity, the governor's staff provides other more political services. The staff:

1. Serves as a research office to provide information and to help shape the governor's position on a wide range of policy issues
2. Serves as public relations specialists to do such things as write press releases and keep the governor posted on political developments that may affect how citizens perceive the governor
3. Handles the important tasks of answering the mail, controlling the governor's schedule, and determining who sees the governor

As with the president, the governor must guard against the dangers of an overprotective staff that isolates him or her from the world beyond the office. According to Martha Wagner Weinberg, reformers have often suggested that if governors would only adopt modern business management techniques, they would be able to manage public affairs much more effectively.[20] She believes, however, that this assumption overlooks some major differences between governors and private-sector chief executives. The governor's management task is much more difficult because the environment in which his or her decisions are made is more complex and less controllable. Even compared with large private businesses, the operations of states such as New York and California, or even Nebraska, are much more complex in terms of budget, number of personnel, and variety of functions.

Differences exist between managing state government and private enterprise that relate more directly to the political process. Governors must share power with legislative and judicial branches, and they must operate with a federal system in which the national government has substantial power. In addition, governors constantly keep in mind how management decisions might affect their future political aspirations.

ADMINISTRATION OF STATE AND LOCAL GOVERNMENT

As discussed in Chapter 1, the scope of state government activities has increased greatly during the twentieth century. As a result, state and local payrolls and numbers of employees now far outstrip those of the federal government. State government employees increased from less than 1 million in 1950 to about 5 million in 2000. There are about 3 million civilian federal employees. Bureaucrats are important because they implement policies that often have been approved by the legislature in skeletal form. As a result, bureaucrats have considerable discretion in the day-to-day administration of programs. This expansion of **bureaucracy** has placed increasing burdens of responsibility on governors and mayors, who historically have been denied strong powers as chief administrators. As noted, and as will be discussed later in this chapter, states have responded by giving governors control of budget preparation and the power to appoint and remove officials. In cities, charters have been amended to give mayors similar powers, and many cities have created the post of city manager.

Reorganization of Government

Despite changes, governors continue to be limited as administrators by the fragmented nature of state government. Most states failed to develop well-organized administrative structures because of the piecemeal growth of bureaucracy. As new functions were given to the states, the easiest response was to create a new state agency as visible proof to concerned citizens and interest groups that the state was "doing something" about the problem. Under these circumstances, the duties of each agency were not clearly defined, and the jurisdiction of new agencies often overlapped with that of already established agencies. Large cities had similar problems of fragmented organization. However, city reform came earlier than did state reform because of the adoption of strong-mayor–council and council-manager plans at the beginning of this century.

Because of the desire to take politics out of state government, many agencies were placed under the control of boards and commissions that acted independently of the governor. Agencies and departments performing similar tasks were nevertheless separated from one another with no one to serve as a coordinator. Communication between agencies was limited, and it was difficult for the governor or the legislature to know what the agencies were doing or who was responsible for their actions. Mergers were opposed by bureaucrats who sought to protect their jobs and by interest groups that were being aided by agencies they had helped create. At their peak in the 1950s, there were more than 100 boards, commissions, and departments in many states. There were even stories of dead men being appointed to serve on obscure boards.

The movement for administrative reform began in the 1890s but did not take hold in state government until after 1920, when administrative **reorganization** in Illinois under Governor Frank Lowden became known around the country. State reorganization commissions were appointed in several states, although there were few instances of substantial reform. The basic goal of the early reformers was to reduce the number of agencies and bring them more directly under the control of the governor. There was a general attempt to upgrade the bureaucracy by creating civil service commissions for merit-appointment and by developing the executive budget. Following World War II and the report of the **Hoover Commission** on the federal level, there was a revival of interest in structural reorganization.

Comprehensive reorganization has occurred recently in Iowa and South Carolina. For example, in 1993 South Carolina reduced the number of state agencies from seventy-nine to seventeen and eliminated many boards and commissions.[21] Typically, reform has been more incremental, with states collapsing boards and commissions into a cabinet model similar to that used by the president.

Since the mid-1970s, reorganization has been the most common response to correcting the problems of bureaucracy. Half the states completed major administrative overhauls from 1965 to 1990, some eliminating as many as 80 percent of their agencies.[22] Typically states consolidate several similar agencies into one larger functional unit, such as transportation or welfare. The goal is to reduce duplication of services and to centralize administration in the hands of fewer department heads. In turn, governors are strengthened by giving them the power to appoint the heads of these reorganized superagencies. Reformers contend that these changes will produce more effective service delivery and that they will increase the accountability of bureaucrats to the public. As Richard C. Elling notes, reorganization is usually supported by governors, the media, and "good-government" groups that long have criticized the lack of businesslike practices in government.

Because state administration is a highly *politicized* process, these apparently logical goals of centralization have met with strong resistance in virtually every state. Interest groups often prefer separation because of the strong control they have been able to maintain over state agencies. State legislators are able to use separate agencies to their political advantage, and they are inherently suspicious of moves to strengthen governors. Finally, by requiring specific allocation of matching funds to support categorical grants, federal grants-in-aid have encouraged the establishment of separate agencies.

Reorganization seldom has resulted in saving states money.[23] However, reorganizers argue that the main benefits will be more efficiency and more effective service delivery. Yet even here studies have shown that some services are provided best by small agencies in which a particular function is not subordinated to the main activities of the larger department. Even collegial administration (organizations headed by boards or commissions) may be as effective as single-headed departments. After his study of Texas, where collegial administration is very common, Charles Goodsell concluded that collegial administration has two major positive justifications.[24] It can improve the demographic and geographic representation of administration, and it has the ability to absorb political heat because of its representativeness. Goodsell believes that both legislators and career bureaucrats can "get off the hook" from constituent or interest-group demands by referring critics to the independence of boards or commissions. Governors can sidestep attacks by arguing that a problem is out of their hands.

Clearly, reorganization does not always lead to greater efficiency or accountability. Centralization of authority may not work well for all organizations. Still, the extreme decentralization of state government, often bordering on chaos, has led to a lack of accountability, and to the extent that problems remain, good-government groups will continue to push for reorganization. Politically, it is in the best interest of governors to be able to consolidate their power through reorganization plans. Most academic observers conclude that the quality of administration has improved significantly, enabling states to respond to new demands placed on them by the devolution of authority from the national government.[25]

Elling has referred to government reform in the late twentieth century as "orthodox reorganization."[26] Orthodox reorganization has been challenged by those who want to "reinvent" government. To them, even reformed bureaucracy is inflexible and ineffective. As we will see later in this chapter, their approach is to replace bureaucratic government rather than to reform it.

Personnel Practices

The personnel systems of government agencies often affect their culture and expectations of employee behavior. Some agencies may discourage awarding middle-management positions to outsiders; others encourage transfers with experience in other types of organizations. When there is a strong preference to promote from within the agency, the bureaucrats who attain supervisory posts tend to be more rigid and less open to new ideas than are relative newcomers to the agency.

An agency's culture (and its policy orientation) is influenced by the **professional ideology** of its employees. For example, many social workers continue to place a strong emphasis on working with individual clients, whereas reformers contend that group political action is a more effective way to deal with the problems of the poor. In addition, professional codes of conduct may serve as a check on the abuse of administrative power.

As in any organization, newly hired employees in government undergo a period of socialization, in which they learn how they are expected to act within the framework of their agency's culture. Those who deviate from established norms usually encounter difficulty in working with their peers, and they may be denied promotions by their superiors. Although some agencies are program-oriented and encourage innovation, many are conservative and oppose change.

Personnel practices also include determining the kinds of people selected for government positions. Since the 1960s, the use of **affirmative action** programs has led to increased hiring of women and minorities in government agencies. Under affirmative action special efforts are made to recruit, hire, and retain employees from groups of people that in the past have been discriminated against and have been underrepresented among government workers. The goal is to make the bureaucracy representative of the sexual, racial, and ethnic groups in the state or community.

In the past, ethnic background and/or political party connections played a major role in creating informal hiring qualifications that effectively screened applicants for jobs in many cities. This tended to exclude women and persons of color. Currently, although women and racial minority employees often are concentrated in certain areas such as social services, and they are less likely than white men to hold administrative posts, the percentage of women and minorities in government is significantly higher than in the private sector. Much of this is due to the use of affirmative action programs.

By the mid-1990s, opposition to affirmative action had become evident in several states. Voters in California (1996) and Washington State (1998) approved statewide initiatives that ended affirmative action in state employment practices. In 2000 the "One Florida" program, supported by Governor Jeb Bush, ended consideration of race in university admissions and state contracts. A federal Court of Appeals decision in 1996 (*Hopwood v. University of Texas Law School*) stopped an affirmative action admissions program, rejecting the notion of diversity as a compelling state interest.

However, in 2003 the Supreme Court found that there was a "compelling state interest" in racial diversity on college campuses, upholding an affirmative action program at the University of Michigan law school (*Grutter v. Bollinger*). The five-member majority supported a "highly individualized, holistic review of each applicant's file" in which race can be used as a factor in admissions. At the same time, the Court by a 6–3 vote struck down a more "mechanical" affirmative action program used by the University of Michigan undergraduate college that awarded 20 points on a scale of 150 (100 points were needed for admission) for membership in an underrepresented minority group.

The majority in *Grutter v. Bollinger* clearly was speaking to the broader society—the military, business, and government—in support of affirmative action programs. A *New York Times*/CBS poll earlier in 2003 found that a majority of Americans supported the concept of affirmative action, but they opposed programs that resembled quotas. Perhaps most would agree with Justice O'Connor's concluding comments in the Michigan law school opinion that affirmative action should "no longer be necessary" twenty-five years from now.

Merit Systems

The value of patronage began to decline as urban residents progressed to better paying jobs in private business and when the reform movement began to press for a **merit system** of civil service. Reformers argued that if workers were appointed by civil service commissions that developed competitive examinations, the system would be insulated from partisan politics and it would lead to "a competent corps of politically neutral civil servants."[27]

Elling notes that states moved slowly to implement civil service reform. It was not until the late 1930s that states were required by the federal government to put employees whose salaries were partially paid by federal grant funds under merit arrangements. Where machines remained in operation, cities moved even more slowly to institute merit appointment. Virtually all states have merit systems for at least 20 percent of their workers and in nearly two-thirds of the states almost all workers are included.

Civil service systems have been broadly criticized in recent years. Although the bureaucratic model worked well to limit specific abuses before World War II, it has created new problems for contemporary government. In the 1930s government employees were not unionized, and courts had not acted to protect workers from wrongful discharge. Much of what civil service was designed to prevent has been ruled illegal or made unlikely to happen by collective bargaining agreements.

Osborne and Graebler contend that civil service rules can hamstring most personnel managers.[28] Unlike private businesses, where interviews and references are used to make hiring decisions, governments often must take the person with the highest score or one of the top three scorers on written examinations, even though they may otherwise be unsuited for the position. Because the process takes so long, the high scorers may accept another job during the six months or so that it takes between testing and hiring. Job classifications, which set pay levels, are determined by how long employees have worked, not by how well they have performed. When employees reach the top of their pay range, they cannot earn more money unless they are promoted into a new classification.

Reinventing government advocates also oppose merit pay systems, arguing that organizations should encourage employees to work together in teams and therefore should provide bonuses for quality group performance. To reward individuals with merit pay would be counterproductive.

Many civil service problems are being addressed by states and cities. The testing process has been streamlined. Questions have been revised to relate more closely to job skills, and departments have been given more freedom to choose among high-scoring candidates. Several states have established "broadband" job classifications in which hundreds of categories are greatly reduced with distinctions made between levels of expertise, or *bands*. As part of the reorganization process, management of the civil service system in most states has been shifted from semi-independent commissions to personnel departments whose heads are appointed by the governor. Similar to changes in the federal government, several states have established a senior executive level in which employees are given less job security but their pay and promotion are based on merit performance. Civil service systems have been abolished in some cities.

Several states have tried to abolish their civil service systems, but strong opposition from labor unions, as in Massachusetts, is a major reason why reform has failed. The most drastic change came when Georgia ended civil service for all employees hired after July 1, 1996. Governor Zell Miller pushed for the change as a way to make the governor more responsible to citizens.[29] The new system was designed to give more flexibility to hire and fire state workers and provide rewards for high-performance service. In 2001, Florida joined Georgia in eliminating most civil service protection for executive-branch employees. Texas has never had a centralized civil service system.

Collective Bargaining

As in the private sector, a group of government employees votes to unionize and usually affiliates with a national union. The bargaining unit then negotiates a master contract that spells out such matters as pay, hours, fringe benefits, and grievance procedures. Most agreements stress seniority rights, meaning that longtime employees are protected from staff reductions. Evidence from across the country suggests that public employee unions have helped increase wages by about 5 percent. They also have helped workers secure better health care and pension benefits. However, public employee unions present a potential threat to merit systems because of their emphasis on seniority. Moreover, their concern for job security may lead unions to oppose changes in personnel rules dealing with hiring and grievance procedures.

Unions often are blamed for protecting the incompetent. Although public employee unions clearly seek to protect job security, **collective bargaining** contracts explain only a small part of the problem as about 70 percent of state workers and 55 percent of city workers are not members of unions. The major reason why it is difficult to fire public employees is that they are protected by a wide range of constitutional guarantees.[30] Oftentimes management is at fault for failing to document an employee's performance, and there is good reason to guard against arbitrary or capricious decisions to fire people.

Only about 10 percent of government employees were unionized in 1960, but nearly one-third were members of collective bargaining units by the mid-1970s. About 60 percent of police were unionized by 1975. These increases occurred because of employee demand, weak employer resistance, the passage of protective legislation, and rulings from the Supreme Court supporting the right of government employees to join unions. Public unionization has leveled off since the mid-1970s as a result of changes in the distribution of public employees, more management resistance, and a decrease in inter-union competition in organizing campaigns. In the 1980s and 1990s public opinion turned against unions, and increasing use of privatization eliminated some public jobs. Recent downsizing has further weakened the bargaining power of unions.

Currently about 80 percent of the states permit collective bargaining in at least one category of public employment. Unionization is most likely to occur in northeastern and Great Lakes states, where private sector unions are strongest. In Connecticut and New York, more than 80 percent of state employees are in bargaining units. At the other extreme, there are about a dozen states (all in the South and West) where no state employees are in bargaining units. The most prominent organizations are the National Educational Association; the American Federation of Teachers; and the American Federation of State, County, and Municipal Employees, which ranks second behind the Teamsters as the largest labor union in the United States. Organizational activities have been particularly successful in large cities. Just over 50 percent of all city firefighters belong to unions, and nearly 30 percent of public hospital workers are unionized. This compares to about 10 percent unionization in private industry.

Although strikes by public employees are illegal in most states, job actions have occurred in many cities when groups such as firefighters and police officers have "sick-ins" (e.g., cases of the "blue flu") as a means of expressing their demands. In many cases, state law stipulates that public employee labor disputes must go to arbitration.

Budgeting

State budget preparations operate in a manner similar to the congressional process. They are executive-centered with responsibility for formulation fixed in an office of budget and management, whose head is appointed by the governor. Governors form a budget as a spending and policy document and send it to the legislature for review and adoption. Since the 1970s legislatures, like Congress, have added staff and have used computerized information systems. Because of their skilled staff, many legislatures are able to develop independent sources of financial information.[31] As a result, appropriations committees and their subcommittees now are able to analyze governors' budgets much more carefully by using their own revenue projections. Hearings are held and negotiations proceed with the governor's office before the budget moves to the house and senate for approval. All states except Vermont require that their budget be balanced at some stage of its preparation or on final passage. Fifty years ago nearly all states prepared a biennial budget, but today thirty-eight states follow the national pattern of annual budgeting. Unlike the federal budget, where large items are budgeted in lump sums, most state budgets are written in specific, line-item form.[32]

As noted in Chapter 1, even newer, more sophisticated budgeting systems in many states failed to forecast accurately the revenue that would be available to governments in 2002 and 2003. This was because the economic recession and federal government policies unexpectedly resulted in less money coming into state coffers.

Effective legislative or executive administrative oversight is strongly influenced by the type of budget process that the state employs. **Incremental budgeting**—the traditional system—provides little opportunity for overall review or program evaluation. Budgeting is based on last year's figures, which were the result of previous political compromises. Agencies make requests for a few new programs, and they routinely overstate the amount of money they need. Governors make some cuts and legislators cut some more. As a result, old programs are seldom reviewed, little innovation occurs, legislators can point to their efforts to keep spending down, and agencies usually get about what they need to run their programs.

In the 1960s, some states and cities attempted to adopt a **program-planning-budgeting system (PPBS),** which was modeled after budgeting in the U.S. Department of Defense. Instead of having to justify specific line items in their budget requests (as in traditional budgeting), under PPBS departments were forced to justify appropriation requests in terms of program objectives. That is, they linked the political ends of their programs to economic means.

Program-planning-budgeting was a very time-consuming process that required accurate data on program efficiency and impact. In the highly political environment of state government, it faced strong opposition from legislators and from interest groups who benefited from incremental budgeting.

Although PPBS was abandoned in the 1970s, experiments with it have produced some valuable spin-off benefits to budgeting. One of the most publicized has been **zero-based budgeting (ZBB),** in which each department must justify all appropriations items each year. The budget is broken down into units, called decision packages, prepared by managers at each level, that cover every existing proposed activity of each department. This approach encourages greater policy orientation, because out-of-date programs are dropped instead of being continued as existing budget items that are not questioned once they become part of a department's established budget. In some cases, departments rank their programs in order of priority and set performance levels for all programs.

Even at its high point in the 1970s and early 1980s, ZBB was less widely adopted than program-planning-budgeting. It was used by Governor Jimmy Carter in Georgia, in Delaware and New Jersey, and in a number of cities, especially in the West. Like PPBS, ZBB continues to be used in modified forms. For example, the governor of Iowa in the early 1990s proposed a complete budget review of every department on a five-year cycle. Aaron Wildavsky noted that in all cases the "zero" is ignored and the base grows to 80 or 90 percent of the last year's budget.[33] As this happens, the process reverts to incremental budgeting.

Today nearly all states require some kind of performance budgeting in which governments first decide what they want to accomplish and then develop their budgets. Programs then are evaluated on the basis of work performance—are objectives being accomplished?—and on how efficiently services are being provided on a per-unit cost basis. This means the focus is on outcomes, or results, of programs. Traditionally, budgeting has focused on inputs—"how much money is spent, how many people are served, what services each person received."[34] This was done because it is much more difficult to measure results. Performance evaluation may also include the level of citizen satisfaction with the program—are streets clean, are people treated with respect by the police?

Urban Bureaucracy

So far we have focused on the administration of state government and the roles of governors and legislators. However, much of what was said about the nature of bureaucracy and about personnel practices applies equally to state and local governments. The leadership role of mayors is discussed at the end of this chapter.

As noted in Chapter 3, much of the impetus for reform and the move to bureaucratic government in the late nineteenth century was prompted by the abuses of urban political machines. However, we also have argued that the adoption of these reforms led to a number of unintended consequences, including an impersonal, middle-class bias in the delivery of government services. As a result, city residents found few bureaucrats who were responsive to their needs. Political scientist Theodore Lowi speaks of the "new machines"—powerful urban service bureaucracies protected by civil service rules, receiving substantial amounts of money from federal and state sources, and thus not responsible to elected city officials or to the general public.[35]

Control of urban government also is made difficult because many street-level bureaucrats have broad discretion in how they perform their jobs. Contrary to what the hierarchical model suggests, people at the bottom of the bureaucracy—those who deal directly with the public—effectively make policy by deciding how public services will be dispensed. As Bernard Ross and Myron Levine point out, because they often are understaffed and must make quick decisions, bureaucrats such as police officers and welfare workers often use shortcuts, including categorizing clients or rationing services to them. Police look for the "wrong" type of person in a neighborhood, and welfare clients often have to wait a long time before receiving services.[36] Bureaucrats see clients in terms of group identification, but citizens seek personal attention to their problems.

The success of many urban programs rests with how well lower-level bureaucrats perform their jobs and how well their supervisors monitor their activities. Major problems include efficiency (how much it costs to produce a service), effectiveness (how well government is able to meet the objectives or goals of its programs), and equity (to what extent services are provided fairly to all residents).

As the number of city managers and strong mayors has grown, city budget making has become more executive-centered. As a result, the budget process in cities is similar to that at the state level—the mayor has a staff office that prepares the budget, the proposed budget is presented to the council for review, interest groups have an opportunity to comment on it, and finally the budget is enacted by the council. While the most common approach is incremental budgeting, many cities have been at the forefront of performance budgeting. As at the state level, city budgets must be balanced.

Criticism of service levels and budget procedures have led to a host of proposals for alternative ways to provide urban services. We turn to some of those in the next section.

Reinventing Government

Best-selling authors David Osborne and Ted Graebler point out that the last times we "reinvented" government in the United States were during the Progressive era early in this century and again in the New Deal of the 1930s. Earlier we evaluated the impact of Progressive reforms on state and local government. Now that we are in a **postindustrial,** knowledge-based, global economy, Osborne and Graebler believe it is time to make major changes in government at all levels.[37] They use the term **"entrepreneurial government"** to describe a new model that uses resources in different ways to maximize productivity and effectiveness. In this new order, the bureaucratic model would be replaced by more flexible, responsive organizations that empower citizens rather than serve them.

Entrepreneurial governments, which are operating to various degrees in many cities across the country, function on the basis of several main principles. In their ideal form, entrepreneurial governments act in the following ways. They encourage competition among service providers by privatizing services or contracting them out. They empower citizens by encouraging them to take control of services through such means as public housing resident advisory boards, ballot initiatives, and community-oriented policing. They focus on outcomes by creating goals for government and measuring how well agencies perform their tasks. They treat citizens as valued customers with individual needs. They earn money by charging fees or by owning businesses, such as cable television systems. They anticipate problems, believing that an ounce of prevention is worth a pound of cure. For example, they believe that fire departments should be rewarded more for fire prevention than for their fast response time after a fire occurs.

Proponents of **reinventing government** (REGO) are critical of "orthodox" bureaucratic reorganization. They call for "flatter" bureaucracies in which the number of intermediate levels of organization between top management and street-level workers is substantially reduced.[38] At the same time they want lower-level workers to have more freedom to make decisions without constant supervision. Managers should be hired on performance contracts. The belief is that if managers have more flexibility to improve services, they will be more responsive to consumers.

REGO principles call for cutting red tape, putting customers first, empowering employees, and getting back to basics—"eliminate what we don't need."[39]

A closely related approach is Total Quality Management (TQM), a business management philosophy identified with American W. Edwards Deming and first put into practice at Deming's direction by businesses in Japan. Major tenets of TQM include the following: The customer is the ultimate determiner of quality; quality results from people working together within systems, not from individual efforts; quality improvement requires effective worker participation; quality requires a total organizational commitment. TQM shares the reinventing government belief in flatter bureaucracies. Some TQM principles have been implemented in a majority of the states.

Critics argue that since TQM was designed for routine manufacturing processes, it is much more difficult to apply to government services, which are very labor intensive. Unlike private businesses, it is not easy to identify who a government's customers are. For example, are the customers of an environmental protection agency the businesses it regulates or the groups that lobby for greater environmental protection? If it is a combination of both, then what weight should be assigned to each of their interests? The public wants clean air and water, but it also wants jobs and it wants to avoid inconvenient government regulation.

Privatization

The Progressives championed service delivery by bureaucracies as a means to eliminate the corruption of payoffs to political machines for contracts awarded by the city to private businesses and to ensure that everyone was treated the same, rather than given preferential attention because of political connections. As a result, we created a series of government monopolies—schools, garbage collection, utilities—to avoid waste and duplication.

Even when they are not conscious of *reinventing government*, many communities have discovered they can save money when service providers compete for public business. As a result, **privatization** has become increasingly common since 1990. As explained by E. S. Savas, it can appear in several forms.[40] Perhaps the most familiar is contracting with private firms to perform a service previously done by government employees. In private business this is referred to as "outsourcing." Public-sector privatization includes managing prisons, providing janitorial services, operating homeless shelters, and collecting taxes.

Privatization also includes contracting with not-for-profit agencies to provide a service such as meals-on-wheels, forming neighborhood security patrols, selling off publicly owned businesses, and giving housing vouchers to the poor. Because competition is central to the ideas of Osborne and Graebler, privatization has been strongly associated with the reinventing government movement. In terms used by Osborne and Graebler, privatization separates steering from rowing in local government. Public officials set policy goals and monitor private providers of services (steer), and nongovernmental employees perform day-to-day tasks (row).

The increase in federal and state mandates is a major factor that has led cities to contract out for services. In particular, environmental mandates for such things as toxic waste cleanup require a level of technical expertise and the use of sophisticated equipment that often are beyond the capabilities of local governments.

Advocates of privatization, such as E. S. Savas, argue that it can substantially reduce service delivery costs. Political scientist James Q. Wilson agrees that private firms usually are more efficient, but he cautions that publicly owned utilities may have lower costs than private organizations.[41] Osborne and Graebler note that where private providers do not have to compete, they may be as inefficient as public monopolies.

Proponents contend that in addition to saving money, privatization is consistent with free market ideology, reduces the size of government, forces providers to be more responsive to customer needs, rewards innovation, avoids the rigidities of civil service, and introduces successful private management ideas to the public sector. Where public agencies have successfully competed for contracts against private businesses, the morale of public employees is greatly improved.

Opponents contend that when the costs of monitoring contracts are considered, service delivery may be more expensive under privatization (as much as 10 percent of the value of the contract). Contracting, they argue, encourages "lowballing," where private firms bid low and then raise their charges to cover the real costs of the service. When costs are lower, opponents believe it often is because providers cut corners in their services and pay workers lower salaries. There are concerns that private companies will not be sufficiently committed to affirmative action in hiring workers and that services may not be provided equitably to minority groups. Although encouraging competition sounds good, it often is difficult to find qualified providers of services when bids are requested.

When law enforcement is privatized (see Chapter 7), there is special concern that civil liberties will be abused. Not surprisingly, public employee unions fear that privatization will lead to a loss of jobs and/or lower wages and benefits. In large cities, such as Chicago, African Americans have taken a substantial hit because they hold a disproportionately high percentage of service and maintenance jobs and those are the most likely to be privatized.[42] As under machine rule, there is still the danger of favoritism in awarding contracts.

Most of the pitfalls of privatization can be avoided by careful wording of contracts and by close supervision of the providers. For example, rather than automatically accepting the lowest bid, cities may use the "lowest responsible bid." City auditors' offices can ensure that bidding is truly competitive and can monitor contractors' performance. But effective monitoring is expensive (perhaps equal to 10 percent of the value of a contract) and time-consuming for governments.

As in Phoenix, cities may wish to retain some public delivery of a service, such as garbage collection, even when the majority of the service is provided by private organizations. Contracts can encourage private companies to hire displaced city workers, or cities can assure public employees that they will not be laid off because of privatization. In a word, cities need to manage competition by defining clearly what they want done, by evaluating performance, and by penalizing those who do not provide services at the expected levels. As Chicago mayor Richard M. Daley stated, "People want services without higher taxes, and they don't care who gives it to them."

More than 90 percent of state agencies have privatized some of their services. The most frequently privatized services are custodial, food, clerical, and security. The number of cities that have hired private companies to manage their water works increased from 400 in 1997 to 1,100 in 2003. About 5 percent of all Americans have their water provided by private companies, some of which are based in Europe. Increasingly, states also are privatizing the professional services of engineers and architects. While over 90 percent of privatization is done by contracting out, states also provide vouchers, especially for social services, and they enter into partnerships with private groups. Exclusive use of public employees is highest in providing public safety operations, such as fire and police, but contracts are used for every service that local governments perform. However, cities have made minimal use of alternative service delivery, other than contracting out.

Reinventing Government Evaluated

Reinventing government strategies seemed to be everywhere in the early 1990s. President Clinton put Vice President Al Gore in charge of the federal program, and hundreds of activists in states, counties, cities, and school districts were eager to change their governments. Although few persons would argue that long-term strategic planning, outcomes-based budgeting, and citizen empowerment are bad, some programs have been reined in by politicians and voters who feel they have been carried to their illogical extremes. Innovation makes some persons uncomfortable, and partisan political concerns may prevent otherwise rational budgeting changes from being implemented.

Curiously, the city in which entrepreneurial government found the greatest acceptance in the 1980s changed direction in the 1990s. As its city manager for eight years, Ted Graebler helped make Visalia, California, the "most entrepreneurial city in America." Aided by a group of well-educated managers, many recruited from other parts of the country, Graebler and his successor as city manager reinvented government in their central California city of 75,000 people. Visalia's mission-driven budget was only two pages long; the city bought a minor league baseball team; and it established an award for "the year's most spectacular failure."

After Graebler left Visalia, the city got involved in a project to build a hotel and redevelop land on the edge of downtown.[43] As the city's share of the project's cost soared, criticism forced the city manager to resign. New city council members who opposed entrepreneurial government were elected, and they appointed a city manager who as police chief under Graebler had not embraced entrepreneurial government.

Even in its heyday, Visalia illustrates the need to take a moderate approach to reinventing government. Although the process was exciting to its professional managers, many townspeople felt cut off from their government (despite constant surveys to listen to the voices of Visalia's customers). The city had more than 100 task forces, which led to a lot of talking but limited government efficiency.

Implementation of REGO by state agencies appears to be significantly less widespread than its proponents suggest. One study found that most REGO proposals have been implemented by only 10 to 20 percent of state agencies. Even the most widespread reform—strategic planning—was fully implemented by less than 40 percent of state agencies. Still, this represents widespread impact on state and local government, often changing the way public officials think about administration even if they do not explicitly refer to "reinventing government." In this regard, we have noted the extensive use of contracting out, or privatizing, public services.

STATEWIDE ELECTED EXECUTIVES

Unlike the national level, where the president and vice president are the only popularly elected officials, most states continue to fill several executive branch positions through election. Only three states—Maine, New Hampshire, and New Jersey—have a single statewide elected official, the governor. North Dakota has twelve and North Carolina and Florida each have ten. Regionally, the South has the most elected statewide officials. Many political scientists argue that the governor and lieutenant governor should be the only statewide elected executives. Electing more creates a **long ballot,** on which voters must vote for offices and candidates they know little about. It also creates agencies that to some extent are independent of the governor because they also have their own executive who has been elected by the voters. Consequently, having a large number of separately elected officials (SEOs) is viewed as reducing a governor's influence in the executive branch. Brief descriptions of officials that are typically elected and their duties follow.

Lieutenant Governor

The basic responsibilities of the lieutenant governor are comparable to those of the vice president of the United States: to be first in line to succeed the governor in the event of the governor's death and in twenty states to be presiding officer of the state senate when it is in session (see Chapter 5). In the eight states that do not have a lieutenant governor, the first in the line of succession usually is the secretary of state. In New Jersey the senate president replaces a governor who leaves office and he or she continues to hold the senate leadership post. This happened in 2001 when Governor Christine Whitman left to become the head of the Environmental Protection Agency. As a result, the new acting governor, Donald DiFrancesco, became the most powerful state official in the United States, because New Jersey gives its governor very strong formal power.

When a governor is out of the state, many lieutenant governors become acting governor. This is an important difference with the vice presidency, because vice presidents do not become acting president when the president is out of the country. A 1992 survey that was responded to by close to half of the lieutenant governors found that many had served as acting governor; the average length of time was forty-six days. During this time, some of the lieutenant governors had signed bills into law, reviewed pending executions, and made other important decisions.[44]

Still, the job of lieutenant governor will be determined largely by what the governor wants the lieutenant governor to do. Governors frequently consult their lieutenant governors when appointing administrators to head executive branch agencies. Often they use lieutenant governors as policy advisers and occasionally as department heads.

Perhaps the most powerful lieutenant governor is in Texas. There the lieutenant governor presides over the senate, appoints committees and committee chairs, and co-chairs the Legislative Budget Board.[45] During his first term in office, Republican Governor George W. Bush worked so cordially with Democratic Lieutenant Governor Bob Bullock that Bullock, who was retiring, endorsed Bush for reelection in 1998.

For a long time states elected governors and lieutenant governors separately, which meant that a governor might have to deal with a politically ambitious lieutenant governor of the opposite party. However, thirty-one states now have joint nomination and joint election of these two officials.

Attorney General

As the state's chief legal officer, the attorney general represents the state in legal disputes and serves as the legal adviser to the governor and other executive-branch employees. Curiously, in about half the states, the attorney general does not have to be a licensed attorney. Attorneys general are popularly elected in forty-three states, chosen by the governor in five states, chosen by the legislature in one state, and chosen by the state supreme court in one state. Although a part of the executive branch, they can become involved in battles with governors. An extreme example is when the attorney general of Arizona was a leader in the move to impeach Governor Evan Mecham in 1986–1987.

In most states, the attorney general is the second most powerful political figure in state office. His or her power stems in large part from the ability to initiate prosecution in well-publicized criminal and civil cases. In addition, when the governor, the legislature, administrative agencies, county attorneys, or city attorneys ask the attorney general for advice regarding an interpretation of state law, the attorney general's opinion generally has the force of law unless challenged in court. The attorney general's office often serves as a state headquarters for consumer complaints about faulty merchandise or misleading advertising.

In 1994, Mississippi Attorney General Mike Moore was the first to sue cigarette manufacturers under the then-novel strategy that the tobacco industry had unjustly benefited from his state's assumption of the costs for tobacco-related diseases and illnesses. So Mississippi sued to recover the Medicaid money spent on smoking-related health care costs. Other states' attorneys general joined Moore and a settlement was reached with tobacco companies in 1998 under which over the next twenty-five years states will share nearly $250 billion. As noted in Chapter 1, since 2000 Attorney General Elliot Spitzer of New York has been a national leader in taking action against Wall Street securities firms. In 2002, a coalition of attorneys general negotiated a $484 million settlement with the parent company of Household Finance.

This activism has created a backlash against the power of attorneys general, led by the Republican Attorneys General Association (twenty states had Republican attorneys general in 2003), against what it calls "government lawsuit abuse."[46] However, there is strong political pressure on *all* attorneys general to join multistate suits that promise large payouts for their states.

In many instances, the attorney general heads the largest law office in the state. This ability to appoint hundreds of young lawyers to serve in state government gives the attorney general a substantial power base should he or she choose to run for governor or senator after those attorneys have gained experience and moved into private practice around the state. Several attorneys general have gone on to become governors and well-known national political figures. They include Robert LaFollette of Wisconsin, Thomas Dewey of New York, and more recently Bill Clinton of Arkansas.

Secretary of State

The duties of secretary of state are to keep records—such as the state constitution, constitutional amendments, legislative acts, and mortgages—and to supervise both federal and state elections. They are elected in thirty-six states and selected by either the governor or the legislature in eleven states; Alaska, Hawaii, and Utah do not have such a position. Secretaries of state receive statements of candidacy for public office, oversee the printing of ballots, and certify election results. Because secretaries of state are basically record keepers, many proposals call for the transfer of these duties to regular administrative departments. Recently, several secretaries of state have become governors. These include Jerry Brown of California, Jay Rockefeller of West Virginia, Barbara Roberts of Oregon, and Bob Taft of Ohio.

Although more than twenty secretaries of state became governor in the twentieth century, many do not have further political ambitions. For example, Thad Eure retired in 1989 as secretary of state of North Carolina after fifty-two years in office. Equally remarkable was West Virginia's secretary of state, Ken Heckler. After leaving Congress in 1977, Heckler tried a variety of civilian jobs. Then in 1984, at age 70, he was elected West Virginia's secretary of state and served through 2000.

Treasurer, Auditor, and Controller

A number of functions involving the handling of money generated from taxes are divided among several officials, and it is difficult to find more than a handful of states that do it the same way. A state treasurer usually is responsible for tax collection, the safekeeping of state funds, and the actual spending of money. Treasurers are elected in thirty-six states and chosen by the governor or legislature in twelve others. Texas eliminated its treasurer in 1996, and in 1998 voters in Minnesota approved an initiative to eliminate the office.

Postaudit, a review after money is spent to see whether it was spent according to legislative intent and without corruption, is the responsibility of the state auditor. Auditors are elected in twenty-five states and chosen by the governor or legislature in others. In a few states, the auditor is called the controller. **Preaudit** is the approval of spending before it actually takes place and is normally done by the controller. The controller is elected in only nine states; appointment by an agency head (such as the department of finance) is becoming more common.

The treasurer, auditor, and controller will not be found in every state, but the functions they perform will be done by some office. The administrative efficiency school argues that all, or most, of these functions should be centralized in one office headed by a gubernatorial appointee. This would make the governor clearly responsible for performing these functions.

EXECUTIVES IN CITIES

Led by Progressive reformers seeking to rid cities of the corruption of political machines early in the twentieth century, many cities acted somewhat sooner than states to centralize authority and strengthen executive authority. However, many mayors continue to be limited by fragmented local organization. In addition, few mayors develop strong party organizations and must therefore depend on the strength of their personal appeal in providing political leadership. As state and federal funds support more local projects, mayors and local administrators are subjected to increased rules and regulations established by state legislators and by members of Congress.

Being the mayor in most large cities is a perilous job with constant political and economic pressure. Few survive well enough to be successful in running for higher office. In small towns, mayors often are main-street merchants who lack the ambition to seek higher office. Even if they perform effectively, mayors often have difficulty becoming well known when seeking statewide office.

City executives function as part of four basic forms of government: weak-mayor–council, strong-mayor–council, council-manager, and commission.

FORMS OF CITY GOVERNMENT

Weak-Mayor–Council Plan

Until the 1870s, all American cities operated with **weak-mayor–council plans** of government. As with early state government, city government structure was strongly affected by skepticism about politicians and about government. At a time when local government performed few functions and city officials were coordinated by party organizations, people were afraid to give substantial power to a single executive.

In a weak-mayor–council system, the council is both a legislative and an executive body (Figure 6-1). Council members appoint administrative officials; they make policy; they serve as ex officio members of boards; and they prepare the budget. The mayor is "weak" because of a lack of effective executive power. The authority to appoint is restricted, and the authority to remove often is altogether lacking. Often, the mayor cannot veto ordinances passed by the city council. In cities with weak mayors, no single person is charged with overall responsibility for government action. Other executive officials are independently elected (there is a long ballot that often is not understood by voters), and a number of boards and commissions are not controlled by the mayor. Because no one is in charge of the overall affairs of a city, voters do not know whom to blame when things go wrong. No one coordinates all public policies in a city, and no one can be held directly accountable when there are service breakdowns.

The weak-mayor system does have some advantages. City departments are free to act without undue political pressure from the mayor. If voters are concerned about the misuse of executive power, the weak-mayor system creates strong checks by the council and by independent boards. In many cases structurally weak mayors have been powerful political forces in their cities, but they must depend on informal factors such as their personal appeal or the strength of their political party.

The number of cities with weak mayors began to decline as early as the 1880s when Boston and some other large cities introduced the strong-mayor form of government. Together with well-organized local political parties, the strong-mayor system effectively used political patronage to centralize power. Other weak-mayor systems also were replaced with city managers and commissions beginning early in the twentieth century.

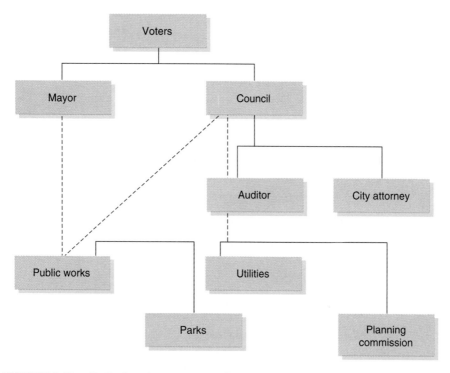

FIGURE 6-1 Hypothetical weak-mayor–council plan. Council has both legislative and executive authority. Council must consent to mayor's appointments of department heads. Mayor's power of removal restricted. Council has primary control over the budget. Some department heads are appointed directly by council.

Still, weak-mayor–council systems survive in many small cities and at some medium-size cities, especially in the South. Despite efforts to reform their charters, Minneapolis and Seattle are notable large cities with weak-mayor systems.

In 1999 voters in Los Angeles handed Mayor Richard Riordan a victory and a defeat for city council members when they strongly approved a new city charter. The reformed charter, which required hundreds of ordinances to implement, gives the mayor power to fire a number of department heads, the ability to issue executive orders, and expanded budget authority. Also, it created a series of neighborhood councils with the power to advise city leaders and enlarge the council membership. The last two provisions were designed, in part, to help keep the San Fernando Valley in the city (see Chapter 1).

Strong-Mayor–Council Plan

Under the **strong-mayor–council plan,** there is a short ballot. The mayor controls the budget, has broad power to appoint and remove city officials, and can veto ordinances passed by the council. Strong mayors are directly elected by the voters and usually have four-year terms with the possibility of reelection (Figure 6-2). The council confirms

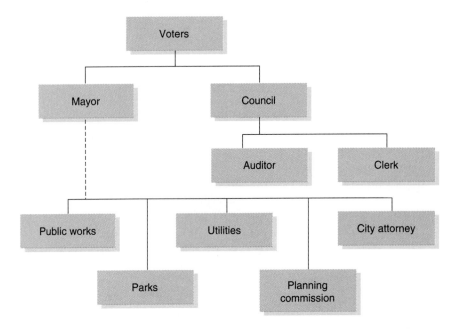

FIGURE 6-2 Hypothetical strong-mayor–council plan. Mayor has strong administrative authority. Mayor appoints and dismisses department heads. Mayor prepares the budget. Short ballot.

appointments, and it usually controls the appropriations process. The mayor's legal position provides a firm base for political leadership, and the mayor is constantly in the limelight. In most cities the "strong" mayor is, in fact, a compromise between a weak and a very strong system.

This plan is used in most large cities where a complex administrative structure requires firm leadership and direction. Most cities with more than 1 million population have a strong-mayor–council system. Problems arise when voters expect too much from the mayor and find it easy to blame that individual for whatever goes wrong in the city. Often, those politicians who are effective campaigners lack the administrative skills to manage the day-to-day affairs of a large city. To offset this shortcoming of the system, many cities with strong mayors have established the position of **chief administrative officer (CAO).** Appointed by the mayor, this professional person is given broad authority to manage the financial affairs of the city. In a few cities the CAO is a permanent position that carries over from one administration to another. In most cases, it is subject to appointment by the mayor. In New York City the mayor selects several deputy mayors who function according to the CAO concept. About three-fourths of all municipal systems of government report having a CAO.

As with governors, "strong" formal powers do not guarantee that mayors will be effective leaders in their cities. They need to have personal leadership capabilities, and even the strongest mayors usually lack some formal powers that they would like to have in an ideal situation. Mayors need to build networks of support in order to compete with private economic power in their cities and to deal effectively with strong government bureaucracies. Likewise, mayors with weak formal power may be "strong" leaders because they are carefully tuned in to the political environment of their cities. This means that to be recognized as the political leader of his or her city, a mayor must exercise power beyond what is provided in the city charters.

Council-Manager Plan

The council-manager plan originated early in the twentieth century as part of the Progressive movement. Reformers sought to eliminate corruption from city hall by removing administration from partisan politics. Their answer was to replace the mayor with a professional administrator appointed by the council. Among the early city reformers was Richard S. Childs, who founded the national short-ballot organization in 1909. A short ballot implied consolidation of elected offices, and in many cases, plans calling for a **city manager** were accompanied by the initiation of nonpartisan elections, civil service systems, and the short ballot. To reformers, the city manager was viewed as a "business director" and the city council as a "corporate board of directors."

In 1914 Dayton, Ohio, was the first city of substantial size to adopt the council-manager plan. By 1918 there were nearly 100 cities with managers, and counties began to adopt the system in the 1930s. Currently a majority of cities with populations between 10,000 and 500,000 have managers and the plan is used in many Canadian cities. Forty-three percent of American cities have a mayor-council form of government. The plan is particularly adaptable to medium-size cities (25,000 to 250,000). Small towns often find it too expensive to hire a full-time manager, and in many large cities the council-manager system is opposed by strong labor unions and minority groups, who often believe the manager has a pro-business bias. Still, an increasing number of large cities, especially in the South and West, have managers.

In most cases a small council elected at large hires a manager (Figure 6-3). In the past, managers often were civil engineers. Now they are likely to be people trained in public administration. The manager serves at the pleasure of the council in a relationship similar to that of a superintendent of schools and the board of education. A mayor may be selected from among the council members to perform ceremonial duties. In nearly half the cities with a manager there is a popularly elected mayor.

Where mayors coexist with managers, the mayor often has more power than the formal model suggests.[47] For example, Robert Boynton and Deil Wright found that mayors of several large cities often played a strong role in appointing department heads and in shaping the council's agenda. When mayors' actions conflict with the model, managers may complain about the overreach of power. More often, however, there is a sense of teamwork between the mayor and the manager.

Where cities have changed from a council-manager system with a weak mayor to a strong-mayor system, it often has been out of frustration that no one really is in charge. For example, Toledo, Ohio, made the switch in the early 1990s in the hope that a strong mayor could halt the long economic decline of the city. Toledo voters approved a charter change after a campaign for a strong mayor was led by the city's major newspaper. As in some other cities, Toledo also moved to a mixed election system for council, combining district and at-large elections, and the position of city manager was eliminated. In 1998 voters in Cincinnati approved a charter change giving the mayor the power to

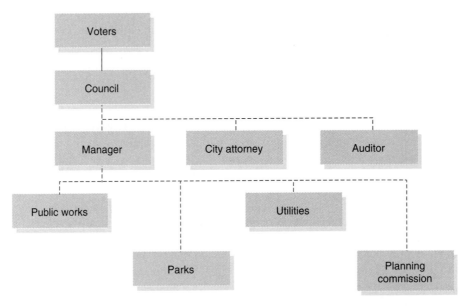

FIGURE 6-3 Hypothetical council-manager plan. Usually small council (5–7 members). Often nonpartisan elections. Council members make policy and oversee city administration. Full-time professional manager. Budget prepared by the manager. Mayor usually has only ceremonial power.

initiate the hiring and firing of the city manager, as well as veto power and significant budget authority. Starting in 2003 Cincinnati's mayor is directly elected, a change from a system in which the councilperson with the highest vote total in municipal elections became the largely ceremonial mayor.

Typically managers are involved in presenting proposals to council members and working for their adoption. Increasingly managers see a policy making role for themselves, and patterns of liberal or conservative policy solutions can be associated with particular managers. The duties of most managers include preparing the city budget, supervising the hiring and firing of city personnel, and negotiating with labor unions. Managers are expert advisers providing information to city councils.

Managers are likely to be found in newer, fast-growing cities with mobile populations. This description fits many suburban communities, and it is there that continuing support for creating council-manager forms of government is to be found. For example, most of the commuter suburbs of Westchester County, New York, have managers.

In general, medium-size cities in the Northeast and Midwest tend to have strong mayors, whereas Sunbelt cities, including Dallas, Phoenix, and San Diego, have managers. In growth areas of the South and Southwest, planning for streets and water lines is a high priority, and the council-manager plan seems to work well. In the Northeast and Midwest, the priority is on responding to a variety of racial and ethnic groups, and the strong-mayor–council system has worked well in those circumstances.

In 2000, about 12 percent of managers were women, up from 1 percent in 1974. The average tenure of managers increased from 5.4 years in 1989 to nearly seven years in 2000. Greater job security and more involvement in the policy making process may affect the kinds of people attracted to what has been a very transitory profession.

Although some reformers have overstated the impact of the manager system (in particular, they fail to understand that "politics" cannot be eliminated and that the struggle for power will not disappear once partisan labels are removed), it has provided efficient, accountable government in many cities. Weaknesses stem from the nature of individual managers—it is difficult to attract competent, experienced people, and the manager must maintain a middle-of-the-road position in which he or she avoids, on the one hand, setting policy and, on the other hand, simply running errands for the council.

Some managers have had a tendency to become very closely identified with business and professional interests in their community. Because of this perceived bias, organized labor in many cities has opposed the creation of a manager plan. There has also been opposition from African Americans and other minorities who believe their interests will be better served in nonreformed cities where the mayor's office may be more responsive to citizen demands. Also cities with managers may lack effective political leadership because of the weak position of the mayor.

In response to criticism that the manager system did not adequately address non-business policy issues, many cities over 50,000 population have modified the original plan to have direct election of the mayor and the election of some council members by district. Under some strong-mayor systems, the manager reports only to the mayor.

Commission Plan

The impetus for the commission plan was a storm that virtually destroyed Galveston, Texas in 1900. So many people were killed that attempts were made to bury people at sea. But bodies washed back on shore and increased the threat of disease.[48] Martial law was declared to stop looting. In response to the crisis, commissioners were appointed to run the city. This became the model for a new form of municipal government.

A **commission plan** has several (usually three to nine) commissioners, elected at large, who exercise both legislative and executive authority. The commissioners are organized as heads of various city departments (public works, parks, finance), and they also act collectively to pass ordinances and control spending (Figure 6-4). Often a mayor is selected from among the commissioners, but his or her duties are largely ceremonial.

After its initiation in Galveston in 1901, use of the commission plan spread quickly, and by 1917 it was in operation in about 500 cities. Dallas, Houston, and Fort Worth were among the first cities that had commissions, and several other big cities, including Pittsburgh and Buffalo, adopted the plan early in the twentieth century. As recently as 1970, about 200 cities had commission forms of government. Only two cities with over 250,000 population (Portland, Oregon, and Tulsa, Oklahoma) reported to the *Municipal Year Book* in 2002 that they had commission forms of government. In all, 143 cities (2 percent of all cities) had commissions in 2002.[49] Most were in the Mid-Atlantic and North Central states. In most states there are no city commissions at all. Even Galveston now has a council-manager form of government. The Voting Rights Act has made the commission form with its at-large voting an endangered species of city government.

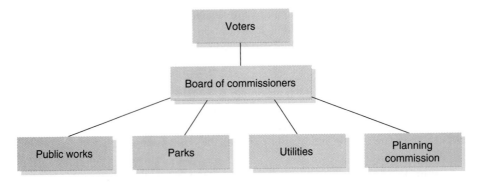

FIGURE 6-4 Hypothetical commission plan. Usually small membership (4–7 members). Commissioners each serve as department heads. Commissioners sit as a legislative body. One commissioner acts as mayor (power equal to other commissioners).

The commission plan has many disadvantages. Because it does not provide for separation of powers, it places little control on spending and administration. In most cities it is difficult to attract top-quality persons to serve as commissioners, and thus government business often is in the hands of amateurs. Without a chief executive, it is difficult to pinpoint responsibility. The small size of the commission does not foster debate and criticism, and it encourages a fraternity of tolerance. City commissioners often practice a mutual hands-off policy from one another's functional areas, and each moves in his or her own direction without overall coordination. The commission has become nearly extinct because of the fundamental flaws noted above and the rise of the city manager form of government as the reform of choice beginning in the 1920s.

THE ROLES OF MAYORS

Mayors, like governors and presidents, play a variety of roles. As the ceremonial head of the city, mayors greet distinguished visitors to the city, attend endless rounds of dinners, and issue proclamations. These activities help give mayors visibility, and they build up political goodwill. As chief administrators, mayors oversee the work of city employees and prepare an executive budget. They may be limited in this function, however, by the presence of independent boards and commissions and other officials who are separately elected. And like governors the mayors can be classified as "strong" or "weak," depending on the nature of their city's charter. As chief legislators, strong mayors exercise strong control over the agenda considered by the council, and they can veto ordinances passed by the council. Increasingly, mayors act as chief city ambassador, devoting a great deal of time to meetings at the state capital and in Washington. Many cities have full-time lobbyists in Washington, and others act through the United States Conference of Mayors and the National League of Cities.

The ways in which mayors carry out their formal duties depend in large part on their style of leadership. At one extreme is the **passive caretaker.**[50] Mayors of this sort take very little initiative, preferring to have private groups agree on projects, which they may endorse. These mayors make little effort to influence policy by offering a vision for the future. Instead, they tend to deal with problems one at a time in terms of whatever "comes up." Their basic concern is to maintain city services and make as few waves as possible.[51] In some instances, the caretaker mayor may excel at ceremonial duties—cutting ribbons, welcoming conventions—and thus improve the image of the city. In some instances, the *only* parts of the job that seem to interest mayors are its ceremonial aspects.

At the other extreme are **entrepreneur mayors,** who have a clear vision of where their cities should go. These mayors surround themselves with large staffs, and they actively seek to build political coalitions to get broad support to implement their programs. Mayors of this sort want to exert strong leadership over their councils and the entire city. For example, Mayor Fiorello La Guardia of New York City (1933–1945) believed that "*his* policies should prevail in *every* area of government activity." Of course, some activist mayors may not be able to accomplish much in the way of substantive policy change.

The **opportunistic policy broker** style of mayor stands between these two extremes. These mayors do not wish to dominate all city activities, but they do not wish to handle only housekeeping responsibilities either. Richard J. Daley of Chicago is described as a classic broker politician who chose from policy proposals put forth by individuals outside city hall. It was, however, only Mayor Daley's "seal of approval" that could put the proposals into operation.

The power of mayors, even more than the power of the governor, rests in their ability to persuade through the use of public relations approaches, the mass media, and bargaining among various urban interests. If mayors are effective persuaders, they can overcome many of the handicaps of weak formal authority, as did Richard Lee of New Haven, Connecticut. In a classic study of political power, Lee was described as "not [being at] the peak of a pyramid but rather at the center of intersecting circles."[52] He rarely commanded. He negotiated, cajoled, exhorted, beguiled, charmed, pressed, appealed, reasoned, promised, insisted, demanded, even threatened; but he most needed support from other leaders who simply could not be commanded. Because the mayor did not dare command, he had to bargain.

Although it is difficult to generalize about the backgrounds and attitudes of mayors, case studies have discovered historical patterns in selected cities. In Chicago, for example, most mayors since 1930 have been Catholic, and all have risen through the ranks of the local party organization. In San Francisco and St. Louis, local businesspeople with outgoing personalities have most often been elected mayor. Until recently, the office of mayor seldom was a stepping-stone to statewide office or to Congress. Mayors of big cities built up too many liabilities, or they were not sufficiently well known across the state even to be taken seriously as candidates for governor. By the 1980s this image of mayors had changed, and several were elected governor. These include Pete Wilson, mayor of San Diego, and George Voinovich, mayor of Cleveland. Still, only three mayors have become president. The last was Calvin Coolidge, who had been mayor of Northampton, Massachusetts.

Mayors of many large cities have been able to take credit for decreasing crime rates and improved local economies. As a result, most incumbent mayors who sought reelection in the 1990s were successful. For example, Richard M. Daley assumed personal control of the failing Chicago school system and was able to improve what looked like a hopeless situation. In New York City, Republican Mayor Rudolph Giuliani took credit for a significant drop in crime in the mid-1990s (see Chapter 7), and he was reelected in 1996 with strong Democratic support. Giuliani's response to the events of September 11, 2001 made him a national figure, but he did not run for reelection because of term limits.

Minority and Women Mayors

Minority mayors constitute an increasingly large category of individuals who, although they have different styles of leadership, face similar problems. Since 1980, African Americans have served as mayors of many of the nation's largest cities—Atlanta, Baltimore, Chicago, Cleveland, Dallas, Denver, Detroit, Houston, Kansas City, Los Angeles, Memphis, Minneapolis, New Orleans, New York, Philadelphia, St. Louis, San Francisco, Seattle, and Washington, D.C. In several cases there were black women mayors in these cities.

The first generation of African-American mayors, led by Carl Stokes in Cleveland and Richard Hatcher in Gary, Indiana, both elected in 1967, served in predominantly African-American cities. The major focus of their administrations was the "**political incorporation** of blacks."[53] That is, they sought to use city government as a means to empower African Americans and other minorities in the political and civic life of their communities. Most studies of cities with first-generation African-American mayors have found that after their election African Americans have gotten more municipal jobs and African-American contractors have benefited from affirmative action programs to award city contracts to minority businesses.[54] In particular, this can be seen in Detroit where longtime mayor Coleman Young began a policy of giving preferential treatment to local businesses over firms outside the city.

The second generation of African-American mayors includes several elected in cities such as Dallas, Denver, Houston, Minneapolis, San Francisco, and Seattle, where African Americans make up less than one-third of the population. In fact, the majority of African Americans elected mayor since the early 1980s have done so in places where blacks comprise less than half the population.[55] Cities in western states with reformed government structures have had less difficulty electing African Americans than have those in the East with a history of machine politics.

In predominantly white cities, African-American mayoral candidates obviously must forge coalitions to get the support of white voters. Once in office, their goals tend to focus more on broad economic development, rather than on African-American incorporation. This means that race is deemphasized in election campaigns, as well as in governing. Even in predominantly African-American cities, such as Detroit and Cleveland, successful second-generation mayoral candidates have de-racialized their campaigns and then altered the focus of their administrations. Mayor Dennis Archer, who succeeded Coleman Young in Detroit, reached out to business corporations and to predominantly white suburbs to help save his declining city. In Cleveland, Mayor Michael White was first elected in 1989 when he defeated another black Democrat by getting about 80 percent of the white vote in the primary election. White was reelected in the 1990s, running campaigns that emphasized his experience and his ability to get things done for Cleveland. After twelve years in office, White chose not to run in 2001. He was succeeded as mayor by Jane Campbell, a white, liberal Democrat.

In virtually all cities, once African-American mayors are in office they need to work with the predominantly white business community to further economic development for African Americans. Some African-American mayors find it difficult to maintain an effective balance between catering to their electoral constituency and forging alliances with upper-class white bankers and merchants. If they seem to be working too closely with the white business community, they are criticized by African Americans for "selling out." If they alienate the white business establishment, African-American mayors risk even more white businesses moving out of their cities. As in Detroit, affluent white suburbs prospered in the 1980s and 1990s, while the city continued to lose people and jobs.

Facing population flight to the suburbs, rising poverty, and a declining tax base, commentators as early as 1969 began to refer to the "hollow prize" inherited by black mayors.[56] Just when blacks began to get elected mayor, their cities seemed to be crumbling. Considering the continuing encirclement of minority central cities by white suburbs and the isolation of cities with black mayors, Kraus and Swanstrom conclude that the "hollow prize problem will only worsen."

After electing African-American mayors in the 1980s, several cities, including Gary, Indiana, Oakland, New York, Chicago, and Los Angeles, have elected white mayors. St. Louis, which is 51 percent black, elected a white mayor in 2001, and in Los Angeles James Hahn, a white candidate, was elected mayor because of strong black support. Richard M. Daley has been elected mayor of Chicago five times, always overwhelming African-American opponents in a city where blacks comprise 37 percent of the population, about the same percentage as the white population. We have noted that Cleveland recently elected a white mayor.

A few predominantly Hispanic large cities, mainly in Texas and Florida, have elected Hispanic mayors. Occasionally, as in Denver and San Diego, predominantly Anglo cities have elected Hispanic mayors. Hispanics are much less segregated than African Americans, and their relatively greater population dispersion lessens their potential for political power in American cities. Only in San Antonio, El Paso, and Miami do Hispanics constitute more than half the population in cities with populations over 300,000. Laredo, Texas, with a population of about 170,000, is 97 percent Hispanic, and it has had Hispanic mayors since 1992.

Although mayors of big cities have overwhelmingly been Democrats—virtually all African-American and Hispanic mayors have been Democrats—an interesting feature of the 1990s was the election of white, Republican mayors in the nation's two largest cities, New York and Los Angeles. And Michael R. Bloomberg, a white Republican, succeeded Rudolph Giuliani as mayor of New York.

A third change has been the election of increasing numbers of women mayors, including several African Americans. Since 1979 women have been elected mayor in such widely dispersed big cities as Chicago, San Francisco, San Diego, Fort Worth, Portland, Minneapolis, Cleveland, Houston, Pittsburgh, Washington, D.C., Salt Lake City, and Las Vegas. Cities with populations between 250,000 and 500,000 had the greatest percentage (31 percent) of women mayors in the 1990s. Small towns, those under 5,000 population, had the smallest percentage (10 percent) of women mayors.

Paralleling the experience of African Americans in cities with African-American mayors, research shows that the election of women mayors has led to more jobs for women in the municipal workforce. Being mayor of a large city seldom offers long-term job security, regardless of race or gender. Kathy Whitmore was reelected mayor of Houston five times, but Jane Byrne in Chicago and Sharon Pratt Kelly in Washington, D.C., served only one term after being unable to respond effectively to the problems facing their cities. Contrary to long-held "conventional wisdom," women mayoral candidates appear to be able to raise money and get newspaper endorsements at about the same rate as men.

SUMMARY

The roles played by governors parallel those of the president. A governor acts as chief of state, commander-in-chief, chief legislator, and chief administrator. The formal (constitutional) powers of governors, including tenure potential, appointment, budgeting, and veto, all have been increased since the 1950s. Although governors increasingly have had to deal with legislatures controlled by the opposition party, they have become effective policy leaders. In addition, the informal powers of governors often are equally important for their success as legislative leaders.

As chief administrators, governors have been given expanded authority to prepare budgets and appoint department heads, but they are hindered as managers by the existence of independent boards and commissions and by personnel practices, such as merit systems and collective bargaining contracts.

Many cities, states, and counties have instituted reforms aimed at "reinventing government," to improve efficiency and service delivery. Techniques include privatization and entrepreneurial activities.

Cities have moved from weak-council plans to strong-mayor–council and council-manager plans in their attempts to centralize power. Managers often are found in newer, suburban communities.

The number of women and minority mayors has increased substantially in the last twenty years, but minorities may find they have won a "hollow prize." In many cases, African Americans and white Republicans have been elected mayor in predominantly white, Democratic cities.

KEY TERMS

administrative efficiency
affirmative action
appointing power
bureaucracy
cabinet
chief administrative officer (CAO)
city manager
clemency orders
collective bargaining
commission plan
entrepreneur mayors
entrepreneurial government
executive budget
formal powers

Hoover Commission
incremental budgeting
informal powers
item veto
Jacksonian democracy era
lame duck
long ballot
merit system
opportunistic policy broker
pardon
passive caretaker
performance budgeting
pocket veto
political incorporation

postaudit
postindustrial economy
preaudit
privatization
professional ideology
program-planning-budgeting system
(PPBS)

reinventing government
reorganization
strong-mayor–council plan
tenure potential
veto
weak-mayor–council plan
zero-based budgeting (ZBB)

SUMMARY OF STATE/LOCAL DIFFERENCES

Issue	State Level	Local Governments
Evolution of executive power	Substantially stronger gubernatorial authority since the 1960s	Change from weak to strong mayors, to commissions, to managers and recent addition of CAO in all systems
Extent of executive power	Governors' ability to veto, appoint a cabinet, prepare budgets is extensive	"Weak" mayors, manager-council, and commission systems all lack central executive authority
Party control	Governors often have to operate with divided party control of state government	Mayors often operate in cities with nonpartisan elections
Separately elected officials	Governors must deal with several separately elected statewide officials, but pick their own cabinets	In most cases, mayors do not face separately elected city officials, but they share power with council members
Administration	Governors are limited by civil service rules and by public unions	Mayors are limited by civil service rules and by public unions
Reinventing government and TQM	Implemented "flatter" bureaucracies and budget reforms	Implemented entrepreneurial enterprises, customer satisfaction measures, such as surveys of service quality

INTERESTING WEBSITES

www.nga.org. An easy to use site sponsored by the National Governors' Association, a bipartisan organization of fifty governors. It has information on important state issues, biographies of the governors, and their inaugural and state-of-the-state addresses. Click on "Site Index" to discover a wide range of topics. For a partisan look see

www.democraticgovernors.org. and

www.republicangovernors.org.

www.icma.org. The International City/County Managers Association website is excellent. Go to "Browse by Topic" and click on "Council-Manager Form of

Government" and "Career Resources." Other topics include "Environment," "Ethics," and "Planning and Zoning."

www.nasbo.org. Website of the professional association of the chief financial advisors to the nation's governors, National Association of State Budget Officers. Online reports that focus on the budgeting process and expenditures are available.

www.usmayors.org. The United States Conference of Mayors maintains this nonpartisan website. "Featured Items" and "Mayors in the Media" contain news stories from a number of cities. "Meet the Mayors" and "Election Center" helps to identify mayors and recent election results. The site also addresses issues of particular relevance to cities.

NOTES

1. Scott Turow, "Clemency Without Clarity," *New York Times* (January 17, 2003), p. A25. Attorney and best-selling author Scott Turow was a member of the study committee.
2. "The Education of Governor Ryan," *New York Times* (January 13, 2003), p. A24.
3. Larry Sabato, *Goodbye to Good-Time Charlie: The American Governorship Transformed,* 2d ed. (Washington, D.C.: Congressional Quarterly Press, 1983), pp. 5–7.
4. Thad Beyle, "The Governors," in *Politics in the American States,* 7th ed., Virginia Gray, Russell L. Hanson, and Herbert Jacob, eds. (Washington, D.C.: Congressional Quarterly Press, 1999), p. 194.
5. Thad Beyle, "Governors: Elections, Power, and Priorities," *Book of the States 2002* (Lexington, Ky.: Council of State Governments, 2002), p. 137.
6. Joseph A. Schlesinger, "The Politics of the Executive," in *Politics in the American States,* 2d ed., Herbert Jacob and Kenneth N. Vines, eds. (Boston, Mass.: Little, Brown, 1971), pp. 222–234.
7. Thad Beyle, "The Governors," pp. 209–217.
8. Alan Rosenthal, *The Decline of Representative Democracy* (Washington, D.C.: Congressional Quarterly Press, 1998), p. 307.
9. David Hosansky, *Congressional Quarterly Weekly Report* (August 9, 1997), p. 1923.
10. Thad Beyle, "The Governors," p. 215.
11. David R. Mayhew, *Divided We Govern: Party Control, Lawmaking, and Investigations* (New Haven, Conn.: Yale University Press 1991).
12. Alan Ehrenhalt, "The Debilitating Search for a Flabby Consensus," *Governing* (October 1996), p. 8.
13. Alan Rosenthal, *Governors and Legislatures: Contending Powers* (Washington, D.C.: Congressional Quarterly Press, 1990), pp. 6–9, 17–20, 24–27. Also see Rosenthal, *The Decline of Representative Democracy,* pp. 294–301.
14. Robert E. Crew, Jr., "Understanding Gubernatorial Behavior: A Framework for Analysis," in *Governors and Hard Times,* Thad Beyle, ed. (Washington, D.C.: Congressional Quarterly Press, 1992), p. 21.
15. Rosenthal, *The Decline of Representative Democracy,* p. 295.
16. Rosenthal, *Governors and Legislatures,* pp. 110–112.
17. Ibid., pp. 26–27.
18. Rosenthal, *The Decline of Representative Democracy,* p. 299.
19. Rosenthal, *Governors and Legislatures,* pp. 18–19.

20. Martha Wagner Weinberg, *Managing the State* (Cambridge, Mass.: MIT Press, 1977), pp. 6, 21–23.
21. Julie C. Olberding, "Reforming State Management and Personnel Systems," in *The Book of the States, 1994–95,* p. 407.
22. Richard C. Elling, "Administering State Programs: Performance and Politics," in Virginia Gray, et al., eds., *Politics in the American States,* 7th ed (Washington, D.C.: Congressional Quarterly Books, 1999), p. 274.
23. James K. Conant, "In the Shadow of Wilson and Brownlow: Executive Branch Reorganization in the States, 1965–1987," *Public Administration Review* (September–October 1988), p. 895.
24. Charles T. Goodsell, "Collegial State Administration: Design for Today?" *Western Political Quarterly* (September 1981), pp. 455–460.
25. Cynthia J. Bowling and Deil S. Wright, "Public Administration in the Fifty States: A Half-Century Administrative Revolution," *State and Local Government Review* (Winter 1988), pp. 52–64.
26. Richard C. Elling, "Administering State Programs: Performance and Politics," p. 273.
27. Ibid., p. 278.
28. David Osborne and Ted Graebler, *Reinventing Government* (Reading, Mass.: Addison-Wesley, 1992), p. 125.
29. Jonathan Walters, "Who Needs Civil Service?" *Governing* (August 1997), p. 18.
30. Jonathan Walters, "The Fine Art of Firing the Incompetent," *Governing* (June 1994), p. 36.
31. Rosenthal, *Governors and Legislatures,* p. 141.
32. Richard F. Winter, "The Politics of Taxing and Spending," in *Politics in the American States,* 7th ed., Virginia Gray, et al., eds., p. 335.
33. Aaron Wildavsky, *The New Politics of the Budgetary Process,* 2d ed. (New York: HarperCollins, 1992), p. 439.
34. Osborne and Graebler, *Reinventing Government,* p. 349.
35. Theodore Lowi, "Machine Politics—Old and New," *Public Interest* (Fall 1967), p. 86.
36. Bernard H. Ross and Myron A. Levine, *Urban Politics: Power in Metropolitan America,* 6th ed. (Itasca, Ill.: F. E. Peacock, 2001), p. 235.
37. Osborne and Graebler, *Reinventing Government,* Preface.
38. Jonathan Walters, "Flattening the Bureaucracy," *Governing* (June 1996), pp. 20–24.
39. Joel A. Aberbach and Bert A. Rockman, "Reinventing Government: Problems and Prospects." Paper presented at the Annual Meeting of the Midwest Political Science Association (April 1999), p. 6.
40. E. S. Savas, *Privatization: The Key to Better Government* (Chatham, N.J.: Chatham House, 1987), p. 3. Also see E. S. Savas, *Privatization and Public-Private Partnerships* (Chatham, N.J.: Chatham House, 2000).
41. James Q. Wilson, *Bureaucracy: What Government Agencies Do and Why They Do It* (New York: Basic Books, 1989), pp. 350–351.
42. Charles Mahtesian, "Taking Chicago Private," *Governing* (April 1994), p. 31.
43. See Rob Gurwitt, "Entrepreneurial Government: The Morning After," *Governing* (May 1994), pp. 34–40.
44. Daniel G. Cox, "Second Thoughts about the Second Banana," *State Government News* 37 (September 1994), pp. 29–33.
45. Jonathan Walters, "The Taming of Texas," *Governing* (July 1998), p. 20.
46. Alan Greenblatt, "The Avenger Generals," *Governing* (May 2003), pp. 52–56.
47. Robert P. Boynton and Deil S. Wright, "Mayor-Manager Relations in Large Council-Manager Cities: A Reinterpretation," *Public Administration Review* (January-February 1971), pp. 28–35.

48. Russell D. Murphy, "Commission Government," in *Encyclopedia of Urban America,* Neil Larry Shumsky, ed. (Santa Barbara, Calif.: ABC-CLIO, 1998), 193.
49. *The Municipal Year Book 2002* (Washington, D.C.: International City/County Management Association, 2002), p. xii.
50. See John P. Kotter and Paul R. Lawrence, *Mayors in Action: Five Approaches to Urban Governance* (New York: Wiley Interscience, 1974), chap. 7.
51. Milton Rakove, *Don't Make No Waves . . . Don't Back No Losers: An Analysis of the Daley Machine* (Bloomington: Indiana University Press, 1975). Also see Adam Cohen and Elizabeth Taylor, *American Pharaoh: Richard J. Daley, His Battle for Chicago and the Nation* (Boston: Little, Brown, 2000).
52. Robert A. Dahl, *Who Governs? Democracy and Power in an American City* (New Haven: Yale University Press, 1961), p. 204.
53. This term was first discussed by Rufus P. Browning, Dale R. Marshall, and David H. Tabb in *Protest Is Not Enough* (Berkeley: University of California Press, 1984).
54. See Peter K. Eisinger, "Black Mayors and the Policy of Racial Advancement," in *Culture, Ethnicity, and Identity,* William C. McReedy, ed. (New York: Academic Press, 1983), pp. 95–109.
55. Rob Gurwitt, "Black, White, and Blurred," *Governing* (September 2001), p. 20.
56. Neil Kraus and Todd Swanstrom, "Minority Mayors and the Hollow Prize Problem," *P.S.* (March 2001), pp. 99–104.

CHAPTER 7

Courts, Police, and Corrections

POINTS TO CONSIDER

- Examine the way in which state courts are organized and the functions performed by courts at each level.
- How have courts been reformed in the past thirty years?
- Compare the methods by which state judges are selected. What are the effects of each system on the kinds of judges selected?
- What has been the changing nature of the relationship between the Supreme Court and state courts since the 1960s?

- Why have crime rates decreased recently in some cities and risen in other cities within the same region?
- What is community policing and how well does it work? Do most people want to "police" their neighborhoods?
- Why did prison populations increase as crime decreased in the 1990s?
- Why do so many more executions take place in southern states than in all other regions of the country?
- What has been the impact of new technology on fighting crime?

State courts deal with those issues that most directly affect people's everyday lives. Most criminal cases are decided in state courts because most crimes are violations of state laws. Virtually all cases dealing with domestic relations—divorce, adoption, child custody—are heard by state courts. Questions of property ownership, contracts, zoning, wills and estates, and automobile accidents all originate in state courts. Yet most people do not know the names of their local judges and they cannot identify any recent opinion of their state's supreme court.

Crime Busters

"It's the mystery of ages," says Jeffrey A. Fagan of Columbia University, why crime goes up in one city and down in another.[1]

By the late 1980s and early 1990s both New York City and Boston were experiencing frightening increases in their homicide rates. In New York, murders increased fourfold from 1960 to 1990, when 2,245 murders were reported. Then murder rates began to fall dramatically in both cities. In New York, the drop was attributed, in large part, to police emphasis on "quality of life" enforcement—focusing on preventing minor property and nuisance offenses that were believed to lead to more serious crime. In Boston, the emphasis was more on "community policing"—building partnerships between the police and community leaders. But crime also dropped in other cities that did not use innovative crime-fighting strategies.

Then in 2001 and 2002 the homicide rate in Boston increased by over 100 percent. Across the country crime rates rose moderately for the first time since 1991.

Where crime has increased, experts point to drug use, the decline in the national economy, and the release of large numbers of people as prison populations decline. In 2003 approximately 1,600 inmates left prison every day, which was four times the rate in the 1980s. This meant that about 250 people were returning from prison to the streets of Boston each month.

Of course, these same factors, plus diversion of police to prevent possible terrorist attacks were present in New York City and crime rates continued to drop. Moreover, by 2003 New York had nearly 3,000 fewer police officers than in the late 1990s.

A skeptic would suggest that as some New York officials tout their sophisticated crime mapping system and police strategies to explain why crime patterns there are defying national patterns, crime rates in the city may start to increase. Should this happen, the crime mystery will remain unsolved.

State courts process more than 26 million case filings each year. This represents more than 90 percent of all litigation in the United States. Next to criminal cases, the largest proportion of state litigation deals with economic issues—government regulation of utilities, workers' compensation, and zoning.

The legal system of the United States is complicated by a federal structure that permits a variety of laws and courts, rather than specifying a unified plan. Throughout the country, state law is the basic law. In the United States, federal law is drafted for specific purposes and **common law** is interpreted individually by each state.* In such a situation, both state and federal courts are bound by state law unless a state statute has been superseded by federal law or is in conflict with the Constitution.

The system is made even more complex by the dual nature of state and federal courts. Unlike many other federal systems, in the United States both the states and the federal government have a complete set of trial and appellate courts. Although federal courts are concerned only with cases that raise federal issues (i.e., involve the interpretation of federal laws or the U.S. Constitution), the jurisdiction of state and federal courts occasionally overlaps. In some civil suits this gives plaintiffs the choice of initiating action in a state or federal court, and in some criminal cases it means the defendant may be tried in both state and federal courts. State courts are inferior to federal courts in the sense that decisions of state supreme courts can be reviewed and overturned by the U.S. Supreme Court. State supreme courts decide over 10,000 cases each year and only a fraction of 1 percent are reviewed by the U.S. Supreme Court.

Although there have been significant organizational reforms in state court systems since the mid-1970s, the judicial branch has not been changed as much as the legislative and executive branches. As we will see in this chapter, current issues being addressed include reduction of delay, selection of judges, the role of women and minorities in the courts, alternative resolutions to disputes, developing performance standards, and the use of new technology.

STATE COURT ORGANIZATION

The historical development of state court systems is strikingly similar to the development of state and local bureaucracy as discussed in Chapter 6. In the nineteenth century, the forces of urbanization and industrialization created a myriad of social and economic problems. Crowded cities led to increases in crime and juvenile delinquency and to the breakup of families. Landlord-tenant relations caused conflicts that were resolved by lawsuits. Questions of employer liability for personal injury and property damage opened new areas in the law. The use of automobiles created traffic law problems; and, of course, accident claims placed a heavy burden on local courts.

---

*Common law is judge-made law that originated in England from decisions shaped according to existing custom. Decisions were reapplied in similar situations (precedents) and, over a period of time, became common to the nation. English common law formed the basis of legal proceedings in the American states—except in Louisiana, where French legal traditions were used—and it has been preserved over the years. Common law also serves as the basis for much federal constitutional and statutory law.

The response of many states was to create new courts, just as new boards and commissions were added to cope with regulatory problems. As with the bureaucracy, courts expanded in an unplanned manner. Their jurisdiction often overlapped, and each court acted independently of others.* New courts included those for juvenile and family relations, small claims, traffic, and, more recently, illegal drugs. Each court had its own rules of procedure, and the nature of decisions varied among courts with similar jurisdiction. As with state administrative structures, much of the history of twentieth-century court organization can be written in terms of reform attempts to unify and streamline complex state court systems.

At the extremes, some states have fully consolidated their courts, and others continue to operate very complex, fragmented court systems. Iowa (Figure 7-1) represents a state that has streamlined its court system to a very basic form. In contrast, New York (Figure 7-2) has thirteen sets of courts. Although many states have simplified their court systems, typically several different types of trial courts remain at the state level.

Court organization is important because it affects access to the legal system and it helps determine the nature of judicial decisions. Justice delayed is justice denied, and the efficient operation of state courts, with the speedy resolution of legal matters, has broad consequences for society.

Trial Courts

Minor trial courts are limited to hearing less serious criminal and civil cases. Municipal courts, for example, often hear only criminal misdemeanor cases where the punishment is a fine or a jail sentence of less than six months. They hear civil suits where there is a limit of $500 to $1,000 in damages being sought. Civil cases relate to the private rights of individuals, and criminal law regulates individual conduct and is enforced by the government. When a case is appealed from these courts, a new trial is held *(trial de novo)* without reference to the first proceeding.

At the bottom rung of **trial courts**, many states have abolished justices of the peace and courts presided over by mayors and magistrates. These have been replaced by county or municipal courts. Justices of the peace settled local traffic law violations, issued warrants for arrest and search, and performed marriages. In some states, they did not receive a base salary but were paid a percentage of fines collected. This led to the classic "kangaroo court," in which the justice and local police officers cooperated in the profitable business of setting speed traps and sharing the fines. Mayors' courts have operated in a fashion similar to those of justices of the peace, with many small-town mayors meting out "justice" in a very personal manner.

In most states minor trial courts are highly decentralized. There are many municipal courts in urban areas and a variety of county courts in rural areas. Then there are separate trial courts to perform specific judicial functions, such as small claims or juvenile

---

*A 1931 study found there were 556 independent courts in Chicago, of which 505 were justice of the peace courts. Cited in Henry R. Glick and Kenneth N. Vines, *State Court Systems* (Englewood Cliffs, N.J.: Prentice-Hall, 1973), p. 25. In such a situation, court costs, reputation of judges, and speed of securing a decision were considered in deciding which court to use. Justices of the peace competed for business and would often trade favorable decisions for continued use of their courts.

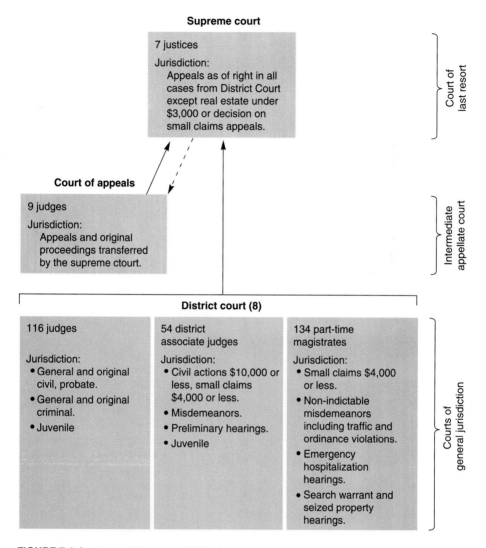

FIGURE 7-1 Iowa court structure, 2003.

Source: Directory of State Court Clerks & County Courthouses—2003 Edition (New York: WANT Publishing Co., 2003), p. 82.

crime. Only a few states have a single set of minor courts. Often where trial courts are consolidated, there are still separate criminal and civil divisions.

"Justice" in minor trial courts often is quick and routine. Defendants appear, they plead guilty or **no contest (nolo contendere)**, a fine is set, and the court proceeds to the next case. When defendants plead "no contest," it is in effect an admission of guilt without stating so formally. The defendant does not admit civil liability. This can be very important in traffic accidents where a civil suit for damages may follow the criminal traffic violation. Although penalties technically are the same as for a plea of guilty,

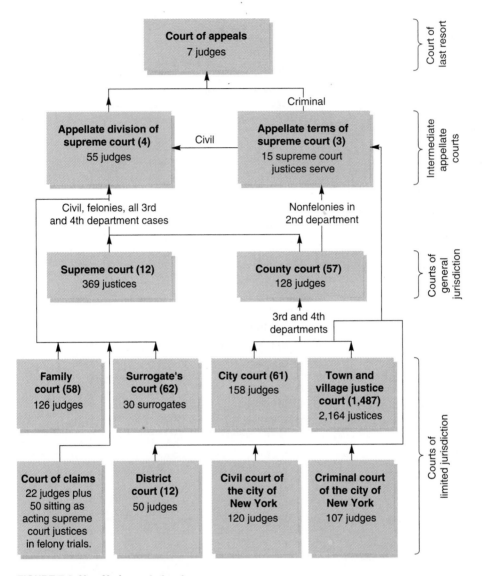

FIGURE 7-2 New York court structure.

Source: Directory of State Court Clerks & County Courthouses—2003 Edition (New York: WANT Publishing Co., 2003), p. 180.

judges may be more lenient when defendants throw themselves on the mercy of the court and explain the circumstances leading to their arrest.[2]

Major trial courts handle felony criminal cases and civil cases involving large amounts of money. Because felony cases place the strongest demands on trial courts, the large increase in criminal filings since 1980 has made effective case management critical if courts are to function well with limits on new personnel. Most often major trial courts—known as district courts, superior courts, or common pleas courts—are established at the county level. Although they are less fragmented than minor trial courts, major trial courts typically have divisions to hear such specialized cases as divorce proceedings and probate of wills. As noted, when cases are appealed from municipal courts, they usually are retried in a major trial court. Some states have grouped county courts into circuit courts, and judges are moved around the circuit. However, that kind of consolidation remains the exception in a system where local control is highly valued. Less than 5 percent of decisions are appealed from major trial courts, and thus for most litigants they are, in fact, courts of first and last resort.

Appellate Courts

Early in the twentieth century most states had only a supreme court to which all cases were appealed. In 2002 thirty-nine states had intermediate **courts of appeal** to deal with the increased volume of cases. Those states without intermediate appeals courts all are geographically small or they have small populations. Some states have one appellate court; in other states there are several regional appellate courts. In a few states, intermediate appellate courts are divided between criminal and civil divisions. Even where these intermediate courts do exist, some cases proceed directly from trial courts to the state supreme court. Appellate court judges usually sit in panels of three to hear cases. Parties to suits (litigants) are successful if they can convince at least two judges that their arguments are correct. In a majority of cases appeals are mandatory, meaning that intermediate court of appeals judges can exercise little control over their docket. In some states intermediate courts of appeal publish few of their opinions and judges often let other colleagues speak for them with little review of the opinion.[3]

All states have a *supreme court* that hears appeals from intermediate courts of appeal and, occasionally, hears appeals directly from major trial courts. State supreme courts have from five to nine justices, who generally sit *en banc* (all together) to hear cases (Table 7-1). Although the highest court in most states is called the supreme court, in a few states it is referred to as the court of appeals, supreme judicial court, or, as in New York, supreme court of appeals (see Figure 7-2). Oklahoma and Texas have separate courts of last resort for criminal and civil cases. Although state supreme courts do not have as much discretion over which cases to hear as the U.S. Supreme Court, their discretion is so broad that most appeals are rejected.

An ultimate power for state supreme courts and for the U.S. Supreme Court is the ability to declare legislative acts unconstitutional. The use of **judicial review** by state supreme courts, that is, to overrule acts passed by state legislatures, is about as frequent as it is for the U.S. Supreme Court to overrule acts passed by Congress.[4] Political scientist Henry Glick points out that the percentage of challenged state laws declared unconstitutional varies greatly among state supreme courts.

Like the U.S. Supreme Court, state supreme courts schedule oral arguments and then meet in private conference to decide cases. Unlike the U.S. Supreme Court, in many state supreme courts opinion assignments are made on a rotating basis among the justices, and this reduces the power of the chief justice. Chief justices in both systems are one among equals in deciding cases, but they may play a dominant role in leading the discussion of cases in conference, and they also have special administrative powers over their court system.

TABLE 7-1 State Courts of Last Resort

State or Other Jurisdiction	Name of Court	Justices Chosen[a] At Large	Justices Chosen[a] By District	No. of Judges[b]	Term (in Years)[c]	Method of Selection	Chief Justice Term of Office for Chief Justice
Alabama	S.C.	★		9	6	Popular election	6 years
Alaska	S.C.	★		5	10	By court	3 years[d]
Arizona	S.C.	★		5	6	By court	5 years
Arkansas	S.C.	★		7	8	Popular election	8 years
California	S.C.	★		7	12	Appointed by governor	12 years
Colorado	S.C.	★		7	10	By court	Indefinite
Connecticut	S.C.	★		7	8	Legislative appointment[e]	8 years
Delaware	S.C.	★		5	12	Appointed by governor	12 years
Florida	S.C.	[f]		7	6	By court	2 years
Georgia	S.C.	★		7	6	By court	4 years
Hawaii	S.C.	★		5	10	Appointed by governor, with consent of senate[g]	10 years
Idaho	S.C.	★		5	6	By court	4 years
Illinois	S.C.		★	7	10	By court	3 years
Indiana	S.C.	★		5	10[h]	Judicial nominating commission appointment	5 years
Iowa	S.C.	★		8	8	By court	8 years or duration of term
Kansas	S.C.	★		7	6	Rotation by seniority	Indefinite
Kentucky	S.C.		★	7	8	By court	4 years
Louisiana	S.C.		★	8[i]	10	By seniority of service	Duration of service
Maine	S.J.C.	★		7	7	Appointed by governor	7 years
Maryland	C.A.		★	7	10	Appointed by governor	Indefinite
Massachusetts	S.J.C.	★		7	To age 70	Appointed by governor[j]	To age 70
Michigan	S.C.	★		7	8	By court	2 years
Minnesota	S.C.	★		7	6	Popular election	6 years
Mississippi	S.C.		★	9	8	By seniority of service	Duration of service
Missouri	S.C.	★		7	12	By court[k]	2 years

Chief Justice

State or Other Jurisdiction	Name of Court	Justices Chosen[a]		No. of Judges[b]	Term (in Years)[c]	Method of Selection	Term of Office for Chief Justice
		At Large	By District				
Montana	S.C.	★		7	8	Popular election	8 years
Nebraska	S.C.		★[l]	7	6[m]	Appointed by governor from Judicial Nominating Commission	Duration of service
Nevada	S.C.	★		7	6	Rotation	2 years
New Hampshire	S.C.	★		5	To age 70	Appointed by governor with approval of elected executive council	To age 70
New Jersey	S.C.	★		7	7[n]	Appointed by governor, with consent of Senate	Duration of service
New Mexico	S.C.	★		5	8	By court	2 years
New York	C.A.	★		7	14	Appointed by governor from Judicial Nomination Commission	14 years
North Carolina	S.C.	★		7	8	Popular election	8 years
North Dakota	S.C.	★		5[o]	10	By supreme and district court judges	5 years[p]
Ohio	S.C.	★		7	6	Popular election	6 years
Oklahoma	S.C.		★	9	6	By court	2 years
	C.C.A.		★	5	6	By court	2 years
Oregon	S.C.	★		7	6	By court	6 years
Pennsylvania	S.C.	★		7	10	Rotation by seniority	Duration of term
Rhode Island	S.C.	★		5	Life	Appointed by governor from Judicial Nominating Commission	Life
South Carolina	S.C.	★		5	10	Legislative election	10 years
South Dakota	S.C.		★[q]	5	8	By court	4 years
Tennessee	S.C.	★		5	8	By court	4 years
Texas	S.C.	★		9	6	Partisan election	6 years
	C.C.A.	★		9	6	Partisan election	6 years[r]
Utah	S.C.	★		5	10[s]	By court	4 years
Vermont	S.C.	★		5	6	Appointed by governor from Judicial Nomination Commission, with consent of senate	6 years

See footnotes at end of table.

TABLE 7-1 State Courts of Last Resort *(concluded)*

State or Other Jurisdiction	Name of Court	Justices Chosen[a]		No. of Judges[b]	Term (in Years)[c]	Chief Justice	
		At Large	By District			Method of Selection	Term of Office for Chief Justice
Virginia	S.C.	★		7	12	Seniority	Indefinite
Washington	S.C.	★		9	6	By court	4 years
West Virginia	S.C.A.		★	5	12	Rotation by seniority	1 year
Wisconsin	S.C.	★		7	10	Seniority	Until declined
Wyoming	S.C.	★		5	8	By court	At the pleasure of the court
Dist. of Columbia	C.A.	★		9	15	Judicial Nominating Commission appointment	4 years
American Samoa	H.C.	★		8[f][u]	[v]	Appointed by Secretary of the Interior	[s]
Puerto Rico	S.C.	★		7	To age 70	Appointed by governor, with consent of senate	To age 70

Sources: Number of judges from Court Statistics Project, *State Court Caseload Statistics, 1999–2000* (National Center for State Courts 2000). All other information from *State Court Organization 1998* (National Center for State Courts); state constitutions, statutes and court administration offices.

Key:

S.C.—Supreme Court

S.C.A.—Supreme Court of Appeals

S.J.C.—Supreme Judicial Court

C.A.—Court of Appeals

C.C.A.—Court of Criminal Appeals

H.C.—High Court

[a]See Chapter 5 table entitled, "Selection and Retention of Judges," for details.

[b]Number includes chief justice.

[c]The initial term may be shorter. See Chapter 5 table entitled. "Selection and Retention of Judges," for details.

[d]A justice may serve more than one term as chief justice, but may not serve consecutive terms in that position.

[e]Governor nominates from candidates submitted by Judicial Selection Commission.

[f]Regional (5), Statewide (2), Regional based on District of Appeal

[g]Judicial Selection Commission nominates.

[h]Initial two years; retention 10 years.

[i]Includes one assigned from courts of appeal.

[j]Chief Justices are appointed, until age 70, by the governor with the advice and consent of the Executive (Governor's) Council.

[k]Selection is typically rotated among the judges.

[l]Chief justice chosen statewide; associate judges chosen by district.

[m]More than three years for first election and every six years thereafter.

[n]Followed by tenure.

[o]A temporary court of appeals was established July 1, 1987 to exercise appellate and original jurisdiction was delegated by the supreme court. This court does not sit, has no assigned judges, has heard no appeals, and is currently unfunded.

[p]Or expiration of term, whichever is first.

[q]Initially chosen by district; retention determined statewide.

[r]Presiding judge of Court of Criminal Appeals.

[s]Initial three years; retention 10 years.

[t]Chief judges and associate judges sit on appellate and trial divisions.

[u]Information is from *The Book of the States, 2000–2001*. No new data was available.

[v]For good behavior.

Source: The Book of the States, 2002 (Lexington, Ky.: Council of State Governments, 2002), pp. 203–204.

In contrast to the U.S. Supreme Court, there are relatively few dissents among judges in state supreme court decisions. Several factors help explain this apparent lack of conflict. First, legal tradition supports unanimity to present clear policy guidelines. Second, some courts assign one judge to research the case and write the opinion. In such circumstances, the other judges are likely to concur, because they have not paid close attention to the case. Moreover, because of the nature of their interaction in a small group setting, with as few as five justices, there is a need to maintain congenial personal relations.

Because the U.S. Constitution often is vague about the nature of governmental power, the U.S. Supreme Court must interpret what it means and this gives the Court substantial power. As noted in Chapter 1, state constitutions are more detailed and therefore more specific than the U.S. Constitution. Still, state supreme court judges exercise considerable discretionary power because state provisions often become outdated and the large number of amendments causes state constitutions to contain inconsistent and contradictory statements.

In contrast to legislators, judges are more likely to be drawn from a homogeneous upper-class or middle-class background, which means they tend to share similar perspectives on many legal issues. Because of a variety of reasons, including open discrimination, until the 1980s there were few women or minority lawyers and proportionally even fewer judges. By 2000, one-fourth of state supreme court justices were female, compared to 3.1 percent in 1980.[5] Racial composition also changed significantly from 0.6 percent nonwhite in 1980 to 11.6 percent in 2000. There were only two African-American justices on all state supreme courts in 1980. In 2000, women were represented on forty-nine of the fifty-two state high courts, and there was at least one racial minority on twenty-six of the high courts.

Political scientists have documented some connection between judges' race and gender, plus party affiliation and religion, and the nature of their decisions. However, there is disagreement about the strength of those connections. The presence of minority and women justices clearly speaks to the representativeness of courts and access to them by all groups of society.

REFORM OF STATE COURTS

The structure of state courts can have an important political impact on a variety of groups. Particularly in urban areas, courts have massive backlogs of cases, a situation that directly influences the administration of justice. Since the mid-1960s, the number of cases filed and disposed of has increased by 1,000 percent. Because they are unable to make *bail* (money or credit deposited with the court to get an arrested person temporarily released on the assurance that he or she will appear for trial), large numbers of people charged with crimes, but assumed innocent until proven guilty, are forced to spend months in county jails waiting for their cases to appear on the court calendar. Forced to exist in overcrowded, outdated facilities, many prisoners have suffered physical hardships, and a variety of suits have been initiated by civil liberties groups to force improvements in jail conditions. These same groups have protested against the bail system, which forces indigents to await trial in jail, and they have complained vigorously about judicial sentencing practices in which different penalties, ranging from probation to several years in prison, are given to individuals who have committed similar offenses. The backlog of cases also has led to the widespread use of **plea bargaining** (discussed in the following section), in which the accused are encouraged to plead guilty to lesser charges in return for the promise of leniency in sentencing.

In most states, the variety of courts operating under different rules of procedure within a single county results in confusion and unequal application of the law. The quality of "justice" may depend largely on how successful attorneys are in steering cases to courts presided over by friendly judges. Trial judges function independently of one another, and there are few effective controls that can be applied to them by appellate courts.

Faced with such a situation, reformers have called for an integrated system in which the number of separate courts would be greatly reduced and the problem of overlapping jurisdiction eliminated. Reformers would place all judges under the general supervision of the chief justice of their state in order to ensure uniform practices and standards of conduct. As will be seen later in this chapter, reformers would also like to eliminate the use of judgeships as political patronage.

Unified Court Systems

Unifying reform includes both the **consolidation of courts** and the **centralization of courts**. Only a few states have consolidated their court system into a single set of courts that handle all trial court litigation. Most continue to have a number of specialized courts with their own procedures. As noted, New York has thirteen kinds of trial courts. States have been more successful in centralizing or unifying their court system under an administrative judge who controls workloads, makes staff assignments, and determines budgets. A majority of states have assumed all or most of the funding of court systems. Only a few states, such as Hawaii, have consolidated *and* centralized their courts.

There is little pattern to which states have unified courts. Unified and decentralized systems occur in all regions and in large and small states. However, unified control by the supreme court tends to be strongest in the western states.

In addition to streamlining the structure of courts, unified judicial systems also include centralizing authority with the state supreme court to budget for all courts; to manage the caseload of courts statewide, including the use of retired judges; and to be responsible for disciplining attorneys and judges. In such cases, the chief justice becomes an administrator responsible for the operation of courts across the state.

Reform is difficult to accomplish because traditional court practices benefit groups, such as lawyers and political parties, that have substantial political influence. Opposition also comes from legislators and judges who believe their existing power would be diminished by the elimination of the current maze of courts and the independence it provides to local judges. In some states reformers have given up trying to change the way in which judges are selected in order to get agreement first on court unification.

Proponents of consolidation argue that fragmented court systems are inefficient and that overlapping court jurisdiction often is confusing. Opponents counter that it is desirable for courts to have the flexibility to adapt to unique needs of the local area.

Proponents of centralized control contend that when each court makes its own procedural rules, "justice" may vary greatly among courts that are independent of each other. State supreme court justices favor centralization because it increases their power, but local judges and government officials want to maintain community control. Most states have a professional court administrator under the control of the supreme court and those administrators have substantial power over the management of lower courts.[6]

Political scientist Lawrence Baum concludes that court unification may not produce the benefits its proponents proclaim.[7] Even in consolidated systems, individual courts and judges may retain substantial autonomy and efficiency may be more closely related to the work habits of individual judges than to court structure. If cases are disposed of more quickly, it may be at the expense of careful review. Many people believe that courts *should* be influenced by external politics to maintain public accountability. Although nearly all state court systems have become more unified in recent years, no state's system is totally unified, and it is unlikely that major changes will occur in the near future.

Access to Courts and Court Management

As noted above, court reform efforts during most of the twentieth century centered on reorganization, or structural reform of state systems. More recently, the focus has shifted to include ensuring racial, ethnic, income, and gender access to courts. Too often people are effectively denied access because of legal costs. Many states do not require public defender systems statewide. Even when they exist, public defender offices often are underfunded, and budgets for paying court-appointed counsel have been cut. Most researchers conclude that public defenders are more effective than court-appointed attorneys, who may have little criminal court experience. In general, however, defending the poor is not a high priority for state and local governments. The United States is the only Western democracy in which civil litigants are not guaranteed legal counsel.

In addition to issues dealing with legal counsel, states have taken a number of other steps to improve access to courts in both criminal and civil proceedings. These include training and certifying court interpreters for those with limited English skills; enforcement of the Americans with Disabilities Act, by applying it to litigants, witnesses, jurors, and spectators; examination of racial, ethnic, and gender bias in the courts; the use of alternative dispute resolution, such as mediation and arbitration; the expansion of night courts; the availability of day care; and the creation of family courts. Family courts consolidate all matters concerning families—divorce, child custody, adoption, and domestic violence—into a single court. Improving access, of course, increases the caseloads of courts that are already crowded.

Access to crowded courts in civil matters is increasingly aided by the use of mediation and arbitration. These and other forms of alternative dispute resolution are less costly and complex than court procedures, and they can be tailored to the specific needs of the participants.

In **mediation** an impartial third party assists the disputants in reaching a voluntary settlement. Usually the process is nonadversarial, meaning that there is no attempt to determine right or wrong, but instead the parties seek to reach a mutual agreement among a selection of alternative solutions. **Arbitration** calls for one or more persons to hear the arguments in a dispute, review the evidence, and reach a decision, or award. The parties agree ahead of time to be bound by the decision. Arbitration is often used in labor disputes. More recently court-annexed arbitration has been used in which judges refer civil suits to private arbitrators, who render prompt decisions. If the losing party does not accept the arbitrator's decision, a trial can be held in the regular court system. In a similar process, a few cities have moved lesser criminal cases to special judges who settle disputes without a jury.

Professional management has been introduced into most state court systems. This includes the use of court administrators and improved budget procedures. Better management can improve access to courts by shifting many more routine functions away from downtown court buildings and neighborhood facilities. Also, drug courts have been established to divert nonviolent drug offenders from the courts to treatment centers.[8]

TRIAL COURT PROCEDURES

As presented in movies and on television, the commonly accepted view of the administration of justice is that of the classic adversary system in which the attorney battles valiantly on behalf of his or her clients. There is always a jury, a narrow-minded prosecutor, and a white-haired judge who wields even control as the attorneys take turns objecting to the irrelevant, immaterial, and leading questions of their worthy opponent. In such a setting, justice always triumphs as the defendant is exonerated and the guilty person is dramatically exposed. In fact, however, most legal issues are settled without a trial when the defendant pleads guilty and the judge issues a sentence.

Plea Bargaining

Only about 10 percent of all criminal cases come to trial. Most are settled in pretrial negotiations among the defendant, the prosecutor, and the judge. This arrangement—*plea bargaining*—in which the defendant pleads guilty in return for a reduced charge and, most likely, a less severe penalty, is dominated by the prosecutor. Defense attorneys typically approach prosecutors to see what kind of bargain they can reach. Because prosecutors and defense attorneys know more about the details of a case, judges often defer to them for factual information and sentencing guidelines. As we would expect, cases most likely to be bargained are those where there is strong evidence against the defendant and the charges are not serious.[9] Still, prosecutors may not want to bargain some cases where they are very confident they will win at trial.

Plea bargaining is a common practice because it appears to benefit each of the interested parties. *Defendants* plead guilty because they receive a reduction of charge (e.g., from aggravated murder to manslaughter); a reduction in length of sentence; a chance for probation; or some combination of these agreements that results in softening the potential damage of the original charge. *Prosecutors* seek to avoid time-consuming trials, and they also wish to keep their conviction rates high. In some cases, the prosecutor may have obtained evidence illegally or may wish to protect informants by keeping them from taking the witness stand; he or she is therefore willing to trade a trial with its doubtful outcome for the sure thing of a guilty plea to a reduced charge. Attorneys for both sides like pretrial settlements because they can control the flow of information. Witnesses are not questioned, and they are not subject to the strict rules of trial procedure. *Judges,* concerned with avoiding delay and backlogs, encourage plea bargaining as a speedy way to dispose of cases. The *police* benefit because they do not have to appear in court as witnesses during their off-duty hours. Plea bargaining also helps the police "clear" cases and therefore bolsters their image as successful crime fighters. This was acknowledged as a judicial fact of life by the U.S. Supreme Court in *Santobello v. New York* (1971). Although the *Santobello* decision recognizes the need for plea bargaining, it also requires that judges make sure that defendants understand the agreements.

Plea bargaining is a quick and efficient means of disposing of legal disputes. Given the existing structure of the courts and the limited number of judges, the legal system in most states would rapidly break down if even half the criminal defendants pleaded not guilty and demanded a jury trial. At the present time, many defendants are convinced that they will be in for a rough time if they do not cooperate with the police and plead guilty rather than having their cases come to trial.

Plea bargaining has been going on for more than one hundred years. Surprisingly, it is not a technique that developed in response to a heavy criminal workload in big cities. Evidence suggests that heavy workloads do not cause plea bargaining.[10] Plea bargaining is widespread in rural counties that have low crime rates, and in some cities with heavy caseloads it is used relatively little. Researchers suggest that the use of plea bargaining is closely tied to the closeness of interaction among members of the courtroom work group—judges, lawyers, and prosecutors.[11] Because these officials often work closely together for a year or more, personal relations develop and they seek more informal solutions for cases. Pretrial settlements in civil cases are a product of the same circumstances that lead to plea bargaining in criminal cases. In both situations settlement helps courtroom work groups achieve several goals. As Eisenstein and Jacob show, plea bargaining reduces uncertainty for all parties, it helps maintain the cohesion of the work group, and it makes the court look good to the general public by showing that it can dispose of cases quickly and that "justice" is done. In other words, criminals are caught and punished.

In spite of its appealing characteristics, plea bargaining has many disturbing consequences. In plea bargaining, the procedures are invisible and informal. Records are not kept of conversations, and decisions seldom are reviewed by higher courts to determine whether the defendant really was guilty as charged. There is a strong potential for coercion as the prosecutor pressures the defendant. Illegally obtained evidence that might be held inadmissible in a court is never questioned. Often the unsuspecting defendant is simply advised by his or her court-appointed attorney to plead guilty, thereby saving the attorney time and allowing him or her to collect an easy fee. Some bargains appear to be too lenient and thus benefit criminal defendants. In other instances, defendants risk much harsher sentences if they insist on their right to go to trial, and thus they may accept a plea bargain even when the case against them is relatively weak.

Given the broad criticism against plea bargaining, it is not surprising that there have been calls to abolish it. Indeed, some state and local governments have experimented with strict limits on plea bargaining. However, most have reinstated it rather quickly. As noted, close-knit courtroom work groups encourage plea bargaining, and in most cases it is clear that the defendant is guilty. Several states and the federal government have passed laws requiring mandatory sentencing for certain crimes. This eliminates plea bargaining in those instances. However, prosecutors often refuse to charge defendants with crimes that require a mandatory sentence because it limits their power to bargain.

In civil cases, there is typically an even greater delay than in criminal cases. In urban areas it may be several years before a case comes to trial. Delay is a major factor leading to out-of-court settlements, in which the two parties agree to a financial resolution of their dispute. Many civil suits involve personal injury for which the plaintiff has accumulated substantial medical bills. Because of the pressure of medical and legal expenses, plaintiffs may choose to settle before a trial date arrives. The defendant (often an insurance company) can usually better afford the costs incurred in delay but may wish to settle privately, being aware of exorbitant awards made by juries in cases where physical injury has resulted in the permanent loss of sight or limb. Putting caps on the amount of damages in civil suits (tort reform) has become a controversial political issue, with liberals (and trial attorneys) opposing limits and conservatives, including President George W. Bush, favoring them.

In the late 1990s several state legislatures approved laws to curtail damage suits. However, the supreme courts in many of those states, including Ohio, Illinois, New Hampshire, and Oregon, have overturned the laws on the grounds that they violated basic constitutional guarantees, such as the right to a jury trial. The battle continues as Republican legislators, backed by business groups, push for limits on the amount of damage awards in civil suits. Labor unions and trial lawyers encourage Democrats to block such legislation.

When the full range of legal procedures is employed, the following patterns in civil and criminal cases can be identified as common among the states.

Civil Disputes

The procedure in a **civil dispute** is as follows:

1. The plaintiff (the complainant, the one who brings suit) approaches a lawyer, who requests the clerk of the proper court to issue a *writ of summons*. This writ, delivered by a deputy sheriff, directs the defendant to appear in court to answer the plaintiff's charges. Increasingly, private process servers perform this task. Failure to appear will result in the defendant losing the judgment by default.
2. Once the summons is delivered, the plaintiff files a *complaint* stating his or her cause of action and establishing that the court has jurisdiction and can provide a remedy in his or her dispute. The complaint is filed with the clerk of courts, who then has a copy delivered to the defendant along with a notice that the complaint is to be answered by a certain date. The defendant may admit to the charges, deny some or all of the charges, or argue that the charges do not raise a sufficient legal issue for the case to come to court. The judge will rule on the defendant's response and, unless he or she has admitted guilt, will allow the defendant to file a more detailed answer. This process of charge and response and possible countercharge by the defendant may continue for an extended time. When all complaints are

answered and all pleadings filed, the issue is "joined" and the attorneys prepare for trial.

3. *Preliminary motions* are made and the case then lies dormant for several months (or years) as the trial date approaches. During the delay, negotiation takes place in an attempt to settle the dispute out of court. More than two-thirds of the cases filed never get beyond the preliminary stages, and in fact many cases are filed with no intention of pushing them to trial. Because lawyers in many civil cases are compensated on a contingency basis (they receive from 25 to 40 percent of the award), they push for out-of-court settlements to be sure of receiving some payment and to save the time and effort of going to trial. Shortly before the trial date, **pretrial conferences** are held in which the judge meets with attorneys for each side in an attempt to clarify and simplify the issues to those in contention.

4. If a settlement cannot be reached privately, the case goes to *trial*. Often a jury trial is waived, although plaintiffs in personal injury cases may prefer a jury rather than having the case heard by a judge, who they believe will be less generous. The judge or jury will decide which party was legally at fault and will also determine the amount of damages to be awarded. It is possible to appeal the verdict to a higher court. Although civil disputes usually involve private (nongovernmental) parties, the results in large damage award cases can have widespread consequences.

Criminal Disputes

The procedure in a **criminal dispute** is as follows:

1. Most arrests are made with a **warrant.** Law enforcement officers become aware that a crime has been committed and begin to identify and locate a suspect. Police need to obtain a search warrant to enter a private home. A magistrate issues the warrant directing a search or apprehension of a suspect, having received a sworn statement that there is probable cause to believe that a crime has been committed by a particular person at a given time and place. If the warrant authorizes a search, it must state clearly the place to be searched and the material to be seized. Still, there are numerous exceptions to the warrant requirement. These include hot pursuit, when a suspect runs into a house, and circumstances where police fear that evidence will be destroyed if they wait to obtain a warrant.

2. After most arrests, the person is taken to a police station for a booking process where reports are prepared and fingerprinting is done.

3. The **initial appearance** occurs the day of the arrest or the next morning. Defendants are advised of the charges and of their constitutional rights, including the right to counsel. If the accused is permitted to enter a plea at the initial appearance, the tendency is to call the process an **arraignment.** Pleas include guilty, not guilty, and no contest (nolo contendere). A plea of no contest is treated essentially the same as a guilty plea. In some states arraignment occurs weeks or months before the trial, in others it is held the day the trial is scheduled to begin. Further, at the initial appearance the court will determine whether the defendant should be held in custody or whether **bail** should be set. Bail money is deposited or bond is posted

as a condition for release from custody and as a guarantee that the defendant will appear at the next stage in the criminal process.

4. In felony cases the defendant is brought before a magistrate (often a municipal judge) for a *preliminary hearing*. The purpose of this hearing is to determine whether the prosecution has sufficient evidence to hold the accused and, if so, to set bail.

5. In many jurisdictions preliminary hearings have been eliminated and the prosecutor (district attorney) simply files a statement (the "information") with the appropriate court, which *indicts*, or formally accuses, a person of the commission of a crime. In other states, the prosecutor presents evidence that a serious crime has been committed to a **grand jury**.* If the grand jury finds sufficient reason to believe the accused committed the crime for which he or she is charged, it will return a "true bill" that indicts the accused, who then is bound over for trial.

6. Pretrial motions regarding the admissibility of evidence or requiring disclosure of information are filed with the court.

7. Pretrial conferences involve meetings of the main players in the criminal process— the judge, prosecutor, and defense attorney. They seek to resolve issues that could delay the trial. Of course, the plea bargaining that occurs at this stage may mean that a trial does not occur.

8. At the *trial stage,* the defendant in most states may waive the right to a jury trial and have the case heard by a judge. If the defendant is found guilty by a judge or jury, it is the judge who usually determines the sentence. Traditionally, judges were given broad discretion between minimum and maximum penalties for specific crimes. As we will see later in the chapter, after passing mandatory sentencing laws in the 1980s that limited the discretion of judges, several states have recently repealed these laws.

Juries

Juries have been mentioned in the discussion of both civil and criminal disputes, and a few words of explanation are in order. A group of potential jury persons (a *venire*) is selected by lot, usually from voting lists or drivers' licenses. These people are called into court as jury cases arise and are examined (*voir dire*) regarding their qualifications to return an impartial verdict in the case at hand.

Charges have been made that the jury system underrepresents minorities. Because African Americans and Hispanics are less likely than whites to be registered to vote, driver's license lists are increasingly used to pick jury members. However, these lists tend to underrepresent older persons, and many who live in large urban areas do not have driver's licenses. Minorities also may be disadvantaged by changes in trial location. In the highly publicized Rodney King trial in 1992 there was a change of venue from Los Angeles, where his alleged beating by police took place, to the nearly all-white

---

*The *grand jury* is a body of twelve to twenty-five members whose purposes are inquisitorial and accusatorial. It is contrasted with a *petit jury*, usually of twelve persons, but at least six, which determines guilt or innocence. The grand jury meets in secret and decides by a majority vote. On occasion, it may conduct its own investigations into official misconduct. The grand jury has the power to subpoena witnesses and records and to compel testimony under oath. It usually follows the dictates of the prosecutor. Because grand juries are expensive and time-consuming, they have been abolished in many states.

suburb of Simi Valley, where it was unlikely there would be any African-American jurors. In 1986 (*Batson v. Kentucky*) the Supreme Court held that prosecutors may not use their peremptory challenges (where potential jury members may be rejected without any reason, as contrasted with dismissal "for cause" where attorneys have reason to believe a potential juror may be biased) to exclude members based on race. In 1994, this ruling was extended to prevent exclusion based on gender in *J.E.B. v. Alabama*. Although all juries in federal trials must have twelve members, several states use juries with as few as six or eight members. Critics of small juries contend that they are more likely than twelve-member juries to exclude minorities and they are less likely to have a minority point of view.[12]

In spite of the importance attached to the jury system, it is not employed as often as one might expect. In some jurisdictions, as many as 90 percent of all people charged with criminal offenses plead guilty. Of those going to trial, roughly half opt to have their cases heard by a judge. Fewer than 10 percent nationwide of those charged with a criminal offense demand a jury trial. Juries are not required for all cases, and typically criminal misdemeanors and various civil actions—divorce, small claims, landlord-tenant disputes—are heard by judges alone. Juvenile defendants are not automatically guaranteed jury trials. The U.S. Supreme Court has held that the Seventh Amendment's right to jury trials in civil cases does not apply to state courts. In criminal cases the Supreme Court has decided that juries are required only if the possible maximum sentence is six months or more.

Compared with judge-tried cases, jury trials are longer, cost more, and involve more people. Most research indicates that judge and jury decisions are remarkably similar. A major study of the American jury system found that judges agreed with jury verdicts 80 percent of the time. When there was disagreement, the jury tended to be more lenient than the judge and more willing to consider a social, as opposed to a strictly legal, definition of guilt.[13]

JUDICIAL SELECTION

The way in which state court systems function is influenced strongly by the quality of judicial personnel. In turn, the type of judge presiding in courtrooms across the country is influenced by the ways in which judges are selected. Judicial selection is a highly political process that directly affects the interests of the most powerful partisan forces in states and communities. Political parties use judgeships as a source of patronage. Lawyers and their bar associations are very much involved in the selection process. Not only are the judgeships themselves prized positions, but judges are able to spread the patronage further by assigning counsel in criminal cases, by naming administrators of estates where a will does not exist, and by appointing numerous minor court officials.

Each of the thirteen original states selected judges by either legislative or gubernatorial appointment. By the 1830s the popular democracy movement associated with Andrew Jackson began pushing states to elect judges. The concurrent rise of political parties meant that the selection and recruitment of judges were done by powerful new political party leaders in many large cities.[14] The Progressive movement in the second half of the nineteenth century reacted against political parties by moving to nonpartisan judicial elections. A feeling of dissatisfaction with both election and appointment of judges led the American Judicature Society, founded in 1913, to propose a plan in which judicial nominating commissions would recommend judicial candidates to governors. From this came the Missouri Plan, which will be discussed later.

Several selection systems are currently used by the fifty states—election, appointment by governors, appointment by legislatures, merit plans, and various combinations of these basic plans (Table 7-2). About a dozen states use one system for trial judges and another for appellate judges, and there may be special systems for minor trial judges. Currently, over thirty states use a merit system to select judges at least at one court level. Trial judges are more likely to be elected than are appellate judges.

Election continues to be the most popular way of selecting judges. Judges are on the ballot along with a variety of other officials, and parties participate by endorsing candidates and managing nominations. Even when nonpartisan systems are used, parties often play a dominant role. In Ohio, for example, judges are chosen in nonpartisan general elections, but partisan primaries are conducted in which judges' party affiliations are clearly stated. Partisan election (election by party label) is most likely to occur in the South. In most cases judicial elections are nearly invisible to voters. Often they are held at odd times during the year and voter turnout is lower than in legislative and gubernatorial elections.

TABLE 7-2 Principal Methods of Judicial Selection for State Courts

Partisan Election	Nonpartisan Election	Legislative Appointment	Gubernatorial Appointment	Merit Plan
Alabama	Georgia	South Carolina	California	Alaska
Arkansas	Idaho	Virginia	Maine[a]	Arizona
Illinois	Kentucky		New Hampshire	Colorado
New York	Louisiana		New Jersey	Connecticut
North Carolina	Michigan			Delaware
Pennsylvania	Minnesota			Florida
Tennessee	Mississippi			Hawaii
Texas	Montana			Indiana
West Virginia	Nevada			Iowa
	North Dakota			Kansas
	Ohio			Maryland
	Oregon			Massachusetts
	Washington			Missouri
	Wisconsin			Nebraska
				New Mexico
				Oklahoma
				Rhode Island
				South Dakota
				Utah
				Vermont
				Wyoming

Source: Council of State Governments, *The Book of the States, 2002* (Lexington, Ky.: Council of State Governments, 2002), pp. 209–211.

In many instances, judges resign before their term of office expires. This allows the governor to make an interim appointment. Typically, incumbent judges stand an excellent chance of being reelected. In addition to low turnout, often there are no opposition candidates in judicial elections.

In nine states, the governor *appoints* some judges in a manner similar to the presidential selection of federal judges. Usually the legislature confirms the appointment, and a strong role is played by interest groups to influence nominations. In a few states, the legislature appoints judges. In those cases, the governor often plays a major role in controlling the legislature's choices and most judges are former state legislators.

One study found no difference among the various systems of judicial selection in the resulting percentages of women and minority judges. Nor was there a difference between the percentages of women and minorities as judges in higher and lower courts.[15]

Merit Systems

Most states adopting new plans of judicial selection since the 1930s have chosen some form of *merit system*. These plans, which have many variations, are based on a selection process first instituted by California in 1934 and made popular by Missouri in 1940. The goal of merit plans is to remove judicial selection from the influence of partisan politics and to select judges on the basis of ability, in large part as determined by lawyers and sitting judges.

The **Missouri Plan** operates as follows. Whenever a judicial vacancy arises, the governor appoints an individual from a list of acceptable names submitted by a commission. There are three commissions in Missouri to nominate judges for three types of courts. The commissions are composed of lawyers, ordinary citizens, and a sitting judge. The lawyers are elected by all the lawyers in the court's district; the lay citizens are appointed by the governor; and the judge is the presiding judge of the court of appeals in that area. In a few states appointment is made by the governor or legislature without a nominating commission. After a judge has served for a period of time, his or her name appears on the ballot and the voters check yes or no. If the vote is no, the selection process begins again. If the vote is yes, the judge's name will appear on future ballots, again without an opponent, and the voters will decide whether they wish the judge to remain in office. In a few states judges run in competitive, partisan retention elections.

In California the governor appoints all supreme court and court of appeals justices. These appointments must be approved by the Committee on Judicial Appointments, which is composed of several judges and the state attorney general. Following appointment, California uses merit-retention elections for appellate judges, similar to those in Missouri. Trial court judges are selected by nonpartisan election.

Contrary to the arguments of good-government groups, most studies indicate that merit plans do *not* produce judges who differ substantially from those who are elected or appointed. They have not had better legal qualifications nor have they decided cases in a noticeably different manner from judges selected by other methods. In the most comprehensive review of the Missouri Plan, the authors note that "governors have used their appointments to reward friends or past political supporters and have implemented the plan very largely from a personal and political viewpoint."[16]

Turnout usually is low in retention elections, and few judges have been voted out of office in states with merit plans. In California, no judge had been voted out of office since the plan was implemented in 1934 until chief justice Rose Elizabeth Bird and two justices were overwhelmingly denied reconfirmation in 1986.

Particularly when considering the results of California retention elections in the 1980s and early 1990s, it was easy to conclude that if interest groups targeted judges for defeat, it would be difficult for judges to defend themselves. However, across the country *fewer* judges were defeated in the 1990s than in the past and voter participation increased.[17]

Merit systems do not remove partisan considerations from the judiciary, nor do they make judicial elections different from elections for other public offices. For example, the 1986 judicial retention election in California was as high-spending and personally contentious as any gubernatorial partisan election.

Regardless of the method of selection, partisan politics plays a major role in the selection of judges. Even in Missouri, governors have appointed most judges from their own party. In nonpartisan elections, parties are usually active in primary elections, and they are often directly involved in general elections. Interest groups are active participants in every selection plan. Governors tend to draw a high percentage of their appointments from current and past members of the state legislature. Under both partisan and merit systems, judges seem equally objective and equally attuned to popular sentiment in their states.

In the 1980s voters in several states defeated proposals to move to merit systems of judicial selection. In general, the proponents and opponents of merit selection among the states have been similar. Proponents include various good-government groups, such as the League of Women Voters; bar associations; and business groups. Opponents include trial lawyers, labor unions, and minorities. Political parties often are split on merit selection depending on how they have fared under an electoral system.[18]

Judicial Elections

We have seen that in practice judges selected by merit plans enjoy a lifetime of service, although they are subject to periodic approval at the polls. As noted in Chapter 4, incumbent judges usually face little opposition. Often lawyers are reluctant to challenge sitting judges, and low-level campaigns favor incumbents running against challengers who are not well known to the general public. Incumbent judges are even less likely to be defeated in nonpartisan elections where party identification cannot be used as a voting clue. When incumbents are defeated, oftentimes there have been allegations of immoral conduct or incompetence that have been played up by the local media.

Unlike federal judges, few state judges are given life tenure in a single appointment and few states give their governors sole power to appoint judges. For appellate courts, the typical length of a term is five to twelve years. Generally, terms of trial judges are shorter, averaging four to eight years. Long terms are believed to be beneficial because they help ensure judicial independence.

Funding judicial elections is troublesome because lawyers often are the major source of campaign contributions. Three states have public funding systems for judicial elections.

For many voters a particularly frustrating aspect of judicial campaigns has been that candidates often are prohibited by codes of ethics from giving their personal opinions about policy issues. As noted in Chapter 4, judicial elections are expected to change following a decision by the Supreme Court to allow candidates to speak more freely on policy issues. In the past, campaigns often have centered around candidates' past experience and how that has prepared them to be "tough on crime" once they are on the bench.

Minority lawyers and politicians prefer that judges be elected from small, single-member districts where it is more likely that a majority of voters will be minorities than is the case in at-large districts that compose an entire city or county. Their position has been helped by the Supreme Court's rulings in *Clark v. Roemer* (1991) and in *Chisom v. Roemer* (1991) that provisions of the Voting Rights Act of 1982 are applicable to judicial elections because judges, like legislators, serve as "representatives" of the people. In *Chisom*, it was contended that Louisiana's system of electing some state supreme court judges from multimember (at-large) districts diluted the voting strength of African Americans. Because 1982 Voting Rights Act amendments prescribe an "effects test" to determine whether government actions have impaired the ability of minorities to influence the outcome of elections (this is most often seen in the way in which legislative boundaries are drawn), if minorities can show that existing electoral systems have had the effect of limiting or excluding the selection of minority judges, states will be forced to change their election districts. The key change in the 1982 amendments was that plaintiffs no longer had to prove that government officials "intended" to weaken the political power of minorities. In *Chisom*, Justice Stevens stated a clear preference for the merit selection of judges. At-large systems for electing judges have been overturned in Missouri and Georgia.

Discipline and Removal of Judges

All state judges serve for at least four years. Terms range up to fourteen years (in New York). In Rhode Island, judges have life appointments, and in a few states appointment is to age seventy. Only in rare instances have judges been removed, or even disciplined, during their term in office. Nearly all states have constitutional provisions for impeachment, but the process (which involves securing valid signatures on petitions and holding trials) is time-consuming and very expensive. Few judges have been impeached and removed from office. Seven states permit judicial recall; but even fewer judges have been recalled than have been impeached.

Not only are these traditional means of removal time-consuming and costly, but they also are often perceived as overly harsh penalties for the alleged offenses. As a result, judges with serious problems frequently escape removal because voters or legislatures are reluctant to take such drastic action. Occasionally judges resign when threatened with impeachment.

A more practical solution to dealing with problems of judicial incompetence or unethical behavior has been the creation of judicial tenure commissions composed of lawyers, judges, and citizens. They investigate complaints, hold hearings, and impose penalties ranging from temporary suspension to removal. More than thirty states have judicial commissions. Most are patterned after the California Commission of Judicial

Performance, which was established in 1960 when voters approved a constitutional initiative. The California Commission has nine members: five judges, two attorneys, and two citizens. The commission investigates complaints against judges and if the allegations have merit, it seeks voluntary compliance through a confidential proceeding with the judge. If the problem cannot be resolved in this way, the commission schedules a hearing and then it can recommend dismissal. Dismissal of a judge must be approved by the state supreme court.

FEDERAL-STATE COURT RELATIONS

We have noted that overwhelmingly litigation in the United States takes place in state courts. Although decisions of state supreme courts may be appealed to the United States Supreme Court, if the case does not raise a substantial federal question or if it has been decided on independent state grounds, the U.S. Supreme Court will not review it.[19] This means that very few state cases are reviewed by the Supreme Court.

In the 1950s and 1960s, the liberal Warren Court overturned a number of state court decisions dealing with school desegregation, rights of criminal defendants, and legislative reapportionment. Since the 1970s, a more conservative Supreme Court has been less intrusive in state judicial affairs. As noted in Chapter 2, since the early 1990s the Court has overturned several laws passed by Congress that were found to infringe on the power of state government.

While the Supreme Court has become more conservative, liberal state supreme courts have become increasingly protective of individual rights and have refused to follow guidelines set down by the Burger and Rehnquist courts. This new **judicial activism** can be seen in several areas of state policy making.

Supreme courts around the country have ruled against their states' funding systems for education. A decade after the Supreme Court upheld Georgia's anti-sodomy law in *Bowers v. Hardwick* (1986), the Georgia supreme court overturned the law as a violation of individual rights in its state constitution. Based on rights provided in their states' constitutions, state courts have rejected Supreme Court rulings dealing with obscenity, gay rights, and rights of criminal defendants.

On a few occasions, the Supreme Court has sought to control state courts by reversing their decisions. For example, the Michigan supreme court overturned a criminal conviction on the grounds that the police search for illegal drugs violated the Fourth Amendment to the United States Constitution *and* the Michigan constitution. In *Michigan v. Long* (1983) the Supreme Court ruled that the Michigan court had relied *exclusively* on the U.S. Constitution and that the search was permissible under rules set by the Supreme Court in its earlier ruling (*Terry v. Ohio,* 1968) establishing principles for permissible searches under the Fourth Amendment.

FIGHTING CRIME

Overwhelmingly, crime control in the United States is the responsibility of states, counties, and cities. The relatively small federal involvement is reflected by statistics that show that New York City's 38,000 sworn police officers are about triple the number of

FBI special agents. About 95 percent of all crime occurs within the jurisdiction of state and local governments. Nearly 90 percent of the money spent to fight crime and house prisoners comes from state sources.

Like other policy making areas we have discussed, crime and corrections reflect the interaction of officials at all levels of governments. Although cities bear the greatest burden of fighting crime, federal, state, and county governments all are involved in passing laws, appropriating money, and making rulings that affect crime fighting at the street level as well as correctional facilities from city jails to maximum security state prisons.

The rate of violent crime tripled from 1960 to 1980. Then it leveled off and declined in the early 1980s, but it increased in the late 1980s. During this twenty-year period politicians at all levels of government tried to use the rising crime rate and subsequent fear of crime to their advantage. State legislators passed bills calling for stricter criminal penalties and mayors tried to instill in their police departments a zero-tolerance for crime. The death penalty was restored in most states and prison populations grew exponentially. Sociologists and political scientists developed a multitude of theories to explain why crime was rising, and they proposed an equally large number of solutions to combat the crime problem.

Beginning in 1992, the crime rate steadily decreased throughout the decade. Rates dropped in every region of the country and in all categories of violent crime as well as burglary and theft. Declines were most significant in the nation's largest cities where crime rates have been the highest. By 2000, the murder rate was at its lowest level since 1966. Rates of violent crimes had declined almost 50 percent since the early 1990s and were the lowest since the government began tracking the crime rate in 1973.

Violent crimes rose slightly in 2001 and in 2002, but they remained significantly lower than in the 1990s. Some criminologists expressed surprise that the crime rate was not higher, given the weak national economy and the recent release of large numbers of people from prison.

As noted in the story at the beginning of this chapter, just why crime rates increase or decrease remains a mystery. Some criminologists credit the drop in crime to the huge number of people in prison (just over 2 million in United States prisons and jails in 2002). Longer sentences imposed in the 1980s clearly helped prevent crimes by keeping convicted felons in jail rather than releasing them to the streets where many would likely return to criminal activity. As we will discuss later in this chapter, and noted at the beginning of the chapter, others credit the drop in crime to changes in police strategy, including the implementation of community policing. Demography also plays a major role in crime rates because males between the ages of 17 and 19 commit nearly half of all violent crimes. As their numbers go up, we would expect more crime to occur.

Curiously, even as crime rates have decreased, *fear* of crime, perhaps heightened by watching local television news, remains high. This helps explain why state legislators and judges continue to find it politically advantageous to be seen as "tough on crime."

Regardless of what causes an individual to perform criminal acts, we can strongly associate violent criminal behavior with young males: Half of the crimes on the annual *Uniform Crime Reports* are committed by males under the age of twenty. Except for larceny-theft, where they constitute about 30 percent of all arrests, women make up less than 15 percent of the arrests for all other *UCR* crimes, and only about 6 percent of all prisoners in the United States are women (this is up from 4 percent in 1981). Arrest rates in cities with populations over 100,000 are nearly double those in rural areas.

There are several reasons why we should be cautious when reading crime statistics. First, the *Uniform Crime Reports*—the major source of national crime statistics, published by the FBI—covers only four types of violent crime (assault, murder, rape, and robbery) and four types of property crime (arson, burglary, larceny, and motor vehicle theft). Most white-collar crimes are omitted. Second, many crimes are not reported to the police. Third, police reports to the FBI may underestimate the amount of crime to make local departments look better. And fourth, although most murders and motor vehicle thefts are reported, other crimes, for various reasons, are vastly underreported to the police. Just under 50 percent of the 6.2 million rapes, armed robberies, and assaults were reported to police in 2000. Many victims do not think the police can solve cases, or they don't think crimes are important enough to report, or the crimes (often assault or rape) have been committed by a relative or friend, or the victim fears retaliation from gang members.

Although the United States has a much higher murder rate than other democratic countries, crime rates are surprisingly high in many Western European nations. For example, Great Britain has a higher rate of burglary than the United States, France has a higher rate of auto theft, and the Netherlands has about the same total crime rate.

As indicated in Table 7-3, the crime rate varies by more than a factor of 3 among the states. In general, New England states have the lowest crime rate. Although six of the seven states with the highest crime rates are in the South or Southwest, several other southern states have very low crime rates. Many "conventional wisdom" beliefs about crime are not supported by these statistics. For example, in urban, racially mixed New Jersey (where gambling is legal in Atlantic City) the crime rate is much lower than in rural, predominantly white Utah. The state with the highest percentage of African Americans (Mississippi) ranks twenty-third in the rate of crime. The states of Washington and Oregon, with their moralistic political culture, have much higher crime rates than Illinois and New York.

The murder rate is much higher in the South than in any other part of the country, a pattern that has been true as long as records have been kept. The lowest murder rates are in New England and Upper Midwest states. Without the South, the U.S. murder rate would not differ greatly from the rate in other democratic nations. Traditional attitudes stemming from slavery, rural isolation, and a historic sense of personal honor seem to account for the especially high murder rates in Louisiana, Mississippi, and Alabama. However, there has been a significant decline in the murder rate in all regions of the country, including the South, since the 1990s.

POLICE ACTIVITIES AND ORGANIZATION

Police make arrests for only about 20 percent of the most serious crimes that are reported to them. However, in millions of cases arrests are made, but the cases are processed as misdemeanors. Thousands more are turned over to juvenile authorities. Millions of urban burglaries are reported to the police largely for insurance purposes, and in most cases there is little hope that arrests will be made. Because urban police are so overworked and because often there are no credible witnesses, in many cases no one seriously expects the police to make arrests.

TABLE 7-3 State Crime and Murder Rates per 100,000 Population, 2001

	Crime Rate*			Murder Rate**	
Rank	State	Rate	Rank	State	Rate
1.	Arizona	6,077.4	1.	Louisiana	11.2
2.	Florida	5,569.7	2.	Mississippi	9.9
3.	Hawaii	5,386.1	3.	Alabama	8.5
4.	Louisiana	5,338.1	3.	Nevada	8.5
5.	New Mexico	5,324.0	5.	Maryland	8.3
6.	Tennessee	5,152.8	6.	Illinois	7.9
7.	Texas	5,152.7	7.	Arizona	7.5
8.	Washington	5,151.9	8.	Tennessee	7.4
9.	Oregon	5,044.1	9.	Georgia	7.1
10.	North Carolina	4,938.0	10.	Indiana	6.8
11.	Maryland	4,866.8	11.	Michigan	6.7
12.	Missouri	4,776.1	12.	Missouri	6.6
13.	South Carolina	4,752.7	13.	California	6.4
14.	Georgia	4,646.3	14.	South Carolina	6.3
15.	Oklahoma	4,607.0	15.	North Carolina	6.2
16.	Nebraska	4,329.6	15.	Texas	6.2
17.	Kansas	4,321.4	17.	Alaska	6.1
18.	Alabama	4,319.4	18.	Arkansas	5.5
19.	Nevada	4,266.0	19.	New Mexico	5.4
20.	Utah	4,243.0	20.	Florida	5.3
21.	Alaska	4,236.2	20.	Oklahoma	5.3
22.	Colorado	4,218.9	20.	Pennsylvania	5.3
23.	Mississippi	4,185.2	23.	Virginia	5.1
24.	Ohio	4,177.6	24.	New York	5.0
25.	Arkansas	4,134.2	25.	Kentucky	4.7
26.	Illinois	4,097.8	26.	New Jersey	4.0
27.	Michigan	4,081.5	26.	Ohio	4.0
28.	Delaware	4,052.8	28.	Montana	3.8
29.	California	3,902.9	29.	Rhode Island	3.7
30.	Indiana	3,831.4	30.	Colorado	3.6
31.	Montana	3,688.7	30.	Wisconsin	3.6
32.	Rhode Island	3,684.9	32.	Kansas	3.4
33.	Minnesota	3,583.7	33.	Connecticut	3.1
34.	Wyoming	3,517.6	34.	Utah	3.0
35.	Wisconsin	3,321.2	34.	Washington	3.0
36.	Iowa	3,301.2	36.	Delaware	2.9
37.	New Jersey	3,225.3	37.	Hawaii	2.6
38.	Virginia	3,178.3	38.	Nebraska	2.5
39.	Idaho	3,133.4	39.	Minnesota	2.4
40.	Connecticut	3,117.9	39.	Oregon	2.4
41.	Massachusetts	3,098.6	41.	Idaho	2.3
42.	Pennsylvania	2,961.1	41.	Massachusetts	2.3
43.	Kentucky	2,938.1	43.	West Virginia	2.2
44.	New York	2,925.1	44.	Wyoming	1.8
45.	Vermont	2,769.3	45.	Iowa	1.7
46.	Maine	2,688.2	46.	Maine	1.4
47.	West Virginia	2,559.5	46.	New Hampshire	1.4
48.	North Dakota	2,417.7	48.	North Dakota	1.1
49.	South Dakota	2,332.0	48.	Vermont	1.1
50.	New Hampshire	2,321.6	50.	South Dakota	0.9
	District of Columbia	7,709.6		District of Columbia	40.6

*Includes murder, rape, robbery, aggravated assault, burglary, larceny-theft, and motor vehicle theft.
**Includes non-negligent manslaughter.
Source: State Rankings 2003 (Lawrence, Kan.: Morgan Quitno Press), pp. 28 and 36, www.morganquitno.com.

In routine patrolling and in responding to calls, police have unusually broad **discretionary authority**. Working alone or in pairs, police officers operate with little direct supervision from police administrators. James Q. Wilson notes that police discretion is inevitable, "partly because it is impossible to observe every public infraction, partly because many laws require interpretation before they can be applied at all, partly because the police can sometimes get information about serious crimes by overlooking minor crimes, and partly because the police believe that public opinion would not tolerate a policy of full enforcement of all laws all the time."[20]

One of the results of having so much discretionary authority is that police often decide to handle situations informally, rather than strictly enforcing the law. For example, police may choose to issue a warning instead of an arrest for possession of certain controlled substances. The ways in which police exercise discretion may depend on the background and personality of the officer, the characteristics of suspects (if they are belligerent or if their style of dress is offensive, they are more likely to be arrested), and the nature of the offense (child sex abuse is unlikely to be overlooked, but certain "victimless" crimes, such as gambling and prostitution, may be tolerated).[21]

Law enforcement takes up only about 10 percent of police time. Most of their shifts are devoted to service (responding to motor vehicle accidents or directing traffic) and to peacekeeping (intervening in family disputes, quieting noisy parties). Of course, if police in cruisers were not "doing nothing," they would not be able to respond quickly to emergencies.

Police discretionary activity and the allocation of their time among the three basic functions noted are influenced by department policy. Some departments target certain kinds of crime to be enforced, some emphasize the service function, and some reduce discretion by keeping in close communication with officers. In turn, department policy may be strongly associated with the style of the department.

Prior to the reform era of the early twentieth century, many police departments were controlled by urban political machines. As a result, law enforcement was applied unevenly across communities. Even where political machines did not exist, corruption was widespread in police departments. Corruption peaked during the 1920s when prohibition was in effect. In many cities, near the turn of the century, a **watchman style** of police behavior emphasized maintenance of order in public places, rather than law enforcement. Police were poorly paid, locally recruited, and minimally trained in virtually all cities and towns.[22]

Political reformers (see Chapter 3) sought to cut the political ties of many police departments. Beginning in the 1920s, the so-called professional movement in policing stressed a formal, hierarchical organization (command structure) and emphasized fighting crime over other police services. This corresponded with changes in technology— automobiles, radios, new forensic techniques—that altered the ways in which police solved crimes. Police were evaluated by such means as the percentage of crimes solved and response time to calls for assistance.

Beginning in the 1970s, criminologists seriously questioned the organization of police departments because it was not effective at preventing crime or limiting disorder. In their classic 1982 work, Wilson and Kelling suggested that community disorder (such as broken windows and graffiti) encouraged more serious crime.[23] They and others proposed that the mission of police departments change from solving crimes to preventing crime. To do this would require changes in both the goals and organization of police departments.

The most widespread response to the need to change police departments has been the introduction of **community policing**. Elements of community policing include the creation of substations across cities, foot patrols, frequent meetings between police and neighborhood residents, and keeping police on the same beats for longer periods of time.[24] A major goal of these departments is to be proactive, rather than simply responding to emergency calls (see the discussion of reinventing government in Chapter 6). In terms of organizational change, more responsibility is directed to the lower ranks as departments become less hierarchical. In turn, residents are given more responsibility to prevent and solve crimes on their own.

As noted in the story at the beginning of the chapter, the use of community policing was given a lot of credit for the drop in crime in Boston in the 1990s. As the city's crime rate began to increase in 2000, some have begun to reevaluate the benefits of community policing and to look more toward New York City's emphasis on "quality of life" law enforcement. This approach focuses on preventing small crimes, such as vandalism, that are believed to lead to more serious crimes in a neighborhood. New York City police commissioner William Bratton said, "I'm from the school of thought that the average citizen doesn't want to be engaged in patrolling their own neighborhood. . . . When I come home at night, I don't want to be looking over my shoulder or coming upstairs to get my flashlight, my armband, and go out and patrol the neighborhood. That's what the police are for."[25]

Still, New York City does not dismiss completely the idea of partnership between police and neighborhood residents. And Boston has moved to strengthen, not abandon, its efforts at involving the community in fighting crime.

Community policing is part of the "reinventing government" emphasis on giving citizens control over public safety and creating anticipatory government. The standard measures of police efficiency were how quickly they responded to calls and how often they "cleared" cases with arrests and convictions. As a result, we hired more police and built more jails as the crime rate continued to grow. In fact, most studies show little connection between the amount of crime and any traditional policy activity.

Every state except Hawaii has a law enforcement agency known as the *state police*, the state highway patrol, or, as in Texas, the Rangers. In a quarter of the states, the responsibility of this central police force is limited to highway duties. In the other states, law enforcement responsibilities include aiding local police in making arrests and controlling riots.

Traditionally, the *county sheriff* has been a central figure in American law enforcement. In addition to making arrests, the sheriff maintains the county jail and serves summonses and warrants. In every state except Rhode Island, which does not have counties, the sheriff is elected. Although sheriffs continue to play a major role in rural counties, *municipal police forces* have assumed most of the sheriff's law enforcement duties in urban areas. However, sheriffs' offices have become very professionalized in many suburban areas where smaller communities may contract with the county for law enforcement service. On the average, about 60 percent of state law enforcement personnel are municipal police, 30 percent work at the county level, and 10 percent at the state level.

CORRECTIONS

The history of prisons in the United States shows that we have gone through a great variety of stages, seeking ways to further public safety and punish offenders. Over the years government officials have followed four basic philosophies to help justify the choice of sentences and to help define the purpose of incarceration.

First, **retribution**, the most ancient goal of sentencing, suggests that offenders deserve punishment and that it is proper for society to seek vengeance for crimes that are normally offensive. In earlier societies punishment often was certain, quick, and brutal, even for what appears now to be a minor offense. Nowadays, long terms of imprisonment are justified by saying the offenders got what was coming to them.

Second, **deterrence** contends that certain, swift punishment of convicted criminals will cause other people not to commit crimes. Because imprisonment is thought to be an especially effective deterrence, this philosophy is compatible with incapacitation.[26] To the extent that crime rates have continued to rise as prison sentences have gotten longer, there are serious questions raised about their deterrent effect. In particular, there has been a long-standing debate (discussed later in this chapter) about the deterrent effect of the death penalty for the crime of murder. Many criminologists argue that it is *certainty*, more than severity of punishment, that deters crime.[27] And as noted, most crimes in the United States go unreported or no arrest is made.

Third, **rehabilitation** became the goal of prison reformers in the 1930s, and it dominated prison philosophy into the 1970s. Rehabilitation was applied to youthful offenders and to adult offenders by Pennsylvania Quakers in the late eighteenth century, but retribution soon came to be the primary goal of adult sentencing in the United States.

As the term *corrections* suggests, rehabilitation seeks to change individual behavior, to make offenders see the evil of their ways, and to prepare them for a productive life outside prison. For those sentenced to prison, there is an emphasis on psychological counseling, education, and job training. It was recommended that prisons should be smaller and should be located close to cities so that family visits would be more frequent. After release, rehabilitation called for halfway houses and more parole officers to better supervise the reentry of former prisoners into society. Psychology offered the opportunity to treat offenders at various stages and to "cure" them of their criminal tendencies.

Of course, the basic test of rehabilitation is how well ex-prisoners behave after their release from prison. The answer is not well. A recent study by the Bureau of Justice Statistics showed that nearly 70 percent of inmates released from state prisons in 1994 were arrested again within three years. Instead of rehabilitation, imprisonment seemed more likely to serve as a training ground for future criminal behavior. With the crime rate soaring, sentences neither deterred crime nor rehabilitated criminals. However, some observers point out that when prisoners attend vocational training classes or take college courses, they are much less likely to return to a life of crime. Yet education programs have been reduced in response to a change in the philosophy of incarceration, as well as to cuts in state budgets.

In response to these realities and in reaction to increased fear of crime, the dominant sentencing philosophy switched to a fourth philosophy, **incapacitation**. This calls for separating people from society, often by long, or at least certain, prison sentences. It is argued that to the extent criminals are taken off the streets, they will not be endangering lives and property. Incapacitation differs from retribution to the extent that its primary objective is not punishment. For example, a convicted criminal can be incapacitated by house arrest using electronic monitoring devices. Still, in recent years this philosophy has supported a "lock 'em up and throw away the key" approach to sentencing, discussed at the end of this chapter.

Even as crime declined in the 1990s, prison populations continued to grow. State prisons held about 685,000 prisoners in 1990 and about 1.18 million in 2000—an increase of nearly 60 percent. In addition, in 2000 about 4.5 million people were on parole or probation. Figure 7-3 shows the steep increase in prison population, including women prisoners, that began in 1970 and continued through the 1990s.

At the turn of the twenty-first century state prison populations began to stabilize, with the 1.5 percent increase in 2000 the lowest in twenty-nine years. The rate of state-sentenced prisoners per 100,000 population was 478 in 2000. This compared to 476 in 1999, 292 in 1990, and 139 in 1980.

In 2002 the total number of people incarcerated in the United States passed the 2 million mark for the first time. Approximately one in every 142 U.S. residents was behind bars. Although the growth rate in the federal prison system from 2001 to 2002 was 5.7 percent, state prison systems grew by only 0.9 percent. In Texas the prison population declined by 3.9 percent, and in California, which maintains the nation's largest prison system (more than 160,000 inmates), there was a 2.2 percent decline. However, the number of people housed in local jails, which includes those awaiting trial, increased 5.4 percent in 2002.

Prison population continued to experience significant growth in the late 1990s in large part because many states had approved longer minimum sentences for a variety of crimes and had ended parole. Arrests for drug-related crimes were especially high in the 1980s, and state legislators responded to the public's demand to get tough on criminals by requiring that convicted felons serve a higher percentage of their prison terms. In some states citizen initiatives required mandatory sentencing. Curiously, drug use declined in the 1990s, but arrests remained high and those convicted got long terms of imprisonment.

A major turning point in sentencing occurred during 2003 when about half the states passed laws eliminating some of their mandatory minimum sentences and restoring early release for parole. Even many conservative legislators concluded that the existing laws were too harsh and too costly. Faced with budget deficits and rising prison populations, Fox Butterfield notes, legislators decided it was more effective to be smart on crime instead of tough on crime.[28] Several states eased "truth in sentencing" laws that required offenders to serve most of their sentences before being eligible for early release.

Criminologists long have pointed out that it is not the *severity* of punishment, but the *certainty* of punishment that deters crime. As we have noted, cities such as New York recently have directed much of their law enforcement to stopping small crimes, thereby putting criminals on alert that the certainty of arrest and punishment has been increased.

When their prisons became overcrowded in the 1990s, several states began to experiment with **alternative sentencing,** creating programs that diverted convicted drug

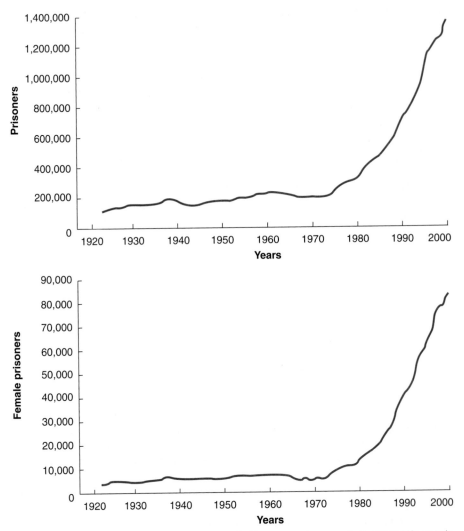

Note: Prison population data were compiled by a year-end census of prisoners held in custody in state and federal institutions. Data for 1925 through 1939 includes sentenced prisoners in state and federal prisons and reformatories whether committed for felonies or misdemeanors. Data for 1940 through 1970 include all adult felons serving sentences in state and federal institutions. Since 1971, the census has included all adults or youthful offenders sentenced to a state or federal correctional institution with maximum sentences of over 1 year.

FIGURE 7-3 Sentenced prisoners under federal and state jurisdiction, 1920–2000.

Source: Kathleen Maguire and Ann Pastore, eds., *Sourcebook of Criminal Justice Statistics, 2000.* U.S. Department of Justice, Bureau of Justice Statistics (Washington, D.C.: USGPO, 2001), p. 505.

users out of the prison system into community-based treatment centers. They also improved supervision of parolees. The secretary of corrections in Pennsylvania noted that before his state improved its parole policies, "Forty percent of the people walking through our prison doors were parole violators, mostly who had relapsed into drug use."[29]

As incarceration rates soared in the 1990s, one effect was to reduce the stigma of imprisonment and its deterrent power on young African-American and Hispanic men. In 2002 about 44 percent of all state prisoners were white, 44 percent were African American, and 11 percent were Hispanic. Among men ages 20 to 34, an estimated 12 percent of African Americans, 4 percent of Hispanics, and 1.6 percent of whites were in prison or jail in 2002. When so many young men are locked up, the social stigma of being in jail has declined. Children are growing up with few male role models and this has had broad-based ill-effects in these communities. But as syndicated columnist William Raspberry asked, "If not jail, then what?"

Although prison populations are stabilizing, the United States still has the world's largest and most expensive prison system. Our rate of imprisonment is eight times that of France and fourteen times greater than Japan.

States spend about $23,000 a year to incarcerate each prisoner and that does not include the cost of building new prisons, which can be close to $100,000 per inmate bed. For example, in Oregon funding for prisons increased 300 percent in the 1990s while funding for education increased by just over 50 percent.

As shown in Table 7-4, the incarceration rate varies greatly among the states. In general, southern states have the highest rates, whereas New England and North Central states have relatively few people in prison. Although the rate of incarceration correlates reasonably well with the crime rate (see Table 7-3), several states, such as Oklahoma and Mississippi, rank much higher in rates of incarceration than in rates of crime. A third of all the nation's state prisoners are in three states: California, Texas, and New York. Much of the disparity in rates of imprisonment can be explained by differences in culture among the states: great variations in degrees of punitiveness, or the willingness to punish people.

More people sentenced to prison, of course, means that states must build more prisons because existing facilities have populations that exceed their capacities. In the first half of the 1990s, states added about 400,000 prison beds at a cost of nearly $15 billion.[30] Spending on corrections increased from 5 percent of state budgets in the early 1980s to 7 percent by the mid-1990s. However, by 1997 there was evidence that the prison-building boom was ending. Although some states, such as New Jersey, continue to have overcrowded prisons, by 2002 several states had an excess of capacity. As a result, states such as Texas and Virginia have been making money by leasing out prison space to other states. Budget shortfalls have caused several states to postpone prison projects. In Illinois, a $143 million maximum security prison stood empty in 2003 because the state did not have the money to run it.

To keep costs down, states have built larger prisons (with up to 5,000 inmates each) that house a wide range of prisoners, from the least to the most dangerous. To help satisfy conflicting political demands to put more people in jail and to keep down state expenditures, many new prisons have a harsh environment—gray walls, no windows, stainless steel tables, and high-voltage wire fences that eliminate the need for patrol. Touch the fence and you're dead.[31] Inmates of several of these new "supermax" prisons have filed lawsuits alleging abusive treatment and racial discrimination.

Perhaps the most popular (and the most controversial) way to reduce the costs of incarceration is to privatize prisons. Although private prisons were used in colonial America, tales of prisoner abuse led to public management of virtually all prisons and

TABLE 7-4 State Prisoner Incarceration Rate, 2001*

Rank	State	Rate
1	Louisiana	800
2	Mississippi	715
3	Texas	711
4	Oklahoma	658
5	Alabama	584
6	Georgia	542
7	South Carolina	529
8	Missouri	509
9	Delaware	504
10	Arizona	492
11	Michigan	488
12	Nevada	474
13	California	453
14	Idaho	451
15	Arkansas	447
16	Florida	437
17	Virginia	431
18	Maryland	422
19	Tennessee	411
20	Ohio	398
21	Colorado	391
22	Connecticut	387
23	Wisconsin	383
24	Kentucky	371
25	South Dakota	370
26	Montana	368
27	Illinois	355
27	New York	355
29	Indiana	341
30	Wyoming	340
31	North Carolina	335
32	New Jersey	331
33	Oregon	327
34	Kansas	318
35	Pennsylvania	310
36	Alaska	300
37	Hawaii	298
38	New Mexico	295
39	Iowa	272
40	Washington	249
41	Massachusetts	243
42	West Virginia	231
43	Utah	230
44	Nebraska	225
45	Vermont	213
46	New Hampshire	188
47	Rhode Island	181
48	North Dakota	161
49	Minnesota	132
50	Maine	127
	District of Columbia**	NA
	Federal System	48

*Prisoners per 100,000 population.

**Responsibility for sentenced felons in D.C. was transferred to the Federal Bureau of Prisons in 2001. In 2000, the D.C. incarceration rate was 971.

Source: State Rankings 2003 (Lawrence, Kan.: Morgan Quitno Press), p. 62, www. morganquitno.com.

jails until the idea was revived in the 1980s. However, state prisons have a long history of contracting out such services as food and psychological testing to private business. Currently more than 70,000 inmates are housed in private prisons in about forty states. Some large businesses, including Corrections Corporation of America, run prisons in several states.

As discussed in Chapter 6, advocates of all types of privatization argue that public services can be produced more efficiently and at lower cost by private industry. Managing some services, such as trash collection, can be evaluated on a cost-efficiency basis. However, running prisons raises more complex issues, including how to ensure the humane treatment of prisoners, how to guard against the possibility of prison contractors keeping inmates in jail longer so that they can make more money, and how to assess legal liability when inmates bring lawsuits. Of course, state on-sight supervision of prisons and careful wording of contracts could prevent more obvious abuses. Moreover, the record in many states shows public management has produced overcrowded prisons, delayed construction of new facilities, poorly maintained buildings, and physical abuse of prisoners. Privately managed prisons have benefited from state and federal mandates to reduce prison overcrowding.

Some critics charge that the widespread privatization of juvenile criminal facilities, such as group homes, has led to longer periods of custody and less emphasis on rehabilitation than in traditional public institutions.

CAPITAL PUNISHMENT

The ultimate penalty, of course, is death. This ancient punishment has a brutal history. In biblical Israel, criminals were stoned to death. In Rome, beheading was the preferred method of death, although arsonists were burned and slaves were strangled.[32] In the Dark Ages those suspected of committing certain crimes were submerged in cold water or placed in boiling oil. Early in the nineteenth century 160 crimes were punishable by death in England. The guillotine was invented in France as an efficient way of beheading criminals. In the United States electrocution replaced hanging early in the twentieth century as the most common form of capital punishment. More recently, lethal injection has become the most widely authorized form of execution among the states.

The Role of the Supreme Court

From 1930 to 1967 about 3,800 persons were executed in the United States. Executions were halted in 1967 by an order of the U.S. Supreme Court as it waited to decide pending cases challenging the constitutionality of the death penalty. The Supreme Court's 1972 decision in *Furman v. Georgia* effectively struck down the way in which the death penalty was administered in thirty-seven states. The majority (5–4) ruled that the Georgia statute, which allowed the jury to decide guilt or innocence and at the same time assign a sentence in capital cases, permitted an arbitrary and capricious application of the death penalty. The Court's decision in *Gregg v. Georgia* two years later upheld the use of the death penalty as modified by the state of Georgia. Based on the Court's 7 to 2 opinion in *Gregg*, death penalty statutes are constitutionally acceptable if there is a two-stage process in which the jury first considers whether the defendant is guilty of murder and then at a sentencing stage the same jury considers any **aggravating** or **mitigating circumstances**. The jury must find the defendant guilty beyond a reasonable doubt of at least one aggravating circumstance, such as that the offense was committed for hire, in order to impose the death penalty. Then the state supreme court must review the death sentence. Mitigating circumstances, such as lack of a criminal record or a mental condition, are used to support a lesser penalty.

Following *Furman* and *Gregg* the Supreme Court held that *mandatory* death sentences for certain crimes are unconstitutional and that capital punishment for rape is excessive. Later, however, a more conservative Court made it easier for states to execute convicted murderers by supporting the death penalty for persons as young as sixteen years old and for those who are mentally retarded. In addition, the Rehnquist Court has limited the number of prisoner petitions from those sentenced to death, and it has permitted victim impact studies at the time of sentencing to help determine the defendant's "blameworthiness."

Two decisions in 2002 restricted the use of the death penalty. In *Ring v. Arizona* the Court struck down laws in five states that had permitted judges alone, not juries, to decide the imposition of capital punishment. In *Atkins v. Virginia* the Court held that the Eighth Amendment bars the execution of the mentally retarded. At the time, seventeen of the thirty-eight states that imposed the death penalty banned executing the mentally retarded. In 2003, the Court refused to accept a case that challenged the constitutionality of executing sixteen- and seventeen-year-olds, but it scheduled a similar case for review in 2004.

In *Atkins v. Virginia* the Supreme Court left it to states to decide how to implement the decision. States need to define mental retardation and to decide whether the judge or jury will determine if a person facing the death penalty is mentally competent.

State Responses

Although some states did not restore the death penalty after the Supreme Court permitted it in 1976, most states rewrote their laws to comply with the *Furman* decision. In 1995, New York State became the thirty-eighth state to have capital punishment. Because of legal restrictions, imposition of the death penalty is time-consuming, costly, and seldom applied.

Several states with capital punishment have not executed anyone since the first states resumed executions in 1977. During the same period seventeen states have executed at least 100 prisoners. Table 7-5 shows the race and ethnicity of prisoners under the sentence of death in 2001. About 1.5 percent of them are female. Only New Hampshire did not have anyone on death row in 2001. Texas, which has executed about one-third of all those executed in the United States since 1977, had the second highest number of prisoners on death row. California, with 592 prisoners under sentence of death in 2001, has only executed eight people since 1977. Because of the complex procedures required before someone sentenced to death is executed, most prisoners on death row die of natural causes.

The ten states that have executed the most people since 1977 are all in the South. Texas executed thirty-three people in 2002, triple the total number executed in the West,

TABLE 7-5 Prisoners Under Sentence of Death, 2001

Jurisdiction	Total	Race, Ethnicity				
		White	Black	Hispanic	Native American	Asian
United States	3,711	1,700	1,593	330	46	40
Federal	24	3	17	3	0	1
U.S. military	7	1	5	0	0	1
Alabama	190	100	87	1	0	1
Arizona	125	88	15	18	3	1
Arkansas	40	16	23	1	0	0
California	592	236	215	111	14	16
Colorado	7	2	2	2	0	1
Connecticut	7	3	3	1	0	0
Delaware	18	8	10	0	0	0
Florida	383	210	134	36	1	2
Georgia	132	67	62	2	0	1
Idaho	20	20	0	0	0	0
Illinois	175	54	111	10	0	0
Indiana	42	29	13	0	0	0
Kansas	4	4	0	0	0	0
Kentucky	42	33	8	1	0	0
Louisiana	92	27	62	2	0	1
Maryland	16	5	11	0	0	0
Mississippi	66	30	36	0	0	0
Missouri	79	45	34	0	0	0
Montana	6	6	0	0	0	0
Nebraska	11	9	0	1	1	0
Nevada	92	45	36	10	0	1
New Hampshire	0	X	X	X	X	X
New Jersey	18	10	8	0	0	0
New Mexico	5	4	0	1	0	0
New York	6	3	2	1	0	0
North Carolina	233	87	130	3	12	1
Ohio	202	95	102	2	2	1
Oklahoma	128	70	42	4	10	2
Oregon	29	24	1	2	1	0
Pennsylvania	242	73	153	14	0	2
South Carolina	73	39	34	0	0	0
South Dakota	5	5	0	0	0	0
Tennessee	103	60	37	2	2	2
Texas	450	158	188	99	0	5
Utah	11	6	2	2	1	0
Virginia	28	16	11	1	0	0
Washington	15	11	3	0	0	1
Wyoming	2	2	0	0	0	0

Source: Kathleen Maguire and Ann Pastore, eds., *Sourcebook of Criminal Justice Statistics 2000.* U.S. Department of Justice, Bureau of Justice Statistics (Washington, DC: USGPO, 2000), p. 549.

Midwest, and Northeast states combined. By early 2003 there had been 846 executions nationwide since 1977 and 299 (35 percent) of them were in Texas. Of the nation's seventy-one executions in 2002, 86 percent were in the South. One explanation for this regional pattern is that southern appellate judges play the key role, seldom granting appeals from death row inmates and not having reservations about imposing the death penalty. Judges in the South are more likely than in other regions to run for political office and being tough on crime helps them. Moreover, we have noted cultural differences by region that influence patterns of imprisonment.

At the beginning of Chapter 6 we noted that before leaving office in 2003 Governor George Ryan of Illinois commuted the sentences of all prisoners on death row. This action was upheld by the Illinois supreme court in 2004. Questions about executing innocent persons are being raised in states across the country.

Race and the Death Penalty

The fact that about 40 percent of all persons who have been executed are African American has led many to oppose capital punishment on the grounds that it is inherently unfair. Just before his retirement in 1994, Justice Harry Blackmun cited racial inequities as a major reason for his opposition to capital punishment in any circumstances. In 1987, the Supreme Court refused to strike down Georgia's system of sentencing, even though a study showed that African Americans in Georgia who killed whites were four times more likely to receive the death sentence than African Americans who killed other African Americans (*McCleskey v. Kemp*). David C. Baldus and colleagues, in the most authoritative study of racial factors in capital punishment, concluded that racial disparities are due more to the *race of the victim* than to the race of the murderer. When the victim is white, the likelihood that the death penalty will be imposed is more than double than when the victim is African American.[33] Before 2003 Texas had not executed a white person for killing an African American for nearly a century.

NEW DIRECTIONS IN THE CRIMINAL JUSTICE SYSTEM

Since the early 1970s, computers have become an important part of all police departments, including those in small towns and rural counties. This followed the creation of the Law Enforcement Assistance Administration in 1968, whose tasks included technological assistance to state and local governments to aid their fight against crime. Computers have given police easy access to nationwide crime information, and they permit checks on stolen vehicles through machines installed in patrol cars. Police can use large computer databases to cross-reference information and to identify suspects. For example, computer models can be used to track the activities of gang members.

Computers can be used in training programs, including shoot/no-shoot decisions and police pursuit driving simulations. And they can be used to generate psychological profiles and in crime scene analysis. Forensic animation, in which computers simulate criminal activity, is useful in both training and crime-solving. Computer imaging can be especially helpful in updating photographs of children who have been missing for several years.[34]

Criminologist Frank Smallenger draws our attention to even more advanced technology used in the criminal justice field that includes laser fingerprint lifting devices, satellite and computer mapping, and chemical analysis techniques.

As highlighted in the 1995 trial of O. J. Simpson, law enforcement officials are developing the technology to use DNA profiling to identify suspected criminals. Only a few human cells from hair or blood samples are needed to provide genetic material to compare with those of the alleged offender. As we saw in the Simpson trial, this technology is not foolproof, and defense attorneys are quick to challenge its authenticity.

A final note of caution. As computer crimes (cybercrimes) expand and pressure mounts to take action against these technically sophisticated offenders, we need to be concerned about protecting the First Amendment right to free speech (a concern when trying to limit indecency or pornography on the Internet) and Fourth Amendment rights to be free from "supersnoop" technologies that listen, record, and photograph.

As more convicted criminals are being sent to prison and overcrowding has become a major problem in many state prison systems, states have been experimenting with numerous alternatives to traditional imprisonment. These include boot camps for young offenders, "shock incarceration," house arrest, electronic monitoring, community service or restitution, drug treatment, and fines.

As an alternative to traditional prisons, several states have experimented with **boot camps** (also referred to as "**shock incarceration**") to scare younger offenders "straight." These camps are based on the military model of discipline and rigorous physical training. Inmates who accept the regimen are released in a relatively short time, while others may be transferred into the regular prison system if they are noncooperative or if they choose to leave the boot camp. By late 1999, accusations of physical abuse in boot camps led officials in several states to end their programs. Charges of abuse have caused other states, including Maryland, to revamp their boot camps. What began as a popular program in the 1970s to get tough with juvenile offenders has become a vehicle for reconsidering the entire juvenile justice system.

Other alternatives to traditional imprisonment include a kind of house arrest in which offenders are monitored by electronic devices on their ankles. Criticisms of house arrest include concern about offenders who are risks to commit violent acts and concern that they are being coddled by staying in their homes. Community service may be done without any time being served in jail, or it may be mixed with a sentence that requires the offender to spend weekends in jail.

In what is sometimes called "creative sentencing," judges have, for example, sentenced slumlords to live in their own buildings. Fines may be an effective way to punish nonviolent first-time offenders.

Following the kidnapping and murder of twelve-year-old Polly Klass in 1993, California passed its so-called "three strikes" law that requires a sentence of twenty-five years to life for a criminal's third felony conviction. Since then twenty-five states plus Congress have passed similar laws. The California law is the most extreme because it allows misdemeanor crimes to be included if they are the third offense. Reviewing two similar cases from California in 2003, the Supreme Court in a 5–4 vote upheld the California law. Writing for the majority in both cases, Justice O'Connor stressed the long criminal histories of both defendants and noted that the Supreme Court had a "long tradition of deferring to state legislatures" on sentencing guidelines. Dissenters on the Court stressed that the sentences (in one instance the defendant's third strike was shoplifting $153 worth of videos and his penalty was fifty years in prison) were "grossly disproportionate" to the crimes.

On the same day the Supreme Court upheld the so-called Megan's Law, which has been enacted in every state. It allows states to post sex offenders' photographs and other personal information on the Internet, or to require some form of registration. These laws are aimed at protecting people from convicted criminals who live nearby. In a second, related opinion, the Court unanimously held that states did not have to hold separate hearings to determine the risk posed by previous sex offenders.

Criminologist Jerome Skolnick believes that three strikes laws will not significantly reduce violent crime because most of these offenses are committed by young men aged thirteen to twenty-three. By the time they are jailed for their third offense, they are, says Skolnick, in the twilight of their criminal careers. Keeping aging prisoners in jail will become, in Skolnick's words, "the most expensive middle-age and old-age (housing and medical care) entitlement in the history of the world."[35] While legislators are lobbied by crime victims groups, who want them to get tough with criminals, and some city and county officials lobby to have new correctional facilities located in their jurisdictions, only a few civil rights groups lobby for more humane treatment of prisoners.

Those, like newspaper columnist David Broder, who accept Skolnick's point of view suggest that states and cities should put their emphasis on crime prevention—dealing with drug and alcohol abuse and reducing access to handguns—rather than on building more prisons. However, it is very difficult for government officials to devise comprehensive solutions to complex problems. Getting at the roots of problems takes time, money, and long-term commitment. Oftentimes elected officials lack all three. As a result, they settle for short-term solutions that may be politically popular but, in the long run, may make things worse.

Earlier we discussed community policing as the most widespread reform of local law enforcement. Privatization of prisons also was discussed as a possible way for states to save money. Both of these policies need further evaluation and longer-term monitoring. Community policing is a concept that could be trivialized as mere jargon or convenient buzzwords that are used to give the appearance of change when real reform has not occurred.

SUMMARY

States typically have three-tiered court systems composed of fragmented trial courts, intermediate courts of appeal, and a supreme court. State supreme courts hear and decide cases in ways similar to the U.S. Supreme Court, but they often differ in that the power of state chief justices is less and there are fewer dissenting opinions.

Reform has centered on consolidating and centralizing state trial and appellate courts. Other reforms include providing better access to the courts and the use of alternative dispute resolution, including arbitration and mediation.

Criminal procedures are strongly influenced by plea bargaining, in which all interested parties seem to benefit. The prevalence of plea bargaining is affected by the cohesiveness of courtroom work groups, whose members seek to reduce uncertainty and avoid time-consuming trials.

Academics have devoted a great deal of time to studying procedures by which judges are selected—election, appointment, and merit. Their conclusions are that the method of selection has, at best, a limited impact on the quality of judges and the nature of their opinions.

Historically, the relationship between federal and state courts has been strained. In the last 20 years liberal state courts often have refused to follow rulings by the more conservative Rehnquist Court.

Criminologists continue to struggle with the mystery of why crime increases and why it decreases in different places and at different times. Various explanations, from the state of the national economy to police strategies, including community policing and "quality of life" enforcement, are explored.

On the job, police have an unusually high amount of discretion. Police behavior can be influenced by the type of organizational structure of their departments. Police behavior also may have an effect on the kind and amount of crime in a city, but how great that influence is remains debatable.

Despite significantly lower rates of crime in the 1990s, longer and more certain prison sentences, especially for drug crimes, resulted in exploding prison populations. Building and maintaining prisons are major expenses for state and county governments. In most states, prison populations have stabilized and often declined since 2000. In response to an increase in crime in the 1980s and 1990s, many states built larger, more secure prisons. Now several states have excess capacity in their prisons.

Although capital punishment is constitutionally permitted in thirty-eight states, implementation of the death penalty since 1977 has varied greatly among the states. In 2002 three times as many people were executed in the South as in all other regions of the country combined.

Crime fighting has been aided by the use of increasingly sophisticated technology, including a wide variety of computer applications.

KEY TERMS

aggravating circumstances	incapacitation
alternative sentencing	initial appearance
arbitration	judicial activism
arraignment	judicial review
bail	mediation
boot camps	Missouri Plan
centralization of courts	mitigating circumstances
civil dispute	no contest (nolo contendere)
common law	plea bargaining
community policing	pretrial conference
consolidation of courts	rehabilitation
courts of appeal	retribution
criminal disputes	shock incarceration
deterrence	trial courts
discretionary authority	warrant
grand jury	watchman style

SUMMARY OF STATE/LOCAL DIFFERENCES

Issue	States	Local Governments
Judicial selection	Appellate judges often selected by merit systems	Trial judges tend to be elected, often on nonpartisan ballots
Judicial philosophy	Appellate judges issue written opinions; may have discretion over which cases they hear	Trial judges deal with narrow issues and seldom give innovative decisions
Law enforcement personnel	State police are relatively small in number and in some states are limited to highway duties	Municipal and county police comprise about 90 percent of total law enforcement personnel
Correctional facilities	Prisons house convicted felons	Jails house those arrested and awaiting trial or convicted offenders serving short-term sentences

INTERESTING WEBSITES

www.ajs.org. Website of the American Judicature Society, a nonpartisan organization interested in judicial independence, ethics, and selection. AJS is a strong advocate of merit selection of judges. Some of their resources are online.

www.ncsconline.org. The National Center for State Courts is an independent, non-profit organization that focuses on providing services to state courts. Find the answer to almost any question concerning state courts by clicking on "Court Information" or "Popular Links."

www.ojp.usdoj.gov/bjs. The Bureau of Justice Statistics, part of the U.S. Department of Justice, has an extensive website. Click on "Courts & Sentencing," then "Court Organization" to access "State Court Organization 1998," a detailed examination of state courts.

www.fbi.gov. At the FBI's website click on "Library & References" and then "Uniform Crime Reports" to view the latest crime statistics.

NOTES

1. John Buntin, "Murder Mystery," *Governing* (June 2002), pp. 20–25.
2. Henry J. Abraham, *The Judicial Process*, 7th ed. (New York: Oxford University Press, 1998), p. 149.
3. Henry R. Glick, *Courts, Politics, and Justice*, 3d ed. (New York: McGraw-Hill, 1993), p. 338.
4. Ibid., pp. 371–372.
5. Chris W. Bonneau, "The Composition of State Supreme Courts 2000," *Judicature* (July-August 2002), p. 28.
6. Lawrence Baum, *American Courts,* 4th ed. (Boston: Houghton Mifflin, 1998), p. 50.
7. Ibid., pp. 53–54.
8. Mary Grace Hume, "Trends in State Justice Systems: Improving Public Trust and Confidence," *Book of the States 2002* (Lexington, Ky.: Council of State Governments, 2002), p. 197.

9. Glick, *Courts, Politics, and Justice*, pp. 230–231.

10. Ibid., p. 232.

11. See James Eisenstein and Herbert Jacob, *Felony Justice* (Boston: Little, Brown, 1977).

12. Kathleen Sylvester, "Putting the Jury on Trial," *Governing* (March 1993), pp. 40–41.

13. Harry Kalven and Hans Zeizel, *The American Jury* (Boston: Little, Brown, 1966).

14. Anthony Champagne and Judith Haydel, eds., *Judicial Reform in the States* (Lanham, Md.: University Press of America, 1993), p. 6.

15. Mark Hurowitz and Drew N. Lanier, "Women and Minorities on State and Federal Appellate Benches," *Judicature* (September-October 2001), pp. 84–92.

16. Richard A. Watson and Ronald G. Downing, *The Politics of Bench and Bar: Judicial Selection under the Missouri Nonpartisan Court Plan* (New York: Wiley, 1969), pp. 338–339. See also Barbara L. Graham, "Do Judicial Systems Matter? A Study of Black Representation on State Courts," *American Politics Quarterly* (July 1990), pp. 316–336.

17. Traciel V. Reid, "The Politicization of Retention Elections," *Judicature* (September-October 1999), pp. 68–77.

18. See Champagne and Haydel, *Judicial Reform in the States*, p. 185.

19. David M. O'Brien, *Constitutional Law and Politics,* vol. 1, 5th ed. (New York: W. W. Norton, 2003), p. 753.

20. James Q. Wilson, *Varieties of Police Behavior* (New York: Atheneum, 1973), p. 7.

21. Frank Smallenger, *Criminal Justice Today,* 5th ed. (Englewood Cliffs, N.J.: Prentice-Hall, 1999), pp. 230–231.

22. Wilson, *Varieties of Police Behavior,* chap. 5.

23. James Q. Wilson and George Kelling, "Broken Windows," *Atlantic Monthly* (March 1982), pp. 29–38.

24. Peter Burns and Matt Thomas, "Fear and Loathing in Five Communities: The Impact of Community Policing," paper presented at the annual meeting of the Midwest Political Science Association (April 15–17, 1999), p. 3.

25. Buntin, "Murder Mystery," p. 25.

26. Smallenger, *Criminal Justice Today,* p. 391.

27. James Q. Wilson, *Thinking about Crime* (New York: Basic Books, 1975), pp. 174–175.

28. Fox Butterfield, "With Cash Tight, States Reassess Long Jail Term," *New York Times,* (November 10, 2003), p. A1.

29. David Firestone, "U.S. Figures Show Prison Population Is Now Stabilizing," *New York Times* (June 9, 2001), pp. 1 & 10A.

30. Penelope Lemov, "The End of the Prison Boom," *Governing* (August 1997), p. 32.

31. Penelope Lemov, "Roboprison," *Governing* (March 1995), pp. 24–29.

32. Herbert A. Johnson, *History of Criminal Justice* (Cincinnati: Anderson, 1988), p. 36.

33. David C. Baldus, George Woodworth, and Charles A. Pulaski, Jr., "Monitoring and Evaluating Contemporary Death Sentencing Systems: Lessons from Georgia," *University of California Davis Law Review* (Summer 1985), pp. 1375–1407.

34. Smallenger, *Criminal Justice Today,* pp. 694–700.

35. Quoted in David Broder, "When Tough Isn't Smart," *Washington Post* (March 23, 1994), p. A21.

CHAPTER 8

Financing State and Local Government

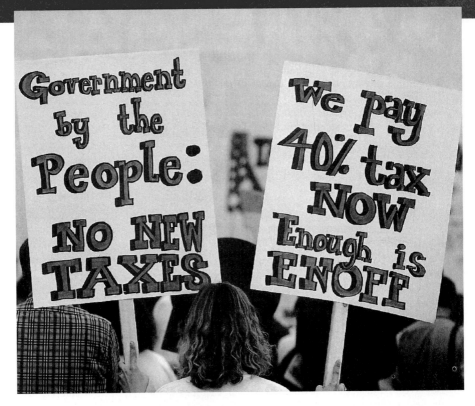

POINTS TO CONSIDER

- Compare the growth of state and local government expenditures to those of the federal government.
- What services do state and local expenditures provide?
- How do the principal sources of revenue for state governments differ from the sources of revenue for local governments?
- What are nontax sources of revenue?
- How and why have state governments become involved in gambling activities?
- Describe the importance of California's property tax revolt in 1978.
- Compare short-term and long-term revenue problems.

HOW MUCH?

State and Local Expenditures

How much money do state and local governments raise and spend? This simple question is not as easy to answer as it might seem. The most accurate picture of spending can be found by examining **direct general expenditures,** a rather complicated name that requires some explanation. The word *general* means that almost all expenditures are covered; a few are excluded, such as spending on unemployment and workers'

Will a Republican Raise Taxes?

If we were to take a poll, how would citizens answer this question: Among state and local elected officials, who would be more likely to raise taxes, a Democrat or a Republican? If you answered that most citizens would say Democrats, you are probably correct. But what if the economy is sluggish, government tax revenue is falling, and the choice is between cutting important government services or raising taxes? That's the situation that faced the Republican governor of Idaho, Dirk Kempthorne, who was in the first year of his second term in 2003.

Governor Kempthorne cut taxes during his first term. He was proud that he had signed forty-eight measures that either reduced taxes or created significant tax incentives for businesses, including reductions in the individual and corporate income tax rates. Even with these cuts, strong economic growth in Idaho and in the nation provided more than enough tax money to maintain and even expand services to the citizens of Idaho. But as the economy slowed in 2002, so did the flow of tax dollars to the state. The governor was forced to reduce state spending, so he cut, among other things, the budgets of most state agencies by 10 percent. Over the next few months the economy did not improve, tax collections did not increase, and the governor was faced with tough choices for his new budget that would start in July 2003: raise taxes or cut services even more. In his state of the state address, presented to the Idaho legislature in early

January, the governor said: "I have labored with all of the options and have come to the conclusion that in order to maintain—not expand, but maintain—the core services to our citizens, it will require additional revenue to the state."[1] Clearly it was not an easy decision. Raising taxes was a last resort, but the Republican governor believed there was no other choice.

To cover an estimated $200 million shortfall in state revenues and keep the budget balanced, Governor Kempthorne proposed to the legislature an increase in Idaho's cigarette tax of thirty-four cents per pack, which would more than double the existing tax. He also proposed a one and a half cent increase in the sales tax; this increase would expire on June 30, 2006. The idea behind the expiration date was that the economy should have improved by then and the higher rate would not be needed. The Idaho legislature, in the longest session of its entire history—116 days—finally gave the governor most of what he wanted to deal with the budget crisis. The cigarette tax was increased by twenty-nine cents and the sales tax by one cent, both set to expire on June 30, 2005. In addition, the legislature created a task force to reassess the state's entire tax structure.[2] Governor Kempthorne is not the only governor—or state legislator or mayor or county or city council member—who has confronted the complex world of government expenditures and revenues that will be discussed in this chapter.

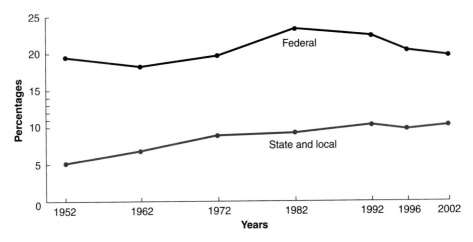

FIGURE 8-1 Federal government and state and local government expenditures as a percentage of GDP, selected years.

Source: Executive Office of the President of the United States, *Historical Tables, Budget of the United States Government, Fiscal Year 2004* (Washington, D.C.: U.S. Government Printing Office, 2003). p. 295.

compensation, which are financed by government-mandated employer and employee contributions. *Direct* refers to expenditures that are actual payments, that is, money paid to government employees, to contractors that governments buy things from, or to beneficiaries of government programs. Another important term is **intergovernmental expenditures,** which are transfer payments from one level of government to another and are particularly difficult to sort out in arriving at how much money state and local governments spend. (See Chapter 2.) It is important to note that these payments are not counted as spending by the government that transfers the funds. These transfer payments become a source of revenue for the government that receives the money and expenditures for the level of government that uses it to make actual payments. Intergovernmental expenditures are an important part of state government spending because states not only receive federal grants and frequently pass the money on to local governments, but states also have their own programs that transfer funds to local governments.

Direct general expenditures in 2000 for state and local governments totaled $1.5 trillion. Dollars per capita (for each person in the U.S.) are a little easier to comprehend; state government expenditures in 2000 were $2,266 per capita and for local governments $3,075. Expenditures by the federal government were $1.8 trillion for the same year, including almost $300 billion in grants to state and local governments.[3]

The real growth of direct expenditures can be identified in Figure 8-1 where government expenditures are viewed as a percentage of the gross domestic product, that is, the total output of goods and services produced inside the United States. The federal government's share is large but has changed little over the years, staying around 20 percent. State and local government expenditures show substantial growth, from almost 7 percent of the GDP in 1962 to 10 percent in 2002, an increase of more than 40 percent!

Limitations on Raising Revenue

In their attempts to raise revenue, state and local governments are affected by a number of factors, most fundamentally, by the level of wealth and personal income within their boundaries. Unless poor states and communities increase tax rates to unbearable levels, they simply cannot raise sufficient revenue to provide services comparable to those in more affluent areas. This is a particularly important problem in large cities and will be discussed later in this chapter.

State and local governments also encounter constitutional limits on taxation. The U.S. Constitution prohibits interference with federal operations by states through taxation, and it protects interstate commerce from direct taxation or undue interference by the states. It also prohibits states from taxing exports and imports without the consent of Congress. Perhaps of more importance are state constitutions, which seriously restrict taxing authority by exempting certain kinds of property and by defining the kinds of taxes that can be used.

The most serious limitations are placed on local governments, which have only those powers of taxation that state constitutions have granted them. State constitutions prescribe what taxes local governments may impose, they often establish the amount of taxation, they specify procedures of tax administration, and they outline the purposes for which tax revenues may be used. The only exceptions are in a few states where constitutions contain home-rule clauses (see Chapter 1) giving cities a general grant of power to levy taxes.

During the 1970s and 1980s, state governments were active in imposing **TELs** (tax and expenditure limitations) that placed limits on revenue or expenditure increases of local governments. Budgets of municipalities in New Jersey, for example, are limited by the state to a 5 percent increase over the previous year's total appropriations or the percentage change in inflation, whichever is less.[4]

WHERE DOES THE MONEY GO?

Table 8-1 presents an overview of twelve major functions on which state and local governments spend the most money. The biggest expenditure item is for elementary and secondary education. The operation of public schools consumes close to 25 percent of state and local spending. The other education category—higher education, which refers to publicly operated universities, colleges, and community colleges—accounts for almost 9 percent of total expenditures. These two categories taken together make up almost 33 percent of state and local expenditures. The second biggest item, 15.6 percent, is for public welfare. This includes, for example, cash assistance to the poor and payments made directly to doctors and hospitals for providing medical care for the poor and elderly. Health expenditures include public health research, immunization programs, and maternal and child health programs, and amount to slightly over 3 percent of expenditures.

Although Table 8-1 presents state and local spending together, this does *not* mean that both levels spend equally across all of these functions. State governments, through the operation of state prisons, spend two-thirds of the total that is spent on corrections.

TABLE 8-1	Major Direct General Expenditures by State and Local Governments, 2000	
Function	Expenditure (in billions)	Percent
Elementary and secondary education	$365.2	24.3
Public welfare	233.4	15.6
Higher education	134.4	8.9
Highways	101.3	6.7
Hospitals	76.0	5.1
Interest on general debt	69.8	4.6
Police protection	56.8	3.8
Health	51.4	3.4
Corrections	48.8	3.3
Sewerage and solid waste management	45.2	3.0
Natural resources, parks and recreation	45.2	3.0
Housing and community development	26.6	1.8
Other spending	248.0	16.5
Total	1,502.1	100.0

Source: "Table 1. State and Local Government Finances by Level of Government and by State: 1999–2000," available at www.census.gov/govs/estimate/00s100us.html (accessed May 5, 2003).
Note: These expenditures include federal grants to state and local governments.

On the other hand, local governments are primarily responsible for police protection and spend over 85 percent of these funds. Eighty-five percent of higher education expenditures are made by state government, only 15 percent by local government. A good example of the use of intergovernmental revenue is in elementary and secondary education spending. More than 50 percent of the money spent by local school districts is actually money that is transferred to them from the state and even the federal government.

WHERE DOES THE MONEY COME FROM?

Intergovernmental expenditures are an important source of revenue, but the taxing policies of state and local governments generate the vast majority of their revenues (often referred to as "own source" revenue). This comes from taxes such as the income tax (both individual and corporate), the sales tax, the property tax, and nontax revenue such as user charges and state-operated or state-regulated gambling activities. Before examining these taxes in some detail, we will look at their relative importance in generating revenues.

Figure 8-2 shows the principal revenues for state governments over the years. The corporate income tax and the sales tax have declined in importance since 1952. At that time almost half of state revenues came from the sales tax. In terms of proportion of total revenues, the individual income tax and nontax sources have increased the most, with the former having almost a threefold increase. Intergovernmental revenue, of which 94 percent comes from the federal government, has become more important—

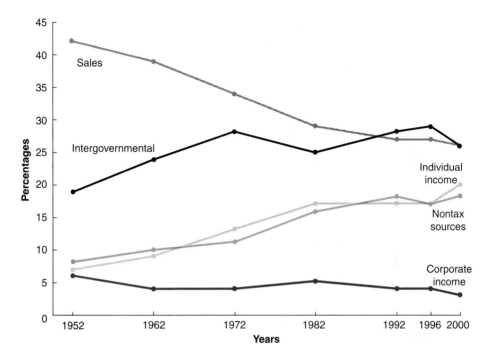

FIGURE 8-2 State general revenues by principal sources, 1952–2000 (in percentages).

Source: Percentage calculations for 2000 were made by the authors from data in "Table 1. State and Local Government Finances by Level of Government and by State: 1999–2000," available at www.census.gov/govs/estimate/00s100us.html (accessed May 5, 2003). Percentages for earlier years were calculated from data in various issues of U.S. Bureau of the Census, *Statistical Abstract of the United States.*

in fact, it was as important as the sales tax in 2000. Overall, in terms of own source revenue, the sales tax is still dominant, 6 percentage points ahead of the individual income tax and nontax sources.

Figure 8-3 has information on principal revenue sources for local governments. Note first of all that two of the taxes that are important to state governments, individual and corporate income taxes, are missing when we look at local governments. These taxes are rarely used at the local level, at least in part because they are so heavily used by the federal and state governments. The proportion of revenue from property taxes has decreased dramatically, although it is still the most important own source revenue. Nontax sources have increased significantly; the local sales tax has also, but it still represents a relatively small contribution to the total picture, only 6 percent. In 2000, intergovernmental revenue, from both the federal and state governments, provided the largest proportion of revenue to local governments, 39 percent.

It is easy to see that the use of particular kinds of taxes follows a pattern in which the national government relies heavily on the income tax, state governments rely on the sales tax, and local governments depend on the property tax. John R. Bartle states that at the local government level, "an important shift is occurring from the property tax towards income and sales taxes, and especially non-tax sources."[5]

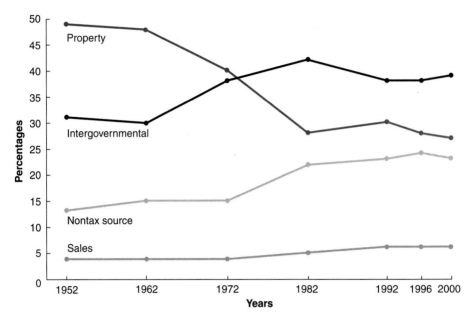

FIGURE 8-3 Local general revenues by principal sources, 1952–2000 (in percentages).

Source: Percentage calculations for 2000 were made by the authors from data in "Table 1. State and Local Government Finances by Level of Government and by State: 1999–2000," available at www.census.gov/govs/estimate/00s100us.html (accessed May 5, 2003). Earlier percentages are from *Significant Features of Fiscal Federalism: Revenues and Expenditures* (Washington, D.C.: Advisory Commission on Intergovernmental Relations, 1994), p. 67, and U.S. Bureau of the Census, *Statistical Abstract of the United States, 1994,* p. 298.

Property Tax

In most states, the **property tax** is a tax on what is termed real property, that is, land and the buildings on it. The property tax is almost exclusively a local tax and the county treasurer usually administers it. It is a fairly complicated process that includes assessment of property values, determination of tax rates (millage), tax computation, and tax collection. A *market approach* is frequently used to assess the value of real property. In this approach, a local assessor periodically evaluates all property in a neighborhood by using the value of property that has been recently sold. Assessors must develop and maintain detailed records of each property. One economist describes the market approach as "similar to neighbors estimating the current market value of their homes based on the sale price of a home on the same street."[6] Tax rates, set by local government officials, are sometimes expressed in mills; a mill is one-thousandth of a dollar. Thus, if a house and the land it is on are assessed at $100,000 and the mill rate is 20, the tax will be $2,000 ($100,000 × 0.020). This rate is frequently reported as $2.00 per $100 of assessed valuation.

In many cities, nearly 25 percent of all property is exempt from taxation. In Boston the proportion is as high as 50 percent; in New York City it is 35 percent. In large part, tax-exempt property is owned by the government or by religious organizations.

General Sales Tax

Mississippi, in 1932, shortly after the start of the Great Depression, became the first state to use a general sales tax. The property tax was the mainstay of state and local government revenue at that time, but during the Depression incomes fell more rapidly than the taxes on the property people owned and many simply could not pay.[7] During the first three years of the Great Depression, incomes fell by 33 percent and unemployment was at 25 percent. Foreclosures to pay property taxes were common, but unpopular. Consequently, twenty-two states, looking for other sources of revenue, quickly followed Mississippi's lead and adopted the sales tax before the end of 1938. During the 1940s and 1950s, ten more states decided to use a sales tax; and in the 1960s, with state governments facing increased responsibilities, eleven states adopted it. Vermont was the last (1969). Currently, only five states—Alaska, Delaware, Montana, New Hampshire, and Oregon—do not use it.

The **general sales tax** is levied on retail sales, and today the rate ranges from a low of 2.9 percent (Colorado) to a high of 7 percent (Mississippi, Rhode Island, and Tennessee). Over half of the states have a sales tax rate at 5 percent or higher. An important element in the sales tax is the tax base, that is, what is actually taxed. The sales tax does not apply to the sale of all goods and services. For example, most states do not tax the sale of food in grocery stores or prescription drugs, and a few even exempt clothing. (However, most states do tax the purchase of nonprescription drugs.) Services are another area that is not usually taxed by states; this includes legal, accounting, and management consulting services as well as barber and beauty services.[8]

More than thirty states authorize local governments to use the sales tax, and about 6,400 do. Of course, the local tax is added on to the state sales tax so local government rates tend to be low, usually 1 or 2 percent. For example, a person making a purchase in Kansas City, Kansas (in 2002) paid 5.3 percent state sales tax, 1.0 percent county tax, and 1.0 percent city tax, for a total tax of 7.3 percent. The state sales tax in California is 6.00 percent, with a statewide local tax rate of 1.25, making a total tax rate of 7.25. In a number of large cities, including Chicago, Dallas, Los Angeles, New Orleans, New York, and Seattle, the combined state and local sales tax rate is over 8 percent.[9]

Income Tax

Forty-three states have a personal income tax, and forty-five have a corporate income tax. Wisconsin was the first state to adopt an income tax, in 1911, two years before the federal government enacted its income tax. Although eight states adopted the income tax shortly after Wisconsin, it wasn't until the Great Depression that it was adopted by a large number of states (sixteen). Beginning in 1961, another eleven states added the income tax; New Jersey was the last (1976). In the late 1950s, many states began for the first time to employ a withholding system to collect income taxes in a manner similar to the federal government. The seven states without an income tax are Alaska, Florida, Nevada, South Dakota, Texas, Washington, and Wyoming. (New Hampshire and Tennessee limit the income tax to dividend and interest income only.)

The **income tax** is levied on individual and corporate income and almost never taxes total income, but rather what is called *taxable* income, the amount left after exemptions, adjustments, and credits have been subtracted.[10] State income tax rates are typically much lower than federal rates. A few states have a "flat tax," which means the rate is the same without regard to income level; Colorado's rate is 4.63 percent, and Pennsylvania's is 2.8 percent. Although most state income taxes are graduated—that is, the rate of taxation increases as income increases—the rate of increase and the maximum rate vary from state to state but are much less than those in federal tax schedules. The tax rate for Iowa is one of the most graduated; it begins at 0.36 percent and increases to 8.98 percent; this top rate is paid on incomes of $54,495 and higher. Many states have tax rates that range from 2 percent to 7 percent.

Wisconsin also was the first state to tax the income or profits of corporations; this tax was adopted at the same time as the personal income tax. As other states adopted the personal income tax, they also adopted the corporate income tax because it was politically impossible to tax personal income and not tax corporate income. Tax rates on corporate income are usually flat and the rate is frequently around 7 percent; however, the amount of revenue produced for the states is relatively low, as noted earlier. (See Figure 8-2.) Corporations in Arkansas have avoided paying their state's corporate income tax, or reduced the size of their payment, by setting up subsidiaries of their corporations in states with lower or no income tax.[11] David Brunori suggests that good tax planning by tax lawyers, along with tax breaks that states give to corporations to encourage economic development, keep the revenue generated from this tax lower than it could be.[12]

Approximately 3,800 local governments in thirteen states also tax income, with especially heavy use in Pennsylvania (more than 2,800 local governmental units use it). Rates tend to be low, 1 or 2 percent.

Other Taxes

All states place an **excise tax,** sometimes called a selective sales tax, on particular commodities such as cigarettes, alcoholic beverages, and gasoline. Taxes on cigarettes and alcoholic beverages are often called *sin taxes* because they tax products that many people consider sinful or harmful. The idea is that taxing these products will raise revenue and may help to diminish consumption. The median tax on a pack of cigarettes is 48 cents; Virginia has the lowest at 2.5 cents and Massachusetts the highest at $1.51. Alcoholic beverages are usually taxed on a per-gallon basis. Tax on beer, for example, ranges from 2 cents a gallon in Wyoming to $1.07 a gallon in Alaska.

The tax on gasoline is considered a *benefit tax* in that there is a relationship between public service benefits received and taxes paid. Gasoline taxes are used to finance the construction and maintenance of highways, so people who use the highways the most will pay a greater share. The median tax on a gallon of gasoline is 22 cents; Georgia has the lowest at 7.5 cents and Rhode Island the highest at 30 cents. During the 1920s and early 1930s, prior to the adoption of the general sales tax, selective sales taxes brought in about 28 percent of state tax revenue (over 50 percent of this amount was from the gasoline tax).[13]

A variety of other taxes are levied—on admissions to entertainment events, inheritances family members receive, and stock transfers, for example. In states that have valuable natural resources—such as coal, oil, natural gas, and timber—a **severance tax** often is levied on their extraction and removal. Although about two-thirds of the states employ some form of severance tax, a few states account for most of the severance tax revenue. In Alaska, North Dakota, Montana, New Mexico, and Wyoming, severance taxes make up 25 percent of all state tax revenue. Fluctuating prices for oil, natural gas, and coal have a strong effect on severance tax revenues. When the price for oil and natural gas declined sharply in the mid-1980s, the accompanying decline in severance revenue caused severe financial problems for the state governments of Alaska, Oklahoma, Texas, and Louisiana.

Nontax Sources

User Charges

A **user charge** (or user fee) is defined as "a payment to government for a specific good, service, or privilege."[14] The definition implies that the payment will equal the actual cost of the service, but that's not always the case. Both state and local governments levy user charges. At the local level user charges are various and include fees paid for the following: rides on subways and buses, trash collection, police services at special events, and water and sewerage systems. A fairly recent user charge by many local governments is the *impact fee*, a one-time fee paid by real estate developers to cover at least part of the cost of extending water and sewer lines and building streets for a new housing development. A significant user charge among state governments is the tuition and fees students pay, frequently with the help of their parents, to attend public-supported colleges and universities.[15] Other familiar charges are tolls for highways and bridges and fees to enter parks and other recreational areas.

Gambling

In 1999, the National Gambling Impact Study Commission observed the following:

> The most salient fact about gambling in America . . . is that over the past 25 years, the United States has been transformed from a nation in which legalized gambling was a limited and a relatively rare phenomenon into one in which legalized gambling is common and growing.[16]

In 2001, Americans bet approximately $700 billion legally—from slot machines to lotteries—and lost $63.3 billion; the difference between these two amounts is what was returned to players as their "winnings." (In 1976, only $17.6 billion was bet legally.) How much money is this? Timothy L. O'Brien, comparing dollars spent on gambling to other activities, notes that "gambling is now more popular in America than baseball, the movies, and Disneyland—*combined*."[17] In casinos alone, Americans spent $25.7 billion, slightly more than they spent on golf, $24.7 billion.

Although there are a number of causes for this dramatic change, there is little doubt that state governments played an important role. The continuing anti-tax mood during the last two decades of the twentieth century, combined with occasional downturns in the economy that reduced state revenues, forced more and more states to turn to state-operated lotteries as a source of revenue. Between 1982 and 1992 the number of states with lotteries increased from fifteen to thirty-six. Today, thirty-eight states operate lotteries; New Mexico and South Carolina were the last two states to adopt lotteries. The District of Columbia also operates a lottery. (See Figure 8-4.) Alabama voters defeated

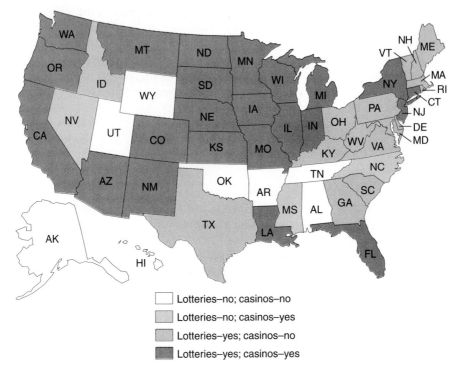

FIGURE 8-4 Gambling in the states, 2002.

Source: National Conference of State Legislatures, "Lotteries in the United States," www.ncsl.org/programs/econ/lotto.html; "United States Gaming at a Glance" www.ncsl.org/programs/econ/00gaming.html (accessed on May 1, 2003).
Note: States with casinos may have state-operated casinos only, Indian-owned casinos only, or both.

a lottery referendum in 1999 (54 percent against, 44 percent in favor), even though it had the strong support of Governor Don Siegelman.

Lotteries are not new in the United States; in fact, they were used in colonial times and during the nineteenth century, but scandals and unethical practices brought federal and state controls. After 1894, when the federal government banned interstate lotteries, no legal lotteries existed in the United States until New Hampshire, hoping to avoid the adoption of a general sales tax, instituted a state-operated lottery in 1964. New York followed a few years later.[18] But it was New Jersey (1971)—by lowering the price of tickets, increasing the number of ticket outlets, giving somewhat better odds, and aggressively marketing the game—that is credited with designing a lottery that proved popular with the public and created more revenue for the state than expected.[19]

In 2000, people spent $35.3 billion buying lottery tickets, and the states captured $12.4 billion as revenue. This is a considerable amount of money, but how much does it contribute to a state's total revenue picture? In 1996, lottery revenues averaged only 2.5 percent of the fifty-state total for own source revenue. The range among the states is from a low of 0.8 percent (California and Iowa) to a high of 4.8 percent (Florida). For most states, lottery revenues are not a big part of the revenue picture; still, if it were not available, the money would have to come from some form of taxation.

When states adopt a lottery the revenues frequently are earmarked for popular programs such as education. Critics contend that the earmarking of revenues is something of a shell game because legislatures often reduce general revenue funds to these programs as soon as they start receiving lottery revenues. In other words, rather than becoming additional funding, lottery revenues become a substitution, more or less dollar for dollar, allowing for a reduction in general fund support. The state of Georgia, which adopted a lottery in 1994, tried to avoid this problem by mandating that lottery revenue should pay for *new* programs—the HOPE college scholarships, prekindergarten classes, and technology in the classrooms—that were being funded for the first time. Thomas P. Lauth and Mark D. Robbins conclude that, in fact, Georgia has been reasonably successful in using lottery revenue as additional funding because of earmarking and a budget process that is "transparent." The Georgia constitution was amended so that these revenues were separately accounted for in the governor's annual budget, and the governor was required to make specific recommendations as to their use.[20] However, Georgia is the exception; in most states lottery revenues are more often used for substitution of existing funding and not for additional funding.

Recently, many states have moved beyond lotteries to casino gambling. (See Figure 8-4.) Nevada was the first to legalize casinos (1931); four decades later (1971), New Jersey did the same. No other state legalized casinos until the 1990s when they were legalized in state after state. By 1999, casinos operated in twenty-six states, including states where casinos are on land controlled by American Indian tribes. The development of Indian casinos is an important factor in the expansion of casinos in the 1990s, along with a strong economic recession (1991–92) that forced states to look for new sources of revenue. How tribes obtained authority to open casinos is an interesting story involving the legal relationship among tribes, the states, and the federal government. Generally, federal and tribal laws, not laws of state governments, control the affairs of American Indians. Indians "retain important sovereign powers over their members and their territory," subject to the powers of the federal government.[21] In several states during the 1980s, tribes started offering high-stakes bingo games and card clubs where draw poker was played, even though these games were not explicitly allowed by the laws of the state. This obvious conflict with state law resulted in a U.S. Supreme Court case, *California v. Cabazon Band of Mission Indians* (1987). The Court ruled against California's attempt to regulate the gambling activities of the Cabazon and Morongo Bands because it infringed on the authority of tribal governments.[22] It was now clear that gambling would expand on reservations. Many observers, knowing the desperate economic conditions on Indian reservations, supported this decision because it offered a way to bring much needed economic development; still there would have to be some regulatory oversight. In 1988, Congress passed and President Reagan signed into law the **Indian Gaming Regulatory Act** (IGRA), which established the National Indian Gaming Commission and tried to clarify the regulatory relationship between the states and tribes for various types of gambling. For casino-style games (slot machines, etc.), tribes and states must negotiate agreements that describe the games that will be played and how they will be regulated. Within a few years of enacting the IGRA, there were more than 150 state-tribal agreements (or compacts) for casino-style gambling in almost half of the states.[23]

States rushed to casino gambling not only because of additional tax revenue but also in the hope that it would be an economic development tool that would create jobs for workers who would build and operate the casinos. Every time a state considers authorizing casinos there is a heated debate over their economic benefits and costs.

The state of Nevada is often described as an example of the benefits of a gambling industry. Tourism is the mainstay of the Nevada economy and tourists come to gamble. Approximately 85 percent of Nevada's gambling revenue comes from out-of-state tourists. Recent estimates are that Las Vegas's 28 million tourists spend $19 billion a year, and the state tax on gambling receipts generates enough revenue so that Nevada does not need an income tax.[24] Can Nevada's success be duplicated? It is clear that in economically depressed communities there are some benefits in terms of increased employment and income and increased tax revenues. For example, a few Indian tribes have had considerable success, notably the Mashantucket Pequot Indians who own and operate the Foxwoods Resort Casino in Connecticut, which has an annual gross revenue of $1 billion. Unfortunately, it is difficult to measure the *social costs* of legalized gambling, that is, the effects on individuals, families, and communities. These costs may be considerable and need serious discussion before states or communities permit casino gambling. For example, bankruptcies in Iowa increased at a rate significantly above the national average after the introduction of casinos. And the cost to individuals and families when gambling becomes addictive is only beginning to be examined. Research sponsored by the National Gambling Impact Study Commission estimates that in any given year there are 2 million adults in the United States who are pathological gamblers.[25]

Just as the expansion of gambling activities seemed to peak, a downturn in the national economy starting in 2002, accompanied by a drop in state revenues, caused many states to consider a number of options to help balance their budgets. Options included expanding existing lottery games, allowing slot machines at horse racetracks, and increasing the state's take from existing gambling activities. The expansion of slot machines, now called video lottery terminals (VLTs), at racetracks has been particularly popular, leading to the term "racinos." Gambling critics dislike VLTs because they are believed to be particularly addictive, but states see them as a source of instant revenue, and they have been taxed at rates as high as 50 percent.[26] The governor of Massachusetts, Mitt Romney, was even more inventive. Political leaders in states with no casinos frequently complain that they lose revenue when their citizens play casino-style games in neighboring states. Massachusetts does not have casino-style gambling— Connecticut and Rhode Island do—so Governor Romney said that his state would continue its no casinos policy if Connecticut and Rhode Island would pay Massachusetts $75 million![27] Critics of legal gambling realize that it's unlikely to go away; many are now proposing that states attempt to regulate its negative effects, such as requiring truth-in-advertising rules for lottery ads, especially emphasizing the odds of winning, which are very low. Another proposal is that states should require casinos to make investments not just in the gambling hall but also in resort development such as hotels, shops, restaurants, and other recreational facilities. This type of investment would have a greater impact on the local economy by boosting tourism, which would provide more jobs.[28]

IS THERE A GOOD TAX?

Criteria

Public finance experts have established a number of criteria for a "good tax": sufficiency, stability, simplicity, and fairness. **Sufficiency** means that state and local taxes must raise enough revenue to fund the programs and policies that citizens want. **Stability** refers to raising a consistent amount of revenue over time, that is, few fluctuations from year to year. **Simplicity** denotes the ease and cost of administering and collecting the tax. **Fairness** reflects the idea that taxes should be equitable.[29] Two of these criteria—simplicity and fairness—will be discussed in more detail here. Let's look at fairness first.

Fairness is based on value judgments and, according to David Brunori, arriving at a consensus on how to achieve it through policy decisions is "perhaps more than any other aspect of sound tax policy . . . subject to substantial disagreement."[30] Many tax experts argue that an important component of fairness is **vertical equity,** that is, taxes should be related to an individual's ability to pay. Another way of putting this is that taxes should be *progressive;* as income increases, the tax paid as a percentage of income also increases. By way of example, a person with an annual income of $60,000 should be taxed at a 7 percent rate, paying $4,200 in taxes; and a person with an annual income of $30,000 should be taxed at a 3 percent rate, paying $900 in taxes. Not everyone agrees with the progressive concept. Opponents argue that taxes should be *proportional.* Everyone should be taxed at the same rate, let's say 5 percent. The person with an income of $60,000 would pay $3,000 in taxes and the person making $30,000 would pay $1,500. Most tax experts agree that taxes should not be *regressive.* A regressive tax is one that taxes those at lower income levels at a higher rate than those with higher incomes. Continuing with our example, this would mean that those with $60,000 incomes would be taxed at 3 percent (paying $1,800 in taxes) and those with $30,000 incomes would be taxed at 7 percent (paying $2,100 in taxes). No state income tax system is set up this way! However, because state and local governments use a mix of taxes in collecting revenues it is possible, in the total tax system, for some taxes to be more regressive than others.[31]

The tax that might earn a failing grade on simplicity is the property tax. All taxes involve some administrative costs, but the record keeping on each property, the hiring and training of assessors, the periodic reassessments, and the handling of appeals make the property tax an expensive tax to administer. Keep in mind that this process is not centralized in a single large office at the state capital but is being carried out in all of the counties in a state.

How fair are the state sales and income taxes? On this criterion, the sales tax is probably the most controversial. Critics argue that the sales tax is regressive because lower-income individuals pay a larger percentage of their income in sales taxes than do middle- and upper-income individuals. However, most states exempt from the sales tax items that people must have, such as food, prescription drugs, and medical services. This means that the sales tax does not take as large a share of money from low-income persons than it otherwise would. These exemptions reduce the regressive nature of the sales tax, making it only *moderately regressive.*[32] Also, a few states such as Connecticut,

Georgia, North Carolina, and the District of Columbia have instituted **sales tax holidays** that provide a temporary sales tax exemption on certain items for a specific period of time. These holidays usually occur during August, the traditional back-to-school shopping period, and exempt clothing, shoes, and school supplies, sometimes even personal computers. As to the fairness of the state income tax, most observers would agree that it is *moderately progressive*.[33] Although some states have a flat tax rate, which is also called proportional, most states have at least a few tax rates with at least small differences between the lowest and the highest rates.

What do citizens think? Surveys have asked the public to evaluate the major taxes used in the United States. In the early 1970s, the property tax was clearly viewed as the "worst tax," that is, the least fair. In the early 1980s, the federal income tax took the lead as the "worst tax," although the property tax was only a few percentage points behind. In a 1999 survey, the federal income tax was still disliked slightly more than the property tax; they were viewed as being the worst tax by 36 percent and 29 percent of the public, respectively.[34] Over the years the state income tax has been viewed as a fairer tax, as is the sales tax.

Although economists still debate the fairness of the property tax,[35] it is clear that a sizable portion of the public has disliked it for some time. Why is that? One reason is that the value of an individual's home is not always tied to his or her annual income. For example, people may live in areas that are growing rapidly, so their property values are increasing dramatically, along with their property taxes, even though their incomes may be increasing modestly at best. Of course, when people retire, their incomes usually drop, but their property values and taxes may continue to increase.

The Property Tax Revolt

Public dissatisfaction with the property tax was particularly acute in California during the 1970s when real estate values doubled and, for many homeowners, property tax bills skyrocketed, sometimes as much as 20 to 30 percent per year.[36] Howard Jarvis, using California's initiative process, led a campaign that succeeded in placing **Proposition 13,** a tax-reduction measure, on the 1978 ballot. With a $7 billion surplus in the state's treasury, voters did not believe dire warnings of cuts in services if Proposition 13 passed. Labor unions, teachers, public employees, the League of Women Voters, and most elected officials urged a no vote, but Proposition 13 passed with nearly 70 percent support in a high turnout election.[37] It had three main provisions:

1. It limited property taxes to 1 percent of assessed value.
2. It "rolled back" assessed values of all property to 1975 assessments. Annual updating increases were limited to no more than 2 percent per year. However, any change of ownership triggers reappraisal based on current value, usually the purchase price, which results in an increase in taxes for the new owner.
3. It prohibited the state from raising any state taxes to make up for lost revenue unless the new taxes are approved by a *two-thirds vote* of the legislature.

The passage of Proposition 13 led to a flurry of tax-cutting activity in more than half the states from 1978 to 1980. Eighteen states approved limitations on taxes and expenditures (TELs, as we called them earlier). The most extreme limits were approved in

Massachusetts, Minnesota, and Idaho. As a result of the passage of Proposition 2 1/2, Boston lost about 75 percent of its property tax revenue. Susan B. Hansen notes that, in general, states with a tradition of using the initiative process were the ones most successful in reducing taxes.[38]

Initially the impact of Proposition 13 was what its supporters wanted; property tax bills declined significantly, and because of the state's budget surplus most public services remained about the same. When the surplus disappeared in the early 1980s, revenue problems began to emerge and continue to plague the state.[39] California, as well as other states, was affected by the 1981–1982 national recession and the reduction of federal aid. As a result, there were cuts in many state programs and communities began to impose user charges for many services. Also, the provision in Proposition 13 that allows property to be reappraised to current market value only when it is sold means that new property owners may pay taxes as much as ten times higher than those of people who have been living in similar houses for years. In 1992, the Supreme Court upheld this system.

States also have enacted property tax relief laws. Arthur O'Sullivan, Terri Sexton, and Steven Sheffrin define property tax relief as any "measure that reduces property taxes below what they otherwise would be."[40] The principal types are homestead exemptions and circuit breakers; both target specific homeowners. **Homestead exemptions,** used in forty-four states and the District of Columbia, are aimed at people who own their home and also are elderly, disabled, or have low incomes. The exemptions exclude from taxation a certain amount of the assessed value of their home. The exemption amount is subtracted from the assessed value of the property before the amount of tax is calculated. **Circuit breakers,** used in thirty-four states and the District of Columbia, limit the percentage of a homeowner's income that can be taken in property taxes. As with the homestead exemption, this program is designed to prevent senior citizens on fixed retirement incomes and low-income households from having to sell their homes because of higher and higher property taxes. The name circuit breaker is appropriate because when an individual's property tax exceeds a certain point relative to income, this program "breaks" the load of higher taxes.[41]

These programs do provide some relief to property owners, especially low-income households. States with the highest property taxes tend to have the most generous programs. In recent years, New Jersey had 2 million beneficiaries, whereas Oklahoma had just fewer than 4,000. Average benefits were $550 in Maryland and $81 in Arizona.[42]

BORROWING AND DEBT POLICIES

When state and local governments wish to finance major capital programs such as highways or schools, they usually must borrow money. Borrowing to meet current expenses is discouraged, although it does occur. Long-term borrowing for permanent improvements is standard procedure. Because of unsound financial management in the nineteenth century, state constitutions place narrow limits on borrowing. Limits are placed on the amount of debt that can be incurred, and borrowing decisions frequently are made by the voters in referenda, rather than by legislators.

Older cities in the Northeast tend to have more debt than other cities because of the variety of services they provide and their deteriorating financial base. State debt occurs because capital spending (e.g., building and repairing bridges) necessitates borrowing. States and cities are rated by private agencies, and if they have low ratings (based on their financial condition), they must pay higher rates of interest. Debt also exists because states form government corporations to finance public works projects, and these corporations can borrow money in excess of state constitutional limits.

A part of state and local debt is in the form of short-term bank loans and tax anticipation warrants, which are paid out of current revenue. To pay for capital improvements, which may involve tens of millions of dollars, governments issue bonds (usually referred to as "municipals"). **General-obligation bonds** are backed by the full faith and credit of the issuing government. In approving this kind of bond, the government agrees to increase taxes to pay the interest and ultimately to retire the bond. **Revenue bonds** are supported by the income from a project such as a toll road. In most cases, voter approval is not needed to issue revenue bonds, and the bonds can often be used to extend the total debt of a government beyond constitutional limits. Generally, both types of bonds are attractive investments, especially to wealthy investors, because the interest they pay is exempt from the federal and state income taxes. Because revenue bonds are somewhat more risky than general-obligation bonds, they usually pay a higher rate of interest.

THE OUTLOOK FOR REVENUES

Short-Term Problems

State and local government revenues are affected by the economic cycle of growth and recession. Periods of economic growth cause an increase in revenue, especially for state governments that rely on the sales and income taxes that result in increased revenue collections when more people are working and spending money. As the twentieth century came to an end, the national economy was strong and state finances were remarkably healthy. The fifty states had a total surplus in 1999 of $33 billion. Governors and legislators were faced with the question of what to do with budget surpluses. They decided on a number of actions:

1. Twenty states cut taxes to reduce excess revenues.
2. Seventeen states made deposits to their "rainy day" funds (These are funds that can be used when state revenues are not as plentiful.)
3. Thirteen states targeted certain programs for extra funding.
4. Thirteen states funded capital construction projects, rather than borrowing money.[43]

But just a couple of years later, economic conditions were not as good and state (and local) government revenues fell with a vengeance, as was noted in the story that introduced this chapter. The relationship between the performance of the economy and state tax revenues can be seen in Figure 8-5; changes in revenue per capita rather closely follow changes in economic growth. The recession that started in the spring of 2001 is different from the previous two in that the drop in tax revenues (−7.4 percent) is much greater than the negative change in economic growth (−0.7 percent). Analysts suggest that this "super-sized" drop in revenues was caused primarily by a decline in *income tax* collections that occurred when investors could no longer realize capital gains from sell-

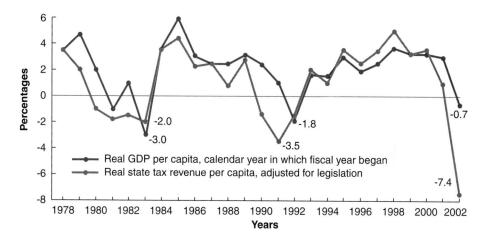

FIGURE 8-5 Comparison of decline in state revenues during three economic recessions: 1980–82, 1990–91 and 2001–02.

Source: Donald J. Boyd and Nicholas W. Jenny, "State Fiscal Crisis Far Worse Than Economy Would Suggest," The Rockefeller Institute State Fiscal News (May 2003), p. 1, fiscal@rockinst.org (accessed May 13, 2003).

Note: "Adjusted for legislation" means that any legislative changes in tax policy that affected revenue collections have been controlled for. "Fiscal year" refers to a financial accounting period of one year, which does not necessarily begin on January 1. State government fiscal years usually begin on July 1 and end on June 30. Reprinted by permission of the Rockefeller Institute of Government.

ing stocks; dramatic stock market price increases not only stopped but they dropped precipitously.[44] (Capital gains—money earned from selling stocks at a higher price than an investor originally bought them for—are reported as income on state tax returns.)

State political leaders were facing the worst budget deficits in over 50 years. The $33 billion surplus of 1999 had turned into a $37 billion deficit in 2002, with similar or larger deficits predicted for at least the next couple of years! As was mentioned in Chapter 6, however, unlike the federal government, state governments *cannot* run a deficit in their operating budgets. In all states but Vermont, constitutional or statutory language requires balanced budgets.

How did state governors and legislators react to this latest economic downturn and unbalanced budgets? Did they reduce spending? Or did they raise taxes? States will usually do both, depending on individual state circumstances. Some specific ideas are offered by Nicholas W. Jenny and Richard P. Nathan; the ideas are arranged, more or less, from the least painful to the most painful:[45]

- Use reserve funds such as "rainy day" funds and refinance debt that would lower interest payments. (Remember, states usually have a capital budget from which they borrow money [incur debt] to buy land, construct buildings, and purchase major equipment.)
- Defer spending and accelerate revenue collections.
- Implement hiring freezes.
- Raise "sin taxes" and close tax loopholes.
- Implement across-the-board or targeted spending cuts.

- Freeze planned tax cuts and spending increases.
- Increase major taxes and adopt substantial spending cuts.

In 2002, twenty-nine states implemented across-the-board or targeted budget cuts; higher education budgets are one of the favorite targets. Political leaders know that colleges and universities can increase tuition and fees to make up some of the reduction. Although specific amounts vary, usually no agency is spared, including corrections, Medicaid, and state aid to primary and secondary education. Many of the steps taken to balance state budgets will have a negative effect on local governments because the amount of their state financial aid may be cut. Fifteen states enacted significant tax increases, increasing tax revenues by at least 1 percent of general fund expenditures. Four states increased their sales tax rate; in Indiana the increase was from 5 to 6 percent. The most popular tax increase was on cigarettes; Pennsylvania more than tripled its tax per pack, from 31 cents to $1.00, bringing in an extra $570 million in 2003.[46]

Some states used the pressure of budget problems to look for ways to do things more efficiently. Virginia Governor Mark Warner, an ex-telecommunications executive, developed plans to merge all information technology workers into a single agency by eliminating three existing agencies and consolidating others. The new agency would buy and maintain the state's "high-tech infrastructure" and in the process save the state $100 million a year.[47]

It is important to note that governors also resorted to what are called "gimmicks," that is, policies that provided a "one-shot injection of revenue or one-time savings on expenditures."[48] Examples include delaying state aid payments to local governments and school districts and delaying state payments to pension funds. Not all of these gimmicks are harmful, but some are. Delaying payments to pension funds means that payments will have to be made later; the payment is simply shifted to future taxpayers.

To be sure, economic cycles will always be with us, and recessions will cause revenue shortfalls. "Rainy day" funds can help to provide some extra money during a recession, but political leaders will be confronted with difficult decisions of cutting spending and increasing taxes to maintain balanced budgets.

Long-Term Problems

Some specialists on state taxes see a long-term problem with state tax systems; they refer to it as a structural deficit. A **structural deficit** exists when money produced by the tax system is insufficient "to maintain existing level of services."[49] Changes in the American economy have affected, in particular, that mainstay of state taxes, the sales tax. Two examples will help to explain this.

It has been widely reported that the strength of the American economy is less in the manufacturing of tangible goods and more in the production of services. The service sector is the fastest growing sector of the American economy. However, the general sales tax, as has been noted, primarily taxes the purchase of tangible goods, not services. During the past fifty years services have grown from 41 percent of household consumption to 58 percent. The Federation of Tax Administrators estimates that there are 164 services that could be taxed. Services provided by accountants, attorneys, doctors, and engineers are the most frequently mentioned examples, but others include barber/beautician, health club, janitorial, lawn care and landscaping, and pool cleaning services. Only three states—Hawaii, New Mexico, and South Dakota—tax roughly the entire list of services; most states tax only a few.[50] It's difficult for states to expand the taxing of services because this is always viewed as a tax increase, and some of the affected groups such as doctors and lawyers are influential interest groups. A comprehensive approach that broadened the sales tax base to include all services and at the same time lowered the tax rate might be successful. Not only is the sales tax affected by the move to a service-oriented economy but so are personal income tax collections, which are lowered, or do not grow as much, because people shift from higher paying manufacturing jobs to lower paying jobs in the service sector.[51]

Another example deals with changes in the way people shop and buy things. Retail sales through mail-order catalogs, the Home Shopping Network, and the rapid growth of sales over the Internet have a negative effect on tax collections. Of course, there is little doubt that e-commerce business in the near future will be larger than anything previously achieved by "remote sellers." Whether state "A" can require remote sellers in state "B" to collect sales taxes on items sold to citizens in state "A" is a complex constitutional and administrative problem. In 1992, the U.S. Supreme Court in *Quill Corp. v. North Dakota*[52] decided that remote sellers were not obligated to collect and remit taxes on sales made to citizens in other states. There was an exception: If a remote seller has a physical presence or nexus (for example, another store or even a warehouse) in the same state as a consumer purchasing an item from the remote seller, then the remote seller is required to collect and remit those taxes. And consumers in states where the remote seller does not have a nexus are to calculate and remit at the end of the year taxes owed to their home states on items that were purchased from remote sellers. (How many times have you done this?) Of course, most citizens are unaware of this requirement, and states have no real way to enforce it.

This is a continuing issue for the National Conference of State Legislatures and the National Governors Association, in particular because large amounts of tax revenue are being lost. In 2001, untaxed e-commerce represented a total loss of $13 billion; by 2006 the loss is estimated to be $45 billion; and the estimate for 2011 is $55 billion.[53] As a practical matter, at the present time it would be difficult for remote sellers to collect sales taxes from all consumers because approximately 7,500 taxing jurisdictions (state and local governments) often define and tax the same products differently. For example, in one state orange juice is defined as a fruit and taxed, in another state it's defined as a beverage and not taxed. A marshmallow may be a food in one state and not taxed, but candy in another state and taxed. It's almost impossible for businesses selling to customers nationwide to keep track of what's what in the various taxing jurisdictions. To overcome this and other administrative problems, state political leaders created the **Streamlined Sales Tax Project,** which has as its goal the simplification and modernization of sales tax collection and administration.[54] Among other things, the project will develop uniform definitions for taxable goods and require state and local governments to have only one statewide tax rate for each taxable product. (However, states can have different tax rates.) Implementation of the project's proposals will not begin until ten states formally approve it and make required changes in their laws. It will then apply to those ten states, with other states being added when and if they approve. Even after all of this, the U.S. Congress or the Supreme Court, because they have power over

commerce between the states, would have to mandate remote sellers to collect and remit the tax on out-of-state buyers.

A study of state tax systems sponsored by the National Conference of State
Legislatures and the National Governors' Association makes the following conclusion:

> State systems are becoming obsolete, inequitable, and unresponsive to changes in the
> economy. Designed primarily during the 1930s for a nation of smokestack industries in
> deep economic depression, state tax systems fall short in the 1990s when services are
> supplanting manufacturing as the economic linchpin, the economy is increasingly
> global, and new information-based industries appear almost daily.[55]

The Revenue Dilemma of Cities

Local governments are not immune to revenue problems, and this is especially true in
large, central cities (population of 500,000 or more) that are surrounded by suburbs.
No one can help but notice the differences between life in the cities and life in the suburbs, and most people with at least moderate financial resources conclude that they
would rather live in the suburbs than the central cities. The percentage of the U.S. population living in these cities declined from 15.5 percent to12.7 percent between 1970
and 2000. More important than this decline is the fact that residents of large cities who
have not moved to the suburbs tend to be poor; from 1970 to 1997, nearly 6 million
middle- and high-income families left the cities. In 1996, median household income in
the suburbs was 31 percent higher than central city incomes, up from the 1989 figure of
22 percent. The difference in median income tends to be higher in cities in the Northeast
and Midwest than in the South and West.[56] Employment growth is slower in central
cities than in the surrounding suburbs. (See Figure 8-6.) Central cities also have more
problems, such as higher crime rates and a declining infrastructure that require higher

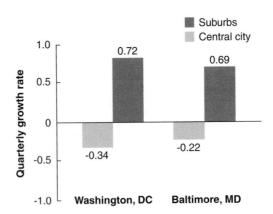

**FIGURE 8-6 Employment growth in Washington, D.C., and Baltimore, Maryland, 1992–1999
(quarterly growth rate).**

Source: "Job Growth in Suburbs versus Cities," *Monthly Labor Review: The Editor's Desk,*
www.bls.gov/opub/ted/2001/Oct/wk5/art03.htm (accessed May 16, 2003).

expenditures by their governments. The resulting higher taxes are another reason for businesses and residents to move to the suburbs, where taxes are usually lower, which further reduces the cities' tax base and increases the likelihood that taxes will be raised.

If taxes are not raised, then the quality of services declines. Because of a wider array of problems, cities have less money to spend on elementary and secondary schools; education expenditures consume "about half of most suburban budgets, but rarely more than a third of most central cities."[57] Many are caught in a downward spiral that can be reversed only by increased financial assistance from the federal and state governments or arrangements that would allow central cities to share in their suburbs' tax base.[58] (See Chapter 9 for a more complete discussion of cities and suburbs.)

Solving long-term financial problems of state and local governments in the twenty-first century will not be easy. The "reinventing government" approach (see Chapter 6) may yield more efficient delivery of services, but it is unlikely to solve long-term problems of the states and large cities. Public aversion to tax increases is strong, even if it is needed to prevent a decline in services.

SUMMARY

State and local governments spend a great deal of money ($1.5 trillion in 2000), and their share of total government spending has increased in the last few decades. Almost one-third of these expenditures is used to finance the public school system (elementary and secondary education, as well as higher education). Other significant expenditure items are public welfare, health and hospitals, and highways.

Intergovernmental funds are an important source of revenue for both state and local governments. In terms of their own taxes, the sales tax is the most important source of revenue for state governments, and the property tax is the most important source for local governments. Both of these taxes have been declining in their percentage contribution to state and local treasuries over the past few decades, and user charges have been growing in importance. In their search for new revenues, more states are operating lotteries. Casino gambling, which is regulated by the states or Indian tribal governments, has spread rapidly. Potential social costs of legalized casinos are frequently pushed aside in the search for new tax revenues and the promise of economic development and jobs.

The public consistently gives low ratings to the property tax because many doubt its fairness, one of the criteria used to evaluate different kinds of taxes. Public dissatisfaction has manifested itself in a number of ways, from California's Proposition 13, which dramatically reduced property taxes, to the adoption in most states of property tax relief laws, which reduce property taxes through homestead exemptions and circuit breakers.

During the late 1990s, state governments benefited from a rosy revenue picture caused by the nation's strong economic performance; but as a recession started in 2001, revenues dropped and states faced one of the worst fiscal conditions to be seen in the last fifty years. Revenue shortfalls were further aggravated by long-term problems—such as lost sales tax revenue from e-commerce—that have created a structural deficit whereby existing tax systems will not generate enough revenue to maintain services in the future. Another challenge is to find revenues to fund services in large cities that have an inadequate tax base.

KEY TERMS

circuit breakers
California v. Cabazon Band of Mission Indians
direct general expenditures
excise tax
fairness
general-obligation bonds
general sales tax
homestead exemptions
income tax
Indian Gaming Regulatory Act
intergovernmental expenditures
property tax

Proposition 13
revenue bonds
sales tax holidays
severance tax
simplicity
Streamlined Sales Tax Project
stability
structural deficit
sufficiency
TELs
user charge
vertical equity

SUMMARY OF STATE/LOCAL DIFFERENCES

Issue	State Level	Local Level
Principal expenditures	Higher education, public welfare, and corrections	Elementary and secondary schools and police protection
Principal own source revenue	Sales tax	Property tax
Long-term revenue problems	Taxing of retail sales made out of state, especially over the Internet	Inadequate tax base in large cities

INTERESTING WEBSITES

www.rockinst.org. This is the website of the Nelson A. Rockefeller Institute of Government in Albany, New York. Click on "State and Local Finances" for analysis of revenues and expenditures. This is a great website for information on a variety of state and local issues; for example, explore "Higher Education" and "Welfare and Jobs."

www.census.gov. This site provides detailed information on revenues and expenditures from the U.S. Census Bureau. Click on "Government" and you will find a list of reports for state and local governments generally, for specific states, and even public school systems. (These reports are not up to the minute; for example, 2002 data should be available in 2004.)

www.taxadmin.org. Website of the Federation of Tax Administrators. Click on "State Comparisons" for the details of each state's tax system such as tax rates, tax collections, amnesty programs, sales tax holidays, and more.

www.ngisc.gov. The National Gambling Impact Study Commission has a wealth of information on a timely topic.

NOTES

1. State of the State Address to a Joint Session of the First Session of the 57th Idaho Legislature, January 7, 2003, www2.state.id.us/gov/mediacenter/sp03/sp_stateofstate.html (accessed May 23, 2003).

2. Bob Fick, "GOP Leaders Seek Votes for Cigarette Tax Hike," Associated Press and Local Wire, May 1, 2003, web.lexis-nexis.com/univ (accessed May 22, 2003).

3. State and local expenditures for FY 1999–2000 are from "Table 1. State and Local Government Finances by Level of Government and by State: 1999–2000," available at www.census.gov/govs/estimate/00s100us.html (accessed May 5, 2003). Federal expenditures are from U.S. Bureau of the Census, *Statistical Abstract of the United States, 2003* (Washington, D.C.: Government Printing Office, 2002), p. 305. Per capita calculations are based on U.S. population of 281,422,000 as of April 1, 2000.

4. *Tax and Expenditure Limits on Local Governments* (Washington, D.C.: Advisory Commission on Intergovernmental Relations, 1995), p. 44.

5. John R. Bartle, "Trends in Local Government Taxation in the 21st Century," *Spectrum: The Journal of State Government* (Winter 2003), p. 26.

6. Henry J. Raimondo, *Economics of State and Local Government* (New York: Praeger Publishers, 1992), p. 138.

7. *Local Revenue Diversification: Local Sales Taxes* (Washington, D.C.: Advisory Commission on Intergovernmental Relations, 1989), 3; J. Richard Aronson and John L. Hilley, *Financing State and Local Governments* (Washington, D.C.: The Brookings Institution, 1986), p. 94.

8. Raimondo, *Economics,* pp. 168–171.

9. John R. Bartle, "Trends in Local Government Taxation," p. 27.

10. Ronald John Hy and William L. Waugh, Jr., *State and Local Tax Policies: A Comparative Handbook* (Westport, Conn.: Greenwood Press, 1995), p. 36.

11. Wesley Brown, "Corporate Income Dwindles as Companies Shift Tax Burden," May 2, 2003, www.nwaonline.net (accessed May 5, 2003).

12. David Brunori, *State Tax Policy: A Political Perspective* (Washington, D.C.: The Urban Institute Press, 2001), pp.109–113.

13. Aronson and Hilley, *Financing,* p. 43.

14. Raimondo, *Economics,* p. 206.

15. Aronson and Hilley, *Financing,* p. 157.

16. *National Gambling Impact Study Commission, Final Report,* 1-1, www.ngisc.gov.

17. Timothy L. O'Brien, "Gambling: Married to the Action, for Better or Worse," *New York Times,* November 8, 1998, p. 3. Also see Timothy L. O'Brien, *Bad Bet: The Inside Story of the Glamour, Glitz, and Danger of America's Gambling Industry* (New York, N.Y.: Times Books, 1998).

18. John L. Mikesell and C. Kurt Zorn, "State Lotteries as Fiscal Savior or Fiscal Fraud," *Public Administration Review* (July–August 1986), p. 311.

19. Frederick D. Stocker, "State-Sponsored Gambling as a Source of Public Revenue," *National Tax Journal* 25 (September 1972), p. 437; Raimondo, *Economics,* p. 212.

20. Thomas P. Lauth and Mark D. Robbins, "The Georgia Lottery and State Appropriations for Education: Substitution or Additional Funding?" *Public Budgeting & Finance* (Fall 2002), pp. 89–100.

21. Office of Tribal Justice, U.S. Department of Justice, *Department of Justice Policy on Indian Sovereignty,* www.usdoj.gov/otj/sovtrbtxt.htm, p. 2 (accessed May 10, 2003).

22. *California v. Cabazon Band of Mission Indians,* 480 U.S. 202 (1987).

23. Roger Dunstan, *Gambling in California,* Chap. 4, "Indian Gaming," pp.1–11, California Research Bureau, CRB-97-003, January 1997, Ferguson.library.ca.gov/CRB/97/03/Chapt4.html (accessed May 10, 2003).

24. Michael Barone and Grant Ujifusa with Richard Cohen, *Almanac of American Politics, 1996* (Washington, D.C.: National Journal, 1995), pp. 815–816.
25. *Gambling Impact,* pp. 7–19.
26. Clyde Haberman, "The Inverse of A.T.M. Is V.L.T.," *New York Times,* May 13, 2003; Alex Berenson, "The States Bet Bigger on Betting," *New York Times,* May 18, 2003, www. nytimes.com (accessed May 18, 2003).
27. Larry Copeland, "Money Woes Drive Some States to Gambling," *USA Today,* usatoday.com (accessed March 5, 2003); "States Look to Gamblers to Boost Sagging Budgets: September 2002 Update," www.ncsl.org/programs/econ/maggam.htm (accessed May 11, 2003).
28. John Lyman Mason and Michael Nelson, *Governing Gambling* (New York: The Century Foundation Press, 2001), pp. 24–28, 52–55.
29. David Brunori, *State Tax Policy* (Washington, D.C.: The Urban Institute Press, 2001), pp. 13–27.
30. Ibid., p. 19.
31. An excellent analysis of the tax systems in each of the fifty states can be found in "The Way We Tax," *Governing* (February 2003), pp. 20–97.
32. Raimondo, *Economics,* p. 180.
33. Ibid., pp. 200–201.
34. Richard L. Cole and John Kincaid, "Public Opinion and American Federalism: Changing Perspectives on Taxes, Spending and Trust," *Spectrum: The Journal of State Government* (Summer 2001), p.16; *Changing Public Attitudes on Government and Taxes* (Washington, D.C.: Advisory Commission on Intergovernmental Relations, 1994), p. 4.
35. See Raimondo, *Economics,* pp. 152–156, for a discussion of two different views of the fairness of the property tax.
36. Arthur O'Sullivan, Terri A. Sexton, and Steven M. Sheffrin, *Property Taxes and Tax Revolts: The Legacy of Proposition 13* (New York: Cambridge University Press, 1995), p. 2.
37. Susan B. Hansen, "The Politics of State Taxing and Spending," in *Politics in the American States,* 5th ed., Virginia Gray, Herbert Jacob, and Robert B. Albritton, eds. (Glenview, Ill.: Scott, Foresman/Little, Brown, 1990), pp. 355–356.
38. Ibid.
39. Jerry Hagstrom and Neal R. Peirce, "The Quake That Didn't Quit," *National Journal,* May 25, 1988, pp. 1413–1416.
40. Sullivan, Sexton, and Sheffrin, *Property Taxes,* p. 26.
41. Ibid., pp. 26–27.
42. Ibid.
43. National Conference of State Legislatures, *State Budget & Tax Actions, 1999: Preliminary Report.* www.ncsl.org./programs/fiscal/presbta99.htm.
44. Donald J. Boyd and Nicholas W. Jenny, "State Fiscal Crisis Far Worse Than Economy Would Suggest: Huge Drop in Capital Gains, Other Investment Income Likely to Blame," *The Rockefeller Institute State Fiscal News* (May 2003), pp.1–4, www.rockinst.org.
45. Nicholas W. Jenny and Richard P. Nathan, "Sizing Up the Shortfalls: The States in Straits," *Government Finance Review* (April 2003), p. 13, www.rockinst.org (accessed May 14, 2003).
46. Nicholas W. Jenny, "2002 Tax and Budget Review and 2003 Budget Preview," *State Fiscal Brief* (March 2003), pp. 2–3, www.rockinst.org.
47. Jason White, "Budget Crisis Spurs Innovation, Reform," *Stateline.org,* March 28, 2003, www.stateline.org.
48. Steven D. Gold, ed., *The Fiscal Crisis of the States* (Washington, D.C.: Georgetown University Press, 1995), p. 47.
49. Ibid., p. 43.

50. Ray Scheppach, "Silver Lining in State Fiscal Crisis?" *Stateline.org,* www.stateline.org (accessed May 4, 2003).
51. *State Taxation of Services: Update 1996* (Washington, D.C.: Federation of Tax Administrators, 1997), pp. 1–6.
52. Quill Corp. v. North Dakota, 504 U.S. 298.
53. National Governors Association, press release, "New Report Shows States to Lose Nearly $440 Billion in Sales Tax from Remote Sales," www.nga.org/nga/newsroom (accessed May 4, 2003).
54. Information on the Streamlined Sales Tax Project is available at www.streamlinedsalestax. org.
55. Ronald Snell, *Financing State Government in the 1990s* (Denver, Colo.: National Conference of State Legislatures, and Washington, D.C.: National Governors' Association, 1993), p. 1.
56. Department of Housing and Urban Development, *The State of the Cities, 1998,* www. huduser.org/publications/polleg/tsoc98/part1-2.html.
57. Peter D. Salins, "Metropolitan Areas: Cities, Suburbs, and the Ties That Bind," in *Interwoven Destinies: Cities and the Nation,* Henry G. Cisneros, ed. (New York: W. W. Norton & Company, 1993), p. 158.
58. Carol O'Cleireagain, "Cities' Role in the Metropolitan Economy and the Federal Structure," in *Interwoven Destinies: Cities and the Nation,* Henry G. Cisneros, ed., pp. 176–183.

CHAPTER 9

Suburbs, Metropolitan Areas, and Rural Communities

POINTS TO CONSIDER

- Why has urban sprawl occurred? What are its consequences?
- How do cities and suburbs differ from each other?
- What is the myth of the suburban monolith?
- Discuss methods of consolidating governments in metropolitan areas. When and why have consolidation efforts been successful?
- Should states and cities limit growth? What are some "smart growth" strategies?
- How has zoning adversely affected cities? How should zoning rules be changed?
- Would you want to live in a town designed by the New Urbanists?

- Why did the population of rural areas decrease in the 1980s and increase in the 1990s?

Throughout this book we have discussed a variety of urban issues—the reform movement, the nature of community power, and the roles of interest groups, mayors, and council members. We now turn our attention beyond central city limits to look at politics in suburbs, small towns, and rural areas. The 1920 census showed that the United States had changed from a predominantly small-town, rural society in the nineteenth century to a predominantly urban society. As noted in Chapter 1, urbanization of the United States has increased to the point where currently about 80 percent of Americans live in metropolitan statistical areas (MSAs).

Clearly, we have become a largely urbanized people. Yet more people live *outside* central cities than within them. The 1970 census showed that for the first time in U.S. history more than half the population of metropolitan areas was suburban. Moreover, because MSAs include whole counties adjacent to a central city or contiguous cities of 50,000 people, many residents of MSAs actually live in small towns that are not suburban, or they live in rural areas. Of course, about 20 percent of Americans live outside MSAs.

Our primary concern in this chapter is to examine politics in suburbia to see how it differs from big-city politics and to see how suburban communities interact with each other. The prevailing view of the suburbs in the 1950s was that they were a homogeneous group of bedroom communities whose white, upper- and middle-class residents

Merger in Bluegrass Country

In the 2000 census Louisville, with 256,000 people, was the sixty-fifth largest city in the United States. In 1960 it had been the thirty-first largest city in the country—nearly as large as Indianapolis. On January 1, 2002, Louisville jumped in size to become the nation's twenty-third largest city.

Louisville's change in status came about because voters in the city and in Jefferson County decisively approved consolidation of most government activity in the county. It was the first time since 1968 in Jacksonville, Florida, that voters had approved city-county consolidation for a major city in the United States. The successful vote in 2000 came after three previous merger proposals had been defeated.[1]

Since World War II Louisville and Jefferson County had merged their schools and water systems, and citizens approved a proportional split of occupational tax revenues. Still, the city-county merger was tough to accomplish. To help get the suburban vote, it was agreed not to spell out all the details of the plan in advance. For example, the eighty-plus municipalities and twenty-one fire districts outside Louisville could remain intact. Interestingly, several small cities chose to merge with each other to have greater power in metropolitan affairs.

The mayor of Louisville, Jerry Abramson, was key to getting the merger approved. After being term-limited as mayor, Abramson was easily elected to the new office of metropolitan mayor. Abramson is described by people in Louisville as a legendary salesman and a "born closer."

voted Republican and limited their concern for social issues to their local schools.[2] This picture was oversimplified even in the 1950s, and suburbs have become increasingly diverse. By the 1970s the idealized version of these communities differed greatly from reality. After examining contemporary suburban life, we will look at ways in which metropolitan areas are attempting to create order where literally hundreds of overlapping governments have fragmented the political process. Then we will travel farther away from central cities to examine life in small-town and rural America.

URBAN SPRAWL: CAUSES AND EFFECTS

As Harrigan and Vogel note, central cities could have grown by annexing areas on their fringes where population was growing.[3] Instead, cities became surrounded by autonomous suburban communities whose residents sought the advantages of a small-town setting close to the economic and cultural opportunities of the central city. As recently as 1950, 70 percent of metropolitan area populations lived in central cities. In 2000, just over 70 percent lived *outside* central cities in the nation's twenty-five largest metropolitan areas. An even higher percentage of voters and the overwhelming majority of elites now reside in suburbs. In addition, most metropolitan residents work in suburban areas.

The mobility afforded by widespread automobile ownership after World War II and the construction of new highways helped to accelerate suburban growth. A host of federal government policies—including the interstate highway system, lower-interest home loans insured by the Federal Housing Administration, tax codes that permitted deductions for home mortgage interest, and grants to build hospitals and sewerage plants—encouraged Americans to move to the suburbs in the 1950s.

The most recent wave of suburbanization has resulted from the creation of new "edge cities" that have developed when office space has been built along interstate corridors on the outer edge of existing suburbs. Some academics argue that the next wave of population movement is beginning to occur as people move beyond suburbs to more distant rural areas where they can telecommute and enjoy open space.

Earlier decisions made by private businesses also facilitated population movement away from central cities. Faced with labor unrest near the end of the nineteenth century, many businesses relocated their plants to the suburbs as a way to isolate workers and to control union activities. Credit institutions often practiced **redlining**, in which they refused to make loans for construction in certain parts of cities they considered too risky. Depressed areas of cities grew worse as new or rehabilitated housing was not funded. The lack of acceptable central city housing led to the exodus of the middle class to the suburbs as government policy made it easier for them to buy houses.

Often these privately made decisions were strongly influenced by racial factors. Redlining made it nearly impossible for many African Americans to get home loans. As more African Americans and Hispanics moved into northern cities after World War II, residential segregation increased. Jobs, shops, and sports stadiums moved to the suburbs and minorities were left behind. In the suburbs, open space was lost to sprawl and exclusionary zoning (discussed later in the chapter) often served to limit housing opportunities for *all* low-income people.

Fragmented Government

As people have moved farther away from the central city, **urban sprawl** has created a maze of government units over which there often is little or no coordination or control by a central agency (see Table 9-1). The New York City metropolitan area, for example, extends over more than twenty counties in three states and contains more than 21 million people. Even though population growth in metropolitan New York has increased less than 10 percent since 1970, the amount of developed land in the area has increased over 60 percent. The Chicago metropolitan area contains more than 1,100 governmental units. Phoenix in 1940 had a population of 65,000 within a ten-square-mile area. Currently the city has a population of 1.4 million in a 475-square-mile area. In addition, suburban sprawl has led to the expansion of Tempe, Mesa, Paradise Valley, and other new cities in the Phoenix metropolitan area.

TABLE 9-1 Political Fragmentation in the 25 Largest Metropolitan Areas

Metropolitan Area	Counties	Municipalities and Townships	Total Local Governments	Local Governments per 100,000 Residents	Population Living in Central City (%)
Pittsburgh	6	412	418	17.7	14.8
Minneapolis–St. Paul	13	331	344	12.3	22.4
St. Louis	12	300	312	12.2	13.8
Cincinnati	13	222	235	12.2	18.0
Kansas City	11	171	182	10.6	34.6
Cleveland	8	259	267	9.2	17.1
Philadelphia	14	428	442	7.4	24.7
Milwaukee	5	108	113	6.9	36.1
Chicago	13	554	567	6.6	31.7
Detroit	10	325	335	6.2	18.4
Boston	14	282	296	5.1	9.6
Dallas	12	184	196	4.2	23.1
Portland	8	79	87	4.1	23.2
New York	27	729	756	3.8	37.3
Atlanta	20	107	127	3.5	11.4
Denver	7	67	74	3.2	21.9
Houston	8	115	123	2.8	41.1
Seattle	6	88	94	2.8	15.9
Tampa	4	35	39	1.8	13.0
San Francisco	10	104	114	1.7	11.1
Miami	2	55	57	1.6	10.5
Phoenix	2	32	34	1.2	42.1
Los Angeles	5	177	182	1.2	23.0
San Diego	1	18	19	0.7	43.7
Washington, D.C.	33	125	158	2.2	17.1

Source: Myron Orfield, *Metropolitics: The New Suburban Reality* (Washington, D.C.: Brookings Institution Press, 2002), pp. 132, 134.

David Rusk notes that 56 percent of Americans lived in 168 "old metropolitan areas" in 1950.[4] The central cities in these metropolitan areas had about 60 percent of the region's population. By 1990, 66 percent of Americans lived in the old metropolitan areas, but their central cities contained only one-third of the regional population. In addition, Rusk identifies another 152 "young metropolitan areas" that had developed, mainly in the South and West, by 1990. Largely because of annexation, their central cities were able to capture much of the area's growth, and as a result they had about 62 percent of the metropolitan population. Rusk reports that the total population of all metropolitan areas increased by 128 percent from 1950 to 1990, while their land area increased by 181 percent.

In 1950 the 172 metropolitan areas in the United States had a population of 85 million, or 56 percent of the total population of the country. In 2000 there were 331 metropolitan areas with 226 million people, or 80 percent of the total population. The ten largest metropolitan areas had a population of about 89 million.

The *fragmentation* of metropolitan government makes it extremely difficult to establish responsibility for metropolitan area policy. In addition, public services suffer because small units are unable to provide many specialized services; there is duplication of services when many governments independently operate facilities such as sewage disposal and water plants; and it is difficult to deal with the many problems—pollution, mass transit, crime, traffic congestion—that extend over several community boundary lines. Affluent suburbs can spend vast sums for education, but central cities face a declining tax base and an increasing demand for services. Property tax *rates* may be higher in a central city than in its more affluent suburbs. At the same time, many suburban governments need to spend relatively little money for crime control or public health. However, many middle-class suburbs increasingly must deal with social and economic problems similar to those confronting central cities. The low-density development of suburbs tends to drive up the cost of infrastructure development and repair.

Fragmentation has numerous other consequences. Significant racial imbalance occurs because outer-ring suburbs remain predominantly white, whereas the central city and, increasingly, inner-ring suburbs have large African-American and Hispanic populations. Suburban land-use regulations drive up the cost of new construction, and this leads to a shortage of housing in central cities when low-income persons are forced to stay within city limits. Suburbs that restrict the growth of *all* types of housing units force development on the suburban fringe, thus adding to the existing urban sprawl. Suburbs that restrict growth push development out farther, and this destroys more green space. Because suburban residents value their independence, they strongly resist metropolitan-wide government or other means of coordination.[5]

Anti-sprawl has become a major political issue across the country. Voters in the 1990s approved numerous state and municipal initiatives to preserve open space. In 2002 voters in the Portland, Oregon, metropolitan area, for the fourth time since an urban growth boundary was established in 1973, rejected an initiative that would have weakened the law.

Cities versus Suburbs

An increasing trend since the 1980s has been the expansion of **satellite (or edge) cities** on the fringes of metropolitan areas.[6] Although cities such as West Palm Beach (Miami),

Scottsdale (Phoenix), and White Plains (New York) are related to the central city, they are employment centers in their own right and often have downtowns and cultural complexes that are quite separate from the core city. The newest edge cities are characterized by low-density, heavily landscaped office campuses, and they are located adjacent to large upper-middle and high-income housing tracts. Always moving farther from the central city, new edge cities, such as Plano, Texas, on the Dallas Tollway, are located several miles beyond the last generation of edge cities.[7]

There have been both push and pull effects regarding patterns of residence. Suburbs have "pulled" residents out of cities with their promise of a better life, but residents of central cities have also been "pushed out" because of a variety of city problems. Migrants from large cities most often mention crime as their major reason for leaving. Rundown schools, drugs, pollution, high taxes, and the rising cost of living are other factors that push people to the suburbs. As the percentage of African Americans and Hispanics has increased in central cities, a clear undercurrent of racism also has influenced whites to flee to predominantly white suburbs. In large cities, people also sense a loss of community feeling and often find it difficult to participate in government decision making.

The movement of racial minorities to inner-ring suburbs has led to resegregation by race as whites move farther away in the metropolitan area. Until 1990, there was general agreement among academics that when a community's African-American population approaches 20 to 30 percent, whites begin to move out in substantial numbers (the **tipping point** has been reached). In the 1990s, some, such as Andrew Hacker, suggested that white exodus can begin much earlier, when the African-American population is as low as 10 percent.[8]

When middle-class families and industry leave, the city's tax base shrinks, and this occurs at a time when welfare, police, and public health expenses are increasing. Yet great *private wealth* remains in the nation's largest cities. Cities continue to attract unskilled workers who seek better lives. But, unlike the early twentieth-century immigrants, today's urban poor find few unskilled jobs, and union control of apprenticeship programs makes it difficult to acquire trade skills. In addition, young blacks are particularly frustrated and alienated when they encounter a substantial gap between real and anticipated social and economic gains. Inner-city neighborhoods continue to deteriorate, even as downtown development projects create spectacular new buildings. For example, Cleveland's poverty rate has remained around 40 percent despite the construction of new sports facilities and new downtown office buildings.

Still, there is increasing evidence to indicate that life in cities has actually improved. In places such as Boston and Baltimore, middle-class people have returned to live in the city, and new shopping areas such as Boston's Quincy Market are flourishing. The Society Hill–Market Street East area in Philadelphia is another example of a successful renewal effort. Cincinnati has banned new surface parking lots downtown and its city planning department has five full-time employees working on historical preservation. Downtowns are being preserved in virtually all cities. This is in contrast to the mid-1960s, when some 1,600 federally supported urban renewal projects in 800 cities often were bulldozing historic neighborhoods. Federal tax laws now encourage preservation, and cities are putting a priority on downtown development. Unfortunately, as upscale renovation has lured white suburbanites back to inner cities, the increased costs have driven African Americans and Hispanics to other urban neighborhoods.

Cities and their suburbs exist in a state of natural hostility. Most fundamentally, there is a substantial difference in lifestyles between residents of the two areas. Although it would be very misleading to picture Grosse Pointe, Beverly Hills, and Scarsdale as "typical" suburbs, suburbanites in northern and western states are better educated, have higher incomes, and are more likely to hold white-collar jobs than are central-city dwellers. In much of suburbia, life still centers around single-family units, and there is a strong emphasis on local schools.

Most large cities have experienced significant white flight since the mid-1970s, resulting in increasing concentration of Hispanics and African Americans in inner cities while many suburbs remain predominantly white. Overwhelmingly, African Americans are likely to live in metropolitan areas. The 2000 census showed that for the first time non-Hispanic whites were a minority of the total population living in the nation's 100 largest cities. Seventy-one of the 100 largest cities lost white population in the 1990s. At the same time those cities had a 43 percent increase in Hispanic residents. Chicago gained 208,000 Hispanics and had its first overall population gain since 1950. Detroit lost 53 percent of its white population in the 1990s and saw its total population drop below 1 million for the first time since 1920. African Americans now comprise about 83 percent of Detroit's population.

Although suburbs remain mostly white, there has been a substantial departure of middle- and working-class minority persons from cities since the 1980s. For example, in the 1980s and 1990s the population of Washington, D.C. declined by nearly 200,000, and the loss of African-American households was nearly three times as great as for whites. Hispanic and Asian-American suburbanization has occurred at even higher rates than for African Americans across the country. Circles of African-American-majority suburbs exist around Washington, Atlanta, St. Louis, Los Angeles, and Chicago. Minorities leaving central cities cite the same reasons as whites for their flight to suburbs—crime, quality of life, property values, and schools.

While the number of all-white suburbs is diminishing, many suburbs are becoming more predominantly white. In suburban Detroit, Livonia was 96.5 percent white in 2000 and Warren was 93.3 percent white. The most racially segregated suburban area in the United States is on Long Island, New York. David Rusk blames its segregation on a mixture of tax, zoning, housing, and education policies that result from Long Island's "frustrating maze of little-box governments; 109 villages, towns, and cities; and 129 school districts."[9] At the other extreme, so-called disaster suburbs such as East St. Louis, Illinois, and Compton, California, are nearly all minority and very poor.

In general, suburbs have not provided a supportive environment for women. When women were more likely to stay home with their children in the 1950s, they often were isolated in suburban communities without public transportation. More recently, working mothers in suburbia may be frustrated by zoning ordinances that restrict the location of child care centers.[10]

In addition to socioeconomic differences, *political differences* between central cities and suburbs can be identified. From our understanding of socioeconomic factors and their relationship to party identification (see Chapter 3), we would expect cities to be strongly Democratic and suburbs to be strongly Republican. In fact, cities, with their concentrations of union members, ethnic minorities, and African Americans, historically have supported the Democratic Party in national and local elections. New York City has cast a majority of its votes for every Democratic presidential candidate since Thomas Jefferson. St. Louis has not had a Republican mayor since 1945. However, New York City and Los Angeles elected Republican mayors in the 1990s and New York City elected another Republican mayor in 2002. Several other large cities—including Cleveland, Indianapolis, Minneapolis, and San Diego—elected Republican mayors in the 1980s. Although predominantly white, upper-class suburbs on the outer ring of metropolitan areas support Republican candidates in state and national elections, overall, as we will see in the following section, suburbs are much more politically competitive than conventional wisdom has suggested.

Suburban Variety

Just as central cities exist along a continuum from those that are weak or declining, such as Detroit and Cleveland, to those that are strong and gentrifying, such as Seattle and Phoenix, we can identify great variety among suburbs. Myron Orfield attacks the "myth of the suburban monolith" by describing three main categories of suburbs that are emerging in metropolitan areas across the country.[11]

Forty percent of the population in metropolitan areas live in what Orfield calls **"at-risk" suburbs.** Some of them are older, inner-ring communities that have been by-passed by metropolitan growth. Others are located on the outer ring of metropolitan areas where there is a transition from rural to suburban. In addition to having some incorporated communities, fringe areas in many regions, such as Atlanta, contain large tracts of unincorporated territory that have high rates of poverty. At-risk suburbs lack a viable business district and they often share many of the same economic and social problems of central cities. Many inner-ring at-risk suburbs, such as those around Chicago, are even more racially segregated than their central cities.

About one quarter of the population of metropolitan areas live in **"bedroom-developing" suburbs.** These communities resemble the 1950s view of the "typical" suburb. Their predominantly white population, living in newer houses, has the most school-aged children of any communities in the region. Because they often lack an adequate tax base, these suburbs face fiscal pressures to build roads and sewer systems and to construct and maintain schools.

Less than 10 percent of the population of metropolitan areas live in suburbs that Orfield calls **"affluent job centers."** These are the edge cities we discussed above. With abundant office space, they have more jobs than bedrooms. For these communities, urban sprawl is advantageous. Still, problems exist. Many workers cannot afford local housing, there is traffic congestion, and it is difficult to resist pressures to develop open space.

Orfield has a series of color-coded maps that clearly show the mix of communities in several metropolitan areas.[12] For example, the San Francisco region has large expanses of at-risk, low-density, unincorporated areas on its fringes and it has an inner ring of at-risk, segregated suburbs near Oakland. Affluent communities are dominant in Santa Clara County, which is at the southeast corner of the region.

Orfield also shows that suburbs are much more politically complex than they have been portrayed in the suburban monolith model. His computer-generated mapping of the twenty-five largest metropolitan areas (home to 46 percent of the nation's population) has produced some surprising results. Orfield found that in 1998 state legislative seats were evenly split between Democrats and Republicans. Many of the country's swing districts, those with no permanent allegiance to either major party, are in the suburbs.[13] Orfield suggests that characterizing suburban women as "soccer moms" misses the suburban reality. Although residents of affluent job centers often vote Republican, the overwhelming number of suburban residents live in at-risk and bedroom-developing suburbs, and it is these swing voters that Orfield believes will play the pivotal role in determining the outcome of upcoming American elections.

THE POLITICS OF METROPOLITAN CONSOLIDATION

Differences in the political, social, and economic composition of cities and suburbs have a direct effect on public policy. In many instances people have moved to suburbs to escape the problems of central cities or, increasingly, to escape the problems of inner-ring suburbs. They do not want to contribute tax dollars to help solve other people's social problems. Meanwhile, cities must respond to a host of pressing issues even as their revenue base declines.

As we would expect, city-suburb differences also have a major impact on the fate of proposals for consolidation of metropolitan governments. In most instances, consolidation plans are opposed by both city and suburban officials, who seek to maintain their community's autonomy and their personal political power. Of the two groups, those in suburbs have been the most opposed to unification. However, the support of residents of central cities also has waned. With population of the central cities declining, metropolitan government would come to mean control by white, middle-class suburbanites. The liberal coalitions of labor and African Americans that control many city governments would stand to lose considerable power if their political strength were diluted in a metropolitan area. In Cleveland, for example, from 1933 to 1959, voters defeated ten referenda to create various forms of metropolitan government. Over the years, African-American support declined from 79 percent in 1933 to 29 percent in 1959. White voter support also declined over time, but the falloff was less dramatic.

African Americans and labor leaders usually oppose consolidation for reasons that are more political, social, and psychological than economic. They contend that the existence of many local governments helps increase citizen *access* to decision making, which produces a greater sense of community and personal effectiveness in dealing with smaller units of government. In such a situation, a variety of groups have the opportunity to make their views heard and to affect public policy.

Fragmentation benefits white, upper-class suburbanites because it allows them to isolate themselves from the problems of cities and to maintain school assignments based strictly on place of residence. In a time when there is strong sentiment for less government, suburban residents may not place a high priority on improved service delivery. Few are likely to believe that metropolitan government, or any government, would improve service and most fear it would increase taxes. Evidence from metropolitan areas where consolidation has occurred—Miami and Nashville—shows that expenditures have risen. In fact, many suburban residents use few government services. They live in gated communities, protected by private security; their garbage is picked up by private providers; and their children attend private schools.

Among academics, those who support the **public choice theory** argue that metropolitan area residents are best served by a fragmented system in which various communities can offer different sets of services that appeal to various tastes of citizens.[14] Public choice theorists contend that those citizens who are willing to pay more for certain services, such as education and recreation, can choose to live in certain communities and those who prefer lower taxes and fewer services can live elsewhere. This is comparable to a free marketplace where consumers shop for the best products at the most appropriate price. As in business, it is contended that competition among suburban communities will lead to innovation and a greater incentive to produce government services more efficiently. Public choice advocates contend that some services can be provided more economically by smaller units of government and that in other cases cooperative metropolitan arrangements can be made.

Critics of public choice theory respond that, although this model might work for those free to move within the metropolitan area, many people do not have the ability to "vote with their feet." Family, finances, and jobs may greatly reduce the mobility of many residents. Of course, this is particularly true for the poor and for minorities. Even if people were relatively free to move, it might result in isolated suburbs pursuing narrow goals to benefit their own residents with little concern for resolving areawide problems.

Those in favor of **consolidation** are most likely to be business and professional people whose perspective is similar to that of early twentieth-century urban reformers. These groups fear that as the central cities are abandoned by the middle class, the poor and less well educated will gain undue political influence. They also believe that metropolitan government would be more efficient because it could achieve the economies of large-scale operations and provide improved public services.

Neal R. Peirce argues that metropolitan areas have become **citistates** that extend over existing city and county boundaries. To compete in a world economy where cities outside the United States have more extensive metropolitan government, Peirce strongly urges residents of metropolitan areas to work together politically to serve their common economic interests.[15]

Contrary to conventional wisdom, some supporters of consolidation argue that it will help minorities. They note that, although African Americans and Hispanics often constitute a majority of voters in large cities, those cities have such weak tax bases that it is nearly impossible for them to respond effectively to the needs of the minority community. These reformers advocate a district system of election in which minority groups would be directly represented in an areawide government. W. W. Herndon, the longtime African-American mayor of Memphis, has been the only mayor of one of the country's fifty largest cities to strongly advocate city-county consolidation. As we noted, Mayor Jerry Abramson in Louisville was a strong advocate of city-county merger, but Louisville had fallen to sixty-fifth place among cities in population. Mayor Herndon believes that Memphis will continue to struggle economically as its suburbs capture most of the region's growth. He also believes that by 2010 African Americans will comprise a majority of the entire county's population.

Plans for Metropolitan Cooperation

Because opposition to consolidation is so widespread and is based on so many different rationales, it is not surprising that proposals to establish metropolitan governments have failed nearly 75 percent of the time they have been brought before the voters. However, a metropolitan area need not make the move from extreme fragmentation to rigid consolidation in one giant step. There are several intermediate options available, such as annexation, special districts, and councils of government. David B. Walker outlines seventeen approaches to regional service problems, ranging from those that are the most politically feasible and least controversial to those, such as city-county consolidation, that have relatively little likelihood of being adopted.[16] We need to remember that, even though comprehensive consolidation of municipalities in metropolitan areas is rare, other approaches are relatively easy to accomplish, and consequently, they are found in most metropolitan areas.

Among the "easiest" to adopt regional approaches to service delivery, Walker includes informal cooperation between two local jurisdictions; interlocal service contracts between two or more local jurisdictions; and joint power agreements in which two or more jurisdictions agree to plan, finance, and deliver a service. About two-thirds of the states permit **extraterritorial powers** in which cities can exercise some regulatory power outside their boundaries in unincorporated areas. This might include zoning and subdivision regulation. In Texas, cities have extraterritorial powers that extend five miles from their corporate limits. The following plans are included in Walker's categories of "middling" approaches and "hardest" approaches.

Annexation

Throughout the nineteenth century, most growth in metropolitan areas occurred through **annexation**. Because annexation was so common, there was little of the suburban fringe fragmentation that marks present-day metropolitan areas. For example, Philadelphia used annexation to expand from two square miles to 136 square miles in 1854, and the city's boundaries have not expanded since then.[17] In 1898 New York City expanded its territory sixfold by adding Brooklyn. By the early 1900s opposition to annexation developed, and large cities in the East and Midwest became surrounded by incorporated suburban communities. Suburban residents wanted to be isolated from large immigrant populations in central cities, and many state legislatures changed annexation laws to require approval by voters in the area to be annexed and by voters in the city.

Annexation has continued to be a useful tool of big-city growth in many southern and southwestern states. In part, this is because in some states—Arizona, Missouri, North Carolina, Oklahoma, Texas, Tennessee, and Virginia—land may be annexed by action of the city alone or by judicial procedures. Often annexation occurs because the owner of a large tract of land wants to develop it and wants city services, such as water and sewers. Texas permits each city to annex up to 10 percent of its territory without any voter approval. In about a dozen states municipalities are permitted by law to veto the incorporation of new jurisdictions forming just outside their boundaries.

In Oklahoma, Oklahoma City has annexed more than 500 square miles of territory since 1959, and Tulsa added 116.8 square miles in a single annexation in 1966. The largest city in area outside Alaska, where three city-county consolidated areas have over 1,000 square miles, is Jacksonville, Florida. City-county consolidation in 1967 gave Jacksonville 774 square miles. Since 1950, Houston has annexed land to grow from 160 to 580 square miles, and Phoenix grew from 17.1 square miles in 1950 to 425 square miles in 2000. Because of its aggressive annexation, Houston still has nearly one-half the population of its metropolitan area. When city-county consolidations are *not* considered, Oklahoma City, with 607 square miles, is the largest city in land area. Houston is second, and Los Angeles (469 square miles) is third. In contrast, most older eastern cities are quite small: Boston has forty-eight square miles, Pittsburgh fifty-six square miles.

Aggressive annexations can lead residents in outlying areas to incorporate new cities in self-defense. Most states require voter approval to create new incorporations, and they set a minimum population that the area must have. In some states the minimum is as low as 300 people. Some new suburban cities are incorporated with very large populations. For example, the largest new cities in the 1990s were Federal Way, Washington (67,535), Lake Forest, California (56,065), and Lakewood, Washington (55,937). Washington, California, Utah, and Florida accounted for 80 percent of the national population in new incorporated municipalities in the 1990s. The largest newly incorporated city in United States history was created in 2001 when voters in Arapahoe County, Colorado, approved Centennial, with a population of 104,000 spread across thirty-six square miles of suburban Denver. In the 1970s and 1980s about seventy places have been incorporated. In the 1990s there were about forty mergers of incorporated places.

In a few cases cities detach property from their boundaries. For example, Oklahoma City detached thirty square miles during the 1980s and is still **overbounded**—that is, large amounts of virtually uninhabited land remain within the corporation.

Annexation is viewed as a means by which metropolitan areas can eliminate some conflicts of authority, avoid duplication of services, and promote more orderly growth. As noted, cities annex land undergoing development to control that development or protect the environment. Opposition comes from suburbanites who fear higher taxes and wish to remain independent of the central city. In some cases, cities may simply add to their problems by annexing areas that lack a strong tax base and are in need of costly services such as roads, water, and sewers. Often these fringe areas have not imposed any zoning laws, and thus they present special development problems to city administrators.

Many large cities—such as Boston, Chicago, Detroit, Minneapolis, and Pittsburgh—long ago became encircled by incorporated areas and have been unable to expand their boundaries. For them, annexation presents no solution to their metropolitan problems. In the Los Angeles area, for example, Beverly Hills continues to resist the annexation efforts of Los Angeles, which completely encircles that affluent suburb. Los Angeles annexed land from 1910 to 1919 to expand its territory fourfold. Pittsburgh is surrounded by nearly two hundred municipalities, and there are nearly one hundred municipalities in St. Louis County. Although some central cities are able to coerce annexation by withholding services such as water to independent suburbs, cities in most states cannot force annexation against the wishes of suburban residents. In addition, some of the largest metropolitan areas, including New York City, Philadelphia, Chicago, and St. Louis, extend into two or more states, and of course no central city can annex land outside its state's boundaries.

Five cities (Detroit, San Diego, El Paso, Brownsville, and Laredo), have boundaries that adjoin urban areas outside the United States.

Thomas R. Dye found that annexation efforts have been most successful when the central city has a substantial proportion of middle-class residents.[18] Where there is less "social-class distance" between city and suburban residents, suburbanites have less fear of unification. Dye's data suggest that cities with managers are more likely to be successful in annexation than cities with mayor-council systems of government. Managers tend to put suburbanites at ease, indicating to them that the influence of partisan politics has been lessened in the city. Size and age have only a limited effect on annexation, and success is slightly greater in smaller urbanized areas and in newer areas.

Special Districts

A politically inoffensive way of providing services on a metropolitan-wide or intermunicipal level is to create a special district government. About 90 percent of special districts provide a single service. **Special districts** are appealing because they are superimposed on the existing structure of government and leave municipal boundaries untouched. As a result, suburbs receive the services they need without losing their independence. Special districts also have the advantage of bypassing taxation or debt limitations imposed on local units by state law. About half of all existing special districts have been created for fire protection, soil conservation, water, and drainage. Others provide sewer, recreation, housing, and mosquito-control services. Since 1942, the number of special districts has grown from 8,000 to nearly 36,000 (although school districts may be classified as special districts, they are considered separately by the Bureau of the Census). Recently there has been a significant increase in the number of special districts on the fringes of metropolitan areas. Often these special districts provide a variety of services to suburban residents and become a kind of junior city.[19] Later the area may be annexed by the central city.

Special districts are established under state law and usually require voter approval. In most states, they are governed by a small board, which has taxing and bonding authority. Board members are most often chosen indirectly, rather than being elected directly by popular vote.

In spite of their wide appeal, special districts have many problems. Governing boards have low voter visibility, and in most cases there is little citizen access to their decision making. One result is that contractors and others doing business with special districts (lawyers, bankers, real estate agents) often operate behind the scenes to their own economic advantage. Special districts are frequently established to meet short-range goals. Once created, they lessen the likelihood that long-range planning will be accomplished to meet problems at their most fundamental levels. Because special districts perform only a single function, coordination of government services is made more difficult and district administrators often view public policy from the narrow perspective of what benefits them without considering the overall needs of their community. Special districts usually encompass only a few municipalities within a metropolitan area, so they cannot be viewed as a suitable substitute for metropolitan government.

In addition to local special districts, there are also regional districts that are area-wide organizations, usually set up by state law. These include the Chicago Metropolitan

Sanitary District, the Bay Area Rapid Transit District (San Francisco area), and the Port Authority of New York and New Jersey. These large units require special action by state legislatures, and because of their size they can become very expensive and quite independent of municipal and county governments.

Transfer of Function

In several places, the county has taken over a variety of public services by entering into contractual arrangements with local governments, a process known as **transfer of function**. For example, Erie County in New York (Buffalo area) provides health, hospital, library, and welfare services to communities throughout the county. Nassau County (suburban Long Island, New York) pursues a program of providing services, including police protection, to towns and villages that have a strong tradition of home rule. Los Angeles County, the largest county in the nation, provides a variety of services to the hundreds of communities in an area that includes over 10 million residents. Large cities also may provide services to neighboring communities. For example, more than a dozen suburbs contract with Chicago for their water supply. The permanent transfer of functions, usually to counties, but occasionally to special districts, has limited potential because fewer than half the states permit transfers, and often voter approval is required.

Councils of Government/Metropolitan Planning Organizations

Councils of government (COGs) are voluntary regional associations of local governments in a metropolitan area that are concerned about a broad range of problems, such as water supply, transportation, sewers, and airports. Each local government is represented in the COG by its own elected officials. Members of COGs meet to discuss problems, exchange information, and make policy proposals. COGs usually conceive comprehensive plans for metropolitan development.

The first COG was created in Detroit in 1954. In the 1960s federal policy (Model Cities Act of 1966) strongly encouraged COGs by requiring local applications for federal funds to be reviewed by a regional agency. There were 350 COGs by the early 1970s and 660 in 1980. In the mid-1970s there were over forty federal programs to promote regional planning and coordination. The regional review requirement was removed by the Reagan administration in the 1980s as the political base of the Republican Party moved to the Sunbelt and suburbs. As a result, COG activity declined in the 1980s, but it expanded with federal help in the 1990s.

A closely related entity, the **metropolitan planning organization (MPO),** was approved by Congress in the 1970s. A major task of MPOs has been to develop regional transportation plans. Like COGs, they suffered a reduction of federal support in the 1980s, but they experienced a resurgence in the 1990s in response to environmental concerns. In some instances, COGs also serve as MPOs.

The most well-developed COGs are in Portland, Oregon, and Minneapolis-St. Paul. The Twin Cities Metropolitan Council was created by the state legislature in 1967 to act as a planning, coordinating, and review agency for the region. The council's seventeen members, appointed by the governor, are nonpartisan and represent geographical districts in the metropolitan area. A bill passed by the Minnesota legislature in 1997 calling for council members to be directly elected was vetoed by the governor. The governor also appoints the head of the Metro Council. It remains responsible to the legislature, which can change its recommendations.

Although the council is not a metropolitan government, it does oversee sewers, highways, transit, parks, and airports in a seven-county area that had more than 300 governments, including 130 incorporated suburbs, with little cooperation between them in 1967. The council supervises metropolitan public policy making through its control of the capital budgets of the operating agencies that provide metropolitan services. Because of its broad authority and taxing power, the Twin Cities Metropolitan Council differs from most councils of government. Although it does not operate public services, it has the power to overrule municipalities, counties, and special districts in its area. The Metropolitan Council also oversees a tax base–sharing program designed to deal with the problem of some communities developing faster than others and creating wide financial gaps between those communities with new businesses and industry and those with declining tax bases.

Because the Metropolitan Council is an MPO, it prepares a metropolitan development guide and it reviews the development plans of local governments in the region. It also reviews applications from local governments for state and federal grants.[20]

The Metropolitan Council has had several successes, including the creation of a tax-sharing plan among the region's local governments. But it has been bypassed in making several important decisions, including the decision to build a domed stadium in downtown Minneapolis. Harrigan and Vogel note that there were several reasons why the council's power declined in the 1980s and 1990s.[21] They include less support for the council from the legislature and business elites, the lack of a power base independent of the governor, and the fact that the major issues the council faced had changed from matters of infrastructure to more politically controversial "social-access or lifestyle issues."

The most ambitious regional authority is the Metropolitan Service District (Metro) for Portland, Oregon, which runs the zoo, the convention center, and the performing arts center and directs regional land use and transportation for nearly 1.5 million people in twenty-four cities and three counties. Metro originated from a federal planning grant in the mid-1970s. A sixty-five-member citizens' committee studied proposals for regional government and recommended the plan to the Oregon legislature with the provision that it be submitted to area voters. As in the Twin Cities, the Portland COG had existed for several years before the new government was approved by Portland area voters and the Oregon legislature in 1978. Metro has a paid, elected executive officer and seven elected council members who are paid an annual salary. Before 1993 they were paid only a per diem allowance. Under a new charter approved in 1993 Metro has increased planning powers and can impose taxes without voter approval. Regional government created by popular vote succeeded in Portland, but failed in Tampa, Denver, and Rochester, which had similar federal grants. Its original approval by Portland voters was due in large part to Oregon's strong tradition of citizen participation. Still, Metro remains largely unknown to most residents in greater Portland. Few know who their Metro councilor is.

COGs are not governments because they can only make recommendations and hope for voluntary compliance by member governments. Their weaknesses include a tendency to concentrate on less controversial physical problems, such as sewers and water supply, and to avoid more controversial socioeconomic problems, such as racism and poverty. Like the United Nations, their authority is very limited, since they can seldom compel participation or compliance with decisions. Since COGs are voluntary organizations, members can withdraw if they wish. Because COG officials also are employed by local governments in the area, there often is conflict among them based on their municipal alliance. In some instances COG membership has been roughly proportional to the population of constituent governments, but others have one-vote-per-government systems. In the former, smaller suburbs are disadvantaged; in the latter the political power of central cities is weakened.

Because of changes in federal government policy and cuts in federal planning grants in the 1980s, over one hundred COGs disbanded. The others have shown more staying power than many predicted. They continue to get federal assistance, and they have gotten more state aid, plus funding from private foundations. In addition, regional planning councils have become widespread.

City-County Consolidation

The most serious attempts at establishing metropolitan government in the United States have come in the form of consolidating city and county governments. Although proposals have been introduced in many cities, **city-county consolidation** has been successful in only a few large metropolitan areas—Louisville, Nashville, Jacksonville, Lexington, and Indianapolis. Voters in Oakland, St. Louis, Portland, Pittsburgh, Memphis, Albuquerque, and Tampa have rejected city-county consolidation referenda. Compared with the other methods of integration, consolidation minimizes more completely the duplication of services and makes possible metropolitan-wide planning and administration. In each instance where such a proposal has been adopted, however, some public services continue to be administered by local units of government whose identities have remained intact. Because many metropolitan areas extend beyond a single county, city-county consolidation offers few possibilities to the nation's largest cities.

In the nineteenth and early twentieth centuries, state legislatures mandated city-county consolidation in New Orleans (1805), Boston, Philadelphia, San Francisco, New York, Denver, and Honolulu (1907). City-county consolidation was common in the nineteenth century, but no consolidations occurred from 1908 until 1947 when voters in Baton Rouge/East Baton Rouge Parish in Louisiana approved a referendum. This was the beginning of consolidations via referenda, with over 120 introduced since 1960. Five city-county consolidations were approved in the 1960s and from 1970 through 2000 voters approved referenda for fourteen consolidations. All but two (one in Montana and one in Kansas) were in southern states, with Georgia the leader. As noted in the story at the beginning of the chapter, since 1968 there have only been two mergers in big cities, Jacksonville and Louisville, that were approved by voters. Success has come in medium-sized (150,000 to 800,000) metropolitan areas and in small, rural western parts of the United States. No consolidated government has ever changed back to its separate forms.

City-county consolidation was unusually high in the 1990s. Wayandotte County and Kansas City, Kansas, consolidated in 1997 and consolidations were studied or proposed in four other Kansas counties. Recently, referenda were defeated in Des Moines, Iowa, Albuquerque, New Mexico, and Knoxville, Tennessee. Leland and Cannon speculate that the increase in consolidation activity is due in large part to the devolution of responsibilities to states and localities and the decline of many inner cities.[22] Residents don't want tax increases and yet they don't want to see public services cut. When some cities have difficulty providing adequate services, reformers argue that voters should approve consolidation as a means to improve government efficiency and reduce metropolitan fragmentation.

Over forty cities operate independently of any county and perform both city and county functions. They include all forty-one cities in Virginia, plus Baltimore, St. Louis, and Carson City, Nevada.

In most cases, proponents of consolidation have been successful only after long battles in which ultimate victory was achieved with the help of unusual political circumstances. Prior political corruption helped gain approval of reform in Jacksonville, Florida, after there were grand jury charges of graft and corruption and the city-county schools lost their accreditation. In metropolitan Nashville, suburban voters feared an aggressive annexation policy waged by the mayor of Nashville.

In 1969, Indianapolis became the first northern city to become part of a city-county consolidation. It is significant that approval came by state legislative action without a popular vote by the residents of Marion County. UNIGOV (as the consolidation is named) operates under a single mayor and a twenty-nine-member council. To a large extent, its creation was made possible because of Republican control of the appropriate state legislative committees and the political leadership of Richard Lugar, the Republican mayor of Indianapolis and currently Indiana's senior U.S. senator. Approval of UNIGOV also was aided by the preservation of most suburban and county offices as well as special service and taxing districts within the county. Three small municipalities and sixteen townships in Marion County chose not to be included in the consolidated government. As in Nashville and Jacksonville, a large council, elected in a combination of at-large and single districts, provides representation for a wide range of groups within Marion County. Republicans controlled UNIGOV, winning all mayoral elections until 2000 and often electing at least twenty members of the council.

Many existing governments have remained separate under UNIGOV. School districts continue to maintain their boundaries, and the county, suburban cities, and special districts continue to elect officials and operate as legal entities. Thus the degree of unification is less than that under most other city-county consolidations.

Because of opposition from suburbanites who fear higher taxes and central city minorities who fear a loss of political control, city-county consolidation will continue to be very difficult to achieve. However, where minorities traditionally have had little power in city government and where reform proposals call for a switch from at-large to district elections, African Americans have supported several city-county consolidations. Clearly, consolidation efforts are part of the overall power struggle in metropolitan areas. In most cases, as in UNIGOV, city-county consolidation has helped economic development, but it has not improved social services, including schools.

Two-Tier Government

Two-tier government is a type of consolidation that meets the desire of local governments to maintain their identity within a metropolitan area. A federal relationship is established between cities and a metropolitan government similar to the relationship between the states and the national government. In this arrangement, areawide functions are assigned to the metropolitan government, and local functions remain with existing municipalities. The existing communities retain their own form of government.

In the United States, Metro Miami–Dade County is the only two-tier system. Elsewhere, such a system has operated in Toronto, Winnipeg, Berlin, and London. The Toronto plan was approved in 1954 by action of the province of Ontario, not the local voters. Originally, half the members of the Metropolitan Council of Toronto were from the city of Toronto and half from the twelve surrounding suburbs. Over time, several suburbs consolidated and the size of the council expanded.

The Metropolitan Council was never able to expand beyond its original boundaries, and by the 1990s Greater Toronto spread over a vast area outside the council's control. By then the city of Toronto made up less than 30 percent of the area's population. The federated system was abandoned, and the City of Toronto and the Metropolitan Toronto government merged into a single government in 1998.

In Miami after World War II, residents were confronted with a host of problems stemming from accelerated growth. In 1957 the voters of Dade County were asked by the Florida legislature to approve a two-tier form of government.[23] Approval came by a slim margin with only 26 percent of those eligible registered to vote. The proposal was supported by the Miami business community, the newspapers, and such good-government groups as the League of Women Voters. Opposition came chiefly from various local public officials and from the wealthier suburbs, such as Surfside and Miami Beach. In metropolitan Miami the usual opponents of unification—organized labor, political parties, and minority groups—all lacked effective organization. As in Jacksonville, the electorate consisted of a large percentage of newcomers to the community. Such a situation is unlikely to exist in any of the older cities of the Midwest or Northeast.

Under a federal-type structure, the twenty-six cities in the metropolitan Dade County area kept control of many local functions, including garbage pickup, street maintenance, and police and fire protection. The reorganized county government, with commissioners and a newly created manager, was given control over countywide services such as mass transit and water pollution.

Since 1957, Miami and Dade County have experienced a huge gain in population, with Hispanics (largely Cuban) making up about two-thirds of the population of the city of Miami in 2000. After African Americans and Hispanics filed suit in the 1980s, charging that the at-large election system diluted their power on the nine-member Metro commission, the commission was expanded to thirteen members elected from single-member districts. In the mid-1990s, voters approved a change to a strong mayor, with veto power, to head the metropolitan government.

Elastic Cities

Former mayor of Albuquerque David Rusk has calculated a "point of (almost) no return" for cities.[24] This point comes when a city's population has declined 20 percent from its peak, when minority population of the city is at least three times the percentage of minorities in its suburbs, and when per capita income in the city has fallen below 70 percent of that of its suburbs. Cities in this category include Detroit and Cleveland, with several other inelastic cities moving in that direction. David Rusk notes that unlike the 1980s when all cities that had passed his "point of no return" declined even further, in the 1990s a few cities on the endangered list improved. The most dramatic turnaround was Chicago, where the city-suburban income gap closed because of improvements in housing and employment in the city. As a result, Rusk now has a set of characteristics of cities that place them *almost* beyond the point of no return.

Rusk says that playing the "inside game," which included federal programs such as enterprise zones and community development block grants, did not work in troubled cities.[25] He notes that "gimmicks" such as new convention centers also have not helped turn cities around.

If large cities in the Northeast and Midwest cannot grow by annexation, and if they are unable to consolidate with their counties, what hope is there that they will benefit from the growth occurring just beyond their limits in the suburbs? Rusk's answer is that cities need to switch to playing the "outside game." That is, by building coalitions with older suburbs (the "at-risk" communities we noted earlier), business organizations, and various nonprofit organizations, central cities should put pressure on state legislators to initiate regional solutions to their problems. As Rusk sees it, "State legislatures *must* serve as regional policy bodies because they are the only ones that can."[26] Without a regional government, such as the Twin Cities Metropolitan Council, which was created by the Minnesota legislature, no group speaks for the entire region.

As a Minnesota state legislator and scholar, Myron Orfield has contended that it is essential for central cities to build coalitions with their suburbs.[27] Among the many bills introduced by Orfield to deal with metropolitan area problems are those calling for the direct election of Metropolitan Council members and calling on suburbs to provide low- and moderate-income housing.

Rusk points out that almost *all* metropolitan areas have grown since 1950. Surprisingly, the Detroit metropolitan area grew by 40 percent from 1950 to 2000, even as the city lost about 1 million people. Although inelastic cities, such as Detroit and Cleveland, have lost population, **elastic cities**, such as Houston (area in square miles up 237 percent since 1950) and Columbus, Ohio (up 385 percent), have greatly increased their populations (Tables 9-2 and 9-3). Elastic cities are able to "capture" suburban growth. As a result, most elastic cities are doing well financially, even though they may be in modest-income areas, and many point-of-no-return cities are doing poorly, even though some are in wealthy areas. Elastic cities are much less racially segregated (only 30 percent of Houston's 2000 population was African American) than inelastic cities (80 percent of Detroit's population was African American) because their central cities are not hemmed in by predominantly white suburbs. Compared to elastic cities, inelastic cities have less job creation, and there is a greater income disparity between them and their suburbs.

PLANNING

Many early American cities, with Savannah, Georgia as a prime example, were carefully plotted and still retain much of their distinctive original design. Most nineteenth-century cities in the Midwest and West were "new towns." As such, the layout of streets, the location of parks, and the placement of businesses were planned in detail. However, as

TABLE 9-2   Elastic Cities Expand Their City Limits; Inelastic Cities Do Not

	City Area (square miles)		Percentage Change	
Central City	1950	2000	1950–2000	1990s
Houston, Tex.	160	579	262%	7%
Detroit, Mich.	139	139	0	0
Columbus, Ohio	39	210	434	10
Cleveland, Ohio	75	78	3	1
Nashville, Tenn.	22	473	2051	0
Louisville, Ky.	40	62	56	0
Indianapolis, Ind.	55	361	555	0
Milwaukee, Wis.	50	96	92	0
Albuquerque, N. Mex.	48	181	277	37
Syracuse, N.Y.	25	25	0	0
Madison, Wis.	15	69	346	19
Harrisburg, Pa.	6	8	29	0
Raleigh, N.C.	11	115	942	30
Richmond, Va.	37	60	62	0

Source: David Rusk, *Cities without Suburbs,* 3rd ed. (Baltimore: The Johns Hopkins University Press, 2003), p. 18.

TABLE 9-3   Elastic Cities Gain Population; Inelastic Cities Lose Population

	City Population			
	1950 (or peak*)	2000	Percentage Change	
			1950–2000	1990s
Houston, Tex.	596,163	1,953,631	228%	20%
Detroit, Mich.	1,849,568	951,270	−49	−8
Columbus, Ohio	375,901	711,470	89	12
Cleveland, Ohio	914,808	478,403	−48	−5
Nashville, Tenn.	174,307	545,524	213	7
Louisville, Ky.	390,639	256,231	−34	−5
Indianapolis, Ind.	427,173	781,870	83	7
Milwaukee, Wis.	741,324	596,974	−19	−5
Albuquerque, N. Mex.	96,815	448,607	363	17
Syracuse, N.Y.	220,583	147,306	−33	−10
Madison, Wis.	96,056	208,054	117	9
Harrisburg, Pa.	89,544	48,950	−45	−7
Raleigh, N.C.	65,679	276,093	320	33
Richmond, Va.	249,332	197,790	−21	−3

*Peak population: Louisville and Milwaukee in 1960; Richmond in 1970.
Source: David Rusk, *Cities without Suburbs,* 3rd ed. (Baltimore: The Johns Hopkins University Press, 2003), p. 29.

city populations rapidly expanded, growth was largely unplanned. Thus by the 1880s, many large cities were crowded, dirty, and unhealthy. The same reform movement that brought changes to the structure and operation of city government (see Chapter 6) also reinstituted planning to beautify cities.

The results of the "city beautiful" movement were especially impressive in Chicago where, after much of the city was leveled in the 1871 fire, a grid system was developed from coordinates downtown. Every eight blocks is one mile and every four blocks in any direction is a wider, commercial street. Many of the suburbs, such as Skokie, continued the numerical system. If you fly into Midway Airport at night you can see the grid pattern, with intense lights every half mile reflecting commercial areas. You can see the grid as you approach O'Hare International Airport, but the newer suburbs have not continued the grid, favoring wavy cul-de-sac patterns—the price of "progress."

Planners created master plans for the overall development of cities to serve as guides to government officials and private business. Comprehensive planning goes far beyond concern early in this century for a set of maps and land-use guidelines. Planners now consider such matters as population projections, transportation, and sociocultural patterns. Although these plans are not legally binding on communities, most cities take them seriously. In most larger cities there is a planning commission, made up of businesspeople and other residents, and a city planner who reports to the mayor or city manager. Often the layout of suburbs has been designed by real estate developers. After incorporation, suburbs may develop a master plan and set up planning offices that are similar to those in central cities. Even most relatively small cities now have planning offices and economic development offices.

More than half the cities in the United States with over 100,000 people have created neighborhood councils that have local control over land use planning and, in some cases, over zoning. In St. Paul, for example, seventeen District Councils exercise significant power over zoning.[28] All adults in each neighborhood can participate and in most instances city governments respect decisions the councils make. Not surprisingly, studies show that less than 20 percent of eligible residents attend council meetings.

We have noted that regional planning is directed by COGs in most metropolitan areas. Seattle and Portland serve as top-of-the-line models for managing regional growth. Both employ regional zoning powers to draw urban boundaries as a means to control sprawl. In essence, they are calling for denser living inside prescribed boundaries. Although sprawl has been contained in the Portland area, the metropolitan population increased by more than 250,000 from 1980 to 2000. Housing prices have risen and developers have pushed for boundary extensions. Metropolitan Council officials respond that while sprawl has been largely uncontrolled in cities such as Denver and Phoenix, housing prices there have risen as much as in Portland.

Oregon has had statewide land-use planning since 1973. Outside of Portland it is managed by county governments. Curiously, the original plan was pushed by conservative Republican legislators, not liberal environmentalists from Portland.[29] Farmers were watching their fields get paved over by urban sprawl and they wanted it to stop. In 2000, sixteen states had some type of land-use planning, with ten of them requiring comprehensive local planning.

In 1997 Maryland became the first state to use the power of state government to manage growth. Its **"Smart Growth"** program decrees that state funding for infrastructure will not go to support projects outside designated growth areas. As Myron Orfield notes, "Smart growth planning accepts that growth is inevitable and even desirable—if it is correctly and intelligently done,"[30] Smart growth strategies include managing growth, as in Portland, Oregon, by creating urban growth boundaries; preserving agricultural land and open space; and using New Urbanist design for cities. New Jersey has developed a "Blueprint for Intelligent Growth" with a map that translates all the state's written environmental rules into visual form.

In the battle to ease urban sprawl, the Sierra Club ranks states in terms of their efforts to buy land around cities, improve urban mass transit, develop green spaces, and revitalize urban spaces. For example, nearly thirty states have so-called "brownfields" programs to clean up abandoned and often polluted urban industrial sites. In 1999 Maryland was ranked first for protecting open space and Oregon was first in land-use planning.

Many communities across the country used the initiative process to limit growth in the 1990s. Throughout the twentieth century, zoning was the most common way for cities, especially suburbs, to limit growth.

Zoning

Zoning ordinances divide a community into districts (residential, industrial, light industrial, commercial, recreational) and prescribe the uses that can be made of the land in each zone. They help maintain property values by separating commercial activities from residential neighborhoods and protecting the environment. Such ordinances are enforced by a building inspector, and a zoning board is created to make exceptions to rules or amend their provisions. In many cities, zoning ordinances have been enacted too late, after commercial and industrial establishments had already misused the land. Zoning ordinances that prescribe the height of buildings or the amount of land necessary for home construction have the effect of keeping minority groups out of upper-class suburbs. Since New York City adopted the first zoning ordinance in 1916, all major cities except Houston have enacted some form of zoning. Beginning in 1926 the Supreme Court consistently has upheld the legality of zoning ordinances as part of governments' police powers.

A particularly controversial use of zoning is when it is used to *exclude* lower-income persons from suburban communities. Zoning can exclude economic groups of people by setting minimum lot sizes and by prohibiting apartments of a certain size or, in extreme cases, prohibiting all apartment buildings. Suburbs also may exclude people through subdivision infrastructure costs that are assessed to builders and passed on to home buyers. As noted, fragmented communities encourage racial and economic segregation. Smaller communities tend to promote uniformity, not diversity, and they make areawide planning very difficult. As housing costs soared in the 1980s and 1990s, even middle-income white people found themselves effectively shut out of many suburban communities.

Even in the absence of metropolitan government, state legislatures, as in Connecticut, can enact **inclusionary zoning** to force developers to include affordable housing in a mix of new homes. The New Jersey Supreme Court ruled in 1975 that all zoning regulations in Mount Laurel were invalid because they failed to provide a range of density levels and building types. The court used a "fair share" concept regarding the location of multifamily housing as well as of houses on small lots. Later, the New Jersey legislature established the Council on Affordable Housing to implement the state's inclusionary zoning policy. Few states have followed the fair share lead of New Jersey.

In 1977 the Supreme Court ruled that communities are not required to alter zoning laws to provide housing for low-income families. The case involved Arlington Heights, a Chicago suburb, and its refusal to rezone a vacant property surrounded by single-family homes to permit construction of a federally subsidized townhouse development. In supporting the Arlington Heights board of trustees, the Court reasoned that predominantly white communities do not have to make special allowances for integration unless there is proof of purposeful racial discrimination. Thus a zoning ordinance was upheld, even though it resulted in a racially disproportionate impact. Two Supreme Court decisions in 1987 overturned no-growth measures that limited land use, supporting the argument that property cannot be taken by local government without fair compensation paid to its owners.

The Mount Laurel decision was challenged and upheld in several cases decided in the 1980s and 1990s by New Jersey courts. Given the conflicting opinions in New Jersey and by the U.S. Supreme Court in Arlington Heights, it seems unlikely that there will be a change in exclusionary zoning laws across the country in the near future.[31]

Recently, widespread opposition has developed against zoning laws that were written shortly after World War II. That was a time when a new generation of urban planners started to use zoning as a means to determine what urban neighborhoods should look like after massive urban renewal bulldozed buildings.[32] New zoning codes created more distance between residential, commercial, and industrial uses. Pedestrians were discouraged as planners tried to create a suburban experience that they thought people wanted in cities.

New Urbanists, such as James H. Kunster, call for an end to existing zoning codes and propose such changes as combining residential and commercial buildings, making streets narrower to discourage automobiles and encourage pedestrians, and bringing back public space in the form of numerous small parks.[33]

Architects and planners Andres Duany and Elizabeth Plater-Zybeck are responsible for several New Urbanist developments, such as Seaside and Celebration in Florida, which are new towns with an old-fashioned look. These communities encourage people to walk and interact with their neighbors by the placement of shops in town squares and by the construction of mixed-income houses set on small lots with front porches instead of garages that face the street. Celebration also micromanages the lives of its residents down to the level of telling them what color curtains (white) they can hang in their windows.

RURAL AND SMALL-TOWN AMERICA

Moving beyond the city limits of suburbs, we come to rural America. Although the Bureau of the Census defines "rural" as the population outside incorporated or unincorporated places with more than 2,500 people and/or outside urbanized areas, few people living in communities of 5,000 or 15,000 and located outside metropolitan areas think of themselves as urban. There is general agreement that small-scale, low-density settlements are "rural"[34] and the study of rural America includes "small towns" with as many as 25,000 people.[35] Even following the census definition, the United States is more rural than we commonly perceive it. For example, forty of Ohio's eighty-eight counties in 2000 had less than 50,000 population and were officially designated as nonmetropolitan, or rural. Across the country there were 2,303 rural counties in 2000. Still, there has been a significant change since 1910 when 62 percent of Americans lived in communities with populations of 10,000 or less. In 2000, it was about 15 percent.

Although urban-rural differences may be declining nationally as a result of such factors as cable television, access to interstate highways, the use of computers, and increased population mobility, many government officials believe that such differences are the biggest dividing line in their state's politics. For example, in Oregon, which is divided east from west by the Cascade Mountains, major differences of opinion are evident on such issues as taxation, land use, the environment, government regulation, and gay rights.[36]

As Foster Church points out, rural Oregonians are distrustful of government at a distance, and they are especially fearful of state- or federal-imposed environmental regulations that can affect their livelihood. At least in Oregon, newspaper endorsements and television advertising seldom affect voting behavior in rural areas, where people are close to their government institutions and where they have direct contact with elected officials. Living in homogeneous communities, rurals often appear less tolerant of diverse lifestyles.

Although rural and farming are not synonymous, a romanticized view of rural America plotted with family-owned farms continues to influence public policy. Legislators are led to believe that if they improve farm life, they will improve rural life. In fact, farming constitutes less than 2 percent of the national economic activity and labor force. Farmers make up less than 8 percent of the *rural* population, and the majority of the income among farm families comes from nonfarm employment.

Agribusiness increasingly dominates, with 20 percent of farms producing 85 percent of the U.S. agricultural output. Yet the growth of corporate farming only serves to make the family farmer a more sympathetic figure to legislators and the general public. Although state legislatures make tax and growth decisions to prevent development of agricultural land, farm policy—price support and acreage allotments—is made by Congress.

Some argue that federal subsidies and transfer payments have played a major role in the decline of rural America. Kotkin suggests that as rural areas have become more dependent on federal aid—farm subsidies ($25 billion in 2002), Social Security, and grants to American Indians—the "spirit of innovation and self-sufficiency," long hallmarks of rural America, have been drained away.[37] Often farm subsidies benefit out-of-state investors and have little impact on improving rural economies.

From 1930 to 1970, rural populations grew very slowly and from 1940 to 1970 most nonmetropolitan counties lost population. Then in the 1970s a rural turnaround occurred in which the nonmetropolitan population gain exceeded the metropolitan gain for the first time in at least 150 years. In the 1980s, the farm crisis, a drop in rural manufacturing, and an urban revival led to a loss of population (about 1.4 million) in the majority of nonmetropolitan counties. Rural population rebounded in the 1990s as three-quarters of the nonmetropolitan counties gained people—a net in-migration of 3.5 million people in all rural counties.

There are several explanations for the recent trends in rural population.[38] In the 1970s the "period effect" of an energy crisis caused many older, less energy-efficient manufacturing plants in cities to close down and many people moved out of cities. We have noted the reasons for a population decline in the 1980s. In the 1990s, several factors can be cited to explain rural growth. These include new manufacturing plants, new prisons, and an influx of retirees.[39] As noted in Chapter 1, there has been substantial growth in rural areas of Colorado, Idaho, and Utah. A significant proportion of that growth has been from white people moving to small towns and rural areas, particularly on the fringes of large cities. Demographer Kenneth M. Johnson, cited by Alan Ehrenhalt, refers to a "selective deconcentration of the American population," in part caused by the fact that new technology allows young professionals to work from their homes in any part of the country. Ehrenhalt suggests that after the 9/11 attacks on New York City and Washington, people may be even more attracted to the safety and security of rural America. There is a particular attraction to those small towns with cultural (universities) and/or recreational (ski resorts) assets.

Another factor has led to a curious pattern of growth and decay across rural America: a distinct economy that has developed along the 46,567 miles of interstate highways.[40] The growth of off-ramp businesses along interstate highways in some towns has more than offset their loss of traditional downtown businesses and helped to stabilize their populations. Of course, many small towns without interstate proximity continue to decline. Interstate business in the South and Southwest hits its highpoint on the outskirts of cities such as Amarillo, Texas, but it also has benefited smaller towns such as Henryetta, Oklahoma.

Because of population growth, many rural governments must deal with the replacement of aging infrastructure and the need to spend more money for education. In addition, new residents expect the same quality of services, such as medical care and garbage pickup, that they had in urban places. And there is more pressure on state government to preserve farmland. For new residents, growth may destroy the "rural way of life" that enticed them to move.

Of course, some rural areas continue to lose population. These tend to be where economies are still strongly linked to farming and mining. In some of those places people have been moving out and there are more deaths than births. Counties losing population are most likely to be found in a line moving north to south from North Dakota through northern Texas. And one of the nation's poorest regions extends from western Texas to the San Joaquin Valley in California.

Earlier we contrasted the roles of council members in cities with their small-town counterparts. Clearly, there are many differences in towns of part-time versus full-time mayors and council members and the scale of government operations as city populations increase.

In many sparsely populated southern and western states the county is the only form of local government. As noted in Chapter 5, townships are a common form of rural government in the Midwest and Northeast. They are less common in the West because the population of many areas has been too low to support them. Although some rural townships fund roads, parks, and even schools, most have lost power as county or regional governments have assumed more of their traditional duties.

Rural special districts, especially for electrification and social conservation, have greatly increased in number in the last half century. At the same time thousands of rural school districts across the country have been consolidated into areawide or single-county districts.

Jim Seroka notes that rural areas have a preference for creating citizen boards and commissions to deal with a specific issue because they distrust existing government departments.[41] The lack of professional administrative capacity makes it difficult for many rural counties to respond to new problems, such as drug enforcement and the needs of the elderly.

Many poor rural areas share a surprisingly large number of similarities with the nation's inner-city neighborhoods.[42] Both have steadily lost population since 1950. Education, transportation, and health care problems in these "other Americas" are equally severe. Rural America has a greater concentration of poor people than does urban America. One-fifth of rural children live in poverty. As noted earlier, people in rural areas have become increasingly dependent on their own form of federal welfare, after having long criticized the residents of urban ghettos for their lack of personal initiative.

At the other extreme, those rural areas with the greatest growth resemble the suburbanization process that began in the 1950s.[43] As we have noted, just as technological and communications innovations have led businesses to move to suburban locations, more recent innovations have encouraged the movement of people to nonmetropolitan areas. People moved to the suburbs seeking more space and improved lifestyles, and now they are moving to rural areas for the same reasons—with the added bonus of a significantly lower cost of living beyond the suburbs.

SUMMARY

Although urban sprawl has been developing for nearly a century, it is largely a post–World War II phenomenon. The movement of people and businesses away from central cities has been aided by federal government policies, private business decisions to relocate, and the social problems of cities. The results are politically fragmented metropolitan areas and a concentration of racial minorities in central cities.

Contrary to the myth that there is a bland sameness to virtually all suburbs, the new suburban reality is that suburbs differ economically, socially, and politically. One categorization identifies at-risk suburbs, bedroom-developing suburbs, and affluent job center suburbs. At-risk suburbs exist on the edge of central cities and at the edge of metropolitan areas. Contrary to conventional wisdom, suburban areas often elect Democratic candidates.

In response to increased metropolitan fragmentation, a host of cooperative solutions have been tried. They range from those that are relatively easy to implement, such as joint power agreements, to "middling" approaches, such as annexation and councils of government, to the extremely difficult, such as city-county consolidation. Although city-county consolidation has been opposed by both suburban and central city residents, many urbanists contend that cities must be "elastic" if they are to grow in population and to prosper. David Rusk believes that central cities must build coalitions with their suburbs and that state legislatures must serve as regional policy bodies if meaningful cooperation is to occur within metropolitan areas.

Zoning was the most common technique by which urban planners attempted to design cities in the twentieth century. Recently, however, zoning has been strongly criticized by the New Urbanists, who want to create more liveable cities by mixing neighborhood uses rather than separating uses.

Beyond suburbs, 20 percent of Americans live in small towns and rural areas. Although rural population has declined significantly since World War II, there was a marked upturn in the 1990s as new technology allowed young professionals to work from home in any part of the country. This trend was particularly strong in the states of the Rocky Mountain West that attracted both young workers and retirees. Although rural Americans are distrustful of distant state government and are opposed to intervention in their affairs by city people, they share a surprisingly large number of social and economic problems with the residents of central cities.

KEY TERMS

affluent job center suburbs
at-risk suburbs
bedroom-developing suburbs
citistates
city-county consolidation
consolidation
councils of government (COGs)
elastic cities
extraterritorial powers
fragmentation
inclusionary zoning
metropolitan planning organizations
(MPOs)

New Urbanists
overbounded
public choice theory
redlining
satellite (or edge) cities
smart growth
special districts
tipping point
transfer of function
two-tier government
urban sprawl
zoning

INTERESTING WEBSITES

www.metroresearch.org. This is the website of the Metropolitan Area Research Corporation (MARC), a nonprofit organization specializing in geographic information systems (GIS) and demographic research. Click on "Explore the Nation's 25 Largest Metropolitan Areas" for more than 400 maps of socioeconomic, fiscal capacity, race, and land use trends. An excellent site!

www.usmayors.org/USCM/sustainable. The website of the Joint Center for Sustainable Communities is a collaborative project of the U.S. Conference of Mayors and the National Association of Counties. Click on "Cities and Counties Working Together." Sustainable communities are those that have programs that will lead to "job growth, environmental stewardship and social equity."

www.narc.org. The National Association of Regional Councils is a nonprofit membership organization serving the interests of regional councils and metropolitan planning organizations. You will find their agenda when you click on "About NARC." The latest information is under "What's Hot."

www.natat.org/ncsc. The National Center for Small Communities website has limited online resources and is oriented to leaders of small communities, but is worth a glance.

NOTES

1. Alan Greenblatt, "Anatomy of a Merger," *Governing* (December 2002), pp. 20–25; Alan Ehrenhalt, "Secrets of Urban Bodybuilding," *Governing* (January 2002), p. 6.
2. For a look at the classic sociological studies of the 1950s, see David Riesman, *The Lonely Crowd* (Garden City, N.Y.: Doubleday, 1956); and William H. Whyte, *The Organization Man* (Garden City, N.Y.: Doubleday, 1959).
3. John J. Harrigan and Ronald K. Vogel, *Political Change in the Metropolis*, 7th ed. (New York: Longman, 2003), p. 234.
4. David Rusk, *Inside Game Outside Game* (Washington, D.C.: Brookings Institution Press, 1999), p. 67.
5. Bernard H. Ross and Myron A. Levine, *Urban Politics: Power in Metropolitan America*, 6th ed. (Itasca, III: Peacock, 2001), p. 357.
6. Joel Garreau, *Edge City: Life on the New Frontier* (New York: Doubleday, 1991).
7. Rusk, *Inside Game Outside Game,* pp. 96–97.
8. Andrew Hacker, *Black and White, Separate, Hostile, Unequal* (New York: Ballantine, 1992), pp. 35–38.
9. Bruce Lambert, "Study Says Long Island Is the Most Racially Segregated Suburb in the U.S.," *New York Times* (June 5, 2002), p. A21.
10. Ross and Levine, *Urban Politics*, pp. 279–280.
11. Myron Orfield, *American Metropolitics: The New Suburban Reality* (Washington, D.C.: Brookings Institution Press, 2002), pp. 28–46.
12. Ibid., following p. 48.
13. Ibid., p. 157.
14. Vincent Ostrom, Charles Tiebout, and Robert Warren, "The Organization of Government in Metropolitan Areas." *American Political Science Review* (December 1961), pp. 831–842. This is the classic work connecting public choice theory to urban politics.
15. Neal R. Peirce with Curtis W. Johnson and John S. Hall, *Citistates: How Urban America Can Prosper in a Competitive World* (Washington, D.C.: Seven Locks Press, 1993).
16. David B. Walker, "Snow White and the 17 Dwarfs: From Metropolitan Cooperation to Governance," *National Civic Review* (January–February 1987), pp. 14–27. Also see Walker, *The Rebirth of Federalism* (Chatham, N.J.: Chatham House, 1995), pp. 272–281.
17. Ross and Levine, *Urban Politics*, p. 379.
18. Thomas R. Dye, "Urban Political Integration: Conditions Associated with Annexation in American Cities," *Midwest Journal of Political Science* (November 1964), pp. 430–446.
19. Ross and Levine, *Urban Politics*, p. 377.
20. Harrigan and Vogel, *Political Change in the Metropolis,* pp. 394–395.
21. Ibid., pp. 398–399.
22. See Suzanne Leland and Christopher Cannon, "Metropolitan City-County Consolidation: Is There a Recipe for Success?" Paper presented for the Annual Conference of the Midwest Political Science Association in Chicago (April 1997).
23. See Edward Sofen, *The Miami Metropolitan Experiment,* 2d ed. (Garden City, N.Y.: Doubleday, 1966).
24. David Rusk, *Cities Without Suburbs,* 3d ed. (Baltimore: The Johns Hopkins University Press, 2003), pp. 78–83.
25. Rusk, *Inside Game Outside Game,* chs. 2 and 3.
26. Ibid., p. 247.
27. Harrigan and Vogel, *Political Change in the Metropolis,* p. 307.
28. Jeffrey M. Berry, Kent E. Portney, and Ken Thompson, *The Rebirth of Urban Democracy* (Washington, D.C.: Brookings Institution, 1993), p. 13.

29. Rusk, *Inside Game Outside Game,* p. 155.
30. Orfield, *American Metropolitics,* p. 115.
31. Lawrence J., R. Herson and John M. Bolland, *The Urban Web*, 2d ed. (Chicago: Nelson-Hall, 1998), p. 300.
32. Alan Ehrenhalt, "The Trouble With Zoning," *Governing* (February 1998), p. 29.
33. James H. Kunster, *Home From Nowhere: Remaking Our Everyday World for the 21st Century* (New York: Simon and Schuster, 1996).
34. David W. Sears and J. Norman Reid, "Rural Strategies and Rural Development," *Policy Studies Journal* (1992), p. 215.
35. Alvin D. Sokolow, "Small Local Governments as Community Builders," *National Civic Review* (1989), pp. 362–370.
36. Foster Church. "County Consequences," *The Oregonian* (July 11, 1993), p. 1.
37. Joel Kotkin, "Grim Acres," *Washington Post* (July 21, 2002), pp. B1, 4.
38. Kenneth M. Johnson, "The Rural Rebound," *PRB Reports on America* (Washington, D.C.: Population Reference Bureau, 1999), pp. 10–11.
39. Alan Ehrenhalt, "Small-Town Prophets," *Governing* (November 2001), p. 8.
40. Peter T. Kilborn, "In Rural Areas Interstates Build Their Own Economy," *New York Times* (July 14, 2001), pp. A1, 12.
41. Jim Seroka, "Government," in *Encyclopedia of Rural America,* Gary A. Goreham, ed. (Santa Barbara, Calif.: ABC-CLIO, 1997), p. 310. Also see Jim Seroka, *Rural Public Administration: Problems and Prospects* (Westport, Conn.: Greenwood Press, 1986).
42. See Oska Gray Davidson, *Broken Heartland: The Rise of America's Rural Ghetto* (New York: Free Press, 1990).
43. Johnson, "The Rural Rebound," p. 17.

CHAPTER 10

State and Local Policy Making: Conflict and Accommodation

POINTS TO CONSIDER

- Compare federal, state, and local roles in funding public schools.
- Why are state courts important decision makers on the school funding inequity issue?
- What are the three general categories of social welfare programs?
- What are the basic features of the Personal Responsibility and Work Opportunity Reconciliation Act? What is its impact?
- Describe incentives that state and local governments use to attract businesses.

- What is the negative side of incentives?
- How are state governments important in environmental policy making?
- What is civic environmentalism?

State and local government is the subject of this book; however, as the opening story illustrates, the complex policy making process in the United States normally involves all three levels of government: federal, state, and local. Generally, the process is one of continual conflict and accommodation between various groups and levels of government, resulting in incremental change in policies. Radical change in policies is unusual. The media tend to focus on the activities of the federal government, but that doesn't mean that it is always the dominant actor in policy making. Four policy areas will be examined in this chapter: education, welfare, economic development, and environmental protection. Education policy is an area in which local governments have been preeminent until just recently; now both the federal and state governments are playing more important roles. Welfare policy is one of the most complicated in terms of sharing power; however, with changes in federal welfare laws the influence of the states has become more important in

Back to School

The start of another school year does not normally involve a courtroom battle over the separation of church and state. But that's what Victoria Pope and her nine-year-old son, Marvin, faced in 1999 in Cleveland, Ohio. Victoria Pope was participating in an experimental program in which the state of Ohio gave her a tuition voucher worth approximately $2,200, and allowed her to choose the school she wanted her son to attend. She decided on St. Francis School, a private Catholic school. Almost 3,200 children, mostly from poor families, participated in the program. Although many people saw it as advancing freedom of choice, others viewed it as using public funds to promote religion, and as a violation of the First Amendment to the U.S. Constitution, which prohibits laws "respecting the establishment of religion." The legal dispute involved the Cleveland Teachers Union, the American Federation of Teachers, the state of Ohio, and even national interest groups such as the Institute for Justice and People for the American Way.

Just before school started, a lower federal court ruled that the tuition voucher program was unconstitutional and had to be halted immediately. A few days later the court ruled that those students who already had vouchers could use them until judicial appeals had been exhausted, so Marvin went back to St. Francis School.[1] And the U.S. Supreme Court resolved the legal battle in 2002. In an important 5–4 decision that will influence the future direction of state and local education policy, the Court decided that the Ohio Pilot Project Scholarship Program was constitutional. The Court reasoned that the program was neutral with respect to religion because it provided aid to parents based on their financial need and allowed them to choose from among private schools, religious or nonreligious. Parents also had the option of having their child continue in public school and receive tutors paid for by the program. In other words, the Court concluded that Ohio's program does not support or "establish" a religion.[2]

the past few years. Economic development policy is controlled by state and local govern-ments, without any federal interference. Finally, the federal government has the strongest voice in environmental protection, but the influence of state and local governments is gen-erally greater than most citizens realize.

EDUCATION

The U.S. Constitution makes no direct reference to education, but state constitutions almost always specify that education is the legal responsibility of state government. The constitution of Maryland, for example, declares that the legislature shall "establish throughout the State a thorough and efficient system of Free Public Schools, and shall provide by taxation, or otherwise for their maintenance." All states have statutes detail-ing the organizational structure of public education, and they delegate considerable con-trol over elementary and secondary education to local school districts.[3] Since the 1980s, however, state government has been increasing its influence on elementary and sec-ondary school policies. State government's importance in providing higher education has grown so much since World War II that today's state universities and colleges almost overshadow the once-dominant private institutions.

Education is a gigantic enterprise. In the fall of 2001, 68.5 million persons were enrolled in elementary and secondary schools and colleges in the United States. About 4.3 million teachers were employed, and administrative and support staff totaled 4.8 million.[4]

The history of public elementary and secondary education in the United States dates from 1647, when Massachusetts's towns were required to establish schools. The Northwest Ordinances of 1784, 1785, and 1787 required that 1 section (640 acres) in each township of 36 sections be granted to the state for the support of public schools. (The Northwest Ordinances provided for the sale of land and governance of territory that was later to become the states of Indiana, Illinois, Michigan, Ohio, Wisconsin, and part of Minnesota.) Connecticut in 1850 was the first state to mandate free education. Mississippi in 1910 was the last. By 1900, most states had compulsory attendance laws and had created a state education officer position, usually called the state school super-intendent. It was not until the Elementary and Secondary Education Act of 1965 that Congress approved the first significant federal intervention in local education.

Before looking at recent education reform issues, a brief description of the tradi-tional roles of the three levels of government is needed.

Local Government's Role

Boards of education in local school districts make many decisions concerning the oper-ations of public schools. Over 90 percent of the more than 16,000 school districts in the United States are classified as **independent school districts,** meaning they are administratively and financially independent of other units of local government. The school board can levy taxes, usually with the approval of the voters, spend money, and hire a superintendent and teachers. In addition, the board oversees the actual operation of schools within its district, but "independent" does not mean that it can do anything it wants. Its policies must be consistent with state and federal laws.

School board members in independent school districts are elected directly by the voters, usually on nonpartisan ballots, in elections held at different times from the more publicized elections for state offices. As a result, school board elections usually have low voter turnout and can be dominated by single-issue groups whose educational concerns may be limited to school policies on sex education or AIDS.[5]

Dependent school districts lack sufficient autonomy or independence in budgetary matters to be considered as a separate government. The school board, even if the voters elect its members, reports to another unit of local government such as a mayor or county council. This board has no taxing authority, therefore, the governmental unit it reports to must approve its budget. The board may or may not have authority to appoint the superintendent, and even if the board does, it may be influenced by the mayor or other political leaders.

The school district's superintendent is important in determining local policies because of his or her expertise in the field of education. The superintendent's relationship to the school board is similar to the relationship between the city manager and council in a small city (see Chapter 6). However, the superintendent typically dominates policy making to a greater extent than a city manager, and council members typically have more experience than school board members. In most instances, there is little conflict between the board and the superintendent regarding school policy.

State Government's Role

With thousands of school districts, it is easy to lose sight of the fact that school districts work within a legal framework established by state government. Aside from education policy making responsibilities of governors and legislatures, forty-nine states have a state board of education that is part of the executive branch and is responsible for the general supervision of elementary and secondary education within the state.[6] The governor usually appoints members of these boards, but voters elect them in a few states. As with local school boards, members serve without salary and are not professional educators.

State boards of education appoint the state school superintendent, although in some states he or she will be elected by the voters or appointed by the governor. The state superintendent is important in determining educational policy and heads a state department of education that averages about three hundred employees.

Traditional activities at the state level have involved teacher certification and standards for the instructional program. All states have regulations governing teacher certification, that is, how a person becomes qualified to teach, and administer these regulations directly.[7] Frequently, states approve higher educational institutions and programs, and graduates of these programs are automatically certified. State legislatures often times delegate the writing of standards for the instructional program to state boards of education. Minimum standards, which must be followed by local school boards, may be established for curriculum, instructional materials, promotion, and graduation requirements.[8]

Federal Government's Role

The federal role in education is based on actions of the Congress and president in making laws and also on decisions by the Supreme Court. In 1979, a separate Department of Education was created in the executive branch; prior to that there was a Division of Education and even earlier an Office of Education, both housed within a department that had broader responsibilities than just education.

Although our emphasis is on education policy making at the state and local levels, the federal government also plays an important role. Early examples are the Morrill Act (1862), which helped states establish colleges of agriculture (the forerunners of many of today's large state universities), and the Smith-Hughes Act (1917), which provided matching funds to assist states in establishing vocational education programs.

Still, it is the **Elementary and Secondary Education Act of 1965** that significantly extended the federal government's role. The most important component of this law, commonly referred to as Title I, provided federal funds to local school districts ($1.06 billion the first year) that had large numbers of children from low-income families. (Children from low-income families are likely to enter school not prepared to learn and have difficulty making normal progress.) Money also was provided for library resources, textbooks, and other instructional materials.[9]

The federal government's impact on schools is most obvious in the adoption of national policies than in the number of federal tax dollars transferred to the states. A few examples are listed:

- The U.S. Supreme Court decision of *Brown v. Board of Education* (1954) declared racially segregated public schools unconstitutional.
- Title IX of the Education Amendments of 1972 forbids sex discrimination in schools receiving federal financial assistance. As a result, courses designed for one sex have been eliminated and the number of girls' athletic programs has increased.
- The Education for All Handicapped Children Act of 1975 (frequently referred to as Public Law 94-142) requires schools to provide appropriate public education for handicapped children that meets their special needs.
- A 1999 Supreme Court decision stated that schools can be sued if they are "deliberately indifferent" to student-on-student sexual harassment (*Davis v. Monroe County Board of Education*).

All of these federal-level policies, including the U.S. Supreme Court's decision in the Cleveland school voucher case that was discussed at the beginning of the chapter, have had a tremendous impact on public schools.

School Financing

When it comes to revenues for operating public schools, the dominance of state and local governments over the federal government is clear (Figure 10-1). State government's share has gradually increased, and in 1998–99 was 49 percent of total revenues. The local share, which was close to 60 percent in 1950, has declined to 44 percent. The federal government's contribution has never been particularly large; it peaked at just under 10 percent in 1971–72 and has declined to just under 7 percent since.

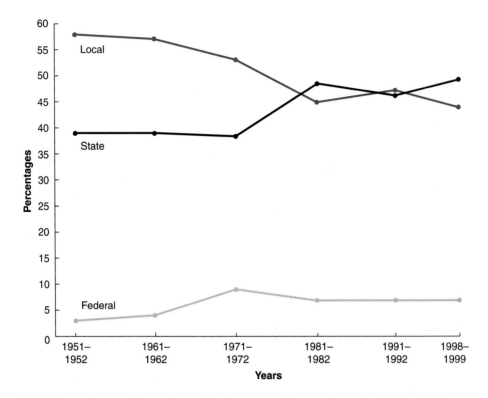

FIGURE 10-1 Source of funds for public elementary and secondary schools, 1951–52 to 1998–99.

Source: U.S. Department of Education, National Center for Education Statistics, *Digest of Education Statistics, 2002,* p. 178, http://nces.ed.gov/pubs2002/digest2001.

The pattern of state-local financing varies greatly among the states. At the extremes, the state of Hawaii finances 90 percent of the cost of public education and North Carolina finances close to 70 percent, whereas in Illinois and Pennsylvania the state share is 30 percent and 38 percent, respectively. In general, political culture is the strongest indicator of the degree of state control.[10] The traditionalistic southern states have a history of more centralized or state control of education. In contrast, the moralistic states of the upper Midwest have stressed local control and financing of schools. But funding in most states is becoming more centralized because of political pressure from special interest groups, greater interest by the governor, and the passage of measures such as California's Proposition 13 that limit the amount of revenues local governments can collect from the property tax.

Even with the growing importance of state governments in school financing, expenditures by local school districts vary considerably because local revenues come from the property tax. As was noted in Chapter 8, the amount of revenue the property tax raises depends to a great extent on the value of property, or the tax base, in the school district. This can result in **funding inequities,** creating "rich" school districts and "poor" school districts literally existing alongside each other within the same state. Districts with valuable residential, commercial, and industrial property have a rich tax base and can easily raise money to finance higher expenditures than districts with a low-valued tax base. African-American school children in inner cities and white school children in rural communities live in districts that tend to have schools supported by low-valued tax bases.

Ohio provides an example. In rural Eastern Local School District, local property taxes raise $1,082 per student; in wealthy Upper Arlington, a suburb of Columbus, local property taxes provide $6,705! Even with federal and state aid Upper Arlington spent $10,000 per student and Eastern spent only $6,000 per student. Although many factors affect student learning, there is little doubt that the funding inequality between the two districts is important in explaining Upper Arlington's success in meeting twenty-five of Ohio's twenty-seven academic performance standards while Eastern met only fourteen.[11]

Inequities in school district funding have led to considerable political controversy. Some argue that the kind of education children receive should not depend on the tax base of their school districts; all children should have an opportunity to an equal education. The other side argues that effort to equalize school funding is a "Robin Hood" approach, taking money from rich areas of the state and giving it to poor areas, and will result in a leveling down of schools. This debate has flowed into the court system, as do many issues in American politics. A national right to equalized funding for education was denied by the U.S. Supreme Court in *San Antonio Independent School District v. Rodriguez* (1973). In upholding the Texas school finance system, the Court argued that education is not a fundamental right protected by the Constitution. (This opinion overturned a lower federal court ruling that the Texas system of school finance did violate the equal protection clause of the Fourteenth Amendment because it discriminated against less wealthy districts. In the San Antonio area, the most affluent school district spent nearly twice as much per year, per pupil, as the poorest district.)

It seemed that this decision would end legal challenges to inequities in school funding, but nothing could be further from the truth. Justice Thurgood Marshall, writing for the Court's minority in the *Rodriguez* case, suggested in a footnote that the unsuccessful plaintiffs might pursue their claims in state courts.[12] Plaintiffs took this advice and turned to state courts, using as the basis for their suits provisions in state constitutions concerning the state government's responsibility to educate its citizens. Over the years, suits have been filed in forty states. Plaintiffs won in seventeen states such as Alabama, New Jersey, and New Hampshire; and lost in ten states, including Georgia, Oklahoma, and Virginia. In most of the other states, plaintiffs lost at the highest court level but further complaints are pending. Even where legal challenges have not been successful, many states (twenty-one according to the National Conference of State Legislatures) have adopted legislation to reduce school district financial disparities by reducing reliance on the local property tax to fund schools.

One of the most far-reaching decisions was made in 1989 when the Kentucky Supreme Court declared Kentucky's educational system unconstitutional.

The court said the Kentucky legislature must provide funding that provides each child an "adequate" education and the schools throughout the state must be "substantially uniform," or equal.[13] The Kentucky court did more than simply direct the legislature to correct funding inequities; it also said that the legislature must improve the management and quality of Kentucky's public schools.[14]

Implementing these decisions, which must be done by a state's governor and legislators, has not always been easy. Ohio is a good example. The first case filed against Ohio's school funding inequities was in 1991, and ended, at least temporarily, more than ten years later in 2002. The controversy appeared to be near resolution in 2001, when the Ohio Supreme Court decided that a state reform plan of $1.4 billion would be constitutional if some additional changes were included. However, the cost of these additional changes was higher than the court expected, adding another $1.2 billion a year to the reform plan. The court then ordered the state and the Ohio Coalition for Equity and Adequacy in School Funding to negotiate a compromise, but the two sides failed to reach an agreement. With this failure, the Ohio Supreme Court again declared that the way the state funds public schools is unconstitutional because it favors rich districts over poor ones, and it ordered the legislature to develop a new funding method. However, the court did not set a deadline and gave up jurisdiction of the case, meaning that legislators and the governor do not have to return to the court for its approval of any new reform plan. Of course, the court could be brought back into the picture if a new suit is filed. Ohio's governor, Bob Taft, believes that with the $1.4 billion reform plan and other increases in state aid to education, the state's funding plan is now constitutional. Overall, state funding has increased by 81 percent since the first suit was filed in 2002, from $3.6 billion to $6.5 billion. Others believe that the system still has not been fixed.[15] The process of conflict and accommodation will continue.

Do Public Schools Provide a Quality Education?

Widespread concern for the quality of education in the United States started with a 1983 report from the National Commission on Excellence in Education entitled *A Nation at Risk: The Imperative for Educational Reform.* In dramatic language the report said: "If an unfriendly foreign power had attempted to impose on America the mediocre educational performance that exists today, we might well have viewed it as an act of war. As it stands, we have allowed this to happen to ourselves."[16]

During the ensuing twenty years, national concern with education has not lessened. A study commissioned by the Hoover Institute at Stanford University argues that the "tide of mediocrity remains high."[17] For example, SAT scores have improved since 1982, but they are still below their 1970s level; students do no more homework than they did in 1982; and in global comparisons U.S. students still fail to score among the top nations. Fewer teachers are specialized in the subject areas they teach than in 1983, and the school year is seven days shorter than it was in the 1970s—other indicators that the quality of education has not changed.[18] Not all professional educators or citizens would agree with this assessment. Most would agree, however, that there is a serious "achievement gap" between schools that produce lower performing students and schools that produce higher performing students.

Education Reforms

All levels of government have been active in debating and adopting educational reforms, but it is state governments that seized the initiative. State politicians have the authority to reduce financing inequities between districts, and they have been sensitive to the demand for accountability, that is, the belief that schools should be held responsible for graduating students who have the reading, writing, and calculating skills needed in today's workplace.[19] By the end of the 1980s, nearly all states had tightened curriculum requirements and increased teachers' salaries; many adopted merit pay that allows larger raises for exceptional teachers. New standards such as a minimum grade point average and minimum scores on standardized tests were adopted for college students seeking to enter the teaching profession.

In the 1990s, some states—Alabama, Kentucky, Ohio, and Washington, for example—adopted "comprehensive statewide reforms," in which specific goals for student performance are identified, curriculum frameworks to achieve the goals are supported by the state, and tests are developed and administered to measure whether the goals are being met. Teachers and administrators in successful schools will be rewarded, and those in failing schools will be given assistance or may even be penalized.[20] In a short period of time, these ideas were accepted by nearly all states and became known as a standards-based accountability system. Simply put, in a **standards-based accountability system** the state emphasizes student achievement by setting goals in the form of standards and creates a statewide assessment plan to measure the academic performance of students, schools, and districts. The state also decides what sanctions or rewards will be provided to schools based on performance or improvement—or the lack of it—over time.[21]

Many educators and political leaders, including President George W. Bush and his brother Jeb Bush, governor of Florida, have advocated more radical reforms under the label of **school choice,** meaning that parents and their children could choose any school, public or private, to attend. This market-oriented reform, its advocates contend, would force schools to compete for students. To engage in this competition, public school principals and teachers would be given more freedom to design their own curriculum and teaching strategies. To attract students, schools would have to establish a record demonstrating that their students actually learn. The frequently cited teacher's expression to an uncooperative student that "I get paid, whether you learn this or not" would no longer be true because if a school's students are not performing, its enrollment will drop. And just like a business in the economic marketplace, a school could fail and the principal and teachers would be out of their jobs. Schools, it is hoped, will compete on the basis of quality. Suggestions for financing a market-based school system include a voucher plan whereby schools, again public or private, receive a fixed amount of public funds from the school district for each student who enrolls.[22]

The first *statewide* plan for school choice, as opposed to limited plans such as the one in Cleveland, uses vouchers and evolved from a campaign promise made by Jeb Bush when he was running for governor in 1998. A year later the Florida legislature approved Bush's A+ Education Plan, a comprehensive reform package that includes expanded testing of students, no social promotion, higher teacher standards, and grading of schools based on the test scores of their students. The voucher program, known as "opportunity scholarships," works this way: If a school receives a grade of "F" for two years within a four-year period, parents can transfer their child from that school to a private school and the state will give them a voucher worth up to $4,000 to help pay the tuition.[23]

Is there evidence that school choice improves student performance? A study of the School Choice Scholarships Foundation in New York City looks at this question. In

1997, the foundation provided 1,300 scholarships (vouchers) to children of low-income families in grades K–4; the vouchers were worth $1,400 annually and could be used at any private school for up to four years. Generally, on standardized tests students offered a scholarship performed at about the same level as a control group of students who attended public schools. African-American students who attended private schools scored higher than those in public schools; there were no differences among Latino students. It should be noted that some researchers have questioned whether this study's data really support the findings concerning African Americans. However, other findings seem well supported by the data. For example, parents of children in this program who switched to private schools were more satisfied with their schools than parents whose children remained in public schools; and private school parents were more likely than public school parents to report that their children were in smaller schools, in smaller classes, and that their schools were generally more orderly, for example, with less fighting. At this stage of the research, the results are mixed. Student performance may not be improved, but parents with children in private schools appear to like their school better than public school parents.[24]

Objections to school choice are many. Some critics do not want any public money going to private schools, as would be the case under most voucher plans. Others wonder where the "good" schools would come from, especially in big cities where the quality of public schools is uniformly low. Starting a new school, renovating a building, hiring teachers and administrators, and buying supplies cannot be accomplished overnight.[25]

The **charter school movement,** which started in Minnesota in 1991, is another approach to improving public schools that has attracted growing interest. The basic concept is that a group of educators will open a school and operate it under a "charter" or contract with the local school board or state for a specified period of time, from three to five years. Charter schools are given the same amount of money for each student that public schools receive, but they are exempt from most state and local regulations that govern public schools. For example, charter schools can decide how to use their time during the school day and how to choose their teachers rather than following the rules of the school district.[26] The idea is that educational innovation and improvement, which will improve student performance, will be greater where there is less regulation. And if that's not the case, their charter will not be renewed. Forty states and the District of Columbia have laws that allow charter schools, and more than 2,500 such schools existed at the start of the school year in fall 2002.[27] Recently opened charter schools are small, most enrolling fewer than 200 students; public school enrollment is more than 450 students per school. At this time, more is known about the characteristics of students who attend charter school than about their academic performance. Although charter schools in a few states enroll a higher percentage of minority students, in most states racial composition is similar to statewide averages. Charter schools tend to have fewer students with disabilities; however, they have a slightly higher percentage of students from low-income families and the percentage of limited-English-proficient students is similar to that of public schools.[28]

A renewed interest in education by the federal government started in 1989 when President George Bush convened the President's Education Summit at the University of Virginia. This conference led to the adoption of national goals, including: All children will start school ready to learn; high school graduation rates will be at least 90 percent;

students will demonstrate competence in a challenging curriculum; and schools will be safe, disciplined, and alcohol- and drug-free. President Clinton and Congress affirmed these goals in two new laws; the most important one was the Improving America's Schools Act (IASA) of 1994, which was actually a reauthorization and revision of the Elementary and Secondary Education Act mentioned earlier. In IASA, the federal government moved from encouraging state educational reform to achieve these goals to general requirements that states had to comply with to continue to receive federal funds. The federal government was now "investing in standards and assessments as a means to hold schools more accountable for the performance of its [sic] students."[29] In other words, subject-matter content standards, student performance standards, and assessment of students and of schools' "adequate yearly progress" in meeting performance standards were going nationwide. Of course, many states had already moved in this direction.

President George W. Bush took office in 2001 and education was one of his top priorities. His proposal for education reform built on IASA and his own experiences as governor of Texas. The bill that Congress passed and President Bush signed into law is called the **No Child Left Behind Act of 2001 (NCLB).** This law requires states to do more in reforming their educational systems and to ensure, as the name of the law implies, that no child will be left behind. Some of the requirements of NCLB that the states must follow are listed below:[30]

- Expand the scope and frequency of student testing.
- Guarantee that every teacher is qualified in his or her subject area.
- Test students annually in grades 3–8 in mathematics and reading or language arts.
- Demonstrate annual yearly progress (AYP) in raising the percentage of students proficient in reading and math.
- Demonstrate AYP in narrowing the test-score gap between advantaged and disadvantaged students.

If schools fail to meet these standards, the state is allowed to replace all or most of the school staff, extend the school day or year, change the curriculum, or restructure the school and reopen it as a charter school.[31] NCLB also increases federal funding to public schools by approximately 24 percent. (Keep in mind that the federal share is very low to begin with.) NCLB increases funding in several areas, including K–3 reading programs and before- and after-school programs, and provides states with greater flexibility to use federal funds as they see fit. Of course, the states have many new requirements to follow.

The Education Commission of the States concludes that the NCLB presents significant challenges to the states. It is an ambitious law that "forces states to move faster and further to improve the achievement of every student."[32]

Higher Education

In response to growing demand for higher education, state support for colleges and universities has expanded greatly since World War II. In 1947, about half of all college students were enrolled in state institutions. By 1968, the figure had risen to 71 percent, and in 2000 over 75 percent. Increased student demand has meant expanded facilities on existing campuses, the creation of new colleges, and a tremendous increase in the number of community colleges. This, of course, was accomplished by a vast expenditure of state funds. In several states, expansion in the 1960s to meet the "baby boom" was followed by declining enrollments in the 1970s and by legislative cutbacks in funding for higher education. During the 1980s and almost all of the 1990s, college enrollment was inching ahead; however, between 2000 and 2012 it is projected to grow from 15 million to almost 18 million students because the traditional college-age population (18–24) will grow by 15 percent during this time period. At the present time, roughly two-thirds of high school graduates attend college compared to only 45 percent in 1960.

The quality of public institutions of higher learning has improved significantly in the last half of the twentieth century. The University of California (especially at Berkeley and Los Angeles) and other major state-supported universities stand on an equal footing with the best private institutions in their states. Several states have established "centers of excellence" at their major universities, and special funds have been created to hire eminent scholars.

Unlike the administration of elementary and secondary schools, state control of colleges is much more diverse.[33] In some states, such as Wisconsin, there is a single governing board for all universities; in other states, such as Illinois, there are several university systems and several boards. In most cases the governor appoints board members, although they are popularly elected in a few states. States with several boards usually have a coordinating panel to review operations of all universities.

State-appropriated funds account for approximately 35 percent of the total revenues public colleges receive; of course, the exact amount varies from state to state. States that appropriate less money charge their students higher tuition (Table 10-1). A geographic pattern of state aid to public colleges is not readily apparent, although the northeastern states rank very low in appropriations per student, in part because well-established private institutions continue to dominate there. Massachusetts has made a determined effort to upgrade its state system of higher education.

Community colleges receive appropriated monies from both state and local governments. Community colleges are strong competitors with four-year institutions for state funds because they are popular with state legislators who like the emphasis on

TABLE 10-1 Average Undergraduate Tuition and Fees in Public and Private Institutions of Higher Education, 2000–2001			
State	Public 4-Year	Private 4-Year	Public 2-Year
United States	$3,506	$15,531	$1,359
Alabama	2,987	9,430	1,671
Alaska	2,936	9,104	2,088
Arizona	2,346	9,185	924
Arkansas	3,006	9,101	1,159
California	2,561	17,590	316
Colorado	2,980	15,962	1,655
Connecticut	4,543	20,151	1,867
Delaware	4,797	8,453	1,680
District of Columbia	2,070	19,310	N.A.
Florida	2,365	13,723	1,438

TABLE 10-1 Average Undergraduate Tuition and Fees in Public and Private Institutions of Higher Education, 2000–2001 *(concluded)*

State	Public 4-Year	Private 4-Year	Public 2-Year
Georgia	$2,698	$13,570	$1,374
Hawaii	2,974	8,024	1,067
Idaho	2,627	13,661	1,316
Illinois	4,177	15,477	1,534
Indiana	3,785	16,080	2,125
Iowa	3,158	14,669	2,149
Kansas	2,637	11,179	1,379
Kentucky	2,898	10,266	1,376
Louisiana	2,773	15,784	929
Maine	4,259	16,433	2,599
Maryland	4,778	18,968	2,271
Massachusetts	4,003	20,586	1,891
Michigan	4,626	11,188	1,739
Minnesota	4,024	16,456	2,512
Mississippi	2,967	9,612	1,134
Missouri	3,878	12,603	1,482
Montana	3,076	9,489	2,007
Nebraska	3,097	11,881	1,425
Nevada	2,349	11,027	1,371
New Hampshire	6,455	17,604	3,935
New Jersey	5,607	16,773	2,295
New Mexico	2,626	14,074	866
New York	4,062	17,434	2,557
North Carolina	2,299	14,277	891
North Dakota	2,938	8,021	1,903
Ohio	4,740	15,475	2,294
Oklahoma	2,257	10,667	1,250
Oregon	3,650	17,711	1,637
Pennsylvania	5,918	17,874	2,285
Rhode Island	4,512	18,415	1,806
South Carolina	4,684	12,788	1,466
South Dakota	3,486	11,250	2,861
Tennessee	2,950	12,921	1,441
Texas	2,803	11,944	931
Utah	2,244	3,730	1,563
Vermont	7,134	15,679	3,004
Virginia	3,723	13,299	1,132
Washington	3,604	15,882	1,745
West Virginia	2,548	13,066	1,667
Wisconsin	3,414	14,994	2,262
Wyoming	2,575	N.A.	1,442

Source: Digest of Education Statistics, 2001 (Washington, D.C.: National Center for Education Statistics, 2002), p. 361, http://nces.ed.gov/pubs2002/digest2001.

Note: Public institution averages are for in-state tuition and fees; out-of-state students at public institutions pay considerably more than in-state students.

technical and vocational education. In addition, community colleges provide an inexpensive way for students to complete their first two years of college close to home before transferring to a four-year institution to complete a bachelor's degree.

Most states give some form of financial assistance to private colleges or to students who are legal residents attending in-state private colleges. Only three states—Arizona, Nevada, and Wyoming, states with few private colleges—do not. Among the more generous states, New York and Illinois have programs for students attending private colleges, and they also make per capita payments to private colleges.

Increasingly, states have developed innovative plans to help parents finance their children's college education. Almost half of the states have prepaid tuition plans that can be purchased in monthly payments while the children are growing up. These plans lock in today's tuition rates. States also have college savings plans (usually called 529 plans, a name derived from Internal Revenue Code Section 529) in which parents can save money that is exempt from federal taxes, and frequently from state taxes.

Affordability of public higher education is an emerging issue in the states. During a recent ten-year period (1991–2001), the cost of tuition, fees, and room and board at public four-year colleges and universities increased by 23 percent, and by 27 percent at private institutions. And as the cost has been going up, state funding of public institutions has actually declined by $23 billion since its peak in 1979. In all states, students and their families are required to pay more of their income to complete four years of undergraduate education and achieve a bachelor's degree. Studies by the National Center for Public Policy and Higher Education report that only a few states offer both low-priced colleges and substantial financial aid targeted to low-income students. Considerable variations exist among the states; for example, the proportion of family income required to pay for higher education at public four-institutions in Vermont is 38 percent, compared with 16 percent in Utah. Among the fifty states, only California, Colorado, Illinois, and Virginia offer both low-cost colleges and high-levels of need-based financial aid.[34]

Concern over accountability, which has been around for several years in elementary and secondary schools, has reached higher education. Governors and state legislators are asking questions about the efficiency and productivity of colleges and universities. Much of the concern is over program duplication and faculty workload. Legislators in Ohio questioned, for example, whether their state really needed thirteen Ph.D. programs in history. Faculty workload, in terms of the amount of time spent in the classroom, is a perennial issue. Many citizens and legislators actually believe that a professor who teaches four three-hour courses is working only twelve hours a week. Of course, the time involved in preparing lectures, grading papers and exams, meeting with students, attending committee meetings, and doing research more than fills a forty-hour week. Upon reflection, government officials usually agree that faculty members are not slackers. A more serious issue is how faculty members divide their time between their two most important duties: teaching and advising undergraduate students and doing research. State legislators think professors are spending too much time on research and not enough in the classroom. Legislation has been introduced in a number of states that would increase the amount of time faculty spend on undergraduate education.[35] Public colleges and universities will be forced in the coming years to prove they are using taxpayer funds wisely.

SOCIAL WELFARE

What is social welfare? **Social welfare** refers to governmental policies "that directly affect the income, services, and opportunities available to people who are aged, poor, disabled, ill, or otherwise vulnerable."[36] Historically, local governments provided services to the poor, but the federal government moved in strongly beginning in 1935. In the 1980s, states started playing a greater role that culminated in 1996 when Congress passed and President Clinton signed into law a major welfare reform bill. Social welfare policy making illustrates better than most other policy areas the complex interrelationships that can occur among levels of government in the United States.

Major Policies

Social services, social insurance, and public assistance are the three general categories of social welfare policy.[37] **Social services** are provided to those with special needs. Examples are day care, job training, mental health care, and vocational rehabilitation.

   Social insurance programs are designed to prevent poverty and are financed by contributions from employees and employers. Employees are then entitled to benefits regardless of their personal wealth. One of the best known programs in this category is **unemployment compensation,** sometimes called unemployment insurance, which provides benefits to regularly employed persons who become involuntarily unemployed and are able and willing to accept suitable employment in another job when one is available.[38] In other words, it provides some income to those who are temporarily unemployed. Wisconsin, in 1932, established the first unemployment compensation program in the United States. The Social Security Act, signed into law by President Franklin Roosevelt in 1935, did not establish one national unemployment compensation program but contained a tax incentive to encourage states to establish and administer their own programs, which the states did. Although there are general federal guidelines that a state must follow, they have some leeway in creating their own unemployment compensation programs. State programs are financed by taxes paid by employers and collected by the states. (The money, however, is deposited in the unemployment trust fund in the U.S. Department of Treasury.) States determine the amount and duration of benefits, establish eligibility requirements, take claims, and pay benefits. The federal government requires that states operate programs that are "fairly administered and financially secure"[39] and offer other services, such as job counseling and placement. Occasionally, during a recession, Congress will authorize and help finance extended benefits for the unemployed who have exhausted benefits under state programs.

   Unemployment compensation, even in the economic boom years of the late 1990s, was still a fairly large program with a weekly average number of insured unemployed persons at 2.3 million. In 2001, when the economy was much worse, the weekly average number of insured employed persons was 3.0 million, and benefit payments for the year totaled $31.6 billion. The average weekly benefit was $238, and the average duration of benefits was 13.8 weeks.[40]

   Public assistance programs pay benefits out of general-revenue funds to people who meet a legal definition of being poor. These programs have been contentious political issues at the local, state, and federal level, and it is these programs that politicians and voters think of when the word *welfare* is used. Examples are food stamps, Medicaid, and the most widely known, and now defunct, Aid to Families with Dependent Children (AFDC).

Congress passed and President Lyndon Johnson signed into law the Food Stamp Act in 1964. **Food stamps** are designed to improve nutrition in low-income families. More than unemployment compensation, this is truly a federal program. Food stamps are coupons that can be redeemed at grocery stores for food. The federal government pays for the entire cost of the coupons and shares the cost of administering the programs with the states. The Department of Agriculture and state and local welfare offices administer the Food Stamp Program, following national eligibility standards and benefit levels. States have much less discretion with this program but are involved in administering it because they certify an individual's eligibility. The average monthly number participating in the Food Stamp Program in 2001 was 17.3 million, and food stamp expenditures were $15.6 billion.

Medicaid, established in Social Security amendments of 1965, provides health care services for persons who have low incomes and limited resources. Children and their mothers, the disabled, and the elderly are the main beneficiaries of Medicaid. Federal and state governments share its cost, which in 1999 totaled $227.8 billion. Overall, the federal government pays approximately 55 percent of the cost; however, a state's average per capita income level determines its share. States that have a lower per capita income pay a smaller share than states with a higher per capita income. The federal share has varied from a high of 76 percent in Mississippi to a low of 50 percent in 11 states. More than 40 million persons received health care services through Medicaid in 1999.[41] Within broad federal guidelines, each state establishes eligibility standards, type of services covered, and the rate of payment for services by health care providers, which is usually below what is charged other patients. In terms of social welfare policies, Medicaid is the most expensive welfare program in the United States, and its cost has been increasing rapidly, posing a difficult problem for states at a time of declining revenues. Medicaid expenditures are projected to grow to $394 billion by 2007.[42]

Even though a new federal law overhauling welfare eliminated the Aid to Families with Dependent Children (AFDC) program, it needs to be described briefly because it served as a flash point in the welfare reform debate of the 1980s and 1990s. AFDC, which originated in the Social Security Act of 1935, provided cash assistance to poor families with only one parent so children could continue to be cared for in their own homes.[43] In its next to last year of operation, 1996, the average monthly number of families on AFDC was about 4.2 million, and the average monthly payment per family was $383. The federal government paid about 55 percent of total AFDC spending; the remainder came from the states.

Each state determined its own standard of need based on estimates of what it would cost families of various sizes to meet the cost of basic food, clothing, and shelter. States also set benefit levels at whatever they wanted, but were not required to pay benefits at 100 percent of need.[44] Because of this discretion, benefit payments varied greatly among the states. New York, with an average payment of $565 per family in 1996, had one of the highest payment levels and Mississippi had one of the lowest, with an average payment of $118 per family.

The public's perception of AFDC was that it not only supported people who should be working but that many women had children simply to receive benefits. Critics of the program pointed to children born to unmarried teenagers who then became dependent on AFDC rather than completing school and finding a job. Many of these popular perceptions were not entirely accurate. For example, teenage mothers made up only 8 percent of AFDC parents. But there was enough truth in the perceptions that they fueled a national debate on reforming the AFDC program.

Ending Welfare as We Know It

"Ending welfare as we know it" expresses the sentiment of many voters and political leaders during the 1990s. Lyke Thompson and Donald Norris put the problem into perspective:

> [Welfare] is a solution to the problem of poverty, but it is also a persistent problem in itself. For welfare is an inadequate response to the problem of poverty; it is perceived to neither increase income enough to end poverty nor encourage its recipients to stand up and leave it on their own. It invites reform.[45]

The road to reform actually started when a few states decided to take advantage of an obscure provision in the 1962 amendments to the Social Security Act. This provision, known as **Section 1115 waivers,** allowed states to experiment with welfare reform through "demonstration projects." States interested in demonstration projects had to obtain a Section 1115 waiver from the U.S. Department of Health and Human Services. States were not encouraged to apply for waivers until the Reagan administration, and they did not appear in any great numbers until the Bush and Clinton administrations.[46] Although the waiver process was slow and cumbersome, by 1995 over fifty demonstration projects were operating in twenty-seven states. These waivers allowed states to try things that federal rules would normally prohibit. Wisconsin with seven projects and Illinois with six were early leaders among the states. Wisconsin, under Republican Governor Tommy Thompson, initiated a number of unusual stipulations for welfare recipients, including "learnfare," which tied a parent's AFDC grant to children's school attendance and "bridefare," which paid the recipient more if she married. Wisconsin Works, W-2 as it was known, was a more comprehensive program to move welfare recipients to jobs.[47] Nevertheless, Section 1115 waivers were not designed for broad-scale reform but only for testing new ideas and strategies.

State reform efforts were important but represented incremental change when compared to the welfare reform bill approved by Congress and signed into law by President Clinton. This law, the **Personal Responsibility and Work Opportunity Reconciliation Act of 1996,** eliminated AFDC and with it the sixty-year-old federal guarantee of welfare checks for low-income mothers. The most important goal of the act was to end welfare dependence by promoting job preparation and work. AFDC was replaced with a program called **Temporary Assistance for Needy Families (TANF),** a block grant of $2.3 billion annually for five years (through 2002). As with all block grants, the states have more discretion in program design and implementation. For example, states can decide the following:

- What families to help and benefits they will receive.
- Whether to adopt financial rewards/penalties to encourage recipients to work.

- Whether to allow the provision of services through contracts with charitable religious or private organizations.

However, some federal strings were attached. For example, states must achieve minimum work participation rates among those receiving aid, and states must require unwed mothers under 18 to live in an adult-supervised setting in order to receive aid. The most significant federal requirement is that of a "lifetime time limit," that is, individuals can receive TANF support for only five years during their entire lifetime.[48]

Jeffrey Katz summarized the meaning of this new law when he said that state and local governments will "now shoulder most of the responsibilities . . . of turning welfare offices into job placement centers and moving people from welfare to work."[49]

What has been the impact of welfare reform? The federal law had an effective date of July 1, 1997, so it has been policy for more than five years. (Congress will consider reauthorizing the welfare reform law in 2003–04.) There is no dearth of studies evaluating the impact of the new law. And it appears that the debate over whether welfare reform has succeeded or failed will be as intense as the debate over its adoption.

Before discussing some of the research, it is important to bear in mind that the economic boom of the late 1990s offered the best possible context for welfare reform and, if welfare reform has been successful, some of that success was caused by an unusually strong economy. One researcher noted that the "employment trends of the 1990s permitted low-skill workers to move into the labor force with relative ease."[50] The most widely cited evidence of success is the dramatic reduction in the welfare caseload, that is, the number of families receiving aid under TANF compared to earlier AFDC years. One of the goals was to reduce the number of families receiving welfare payments, and this has happened. Table 10-2 shows a national reduction from August 1996 to September 2001 of more than 50 percent.

TABLE 10-2 Change in Welfare Case Loads by State: Total AFDC/TANF Families, 1996–2001			
State	AFDC August 1996	TANF September 2001	Percent Change
U.S. Totals	4,408,508	2,102,608	–52.3%
Alabama	41,032	18,195	–55.7%
Alaska	12,159	5,637	–53.6%
Arizona	62,404	36,497	–41.5%
Arkansas	22,069	11,906	–46.1%
California	880,378	459,736	–47.8%
Colorado	34,486	10,855	–68.5%
Connecticut	57,326	25,692	–55.2%
Delaware	10,585	5,476	–48.3%
District of Columbia	25,350	16,291	–35.7%
Florida	200,922	59,183	–70.5%
Georgia	123,329	51,482	–58.3%
Guam	2,243	3,061	36.5%
Hawaii	21,894	12,244	–44.1%

TABLE 10-2 Change in Welfare Case Loads by State: Total AFDC/TANF Families, 1996–2001 (*concluded*)

State	AFDC August 1996	TANF September 2001	Percent Change
Idaho	8,607	1,286	−85.1%
Illinois	220,297	55,679	−74.7%
Indiana	51,437	45,230	−12.1%
Iowa	31,579	20,775	−34.2%
Kansas	23,790	13,647	−42.6%
Kentucky	71,264	35,553	−50.1%
Louisiana	67,467	24,159	−64.2%
Maine	20,007	9,418	−52.9%
Maryland	70,665	27,207	−61.5%
Massachusetts	84,700	44,342	−47.6%
Michigan	169,997	74,081	−56.4%
Minnesota	57,741	39,893	−30.9%
Mississippi	46,428	16,835	−63.7%
Missouri	80,123	45,185	−43.6%
Montana	10,114	5,225	−48.3%
Nebraska	14,435	9,795	−32.1%
Nevada	13,712	8,547	−37.7%
New Hampshire	9,100	5,786	−36.4%
New Jersey	101,704	43,380	−57.3%
New Mexico	33,353	17,438	−47.7%
New York	418,338	212,581	−49.2%
North Carolina	110,060	42,692	−61.2%
North Dakota	4,773	3,150	−34.0%
Ohio	204,240	82,946	−59.4%
Oklahoma	35,986	14,157	−60.7%
Oregon	29,917	20,010	−33.1%
Pennsylvania	186,342	81,933	−56.0%
Puerto Rico	49,871	25,024	−49.8%
Rhode Island	20,670	14,778	−28.5%
South Carolina	44,060	18,308	−58.4%
South Dakota	5,829	2,706	−53.6%
Tennessee	97,187	61,583	−36.6%
Texas	243,504	132,292	−45.7%
Utah	14,221	7,492	−47.3%
Vermont	8,765	5,165	−41.1%
Virgin Islands	1,371	664	−51.6%
Virginia	61,905	29,238	−52.8%
Washington	97,492	53,190	−45.4%
West Virginia	37,044	15,831	−57.3%
Wisconsin	51,924	18,674	−64.0%
Wyoming	4,312	478	−88.9%

Source: U.S. Department of Health and Human Services, Administration for Children and Families, "Percent Change in AFDC/TANF Families and Recipients, August 1996–September 2001," www.acf.hhs.gov/news/stats/afdc.htm (accessed June 2, 2003).

The national government and the states have conducted follow-up studies to determine whether those who have left the welfare rolls (usually called "leavers") are moving toward self-sufficiency. Studies of mothers who left welfare show that 60 percent are working at the time they were interviewed and 75 percent were employed at some point. Most welfare "leavers" report working in low-paying service industry jobs such as cooks, janitors, bus drivers, and sales clerks, earning between $6.50 and $7.50 per hour and working 35 hours a week. Although employment definitely increases their income compared to when they were on welfare, it is still below the federal poverty line, which in 2001 was $14,630 for a family of three.[51] Harrell Rogers concludes that those who leave welfare and work "tend to be financially better off than they were while on welfare but are still either poor or very close to poverty."[52] This is certainly true, but many researchers have pointed out that "leavers" are still eligible for noncash benefits such as Medicaid and food stamps that they received while on welfare, and if these benefits are calculated into their income, then they actually may move above the federal poverty line. Unfortunately, there is evidence that many families have not taken advantage of these benefits because of difficulty in obtaining them once they have a job and lose contact with the local welfare office.[53] The actual cash low-income families have can also be increased by the earned income tax credit (EITC). This credit reduces the amount of federal tax owed on money earned and can even result in a tax refund to those who claim and qualify for the credit. It is important to note that the EITC program, which cost $30 billion in 2001 and is a real boost to the income of the working poor, was a policy already in existence at the time welfare reform was adopted. Another effect of welfare reform, and perhaps an unanticipated one, is a decline in state spending on cash assistance and a substantial increase in spending on work support services such as child care, transportation, and job placement. This type of assistance makes it considerably easier to get a job and to keep it.[54]

A fair assessment of the welfare reform law is offered by Isabel Sawhill, Kent Weaver, and Andrea Kane: "Although the 1996 law has been far more successful than many people expected, problems remain, and an opportunity exists to further improve the broad range of policies targeted at low-income families."[55]

ECONOMIC DEVELOPMENT

At first glance, economic policy appears to be completely dominated by the federal government. After all, state and local governments do not have an equivalent of the Federal Reserve Board that sets interest rates. They are not allowed, legally, to carry budget deficits that could help stimulate their economies during a recession. They cannot, as President Bush did in 2002, use temporary tariffs and quotas to assist the domestic steel industry, which had been hurt by a surge of imported steel from foreign producers. It is true that the federal government is a dominant actor in economic policy, but state and local governments also play an important role.

At various times in American history, states have taken an active role in stimulating economic growth. Perhaps the best known period is the early nineteenth century when state governments financed a transportation network, especially canals, that opened up states in the interior of the country (Illinois, Indiana, and Ohio) to trade with the Northeast and South. The state of New York spent $7 million to build the Erie Canal, the most successful of many similar ventures by state governments.[56]

In the early part of the twentieth century, many states moved to protect their workers by establishing minimum labor standards and providing unemployment insurance and workers' compensation programs. Southern states, beginning in the 1930s, adopted policies to diversify their agricultural economies by attracting northern industry. Mississippi created the Balance Agriculture with Industry program, which lured companies from the North by offering tax incentives and low labor costs.[57]

During the post–World War II period, a vibrant American economy dominated the world for at least twenty-five years, economic growth was reasonably widespread within the United States, and generally there was little state intervention to promote economic growth. The fact that investment decisions were made by private businesses free to locate in any state was of little importance. During the late 1980s, however, increasing economic competition from abroad and slow growth in the national economy created a situation that continues even when the economy is strong, where "state effort to sustain growth could be instrumental for economic progress."[58] State governors now rank economic development as important as more traditional state issues, such as education, welfare, and highways.

Location Incentives and Bidding Wars

The demand for businesses that provide factory or service jobs exceeds the supply, resulting in competition between state and local governments. To win this competition, they have adopted a **maintenance/attraction strategy.** Businesses are offered incentives to maintain existing industries where they are or to induce out-of-state businesses to relocate or build branch plants within their boundaries.[59]

An example of this approach is the use of **tax incentives,** which give tax breaks to recruit and retain businesses. Since the mid-1980s, the number of states using tax incentives for job creation increased from twenty-seven to forty-four.[60] The nature of this incentive varies from state to state; North Carolina offers a $2,800 income tax credit for every new manufacturing job created above a threshold of nine. The creation of specific jobs is only one item that qualifies for tax breaks. Others include the purchase of equipment and machinery, raw materials used in manufacturing, and money spent on research and development. The total number of different tax incentives offered is over fifteen, although not all of them are used by every state.

Local governments frequently exempt a new business from the local property tax for a number of years, an incentive known as *tax abatement.* Property tax abatement is the most popular incentive used by local governments. Gaining in popularity is another incentive called *tax increment financing* (TIF). A geographic area within a city must be designated as a TIF district; with this designation the city improves the district with site clearance, utility installation, and street construction, and also offers subsidized financing to encourage businesses to locate there. Money is borrowed for the improvements and is paid back from future growth in property tax revenues that the improved district generates. If everything works as planned, this development will pay for itself and the money will not have to be taken from current local budgets.[61]

Financial incentives are low-interest loans that have the backing of state or local governments. More than forty states offer loans for plant construction, purchasing equipment, existing plant expansion, and establishing plants in areas of high unemployment.

Both of these incentives lower a business's costs, which should translate into increased sales and profits.[62] Generally, states in the South have the highest number of tax and financial incentives to attract businesses.

Unfortunately, today's global economy, in which jobs can move abroad almost as easily as they move from state to state, has intensified competition. States and communities are now putting together **customized incentives,** a package of a large number of firm-specific incentives used to recruit a major new business or retain an existing one. Customized incentives are usually associated with a bidding war where one state after another ups the ante, hoping to win a new automobile manufacturing plant or an equivalent prize. In this environment, companies see a chance to ask for more and more. Recently, Intel Corporation made available to states interested in a new computer chip factory a 104-item wish list of the kind of incentives they were looking for. (Intel called it an "ideal incentive matrix.") In addition to the usual tax and financial incentives, the list included an item requesting immediate resident status for its employees and dependents so that they could take advantage of lower in-state college tuition.[63]

Perhaps the most intense bidding war occurred in 1993, when states and cities vied for a new Mercedes-Benz plant that would build sport-utility vehicles. At first, 170 cities and thirty states were in the running. It then narrowed to sixty-four sites in twenty-one states, then eleven states, and then seven states, with Alabama emerging as the winner.[64] Alabama's incentives package, which totaled over $250 million (some estimates were as high as $300 million), cost approximately $200,000 for each job created at the plant.

DaimlerChrysler's announcement that it planned to build a manufacturing plant, this one for Mercedes-Benz vans, set off another round of bidding wars in southern states. (Foreign car makers appear to like the South because of low cost, nonunion labor.)[65] South Carolina's legislature passed a bill allowing it to borrow more money for economic development, including $110 million for DaimlerChrysler. Florida lawmakers approved new worker training funds and a corporate tax cut. A news reporter in Louisiana wondered why state officials did not make an effort to bring the plant to Louisiana.[66] At the same time, Arkansas legislators debated whether, in a tight budget year, money should go to public schools or economic development by pursuing a new Toyota automobile plant.[67] The state of Georgia, with a $320 million incentives package, was the eventual winner of the Mercedes-Benz plant; with a potential 3,000 jobs, the cost per job is approximately $100,000, considerably less than the cost of Alabama's Mercedes plant.

Bidding wars also occur when a business announces that it may leave its present location. For example, Marriott International, Inc. recently considered moving its headquarters from Montgomery County, Maryland, to Virginia. To keep Marriott in Maryland, the state and county put together a package of grants and tax breaks of close to $44 million. After months of intense negotiations, Marriott decided to stay in Maryland, and to add 700 headquarters jobs in exchange for the incentives package.[68]

It's not clear if the high cost of incentives has peaked, but some observers are questioning whether the economic benefits a state and its citizens receive from acquiring a new facility actually outweigh the costs. States are being cautioned that before offering an expensive package of incentives they should look at it from the perspective of cost-benefit analysis. But this is hardly an exact science. In the case of the Mercedes-Benz plant, what benefits does it offer the state of Alabama and its citizens? Of course, the principal benefit is that new jobs are created. Estimates were that when the plant was in full production it would employ 1,500 workers making about $12 an hour for the first two years and after that $16 an hour.

What are the costs for states and their citizens? A number of costs such as those in Alabama that involved purchasing the site and conducting training sessions are an exact amount of money that is easily known. And taxes not collected because of various tax breaks can be estimated with some reliability. However, *development impact costs* are usually ignored or seriously underestimated. Research on the relationship between job growth and population growth shows that for every five jobs created, four of them go to new residents who, if not for the presence of a new plant, would be living someplace else. And new residents require "new schools, wider roads, extra police and other governmental expenses that come with population growth."[69] Because costs are particularly difficult to estimate, states and communities should be careful in offering incentive packages that exceed their realistic appraisal.

Head-to-head competition in the bidding wars has increased in intensity and is frequently being called an "economic civil war" between states and communities. In addition, it is increasingly clear that businesses are playing one state or community against another, trying to get the best deal they can. Marriott executives, in the example mentioned above, decided well in advance of final negotiations that they would stay in Maryland. They even asked Virginia officials to keep their decision confidential so they could negotiate the best possible package of incentives from officials in Maryland.[70] As in most wars, ethics are too easily set aside by the participants.

Some state leaders have called for a truce. The National Governors' Association has adopted voluntary guidelines that encourage governors to improve the general business climate in their states rather than using customized incentives packages. Under these guidelines, incentive packages would be used primarily to encourage investment in economically depressed areas.[71] With the budget crisis that started in 2002, states were forced to cut back on incentives and to consider reforms. For example, Nebraska looked at legislation that would require businesses receiving tax incentives to pay workers at least $8.25 an hour. Illinois and other states considered "clawback" provisions that would require companies to repay the state for incentives if they decide to leave. Illinois legislators were outraged with Motorola when it decided to close a nine-year-old cell phone plant after the state had provided $36 million in tax credits and road improvements.[72]

Alternative Approaches

A few states are trying a different approach to promote economic development. Rather than trying to attract business to the state, this strategy develops "new growth opportunities for local entrepreneurs and businesses."[73] John Jackson calls this a **creation strategy** that relies on increasing the availability of capital for entrepreneurs, educating the workforce, and promoting innovation.[74] This approach may help take states out of the bidding wars because political leaders will focus on their state's economy as it is, evaluating strengths and weaknesses, establishing economic goals, and building on economic strengths. In Pennsylvania, for example, the Ben Franklin Partnership program provides matching state funds to encourage local businesses and universities to work "together on research that might result in a marketable (or improved) product or process."[75] State-sponsored venture capital funds, which are used to give financial backing to high-risk companies in the early stages of developing and marketing a new product, exist in over thirty states. Many states also are actively seeking overseas markets for local firms.

David Osborne emphasizes another approach to economic growth. He suggests that in today's world of high-tech industries and global competition, states must have, among other characteristics, a skilled, educated workforce, an intellectual infrastructure of first-rate universities and research facilities, and an attractive quality of life.[76] In other words, the expenditure of public revenues on traditional government functions is important in the long run in determining a state's or a community's economic prosperity.

A study of executives of 118 internationally owned firms in North Carolina lends some support to this view. Dennis Rondinelli and William Burpitt asked these executives to rank the factors they considered when deciding where to locate their business. The top factors affecting their decisions were *labor force* (labor availability and wage rates), *transportation* (interstate and highway systems), and *quality of life* (quality of education facilities, cost of living, and climate). Tax incentives and government financing programs were among the least important factors.[77] (See Table 10-3.) The authors conclude that "states and localities offer incentives primarily because others do and because they overestimate the importance of incentives in business locations."[78] Still, in these bidding wars no political leader appears willing to "disarm unilaterally," for fear of losing a new plant to a neighboring state or city.

TABLE 10-3 Ranking of Location Factors by Executives of Foreign-Owned Firms in North Carolina

Location Factors	Mean
Labor force factors	8.839
Transportation factors	8.144
Quality of life factors	8.000
Business climate factors	7.627
Education factors	6.711
Proximity factors	6.678
Plant location services	5.711
Tax incentives factors	5.550
Government agency assistance	4.076
Government financing factors	2.898
State marketing efforts	1.694

Source: Dennis A. Rondinelli and William J. Burpitt, "Do Government Incentives Attract and Retain International Investment? A Study of Foreign-Owned Firms in North Carolina," *Policy Sciences,* no. 3 (2000), p. 188. Reprinted by permission of the publisher.

The Effect of Political Culture

State economic problems cause states to adopt economic development programs, but political culture is an important determinant of the kind of programs they adopt. Research by Keith Boeckelman and Russell Hanson examines several hypotheses concerning the effects of political culture.[79] Boeckelman concludes that moralistic states are less likely to offer tax and financial incentives that primarily serve business interests and are more likely to focus on the protection of workers (workers' compensation benefits and efforts to encourage labor–management cooperation) and programs that are part of the creation strategy. Hanson also finds evidence that moralistic states, with their concern for the "good society," for example, protect the interests of workers with liberal minimum wage and workers' compensation laws.

In states with individualistic political cultures, governing is conceived of as a marketplace. Government is more directly concerned with commercial considerations and economic matters, and it engages only in activities that are specifically demanded of it. Business leaders are well organized to make demands, and resulting policies favor the use of incentives, which means states emphasize a maintenance/attraction strategy for economic development. Loans for building plants and purchasing equipment and machinery, whether made directly or guaranteed by the state, are prominent incentives.[80]

Traditionalistic states, which include most southern states, regard governing as an activity solely for those at the top of the social structure who use their power to preserve their elite position. Development policies were designed (1) to provide businesses with low labor costs through the adoption, for example, of "right-to-work" laws that made labor union organizing difficult and (2) to offer tax incentives such as tax exemptions for new equipment and machinery. Many policies that kept labor costs low prevented labor from organizing and gaining power, and thus threatening the position of the existing elites. However, since the mid-1980s traditionalistic states have abandoned some of their policies that were against the interests of labor. Hanson suggests that economic changes and growth in these states are beginning to "alter traditional social structures, loosening the hold of elites on public policy, and increasing the number and power of groups previously excluded from politics."[81] Of course, the traditionalistic political culture of these states may change as a result.

ENVIRONMENTAL PROTECTION

Prior to the first Earth Day in 1970, environmental protection was primarily a state and local responsibility. In the late nineteenth century, Chicago and Cincinnati had laws regulating smoke emissions, and the first state law regulating air quality was passed in Ohio about the same time. In 1952, Oregon was the first state to pass statewide air pollution legislation and to establish an air pollution control agency. Generally, however, state and local governments paid little attention to environmental protection. Increased public concern about the issue caused the federal government to assume a leadership role in the early 1970s that led to the passage of two significant laws: the Clean Air Act of 1970 and the Federal Water Pollution Control Act of 1972 (usually called the Clean Water Act). Both laws, which have been amended several times since their adoption, are basic to environmental protection today.

The Role of Federal and State Governments

Evan Ringquist describes the role of federal and state governments by identifying five government activities in environmental policy making: setting goals and standards, designing and implementing programs, monitoring and enforcement, research and development, and funding.[82]

The federal government tends to dominate in *setting goals and standards.* For example, the Clean Air Act required the U.S. Environmental Protection Agency (EPA) to set uniform, nationwide emission standards for a number of hazardous air pollutants. The Clean Water Act, however, did not take a strong top-down approach. The federal goal was to classify most waterways as suitable for recreational activities (or "fishable-swimmable," as it is usually called), and states were given authority to define specific water quality standards to meet this goal. Actually, the air quality standards are not completely uniform either because many states have enacted standards that exceed those of the federal government. In 1991, eleven northeastern states and the District of Columbia adopted California's strict standards for new car emissions. On the other hand, a few states have laws that prohibit exceeding federal air quality standards.

States play a larger role in *designing and implementing programs* and *monitoring and enforcing regulations.* This means that states, to some extent, can determine techniques to achieve federal goals and standards, monitor air and water quality, inspect facilities, and levy fines when violations are discovered. In 1999, states performed almost 300,000 inspections to determine compliance with environmental laws. Over 11,000 "significant violations" were discovered and 5,000 consent agreements were negotiated to correct the violations.[83] Approximately 75 percent of federal environmental programs that can be delegated to the states have been assigned to them. For a program to be delegated to the states, the state must pass authorizing legislation that is at least as strong as the federal law and demonstrate that it has adequate resources to run the program. The state then petitions EPA for approval. Clean air programs have been delegated to forty-two states and clean water programs to thirty-four states.[84]

Through the process of implementing these laws, states have occasionally developed innovative ideas. For example, states pioneered the "bubble" concept of air pollution control. This approach, rather than strictly regulating each emission source, allows an imaginary bubble to be placed over a plant, and as long as emissions within the bubble do not exceed air quality standards, the plant's owners can decide how to best regulate each source of emissions. Perhaps the standards can be met by installing very sophisticated pollution control equipment on one emission source and less sophisticated equipment on others. With the bubble concept, it may be possible to meet air quality standards at less cost to the plant's owner.[85] Also, some states, Minnesota and New Jersey, for example, have an "environmental bill of rights," which allows citizens to file enforcement suits against polluting firms.[86]

The last two activities are *research and development* and *funding.* Questions about acceptable levels of pollution and the best strategies to control pollution still do not have definitive answers, and research continues to be important. Few states have elaborate research programs, and most of the research money comes from the federal government.[87]

Federal funds for environmental protection and natural resources peaked in the mid-1980s. In 1986, states spent a total of $8.3 billion, with $3.4 billion (41 percent) coming from the federal Environmental Protection Agency. Between 1986 and 2000,

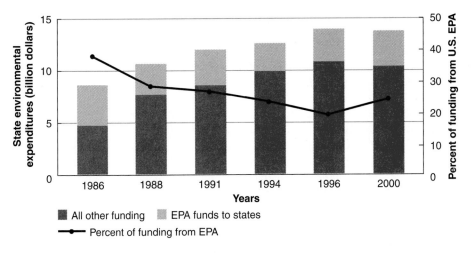

FIGURE 10-2 Trends in state environmental and natural resource spending, 1986–2000.

Source: R. Steven Brown, "States Put Their Money Where Their Environment Is," p. 25, www.sso.org/ecos/ECOStatesArticles/rsbrown.pdf. Reprinted by permission of the Environmental Council of the States.

state spending more than doubled, and EPA funding to the states declined by 4 percent. In 2000, states spent more than three times as much ($10.3 billion) as they received from the EPA ($3.3 billion).[88] (See Figure 10-2. Please note that these dollar figures are adjusted for increases in the cost of living to the year 2000.) A few states, such as Arizona, found innovative ways to fund environmental programs. Arizona enacted a $1.50 surcharge on annual motor vehicle registrations to provide money for air pollution control improvements.

Still, it should be remembered that in the most important activity—setting goals and standards—it is the federal government that is dominant and not the states. States are important in administration and are playing a greater role in funding, but the states have been following the federal government's lead.

Civic Environmentalism

The approach to environmental protection that has just been discussed is frequently referred to as command-and-control regulation. In general terms, this regulatory approach frames "rules of behavior that are applied to specific individuals or organizations through an enforcement process."[89] Quite recently, another approach has emerged. It is called **civic environmentalism,** which is the idea that in some instances "communities and states will organize on their own to protect the environment, without being forced to do so by the federal government."[90] It is a bottom-up approach to environmental protection. A leading expert on civic environmentalism, DeWitt John, has identified the key features of civic environmentalism by examining environmental initiatives in Iowa, Florida, and Colorado.

First, civic environmentalism *focuses on unfinished business* in environmental protection—those pollution issues that are not receiving adequate attention from the federal government. Examples are **nonpoint pollution,** pollution that comes from many sources and covers a large area such as fertilizer runoff from agricultural activities and runoff from urban storm water systems. (Point pollution comes from a single, easily identifiable source, such as a smokestack.) Other examples are pollution prevention (trying to prevent at least some pollution before it occurs rather than trying to clean up after it happens), and ecosystem protection (concern for an entire ecosystem rather than protecting a single species or controlling a single polluter).[91]

Nonpoint pollution is an important issue in Iowa, where large quantities of herbicides and chemical fertilizers are used to increase corn yields. Iowans took steps to reduce the use of these chemicals, thereby protecting the drinking water supply from contamination. Florida's Governor Lawton Chiles (1991–1998) led the way in negotiating an end to a three-year battle between local, state, and federal officials over water quality in the Everglades. The result was an agreement on initial plans to protect and restore the Everglades. In Colorado, the state's Public Utilities Commission made a commitment to energy conservation by encouraging "demand-side" management from companies generating electric power. (Reducing demand for electricity reduces the amount of electricity produced, which reduces pollution from the generation of electricity, especially from coal-fired electric power plants.) Demand-side management means utility companies encourage consumers to take measures to use less electricity, which they would normally see as counter to their interests because less consumption could reduce company profits.

Second, civic environmentalism makes *extensive use of nonregulatory tools,* such as educating the public at large about environmental concerns, technical assistance, and grants along with tax credits and loans to correct pollution problems. The Groundwater Protection Act in Iowa emphasized educating farmers about new ways of cultivating and rotating crops as well as reduced use of chemicals. Funds were provided to help farmers pay for improvements that would reduce chemical pollution of waters. This nonregulatory approach may be better than command-and-control regulation when there are a large number of polluters (90 percent of Iowa is farmland and there are 100,000 farmers) and when it is difficult to monitor how much pollution each individual contributes such as in groundwater contamination.[92]

Third, *interagency and intergovernmental cooperation* is emphasized because environmental problems usually involve many governmental agencies and little can be accomplished without cooperation. In Florida, agencies regulating the Everglades included the South Florida Water Management District, the state Department of Environmental Regulation, as well as the governor, and various individuals at the federal level including the superintendent of Everglades National Park and the secretary of the interior. It is unlikely that a single agency can improve most environmental problems, especially those dealing with ecosystems; long-term relationships and trust among these groups are needed.

Fourth, *alternatives to confrontation* are sought in an attempt to ameliorate the white hat–black hat arguments between environmentalists and polluters over who is responsible for a particular environmental problem. To do this, both sides need to agree that there is a problem. If this can be accomplished, negotiations may bring some success in protecting the environment.

Fifth, a *new role for the federal government* will be created. With states providing leadership on the "unfinished business" agenda, the federal government should assist by continuing to provide information from environmental research and more funds for environmental protection. Both can help states initiate new programs.

Civic environmentalists, however, do not want the federal government out of the environmental protection business entirely. They see the bottom-up approach of civic environmentalism as a complement to existing federal laws and regulations.

SUMMARY

Providing elementary, secondary and higher education is a major governmental activity. Historically, elementary and secondary education policy has been made by more than 16,000 local school districts, within the general guidelines of the state boards of education, governors, and legislators.

School funding inequities and public concern over the quality of education in public schools have caused the federal government and especially state governments to become more active participants in the making of education policy. Overall, states are assuming a larger role in financing school systems. They now contribute close to 50 percent of the total revenue for public elementary and secondary schools. And some states, such as Kentucky, have undertaken major reforms to eliminate funding inequities and improve the management and quality of public schools. Almost all states are adopting more and more laws and regulations that school districts must follow. For example, many states have established specific goals for student performance and have developed tests that measure whether the goals are met. The charter school movement advocates the creation of new schools that are financed by public funds but are independent of the rules and regulations that govern traditional public schools. School choice, a more radical reform proposal, is being discussed and tested. The federal government, through the No Child Left Behind Act of 2001, sets new requirements for educational reform that the states must meet.

States have played an important role in meeting the demand for higher education by creating public two- and four-year colleges and universities. Although state funds on the average account for about 35 percent of the revenue of public higher educational institutions, the amount of state support and student tuition varies considerably from state to state. The quality of public higher education is frequently praised, but more critical questions dealing with efficiency and productivity have been raised recently.

The federal government is the principal developer and funder of social welfare programs. But state and local governments are important because they assist in financing and play a meaningful role in their administration. Social services, such as day care, and social insurance programs, such as unemployment compensation, are much less controversial than public assistance programs that pay benefits to people who meet a legal definition of poor. In 1996, Congress passed a welfare reform law called the Personal Responsibility and Work Opportunity Reconciliation Act, which eliminated the politically unpopular Aid to Families with Dependent Children and established a goal of ending welfare dependence by promoting job preparation and work. A new block grant, Temporary Assistance for Needy Families, gave the states greater leeway in designing programs to aid needy families. The welfare caseload has dropped dramatically, but debate continues as to whether or not welfare "leavers" are moving out of poverty.

State and local governments adopt economic development policies to encourage business investment in their particular state or community. The traditional approach to economic development is the maintenance/attraction strategy that uses a variety of tax and financial incentives to attract new businesses and keep those that they have. Increasing competition for private investment, especially large automobile manufacturing plants, has caused bidding wars between states. However, development impact costs, which are usually ignored by state and local officials, sometimes exceed economic benefits of a new manufacturing plant. A newer approach to economic development, called a creation strategy, provides resources for existing local entrepreneurs and businesses to develop new products or processes that have the potential for growth.

State government's role in environmental protection has been primarily in designing and implementing programs, along with monitoring and enforcing them, to achieve federally determined goals. State governments have been spending more and more of their own funds on environmental protection. A new civic environmentalism emphasizes state and local initiatives to solve some environmental problems, especially nonpoint pollution.

KEY TERMS

charter school movement
civic environmentalism
creation strategy
customized incentives
dependent school districts
Elementary and Secondary Education Act
of 1965
financial incentives
food stamps
funding inequities
independent school districts
maintenance/attraction strategy
Medicaid
No Child Left Behind Act of 2001 (NCLB)

nonpoint pollution
Personal Responsibility and Work Opportunity Reconciliation Act of 1996
public assistance
school choice
Section 1115 waivers
social insurance
social services
social welfare
standards-based accountability system
tax incentives
Temporary Assistance for Needy Families
(TANF)
unemployment compensation

SUMMARY OF STATE/LOCAL DIFFERENCES

Issue	State Level	Local Level
Education	Growing influence in policy making and funding. However, states must follow the federal government's NCLB Act.	Influence in policy making and funding is still important but has been declining in recent years.
Welfare	Expanded policy role under federal government's TANF program.	Administer new state-designed welfare program.
Economic development	Aggressive competition for new businesses using tax and financial incentives.	Aggressive competition for new businesses using tax abatements and tax increment financing.
Environmental protection	Important role in funding and implementing programs and enforcing regulations.	Provide services such as water, disposal of solid waste, and sewage treatment according to federal and state guidelines.

INTERESTING WEBSITES

http://movingideas.org. The Moving Ideas Network provides access to ideas and resources from leading progressive research and advocacy institutions.

www.heritage.org. This is the website of the Heritage Foundation, a research and educational institute whose mission is to promote conservative public policies.

www.sso.org/ecos/. The Environment Council of the States' website describes the role of state governments in environmental protection. Great site; click on almost anything for useful information.

NOTES

1. Mark Vosburgh and Scott Stephens, "Judge Suspends School Vouchers," *Cleveland Plain Dealer,* August 25, 1999, 1A; Scott Stephens, "Judge Eases Own Ban on School Vouchers," *Cleveland Plain Dealer,* August 28, 1999, p. 1A.
2. Zelman v. Simmons-Harris, 536 U.S. 639 (2002).
3. Roald F. Campbell and others, *The Organization and Control of American Schools* (Columbus, Ohio: Merrill Publishing Company, 1990), p. 50.
4. *Digest of Education Statistics, 2001* (Washington, D.C.: National Center for Education Statistics, 2002), http://nces.ed.gov/pubs2002/digest2001/introduction.asp.
5. Jacqueline P. Danzberger and Michael D. Usdan, "Strengthening a Grass Roots American Institution: The School Board," in *School Boards: Changing Local Control,* Patricia F. First and Herbert J. Walberg, eds. (Berkeley, Calif.: McCutchan Publishing Corporation, 1992), pp. 98–99.
6. Campbell and others, *Organization and Control,* p. 81.
7. Ibid., p. 93.
8. Ibid., pp. 91–92.
9. The U.S. Department of Education's Office of Elementary and Secondary Education has information on current programs and funding at its website: www.ed.gov/offices/OESE/.
10. Frederick M. Wirt, "Does Control Follow the Dollar? School Policy, State-Local Linkages, and Political Culture," *Publius* 10 (1980), pp. 69–88.
11. "School-Funding Deadline Looms for Ohio," *USA Today,* June 20, 2001, www.usatoday.com/news/nation/june01/2001-06-11-ohio-school (accessed May 29, 2003).
12. William J. Fowler, "Introduction to Achieving Equity in School Finance, Overview," http://nces.ed.gov/edfin/litigation/introduction (accessed May 23, 2003).
13. Malcolm E. Jewell, "The Supreme Court, Kentucky's School," *Comparative State Politics* 10 (August 1989), p. 1.
14. Ibid., pp. 4–5.
15. Spencer Hunt, "Ohio Supreme Court Ruling Muddles School-Fund Issue," *Cincinnati Enquirer,* December 12, 2002, www.enquirer.com/editions/2002/12/12 (accessed May 29, 2003).
16. National Commission on Excellence in Education, *A Nation at Risk* (Washington, D.C.: Department of Education, 1983), p. 5.
17. Majorie Coeyman, "Twenty Years After 'A Nation at Risk,'" *Christian Science Monitor,* April 22, 2003, www.csmonitor.com/2003/04p13s02-lepr.html (accessed May 29, 2003).
18. Ibid.
19. Campbell and others, *Organization and Control,* p. 82.
20. Paul T. Hill, *Reinventing Public Education* (Santa Monica, Calif.: Rand, 1995), pp. 75–78.
21. National Conference of State Legislatures, "Education Policy Issues: Accountability, Standards, and Assessments," www.ncsl.org/programs/educ/ahomepage.html (accessed May 27, 2003).
22. A concise statement of the market-based approach to education can be found in John E. Chubb and Eric A. Hanushek, "Reforming Educational Reform," in *Setting National Priorities: Policy for the Nineties,* Henry J. Aaron, ed. (Washington, D.C.: The Brookings Institution, 1990), pp. 213–247.
23. Diane Rado, "Bush Signs, Defends Voucher Bill," *St. Petersburg Times,* June 22, 1999, p. 1A; Mike Clary, "Florida to Be First to Launch Statewide School Vouchers," *Los Angeles Times,* April 29, 1999, p. A1.

24. Daniel P. Mayer, et. al., "School Choice in New York City After Three Years: An Evaluation of the School Choice Scholarship Program, Executive Summary," Mathematica Policy Research Group and Program on Education Policy and Governance, Harvard University, MPR Reference No. 8404-045, February 19, 2002, pp. 1–2.
25. Hill, *Reinventing Public Education,* pp. 82–83.
26. Paul T. Hill and Robin J. Lake, *Charter Schools and Accountability in Public Education* (Washington, D.C.: Brookings Institution Press, 2002), pp. 4–5.
27. Education Commission of the States, *StateNotes,* "School Choice: State Laws," May 2003, pp. 2–3, www.esc.org.
28. National Conference of State Legislatures, "Education Program, Charter Schools," www.ncsl.org/programs/educ/charter.htm.
29. National Conference of State Legislatures, Education Program Education Issues, "NCLB History," www.ncsl.org/programs/educ/NCLBHistory.html (accessed May 27, 2003).
30. Education Commission of the States, Issue Site: No Child Left Behind, www.ecs.org (accessed June 2, 2003).
31. NCSL, "NCLB History."
32. ECS, "No Child Left Behind."
33. Frederick Wirt and Samuel Gove, "Education," in *Politics in the American States,* 5th ed., Virginia Gray, Herbert Jacob, and Robert B. Albritton, eds. (Boston: Scott, Foresman/Little, Brown, 1990), p. 471.
34. National Center for Public Policy and Higher Education, "Measuring Up 2002: The State-by-State Report Card for Higher Education: Affordability," http://measuringup. highereducation.org/2002/Affordability.cfm.
35. Charles Mathesian, "Higher Ed: The No-Longer-Sacred Cow," *Governing* 8 (July 1995), pp. 20–26.
36. Diana M. DiNitto, *Social Welfare: Politics and Public Policy,* 4th ed. (Needham Heights, Mass.: Allyn & Bacon, 1995), p. 3.
37. Ibid., pp. 3–4.
38. "Unemployment Insurance," *Social Security Bulletin* 56 (Winter 1993), p. 19.
39. Ibid.
40. *Social Security Bulletin, Annual Statistical Supplement, 2002* (Washington, D.C.: Social Security Administration, 2002), p. 6.
41. Ibid., pp. 55–56.
42. Ibid., pp. 52–55.
43. DiNitto, *Social Welfare,* p. 167.
44. Clarke E. Cochran and others, *American Public Policy,* 4th ed. (New York: St. Martin's Press, 1993), p. 223.
45. Donald F. Norris and Lyke Thompson, eds., *The Politics of Welfare Reform* (Thousand Oaks, Calif.: Sage Publications, 1995), pp. 3–4.
46. Kitty Dumas, "States Bypassing Congress in Reforming Welfare," *Congressional Quarterly Weekly Report* (April 11, 1992), pp. 951–952; "Welfare by Waiver," *Public Welfare* (Winter 1995), p. 4.
47. Jason DeParle, "Getting Opal Caples to Work," *New York Times Magazine,* 24 August 1997, pp. 33–61.
48. Vee Burke, CRS Report for Congress, *The New Welfare Law: Temporary Assistance for Needy Families,* Congressional Research Service, The Library of Congress, 1997.
49. Jeffrey L. Katz, "After 60 Years, Most Control Is Passing to States," *Congressional Quarterly Weekly Report* (August 3, 1996), p. 2196.
50. Courtney Jarchow, "Employment Experiences of Former TANF Recipients," National Conference of State Legislatures, The Welfare Reform Series, May 2002, p. 4.

51. Ibid., pp. 5–6.
52. Harrell Rogers, "Welfare Reform: Making Work Really Work," *Policy Studies Journal,* no. 1 (2003), p. 91.
53. Isabel Sawhill, R. Kent Weaver, and Andrea Kane, "An Overview," in *Welfare Reform and Beyond: The Future of the Safety Net,* Isabel Sawhill, et al., eds. (Washington, D.C.: Brookings Institution, 2002), pp. 4–5.
54. Ibid.
55. Ibid., p. 5.
56. Paul Brace, *State Government and Economic Performance* (Baltimore, Md.: Johns Hopkins University Press, 1993), p. 19.
57. Ibid., pp. 24–25.
58. Ibid., p. 31.
59. John E. Jackson, "Michigan," *The New Economic Role of American States,* R. Scott Fosler, ed. (New York: Oxford University Press, 1988), pp. 105–111.
60. The Council of State Governments, "State Business Incentives," *State Trends and Forecasts* 3 (June 1994), p. 3.
61. Richard D. Bingham, "Economic Development Policies," in *Cities, Politics and Policy: A Comparative Analysis,* John P. Pelissero, ed. (Washington, D.C.: CQ Press, 2003), pp. 248–251.
62. Charles J. Spindler, "Winners and Losers in Industrial Recruitment: Mercedes-Benz and Alabama," *State and Local Government Review* 26 (Fall 1994), p. 192.
63. Charles Mahtesian, "Romancing the Smokestack," *Governing* (November 1994), p. 37.
64. Council of State Governments, "State Business," p. 12.
65. Stewart Yerton, "Louisiana May Pass on Bidding for Plant: DaimlerChrysler to Pick Site in 2003," *Times-Picayune,* August 2, 2002, p. 1, http://web.lexis.com/univ.
66. Ibid.
67. Melissa Nelson, "Legislators Consider Possible Incentive Packages," Associated Press State and Local Wire, December 4, 2002, http://web.lexis.com/univ.
68. Timothy B. Wheeler and Jay Hancock, "Marriott Decides to Remain in Md.," *Baltimore Sun,* March 12, 1999, p. 1A.
69. Jay Hancock, "Officials Base Subsidies on Flawed Model," *Baltimore Sun,* October 12, 1999, p. 9A.
70. Jay Hancock, "Marriott Used Virginia as Ruse to Raise Maryland Bid," *Baltimore Sun*, March 27, 1999, p. 1A.
71. Council of State Governments, "State Business," pp. 18–19.
72. Christopher Swope, "Economic Development: States Tighten Up Tax Lures," *Governing* (May 2003), p. 80.
73. Gray and Eisinger, *States and Cities,* p. 286.
74. Jackson, "Michigan," pp. 105–111.
75. David Osborne, *Laboratories of Democracy* (Boston, Mass.: Harvard Business School, 1990), p. 49.
76. Ibid., pp. 4–11.
77. Dennis A. Rondinelli and William J. Burpitt, "Do Government Incentives Attract and Retain International Investment? A Study of Foreign-Owned Firms in North Carolina," *Policy Sciences* 33, no. 3 (2000), pp. 188–195.
78. Ibid., p. 200.
79. Keith Boeckelman, "Political Culture and State Development Policy," *Publius* 21 (Spring 1991), pp. 49–62; Russell L. Hanson, "Political Cultural Variations in State Economic Development Policy," *Publius* 21 (Spring 1991), pp. 63–81.
80. Hanson, "Cultural Variations," p. 77.

81. Ibid., p. 81.
82. This discussion relies heavily on Evan J. Ringquist, *Environmental Protection at the State Level* (Armonk, N.Y.: M. E. Sharp, 1993), pp. 67–76.
83. Environmental Council of the States, "State Information," p. 2, www.sso.org/ecos/states/StateInfo.html.
84. Ibid., p.1; Environmental Council of the States, "The States Protect the Environment," p. 2, www.sso.org/ecos/states/StateInfo.html.
85. Walter A. Rosenbaum, *Environmental Politics and Policy* (Washington, D.C.: CQ Press, 1985), pp. 292–293.
86. Ringquist, *Environmental Protection,* p. 73.
87. Ibid., p. 74.
88. R. Steven Brown, "States Put Their Money Where Their Environments Is," www.sso.org/ecos.
89. DeWitt John, *Civic Environmentalism Alternatives to Regulation in States and Communities* (Washington, D.C.: CQ Press, 1994), p. 309.
90. Ibid., p. 7.
91. Ibid., pp. 260–261.
92. Ibid., p. 10.

Appendix

State Fast Facts

State	Nickname	Capital	Population*	Area**
Alabama	Heart of Dixie	Montgomery	4,464,356	52,237
Alaska	The Last Frontier	Juneau	634,892	615,230
Arizona	Grand Canyon State	Phoenix	5,307,331	114,006
Arkansas	The Natural State	Little Rock	2,692,090	53,182
California	Golden State	Sacramento	34,501,130	158,869
Colorado	Centennial State	Denver	4,417,714	104,100
Connecticut	Constitution State	Hartford	3,425,074	5,544
Delaware	First State	Dover	796,165	2,396
Florida	Sunshine State	Tallahassee	16,396,515	59,928
Georgia	Peach State	Atlanta	8,383,915	58,977
Hawaii	Aloha State	Honolulu	1,224,398	6,459
Idaho	Gem State	Boise	1,321,006	83,574
Illinois	Land of Lincoln	Springfield	12,482,301	57,918
Indiana	Hoosier State	Indianapolis	6,114,745	36,420
Iowa	Hawkeye State	Des Moines	2,923,179	56,276
Kansas	Sunflower State	Topeka	2,694,641	82,282
Kentucky	Bluegrass State	Frankfort	4,065,556	40,411
Louisiana	Pelican State	Baton Rouge	4,465,430	49,651
Maine	Pine Tree State	Augusta	1,286,670	33,741
Maryland	Free State	Annapolis	5,375,156	12,297
Massachusetts	Bay State	Boston	6,379,304	9,241
Michigan	Great Lake State	Lansing	9,990,817	96,705
Minnesota	North Star State	St. Paul	4,972,294	86,943
Mississippi	Magnolia State	Jackson	2,858,029	48,286
Missouri	Show Me State	Jefferson City	5,629,707	69,709
Montana	Treasure State	Helena	904,433	147,046
Nebraska	Cornhusker State	Lincoln	1,713,235	77,358
Nevada	Sagebrush State	Carson City	2,106,074	110,567
New Hampshire	Granite State	Concord	1,259,181	9,283
New Jersey	Garden State	Trenton	8,484,431	8,215
New Mexico	Land of Enchantment	Santa Fe	1,829,146	121,598
New York	Empire State	Albany	19,011,378	53,989
North Carolina	Tar Heel State	Raleigh	8,186,268	52,672
North Dakota	Peace Garden State	Bismarck	634,448	70,704
Ohio	Buckeye State	Columbus	11,373,541	44,828
Oklahoma	Sooner State	Oklahoma City	3,460,097	69,903

(continued)

State Fast Facts *(concluded)*

State	Nickname	Capital	Population*	Area**
Oregon	Beaver State	Salem	3,472,867	97,132
Pennsylvania	Keystone State	Harrisburg	12,287,150	46,058
Rhode Island	Ocean State	Providence	1,058,920	1,231
South Carolina	Palmetto State	Columbia	4,063,011	31,189
South Dakota	Mount Rushmore State	Pierre	756,600	77,121
Tennessee	Volunteer State	Nashville	5,740,021	42,146
Texas	Lone Star State	Austin	21,325,018	267,277
Utah	Beehive State	Salt Lake City	2,269,789	84,904
Vermont	Green Mountain State	Montpelier	613,090	9,615
Virginia	Old Dominion	Richmond	7,187,734	42,326
Washington	Evergreen State	Olympia	5,987,973	70,637
West Virginia	Mountain State	Charleston	1,801,916	24,231
Wisconsin	Badger State	Madison	5,401,906	65,499
Wyoming	Equality State	Cheyenne	494,423	97,818

*2002 Census resident population estimates.

**Total of land and water area in square miles.

Source: Kathleen O'Leary Morgan and Scott Morgan, eds., *State Rankings 2003,* 14th ed. Lawrence, Kans.: Morgan Quitno Press, 2003, p. vi.

Date Each State Admitted to Statehood*

	Alpha Order			Rank Order	
Rank	State	Date of Admission	Rank	State	Date of Admission
22	Alabama	December 14, 1819	1	Delaware	December 7, 1787
49	Alaska	January 3, 1959	2	Pennsylvania	December 12, 1787
48	Arizona	February 14, 1912	3	New Jersey	December 18, 1787
25	Arkansas	June 15, 1836	4	Georgia	January 2, 1788
31	California	September 9, 1850	5	Connecticut	January 9, 1788
38	Colorado	August 1, 1876	6	Massachusetts	February 6, 1788
5	Connecticut	January 9, 1788	7	Maryland	April 28, 1788
1	Delaware	December 7, 1787	8	South Carolina	May 23, 1788
27	Florida	March 3, 1845	9	New Hampshire	June 21, 1788
4	Georgia	January 2, 1788	10	Virginia	June 26, 1788
50	Hawaii	August 21, 1959	11	New York	July 26, 1788
43	Idaho	July 3, 1890	12	North Carolina	November 21, 1789
21	Illinois	December 3, 1818	13	Rhode Island	May 29, 1790
19	Indiana	December 11, 1816	14	Vermont	March 4, 1791
29	Iowa	December 28, 1846	15	Kentucky	June 1, 1792
34	Kansas	January 29, 1861	16	Tennessee	June 1, 1796
15	Kentucky	June 1, 1792	17	Ohio	March 1, 1803
18	Louisiana	April 30, 1812	18	Louisiana	April 30, 1812
23	Maine	March 15, 1820	19	Indiana	December 11, 1816

(continued)

Date Each State Admitted to Statehood* *(concluded)*

ALPHA ORDER			RANK ORDER		
Rank	State	Date of Admission	Rank	State	Date of Admission
7	Maryland	April 28, 1788	20	Mississippi	December 10, 1817
6	Massachusetts	February 6, 1788	21	Illinois	December 3, 1818
26	Michigan	January 26, 1837	22	Alabama	December 14, 1819
32	Minnesota	May 11, 1858	23	Maine	March 15, 1820
20	Mississippi	December 10, 1817	24	Missouri	August 10, 1821
24	Missouri	August 10, 1821	25	Arkansas	June 15, 1836
41	Montana	November 8, 1889	26	Michigan	January 26, 1837
37	Nebraska	March 1, 1867	27	Florida	March 3, 1845
36	Nevada	October 31, 1864	28	Texas	December 29, 1845
9	New Hampshire	June 21, 1788	29	Iowa	December 28, 1846
3	New Jersey	December 18, 1787	30	Wisconsin	May 29, 1848
47	New Mexico	January 6, 1912	31	California	September 9, 1850
11	New York	July 26, 1788	32	Minnesota	May 11, 1858
12	North Carolina	November 21, 1789	33	Oregon	February 14, 1859
39	North Dakota	November 2, 1889	34	Kansas	January 29, 1861
17	Ohio	March 1, 1803	35	West Virginia	June 20, 1863
46	Oklahoma	November 16, 1907	36	Nevada	October 31, 1864
33	Oregon	February 14, 1859	37	Nebraska	March 1, 1867
2	Pennsylvania	December 12, 1787	38	Colorado	August 1, 1876
13	Rhode Island	May 29, 1790	39	North Dakota	November 2, 1889
8	South Carolina	May 23, 1788	39	South Dakota	November 2, 1889
39	South Dakota	November 2, 1889	41	Montana	November 8, 1889
16	Tennessee	June 1, 1796	42	Washington	November 11, 1889
28	Texas	December 29, 1845	43	Idaho	July 3, 1890
45	Utah	January 4, 1896	44	Wyoming	July 10, 1890
14	Vermont	March 4, 1791	45	Utah	January 4, 1896
10	Virginia	June 26, 1788	46	Oklahoma	November 16, 1907
42	Washington	November 11, 1889	47	New Mexico	January 6, 1912
35	West Virginia	June 20, 1863	48	Arizona	February 14, 1912
30	Wisconsin	May 29, 1848	49	Alaska	January 3, 1959
44	Wyoming	July 10, 1890	50	Hawaii	August 21, 1959

*First thirteen states show date of ratification of Constitution.
Source: State Rankings 2003, p. 1.

State Population—Rank, Percent Change, and Population Density: 1980 to 2001

[As of April 1, except 2001 as of July 1. Insofar as possible, population shown for all years is that of present area of state. Minus sign (−) indicates decrease]

State	RANK				PERCENT CHANGE			POPULATION PER SQ. MILE[1] OF LAND AREA		
	1980	1990	2000	2001	1980–1990	1990–2000	2000–2001	1980	1990	2001
United States	(x)	(x)	(x)	(x)	9.8	13.1	1.2	64.0	70.3	80.5
Alabama	22	22	23	23	3.8	10.1	0.4	76.7	79.6	88.0
Alaska	50	49	48	47	36.9	14.0	1.3	0.7	1.0	1.1
Arizona	29	24	20	20	34.8	40.0	3.4	23.9	32.3	46.7
Arkansas	33	33	33	33	2.8	13.7	0.7	43.9	45.1	51.7
California	1	1	1	1	26.0	13.6	1.9	151.8	191.1	221.2
Colorado	28	26	24	24	14.0	30.6	2.7	27.9	31.8	42.6
Connecticut	25	27	29	29	5.8	3.6	0.6	641.4	678.5	707.0
Delaware	47	46	45	45	12.1	17.6	1.6	304.2	341.0	407.5
District of Columbia	(x)	(x)	(x)	(x)	−4.9	−5.7	(−Z)	10,396.3	9,884.4	9,313.1
Florida	7	4	4	4	32.7	23.5	2.6	180.7	239.9	304.1
Georgia	13	11	10	10	18.6	26.4	2.4	94.3	111.9	144.8
Hawaii	39	41	42	42	14.9	9.3	1.1	150.2	172.6	190.6
Idaho	41	42	39	39	6.7	28.5	2.1	11.4	12.2	16.0
Illinois	5	6	5	5	(Z)	8.6	0.5	205.6	205.6	224.6
Indiana	12	14	14	14	1.0	9.7	0.6	153.1	154.6	170.5
Iowa	27	30	30	30	−4.7	5.4	−0.1	52.2	49.7	52.3
Kansas	32	32	32	32	4.8	8.5	0.2	28.9	30.3	32.9
Kentucky	23	23	25	25	0.7	9.6	0.6	92.1	92.8	102.3
Louisiana	19	21	22	22	0.4	5.9	−0.1	96.6	96.9	102.5
Maine	38	38	40	40	9.2	3.8	0.9	36.4	39.8	41.7
Maryland	18	19	19	19	13.4	10.8	1.5	431.5	489.1	550.0

Massachusetts	11	13	13	4.9	5.5	0.5	731.8	767.4	813.7
Michigan	8	8	8	0.4	6.9	0.5	163.1	163.6	175.9
Minnesota	21	20	21	7.4	12.4	1.1	51.2	55.0	62.5
Mississippi	31	31	31	2.2	10.5	0.5	53.7	54.9	60.9
Missouri	15	15	17	4.1	9.3	0.6	71.4	74.3	81.7
Montana	44	44	44	1.6	12.9	0.2	5.4	5.5	6.2
Nebraska	35	36	38	0.5	8.4	0.1	20.4	20.5	22.3
Nevada	43	39	35	50.1	66.3	5.4	7.3	10.9	19.2
New Hampshire	42	40	41	20.5	11.4	1.9	102.7	123.7	140.4
New Jersey	9	9	9	5.2	8.6	0.8	992.9	1,044.5	1,143.9
New Mexico	37	37	36	16.3	20.1	0.6	10.7	12.5	15.1
New York	2	2	3	2.5	5.5	0.2	371.9	381.0	402.7
North Carolina	10	10	11	12.8	21.4	1.7	120.7	136.2	168.1
North Dakota	46	47	48	−2.1	0.5	−1.2	9.5	9.3	9.2
Ohio	6	7	7	0.5	4.7	0.2	263.7	264.9	277.8
Oklahoma	26	28	28	4.0	9.7	0.3	44.1	45.8	50.4
Oregon	30	29	27	7.9	20.4	1.5	27.4	29.6	36.2
Pennsylvania	4	5	6	0.2	3.4	(Z)	264.7	265.1	274.2
Rhode Island	40	43	43	5.9	4.5	1.0	906.4	960.3	1,013.4
South Carolina	24	25	26	11.7	15.1	1.3	103.7	115.8	134.9
South Dakota	45	45	46	0.8	8.5	0.2	9.1	9.2	10.0
Tennessee	17	17	16	6.2	16.7	0.9	111.4	118.3	139.3
Texas	3	3	2	19.4	22.8	2.3	54.4	64.9	81.5
Utah	36	35	34	17.9	29.6	1.6	17.8	21.0	27.6
Vermont	48	48	49	10.0	8.2	0.7	55.3	60.8	66.3
Virginia	14	12	12	15.8	14.4	1.5	135.0	156.3	181.5
Washington	20	18	15	17.8	21.1	1.6	62.1	73.1	90.0
West Virginia	34	34	37	−8.0	0.8	−0.4	81.0	74.5	74.8
Wisconsin	16	16	18	4.0	9.6	0.7	86.6	90.1	99.5
Wyoming	49	50	50	−3.4	8.9	0.1	4.8	4.7	5.1

X Not applicable. Z Less than 0.05 percent. ¹Persons per square mile were calculated on the basis of land area data from the 2000 census.
Source: U.S. Census Bureau, *Statistical Abstract of the U.S. 2002,* 122nd ed. Washington, D.C., 2001, p. 23.

	Personal Income (in millions)	Personal Income Rank	Personal Income Per Capita	Per Capita Rank	Gross State Product (in millions)	GSP Per Capita	GSP Per Capita Rank
Alabama	$112,737	25	$25,128	43	$119,921	$26,966	45
Alaska	20,699	46	32,151	14	27,747	44,258	4
Arizona	142,868	23	26,183	38	156,303	30,465	36
Arkansas	63,720	34	23,512	49	67,724	25,333	47
California	1,158,679	1	32,996	10	1,344,623	39,698	7
Colorado	149,958	21	33,276	9	167,918	39,039	9
Connecticut	147,784	22	42,706	1	159,288	46,773	1
Delaware	26,465	44	32,779	12	36,336	46,371	2
Florida	494,648	4	29,596	23	472,105	29,539	39
Georgia	246,720	11	28,821	28	296,142	36,175	16
Hawaii	37,348	40	30,001	20	42,364	34,967	20
Idaho	33,605	42	25,057	44	37,031	28,619	41
Illinois	420,913	5	33,404	8	467,284	37,626	11
Indiana	173,932	16	28,240	32	192,195	31,608	30
Iowa	83,051	30	28,280	31	89,600	30,619	35
Kansas	79,144	31	29,141	26	85,063	31,641	29
Kentucky	104,691	26	25,579	39	118,508	29,321	40
Louisiana	114,064	24	25,446	41	137,700	30,812	32
Maine	35,913	41	27,744	33	35,981	28,222	44
Maryland	198,119	15	36,298	4	186,108	35,138	18
Massachusetts	252,252	10	39,244	3	284,934	44,878	3
Michigan	304,490	9	30,296	18	325,384	32,740	26
Minnesota	171,026	17	34,071	7	184,766	37,558	12
Mississippi	64,248	33	22,372	50	67,315	23,664	49
Missouri	164,143	18	28,936	27	178,845	31,964	28
Montana	22,755	45	25,020	45	21,777	24,138	48

Nebraska	51,480	36	29,771	22	56,072	32,766	25
Nevada	65,596	32	30,180	19	74,745	37,405	13
New Hampshire	43,778	38	34,334	6	47,708	38,605	10
New Jersey	338,912	7	39,453	2	363,089	43,151	5
New Mexico	44,412	37	23,941	47	54,364	29,886	38
New York	690,488	2	36,043	5	799,202	42,115	6
North Carolina	230,556	13	27,711	34	281,741	35,002	19
North Dakota	17,109	49	26,982	36	18,283	28,469	42
Ohio	335,841	8	29,405	25	372,640	32,823	24
Oklahoma	89,350	29	25,575	40	91,773	26,596	46
Oregon	101,176	28	28,731	29	118,637	34,675	22
Pennsylvania	391,354	6	31,727	15	403,985	32,895	23
Rhode Island	33,503	43	31,319	16	36,453	34,773	21
South Carolina	104,320	27	25,400	42	113,377	28,259	43
South Dakota	20,468	47	26,894	37	23,192	30,724	33
Tennessee	160,414	20	27,671	35	178,362	31,351	31
Texas	621,832	3	28,551	30	742,274	35,598	17
Utah	56,299	35	24,306	46	68,549	30,696	34
Vermont	18,231	48	29,567	24	18,411	30,240	37
Virginia	240,115	12	32,922	11	261,355	36,922	15
Washington	198,317	14	32,677	13	219,937	37,315	14
West Virginia	42,682	39	23,688	48	42,271	23,376	50
Wisconsin	162,818	19	29,923	21	173,478	32,343	27
Wyoming	15,249	50	30,578	17	19,294	39,074	8
D.C.	24,046	—	42,120	—	59,397	103,830	—
U.S.	8,922,320	—	30,941	—	9,941,552	35,326	—

Source: State and Local Sourcebook 2003. Supplement to *Governing*, p. 3.

Map of the United States, Showing Census Divisions and Regions

Source: U.S. Census Bureau, *Statistical Abstract of the U.S.*, 122nd ed. Washington, D.C., 2001, inside cover.

Index